Orientation
in Social
Psychology

Carolyn Wood Sherif

The Pennsylvania State University

Orientation in Social Psychology

Harper & Row, Publishers
New York, Hagerstown, San Francisco, London

Sponsoring Editor: George A. Middendorf
Project Editor: Cynthia Hausdorff
Designer: Emily Harste
Production Supervisor: Francis X. Giordano
Compositor: University Graphics, Inc.
Printer and Binder: The Murray Printing Company

Orientation in Social Psychology

Library of Congress Cataloging in Publication Data

Sherif, Carolyn W
    Orientation in social psychology.

    Bibliography: p.
    Includes indexes.
    1. Social psychology.   I. Title.   [DNLM: 1. Psy-
chology, Social.   WM251 S551o]
HM251.S53   301.1   75-25625
ISBN 0-06-046104-7

Contents

Preface, xi

1. Social Psychology in Challenging Times   1

Where Do Social Psychologists Get Problems to Study?, 2
The Focus of Social Psychology, 4
How Social Psychology Grew, 5
Pointing at Social Psychology, 6
An Experiment on Obedience to Prestigious Authority, 6
Human Consciousness and Little Black Boxes, 13
Human Awareness and the Social Psychology of Research
    Situations, 14
Ethical Values and Research Conduct, 15
What Is a Social Situation?, 18
An Overview of Where We're Going, 19

2. Interacting in Brief Encounters   24

Social Psychologists' Fascination with Strangers Meeting
    Briefly, 25
What Is It That Affects Behavior in Social Situations?, 26
Paying Attention to Something Involves Ignoring Something
    Else, 29
First Impressions of Strangers, 32
The Action Affects What We Notice About Others, 37
Social Situations as Problems for the Individual, 41
If Others Differ from Us, Do We Do as We Would Have Them Do
    unto Us?, 48
Getting It Together, 49

3. Becoming Related to Others   52

Getting the Problem into Focus, 53
Forming Bonds of Relatedness, 54
Social Norms as Personal Ties, 55
Social Norms and Realities, 57
Mutual Expectations as Interpersonal Ties, 59
Power Differentials and Socioemotional Roles, 61
Naturalistic Experiments on the Formation of Mutual Bonds, 65
The Earmarks of Becoming Related as a Unit (Group), 69

Real-Life Confirmation of the Experiments, 70
Mutuality and Self-disclosure in Interpersonal Ties, 72
The Impact of the "Outside World" on Private Affairs, 74

4. **When a Person Belongs to a Group   82**
Social Desirability and the "Lie Detector," 84
Studying Behavior in Groups, 86
Group Norms as Regulators of Individual Differences, 96
Position in the Group Affects the Kind of Conformity
    Expected, 100
Role-Status of Members, 101
Leadership in Interpersonal Relations, 104
Leadership Roles and Techniques, 105
Leadership Style Is Contingent on Other Aspects of the Group
    Situation, 107
The Leader as a Group Member, 109
Group Solidarity, Unity, or Cohesiveness, 110

5. **When Persons Belong to Different Groups   112**
Reminiscence of an Eyewitness: How the Research
    Happened, 114
Experimental Plan, 119
How the Experiments Differed from Any Old Summer Camp,
    120
If It's Inter*group* Behavior, There Have to Be Groups, 121
"Irrational" Behavior by Normal Persons, 122
What Is *Sufficient* Cause?, 124
The Sufficient Cause for Intergroup Hostility and Prejudice, 129
Changing Intergroup Relations and Changing Intergroup
    Attitudes, 130
What Kinds of Human Contact Will Reduce Conflict?, 132
Superordinate Goals in Reducing Intergroup Conflict, 133
What Intergroup Relations Can Tell Us About Changing
    Intergroup Behavior, 135
Machiavellianism, Small-Scale and Large-Scale, 139

6. **Asking Questions About the Human Person:
Ape, Angel, or Cultural Robot?   141**
Where We've Been and Where We're Headed, 141
You and I as Everyday Social Psychologists, 142
What Is Human Nature Anyway?, 143
Linguistic Process as Human Nature,
Male and Female "Natures" as a Case Study, 155
Can Society Define Anything as "Right"?, 163

7. The Self-system: Organization of Social Learning and Anchor for Experience   170

Bumping into Self While Studying "Cognition", 172
Remembering, 173
Can We Make "Objective" Social Judgments?, 178
Attributing Causes for Our Own and Others' Actions, 183
Where Does the Self-system Come From?, 188
The Role of Age-Mate Interaction in Self-regulation, 193
Consistency in Social Behavior and Consistency in Social
    Situations, 197

8. Reference Persons and Groups: Social Anchors for Self   200

The Concept of Reference Groups, 201
When Does the "We" Move Me?, 209
Society Sets Reference Group Standards, 215
Personal Satisfaction and Choice of Reference Groups, 220
Social and Psychological Marginality, 222
Self-esteem: Do I Like Myself?, 225

9. People's Attitudes and Their Involvement   229

The Attitude Concept in Social Psychology, 230
What Is an Attitude?, 238
How Are Attitudes Measured?, 240
Attitude Structure: Latitudes of Acceptance, Rejection, and
    Noncommitment, 245
A Person's Own Categories for Evaluation, 251
The Degree of Involvement in a Person's Reference Group, 255
The Degree of Involvement and the Importance of Reference-
    Group Norms, 256
Brief Encounters and Attitude Assessment, 258
Indirect and Unobtrusive Techniques, 259
Predicting Specific Actions Related to Attitudes, 260

10. Attitudes Toward "My Kind of People" and "Those Others"   266

"Explaining" by Definition: The Case of Prejudice and
    Stereotype, 268
Attitudes as Self-Other Relationships, 271
Social Distance from Other People, 272
The Bogardus Technique for Assessing Social Distance
    Norms, 273
White Norms for Keeping Blacks at a Distance, 277

What Differences Among People Become Important?, 279
What Kinds of Behavior Make Role Relationships
    "Intimate"?, 282
Attitudes Toward "Other Kinds" and the Psychology of Social
    Judgment, 284
Reference Group Premises and How Peoples Are
    Categorized, 285
Attributing Traits to "Those Others": Social Stereotypes, 290
Mutual Acceptance of Stereotyped Traits: The Remarkable Sex
    Case, 296
Glorifying Stereotypes into "Scientific Explanations," 299

11. **Stability and Change of Attitudes and Actions**   301
Stability and Change in the Social Environment, 302
Technology and the Radius of the Self-system, 304
Psychosocial Scales and Attitude Change, 307
Cultural Lags and Contradictions, 309
The Power of a New Reference Group: Bennington College
    Students, 310
The Impact of "the Times" on College Students and Older
    Folks, 312
Back to the Thirties: Moreno's Role-taking and Role-playing,
    316
The Power in Deciding to Act Together, 320
Group Decisions About *Whose* Problems?, 326
Institutional Decisions and Personal Decisions, 327
When a Social Psychologist Becomes a Technician of Attitude
    Change, 328

12. **Reactions to Communications When
    We Can't Answer Back**   330
Hypocrisy About Research in High Places, 331
The Selectivity of Audiences, 332
Who Says What to Whom, How, and with What Effect: A
    Rhetorical Question, 333
Communication Flow: Is It One-Way, Two Steps, or Several?,
    339
When Is a Person Likely or Unlikely to Change?, 342
Sizing Up Communications Discrepant from Our Attitudes, 345
What Do We Know About Attitude Change in Response to
    Discrepant Communications?, 351
What Do We Know About Attitude-Communication
    Discrepancy?, 358
Personal Involvement and Susceptibility to Change, 360

13. Social Movements as Generators of Social and Personal Change   361

Social Psychology and Social Movements, 362
What a Social Movement Is Not, 364
What Social Movements Are, 366
Why Social Psychologists Cannot Ignore Social Movements, 367
Social Problems and the Motivational Base They Generate, 368
Background to the Revival of the Women's Movement, 371
Motivational Base for Rebirth and Its Early Phase, 373
Organizational Growth: Group Formations, 379
Counterreactions and Intergroup Conflicts, 383
Movement Goals and Attitude Change, 385
Identity Search and Scope of Change, 387
Conflict, Tactics, and Violence, 389
Last Words, 391

References, 393
Index of Authors, 425
Index of Subjects, 432

Preface

I started writing this book because I wanted to help newcomers find their bearings in social psychology. *Orientation in Social Psychology* is a pragmatic title, but it reflects that high aim. One meaning of orientation is "to ascertain the bearings." I did not want to *point at* social psychology or *tell about* it, but to write so that others could ascertain their bearings *in* social psychology.

During the last decade, more and more students of diverse ages, backgrounds, and interests have turned to books and courses on social psychology with eager questions. Some intend to pursue careers in one of the human sciences or in related applied specialties, but most do not. All seek insight into issues that are at once the most personal and the most social—those pertaining to human individuals in their relations with one another. I felt a growing urgency to communicate seriously with all students at a level that neither condescends to them nor compromises my own integrity as a working social psychologist. My problems in translating that urge into this book were not merely difficulties in writing "good, plain English."

In all conscience, I could not write about social psychology as an established, coherent body of "knowledge" that I could parcel out in neat bundles. That qualm of conscience is enough to turn off those who come to social psychology seeking answers from its oracles. Social psychology is actually much more exciting than a bunch of pronouncements from stuffy oracles. It is more like a sprawling arena filled with people busily engaged in diverse activities that all have to do with ourselves.

Typically, the main events in social psychology's arena are research activities of one kind or another inquiring into persistently troublesome problems about human existence and action. I knew that I could not put them all between book covers, much less all the intriguing side events, so I did not try. I did try to shed light on why and how major research activities came into being, linking them and the problems they explore both with historical events in society and with their precedents in social psychology. I tried to point to accomplishments toward integrating diverse activities by tracing their relationships with one another and with a few central concepts. Such links become particularly useful when a newcomer decides to read more in the current literature. He or she has some framework as background for the new reading.

As a fascinated and enthusiastic participant, I wanted to share my understanding of why and how research is done, without insisting that newcomers learn its litanies by heart. Instead, we would go together through the sequence of events, starting with clear understanding of why they were undertaken and what was actually done, as well as the findings. Out of context, issues of research methods can easily appear to be nit-pickings, or worse yet "technical matters" of concern only to technicians. They come alive within their proper contexts, which are efforts by human beings to inquire into mysteries and significant issues of the human condition—theirs and ours. Newcomers can form critical standards for evaluating research findings. I am convinced that they do so more readily through clear examples of good research processes than by reading about research techniques and issues in the abstract. Instructors can incorporate the latter kind of information within discussions of the research process.

The only way that I could translate my aims into this book was to regard the challenge as personal. In writing, I am very much there in first-person singular. The experience was at times disturbing to someone like me, accustomed to writing impersonal journal articles and books, often behind the doubly protected façade of coauthorship with Muzafer Sherif. I survived by writing for imaginary audiences composed mostly of students and friends, many of whom know me without knowing much about social psychology, an important part of me that I wanted to disclose.

With that prime audience in mind, I wrote chapters of increasing difficulty to be read in order. Orientation in social psychology is to be gained by going from one to the next. For example, the later chapters on attitude change assume that the reader has made it in one piece through the earlier chapters. The last chapter on social movements should have quite different implications for the reader who has read it last than for someone who has not read the preceding dozen chapters first.

The book can be read as a self-contained introduction to social psychology, but I hope that reading it whets the appetite. In fact, I hope that instructors in courses will supplement it with a book of selected readings, with reprints, research or practicum exercises, or other smaller books that cover additional topics, explore particular problems in depth, or contrast possible theoretical interpretations on the topics covered. The references at the end of the book include a number of good supplements, their relevance being indicated in context of the chapters.

One of my greatest struggles in writing was to ignore insistent voices from more knowledgeable faces who kept popping into my imaginary audience, asking questions: "Why didn't you include *this?*" "You can't leave *that* out!" "But you know that *this* is a special interest of mine!" In order to ignore such claims while writing, I had to conjure up additional faces among the newcomers. Their puzzled expressions sustained my belief that orientation in social psychology is their primary need, giving me strength to continue as planned. However, if those more sophisticated questioners were at all representative of instructors who may use the book, they will find much opportunity to add, expand, elaborate, and criticize. That, too, is as planned.

Another confession: In an effort to sustain contact with my imaginary newcomers, I may have drawn too pretty a picture. Captured by my own enthusiasm to involve them, it was easy to err in the direction of exaggerating the clarity of forms, the balance of design, and the completeness of vision. To counteract such distortions in the direction of symmetry and closure, I've not hesitated to bring up controversial issues that will probably continue to be important or to pass my own judgments about them. Here the first-person singular may be a distinct advantage for the reader. It should be easier to take issue with my personal statement than with a judgment rendered implicitly through impersonal discourse or attributed to a mythical collective wisdom. I have tried to make issues clear and to indicate why I've taken a stance, in such cases.

I am content if readers use what is offered here as a point of departure, whether in similar o different directions. I have been concerned with major perspectives in the field, but I have no expectations that all or most readers will share my judgments or my scruples. Of one thing I am confident: It is impossible to achieve a perspective of one's own without appreciating that *some* orientation in social psychology is possible. Once that possibility is glimpsed, a student begins to understand why different viewpoints exist and gains the freedom to select or to propose alternative perspectives.

Readers acquainted with *Social Psychology* (Sherif and Sherif, 1969) will recognize by now that this smaller book is not a revision of that text. It was written with different aims and without the invaluable guiding hand of the senior author of that book, Muzafer Sherif. He fully appreciated and supported my efforts in writing this book, making detailed comments on most chapters in the next-to-final draft. Many of his suggestions led to revision and rewriting. He did his best to persuade me to excise from the manuscript the personal context for his work. Unfortunately, I could not do so without severing part of the first-person singular from my narrative. Despite this and other exceptions to his judgment, I trust that he may find this book as much a product of our joint work during three decades as others in the past.

The chapters have been through several drafts, and I want to thank the person who did most of the hard work of getting them onto paper.

Mary Frank is one of the best manuscript typists I've known in a fairly long line of excellent ones. Esther Beittel also typed portions with unfailing care. For much of their help, I am indebted to arrangements for faculty scholarship in the Department of Psychology at the Pennsylvania State University made by its chairman, Merrill Noble.

Four reviewers of the near-final draft were procured by George Middendorf of Harper & Row, for which I am grateful. Though unknown to me, I hope that the reviewers will read here that they contributed constructively to my efforts in the final revision of the entire manuscript. Their reactions were encouraging in moments of discouragement and thought-provoking beyond the confines of this particular book.

While writing I have been fortunate to be living in a stimulating academic setting. I will be happy if my colleagues recognize in these pages that I have learned through them, especially Leigh Seaver, Lance Shotland, Richard Bord, George Guthrie, and Charles Cofer here and, elsewhere, Joan Rollins, Donald Granberg, and Lawrence La Fave. I am particularly glad to remind several former and current graduate students of dialogues we've had in these pages and where some of their direct influences are to be found: Gerald Gorn on attitude change; Leigh Shaffer on my decision to discuss the self-system as a basis for understanding attitudes; Helen Kearney in the treatment of factionalism and other aspects of social movements; Luis Escovar on group cohesiveness and the Chicano movement; Elyce Milano for thinking about the concept of social distance as it relates to the sexes; Michael White on reference groups; Richard Quarton and Rand Spiro on cognitive development and functioning. Others who may recognize conversations in these pages include Sharon Houseknecht, Edith Grey, Beth Rom, and Lewis Jenkins.

I have learned a great deal of social psychology in graduate seminars since 1972, especially from participants in the first graduate seminar at Penn State on the psychology of women, who included Judy Abplanalp, Margaret Bailey, Phyllis Berman, Trudy Bush, Donna Chmielewski, Pamela Cooper, Helen Kearney, Vicki McGillin, Stephanie Shields, and Aletha Stein. Members of other seminars on interaction processes within and between groups and other special topics in social psychology may also see that they influenced me as much as I affected them. Sandra Brooks' comments on the drafts of Chapters 3 to 5 and in other contexts were particularly helpful.

As I wrote I invariably pictured Sue, Joan, and Ann Sherif in my imaginary audience. I am eager to learn more from them when they read the book. Along with other friends who were always there when I wrote, they have already taught me more than I have yet learned to communicate in writing.

Carolyn Wood Sherif

**Orientation
in Social
Psychology**

Social Psychology in Challenging Times

1

When new acquaintances find out that I am a social psychologist, they often say something like this: "Oh, *social* psychology sounds interesting ... I hope you won't think I'm stupid, but just what is social psychology all *about?*"

Of course, the question is not stupid nor is the person stupid for asking it of a social psychologist. It's I who feel stupid, when I try to answer it. Being a teacher, I can toss off a stock answer, something like this: "Well, social psychology is a field of study—of research. We study individual behavior in relation to its social context— you know, other people, groups, culture, things like that."

I feel stupid when I say something like that because I don't believe it answers what the person is really asking. Sometimes I can tell it hasn't because another question follows: "Well, that's just about everything, isn't it? I mean, just what do you study?" The person is asking for orientation: What is it, out there in the real world and in my own life, that social psychology explores?

Another way to answer is to point to some of the problems that social psychologists have studied, to tell how they went about it, and then to toss in some interesting research findings. I will do quite a bit of "pointing" at social psychology, especially early in this book. However, I have to take the question of what social psychology is about more seriously. The "facts" do not necessarily speak for themselves. At least I have found that pointing to social psychologists and their varied research activities sometimes simply confuses people. It's a little like going to another country where people are busily engaged in doing lots of different things that, you are told, all have something to do with one huge project. You can learn a great deal about what several work teams are doing without ever finding out what the activities of one team have to do with those of other teams, much less what the project is about.

This book is called *Orientation in Social Psychology* because I'd like to be a sort of native guide in locating paths from one part of social psychology to another. As we go from one kind of problem to another, my aim is to help you know what you've seen, where we're going, and how one trip relates to the others. I won't assume that you'll want to go native and join the social psychology tribe. But, if you become interested in learning more about social psychology, I hope that you'll have your bearings and enough perspective on its varied activities so that you can take off without fear of future shock. That's what I mean by orientation *in* social psychology.

WHERE DO SOCIAL PSYCHOLOGISTS GET PROBLEMS TO STUDY?

The problems that social psychologists study grow out of questions about how people act and about the experience of being human within a social environment. For example:

How do other people influence me and how do I influence them when I work, study, play, try to decide what to do, choose friends, take sides in a controversy, try to help others, or get in a fight?

Why do I feel at ease with some people and know pretty much what to expect of them, whereas others put me on guard and leave me with a cold feeling in my stomach or wondering what on earth they will do next?

Why are some people so smug and self-satisfied within their own groups that they seem to think they're always right?

How do leaders lead and why do followers follow them?

How do customs get started?

Why do people draw lines between "my kind of people" and "those others," at times viewing "those others" with a hostility that places them beyond the pale of humanity?

How did I get to be "me"? If I had been born a boy, would I still be "me"? Suppose I'd been born in a Mexican village: Who would I be? Why is it sometimes so difficult to *know* who I am and where I stand?

Why do some people seem apathetic about things that I care about a great deal?

When I try to explain things to some people, being very careful to make my viewpoint clear and be sure of my grounds, why are they so stubborn and mule-headed? Sometimes it's hard to get them to listen, and even when they do, they don't accept what I say. Why?

How does an individual change, if anyone ever does? Is it possible for my friends and me to decide we want to change something about ourselves, and do it? Will having new friends change *me*?

Why do some people who seem to have the necessities of life get so excited about their "rights" and act as though they were "deprived"?

What can individuals do to change their relationships with other people who restrict their lives, liberty, and pursuit of happiness?

These are big questions. They've been asked for ages by social philosophers, religious leaders, writers, educators, and politicians, as well as by you or me. If we had all the answers, social psychologists would be unemployed. If social psychology could give all the answers, many other kinds of psychologists and lots of anthropologists, sociologists, political scientists, and other social scientists would have less to do. None of this is likely to happen in the foreseeable future.

Human beings have been watching one another and thinking about themselves and each other for a long time. Efforts to study and research each other in ways that can be communicated, checked by others, verified, or found in error are all relatively recent in human history; humankind had already learned a great deal about the planets and stars, about the earth, about flying objects and falling bodies, about the composition of physical matter, about the plants and other animals around them.

During the last century our forefathers and some foremothers began to look upon one another with the serious intent of research on human behavior. That seems a long time ago to you and me. It is not very long considering the centuries it had already taken for the physical sciences to gain the high prestige they began to enjoy in the nineteenth century. By the end of that century, the physical sciences, biology, and their applications in technology and medicine had such an aura that to many people they seemed the key to progress toward a better world. Through "science," it was said, human beings would conquer and transform their environment. Poverty, hunger, disease, and early death were all to be vanquished.

What has happened? Science has brought changes to the environment, lifted people from poverty, taught us how to feed more people, made the sick well, and prolonged life. It has also been used to kill millions, to destroy cities, to destroy land that grows plants and supports animals, and to shorten lives. We have new problems, undreamed of in earlier times. Many people who once believed that progress toward an ever-better world was our future, with science its magic key, are disillusioned or bitter.

The irony is that the physical sciences and the technologies they spawned have reached levels far beyond those promised a hundred years ago. They do offer the potentiality of equal opportunity for most people on earth to live, as well as equal opportunity to die a manmade death. They can be used to maintain and improve the physical environment as well as to destroy it as a human home. Our vast ignorance of each other as human beings is demonstrated in the fact that neither you nor I have much basis for knowing whether human beings will take either course or will muddle along until we are as extinct as dinosaurs. The great challenge of our times is whether we can gain enough understanding of ourselves and other people to act effectively before decisions are made that spell mutual destruction, quickly or slowly, and to support those that spell mutual survival.

The social sciences, including social psychology, have no magic keys to the present or future. I do not believe that we would have magic keys even if (by some fluke of history) we had worked as long and as extensively as the physical sciences. The problems of human affairs are much more complex and difficult than those whose solutions led to putting men on the moon. We who are studying them are human beings ourselves, hence can be part of the problems as well as their solutions. All the more reason, I should think, why we should find out what we are about, and why we should share whatever we know in ways that we can both understand and evaluate. There are plenty of problems in human affairs to challenge all of our efforts.

THE FOCUS OF SOCIAL PSYCHOLOGY

Social psychology has a distinctive focus in studying human affairs, and it's important to recognize that there is a *focus*, not a wide-angle lens that can take a picture of everything at once. It concentrates on the actions of human individuals in relation to the social environments in which the individuals develop and act. Such a focus differs from the ways that a sociologist, an anthropologist, a political scientist, or an economist would typically explore the same human affairs. Any one of them might become interested in the activities of a human individual in the course of their study, and they often do. However, their major focus is on regularities and patterns in the way human beings deal with one another and with their physical and social environment. They are concerned with changes in those patterns. But social change can also be studied on a broad scale without bringing particular individuals into the picture.

For example, sexual customs and their change, forms of family relationships, political parties, patterns of human fertility, patterns of the import and export of goods, or what is valued in a culture can be studied meaningfully without paying particular attention to the individuals involved in them. Suppose that we wanted to know how these social forms affect particular individuals or what happens when individuals try to ignore them or to change them. That focus is social-psychological.

There is more to social psychology than simply the impact of social life on the individual, however. An individual is not merely a "building block" of social life, but an active human being. All of the human affairs, objects, and events that other social scientists study involve human individuals at one time or another. Human individuals create customs, myths, belief systems, and exchange patterns. Social psychology is concerned with how individuals create and change their social conditions, as well as how they respond to them.

You may object that human affairs are not separated into neat little compartments so that we can focus on one part while ignoring another. You are right, of course. Social psychologists are dependent on other social scientists for information about the forms, the customs, the social institutions, the technologies, the trends and changes in social environments within which individuals act. Other social scientists, in turn, become dependent on social psychology when they try to make general statements about individuals.

HOW SOCIAL PSYCHOLOGY GREW

Those of you who have become acquainted with the varied departments in colleges or universities are bound to have another question: Aren't social psychology courses sometimes offered both in departments of psychology and sociology? Yes, they are. Like any bureaucracy, the organization of university departments is a matter of history as well as logic. Social psychology appeared on the scene about the turn of the century as a small social movement within academia, in both psychology and sociology. The first two textbooks that were widely used appeared in 1908, one from a psychologist (William MacDougall) and one from a sociologist (E. A. Ross). In both cases, social psychology grew in reaction against what was being taught as psychology at that time. Many psychologists were absorbed in a search for the "elements" that composed human consciousness or mind in a highly abstract sense, a problem that had concerned philosophers before them. Whatever its merit, the search took academic psychology in directions that seemed to many irrelevant to problems of genuine concern to human beings in their relationships with one another. Social psychologists began to explore problems they considered more relevant, at about the same time in the sociology and psychology departments that were themselves new on the university scene.

The focus of social psychology is on activities of individuals in relation to their social context. Does that mean that social psychologists in psychology departments look at individuals and those in sociology departments study their social context? There have been attempts to talk about "sociological social psychology" and "psychological social psychology" in such terms. Frankly, I think that differences hiding behind such fancy labels are likely to become unimportant. Substantial differences almost always acquire simple, clear-cut labels.

No matter where social psychologists work, they have to include both the person and the social context within the focus of study. In my experience, differences between the working practices of social psychologists in different departments have at times been smaller than those between two social psychologists in the same department. Common to them all is their interest in problems that cut across the traditional lines between psychology and sociology departments. Most of them think of themselves as social psychologists, *period*.

The growth of social psychology in this century has been rapid. The interest in social psychology was sufficiently great that by the early 1930s the small band of intrepid pioneers already had an encyclopedic survey of experimental social psychology (Murphy and Murphy, 1931; revised with Newcomb, 1937) and two handbooks (Murchison, 1935; Young, 1927). These are signs of academic respectability, if not success. During the thirties, growth was nourished by events outside the ivy walls of academia. The severe human problems and dislocations of the Great Depression, followed by a second world war, sustained its rapid development. Since then, social psychological research has been greatly boosted by financial support from governments, business, and research foundations. In most universities social psychologists are found in half a dozen different departments.

POINTING AT SOCIAL PSYCHOLOGY

The focus in social psychology is most directly on the actions of individuals in relation to social situations that precede the actions and in which they occur. How do we go about studying the individual's actions in relation to social situations? Let's consider an example of how one social psychologist went about it. The example that I've chosen will also help in clarifying our definition of a "social situation." It is not intended as a "typical" or "representative" study, but it will serve well as a framework for several general points about how a social psychologist works and evaluates research findings.

AN EXPERIMENT ON OBEDIENCE TO PRESTIGIOUS AUTHORITY

How does a social psychologist ask questions that can be answered by observing behavior in a social situation? One interesting example is Stanley Milgram's research on reactions to orders from an authority figure (Milgram, 1963, 1965). Milgram's interest in the problem grew from events after World War II when officials of Nazi Germany were put on trial for actions that would be defined as criminal by judges in almost any country if committed by one private person against others. The difference was that the judges were from other countries and the deeds were not "private." From the deeds themselves, many people concluded that the perpetrators of such terrible deeds must be totally devoid of feelings for others or of values for human life. However, some of the officials declared that this was not the case: They were simply obeying orders from superiors in the government of their own country, who they had been taught should be obeyed. Milgram set out to investigate whether individuals in the United States, where human life is valued, would inflict pain on fellow citizens when ordered to do so. Furthermore, he was concerned about the circumstances in which they would be more likely and less likely to obey orders or to defy them.

Clearly, a young social psychologist at Yale University could not study actual harm to other persons. He could have tried to study all of the situations in which persons obey orders in real life. That effort might take a lifetime and probably would be impossible. For one thing, a social psychologist is not readily admitted to situations where authorities are giving orders that might harm someone else. For another, people's memories of such incidents in the past are likely to differ from the actual events.

So Milgram proceeded to do what a social psychologist often must do to explore a problem, either in a laboratory or in real-life circumstances. He found the problem in real life, but he studied it in miniature. He built a model situation that included essentials of a real-life problem. When the social situation in which behavior occurs can be specified very carefully, or when some parts of it can be kept the same while other parts of it are varied, clearer conclusions can be drawn about how the social environment affects individuals, and vice versa. The difficult tasks of constructing a model for the problem to be studied and of trying to see how the different aspects relate to an individual's behavior are equally important for research conducted in real-life situations and in a laboratory. No one can study all possible examples of the behavior in question or every situation in which it has occurred.

Milgram worked in a laboratory for a good reason. It occurred to him that an experimenter in a "scientific laboratory" has considerable prestige and authority over those who are studied in it. As an authority figure, an experimenter requests that individuals perform certain activities "to help science."

A Laboratory Model for Authority

Milgram used the research laboratory to build his model for authority. The way that he did so was ingenious and very important, for it tells us that every social situation embodies parts of the larger society or culture in which it occurs.

In Milgram's case, the parts of culture included a prestigious institution (Yale University), a specific building and rooms in it, certain equipment with social meaning, and the social values and prestige associated in our society with scientific research. Milgram also used two cultural roles to build an "authority": the role of researcher at a high-prestige university, who appeared wearing a white laboratory coat and assumed an authoritative manner, and the role of employer. He paid people to participate in the research, thereby incurring their obligation to carry out specified tasks (although he did not use nonpayment as threat). The participants were mature men, from both blue-collar and white-collar occupations.

When a man came to the laboratory, he was introduced to another man. One was to be a "teacher" and one the "learner" in an experiment. Though it appeared to be chance, the first man was always the teacher. He was to give a shock to the learner every time the learner made a mistake. The fancy equipment was presented as a shock generator, marked from 15 volts (labeled "slight shock") to 450 volts (labeled "danger: severe shock"). The "teacher" was instructed to drill the learner in reciting a list of paired words. Each time the learner made a mistake, the teacher was to administer a shock to his hand, increasing the shock one step on the marked intensity scale for each successive mistake he made.

No one actually experienced pain in the experiment. The only electric shock ever emitted by the equipment was a very light one given to the "teacher" to demonstrate that the equipment "worked." The "learner" never received any shock.

The learner was actually assisting Milgram. He had been told previously when to make mistakes and how to react to the supposed shock. He followed a prepared scenario when the teacher pushed the button, indicating discomfort, pain, groaning, beating with his free hand, and becoming increasingly insistent that the experiment be stopped. Finally, when and if the scale registered 300 volts, the learner demanded to be freed from the apparatus and refused to answer any more questions. The researcher confined himself to giving orders, even in this last instance commanding the two to continue. This was Milgram's model situation and, as I will indicate later, he changed it only in carefully specified ways to assess how these changes affected the outcome.

The man who was the "teacher" was the one whose actions Milgram studied. In addition to anything else he might do, such as protesting or arguing, he either did or did not use the shock apparatus. Milgram got an automatic record of the setting on the apparatus that was the maximum (supposed) shock each man delivered. He could also report the percentages of the men who did and did not deliver a shock at each step of increasing intensity. There were thirty steps of increasing electric shock to be delivered to the learner in succession, each time he made a mistake. What percentages of the men do you think delivered that maximum shock?

If the feelings of another person are very important in determining behavior in this situation, we could reasonably expect that only a tiny minority of the men would actually deliver the maximum. When this situation was described to forty psychiatrists at a medical school, they expected likewise, estimating that, on the average, less than a *one-tenth of 1 percent* of the men would deliver the maximum shock. Would you agree? If you do, you are also in agreement with college students at Oregon State University, who estimated, on the average, that the maximum shock delivered in this setup would be about 113 volts (Larsen, Coleman, Forbes, and Johnson, 1972).

If you did agree, like these particular psychiatrists and students, you have underestimated the impact of this social-cultural situation on a person's actions. Milgram reported that 62 percent of the men actually did deliver the maximum shock. Of course, this also means that 38 percent refused. However, about 80 percent administered shocks labeled of intermediate intensity (where the psychiatrists were predicting that less than 20 percent would) and over 95 percent administered the shocks labeled as low intensity.

What were the features in the situation that produced the somewhat surprisingly high level of obedience to the authority? I have indicated some of them in describing Milgram's model. He was able to specify others by changing the situation systematically. One very important feature was the researcher's actual presence in the room. When he was out of the room and gave orders by telephone, obedience to his commands fell off markedly. Some men even reported dutifully that they had administered shocks when the records showed that they had not.

Even more interesting was the effect of changing the men's proximity to the learner. The maximum shock was delivered to the learner most frequently (by a little less than two-thirds of the men) when the learner was in the next room and could only be heard occasionally pounding on the wall. Somewhat more men failed to deliver the maximum shock when the learner's voice also could be heard protesting from the next room. When the learner was only 1½ feet away in the same room, still more men failed to deliver the maximum shock. When ordered to force the learner's hand back onto the shock apparatus after he had removed it, 70 percent refused to give the maximum shock.

Another change that dramatically changed the frequency of obedience was to have another person in the room who (by instruction) refused to follow orders. Ninety percent of the men also refused. On the other hand, the later research at Oregon State by Larsen et al. (1972) showed that merely watching another person ostensibly delivering the maximum possible shock strikingly increased the voltage delivered by the observer when it became his turn to be the "teacher."

Milgram studied how the prestige of the institution affected obedience by repeating the same procedures at Yale and at an office building in another city, the office being labeled Research Associates. Whereas 62 percent gave the maximum shock at Yale, only 48 percent did at the office building. This difference suggests only that Yale's prestige added to the researcher's authority. There was still a substantial proportion impressed enough by scientific research with its white-coated researcher to fulfill the unpleasant obligation in less awe-inspiring surroundings.

It would be difficult to contend, I think, that most of the men Milgram studied were cruel individuals or belonged to a society where no value is placed on sparing others from pain. Apparently, some of the men were affected more by their values than by the authority situation since some refused in every condition. Yet, the findings cannot be fully accounted for in terms of individual differences in value commitment or sensitivity among the men. Milgram had assigned men to his different conditions randomly, so that the chance that men with high value commitments would participate in the various conditions was about the same. Yet, the proportions who defied authority varied greatly according to the specific conditions faced.

It might occur to you that the men who delivered maximum levels of shock had already developed into more highly aggressive, hostile, punitive, or cynical personalities that predisposed them to such an action. In the Oregon State study (Larsen et al., 1972) five paper-and-pencil tests of such personality dispositions were given to students participating in the research. Each person's score on each of the five tests was compared to the voltage he or she administered in the experiment. However, there was little or no relationship between the test results and the level of shock administered. Nor have Milgram and his associates found clear evidence for consistent differences between the men who did and did not give the maximum shock (see, for comparison, Elms, 1972).

Of course, these findings do not mean that a person's past experiences and personal tendencies in these respects are totally unimportant in affecting whether he will obey or defy authority. They could indicate that the nature of the social situation aroused attitudes toward science and authorities that override individual differences in hostility and aggression. Confirming this conclusion, the students at Oregon indicated after the experiment that they had acted as they did because they wanted to contribute to scientific research and had been asked by an "experimenter" who "knew what he was doing." With such faith in the authority, one did not need to be personally hostile to obey. Milgram's men gave similar reasons for their behavior (see Elms, 1972).

Could it be that such obedience to authority or readiness to inflict pain is merely typical of males in our society? Certainly we hear women described as the "gentler sex," reluctant to inflict or observe discomfort in others. Milgram repeated his research with women.

There were no significant differences from the major findings for men. Similarly, male and female students at Oregon State responded to the social situation in much the same ways. The only significant differences were that, on the average, men administered shocks lasting a *total* time (summed over 60 trials) that was 10 seconds or so longer, a pretty inconsequential difference. Men who had watched a "model" following directions to the letter did deliver a slightly higher maximum voltage than women on the average (Larsen et al., 1972).

What Milgram's Experiment Can and Cannot Tell Us

There is a great temptation to jump to conclusions about people in general on the basis of a single study, especially when it is well done and interesting like Milgram's. These days, it is easy enough to think of real-life examples of people obeying authority in what seems a blind and cruel way.

For example, since Milgram's experiment, an officer in the United States army was convicted for deliberately killing civilians in a village in South Vietnam. He testified that he had been ordered to do so by superiors. So far, it sounds like Milgram's experiment. But was it? His superiors were not present at the massacre. The officer also testified that he had not only been trained to kill the enemy, but had been intensively trained to regard all civilians in such villages as enemies or potential killers. He had seen civilians killed many times before. The men who participated in Milgram's experiment had no such training. Are the situations comparable?

Let's look at the other side of the coin: Those who defied the experimenter in Milgram's research had to bear no consequences for their refusals but the continuing orders of the experimenter. Many young men during the Indochina war defied authority when such defiance meant jail, punishment, or exile. Others entered the armed services and followed the directives of authority despite objections to the war, enduring considerable emotional conflict as a result. Their obedience was directly related to fears and anxiety about punishment and, at times, to what parents, relatives, or friends might think of them if they refused.

As you can gather, I think that we should be cautious in interpreting these particular cases of obedience or defiance of authority as exact parallels to the model that Milgram studied. What Milgram's experiments do show is that once a person has agreed to participate in an activity and has accepted the authority of someone in that situation, directives given on the spot have great impact on actions, provided also that the social situation in which the person is enmeshed is firmly stacked to minimize other alternatives (no one else is present but the authority, and so on).

You may feel dissatisfied with such a generalization, preferring instead a general statement about all reactions to authority. However, it is the social psychologist's dilemma that such broad generalizations can seldom be made on the basis of one or a series of miniature experiments. The experimental model can help sharpen our analysis of a real-life event, especially by sensitizing us to all of the aspects of the social circumstances.

The research is not diminished by such qualifications. What was found was of great importance. The findings lead us to inquire why a particular authority is accepted, and why people enter into situations with such potential for shaping their actions, even against their own "best judgment." Certainly, the findings in the different experimental conditions direct us to look at the various components of the situation, in addition to the authority figure (the location, the victim's proximity, what another person does in the situation).

Does this mean that the social situation Milgram constructed solely and directly "determined" the men's actions? Surely not. Despite the negative results of attempts to find personal differences between those who obeyed and did not obey, we are still faced with the undeniable fact that substantial proportions refused to follow orders as the (supposed) shock increased. Maybe we have concentrated too much on just one of their actions during the experiment, namely, delivering the shock. That is not all that happened, and we may find the men's other reactions enlightening.

Somewhat to Milgram's surprise, some of the men simply carried out the requests, with no further ado. However, a good many who obeyed also asked questions, protested orders at different points, and some showed considerable emotional arousal, even trembling. Some said that they did not like the task and would take no responsibility for what might happen to the other fellow. Afterward, as I noted, most of those who obeyed indicated their trust in the researcher: Nothing was going to go really wrong under the auspices of science. Those who refused to obey clearly did not accept that premise. Like some who obeyed, they refused to take responsibility for what might happen but they had less faith in the researcher.

Such reactions tell us that the men were not responding mechanically and directly to orders or to the rest of the situation. They were feeling and thinking. Certainly, we cannot always take a person's words as accurate descriptions of his or her private experiences. The men who said they gave the shock when the experimenter was out of the room were contradicted by his records. I don't suppose that any of us would doubt that these particular men *did* have private thoughts related to their contradictory actions.

We cannot assume that a wholly accurate report of what a person experienced during the experiment would "explain" the actions observed. Since the same men did not participate in different conditions, none could have said that having the learner some distance across the room or in the next room made it easier to deliver the shock. The findings show that it did, however.

My point is that without looking at the men's other actions, in addition to whether or not they obeyed, the entire affair looks like a convention of robots. Knowing something of what they were thinking and feeling, on the basis of their words and other actions, reveals them as the human beings they are, even if we are shocked and dismayed at what some of them believed they were doing. Knowing what they thought and felt helps us explain better all of the influences that led them to obey or to defy the authority.

HUMAN CONSCIOUSNESS AND LITTLE BLACK BOXES

Some of the research in this book and some of the controversies about interpretation of the findings are going to seem puzzling to you without another word from history. About half a century ago, some psychologists within academic psychology became dissatisfied with the state of the field. They emphasized that if psychology was to proceed on a sound basis, psychologists would have to agree that neither they nor anyone else could study human consciousness (awareness) directly. All that can be studied, they said, is what we can observe, including what can be measured indirectly (with instruments, as a thermometer indicates body temperature), if we are clever enough. In other words, a researcher's actual *data* are observations or measurements of a person's actions and of the environmental conditions before and during the actions. When we speak of another person's consciousness or awareness or feelings, *we* are making inferences from the actual data. If there are no such data, such inferences are pure speculation on our part.

This little revolt within psychology was termed *behaviorism,* and there have been many different kinds and brand names since then. Of course, the early behaviorists were right in stressing the difference between the "hard facts" and our speculations about what goes on in another person's mind. No one has ever observed directly someone else's feelings of being afraid, elated, or depressed. No one can watch another's thinking. No one can participate in another's dream. All that we can observe or measure is a person's behavior: words, deeds, "body language," failure to act, trembling, and so on.

In the sense that they agree with these definitions of their data, all social psychologists today are behaviorists. However, the term *behaviorism* has acquired several other meanings, one of which implies that it is a waste of time, or even "unscientific," to make inferences about what a person thinks, feels, or imagines. In this sense, most social psychologists are not "behavioristic." Here, I can only caricature the extreme behavioristic position to illustrate why I bring up the topic at all. One interpretation compared the human individual to a black box—black because no one can see what goes on inside: Since we do not know enough about the human nervous system, especially the brain, we should not make inferences about what goes on inside the black box. Such inference smacks of loose "unscientific" terms such as consciousness or mind, which we have to get rid of. So, all we can do is to observe what goes into the box (the stimulus) and what comes out (the response). For such a behaviorist, the job is to establish laws relating input to output, or stimulus to response.

I doubt very much that anyone who held such a view would have done an experiment like Milgram's. If someone had, a problem would arise in finding a law to explain why one little black box refused to obey while others in the same situation did. The available evidence does not suggest that the obedient and defiant men were entirely different types of boxes apart from the research situation. Their words and actions indicate that the men were sizing up and experiencing the situation differently. The assumption that human consciousness is irrelevant to the study of behavior blinds us to such evidence. We can never find what we refuse to look for.

Inferences about what a person is experiencing during a social event can be based on behavior (verbal or nonverbal) in addition to the "response" that is of greatest interest in the study (in Milgram's, the act of delivering shock). What we infer about a person's conscious experiences will not necessarily "explain" all of the actions of focal interest, but it will certainly help in understanding more about the entire event.

Both the way a person experiences a situation and the way the person acts are jointly affected by what is "out there" in the situation and by influences from within the person, including relevant past experiences. Making inferences about what a person is experiencing inside is a great deal more difficult than ignoring the problem. We have to be sure of our evidence since there is always the danger of putting our own ideas and feelings into another person's head.

The social psychologist's job is to study a person's conscious experiences (indirectly, making inferences from verbal and nonverbal behavior) and related activity, in connection with preceding and ongoing social situations. The job would be a great deal simpler if human individuals were boxes, but it wouldn't be nearly as exciting.

HUMAN AWARENESS AND THE SOCIAL PSYCHOLOGY OF RESEARCH SITUATIONS

One reason that social psychologists have to make inferences about what people are experiencing is that otherwise they cannot understand the problems encountered in observing behavior. In later chapters of the book, I will give numerous examples of how a person's actions are affected when that person knows he or she is being observed. There are some things that we simply do not *do* when we know someone is watching us. When we also think that *what* we do may tell a researcher something important about us, we get ourselves into shape to look our best. If the proceedings are at all interesting, we try to figure out what the researcher is trying to find out and to react accordingly.

At times, as we shall see, some behaviors simply cannot be studied if the person is aware of the fact. Being human, he or she responds to that fact so strongly that the entire course of events is changed. At other times, the behavior of interest can be studied when the person is fully aware that he or she is a "subject" in research, but only if the researcher disguises the purpose of the study, as Milgram did. The men thought the study concerned learning, whereas he was interested in whether they would obey orders.

If Milgram had told the men the purposes of his study, and what was going to happen beforehand, they would have acted very differently. If they had known that there was no shock, that the learner was acting a part and did not suffer discomfort, the problem he wanted to study would have disappeared. As Milgram's research shows clearly, the researcher is part of the experiment. The scenario devised and what happens over time cannot be understood apart from the researcher's relationship to the person being studied, apart from the place where the action occurs, apart from other persons who are present, or from the task that the researcher devised, all of which are often under the researcher's control.

Whereas this is quite obvious in the Milgram experiment, it is not always so obvious in other research, particularly in studies done in more natural settings—in homes, schools, summer camps, or on the street. Still, it is true of any research on human beings that the researcher and research paraphernalia are parts of the social situation to which an individual is responding. We shall have to learn quite a bit about how researchers have tried to minimize, to overcome, or to circumvent the impact of the research situation itself on behavior.

ETHICAL VALUES AND RESEARCH CONDUCT

As I said earlier, Milgram's research is not "typical" in social psychology. For one thing, many more variations of the experimental situation were explored than most researchers have energy and foresight to attempt (Milgram, 1974). For another, it placed the participants in an unusual and potentially stressful circumstance.

After the experiment was over, each participant was told that the learner had not actually suffered, and Milgram went to considerable length to ensure that no one left feeling bad or guilty about how he had behaved. Later, each participant in the experiment received full information about the purpose and findings of the experiment. They filled in questionnaires, indicating among other things, whether or not they regretted the experience. Only 1.3 percent of a large number of men who participated in the research responded that they wished they had not taken part in the experiment.

To me, as a social psychologist, these actual data indicate that possible ill effects of the experiment from the participants' point of view were confined to a very few. As I read the follow-up results, the experience turned these few off about participating in research and left a sour taste about being deceived. To me, that is regrettable, but a minor side effect from a significant research. What is more regrettable is that over time so many college students have been deceived about the purposes of research, often unnecessarily and for less important research problems, that a good many now expect to be deceived the minute that they see a researcher.

Almost all social-psychological research done in academic settings has studied persons who volunteered to participate and whose identities have been fully protected by researchers. Many of the volunteers are students. In my opinion, any stress endured in most of the research does not begin to compare with the ordeals that students face in studying and taking examinations. However, I think that you, as reader of this book, have quite as much right as I to make ethical judgments on such issues. I would much rather that you meet social psychology as it is and make up your own mind.

One thing worries me, however. Today there are guidelines for researchers published by the American Psychological Association to help them ensure the well-being and privacy of the persons they study. The Department of Health, Education and Welfare has also set up requirements that universities receiving federal funds must follow in monitoring their research activities involving human beings. This may be well and good to ensure that all academic researchers behave as conscientious researchers always do. However, little of this activity and the bureaucracy that it spawns will touch those areas where, it seems to me, there is the greatest danger of invasion of privacy and disregard for human beings.

I am concerned about the *purposes* for which research is done and the *uses* to which it is put as well as about respect for the persons studied. The purposes of research have a great deal to do with how human beings are treated and whether or not their privacy is respected. Especially since World War II, much social-psychological research has been sponsored by federal or state governments and their agencies, by business, industry, and private foundations with ideas about what kind of research is worth supporting and what is not. (For example, during the 1950s, finding an organization eager to lend financial support to study problems of desegregation in the United States was nearly impossible. The Office of Naval Research supported many studies of "small groups" for some years, then shifted its support chiefly to studies carried out abroad on people's attitudes.) The long-range effects of such sponsorship on the kinds of problems studied would make a fascinating study in itself, which, unfortunately, remains to be done.

Some of the sponsored research allowed the researchers freedom to execute research of their own choosing without sponsor interference, once the grant was awarded. However, a great deal of research was "made to order" by a researcher for a sponsoring organization in pursuit of its own purposes, with little concern for any lasting contribution that the activity might make to understanding human beings or their affairs. Such a researcher is, in effect, functioning as a technician in the service of the organization. Any research skills he or she has become a bag of tricks that earn a living through getting information useful only to the sponsor. The work may be quite justifiable ethically or at least harmless. However, in these days of big government, big business, big public opinion surveys, and big advertising by both business and government, we may quite properly raise some questions about the purposes and consequences of such research.

If, under the name of "science," research is used to gain information about the private activities or lives of individuals to be used for the purposes of government or institutional control and punishment, ethical questions should be raised immediately. Such use of research data has nothing to do with understanding social behavior. There are older, more reliable names for such activities, including coercion and spying. It has been and still is the rule in social-psychological research in universities that the identity of particular persons and groups studied remain anonymous, both to readers of research reports and to research sponsors. The rule is not respected in much research done in the name of government and private agencies.

Even if the researcher adheres to such elementary rules protecting individual privacy, there are other ethical dilemmas in sponsored research that should be considered. For example, not very long ago, a number of social scientists began a research project in a South American country on the "roots of revolution," which was called Project Camelot. Because the sponsoring agency told the researchers they had a "free hand" as to what to study, the undertaking seemed ethical and justified to several U.S. researchers. Some of their colleagues in the United States and South America protested that the U.S. Department of Defense could have no impartial reason for sponsoring such research. They might well have added that the CIA has little respect for protection of privacy, even if the researchers did. The project was terminated with some embarrassment. Subsequent events in South America involving the U.S. government have justified raising the ethical issues.

Or consider a made-to-order research project that involved social psychologists: When, if ever, is it ethical for social psychologists to use their research findings about group persuasion and commitment to induce workers in a factory to raise their production rate? What ethical issues are at stake when researchers try to discover how to sell a product that a manufacturer wants to introduce primarily to make a larger profit?

In reading this book and considering ethical issues in research, I hope that you will keep in mind the purposes for which research was done as well as how it was done. Such issues are particularly salient when researchers observe others without their knowing they are being watched. Of course, it can be maintained that people watch other people all of the time. However, it seems to me that the purposes and sponsorship of such research are crucial. If the problem of research is important and the researcher can study it in no other way, the conscientious researcher destroys evidence on the identity of individuals or groups observed. If identifying persons, places, and actions is the purpose of the sponsor, there can be no ethical justification for calling such methods "research." The activity should be given its proper name—spying, for example.

WHAT IS A SOCIAL SITUATION?

In different contexts, I have said that social psychology is the study of the individual's personal experience and associated actions in relation to social situations. This definition clearly specifies what is psychological and what is social about social psychology. It also indicates the social psychologist's major task: to relate the two. Now let's consider for a moment what is meant by a "social situation." One reason that I pointed at social psychology through Milgram's research is that it shows very clearly that social situations are not as simple as we might think. In addition to the other persons present in the experiment, the social situation in his research included apparatus, an elaborate laboratory room, instructions about the task that was to be done, and an impressive physical location: a prestigious university, which endowed the researcher with respectability, responsibility, and authority. Through its doors the men carried their own cultural backgrounds along with their individualities; the hallowed grounds and the aura of scientific endeavor produced a willingness to carry out the task.

Throughout the book, we will be learning more and more about social situations. Of course, *other individuals* are their most frequent and significant earmark. However, every social situation also embodies *aspects of the culture* in which it occurs: not only those human-made locations with their facilities and arrangements, but rules for conduct in those locations and with those persons also engaging in the activity or present in other capacities. Since individuals are often pegged as higher or lower in prestige, as dominant or subordinate, or as equals, it is seldom sufficient simply to describe their personal characteristics (height, weight, attractiveness, smiling or frowning countenance, and so on). In fact, another person is not even necessary to a social situation: Since culture refers to that part of the environment constructed by human beings, you are in a social situation right now, reading this book.

Defining what constitutes the social situation will serve as a major theme in this book, helping us to get our bearings in relation to a wide range of apparently diverse problems in social psychology. As I said at the outset, I see my role is that of guide for gaining orientation in the field, rather than telling you all that I know and don't know about specific research topics (such as reactions to authority, helping other people, or hostility toward other groups). You can pursue interests in such specific problems on your own or through special courses, wisely and well, if you first know what social psychology is all about. So, how are we going about seeking orientation in social psychology?

AN OVERVIEW OF WHERE WE'RE GOING

There is no doubt about it: Other human beings are the most significant and consequential parts of the social environment. Unlike other aspects of a social situation, other persons respond to us, and we to them, and they to us, and we to them, and so on. Such give-and-take among human individuals is what is meant by *social interaction*, the theme with which we shall start.

In the next chapter, research on a variety of specific problems will be summarized to focus attention on the interaction process among persons in brief encounters. Such research is useful, as well as interesting, in understanding individual experience and behavior during interaction with others, especially the impact of the other aspects of the social situation: the cultural components, the location, and the activities being engaged in. One reason is that the *relationships among participants* in brief, casual encounters are often not very important. Therefore, the impact of cultural prescriptions, the structure of activities, and the immediate problems faced by the individuals is sometimes striking. Much of the research in Chapter 2 was done in natural environments rather than in the laboratory.

In Chapter 3, the focus continues by considering what happens when individuals continue to interact over enough time that they begin to be "related" to one another. What is happening *between* individuals as they relate to one another? What is meant when we speak of "bonds" among us? What difference do those beginnings of "relatedness" and "bonds" make in our own actions, in actions by the others, in the *relative* impact of the location and the problems we face? Chapter 3

("Becoming Related to Others") includes laboratory studies as well as observations in a prison camp and research in human relations workshops.

Next, we shall turn to interactions among persons that have become sufficiently predictable over time that we can speak of them as a "group." Chapter 4 explores what happens when a person belongs to a group, including what happens to social psychologists who try to study what goes on among members. The major issues of concern will include the regulation of interactions among individuals by group "norms," which define what is considered "conformity" and what is considered "deviant" in their activities and relationships with one another. Their interpersonal relations will be of particular interest, for these become stabilized during interaction so that we can speak of a member's "role" relative to others and his or her relative "status" in power plays among members. One reason that research on interaction among members of small groups can be enlightening is that it specifies more exactly just what is meant and what is involved in concepts that are widely used in discussions of the larger social and cultural scene: concepts such as norm, role, status, leadership-followership, solidarity or cohesiveness, and, above all, issues of conformity and deviation in all of these respects.

Chapter 5 will take us from *within* a group to what transpires as members of *different* groups interact. I wish here that I could take time to tell you all I know and don't know about this topic because it bears on some of the most consequential social and personal problems of the day and of the foreseeable future. However, I am going to hold firm to our purpose: orientation in social psychology. Therefore, the chapter concentrates mainly on experiments in natural settings that trace the interactions when persons belong to different groups from their inception to an outbreak of conflict between them and, at last, the resolution of that conflict. By learning why interactions among members of different groups are *not* the same as interactions among strangers or friends, we will be prepared in later chapters to deal with the important social issues of prejudiced attitudes and stereotypes toward other groups (Chapter 10) and of the encounters that invariably arise as a new social movement takes shape, seeking to change some important aspect of human relationships (Chapter 13).

Chapter 6, "Asking Questions About the Human Person," may appear to be a break in our cumulative excursions through different forms of interaction among persons. You will find that it is really a continuation. Having learned about the importance of interaction in social situations, we should be in the position to assess more accurately what kind of a human creature we are studying. Do we have here an "ape, an angel, or a robot"? We will use evidence about how human beings interact as the basis for assessing generalizations about "human nature" and various *kinds* of "human nature" ("superior-inferior," male-female, and the like). Such data will serve as a check to speculations about what is "given" in the human individual, insofar as social behavior is concerned. Conversely, they indicate limitations on the extent of social influences related to human psychological functioning. Can society really make anything "right" in a member's eyes? In my opinion, many of the age-old controversies on such issues can be settled only by keeping a close eye on evidence about the interactions among persons and the impacts of those interactions on their respective actions.

The discussion and survey of evidence in Chapter 6 will prepare us for closer attention to the human person, particularly on how a person's past experiences become organized over time in his or her "self-system" (Chapter 7). Once formed, the self-system anchors and gives direction to a great deal of the individual's private (subjective) appraisals of what goes on in social situations. If such a concept sounds pretty speculative to you, let me add that we will start by showing very concretely how the self-system keeps popping up in the most unlikely places—for example, in laboratory research on mental processes of the "highest" order, such as thinking, remembering, and judging. A concept like self-system also proves useful in finding our way into social-psychological research about how we decide what "causes" our own behavior and that of other people during interaction ("attribution processes"). Chapter 7 includes a flashback into human development, summarizing some important orientations to what we know about the formation of self-systems. The concept of self-system is also needed to pull together a lot of scattered and fragmentary "facts" about human motivation, as we shall see.

Chapter 8 hinges on how the self-system is related to other persons and groups, thereby ensuring that social interaction continues to be focal in our attention. The concepts of "reference person" and "reference group" were designed to link the person's self explicitly to those significant others to whom he or she relates psychologically. As we shall see, these concepts are useful even when the individual answers a simple question such as Who am I? They are more essential as we continue into problems of the person's motivation to attempt activities, on what happens when the person does well or poorly, and whose terms make the efforts "success" or "failure." Together, the concepts of self-system and reference persons (or reference groups) bring better order to a large amount of scattered data on personal aspirations and motives, on personal satisfaction or distress, on experiences of uncertainty about self, and about whether and how well the person likes himself or herself. They are applied in Chapter 8 to the person's experiences as marginal to organized groups in society and to experiences during adolescence.

Chapters 9 and 10 should prove helpful in getting some bearings relative to the masses of research on social attitudes—attitudes we have toward social objects and controversial issues as well as toward each other (Chapter 9). Chapter 10 concerns attitudes toward "those other kind of people," namely, those not regarded as "our kind" or kept distant from "us." Such attitudes can amount to viewing others with hostile prejudice through lenses that encourage the continuation of social stereotypes. Who "those other kinds" are depends, of course, on the viewer. Most of the research in Chapter 10 concerns attitudes toward persons of different race, nationality, or sex. It will become clear that orientation in research on attitudes is possible only when we consider their relation to the person's self-system and its links to significant reference persons and groups.

Once we have found our way around the attitude research literature, we should be ready to tackle the most difficult problem of all: how and when a person's attitudes are likely to change. The problem of changing attitudes cannot be separated from issues of the person's self-system at the time, nor from the stability or change of the larger social environment. Chapter 11 puts the problem of personal change in such a perspective. Starting with some salient features of social change, including the cultural lags and contradictions it can produce, that chapter uses the orientation already gained from our earlier focus on the interaction process, especially in Chapters 3 and 4. In discussing "Stability and Change of Attitudes and Actions," Chapter 11 considers the options that times of rapid and uneven change present to individuals: becoming a member of a new group, dealing with the compelling events of the times by changing one's relationship with important other persons (role changes), deciding together with one's group to commit oneself to new actions.

Chapter 12 turns to the possibilities of attitude change in response to communications that come our way that we can't answer back. The air is full of such communications directed at us every day. There must be literally tons of research data on reactions to such one-way attempts at persuasion. Again, it would be nice if we had more time to spend on such challenging but confusing topics. I believe that you will find the emphasis on the social situation as the context for the communication, as well as all that we will have learned about human persons, useful in guiding your further explorations, especially those into the mass media.

Finally, Chapter 13 considers social movements (whose purpose is to generate social change) as contexts for significant personal change—not only for its participants but for nonparticipants as well. Because I am a woman and because the women's movement is well documented and contemporary, I have used its older and recent history to illustrate the various topics in social psychology that are readily included in the study of social movements. I have also brought in other social movements in appropriate contexts, as well as findings from research on social networks, the spread of information, and group formation. The primary aim of the chapter is not merely to inform you on the women's movement (which I am delighted to do), but to point to some common features in all social movements that make them such rich contexts for studying almost every problem in social psychology that we shall have discussed by then.

Now we begin. I hope that you find orientation that will be useful in bringing social psychology to bear upon the problems of these challenging times. I hope that some of you will want to explore social psychology further and that a few may decide to join social psychologists in their efforts. Of one thing I am certain, however: The challenges of our times are not for social psychologists alone. The orientations that you gain and the actions that you take are more important.

Interacting in Brief Encounters

Have you ever watched someone who believed that he or she was truly alone? It is difficult because the minute that person knows you are watching, the situation is changed. If you are lucky, you'll see the change happen. Eloquent posing and careful study of the mirror cease abruptly. Blank eyes staring into space shift rapidly to the book on the table. A finger leaves the nose, the hand groping for a handkerchief. Scratching shifts suddenly to another part of the body. Sprawling legs come to attention.

Long ago, social psychologists demonstrated that just being in the presence of another person changes our behavior, compared with being alone (Allport, 1924). The changes are for the better at times, for the worse at others, and sometimes are simply "different." In this chapter, we start trying to discover what produces such changes in behavior, and why the same person may act so differently from one social situation to the next.

A considerable range of activities and situations studied in research is sampled here: laughing with another person, efforts to maintain privacy, blind dating, reactions to emergencies, and helping others needing assistance. Such diversity becomes an advantage when we seek to answer the question *What is it,* out there in the social environment, that affects the way I feel and act? We don't want a list a mile long enumerating every single thing that might affect us over a year. Much more useful is a general framework that we ourselves can apply in analyzing particular situations that we encounter. What do we look for and where do we look? A diversity of examples helps to ensure that we don't overlook some important classes of social stimulation.

Wait a minute! The chapter title says "interacting in brief encounters." Brief encounters with *whom*? If this question occurred to you, you're right up front. *Who* we encounter makes all the difference in the world. The chapters to come concentrate on the tremendous significance of human ties that bind or divide us. Such ties take *time* to form. They link or separate us in far more than one brief episode. They can dominate our thoughts and deeds so much that at times we forget where we are, who else is around, or what is going on.

Perhaps the great personal significance of human relationships that endure for a while is one reason for looking at give-and-take among persons who are not involved with one another on highly emotion-laden and continuing terms. We may more clearly see other influences in social situations that are obscured when interpersonal relations count so much, even though those influences are important parts of the total picture. That is one reason why I'm starting with research on brief encounters chiefly among *strangers*. There are others.

We spend a lot of time encountering strangers. We size them up and form impressions about them that may influence the course of any future contacts. How we do so and how we react to strangers in different circumstances can tell us quite a bit about what manner of critter we human beings are. We will look for general guidelines about how human beings see, feel, weigh, and respond to social situations. Such guidelines can be useful as we venture into the complex flow of give-and-take among persons who *count* with one another.

Finally, we focus on brief encounters among strangers here because, in fact, a great deal of the research in social psychology consists of snapshots of such transitory contacts.

SOCIAL PSYCHOLOGISTS' FASCINATION
WITH STRANGERS MEETING BRIEFLY

As a social psychologist, I can give some good reasons for the enormous proportion of available research that concerns brief encounters among strangers. By studying strangers, the effects of past experiences together are eliminated. For a short time, the researcher can study a social situation in considerable detail, controlling certain aspects of it and systematically varying others (the *stimulus variables*) to assess their influence on behavior. Or the researcher can introduce the same stimulus conditions (situations) to persons with different past experiences (say, as males or females), thereby comparing the effects of *personal variables* in reactions to the situation. Such controls permit the experimental study of social behavior. The plan and logic for controlling certain factors and deliberately varying others is what researchers refer to as *experimental design*.

Does it follow that experiments in social psychology have to take place in a laboratory? Not at all. A place where the researcher has virtually complete control over what happens may be advantageous in studying certain problems, particularly if special equipment is required. However, as Milgram's research in Chapter 1 suggested, the laboratory location and fancy equipment may be disadvantageous in studying other problems: They arouse certain expectations that make it a very different place from, say, the library, the coffee shop, or the subway. This chapter includes several experiments that did not take place in a laboratory. Does it follow that only brief encounters among strangers can be studied experimentally? Not at all. In later chapters, we shall see examples of experiments involving friends, group members, family members, and enemies, as well as events occurring over periods of time. We shall also learn that there is value in research that is not an experiment.

There are also poor reasons for research on strangers during brief encounters. These include the assumptions that nothing of great consequence happens when interaction continues over time, that encountering a stranger is equivalent to encountering an individual one knows, or that a researcher's convenience or personal preference for working in a laboratory with student "subjects" justifies application of the results to other social situations. You have a right to adopt a "show me" attitude as to whether research findings on brief meetings of strangers are applicable to other situations or to real life. You might ask questions about them similar to those posed about Milgram's research model in Chapter 1. If you come across a study in which the reasons for using the brief-encounter-among-strangers model seem poor, you will be correct in asking for better justification.

WHAT IS IT THAT AFFECTS BEHAVIOR IN SOCIAL SITUATIONS?

A social situation is a complicated affair. There is more to even a brief encounter than meets the eye. The participants define the situation, themselves, and each other in terms that reflect their cultural backgrounds, their social roles and positions—for example, as an important man of power and a glamorous woman; a poor, lowly student and an authoritative professor. Each participant is affected by the physical and social character of the location where the encounter occurs, including that of other people who happen to be there also. The activity under way, or the problem posed by the situation to participants, also affects the actions of each individual. His or her actions, in turn, become part of the situation for the other participants. Such *interaction* among *persons* in *activities* in sociophysical *locations* is the earmark of any social situation.

Before we enter a situation, boundaries for our actions are set by cultural rules that we take so much for granted that they are likely to be neglected, even by researchers. Such rules concern the particular role we take relative to others and what we expect of them, as well as definite boundaries for how each should and should not behave in the situation (social norms). For example, consider this situation: You enter a room and a stranger of the opposite sex tells you to go to the adjoining room and remove your clothes, adding that he or she will join you in a moment. Would.you do so?

Almost certainly you would if the stranger was a physician and you were in the office for a physical examination. When you have undressed, suppose that another stranger of opposite sex dressed in work clothes enters suddenly. I would guess that the chances are fairly high (especially if you are female) that you would grab something to cover your body, dive for the nearest shelter, sharply question the person, or all three.

Neither the physical features of the situation nor the personal characteristics of the strangers can fully account for your actions in that situation. Their logic presumes certain rules for appropriate behavior and role relationships (doctor–patient, strange intruder–private person) that relate to the function of the location and its equipment as well as your purpose for being there. We could test the cultural influences on behavior by comparing what happened in a society where the doctor-patient relationship was unfamiliar or there were different rules about personal modesty.

Social psychologists need to learn a great deal about the cultural setting of behavior in order to make correct inferences about a person's actions. Otherwise, we are likely to come to ethnocentric conclusions implicitly based on standards, values, and other conditions of our own culture, as though they were universal. In years past, social psychologists have made such ethnocentric errors, positing as universal such psychological tendencies as individualistic competitiveness to excel others, masculine dominance, female submissiveness, socially destructive violence, or the profit-margin mentality simply because these were to be found in the culture or social class they studied.

Ethnocentric conclusions have practical implications as well as scientific weaknesses. It is far too easy to justify and do nothing about a state of human affairs that we label a universal tendency of the human animal or certain kinds of human beings. The practical implications are vastly different if we conclude that the tendency is contingent on specified sociocultural arrangements, which are subject to change. The only procedure that can safeguard us from errors of ethnocentrism is comparison of behaviors in widely different social contexts, such as different cultures, social classes, sex roles, and historical periods.

Because the locations of social interaction frequently embody cultural definitions of the roles and appropriate actions of individuals, research comparing interaction in different locations illustrates the ways culture permeates a brief encounter.

Physical Location as Cultural Framework: Laughing Places

We can find locations where the same behavior is evaluated quite differently without going outside of our own culture. Vidulich and Wilson (1967) selected two such locations at Louisiana State University: the library and the coffee shop in the student building. Into each, they dispatched an attractive, outgoing young woman. Her mission: to sit next to the first undergraduate she saw seated alone at a table, to start a conversation, and then to show that person selected cartoons to see whether or not she could get the student to laugh.

The young woman's actions were rehearsed and the cartoons selected well in advance. The ten cartoons were scattered through a book and had been selected because students who looked at them earlier had *not* found them amusing. Vidulich and a coworker had previously developed a rating scale for reliably classifying behavior into seven degrees of amusement, ranging from no manifestation (no movement of face muscles, facial or verbal expressions indicating "not funny") to high-intensity roars (loud sustained laughter, vigorous body movements). In each location, two raters inconspicuously observed what transpired so that they could rate reactions to the cartoons independently. Their ratings were in close agreement. Librarians had been forewarned that research was in progress since what happened would be frowned on in most libraries.

At each location the young woman entered carrying books. She started a conversation with the student in a way appropriate to the location, for example, by asking about the student's book or by asking for a match (in the coffee shop). Shortly, she introduced herself. To half of the students in each location, she was Dr. Bales of the English department (wearing faculty-type clothes) and to the rest she was Sandra Bales, an English major (wearing student apparel). After starting the conversation, she began to flip the pages of the cartoon book, laughing occasionally, and commenting that she had just borrowed the book. Then she casually showed five of the cartoons to the student, one at a time, with neutral comments such as "Look at this one" or "How about this?" She avoided acting amused at these first five cartoons, but began to laugh at the next five at an intensity classified as "medium" (clearly audible laughter and moderate bodily movements).

In all, Dr. Bales or Sandra talked to 40 male and 40 female undergraduates, who never suspected that they were being studied. The researchers' question was whether the location and/or the status of the confederate would affect the amount of amusement expressed by the students. Typically, students responded to the first five cartoons with a polite smile of the "pasted-on" variety. When the confederate began to laugh at the last five cartoons, their amusement intensity increased in all conditions, the average increase representing a change from the pasted-on smile to a "high-intensity smile with positive comment" ("that's good" or "very funny"). Only two of the students in the library laughed aloud, however, both to the higher status faculty member. Over half of the students in the coffee shop exceeded the confederate's medium-intensity laugh.

The relative impacts of the confederate's status and the location were inferred from the *difference* between each student's amusement level for the first and the last five cartoons. In each location, Dr. Bales produced about three times the change achieved by Sandra, the student. In the library, the change in amusement level was about one-half that in the coffee shop. So, if you like to leave them laughing, find a laughing place and you will have twice the effect, even with poor material. The place and your status set rules for the game that is played.

However, take caution: The merriment was produced by a young woman described as attractive, outgoing, and socially facile. You or I might bomb with such poor material. Dr. Bales and Sandra were equally successful with male and female students. Other research has shown that the sex of the researcher frequently affects the results (Stevenson and Allen, 1964; Rosenthal, 1966). For example, a high-status male often is more effective with women than another woman (which, of course, tells us something about the women who were studied). We have to conclude that the outcome of the Vidulich study was dependent on a highly personable confederate. Of course, this conclusion does not erase the impressive effects of location and status in influencing behavior, but it raises new issues.

In the two locations studied, all kinds of other activities were going on. The situations were much more complex than the descriptions suggested. How can we specify what influenced behavior in such complicated situations? Why did the students pay such attention to the confederate? Some general principles of psychological functioning will help a great deal in dealing with such questions. The next sections illustrate some of them through research on how we size up other people whom we encounter for the first time.

PAYING ATTENTION TO SOMETHING INVOLVES IGNORING SOMETHING ELSE

If everything in a social situation were equally important in affecting behavior, it would be next to impossible to make sense out of social behavior. We would always have to consider every aspect of the situation, no matter how minuscule. However, at a given time, neural processing of input from the stimulus world and from within ourselves is *selective*. What we notice, see, or hear is necessarily limited, in the first place, by our sensory and neural equipment. Within those limits, we usually notice and respond to only a fraction of what we could potentially. This is not to say that what we ignore is totally unimportant. It forms a backdrop and context for what we attend to, whether we are aware of it or not. The quiet of the library or the buzz of conversation in the coffee shop created quite different backdrops for the confederate's laughter in the Vidulich study. Unconsciously, we adjust our gestures to such contexts, for the laugh that is quite natural in the coffee shop would sound like a maniacal roar in the library.

If we can determine *what* the person is attending to in the situation, we have a much easier task in analyzing behavior. However, this problem turns out to be more easily stated than solved. Our selectivity at a given time is guided by our concerns, interests, motives, and anxieties, but it is also at the mercy of compelling events in the situation itself. Such joint determination of psychological selectivity was strikingly illustrated the one time I experienced an earthquake.

It was in Oklahoma, where earthquakes are not common. The first distant rumble was disturbing. As it grew to the roar of an approaching train, the floors began to shake, the chandelier swung about, and the furniture slid across the floor. I felt shaky, too. In one classroom at the university, class members shared the common experience, growing increasingly disturbed as the wall plaster cracked. Everyone looked around in distress, some talking, to find out what was happening and what to do. Fortunately, the quake was short. Had it lasted longer, it might have disturbed the professor, who was so absorbed in the notations he was making on the blackboard that he missed the entire event.

Selectivity for Other Persons: Personal Space

Human beings are more likely to attend to another human being than to pebbles, dust, or pieces of wood. Research has found that by the early months of life, human babies look longer at a rather poor picture of a human face than at abstract patterns that in themselves are quite as interesting. We can and certainly do ignore a lot of other people, but some of our reactions to people show this special selectivity quite well. One line of research indicating a special selectivity concerns what Robert Sommer (1969) called "personal space."

Psychologically, the boundaries of our bodies do not stop at the skin. There is space around us that, by virtue of our being within it, is *personal*. Entrance by another person into that space occurs comfortably only in certain places and situations, and with certain people;

otherwise it is viewed an an "invasion." Research has shown that there are rules governing how much personal space is deemed comfortable in different cultures and in different situations within the same culture. In some studies, South Americans appear to require less personal space than their Yankee neighbors; children exhibit less than adults; and, of course, personal space varies with relationships among persons. Sexual love involves the mutual exploration and conquest of personal space.

All of this seems perfectly natural until we realize that personal space indicates a special ·selectivity for another human being. For example, imagine yourself in the library seated alone at a table with empty chairs a few inches away on either side. Those empty chairs are no bother, right? You scarcely notice them. However, now a stranger (same sex) sits down so that your shoulders are about 12 inches apart. Would that bother you?

Felipe and Sommers (1966) studied exactly this situation and found numerous signs that the person whose space was invaded *was* bothered. Some slid to one side of their chair. Others moved their chair away. Still others turned their back on the invader or set up barriers of books and coats. Within 30 minutes, 70 percent of the persons subjected to such invasions pulled up stakes and left (as compared with about 25 percent of persons also reading alone who were joined by a stranger seated one chair away and 13 percent of persons who were left alone for 30 minutes). But, of course, we can say that no one likes to be crowded! Note, however, that readers whose space was violated crowded *themselves* even more by sliding against the chair or piling up books and belongings. Other people crowd us more than objects.

Our special selectivity for other people includes attentiveness to what they are doing—their activities and what these implicitly convey about their purposes. In another study, Sommer and Becker (1969) found that the sight of a single girl studying at an empty table in one of several small eating rooms at a popular soda fountain was sufficient to deter others from sitting at "her" table, even when the soda fountain was so crowded that they had to enter the room to have a place to drink. In comparison, "reserving" a seat by leaving objects (food or books) on the table in front of a chair was not as effective in deterring others from sitting at the same table. (The unwritten rules for privacy in such situations are quite different, of course, in other societies, where the use of available space may be taken for granted except in the most expensive restaurants.)

Personal space is a *relative* distance—relative to our personal-cultural backgrounds, to who-I-am and who-you-are, what we are doing, and where we are. It is even relative to the physical space in which we interact, as Michael White (1972) showed. In the course of orientation activities for incoming college freshmen, he arranged for short interviews to occur in either a quite large or a smaller room. Only one chair was in place, near the middle of the room, so that the student had to carry a chair placed against the wall to be seated for the interview. By taking advantage of the square room tiles and the student's seated position, White was able to estimate the distance between the student and the interviewer quite accurately, without arousing the student's suspicion that where he sat was of any interest. He found that the students sat closer to the interviewer in the large room—where more space was available—than in the small room. (Women students also sat closer than male students, whether the interviewer was male or female.)

FIRST IMPRESSIONS OF STRANGERS

How do we size up another person who becomes focal to our attention? How does that person form an impression of us? Popular books and articles on personal encounters are full of advice about how to present ourselves so that we, too, can "win friends and influence people." Often the advice is sound enough, in that researchers who have bothered to test it have found that, yes, we tend to like others who seem to like us, who have something in common with us, who are warm, and who agree with our important beliefs. We do not like as well others who are unlike us in important respects, who appear to ingratiate themselves to gain some private end, or who appear interested in order to manipulate our behavior, and so forth (see Huston, 1974, for a review of the copious research supporting these conclusions).

How a person acts and treats us do count in forming impressions, but seldom if ever do we wait for the evidence to roll in, suspend judgment, and keep an open mind about the other person. We form impressions in brief encounters on the basis of very little evidence. We come to such encounters with a rich store of classifications just waiting to hold individuals whom we meet—many of them social categories defined in our society (man-woman, young-middle aged-old, rich-poor, doctor-lawyer-merchant-chief, a girl I could marry-a good lay, black-white, and so on).

We have pretty clear-cut notions of what personal characteristics go with each category, what personal qualities are prized, and what kind we like. Such notions reflect our culture and our viewpoint from the particular niche we occupy or wish we occupied—as well as personal experiences, worries, and longings. The framework of pigeonholes affects how we approach others, what we expect of them, how much and what kind of contact we want from the start. The particular pigeonhole also shapes the kind of motives, intentions, and purposes we attribute to others. It is the lack or inaccuracy of such pigeonholes that makes a little child's reactions to strangers so refreshing, once initial shyness is overcome. (A 3-year-old at a day-care center where our 17-year-old daughter, Ann, was a "teacher," learned that I was Ann's "mother" and asked her, "Are you a little girl?")

Stress on the importance of social classifications for first impressions of strangers runs counter to prevailing ideologies that urge the importance of reacting to others on strictly *human* terms and not jumping to conclusions. However, stating such beliefs and studying what happens when people meet are two different activities. Do you react to a male and a female in the same way? Can you honestly say that you ignore a person's age, skin color, accent, or dress?

I believe that it is possible for a person to be aware of the constricting influence of social categories on response to others and to alter his or her own conceptions to include "humanity" in each. But I can find no research evidence suggesting that it is possible to react to a stranger using no categories at all. In fact, demonstrations on college campuses of reactions to a human being completely ensconced in a black bag indicate that it is difficult to interact at all when the other person does not "fit" any place or is, at best, simply "person in a bag."

When we interact with a stranger for more than a minute, we have an itch to place the person, probably all the more so if that person has some attractive qualities. (Is she married? Does he have a good job?) My husband has a collection of anecdotes about efforts to place him. He's a good candidate because, besides being attractive, he speaks English with an accent that few Americans can identify (there aren't that many Turks here) and he could be one of several nationalities. His favorite anecdote is about the time we went to a high school where most of the students were Navaho. I was giving a questionnaire to students and he assisted in distributing forms and answering questions. At the close of one session, seven or eight pretty young women hung around my table giggling and finally got up nerve to ask me: "That man who's helping you: what tribe is he?" (When I told him about the incident, he was elated: "Good, they like me." The important categories for the students were being native American or not, and they had placed him into their preferred one.) They also had preferred tribes, so I said he had no tribe. I don't think they believed me.

The effects of social categorization on impressions of persons belonging to different ethnic and national groups have been widely studied, as we shall see in Chapter 10. Probably to the detriment of a general theory on how we form impressions of others and come to attribute motives and purposes to them, that research on "group stereotypes" has seldom been linked to research on reactions to people belonging to other social classifications. To the prejudiced white person, for example, the designation of a person as black affects appraisals of the person's industry, honesty, aggressiveness, sexuality, and other traits contained in the racist stereotypes for blacks. Such attribution by the white person depends only on classification as "Negro," as shown by Secord (1959). Photographs of black faces were selected to vary greatly with respect to how negroid their features were (for example, skin color, facial features, hair). Despite these differences, white raters (especially those who were more prejudiced) assigned racist stereotypes about equally to each picture.

Such blanket reaction to individuals in a social category is by no means confined to racism. For example, being female is linked to a variety of stereotypes, including excessive emotionality, lack of aggressiveness, and less competence in certain respects. Goldberg (1968) reported that identical written passages were evaluated lower when attributed to a woman (Joan X) than to a man (John X), and the raters were college *women*. In another study, the technical skills of the artist who had entered abstract paintings in a contest were rated higher when the artist was designated as male than as female. The male artist was also voted more likely to succeed, which perhaps contains a grain of realism in this nonabstract world where merit is not the sole criterion of success (Pheterson, Kiesler, and Goldberg, 1971).

There is also a curious inverse relationship in many people's minds between feminine beauty and intelligence, as a beautiful actress turned businesswoman complained in a recent magazine article. Her beauty, she found, had its handicaps because most people assume that a beautiful woman is stupid. The converse is also widely entertained: Matina Horner (1970) found that college students who were asked to tell a story about a woman who achieved first rank in her class at medical school frequently went to great pains to describe the woman as homely, excessively tall, or ungainly.

Now for the point of this discussion: How we appraise or "define" a situation is always a selective process. For a variety of reasons, we are keenly tuned to notice other people. How we size up the individuals, however, is also guided by what we bring to the situation, particularly social classifications into which we place them with the accompanying preconceptions about "what kind of people" fit into each. In fact, what we notice about others may tell almost as much about ourselves as it does about them.

Whatever we do notice or emphasize, whether from our preconceptions or in their behavior, affects our subsequent reactions to the person. Such selectively chosen characteristics become *anchors* that stabilize our impression of the person. As an anchor limits a boat's movement by wind or tide, such key characteristics affect the processing of additional information about the person.

Anchor Effects on Impressions of Strangers

Harold Kelley (1950) demonstrated the effect of an important personal characteristic in anchoring reactions to an instructor in a college classroom. His naturalistic experiment was based on earlier research by

Solomon Asch that had shown personal "warmth" or "coldness" to be regarded as a salient quality in social interaction.

Students in several sections of a psychology course were informed that they would have a guest instructor and would be asked to evaluate his performance for the university. In order that the instructor not get wind of this evaluation, students were asked not to discuss the matter. This caution permitted Kelley to distribute two different sets of introductory information randomly among the students. Each described the instructor's background and qualifications, including the information that he was regarded as industrious, critical, and determined. However, in one set, these last adjectives were preceded by the word "warm," and the other set substituted the phrase "rather cold."

The instructor entered and led a 20-minute discussion. After he left, each student rated him on 15 rating scales. Each scale allowed one of several possible ratings between extremes—for example, from "knows his stuff" to "doesn't know his stuff," "informal" to "formal," "good natured" to "irritable." Unknown to the students, during the discussion, a tally was kept of the frequency of their participations in the discussion, according to whether they had received the information that the instructor was "warm" or "cold."

During the class discussion, there was a tendency for more students who had been informed that the instructor was "warm" to participate (56 percent of them) than those told that he was "cold" (32 percent). The difference is statistically significant at a level often considered borderline in reliability, in the sense that repetitions of the experiment could by chance alone yield smaller differences in about 10 out of 100 repetitions. However, the differences in the students' ratings of the "warm" and "cold" instructor were in line with this difference in their frequency of participation and were highly reliable.

The "warm" instructor tended to receive higher ratings on all 15 rating scales, as one might expect if the "warm" trait acted like a halo radiating on all other qualities. However, for a number of the 15 traits, the differences between ratings of the "warm" and "cold" instructor were not large or statistically reliable. For example, each was rated about the same on how much he "knew his stuff," intelligence, and probable success as a psychologist. Those qualities that were rated significantly higher for the warm than the cold instructor were qualities that, in earlier research, had been found related to the warm-cold variable. They included being more considerate, more informal, more sociable, more popular, better natured, humorous, and humane.

Didn't the way the instructor actually behaved have any effect on these ratings? Kelley had two instructors, each of whom was identified as warm and cold to different students, but instructed to behave as nearly the same as possible in every class. The differences between ratings of "warm" and "cold" teachers were obtained for both instructors; however, they were more marked for one role player than the other, suggesting that yes, indeed, actual behavior did make a difference. The 20-minute episode was a brief encounter, and a longer time might have emphasized the difference.

The effect of the warm or cold anchor in Kelley's experiment is an *assimilation* effect, that is, evaluation of other traits were assimilated *toward* the anchor. The warm anchor pulled other judgments up to be more favorable and the cold anchor pulled them down toward more unfavorable ratings. Such assimilation effects are also frequently found in laboratory research in which a person is given successive bits of information about an unknown personality. If the first information presented concerns salient personal characteristics, these first impressions tend to anchor the processing of subsequent information about the person (the so-called primacy effect). Any further information that speeds the formation of a category describing "what kind of a critter" this stranger is or that strengthens the person's confidence in his ratings increases the anchoring effect of such first impressions. Subsequent information is assimilated toward it or, if it concerns less important characteristics, is discounted or ignored (Jones and Goethals, 1971).

However, the assimilation effect of an anchor is not absolute: It is dependent on new information coming in that is not *too* discrepant from the anchor. The tendency to assimilate new information into the existing category for the person as "warm" begins to break down when, for example, an instructor rudely cuts off a student's remarks or shows indifference to a student's discomfiture. The more discrepant from the anchor such new information becomes, the more it is subject to another effect—namely, *contrast* or the exaggeration of differences. Owing to its larger discrepancy from the anchor *(warm)*, the new information is assessed as *more* divergent than it might be under other circumstances. Thus, the cutting instructor might be regarded as extremely abrupt for a relatively moderate action simply because the anchor being used to assess him was "warm." The same cutting remark by a "cold" instructor may be judged as less extreme.

Such assimilation-contrast effects arising from the relation between an anchor or standard used in sizing up persons, events, or other social objects were studied systematically by Sherif and Hovland (1961). A recent review of the research on forming impressions of strangers indicates that assimilation-contrast also accounts for the effects of the order in which information about another person is received on our impression of that person (Jones and Goethals, 1971). The first information tends to anchor the assessment of later information, resulting in its assimilation toward the first information. This early anchor also produces a contrast effect for new information that deviates from it too greatly. But repeated information that is discrepant from that anchor may weaken the anchor. A new anchor is formed based on the more recent information (recency effect). Such a sequence of contrast effects, followed by a new anchor, is summed up in folk wisdom about the wrath directed to a lover or friend who betrays through actions that might seem minor transgressions in one whose image had not once glowed so radiantly. However, in a brief encounter, there is seldom time for such dramatic changes to occur.

When we size up other persons, we inevitably make comparisons between them and someone else. George Bernard Shaw defined masculine romantic love as the gross exaggeration of the differences between one woman and others. The characteristics of the loved one are taken as standard (anchor), even slight differences in others are displaced and seen as more different than they are (contrast). Such variations in love or hate relationships are usually attributed to emotional intensity (love is blind). It is important to emphasize that the assimilation-contrast effects are not *caused* by such emotions, even though personal investment strengthens the potency of the anchor. They are a result of comparing things (here, personal characteristics) that differ in varying degree from whatever we have chosen as a standard. The anchoring effect of the standard is such that small differences tend to be assimilated toward it and larger differences exaggerated (contrasted). These systematic displacements occur in comparisons that are no more emotionally arousing than lifted weights, sound frequencies, or colors (Sherif and Hovland, 1961; Helson, 1964).

A good example of contrast effects in sizing up persons is a study of clinical judgment, in which the task was to rate how disturbed or normal a person seemed on the basis of a description of the person's behavior (Bieri, Orcutt, and Leaman, 1963). Three descriptions were presented for judgment each time, a description composed of symptoms for "moderate" pathology being preceded by two other descriptions. The two preceding descriptions were composed of symptoms of "severe" pathology or were relatively symptom free. In this study, judgments of how pathological the "moderate" case was depended on whether the two cases that preceded it were low or high in pathology. When preceded by severe cases, the moderate case was seen as less pathological. When preceded by low cases, the moderate case was seen as higher in pathology. In both cases, the differences from the preceding cases were exaggerated, which is a contrast effect.

THE ACTION AFFECTS WHAT WE NOTICE ABOUT OTHERS

What people are doing, the purposes of the activity, and the demands of the problems at hand are quite as much a part of the social situation as its location and the social-personal characteristics of those present. We can appreciate their importance in affecting our own behavior

when an individual does something out of line with activity in progress—for example, falls asleep at a party, starts doing push-ups during
a class discussion, or stops to watch birds during a tennis match.
Conversely, our expectations of others are so closely tied to what we
consider their customary activities and problems that we may be unable to imagine them doing anything else. Each of my daughters has
gone through a process of reconciling the mother they know at home
with that mother at work. As a teenager, one of them exclaimed: "I
know what you do but I just can't *imagine you teaching.*"

Activities and problems at hand have their own structures, which
place certain demands on the individual—a fact that we shall make
much of in later contexts. Along with the location and other persons
participating, activities also engender expectations for self and others.
Take, for example, the traditional medium for unmarried males and
females to become acquainted—the date. What expectations does a
date engender? Of course, expectations will vary depending on the
specific activity, whether a dance or a ball game. Expectations for
heterosexual meetings are also changing as the "date" becomes a
historic institution scorned by some youth. Nevertheless, research on
what personal characteristics make a first date attractive to the partner
can tell us quite a bit about the expectations that such an event
engenders.

At the University of Minnesota, Walster, Aronson, Abrahams, and
Rottman (1966) had the opportunity to study the reactions of 752
freshmen who signed up for blind dates supposedly matched by computer but actually paired on a random basis. The university files were
full of information on the students' grade records, achievement tests,
and several personality tests from a state-wide testing program. Each
student filled in a questionnaire when applying for a date, rating his or
her own self-esteem, popularity, and other personal concepts. When
the student came to pick up a ticket for the dance, several college
sophomores rated him or her for physical attractiveness. (Incidentally,
their ratings did not agree very closely, suggesting that beauty is partly
in the eyes of the beholder. Their average rating for each student was
used in analyzing the data.) At the dance itself, everyone took time out
at intermission to rate his or her own partner on physical attractiveness
and as to how much the partner was liked.

Whether the date was a success in school, regarded self as popular,
was high or low in self-esteem, got scores indicating high social skills,
introversion, or extroversion had almost no relationship to how much
he or she was liked. What was related to how much one's date was
liked was physical attractiveness, as rated by the sophomores. When
the person's own rating of his or her partner's attractiveness was used
as the criterion, the partner's attractiveness was even more highly
correlated with how much the partner was liked.

Taken alone, these findings may indicate merely that beautiful people are always liked better on a date; however, later research by some of the same investigators suggests that such a conclusion is oversimplified (Bercheid, Dion, Walster, and Walster, 1971). What is not at all obvious is that the high relationship between physical attractiveness and liking for a date reflects expectations about the dating game itself.

Byrne, Ervin, and Lamberth (1970) set up an experiment comparing a computer dating situation with a laboratory study in which students judged verbal descriptions of "evaluations of strangers." Students' expectations for the computer dating situation were revealed before the research got seriously under way. The investigators had intended to assign students randomly to participate either in the dating situation or the laboratory study. However, word about the computer dating started through the campus grapevine. Students came to participate dressed much more attractively than for an ordinary academic activity, wafting unmistakable odors of perfume and shaving lotion. (The researchers went ahead with the dating study, but had to wait until later in the year when the excitement had died down to study the evaluation of strangers.)

Their findings support the notion that the students' expectations for a computer date were different than for a laboratory experiment on evaluating strangers and, furthermore, that the activity of dating was associated with fairly specific expectations. In the first place, ratings of strangers described in the laboratory were consistently lower than ratings of dates, even though the actual date consisted only of half an hour visit over a soft drink. In addition, the dates rated each other higher than strangers in a variety of respects that the half hour contact scarcely allowed time to explore, such as knowledge of current events, personal adjustment, and desirability as a marriage partner.

In the dating situation, how much the date was liked was not closely related to ratings of physical attractiveness made by the male researchers (who apparently did pretty well in rating the attractiveness of female students but poorly on male students!). However, when each participant's rating of his or her date's attractiveness was correlated with how favorably the date was evaluated, there was a substantial relationship. This could mean that we simply regard a date as more attractive if we like the person or vice versa; but the results suggest that the matter is not that simple.

The highest correlation was between how the participant rated the date's physical attractiveness and sexual attractiveness, both of which were correlated with how much the date was liked. Relationships between physical attractiveness and how desirable the date was for a future meeting or for possible marriage were lower. These findings are not surprising if we assume that blind dating has something to do with sexual anticipation and that physical attractiveness has something to do with immediate sexual turn-on. Such expectations are apparently pretty specific to the date situation, as they do not necessarily lead to wanting to date the person again and are even less likely to point immediately to possibilities of marriage.

This interpretation of the dating results is supported by an additional finding by Byrne and his coworkers. Overall, they found that when a student had reason to believe that the date was similar to himself or herself, the date was liked more than when the student had been led to believe that the date was dissimilar in several personal characteristics. But in the computer dating situation, sexual attraction to the partner was rated higher when the student believed the date was quite dissimilar. Since sexual attraction and liking were the most closely related variables, the findings suggest that, at least for a blind date, variety is the spice of life.

When Beauty Is More Than Skin Deep

Physical attraction and sexual titillation may be the best and most to hope for on a blind date. Surely, however, there are circumstances when acceptance by another person is more important than appearance. Sara Kiesler and Roberta Baral (1970) reasoned thus and set out to test the hypothesis that blows to self-esteem can make a man more eager for the company of a companionable but less attractive woman than of an equally friendly beauty. Undergraduate and graduate student males, all single, agreed to participate in an effort to standardize a new intelligence test that had, it was said, already shown its accuracy in predicting success in life. To half of the students, a male experimenter commented approvingly at their responses on the test, comparing them favorably with results he had already obtained. For the other half, he frowned frequently, making unfavorable comparisons and asking the student if he felt "relaxed enough" to take the test. As the test had several parts, the experimenter stopped between parts to get a cup of coffee, inviting the student along.

In the coffee room, the two men encountered a young woman introduced as the experimenter's assistant. When the experimenter left to make a phone call, the student and woman remained at the table, but were rejoined shortly by the experimenter, who said that he had to discontinue the research session as his car was needed at home.

The behavior of interest was the student's romantic intentions to the woman after the experimenter left—namely, the frequency of such actions as offering refreshments, asking for her phone number, complimenting her, ignoring her remarks that she had to leave, or asking to meet her again. In half of the cases, the lovely young woman wore heavy glasses, no makeup, pulled her hair back tightly with a rubber band, and wore a sloppy outfit of clashing colors and designs. For the other half, she was suitably dressed and at her best. The issue at hand was whether the men who had just suffered a blow to self-esteem on the test and the men who had been approved by the experimenter would pay equal court to the girl at her worst and at her best.

The men who had succeeded on the test were definitely more attentive to the girl at her best than at her worst. Those with drooping egos, however, were much more likely to compliment and court the sloppy girl. Possibly the slings and arrows of outrageous fortune made them less willing to run the risk of refusal that similar attention to the bandbox beauty might have entailed. Since the two girls who alternated in both roles did not know whether a man had succeeded or failed on the test, it is unlikely that their treatment of the men differed sufficiently to account for the men's reactions. Apparently the physical attributes of another person are sized up relative to the possibilities of a relationship between ourselves and that person. There is comfort in finding that "friendly, accepting, and interested" behavior at a time when another person feels low is appreciated even when it comes from an unlikely candidate for Ms. or Mr. Universe.

The real moral of the story, however, is that it is nearly impossible to predict how a person will behave in a social situation solely on the basis of the physical characteristics of other persons. The place where interaction occurs, the expectations the participants bring to the situation, and their activities form a pattern or structure that shapes the individual's behavior.

SOCIAL SITUATIONS AS PROBLEMS FOR THE INDIVIDUAL

Social life is so organized that an individual passes in and out of different and fairly complicated social situations in a routine fashion much of the time, particularly if cultural expectations for behavior are rather clear-cut and shared by the participants. When any of these constituents break down, become uncertain or conflicting, the individual faces a problem as to how to act.

How does a person tackle a social situation that poses a problem through ambiguity or lack of clear guidelines? It is psychologically unsettling to face such a situation. There is a tendency toward psychological structuring, even when the world "out there" is not very clear-cut. This tendency for the person to try to define a situation clearly even when the situation itself is not clear-cut is particularly impelling when something in the situation commands action of some kind, for example, another person apparently in need of help. Two general kinds of such situations have been studied: situations in which an emergency threatens a person's welfare and situations in which a person interrupts another's daily routine to ask for assistance to achieve some end of his or her own. The research is particularly interesting since cultural expectations are strong that help should be rendered in such situations. Therefore, if a person does not come to the assistance of another, we are likely to attribute inaction to deliberate flaunting of the cultural value, moral callousness, apathy, or some combination of personal deficiencies. However, the research shows very clearly that such need not be the case.

Help!

We owe to Latané and Darley (1969) the analysis of emergencies in which another person faces sudden and unexpected threat; they became concerned with the problem after reading newspaper reports of dangers or attacks to persons in large cities that were witnessed by bystanders who made no move to offer aid or assistance. One such report concerned the murder of a young woman late at night in full view of neighbors wakened by her cries and watching from their apartment windows. Journalists and readers were prone to attribute the tragic inaction to apathy or alienation from the plight of one's fellow human beings promoted by big-city life. These two social psychologists, however, wondered whether or not the causes of inaction might be rooted in the immediate *conditions* of city life in which such emergencies are encountered, rather than in the apathy or indifference of the onlookers.

Latané and Darley noted that such an emergency is sudden, unexpected, and ambiguous in several ways, especially at night. Amid the clamor and furious activity of city life, there is a problem in even recognizing an emergency unless the victim can cry for help. The event must be powerful enough to seize the bystander's selectivity before there can be any question of helping or not. Once the person has noticed the emergency, however, there is immediately a problem of interpreting what the emergency is all about. (A person who stumbles and falls in a diabetic coma is not immediately distinguishable from one in an alcoholic coma.)

In their research, Latané and Darley circumvented initial steps by ensuring that the emergencies they simulated could not be overlooked. They did not simulate all of the conditions in urban life in which individuals might encounter emergencies, notably the actual threat posed to potential helpers by an attacker or the fear of consequences in reporting the event to police (such as being accused of false report, facing possible revenge by the perpetrators, or long court proceedings). What Latané and Darley did do was to show very clearly that when an emergency situation outside of the customary routine is highly unstructured in that several interpretations of the event are feasible, the individual is prone to attend to the behavior of other persons in dealing with the problem of how to react.

Their main hypothesis was that in an emergency situation, the presence of inactive bystanders inhibits the tendency to respond with assistance, this decrease in assistance becoming more frequent as the number of inactive bystanders increases. Since subsequent research has indicated that this hypothesis holds only under certain conditions, it is important to examine with some care the situations they studied. As we shall see, the situations had in common a relatively high degree of ambiguity with respect to interpretation of the emergency.

In the experiments, the participants were voluntarily serving as subjects in research ostensibly concerned with other purposes, such as evaluating games for a market survey or "life in an urban university." Incidents were created in the midst of their research activities. For example, in one study, a female assistant in the next room was heard to cry out and moan in pain following a loud crash. In another, subjects hooked into an intercommunication system heard one of their number apparently undergoing an epileptic attack.

In assessing the findings, it is important to note that post-experimental interviews revealed that the situations allowed the conclusion by participants that the incident was deliberately introduced to test their reactions or, even more frequently, that the researcher was in command of the situation and probably would respond appropriately to render assistance to the distressed person. Most participants in laboratory research assume that personal safety is guaranteed by the researcher. Their interview results illustrate why social psychology has to be concerned about the person's immediate experience as well as his behavior in interpreting research findings. This personal experience involved conceptual functioning at a fairly complex, problem-solving level, such as forming hypotheses about what was happening and why.

Overall, individuals who faced the emergencies alone typically attempted to render some kind of assistance (70 to 100 percent of them depending on the particular emergency situation). On the other hand, when passive bystanders who had been instructed not to offer help were present, significantly fewer naive bystanders offered help (only about one-third did). There was a tendency for this inaction to be more frequent as the number of passive bystanders increased. Those who rendered no assistance usually said afterward that they were unsure what was happening, but had decided that the situation was not very serious, that their assistance might embarrass the victim, or that someone else would render help.

In these ambiguous problem situations, the heightened influence of others' behavior (inaction or action) was revealed in still another experimental variation. Two naive strangers, who were not instructed as to how to respond, encountered an emergency. In about 40 percent of the pairs one of the two offered help. However, two friends, also uninstructed, offered assistance almost as frequently as individuals facing the problem alone (70 percent of the pairs). The difference between strangers and friends is correlated with the finding that there was more conversation between friends. The established flow of inter-action between the individuals afforded opportunity for quick defini-tion of the emergency that was not readily present between strangers, namely, ascertaining that neither party knew what was going on nor had great confidence that the situation was not dangerous.

While the Latané-Darley research has been interpreted as an exam-ple of the "diffusion of responsibility" among bystanders (the "let George do it" idea), their findings are most parsimoniously understood as examples of the heightened effect of others' behavior (inaction or action) in defining an unstructured problem situation. This interpreta-tion also squares better with subsequent findings in which the problem situation was *less* ambiguous and the number of inactive bystanders had no appreciable relationship to whether or not help was offered.

Clark and Word (1972), for example, studied the reactions of Florida State University students to the sounds of a falling ladder, a venetian blind, and the body of a maintenance worker whom students had seen enter an adjacent room to begin work. In one condition, the worker called for help and groaned. In another condition, the worker made no sounds. Whereas all students responded to the first situation, the worker received help in only 20 to 40 percent of the cases when he made no sound, an event that was frequently interpreted by the stu-dents as not serious ("maybe he dropped his equipment"). Further-more, in the latter situation, the presence of others reduced the likeli-hood that the individual would respond. An ambiguous situation heightens the effect of others' behavior, whether that behavior is to act or not to act.

A Terrible Thing Happened in the Subway . . .

In contrast to the situations studied by Latané and Darley, a subway car in a large city is a "closed" situation. While the train is in transit, no immediate escape or outside assistance is possible. Suppose that you are on your way downtown when, suddenly, a fellow passenger falls to the floor and lies there on his back.

For adjacent passengers, such an emergency is certainly a problem and only they can render assistance. Piliavin, Rodin, and Piliavin (1969) showed that in the New York subway such a victim usually did receive assistance, the likelihood of assistance bearing no relation to the number of bystanders present. However, their research indicates another source of ambiguity in emergencies. This ambiguity concerns the causes of the emergency and the possible consequences of offering assistance.

Teams of Columbia University students enacted the scenario and systematically observed reactions on a long subway run. Repeatedly, the students boarded the train as individual passengers, one of them stopping at a central location. This person sometimes walked with a cane. On other trains, the central character carried a bottle tightly wrapped in a brown bag and exuded a heavy odor of liquor. In any event, after the train started, the victim fell to the floor, remaining on his back. Since the research plan was not completed (owing to a strike of Columbia students that occupied the student assistants and the reluctance of some assistants to play a drunk), I will report only the main findings.

In the closed subway car, the apparent invalid with the cane received help on 95 percent of the trips. The drunk, as you might expect, received spontaneous help less frequently (about half of the trips). The sensitivity to behavior of others could only appear, of course, in the case of the drunk where there is some issue about how much help the victim "deserves," how he *can* be helped, or about the consequences of helping. In this case, such sensitivity was found: Just one other person offering help (an instructed model) increased the frequency of aid to the drunk (over 70 percent of the trials). The riders on the train were about half male and half female, but helpers were more frequently male than would be expected by chance. This finding is not surprising at all: The victims were male and the problems facing a female helper in actually giving help and dealing with possible consequences are quite different.

A later study by Piliavin and Piliavin (1972) in Philadelphia subways generally supports the proposition that definition of what help is appropriate and the consequences of helping complicate the situation. The plan of this study was similar to that in New York, so that findings could be compared with the case of the drunk and the invalid in New York. In this case, however, the man with the cane collapsed on half of the trials, and on the other half he also (apparently) bled from the mouth. Apparently the Piliavins did not anticipate that the release of food-dyed contents from an eye dropper secreted in the victim's mouth would arouse such a stir as it did. They reported reactions to the sight of "blood" that included attempts to pull the train's emergency cord and "impending panic" among passengers. (They noted that their procedures were "harrassed" by subway attendants and police. To the latter, the harrassment may have seemed the other way around. I leave it to you to decide whether or not the limits of research realism were exceeded since, as I stated in Chapter 1, I believe such matters are not the exclusive concern of researchers.)

The victim with the cane was given assistance almost invariably, whether he "bled" or not. The frequency of "indirect" help plus "no help" was significantly greater with the bloody victim, but numbers were too small to conclude that assistance of some kind was more likely in one condition than the other.

The finding of importance here was that decisions about helping caused a delay in helping the bleeding victim. Within 70 seconds after he fell, the victim with the cane was helped in approximately 90 percent of the trials, but only a little over half of the bleeders and 20 percent of the drunks (in New York) were helped in the same time span. Delays in helping the bleeder and the drunk (which were even longer than 70 seconds for an additional 30 percent exposed to each) are indicative of the uncertainty experienced by the onlooker. It is precisely under such circumstances that the behavior of others is most effective in reaching a decision to act or not to act, with the risk of appearing apathetic, callous, or unconcerned.

The practical implications of the analysis of helping in emergencies are great. On the one hand, apathy and indifference can be countered only indirectly, by appeals to moral values, humanity, and the like. On the other hand, this analysis would suggest that the best ways to guarantee bystander assistance in emergencies are by providing quick means to assess the need for help and possible resources, providing role models for effective action, and reducing fear of possible consequences. Needless to say, none of these is easy to come by in modern urban life but at least implementation is possible.

Please!

A simple request for information or another small service by a stranger is responded to quite differently from the cry for help in an emergency. In fact, the giving of help appears to be so frequent under ordinary circumstances that it surprises many people. For example, in 1972 students in the psychology honors seminar that I was teaching wanted to do a field experiment. Through interviews with students they determined that a widely shared view of the university was of a large, impersonal institution where even students would not go out of their way to help one another. We devised a research plan in which pairs of students posed as visitors and requested directions to distant points on the campus from students of the same or opposite sex and at different locations. To their great surprise, the response was overwhelmingly helpful, even to drawing maps on request and taking the visitors to the distant location. My point is that much of the impression about how unfriendly or unhelpful strangers are stems from failure to request help rather than actual experience in being refused.

Harvey Allen (1972) studied requests for help on the New York subways by having a pre-instructed bystander give erroneous directions, so that the innocent bystander who wanted to help had to "go out of his way" by contradicting that fellow passenger. For example, he addressed several fellow passengers "at large," asking if the train on which they were all riding was headed downtown. His pre-instructed confederate immediately answered that yes, it was, despite the fact that the train was going uptown. Would other bystanders intervene to correct the error? Only in somewhat over half of the cases. Why? Well, it was at least possible that the remark was not addressed to oneself and that contradicting the misinformer would lead to some difficulty.

Allen checked out the first possibility by addressing his inquiry directly to one bystander and having the confederate blurt out his erroneous reply before the bystander had a chance to answer. In this case, 93 percent of the bystanders who had been addressed directly corrected the error ("No, it's going uptown").

The possibility that contradicting a misinformer might lead to difficulty was checked in another series of trials. This time the request was put to both an innocent bystander and the misinformer at the same time. The misinformer answered quickly and erroneously to each case, but on some of the trials he behaved in a mild manner or displayed uncertainty while answering. In the other trials, he had already established himself as either a pugnacious or noisily sarcastic individual by his behavior to fellow passengers. When this disagreeable fellow gave wrong information, only about one-third of the bystanders who had also been addressed dared to correct him. On the other hand, 84 percent of the bystanders corrected the errors of the mild or uncertain misinformer.

Allen's research points to another important source of possible ambiguity in a social situation, namely, the question of *who* among a gathering of individuals is expected to respond. This issue is particularly problematic if everyone present appears to be "equal." In one experiment (Levy, Lundgren, Ansel, Fell, Fink, and McGrath, 1972), students were participating in a study on mathematics when a stranger appeared and made a variety of requests. If the student was alone at the time, the stranger was responded to more quickly than when the student was working with others instructed beforehand not to respond to or to express opinions about the request. The authors suggest that the implicit "equality" of research subjects made the question of taking the initiative to respond to an outsider highly problematic. As a teacher, I have observed the same phenomenon in early meetings of very large classes. Conversely, the differentiation of persons according to their status and roles in life serves to reduce the ambiguity of whether or not to act in a variety of situations, even among strangers.

As in the study of emergencies, it is apparent that when a social situation lacks structure in some important respect, we are particularly prone to be influenced by others. Their *failure* to act can affect us quite as much as their positive actions or their attempts to persuade us to behave in a certain way.

IF OTHERS DIFFER FROM US, DO WE DO AS
WE WOULD HAVE THEM DO UNTO US?

Although the data were incomplete, the study in the New York subway suggested that, especially when the effectiveness and consequences of help were questionable (the drunk), help was given more often to a victim who was readily identifiable as belonging to the same social group—in that case the same race. A similar implication in a nonemergency situation was found by Bryan and Test (1967). White shoppers more frequently put money in a Salvation Army kettle for a white solicitor than a black solicitor.

Gaertner and Bickman (1972) made over a thousand phone calls to investigate whether people do a bit better for persons of their own race who request help than for persons of another racial group. Males speaking in either "standard" or "black" English called numbers located in segregated black or white sections of Brooklyn. In each area, the caller pretended to have reached a wrong number while trying to get his auto mechanic to come to his aid on the highway, where his car had broken down. Stating that he had used his last coin, the caller asked the telephone respondent to call his mechanic for him, giving a number that reached the researchers.

In the different classifications according to the sex and race of the caller and respondent, the proportions actually making the phone call ranged from approximately one-half to nearly three-fourths. Men in both races placed significantly more calls than women. White respondents more frequently helped white motorists than black motorists. However, black men and women called the garage with about equal frequency for white or black callers. So the answer to the question of whether we do unto others as we would have them do unto us depends on how the person defines "we." Some white men and women defined "we" in a way that excluded helping blacks. Black men and women defined "we" in a way that, in this situation, included whites.

A study by Feldman (1968) bears on the definitions of "we" in terms of nationality. Feldman studied responses to requests for help by foreign and compatriot couples in Boston, Paris, and Athens. The effort required interaction with over 3000 persons in these cities, following definite rules about which individual to pick (for example, every fourth person who walks toward you on a crowded city street) and a definite scenario for the interaction.

In five experiments, the situations varied considerably. Some required the tourists to make a direct request for assistance to a passerby, for example, asking directions to a well-known location in the city or asking that a stranger mail a letter (with or without a stamp) on the grounds that they had to wait for a friend. Other situations involved a native in an occupational role who was given the opportunity to assist or cheat the tourists—for example, by returning or keeping overpayment on a purchase, by driving a taxi directly to a requested location for proper fare or by taking a longer route, overcharging, or otherwise taking advantage of the tourists' ignorance. An American couple served as tourists in all three cities, a French couple served as foreign tourists in Boston, and native couples played native tourists in France and Greece.

Feldman's primary questions concerned whether differential treatment would be given native tourists and foreign tourists in the three cultures. The results indicated that the answers depended very much on whether the encounter was among passers-by on the street or involved occupational-customer roles. In the latter case, there was less differential treatment according to whether the customers were native or foreign. In those situations where occupational expectations were not operative, however, differential treatment of natives and foreigners occurred approximately half of the time, typically to the disadvantage of the foreign visitor. A notable exception occurred in Greece. In general, Greeks treated the American couple with more helpfulness than they treated their compatriots, a finding that may be traceable to the Greek cultural norms governing hospitality. According to Feldman and Harry Triandis (a social psychologist of Greek origin), any guest in Greece is regarded and treated as within the hospitality circle ordinarily reserved for family members and their close friends. Foreign visitors are defined as guests, therefore within the "we" of hospitality. Strange fellow-Greeks are not, hence were not helped as often. More recently, Americans in Greece have discovered that they are unwanted "guests."

The cultural frameworks quite clearly affected the definitions of the several situations in which assistance was requested. For example, Bostonians were extremely helpful to foreigners asking directions, giving correct instructions over 80 percent of the time, as they also did for fellow Americans. Parisians, on the other hand, gave correct directions to foreigners less frequently but were more helpful than Bostonians in agreeing to mail a letter. Everywhere, the kind of activity called for by the request for help and the extent to which the options were clearly defined by cultural or occupational norms affected the frequency of helping.

GETTING IT TOGETHER

The research in this chapter has concerned interaction in brief encounters, most of it among strangers. It was chosen selectively from a great bulk of research on brief encounters and interaction among strangers. Most of it was naturalistic as far as the participants were concerned. What is the upshot and where does it lead us?

First, the research has shown how complex even a brief episode of interaction is. Our focus in social psychology is on individual experience and behavior. In order to understand it, we have to consider the characteristics of *other persons present,* but also how they behave and their actual or potential relationships to the individual. But that is not enough: The location of the interaction and its facilities with their unspoken connotations and the *activities* under way or the *problem* posed by the situation have to be studied in their own right, for they, too, provide the frameworks for individual action. Together, the location, the activities or problem, and other participants form a pattern of which the individual becomes a part when he or she enters the situation. The relationship of the individual to the patterned context of the social situation depends on his or her past experiences, the ingredients of the immediate situation, and future implications of acting or not acting that the human participant may forecast.

Second, since even a brief interaction situation is complex, we are desperately in need of guidelines to orient our study of more complicated problems in social psychology. Such orientation has been embedded in this chapter. It bears repetition and summary because it will be useful in chapters to come.

Individual behavior is always affected both by the characteristics of the social situation in which the person participates and by what that person brings into the situation (including past experiences, ideas, beliefs, motives, temporary moods, or feelings). These inputs are processed *selectively,* for the human organism is not able to attend equitably to them all at any given time. Therefore, at a given time some aspects of the situation itself and of the person are more salient than others.

One advantage of specifying the salient anchors in the situation is that they have certain predictable consequences for the way in which the person sizes up the situation and reacts to it. For example, earlier in this chapter, assimilation and contrast effects in forming impressions of strangers were illustrated as predictable consequence of the relationships among anchor values (for example, personal "warmth") and other aspects of the person to be sized up.

The individual's desires, fears, past experiences, and culturally shared schema often anchor the way situations are defined and reacted to. However, social situations themselves have properties that the individual can ignore only at considerable risk. The objective physical and cultural properties of some situations limit the alternatives for action. To the degree that such clear-cut structure is lacking, the individual faces a problem in sizing up the situation and deciding what to do.

There is a psychological tendency toward experiencing stability and continuity in ourselves and in the world around us. Uncertainty and instability for any length of time are discomfiting. Thus, when the environment lacks structure in some important respect, the individual actively seeks or tries to provide some stable guidelines for sizing it up. If the individual's past experiences are not applicable to the situation, he or she becomes highly susceptible and sensitized to the actions and interpretations of others. It is the lack of external structure in a social situation that sensitizes the individual to the behavior of a "model" and to suggestions made by another person. It is a sobering realization that in ambiguous problem situations our *failure* to act may reflect the influences of another person's inaction, just as our choice of a line of action may be influenced by another person's urgings.

Finally, research in this chapter and the guidelines just summarized pose an enigma: In the study of social behavior, the researcher becomes part of the social situation confronting the person being studied. The person's definition of a situation as *research*, the researcher's role in it, the instructions, research tools and techniques all may affect the very behavior that the researcher wants to study. Much of the research in this chapter was planned and executed so that the researcher and the research tools were embedded as natural parts of the situation. However, we shall have to take into account the undeniable fact that if a person knows that he or she is being studied, this awareness may be more important in affecting behavior than other aspects of the situation that the researcher carefully controls and varies, because their impact is the problem the researcher wants to study.

A research situation is a social situation. Rather than writing a special chapter on the social psychology of research situations, which has been a flourishing area for research during the last decade, I will bring up the enigma and its consequences as we go along. Research methods and techniques are not terribly interesting in the abstract except to specialists. It is easy enough to discard their impact on behavior as "artifacts." On the other hand, if we look upon them in the context of important human problems, the reasons for the "artifacts" bear on matters of importance in understanding social behavior. And that is ultimately what social psychology is all about.

Becoming Related to Others

As I mentioned, one reason for studying how unacquainted persons act in various social situations is to eliminate the possible effects of past history on interactions between people. Looking at it another way, such experimental "control" is also admission that people who know one another might define a social situation quite differently than strangers and might go about their transactions with each other and the activity at hand in ways that we could understand only if we knew what was between them.

The research literature on the topics that pertain to transactions among individuals gives impressive evidence of the pains that researchers sometimes take to control, limit, or prevent their communication. Individuals are separated into cubicles; at times they are restricted to passing written notes or pushing buttons that control electronic signals. Such measures are not intended as analogs with solitary confinement in prisons or life in space capsules. Aren't such stringent methods to "control" an admission that *something can happen* among individuals over time that is quite powerful, quite important?

In this chapter, we will examine evidence that *something does happen* among individuals when they interact beyond a brief encounter. *Something may develop among them* that affects their perception of one another, their attraction to one another, and how they behave.

In short, we will start looking at the

formation of human ties that come in time to bind individuals as friends, as enemies, as lovers, as family members, fellow-workers, or members of something or other. Such human ties are woven throughout human lives and the social fabric. To each of us, their lack is experienced as deprivation and their disruption as loss. Such rudderless drifting in personal experience is painful, in proportion to the weight of the anchor that is missing. We have to *do* something about our lack.

Such facts alone make it important that we inquire into the nature of human ties. Research findings about brief encounters among strangers cannot be applied directly to social situations where participants have interacted over a period of time. The social space between the latter is not a vacuum. The great challenge is to discover what kinds of powerful ingredients it contains.

GETTING THE PROBLEM INTO FOCUS

In reviewing research on interpersonal attraction, Levinger and Snoek (1972) emphasized that the bulk of the research was "limited to an early stage of relationship" when very little information about the other person or trivial rewards have maximal effect on how one regards the other. Also, they criticized the narrow focus of research on "unilateral evaluations of others considered as social objects" (p. 14). Viewing the individual as an atom, the research models have neglected how persons feel about and treat each other, how each regards their association, how each views outside conditions affecting their relationship, and, one might add, how each believes the other feels about each of these aspects and how each expects the other to feel and respond.

Finally, Levinger and Snoek (1972) observed that the research models too frequently assume that liking another person is the equivalent of choosing to associate or actually affiliating with that person, which of course it is not. They pointed out that most of the research has concerned a minimal relationship among persons, starting with zero contact or simple awareness of another person without interaction, and most frequently extending only to "surface contact" during restricted interaction, with little interdependence among the persons. Beyond that surface level of relationship, they emphasized that many consequential human contacts involve differing levels of "mutuality." By mutuality, they meant that the parties become interdependent through overlap or intersection in various aspects of their lives. (Their "fantastic extreme" of such mutuality would be total overlap and interdependence in all spheres of living.)

In one of those rare and happy coincidences in social psychology, Levinger and Snoek's "levels of mutuality" in interpersonal relations overlaps with similar conceptions that we reached on the basis of reviewing an entirely different body of research, namely, that called "small groups" (Sherif and Sherif, 1956, 1969). There we found generalizations about interpersonal relations, leadership-followership, conformity-deviation, performance, and productivity based on research among total strangers interacting for short periods. We called such transitory proximity or interaction among unacquainted individuals "togetherness" situations (corresponding to "surface contact"). We focused then on what happens among persons as their personal motives and the activities they engage in together bring them into greater and greater interdependence. This is the focus in this chapter.

FORMING BONDS OF RELATEDNESS

I will start in the simplest way possible by summarizing laboratory research in which interaction has continued for sufficient time that the beginnings of a relation among individuals can be detected. Such laboratory experiments are stripped-down models of reality, but they are suggestive for understanding experimental studies over time in natural settings and the more complex flow of interaction in real life that will concern us later in this chapter.

Over forty years ago, a graduate student in psychology at Harvard began to ponder problems that concern us here. Muzafer Sherif came to the United States from Turkey and was struck by the contrasts between the two cultures. Before completing the experiments that I shall summarize, he was to return to Turkey to teach, there beginning preliminary work that grew a few years later into his doctoral dissertation at Columbia University (Sherif, 1935). The dissertation, in turn, grew into a small and fascinating book, *The Psychology of Social Norms* (1936), which I read in the library of the University of Iowa as a graduate student about eight years later. (I was quite excited by the book, which was an inspiration for my own research at that time. I could not have imagined then that a couple of years later I would leave my job in survey research to become Sherif's research assistant at Princeton University and then marry him.)

What was Sherif pondering? He started by observing that "irrespective of the race, level of culture, religion, or social class to which an individual may belong," he or she is born with certain needs, including those "for nutrition, shelter, and, later, mating" (p. 1). However, "how and under what circumstances they will eat, mate and enjoy shelter are, to a great extent, regulated by customs, traditions, laws and social standards. This is true for every individual, living in every society we know, primitive or highly developed" (p. 1). Furthermore, every enduring human grouping and the new formations that come into existence develop "a system of customs, values, laws and standards that regulate the relationship of the individuals to one another and the life activities in which they engage" (p. 2).

All such bonds linking individuals together and relating them to the business of living "presuppose as a necessary condition the getting together or coming into contact of individuals in pursuit of satisfaction of their needs." But once the complex structure of "social organization, customs, values and standards (or even trifles of etiquette) starts its history, *it has something very important to say about the operation of those very basic forces that have contributed to its rise*" (pp. 2–3). Therefore, Sherif came to consider the problem of the formation of "rules, customs, values and other sorts of norms" as basic to understanding how individuals relate to one other and to activities of mutual consequence. But how can a person study such a huge problem?

SOCIAL NORMS AS PERSONAL TIES

Sherif developed the idea for his experiments from an observation made by the French sociologist Emile Durkheim that whenever individuals collectively face an out-of-the-ordinary situation or problem that allows for numerous alternative interpretations or modes of attack, they develop a common interpretation or a common way of meeting the problem. Such *représentations collectives*, as Durkheim called them, subsequently affect the experience and outlook of the individuals with reference to the situation or the problem. So Sherif set about looking for a novel, unusual situation that lacked objective structure and was ambiguous in some important respect.

He actually tried out several possibilities before settling on the autokinetic phenomenon, then a little-known visual phenomenon of apparent movement discovered by astronomers through their own errors in reading the location of a single star on a dark night. In a totally dark location, a tiny stationary pinpoint of light appears to move, universally so far as we know. (Later, during World War II, autokinetic movement was to cause airplane accidents on dark nights before pilots learned that they could seriously misjudge the location of a single light on another nearby airplane.)

First, Sherif brought individuals alone to the laboratory to judge how far the light (apparently) moved. Since there was really no movement at all and the subjects had no way of knowing whether they were right or wrong, it would be reasonable to suppose that an individual would make very erratic and inconsistent judgments. At first this was true; but over a hundred trials at judging the extent of movement, the individual settled down to making judgments within a fairly definite range of distances, many judgments clustering about a modal distance within that range. In short, faced with this novel and puzzling situation, individuals tended to create a fairly stable pattern of their own, even though none was "out there." As a result, different individuals arrived at quite different ranges for judging the apparent movement. As noted in Chapter 2, the psychological tendency in ambiguous situations is toward stability in personal experience, even though the environment lacks objective structure.

Next, Sherif brought different individuals together who had formed divergent psychological scales when each had judged the movement alone. Two or three of them made their judgments together aloud, in any order they wished, each for a hundred trials on each of three different days. There was time for something to happen between them, even though all that could happen in the experiment had to do with the extent of movement. Sherif did not ask the individuals to reach an agreement but, over the time period, the once divergent judgments of the two or three persons converged to a common range or mode for judgment. In some pairs, the common norm for judgment represented a kind of averaging over time of their initial individual responses, but in other cases, the convergence represented judgments of greater or less movement than had been reported individually, on the average.

This sequence was in contrast to what transpired when individuals faced the light together for the first time. They arrived at a common range and mode for judgment during the first session and maintained the common norm together on succeeding days. More important, when each individual subsequently returned to the laboratory alone, each made judgments within the range established together with the earlier partners. The social norm had become personal for the individual.

Personal Ties and Their Limits

Psychologically, the personal acceptance of the social norm as one's own is one of the most intriguing findings. Subsequent studies have shown that personal acceptance of the social norm does not occur solely through "yielding" to the other persons. The same results are obtained when the person is not required to utter judgments aloud in the presence of other judges, but overhears them and subsequently reports his or her own judgments alone (Hood and Sherif, 1962). Studies that have followed the effect of the social norm in the individual's judgments alone over intervals of time have reported persistence of the personal acceptance of the norm for periods of 28 days to one year (Bovard, 1948; Rohrer et al., 1954). In fact, norms formed through interaction with peers in the research were maintained better than norms that had been formed by exposing the person to actual light movements (Rohrer et al., 1954) or by the experimenter reinforcing "correct" judgments within a prescribed range (Stone, 1967). Something had happened between the persons that was more binding than simple habit formation or reinforcement by an authority figure.

If the major findings on norm formation were specific only to autokinetic movement, they would be somewhat esoteric. They are not; the findings have been confirmed using a variety of other stimuli for judgment—for example, numerosity of dots, size of figures, experienced warmth, visual illusions, esthetic judgments, the frequency and rhythm of sounds (see Sherif and Sherif, 1956, pp. 264–267). Note, however, that all of the supporting evidence occurs in situations that are in some respect ambiguous or *lacking in objective structure*. It is tempting to conclude, as some writers have, that this experimental model applies only when individuals have no "information" about external events and that, therefore, in such situations they can be led to see or interpret them in any way whatsoever. Such is not the case. By examining why, we can correct our own tendencies to be glib about how individuals go about dealing with puzzling situations, about their capacity to utilize objective cues, and about their susceptibility to social influence.

In fact, a laboratory situation with an autokinetic light contains more "information" than the light, and individuals do utilize those clues in making judgments. They have, after all, walked into a building and a room. Although dark, the room provides indirect clues as to its size through its location, doors, reverberations from one's voice, distance away from the light, and the like. Without any social influence at all, judgments of autokinetic movement vary in magnitude as a function of such clues. The norm formed through interaction in a small room is smaller in magnitude than one formed in a huge, empty auditorium, where observers may report movement of several feet (see Sherif and Harvey, 1952). Thus, it should come as no surprise that there are limits to how greatly a person will be influenced by judgments from others that deviate increasingly from his or her own (Whittaker, 1964). The individual simply pays little heed to judgments a dozen times the length that he or she has found more "natural" in terms of the clues provided by the location and setup.

SOCIAL NORMS AND REALITIES

Sherif never proposed that the autokinetic situation was "typical," in the sense that social norms are formed only in such highly ambiguous situations. After the autokinetic experiments were done, Tresselt and Volkmann (1942) pointed out and demonstrated that one of the simplest ways to bring individuals with divergent viewpoints into consensus was to expose them to the same limited range of concrete, well-structured stimulus events. In other words, if we all know only the same limited slice of life, we reach agreement on it quickly and our ignorance is bliss.

At almost the same time, Sherif was back in Turkey conducting with his students a comparative study in five Turkish villages isolated in varying degrees from urban centers and modern technology. Since the more isolated villagers lacked standardized units for distance (for example, meters), clocks, or common modern conceptions for judging a standard of living, how could they communicate in practical situations about concrete events involving distance, time, or poverty–riches? They found that consensus in dealing with these problems was established among residents of each village, their most common basis being the effort expended in activities or the periodicity of natural and social events (Sherif, 1948, pp. 369–401; Sherif and Sherif, 1956).

For example, villagers would speak of "the time it takes to work a plot of land," "as long as it takes to smoke a cigarette," "one day on the road" (for distance). They agreed on the crops, possessions, or surplus that indicated being "rich." These conceptions differed in different villages, and amusing misunderstandings arose when residents of one village tried to communicate specific experiences to others. Their different norms were traced to differences in the actual life experiences and surroundings in the villages (for example, the presence of mountains to mark sunrise, the availability of roads or water with respect to distance, the actual ranges of poverty–surplus).

Rather similarly, I did a study with preschool children in 1947 in which their problem was to communicate which of several attractive but novel toys they chose to play with together. Although I responded to any reasonable description of a toy, each group of children reached consensus on labels for the most attractive toys fairly quickly. For different groups of children, different labels were adopted for the same toy. All children within a group used its labels in talking about the toys. Interestingly enough, the consensus on different names in different groups prevented conversation between the groups about the toys. Some children concluded that they were playing with different toys than were children in other groups. The normative character of the labels was revealed in the reactions to children who tried to use a different description or name. The deviant child was corrected, the request ignored, or, in a few cases, the child was chastised for using the "wrong" label.

It is probably impossible to specify "typical" situations for norm formation in real life with respect to how ambiguous or how clear-cut are the objects or events with which the norm deals. However, the issue of whether norms formed during interpersonal interaction are closely linked to concrete environmental events or are primarily based on consensus among persons with a minimum of other environmental feedback is certainly significant.

For one thing, environmental events change. Social consensus formed in earlier periods may be passed on to new generations, even though it is a historical relic with little direct relevance to contemporary problems. It still has the force of "you *ought* to . . .," largely because people agree. For example, the old social dictum that women should keep silent when business dealings are discussed became a relic as women entered into the conduct of business. Such clash between social viewpoints, on one hand, and contemporary events, on the other, should hasten a change in the viewpoints. Norms pertaining to human problems with many or highly ambiguous possible outcomes may persist much longer since actual events are unlikely to clearly confirm or deny their efficacy. Who was to say whether or not human sacrifice propitiated angry gods?

Other aspects of becoming related to others must concern us now, however, especially those concerning the particular individuals involved and relationships among them. Research utilizing the autokinetic phenomenon or other highly ambiguous situations confirms the importance of interpersonal relationships for whether or not norms develop among persons and how binding they become. For example, persons who have been seen to succeed (Kelman, 1950) or demonstrated competence in another task (Mausner, 1954) have greater effect on social norms that develop than persons who have failed or proved incompetent. Preexisting friendship, affection, or esteem hasten norm formation and strengthen the norm, whereas preexisting hostility or rejection of another's authority prevents norm formation altogether (Sampson, 1968). We can learn more about how such interpersonal ties begin to form by turning to research that studied their beginnings.

MUTUAL EXPECTATIONS AS INTERPERSONAL TIES

At many of the larger universities in the United States, there are laboratories devoted to the study of interaction processes among individuals, many of them impressive rooms that have been wired for sound and equipped with hidden cameras and one-way mirrors. One might think that such a location would so inhibit or terrify individuals that their interaction would be stilted, reluctant, or infrequent. As such laboratories sprouted in increasing numbers, however, their utilization was enhanced by a variety of outside developments that provided persons willing, or even eager, to interact for purposes of study and/or self-enlightenment. In community, educational, and business settings small social movements had developed to "improve human relations," to "train" people in interacting with others (T-groups), to sensitize people to each other (sensitivity groups), to get people to know others openly (encounter groups) and to attain various "self-analytic" and therapeutic aims. Whatever their other results, the movements furnished a milieu in which business and community leaders as well as college students would willingly participate in discussions for study purposes.

At mid-century, a young sociologist, R. Freed Bales, proposed methods for observers behind one-way mirrors to keep a running record of what happened among people during discussions (Bales, 1950). There had been a number of earlier schemes for observing interaction and numerous others have been used since (see Weick, 1968). But at the time, Bales's proposals were distinctive in providing means to obtain a running record of what transpired during interaction, including a classificatory scheme for coding its content. Observers were trained to use Bales's categorical system so that, as discussion ensued, each act by each participant could be classified into an appropriate category (for example, "gives suggestion" or "asks for suggestion," "agrees" or "disagrees"), punched into a running time sheet, and recorded for posterity. The records could be analyzed later in terms of the frequencies of individual participation, who spoke to whom, who replied to whom, and so forth. In addition, such analysis could be related to ratings made by the participants as to who was more effective in the discussion, whom they liked and did not like, and so on.

Large quantities of data have been collected by Bales and his coworkers on successive sessions among virtual or total strangers who discussed and attempted to offer solutions for problems in human relations. What went on among the participants? It is well to keep in mind that the individuals were not only meeting in laboratory situations with no appointed "leader," but also that all they *did* was discuss problems. In a great many interpersonal relations, individuals do lots of things besides talk to one another. What happens between persons is inevitably affected by the activities they engage in together.

One general finding in Bales's research was that individuals did not participate with equal frequency. This apparently trivial fact is important. Owing to individual differences related to activities in progress, complete equality in interpersonal relations is highly unlikely unless it is imposed on participants by systems of privilege and forfeit (as some small "consciousness-raising groups" in the woman's movement tried to do in the late 1960s). Bales (1953) found that the relative frequencies of participation by individuals formed a gradient (from more to less) that became increasingly steep as the number of participants increased from 3 to 12 or more. In other words, the effect of increasing numbers was to increase the differences among them in how frequently each participated.

Amount of participation was related, in turn, to how a person was rated by others on the quality of ideas offered toward solution of problems and on how much that person was liked. The tendency was for the high participators to be seen as more effective in the discussions (Bales, 1965). Thus, one thing that happens among individuals over time is the building of *expectations* about one another, related to their ongoing interactions, such that some persons are seen as contributing more to the activity than others. The ties that start to form are becoming *differentiated*. Expectations are not identical for every individual.

Just how mutual expectations among participants become differentiated and stabilized is complex, but we do know that sheer amount of talking is not the only or even necessarily the most important part of the process. The importance of conversation or any other aspect of interaction depends on the nature of the tasks or problems faced. In Bales's research, the problems and tasks were verbal.

POWER DIFFERENTIALS, LIKING, AND SOCIOEMOTIONAL ROLES

A large amount of research conducted by the armed services and in various research laboratories clearly showed that when complete strangers are brought together to perform a variety of tasks, their relationships become differentiated fairly quickly in a *specific task* (see, for example, Gibb, 1968). *Who* was more or less effective depended very much on the kind of tasks in which they engaged (Carter, 1953). The point here is that the development of mutual expectations about how effective various persons are in performing a task introduces into their personal relationships a differentiation according to the relative *power* of the participants to affect the course of interaction. For example, some persons are able to interrupt others more successfully, to keep others from interrupting, and the like (Meltzer, Morris, and Hayes, 1971).

One aspect of becoming related to others, then, is the development of mutual expectations concerning the individuals' relative effectiveness in initiating, controlling, and affecting the course of interaction. Such effective initiative represents social power. The relative power of individuals in a developing relationship is a highly significant aspect, for it provides a handle in understanding a lot of what will happen among the persons (for example, what activities they will choose to engage in, how decisions are made, and their mutual capacities to reward or to punish one another).

In Bales's research, participants who were perceived as being more effective were also likely to be rated higher as being liked *and* as being disliked than less active participants. All of this sounds a bit confusing until we note two additional facts: First, considerable research has indicated that there is not a perfect correlation between one's social power and how well one is liked (see, for example, Norfleet, 1948; Carter, 1953; Gibb, 1969; Sherif and Sherif, 1953). Second, the tendencies noted by Bales were detected by averaging ratings of liking and disliking for high and low participators over a number of separate experiments and did not, therefore, reflect exactly what transpired in particular discussions.

Probably the most controversial finding that Bales reported was that on the average, *the* most active person was typically disliked more and liked less than the *second* most active person in a discussion (1953). In a later analysis by Bales and Slater (1955), the kinds of actions frequently engaged in by the most active persons with "best ideas" were compared with those engaged in by the best-liked persons in all the discussions. There seemed to be a tendency for the best-idea person to perform more actions having to do with getting the task accomplished and for the best-liked persons to have higher concentrations of activity in less directive, "social-emotional" areas (such as "gives support"). From such global data, many writers concluded that being more powerful meant giving and getting less affection and that, because of this, someone else was needed in all interpersonal relations to smooth things over, attend to hurt egos, and generally make people feel better about what was happening.

Although the two specialized roles (the more powerful "instrumental, or task," role and the less powerful "social-emotional" role) were based on data in male discussion groups, the notions were quickly picked up by specialists working on other human relationships, especially the family. The whole idea fits nicely with conventional notions about men and women (the powerful, tough male, who rides roughshod over everyone's feelings to get the job done, and the less powerful, sensitive, and nurturant female, who picks up all the pieces). The research findings seemed just dandy: They were interpreted to mean that things *had* to be that way. Every human relationship needs an "instrumental" role and a "social-emotional" role, and men and women, respectively, fulfill these roles.

Well, there were a few things wrong. Bales (1965) found some himself when he analyzed data on discussions again, bringing into the picture the question of how much attention was *received from others* by the most frequent participator. He divided the discussions in terms of the "feedback ratio," that is, the ratio between the frequency of remarks the most active person *received* from others and the frequency of remarks he *made*. A low ratio meant that a person was talking a lot but receiving little feedback from others. Lo and behold, it was only in discussions where there was a low feedback ratio that the most active person was liked less than the second most active person. In fact, in those discussions, the most active person's *ideas* were rated lower, too.

In short, in some of Bales's discussions a number of blabbermouths who did not get feedback from others and who were liked less were unduly affecting the overall analysis of the most active participants. In discussions with moderate or high feedback ratios, the person who was most active was rated best in ideas and liked more than the second ranked person. The distinction between "instrumental" and "social-emotional" roles disappeared.

More recently, researchers started looking to see how many *discussions* produced two clearly differentiated roles that could be called "instrumental" and "social-emotional." Somewhat to their surprise,

Lewis (1972) reported that the same individual took both of these roles at least as often as one would expect by chance, which means that the roles were separated only at about chance level, too. By this time, fortunately for the state of marriage counseling, some researchers on the family (for example, Levinger, 1964) were pointing out that it was nonsense to identify the role of a husband as instrumental and that of a wife as social-emotional. True, most husbands work and earn money, but if they get along with their family and coworkers, they perform social-emotional activities as well. True, many wives do not work outside the home, but anyone who thinks that wives spend all or most of their time in social-emotional activities ought to try taking over the household for a week. (Of course, wives' instrumental activities at home do not bring in a paycheck.) And many wives work both inside and outside the home.

Still more recently, Bonacich and Lewis (1973) analyzed data from 24 discussions, 16 among females and 8 among males. Each contained 5 members and continued for 4 sessions. On the basis of previous research findings, they predicted that the person with the highest proportion of acts in the task or instrumental area would be identified by other participants as the most effective or powerful. There was a tendency for this to be the case. The second hypothesis was that the person whose actions were more frequent in the social-emotional area would be liked best. This hypothesis was not supported, particularly when participants were women.

We can conclude that mutual expectations among individuals start to be differentiated and stabilized even in as short a time as four discussion meetings, provided of course that the participants want to discuss. The participants' relative effectiveness in initiating and controlling interaction is one aspect of the differentiation, but such exercise of social power need not preclude attention to social-emotional problems among individuals that arise. High social power or highly frequent social-emotional activities do not guarantee how much the individual exhibiting them will be liked, but social power and being liked go hand in hand as frequently as not.

Burke (1974) has suggested that relative frequencies of participation in discussions by members may not yield a very accurate picture of the participants' roles, even when broken down into task or socio-emotional categories. In analyzing data from 80 discussions, each among 3 to 5 male students, he also analyzed the "turn-taking" among participants. He interpreted the findings as showing that high social power in discussions is not simply a function of "individual propensity to talk" or of task-oriented content, but also of the control gained in taking and passing along "turns." Further studies focusing on the interpersonal tactics of participating and regulating the turn-taking of others may clarify the concepts of role and social power.

Mutual Bonding

Our most immediate personal experiences of how we become positively related to others center around an initial attraction to them that
grows into liking, affection, or love, which, if mutual, forms the bond
relating us to one another. This sequence, and the primacy of mutual
liking in it, is at the heart of most research on interpersonal relations. Its
study was fostered by the pioneering work of J. L. Moreno (1934, 1953),
particularly after he came to the United States from Austria to demonstrate with his coworkers the great importance of interpersonal relations in problems ranging from runaways among institutionalized
delinquent girls to the diagnosis and therapeutic treatment of psychiatric cases.

Social psychology owes a great deal to Moreno's work. He developed the techniques of "psychodrama," or role-playing, for understanding and treating personal problems. With coworkers, notably
Helen Jennings (1950), he devised techniques of "sociometry," the
mapping of individual preferences for association in the form of charts
that revealed mutual ties, networks, or clusters, and interpersonal links
between the clusters. Moreno's simple technique of asking people with
whom they would choose to engage in various activities is still widely
used. Most of the refinements have concerned analysis of the data,
including the applications of probability theory, matrix algebra, and
mathematical theory of graphs. The actual behaviors studied are still
interpersonal choices and preferences.

Moreno's early work emphasized that the world would be better if
individuals were allowed to choose whom they associated with,
worked with, and lived with. Theoretically, he was fascinated by the
power of *tele* (influence through distance, as in *tele*communication,
*tele*pathy, *tele*phone), which he conceived as the mutual and reciprocal influence among interacting persons. *Tele* was the "cement that
holds individuals and groups together" (Moreno, 1960, p. 17). Unfortunately, through no fault of Moreno's, most of the research investigating
the "cement" translated into studying individual perferences or liking
for one another (see Lott and Lott, 1965). Moreno himself recognized
that the problem encompassed "hostile and threatening relationships"
as well as mutual affection and love (p. 15).

Are mutual attraction and liking (or mutual hostility and dislike) the
primary raw stuff of becoming related to others, or are these cementing
"substances" themselves products of more basic conditions of the
human encounter? Sherif's proposal in *The Psychology of Social
Norms*, which I quoted earlier, suggests a testable proposition with the
latter possibility. As you may recall, he proposed that when coming
together is necessary for the attainment of individual needs and goals,
participants invariably develop a system of rules, criteria, and values
that "regulate the relationship of the individuals to one another and the

life activities in which they engage." If this is true, then mutual expectations among persons and social norms regulating their activities are quite as much a part of the bonding process as the experiences of liking or disliking, loving or hating that occur during the process. This proposition was tested in three separate experiments conducted by Sherif and his associates.

The experiments were among the most naturalistic in social psychology, each being conducted in a summer camp organized for purposes of the research and completely under the control of the research staff (Sherif and Sherif, 1953, 1956, 1969). Since full accounts of their larger purposes and conduct will be given in Chapter 5, here I will summarize only the essentials. Suffice it to say that for the larger purposes, each study had to begin with the development of cohesion among individuals who were previously unacquainted.

NATURALISTIC EXPERIMENTS ON THE FORMATION OF MUTUAL BONDS

In each study, 20 to 24 boys 11 and 12 years of age were selected to participate in a summer camp lasting approximately three weeks. American boys of this age are highly motivated to go camping and to engage in the various activities available in such an outdoor setting. The boys were carefully selected to ensure that they had no previous interpersonal ties and were healthy boys from stable, middle-class backgrounds (see Chapter 5). Although parents were informed that the camp was for study purposes, the boys themselves were unaware that they were involved in an experiment and would be observed and studied systematically. Everyone in the camp appeared to them as regular camp personnel. Techniques for observing and collecting other data were "unobtrusive" to the boys; they were not made aware that their behavior was of primary interest.

The first major hypothesis tested in the research concerned conditions in which the unacquainted boys would develop interpersonal ties and become related to one another psychologically. In brief, we predicted that when the boys interacted repeatedly in activities that were *highly appealing* and that *required interdependent actions* among them, at least three things would happen:

1. Mutual expectations would arise among them about how they *would* and *should* act relative to one another, including their respective roles in performing various tasks and the exercise of *effective initiative (social power)* in making decisions, choosing activities, seeing that tasks got done, and regulating frictions among them.
2. A variety of criteria, or standards, would be formed defining what was valued, what was to be rewarded or punished, and how to go

about various activities of some consequence to members *(social norms).*

3. A we-feeling would develop over time, defining the individuals to themselves and to others as a *social unit,* as members in a group.

Given the motivational appeal of the camp and the opportunities for highly attractive activities, the test of these expectations was straightforward: Allow the boys themselves to choose their activities and provide the wherewithal to engage in them, with a minimum of direction or assistance. They would have to pull together, divide up tasks and responsibilities, and take initiative if they were to enjoy themselves and, indeed, in some instances, if they were to eat when hungry and drink when thirsty. The adult staff functioned, therefore, in a highly permissive, unauthoritative fashion—with one restriction: They were actively to encourage and at times arrange the *choice* of those activities that required cooperation of all individuals and to discourage prolonged activities that could be pursued separately or in smaller clusters.

Probably it is not possible to emphasize too strongly the importance of the structure of activities that we engage in with other people for the entire course of our relationship with them. Steiner (1972) has analyzed research on small groups from this viewpoint, showing that the *requirements of tasks* differ a great deal, with varying consequences for the persons who perform them together. A similar analysis would be most useful in other research areas. It has been said that we do not really know another person until we've competed with him or her; the same thing might be said about working side by side, cooperating, or living with another person.

In the first two experiments, the boys all came together to the camp and, for several days, lived in one big cabin. They were quite free to choose bunks, to come and go, and to engage in activities together as they pleased. As might be suspected, the boys soon began to associate in little clusters of two, three, or four. Budding friendships began to form. (One such cluster even called themselves "the Three Musketeers.") At the end of three days, the staff began to ask them questions about whom they preferred to associate with in a variety of camp activities and whom they liked best (Moreno's sociometric questions). They found that the answers confirmed what they had seen: Mutual liking and preferences were developing among pairs, threesomes, and foursomes.

At this point, the test of the hypotheses began: The researchers studied the sociometric choices (preference, liking) and split the boys into two cabins, so that about two-thirds of the boys chosen by any given boy would end up in the other cabin, not his own. If among the most fortunate, he found himself in a cabin with boys including only one-third of his choices. (If he chose three boys, only one would be in his cabin.) The announcement of this split made in the name of practicality was distressing to a number of boys. Anticipating that it would be, the staff announced at the same time that the two cabins would leave immediately, though separately, on a hike and campout in the woods, which was the single most attractive activity to all of them.

For about the next five days, each cabin had its own choice and schedule of activities. The staff was helpful but nondirective. For example, if the boys wanted to eat out in the woods, food was supplied but it was in raw, unprepared form—six pounds of ground meat, bread, unmixed fruit drink, a whole watermelon—and a fire had to be built.

During the days that followed, the staff each day made ratings of the boys in their cabin as to who got activities started, who made suggestions, which suggestions were adopted, who got things done, what correctives were made on whose behavior and with what reactions from others—in short, ratings of the boys' *relative effectiveness in initiating and controlling interaction*. At first, the ratings of individual boys varied a great deal, depending on what activities they engaged in that day and how things were going among them. There was a great deal of testing among the boys, of attempting to shine or dropping out, of direction and resistance to direction, and so on. With successive days, however, an observer's ratings began to take on a pattern: The boys' behaviors with one another began to be more consistent so that the same individuals were rated as high or as low in effective initiative from day to day in a variety of different activities.

Of course, one observer could be seeing the picture all wrong, so another independent observer who did not know the first observer's ratings then stayed with the boys and made ratings. By the end of five days, such an independent observer made ratings closely resembling those of the regular observer. At this point, the sociometric questions that had been used to split the boys into two cabins were asked again, making it very clear that a boy could make his choices from others in the entire camp. There were two important outcomes:

1. When the questions put to the boys asked for their perceptions of effective initiative (Who usually gets things started? Who gets things done?), their answers revealed that their evaluations and expectations of each other resembled the ratings made by observers.

2. When the questions concerned personal perference and liking, an astonishing reversal had taken place since the division into two cabins: Whereas initially only one-third of their preferences were for other boys in their own cabins, by now 88 to 95 percent of their choices were for boys in their own cabin. The experiences of the week, during which interpersonal expectations and dealings with one another became stable, had also produced almost exclusive liking within the bounds of their own cabin group. (You might remember this finding the next time

you are tempted to say "I belong to my group *because* I like the members." It is at least possible that you like the members because you belong to the group!) In the third experiment, the two groups came to the camp separately and did not encounter each other for nearly a week. By that time, each was firmly convinced that its members were the best and their friendships warm and enduring.

A critical test was made of the hypothesis that the development of power relations among the individuals would be accompanied by stabilized expectations among them. This test was based on the general principle that in situations with ambiguous outcomes, individuals will structure the outcomes in line with their previously established expectations of one another. A ball practice was arranged preparatory to a baseball game, individuals in each cabin taking turns at throwing the ball at an unmarked target that, unknown to them, recorded the location of the hit for the researchers. To make the practice "more fun," the individuals judged each other's performance in terms of how near or far the balls hit from the bull's eye. The performance by those rated high in social power was *overestimated* by other members, whereas that by individuals rated lower in social power was judged more accurately, or even underestimated (Sherif, White, and Harvey, 1955).

These tendencies were much clearer at the top and bottom levels of power in the group. Indeed, both the observers and the boys themselves were much more consistent in assigning top and bottom levels than the intermediate ones. These findings were later substantiated by Koslin, Haarlow, Karlins, and Pargament (1968) using several different tasks and controlling their data to show that the outcome did not reflect simply associations between a boy's status and his skill in one task. In short, when our ties with others are formed through participation in significant activities together, we come to expect more of some individuals than others, to legitimize their greater social power in several relevant activities, and to find ourselves and evaluate ourselves relative to them.

The camp experiments also found that as the relationships among individuals became patterned through more or less consistent give-and-take and mutual expectations among them, a host of social norms were developed and shared: Individuals were given nicknames. Places were improved and appropriated as "ours," with names given to them. Sanctions were agreed on for less than willing or recalcitrant members ("Take ten rocks out of the creek"). "Standard operating procedure" was developed for carrying out the common tasks. Individuals referred to their own cabin as "us," "we," even "home." When preparing for sport contests with each other, each group readily adopted a name to epitomize their unit relationship and we-feeling.

In some cases, the very personal qualities that members exhibited became distinctive to the group. The boys in one cabin developed a social norm prizing "toughness," which apparently started when one member with high standing suffered an injury to his foot while on a hike and refrained from telling anyone about it. Henceforth, the members were "he-men," bearing pain, rough and tough, turning the air blue with curses. The other group in the same camp was at the same time forming norms that emphasized consideration, humility, good language, and prayer. All members in each group regulated their behavior accordingly. There were no differences in the boys' backgrounds that could explain the striking contrast.

THE EARMARKS OF BECOMING RELATED AS A UNIT (GROUP)

Over time as individuals interact, they may relate to one another in a "unit," or group, relationship. Between two individuals, such a relationship may be called that of friends or rivals, lovers or family, comembers or coworkers—its scope and degree of mutuality varying both with time and with the number of consequential activities it encompasses. When more than two persons are involved, the word that comes to our tongues is more likely to be "group." Perhaps it is well to recognize that this vocabulary difference (pair versus group) may be less important than it seems. True, the societies in which we live define their own norms; they have their own labels and even laws that regulate the bounds of such relationships differently. But sheer number is not definitive in these cultural differences. Many societies have much more rigid regulation of the small, intimate, married couple than the social groups that are larger, whether intimate or not. For our purposes in this book, we can call any such relationship among two or more persons a *group*, designating thereby its unit character and the ties that, in varying degree and to varying extent, bind its members to one another, at least in matters of mutual consequence. Of course, in any specific group, it does make a difference how many persons belong.

What are the earmarks of such unit, or group, relationships as compared with more transitory and brief encounters (surface togetherness)? First, the ties among individuals are products of their interaction in *interdependent activities related to significant motives or needs of the participants*. Second, over time, their behavior and expectations relative to one another become *more or less* stabilized and consistent across different specific situations, particularly with regard to the exercise of social power (*status and other role relationships* developing among them). Third, and closely related to the differentiation of interpersonal ties, a *set of social norms* is standardized among them pertaining specifically to *their* relationships, *their* conduct of activities, and to what *they* consider as valued and as *their own*. Finally, once role relationships and social norms have come into existence, they link participants with one another, defining the association and regulating its conduct. Such ties are invested with *mutuality* in some degree.

Once formed, the ties and the unit character of the association are themselves a framework for individual experience and behavior. Actions, feelings, reactions to others, and what the person sees as rewarding or as punishing can be understood better within that framework. The person strives to develop the relationship and protect it from outside threat. The coming into existence of the social unit can even take precedence over the motives that brought the individuals together: in extreme cases their personal attainment will be sacrificed in order to uphold the unit. When mutuality develops, the *relationship itself* is valued by participants.

REAL-LIFE CONFIRMATION OF THE EXPERIMENTS

The formation of ties that bind does not happen every day. When it does, it is seldom possible to document the events in sufficient detail. There are, however, some well-documented cases of people thrown together by circumstance (such as war or other catastrophe), of which one will have to suffice here.

When World War I broke out in 1914, the German government detained 4000 British males from all walks of life, herded them into the horse stalls and lofts of a racetrack near Berlin, and kept them there for four years. This political incident would perhaps have remained a footnote in history were it not that among the prisoners was a young Canadian music student who later became a psychologist. Ketchum recorded observations at the time, but later became almost obsessed in collecting data on the experience. Like many other participants, he was caught in an apparent contradiction: The experience was traumatic and yet the years in camp were unforgettable, recalled warmly by many of the participants. He collected documents, diaries, letters, and reports from former inmates over the years until his death (Ketchum, 1965).

The German military at the time had few precedents and had made almost no preparations for the 4000 men. They imposed few rules, except that order had to be preserved and that prisoners had to answer roll call. The needs of prisoners were many and intense: Each had been suddenly snatched from a normal life and imprisoned "for the duration," with absolutely no idea of what the immediate or distant future might hold. In addition, there were inadequate food, cold, crowded conditions for living and sleeping, and problems in keeping clean and eliminating.

Ketchum described the early days of the camp as periods of intense, almost bizarre interaction among the men at every opportunity: Everyone wanted to tell exactly how he happened to be there, to gripe against the Germans, and to speculate about what would happen. The "flood-gates" of conversation were open far into the night. But there were serious problems to be dealt with, first in the horse stalls, or "boxes," where, somehow, the men had to live together in cramped quarters with no facilities. It was there that interpersonal ties and norms were first formed during the highly practical business of securing space for everyone, keeping clean, and surviving with as little pain as possible. Ketchum compared the ties that grew up within the boxes to family relationships, affectionate but marked with petty conflicts of those living in intimate contact. Men who would not do their part, be considerate of others, or "fit in" were chastised. In some cases they moved to another box. Each box had its own nicknames, catchwords, and private jokes reflecting outstanding events in its life together.

The Germans paid little attention to the boxes, but expected law and order within the barracks. Ketchum documented in fascinating detail the distinctive ways of life and reputations that the various barracks formed during the camp. Years later, one of his respondents wrote about the various barracks and their reputations (as "pro-German," "supermen," or "old school"), adding that he had been in a "good" barrack but that if he had not "I would have chosen Barrack Eleven" (p. 124). Imagine, if you can, having such a strong preference that you remember later which prison you would substitute for your own!

As time dragged by, interest groups of wide variety began to develop among those interested in sports, music, theater, social problems, art, and technical training of various kinds. School classes were offered from high school through university—all organized by prisoners. Amazingly enough, those few who were imprisoned with relatives or work associates (for example, British sailors in port at the time) found their former ties less sustaining than one might expect. "Ship's crews lacked any further function and broke up fairly quickly; kinship was similarly affected . . . and, though many pre-war friendships survived internment, a surprising number disintegrated" (p. 33).

The strength of the new ties that developed, in turn, was proportional both to the intense trauma of uncertainty that internment brought and the basic needs that had to be dealt with, and to their effectiveness in dealing with problems faced together. At last, the ties extended to pride at being residents of Ruhleben. Ketchum's colleague, Robert MacLeod, who completed the account of Ruhleben and introduced it after Ketchum's death, wrote: "Ruhlebenites felt themselves as Ruhlebenites, were proud of what they made of the camp, and in some cases were grateful for having had a priceless experience" (p. 365). This astounding outcome of an otherwise shocking experience is good evidence that *something happens* among human beings who become interdependent in dealing with consequential problems. That some-

thing can occur only when reciprocal behavior and expectations as well as shared values (norms) are sufficiently stabilized to define oneself as part of a developing social unit facing common problems. The "group-ness" of an association among individuals is proportional to the stability of these ties among them.

MUTUALITY AND SELF-DISCLOSURE IN INTERPERSONAL TIES

In search of what binds individuals in mutual relationships, researchers have studied how much the participants disclose of themselves, how open they are in revealing personal data. Today we emphasize the lack of openness among individuals, the lack of genuine sharing and concern. It might even seem that self-disclosure is *the* needed "psychic cement" for interpersonal relationships.

A moment's thought cautions us, however. Self-disclosure to others can cement misfortune as well as fortune. Who among us has not shared a thought or deed with another person that we wish that person did not know? Just how regretful we are depends, no doubt, on the significance of our disclosure for the relationship and how large the scope of our mutual ties is in our lives. Mutuality in the relationship need not be equated with mutual affection, nor is affection an inevitable by-product of self-disclosure. Thus, researchers have found that persons disclose different things about themselves to mother or father, best male friend or best female friend, associates at work, husband or wife (Jourard and Lasakow, 1950; Rickers-Oviankina, 1956). Taylor (1968) reported that college roommates who revealed a great deal about themselves, especially early in their relationship, frequently came to dislike one another in time.

What is disclosed about oneself during interaction with others varies enormously over time and in terms of what individuals conceive as private to that relationship. Yalom (1970) observed that in group therapy these days, sex is not the difficulty in discussion that it once was, coming up "with abandon in early meetings," but that money and income are "threatening subjects" to the same people (p. 272). Sex, on the other hand, may be regarded a very private affair to be excluded from conversation between, say, mother and son, the latter reluctant to strain the parental relationship and really not wanting to hear how it is with his parents in bed, and the former being guided by the custom of her own earlier generation.

Nevertheless, there is some consensus in a society about what people regard as highly personal information and what is not when disclosed to a casual acquaintance, on one hand, or to a "best friend," on the other. It is the "in between" matters on which wide differences occur in judgments of intimacy (Taylor and Altman, 1966). So it is meaningful to speak of "high" and "low" levels of intimacy in self-disclosure with a best friend and of some individuals being characteristically more or less disclosing in that context. Using such data as their standard for comparison, investigators at the Naval Medical Research Institute have compared the amount and "level" of disclosure over time among strangers (naval trainees) living in pairs in isolated rooms for about a week (Altman, Taylor, and Wheeler, 1971; Taylor, Altman, and Wheeler, 1973).

The isolation rooms were small (12 by 12 feet), windowless, and furnished with only the bare essentials for living together. If either person opened the door, an alarm sounded "aborting" the experiment. Except for a few experimental tasks to perform at intervals and the business of living in close quarters, the men had little to do but talk. They were aware of being studied and that closed circuit television cameras were trained on them. Under such circumstances, how much and when did they reveal personal experiences during the week, and with what results?

Those pairs who stopped the experiment before its completion went about the activities of dealing with the somewhat stressful isolation differently than pairs who completed the experiment. The former tended to neglect procedures the others went through in defining areas of privacy and dividing responsibilities, experiencing interpersonal difficulties as a result (Altman et al., 1971). But also, those who aborted had deviated significantly from their more customary level of self-disclosure with a "best friend." The man typically low in disclosure even with a friend became a virtual sieve, spilling out more about himself than the customary high revealers who completed the experiment. At the same time, those customary high revealers who eventually aborted spilled out more than any of the other men during the first day and then began to clam up, revealing far less about themselves than their customary level with friends (Taylor et al., 1973). Those who completed the experiment more gradually revealed themselves to one another, at first at a high rate, especially on topics of less intimate nature, and then at a decreasing rate. Over time, they gradually disclosed more and more about themselves both at low and high levels of intimacy.

It would seem that "openness" in encounter is not the universal cement of human relations, but rather a product of the gradual stabilization of reciprocal expectations about one another and about the relationship, or mutual acceptance of its workings, and of satisfactory rules for conduct in activities consequential to the relationship. Mutuality in the interpersonal relationship depends on such joint definition and, among other things, on the degree of interdependence in its actual conduct.

THE IMPACT OF THE "OUTSIDE WORLD" ON PRIVATE AFFAIRS

Interpersonal give-and-take among friends or members of other groups is not detached and immune from the outside world. To some degree, such units are "open" systems. It is easy enough to see the effects of the larger society and smaller milieus within it in the research cited in this chapter. It is not as readily apparent, but just as true, that some of our most private and intimate relationships are under constant barrage from "outside" influences. We have other relationships outside of the private circle that affect it. Many of the problems we confront are problems defined by the outside world. Such "outside" influences are particularly compelling in the family unit, whose members typically work, study, acquire life's necessities, seek entertainment, find friends, and spend much of their time outside of the home.

In large, modern societies, interpersonal relationships are continually impregnated with the problems and conflicts of the larger scene, often with distressing consequences. Large numbers of individuals regard the "personal" and the "social" as two separate spheres of living, so they fail to see this impact on their personal lives. They attribute their problems to themselves alone or to the particular individuals they deal with directly, becoming more dissaffected and alienated from each other. In contrast, the feeling of helplessness in the face of problems that come from "outside" leads other individuals to attribute all responsibility for personal affairs to "society" or the "culture." They neglect the fact that if some aspect of a society or culture is to change, particular individuals will have to reinforce or even to initiate that change.

One product of problems accumulating at the juncture of what individuals see as personal and social has been the formation of a variety of movements for "training" in interpersonal, or group, relations (T-groups), increasing "sensitivity" to others, "consciousness raising," and various kinds of group therapy. Whatever their aims (which are diverse) or their methods (which include many variations) all such efforts reflect a widespread longing for a "cultural island" removed from the problems the individuals face in daily life. They also reflect strong feelings that something is terribly wrong with human relationships and fervent hopes for their improvement.

With quite a few variations in stated purpose and methods, the group dynamics, or sensitivity training, movement does offer a "cultural island" where one may come for a period of time with others who are initially strangers, away from the immediate pressures and problems of everyday life. Whatever the variations in emphasis, the focus in such encounters is on getting away from habitual grooves in dealing with others, on openness, self-disclosure, and on learning from what transpires among people in the "here and now." They are not, however, insulated from the outside. They can be viewed as phenomena created by the world outside of their confines, reacting both against and in terms of different aspects of the larger society.

"Group Dynamics," or T-Groups: An Example

Perhaps I should explain to you my own interest in the research on training groups. Among my own colleagues, I had observed for years that the group dynamics movement aroused some to strong partisanship, almost as though they had joined a cult, whereas others were equally vehement in denouncing it. One day a few years ago, I gave a lecture on group formation, emphasizing its "earmarks" as pointed out earlier in this chapter. Afterward, a student challenged me with vigor, saying that he had participated in several T-groups or sensitivity groups and that there had been no social norms and no differentiation of member roles, even though the groups continued for some time.

Now a student knows (or should know) that such a challenge can be taken by a teacher as an opportunity to learn something. Fortunately, the student welcomed my suggestion that he undertake a review of the research and descriptive literature. He hoped to see whether his personal experience (that there had been no structure among participants) corresponded to what more practiced observers had found. At the end of the term, he turned in his report, full of evidence on the earmarks of group formation in human relations workshops as well as the frequent formation of subgroups or factions within them. He had found the reading an eye-opening experience and, on reflection, could supply incidents from his own participation to illustrate the research evidence.

More recently, I have been reading the literature on what happens in these encounters, partly to assure myself that we were not superimposing concepts on it that were not supported by the data. This reading has convinced me that group formation can occur in workshop and training sessions over time, but not that it always does. Some such experiences continue over time with little or no stabilization of interpersonal relations and little other structure. Such fluidity seems to characterize situations that are short in duration, where membership is not voluntary or changes continually, or where the formal "leader" (trainer) deliberately prevents the establishment of regularities in interpersonal dealings with the ideological conviction that such intervention is desirable, therapeutically or otherwise. (The latter may be justified. My point is that such intervention can prevent or delay group formation).

It is instructive to review what I have found from the viewpoint of the interplay of "outside" influences and what participants produce themselves during interaction. For convenience, the following sections are divided in terms of the earmarks of unit (group) formation cited earlier. No doubt the review will leave some of you with questions about what happens during these encounters and their effects. If so, you can find some of the answers in recent books by Cooper and Mangham (1971, for research summaries), Golembiewski and Blumberg (1970, for articles on all sides), Aronson (1972, Chapter 8 for views of an enthusiastic but cautious partisan), and Yalom (1970, for a balanced assessment of both therapeutic and training groups). In this discussion, groups with personal therapy as their aim are introduced only when research evidence on them was clearer than that on T-groups.

Motives Conducive to Interaction in Interdependent Activities

The chief impetus propelling individuals toward human relations workshops of varying kinds is, according to Yalom (1970, p. 359), the "common social malady" of alienation, disaffection, loneliness, and discontent characterizing much of modern life. To that broad statement should be added the growth of widespread conviction among people that such experiences with others will promote skills to do something positive about the malady. The importance of that belief is evident from the outcome when individuals, for some reason, are coerced into attending. The typical reactions are long periods of silence and expressions of hostility (Tuchman, 1965), which are inimical to positive outcome. Their active participation is unlikely unless they become convinced that "some good may come of it" during the meetings.

So strong and widespread are these twin aspects of the motivation to attend workshops that Yalom reports the phenomenon of becoming "addicted," citing an extreme example of persons participating in their third "marathon" session in a week. I have known college students so involved in sensitivity groups that school work became secondary to them. When I suggested to one such student that he drop all but one of the groups he attended regularly in order to prevent his failure in school, he replied "But they are my *friends!*"

If there is little doubt about the importance of prior motivations to attend, there is also ample evidence of other motivations arising during interaction, as they had for my student. Yalom (1970) refers to the powerful effect of discovering through interacton that one's private problems or experiences are, in fact, common to others. This experience of "common fate," or "universality" ("I'm not the only one"), promotes interaction at a rapid rate. For a movement such as Alcoholics Anonymous (which developed earlier and quite independently of the T-group, or sensitivity, movement) the common experience and definition of being alcoholic provides the pivot for all continuing interaction among members.

In T-groups, the formal "trainer" (who typically attempts *not* to lead) imports the movement's egalitarian norms into the situation by requiring that the participants decide what to do. The nearly complete lack of structure about "what we are supposed to do" is distressing at first. Some individuals rebel against it as disturbing or a "waste of time." Others seek actively to create some structure by taking initiative, securing agreement on procedures and objectives. The initial fluidity and ambiguity of the situation with its ensuing personal discomfort become a motivational basis shared by participants to "make *something* happen."

The sequence of events described in the research proceeds from the initial lack of structure among participants (who are typically unacquainted at that time) to the formation of more stabilized patterns of interaction among participants. The rise of subgroups or factions dividing members is frequently reported. The point is that research from various sources indicates that some such sequence does occur typically (Cooper and Mangham, 1971; Mann, 1971; Mills, 1964; Tuchman, 1965; Yalom, 1970). Included at some point in the sequence are invariably the other earmarks of group formation that we have noted—namely, the formation of social norms in matters of consequence, the stabilization of interpersonal give-and-take along with expectations of one another, and the growth over time of a unit character (we-feeling) with some degree of cohesiveness.

The Formation of Norms in Matters of Consequence

The social norms that come to prevail in such sessions according to all reports are imported into the situation by the formal trainer (however tacit the method) and the written culture of the movement. These norms run counter to habitual everyday behavior in encouraging "openness," "self-disclosure" (Yalom, 1970, p. 50), and the expression of personal *feelings* about others and what is going on, as contrasted with personal judgments about others, which are disapproved. (Aronson, 1972, pp. 245–246). The normative character of such positively valued behaviors is revealed in reports that participants are corrected , and then come to correct one another, for behavior deviating from the rules.

Concrete data on the formation of norms peculiar to the interaction situation and generated by participants themselves are more sparse. Apparently, in group therapy such norms are regarded as "antitherapeutic" (Yalom, 1970, p. 125) or otherwise contrary to movement aims. Such norms generated during interaction have included decisions to "take turns" in speaking and "stick to the subject" of discussion and definitions by participants of the group's "privacy," which, when violated, become of great concern to members. Almost every report on the sequence of events includes description of the time and effort spent in arriving at rules of procedure and ways of dealing with interpersonal problems. Such time and effort may generate social norms peculiar to particular groups. For this reason, as well as because of the differing personalities of participants, researchers refer to the different "atmospheres" in different groups.

The Stabilization of Reciprocal Patterns of Behavior Among Participants

Typically, participants in T-groups do not disclose their outside status in life, although it is occasionally known. Thus, what happens among individuals may not reflect their respective statuses in the outside world until the information becomes shared. In any event, the most unanimous agreement in the research evidence is that the participants soon become involved in dealing with their relationship to the formal leader (trainer), who immediately attempts to reduce or eliminate the authoritative aspects of that role (yet is initially seen as "expert" if only because he or she is "paid" to perform a function).

The pervasive ideology of the movement starting with its earliest Center at Bethel, Maine (the National Training Laboratory), has been determinedly antiauthoritarian. To some trainers, therefore, the ultimate success of their efforts occurs when participants actively rebel against the trainer or at least succeed in defining for him the extent and manner of his participation (Yalom, 1970, p. 238). In the early days at Bethel, the movement's ideology went so far as to define "democratic" procedure as lack of structure (differentiation) among participants. As one observer at the time found (Whyte, 1953), this commitment meant that the trainer (despite his antiauthoritarian stand) would subtly secure normative agreement among participants that prevented the stabilization of interpersonal relations. Attempts to take initiative or any evidence of power differentials were sanctioned as "wrong." Observing such events, Whyte (1953) commented on the power gains that such a norm gave to the formal leader, who had, in effect, manipulated its acceptance. Whyte found that structure did arise but less and less through the initiative of members.

The more recent research reveals clear indications of the differentiation among participants according to their effectiveness in initiating interaction and dealing with problems among participants (power differentials). Several writers who have summarized the sequence of workshops describe a period during which participants concentrate on reaching some stable expectations of one another (for example, Tuchman's role formation; Yalom's concerns with "who is top and bottom"). Research evidence shows that one kind of behavior that leads to popularity (sociometric choices) is initiating structure in the proceedings. Other aspects of achieving popularity that have been studied are, not surprisingly, related to individual differences in adhering to the most important norms, such as participating in discussion and skill in introspecting about one's own "feelings" and in self-disclosure (Yalom, 1970, pp. 49–51).

The personal importance of status in such a group was shown in research by Lundgren and Miller (1965), whose data were collected on T-groups at Bethel. The individual's rating of self-esteem, they found, was related to his or her status in the group. Members chosen more frequently by others rated their own self-esteem higher than did members chosen less frequently. At the same time, they found that the more popular individuals underrated themselves in comparison with the esteem in which they were actually held by the group. Such downplaying of their own worth suggests that their actual behavior was likely to reflect a measure of personal modesty and humility rewarded by the norms in these groups.

The "Social" Becoming Personal: Effects of Group Formation

What you, as reader, probably want to know about these groups is whether or not they really do help people in some specific ways after they leave the group. Well, the evidence is far from clear-cut. We can find flat conclusions that there is not a single study demonstrating carry-over of anything from a workshop to daily life (Odiorne, 1970) as well as more cheerful estimates by researchers that "it is reasonable to conclude that there is moderately strong evidence of lasting and effective change in individuals participating in T-group training" (Cooper and Mangham, 1971, p. 10). The latter conclusion, however, is prefaced by the phrase "with these reservations." The reservations refer to a full page of serious criticisms and limitations they found in existing research into the question.

This fuzzy picture is not very surprising when we realize that most of the research has attempted to vindicate the group experiences in terms of goals, which are very broad, nonspecific, and, in some cases, simply too much to hope for from a short-term experience that individuals leave for quite different ones in daily life. Far too little research has concentrated on the more modest, but theoretically important, aim of seeing whether or not the properties of the groups (their interpersonal role relations and norms) are stabilized in some degree and, if so, whether they do indeed affect the behavior of individual members.

There is a lot of evidence that individuals report "feeling better" after training. While this finding may be important we really have little basis for understanding "why." The study most frequently cited as demonstrating positive effects of T-group experience is also one that relates to a structural property of the groups, namely relations among members and the formal leader. Dunnette (1969), in a carefully planned project, compared groups led by well-trained leaders (hence presumably skilled in inculcating the norms and encouraging interpersonal relations) with groups led by less experienced leaders, and groups that simply discussed current events and played games. Dunnette chose behavior to test the comparative effects of these experiences that was relevant to group properties, namely, the ability of participants to predict each other's preferences in a variety of respects (their "empathy"). The groups led by well-trained leaders did excel the others in making such predictions. This outcome is not surprising if we consider that better mutual understanding is what we would expect when individuals become related to one another in some significant respect. They know better what to expect of one another. These are signs of stabilized role relationships.

Another area pertinent to whether such groups have impact on individual members beyond their immediate interaction together concerns the development of a "unit character," "we-feeling," or "group identity." The frequent report of an individual's "feeling" better may be related to such a development. Here, the important finding is that a we-feeling or cohesiveness strong enough to lend support to the participants from the others appears *late* in the interaction process over time, not early (Yalom, 1970, pp. 240–241, 244). This finding suggests strongly that the "cement" binding participants together is dependent on prior interactions during which interpersonal relationships and norms for conduct are stabilized in some degree. It would seem that the strength of such ties would, in turn, be closely related to whether or not the experience would carry over into daily life outside the workshop.

In this respect, "self-help" groups modeled on Alcoholics Anonymous have an advantage over discrete, short-term "training" or "encounter" experiences. Such groups actively encourage continuing interaction in repeated meetings as well as contacts among participants outside of formal sessions.

However, self-help groups also differ in other important respects, notably by their focus on quite specific personal-social problems (such as drinking or other drug usage) and by their providing each new group or new member with a "history" of accomplishments by earlier members, including rituals, traditions, and slogans uniquely summarizing how and why the accomplishments were attained. Those modeled on Alcoholics Anonymous are also determinedly antiauthoritarian, but provide rules and values (norms) that emerged during the interaction of earlier members (for example, "Don't take the first drink"; "Twenty-four hours at a time"; "Principles before personalities"). Adhering to such norms and enabling other members to grasp and maintain them become the criteria for gaining status and for stable role relationships among members.

In order to discuss further how and to what extent groups of the kind we have been discussing affect their members personally, I would have to explore the literature on the many and proliferating kinds of "group therapy." Frankly, I have not done so, nor would my colleagues in clinical psychology (whose province is therapy) necessarily agree that I am qualified to grasp what they see as important issues in therapy. (Some psychiatrists, that is, M.D.s, also practice group therapy; see, for example, Yalom, 1970.) What a social psychologist has to offer those concerned with such issues is a better understanding of the workings of groups. In any event, such an excursion would also be inappropriate in the context of discussing the group dynamics, or T-group movement since personal therapeutic outcomes have been explicitly excluded from its aims, all of which pertain to the development of skills in interaction processes.

Therefore, I will postpone further discussion of how binding interpersonal relationships within a group become for members until we consider membership in established continuing groups, a topic to which we now turn.

When a Person Belongs to a Group

In the English language, *group* is about as specific as the word *thing*. We talk about a group of people waiting to cross the street, a classroom group, a group of children playing, a women's group, a national group, a discussion group, a "control" group (in research). About all that these have in common is that they refer to more than one person. Please bear with me for a little hair-splitting, so that we shall mean the same thing when we speak of a group.

I am going to use the term *group* in a special way. This usage applies to a wide variety of human associations, but not to many others. Here is the definition: A human group is a *social unit* consisting of two or more individuals who have formed *role and status relationships* with one another and who have a set of *values* or *norms* applying to their behavior, at least in *matters of consequence* to their relationship.

The "group-ness" of a group is proportional to the stability of the social unit defining membership, of the interpersonal ties among members, and of the norms regulating their behavior. Therefore, deciding whether a particular situation is a group situation need not be a simple yes or no matter.

This definition of a group applies to many of our consequential associations, including our family, friends, clubs, work groups, and groups with particular interests in community, culture, religion, politics, sports, or music. Some of these may be more "groupy" than others. Some are formally organized and some are informal, even casual. It also includes many groups that the English language labels with disapproval: gang, clique, outfit, Mafia, and so on. The definition does not include a great many casual or chance encounters on street corners, in audiences, in classrooms, or among complete strangers in a research laboratory. It need not apply to many important social classifications used to enumerate individuals for the census (sex, socioeconomic class, age, and so on), although groups may form on such bases.

You can readily see that the major terms defining a group are those discussed in Chapter 3 as ties formed when persons become related to one another. *Role relations* refer to characteristic patterns of give-and-take among persons and the mutual expectations associated with them. Included in such role differentiation among persons, there is invariably a dimension of *social power*: A member's rank position in that respect is called his or her *status* in the group. (Social power refers to the exercise of effective initiative in dealings with others, in activities decision making, including the effective application of sanctions to other members. Force or threat of force is not essential to such social power, although it may be used.) Social *norms,* in turn, refer to mutual criteria or measuring rods for *evaluating* activities, events, beliefs, or objects as acceptable (even ideal) or as objectionable (even to be stamped out).

Social situations involving members of one's group are simply not identical to those that do not. As we found in Chapter 2, any social situation provides a complex pattern, an atmosphere, a structure that, together with the person's internal state at the time, profoundly affects the person's conscious experience and actions. Any social situation is composed of diverse ingredients related to the location (with its cultural definitions and facilities), to the activities or tasks to be performed there, and to other individuals present.

Group situations are no exception; but in group situations, the *relationships among participants* become major anchors for the person at times overpowering other ingredients. Lovers do dance in public parks and embrace on city streets. A quiet library can be turned into buzzing confusion by an absorbed group of youngsters. High school friends do exchange notes during classroom activities. Rival gangs appropriate entire floors of a school building as *theirs*, and what happens is a mystery only to outsiders like teachers (as actually occurred in Philadelphia). The orderly procedures of a volunteer fire company continue amid the utmost confusion.

In this chapter, we consider those properties of interpersonal relations that characterize a group. The "reality" of these properties does not reside solely within a single mind or in the deeds of a single participant. They can be deduced over time from regularities in the interactions among members as they deal with events, objects, and other persons. The study of such regularities in social life is a major task for sociologists, anthropologists, or other social scientists. A psychologist who neglects the characteristics of a group is ignoring a significant portion of the effective stimulus situation that an individual faces. The structure of a group includes rules governing when and for what an individual will receive rewards or punishments, for example. In fact, *what* will be considered as rewarding or punishing is in large measure defined by the properties of the group to which an individual belongs. The structure of interpersonal give-and-take is thus a key to understanding group dynamics as well as to predicting behavior of members during the ongoing activities in which they engage and often outside of the group as well.

SOCIAL DESIRABILITY AND THE "LIE DETECTOR"

Any interpersonal relationship becomes private in the eyes of its participants, in some respect and in some degree. Every group develops its secrets—big ones or small ones—whose exposure to public view would affect members personally, their relationships, or at times the maintenance of the group as a unit. Just as an individual protects personal secrets, group members protect the privacy of their interpersonal ties, at times reacting to outsiders as intruders.

A researcher by definition is an outsider and may be seen as an intruder even when the intent is harmless. Wittingly or unwittingly, group members take measures to protect areas of their privacy in which they have an important stake. We discovered this fact early in a research project on adolescent groups. An observer had been in contact for several months with a small group of adolescent boys. He was on good terms with the members and was permitted into their privacy in many respects, including secrets about their undetected scrapes with the law. A part of the project was to secure sociometric choices (Chapter 3) from each boy, as to "who gets things started" when you're together, "who gets things done," and "who do you want for sure to be there" in certain important activities.

When the observer started asking such questions, he was astonished at the responses of the individual boys. Despite the fact that he had seen them together repeatedly for a considerable period, they seldom named each other. Many of the names were unfamiliar to him. Some of these turned out to be younger brothers and their friends. What he did not know at the time was that on the preceding weekend, there had been a fight with members of a rival group in which a boy was killed. Even though the observer had no connections with police, the boys were taking no chances with their friends' names just then.

This striking example of mutual protection indicates a difficulty in interpreting responses made in a research setting on matters that touch on a person's close relations with others. The person may respond quite as much to the researcher as about the matters the researcher wants to study. Clark and Tifft (1966) demonstrated how complex the determinants of responses to a researcher can be in a study of male college students. The students were asked to report whether or not and with what frequency they had engaged in certain socially undesirable or illegal social behaviors (such as being in a fist fight, stealing, using drugs, or engaging in certain sexual activities).

For a moment, think of yourself in this situation: Clark and Tifft have asked you to read a list of actions and check off which you have performed, indicating how often. The actions are all deviations from some cultural norm or law. You have agreed to fill in the questionnaire, perhaps believing that your answers will have some value for research. You have been assured that your questionnaire will be identified only by a number assigned to you. Presumably, you decide to be as honest as you can, but. . . .

Two weeks later the researchers are back. They say they are checking reports for accuracy. (You know, everyone forgets things, and you might have some second thoughts since you filled in the questionnaire.) You have the number assigned you, so pick your form out of the stack, check it over and change anything you want in the interests of accuracy. Now you think you have finished. But no, the researchers say that next you are going to take a polygraph examination, a "lie detector." Like many people you think the test is probably accurate. (We will assume that you do not know how to "fake" such a test, which can be done.) In view of the upcoming polygraph exam, would you like to change anything else on the questionnaire?

Every college student in Clark and Tifft's study made changes on their initial reports. About 58 percent were made at the interview, and the other 42 percent at the time when the polygraph was mentioned. As you also might expect, most changes were reporting increased frequency of deviant actions. Apparently, the students had been trying to "look good" to the researcher. These particular changes concerned actions that the students rated as "never permissible" in the eyes of "the group of boys you have generally done things with" and in their own eyes as well.

But that was not the whole story: Some of the changes were in the direction of *lesser* frequency of actions that the student had reported earlier. Why had he wanted to appear "worse" to the researcher than he was? In 88 percent of these cases, decreased frequency was reported for actions that his *friends* would have regarded as quite acceptable, such as fist fights or premarital sexual intercourse. He had been "looking better" for the researchers according to norms shared by his *friends*.

Psychologists have become keenly aware that persons responding to direct questions or tests requiring reports on their personal behaviors are likely to bias their responses in the direction of "social desirability" (Edwards, 1957b). Since *what* is socially desirable is a normative issue, responses of group concern made to a researcher who is also evaluating behavior in some way are exceedingly difficult to interpret. This dilemma is acute when the behaviors in question relate to matters of some consequence in the interpersonal dealings of group members. The person is inclined to "put the best foot forward," and that foot may be wearing a shoe selected just for the occasion of the research.

In a way reminiscent of the adolescent boys mentioned earlier, Yananamo Indians in remote parts of Venezuela improvised responses for the anthropologist Napoleon Chagnon when he was gathering the names of their relatives in order to construct a geneology. In his motion picture *A Man Called Bee* (1975), Chagnon relates that he was unaware of a taboo on naming dead relatives, which led his cooperative informants to manufacture names in response to his queries. When he discovered the taboo, he had to discard a whole year's geneological work that represented chiefly the imaginative ingenuity of his respondents!

The researcher who brings individuals to a laboratory to watch their social interaction runs the risk of seeing them at their social best, when they know the researcher, or a research instrument, is observing them. Thus, teachers interact with pupils with greater frequency when they know they are being observed (Mercatoris and Craighead, 1975). Suppose the researcher hides behind a one-way mirror. Leigh Shaffer and I confirmed that an unknown observer concealed behind a one-way mirror had more, not less impact on students' behavior than an observer face to face with the person. Furthermore, males and females reacted differently to the hidden observer, who, in this case, affected the females more. Strange but true, an observer silhouetted by a light behind the one-way mirror had *less* effect on behavior than the carefully concealed observer when the mirror was used correctly (Shaffer and Sherif, 1973). Nor did these effects of the one-way mirror or the sex differences dissipate over time as the students became "used to" the situations.

STUDYING BEHAVIOR IN GROUPS

A great deal of social behavior is public and can be observed in unobtrusive fashion, as we learned in Chapter 2 (see Webb, Campbell, Schwartz, and Sechrest, 1966; Weick, 1968). Fairly accurate and reliable methods can be devised to estimate, for example, how closely members cluster while interacting in free play (Aiello and Jones, 1971) or whether there are patterns in who sits with whom in a classroom (Campbell, Kruskall, and Wallace, 1966). In our own research on informal groups of adolescents, groups were chosen for more intensive study by watching from some distance to see who congregated at various recreation centers, corners, vacant lots, or eating establishments in a neighborhood (Sherif and Sherif, 1964). It turned out, as earlier theoretical statements had predicted, that the relative frequency and regularity of *voluntary* association among particular individuals are excellent indications that a group exists, in the sense defined in this chapter.

If a researcher gains entry into more private areas of interaction, needless to say we can learn a great deal more. The manner in which such entry is achieved is often called *participant observation*, a term that is widely misinterpreted and covers a great many variations in actual practice. Among contemporary anthropologists, for example, the term is often used to indicate that the researcher lives among the people studied without the condescending superiorities of erstwhile colonialists reporting on exotic and distant cultures (see Wax, 1972). Beyond that, the extent of "participation" in group life ranges all the way from merely pitching one's tent nearby in order to talk to individuals to various degrees of participation in the people's activities, including ostensibly sharing in the mystic experiences of the group's spiritual specialists.

The critical issue in participant observation is the establishment of rapport and trust with group members, and not how closely one's participation corresponds to that of an actual member. For example, W. F. Whyte lived for three years in a Boston slum, taking part in family, group, and community life in order to study the "street corner" groups of young men. He confided to at least the more significant persons with whom he had dealings that he, an outsider, was interested in studying and understanding their community. The result of his labors, *Street Corner Society* (1955), is one of the most rewarding studies of groups and their relationship to the community and society in which they functioned. Whyte lived in the slum, but he did not and could not become an Italian-American, nor did he abide by all of the customs and norms of the groups he studied. He was participant in the sense that he became accepted into much of the community life *despite* the fact that he was a Harvard Fellow.

The Observer Being Observed

In Chapter 2, we found that when confronted with a stranger, individuals invariably attempt to "place" the strange person in social life and in terms of his or her purposes and intentions. An observer is no exception to this general tendency. Suppose that a researcher tells the person that he or she is a researcher, a psychologist, or social scientist. Polsky (1962) did so when he moved into a cottage for delinquent boys, frankly telling them that he was a sociologist doing research on cottage life. Despite his candor, there were still rumors to the effect that he was a newspaper man, that he was going to write a book exposing the administration of the place, that he was a spy for the administration, and so on.

Even when rumors are dead, the researcher is assessed in the light of stereotyped expectations about his or her occupational role, just as persons with other cultural roles and titles are likely to be. Such expectations are potent and widespread, as illustrated by an incident reported by Segall (1965) in a remote district in East Africa. He was introduced to the hereditary ruler of a major tribal group, who held out his hand, saying, "Well, Dr. Segall, I understand you are a psychologist; I suppose before this party is over you will have psychoanalyzed me" (p. 63). (I once overheard our youngest daughter clearing up a small friend's preconception about my title of "doctor." "No, no! She's not the kind of doctor that does anyone any *good*.")

For such reasons, when Muzafer Sherif started a project studying informal groups of adolescents in 1958–1959, each observer's background was conducive to good "fit" into the neighborhoods he studied (in terms of language, skin color, social class, and so on), but his public role was not that of a researcher. The observer did not act like a researcher—he took no notes and asked no challenging or personal questions in the presence of group members. His task was to develop a purpose for being in the neighborhood that was nonauthoritative, helpful, and friendly to adolescent boys he had spotted associating there. For example, depending on the locale, he might appear as a trainee in recreation work, a frequent visitor to a local hamburger stand who was also a college student, or a worker in a park. (Community authorities were cooperative in arranging such opportunities for the observer and also in agreeing that any data collected would be for the researcher's eyes only.)

Particularly on early encounter, group members watched the observer, testing him to see whether confidences would be kept or information leaked. Members of one group went so far as to drive to his neighborhood to see whether he actually lived there. An outsider, even a harmless one, constitutes a *problem* for a group. Developing rapport and trust with members means building mutual expectations with them that one's presence constitutes no interference or betrayal of what they regard as private and, in fact, may be rewarding.

As noted in Chapter 1, the development of trust between researcher and those studied is a two-way street. The researcher, in turn, is obliged to respect the privacy of members' relationships and activities in collecting and reporting the findings. In my opinion, the only possible justification for gaining confidence for study purposes is if important data cannot be obtained in another way, and the only possible justifiable use of the data is for increased understanding of human behavior, with complete confidentiality of information about individuals and their groups.

Participation and Observation

We face the problem that participation in a group may greatly affect what goes on among members. Whyte reported that one of his prized confidantes (the leader of one group, Doc) confessed that he often thought about what Whyte would think of his actions. Some such effects of having an observer around are inevitable. The problem is not to eliminate but to control them.

In our research, observers were told *not* to consider themselves participants in the groups they studied. As they were a few years older than the members, their relations to the members could be established as a friendly, nonauthoritative person who was not around to judge or influence them. They were to avoid entering into the status strivings of members, as well as yielding to any group pressure to comply with their norms for behavior. Once an outsider succumbs to temptations to compete for status, particularly with the group's leadership, and to conform to its customs, he or she is likely to be co-opted into the group. If the observer is thus co-opted, his or her perspective and selectivity in reporting are bound to be affected (for such is one consequence of group membership). It is interesting that one of the major reasons given for the paucity of careful accounts of ongoing interaction in T-groups and sensitivity groups (Chapter 3) is the researcher's growing identification with the members (Cooper and Mangham, 1971).

Can Observation Be Reliable and Valid?

With a single observer, there is always the possibility of a biased view of events. The only way to ensure that the observation is reliable is to compare it with that of an independent observer who does not know what has already been reported. We faced this problem keenly in our research because observers were instructed not to make notes in the presence of group members, but immediately on leaving them. Thus, forgetting was bound to occur. However, we did not ask that the observer look for *everything* that happened, but to focus on certain aspects of interaction at a given time. We found observers able to perform that task. Another observer was introduced for a special occasion (a ball game or picnic where he could be a guest) and these independent observations provided a check on reliability of the evidence.

The problem of validity—namely, whether what is reported accurately represents what transpired—can be ensured only by using as many different and independent means of collecting data as possible. For example, when confidence of members was attained, then an observer could secure answers to direct, preplanned questions (for example, sociometric questions about "who gets things started," and so on). Data from public and school records could be found to check certain information gained during observation. At times, special test situations were introduced in which members' actions provided verification for important group properties. For example, you will recall in the last chapter that at a summer camp the boys' judgments of each other's performance in target practice revealed their mutual expectations related to status in the group.

Ultimately, the validity of conclusions about behavior and events can be checked through a variety of methods for data collection, not all of which are subject to the same source or manner of bias. When several methods yield similar conclusions, we can have more faith in their truth value. The use of a combination of independent research methods is, in fact, needed in almost any social-psychological research. In this process, time is a great ally, particularly in group life. The recurrence over time of not one episode but many episodes of members dealing with each other, choosing certain activities, praising some actions and objecting to others provides a firmer basis for conclusions.

A Group in Action: Structure in "Dynamics"

A capsule account of one of many groups studied intensively over periods of several months to a year will bring us to realities of group interaction. I have chosen this particular example because it illustrates several important points about group membership, especially that the group itself is an ongoing dynamic process that may change over time (Sherif and Sherif, 1964). Specific episodes illustrate what the observer was looking for, namely: (1) regularities in various situations as to who was able to initiate activities effectively, to influence decisions, and to control interaction among members; and (2) similarities in what was regarded as important by members, what was acceptable among them, and, conversely, reactions to deviations from the bounds of acceptable behavior.

The Locale and the Observer

Our observer (Joel Garza) was a graduate student in social work who had grown up in the southwestern city of over half a million population where he observed. The neighborhood was not familiar to him but, like its population, he spoke Spanish as well as English and shared a common cultural background. The area had high rates of crime and delinquency for the city. Its inhabitants were chiefly first or second generation in the United States from Mexico. Family incomes were low, particularly for the support of the large families living there in small frame houses. However, the adolescent boys whom the observer studied were all children of hard working parents, only one being supported solely by his working mother.

The observer went to a city park bordering the neighborhood. On a typical weekend it was full of children of all ages, couples, and young adult males who hung around to talk and play basketball or baseball. Everyone seemed to know everyone else. The observer saw a good many adolescent boys, but he decided that before talking to them, he first had to resolve the problem that his presence as an outsider in the park created. So he took a ball to the park and worked out near the *adult* men, who joined him shortly. Over several days, he explained to them that he would like to be a coach for teen-agers, because that was where jobs could be found coaching, but he had no experience. If he found a team that wanted to play, he could get games with other teams outside of the neighborhood.

The grapevine was at work. After weeks of playing in the park with the adult males, a 16-year-old boy approached the observer to check the rumor that he could get basketball matches. The observer was wary: "Why don't you fellows play in St. Anthony's with the church league?" "We tried that, but we can't get along with the coach." So the observer made a date to meet the boy's friends the next day. No one showed up.

It was several days before the observer finally made connections with the boys, eight of them. (Another boy, Dompe, was recruited later as a good ball player. Despite that fact, Dompe was considered a marginal member of the group because he had a girl and was unreliable about showing up for practice.)

Roles and Status of Members

The observer was introduced by his contact with the explanation that "this man can get us games with other teams." There were questions: "Who would we play?" "Why don't you get fellows some place else?" (All communication was in Spanish).

The observer explained that he had happened to see them play and that he wanted to be a coach. Che, a short sturdy 17-year-old, turned to Juan, a tough looking fellow of 18: "Do you want to play, Juan?" Juan answered: "Hold on, let him finish talking." The observer continued that it was important for him to start with boys who played well, so that he might get a winning record right from the start. Juan said, "I'll play," turning to an attractive boy of 17: "Rogelio?" "I will. How about you Wero?" Wero replied: "Hell, yeah. We'll all play and we'll all give hell to those damn guys." Everyone else volunteered.

Juan said to Che: "You and Lalo will play in front and me, Wero and Rogelio under the basket." (Lalo was the largest of three 15-year-olds, so Juan was leaving out two other younger boys as well as the boy who had introduced the observer.) Wero asked Rogelio if they should practice now. He did not answer, so Wero turned to Juan: "No, I'm tired. I've been here all afternoon and want to go home to eat." Che, Rogelio, and Wero said that would be best, Wero adding that they could practice tomorrow. The boy who had introduced the observer spoke: "Tomorrow night will be best for me.'' Rogelio said: 'We'll be too tired at night to practice.'' Che added: ''It's best in the afternoon—right, Juan?'' Juan said they would meet at two in the afternoon.

Conformity and Deviation

The observer was puzzled at their treatment of the boy who was his initial contact. When they met the next afternoon, the boy was not there. The observer asked about him. Juan said: ''I don't know if he will play. Anyway, *el puto* (fag) doesn't rate any more.'' (Later, the observer found out why. Another bunch of boys had jumped the group, and the boy had run away. The fact that he ran from a drawn knife was no excuse, and these boys were in the process of excluding him completely. He had violated the norms of masculine bravery and loyalty to the group. His exclusion was finally so complete that even the neighborhood girls avoided him.)

The observer could tell that the boys had played together before. They worked as a team, anticipating when a teammate was going to shoot, fake, make a fast break. He followed the practice of mapping out plays on paper without assigning positions. Juan would take the paper and tell each fellow what position to play, how to execute the movements, and so on. He praised their successes. When Lalo (the one 15-year-old regularly on the team) made an error, Juan cursed him strongly. Once Wero made an error and Juan threw the ball hard at his upper back. Wero turned in a fury, which he contained when he saw who had thrown the ball. Juan was never hard on Rogelio or Che, however. He accepted their suggestions on the starting lineup and substitutions, seeming to trust their judgment more than his own.

Together, off the field, the boys acted like tough ruffians. They made much of their fighting exploits, in which Juan and his younger brother Pete (16 years old) were invariably the toughest and most fearless. They had utter scorn for the police, whose attitude, in turn, was expressed when a policeman asked the observer: ''What are you going to do with those monkeys?'' On the reply that they would play basketball, the policeman laughed: ''*This* I want to see!'' (Despite this attitude and the fact that the observer learned in the course of observations that the boys went joy-riding in stolen cars, rolled drunks, took money from younger boys at knife point, smoked marijuana, stole soft drinks and other sundries, only two of the boys had been caught. Che had been put on probation for theft of a local church, three years previous. Juan had been found in a grocery store after closing hours, but was simply discharged since he worked there.)

The team was good. They won several games and chose a team name, after their park. Then Rogelio began to explore the possibility of getting in the City Recreation League, the day before the deadline. The fee was ten dollars. Juan had all of them pool their money. It totaled

$1.18, of which Juan gave 55¢. After the game that day, Pete suggested buying cold drinks, but Rogelio, with Juan's assent, insisted that the money was "down payment" on the entry fee. Then Rogelio asked the observer if he could help them out with the difference.

Change in Leader-Follower Relations

The team entered league competition, and winning became even more important to them. (Their greatest worry at the thought of losing was what other teen-agers and young men in the neighborhood would say. They lost only three games.) The observer bought them T-shirts for playing, watching to see who would get his choice of numbers and how they were distributed. Again, the power structure that he had observed previously was clear. Juan took charge and got first choice. Then Che and Rogelio chose. Wero and Pete (Juan's tough brother) were next, followed by Dompe (the newly invited good player), Lalo (the playing 15-year-old) and the two 15-year-olds hanging on.

Basketball was the league activity at the time. Now Juan, the indisputably tough leader, was not as good at basketball as he was baseball. One day, a game was called at the last minute. The two younger boys were in school and did not learn about it and Dompe did not show up. There were six fellows for the five man game. Who would start?

Juan, who was rather uncertain about lineups anyway, kept quiet. Che asked the observer who should sit out first. When the observer declined to decide, Rogelio asked Che to choose five players. Che eliminated Wero, who protested that his position was indispensable against the particular opponent. Rogelio asked Juan, please, to decide. Juan thought a moment, then said that he did not feel very well and would sit out. The game started. Juan's "illness" did not last long: He played when Pete took himself out. Then Che and others followed suit so that Juan could play. They won the game.

During the next month Rogelio's words began to count more and more in making decisions. He never left Juan out of the lineup, but Juan often volunteered to sit out when the team was in a tight spot. Something else was happening during the league competitions of the next ten days. Realizing that if they "got into trouble," they would be eliminated from the competition, the members became increasingly cautious in avoiding trouble with other groups.

Juan's leadership had been closely tied with his toughness and skill in fighting. One evening, while the boys were watching a ball game between two rival church teams, the boys sensed open conflict arising. Two priests came out on the floor to quiet the crowd, but their pleas went unheeded. The boys began to talk about what to do if they were attacked. Juan said they should attack first. Rogelio, backed by Che and Wero, told Juan in no uncertain terms *not to start anything*. On the way home, they explained how seriously they could get into trouble if he did not stop looking for a fight. Later Wero remarked that Rogelio was the best person to keep them out of trouble.

In two months time, the shift in focus to sport competition in the league (which in turn necessitated keeping out of trouble) was accompanied by change in the power structure of this small group, without severe interpersonal struggles or loss of members that may accompany such change at times. The change is illustrated by the observer's average ratings of the members' ranks in effective initiative during several observation episodes during the period.

In the weeks preceding December 30, the observer's ratings of effective initiative had become quite stable, with Juan, Che, and Rogelio occupying ranks one, two, and three and the two 15-year-olds tying for low men on the totem pole, with Dompe (the good but unreliable player) just above them. In between, Pete (Juan's tough younger brother) and Wero were tied in fourth rank, each with quite different roles, as Wero was better in sports and was one of the few older boys still attending high school. Lalo, the 15-year-old who played well, ranked just below them.

In January, the observer became unable to distinguish a "top man" in the group. Juan and Rogelio were tied in that position, the observer noting that Juan's influence was declining as Rogelio's increased. At the same time Pete (Juan's tough younger brother) was losing power. By the first of February, the power structure was realigned and stable once more, with Rogelio an unchallenged leader, followed by Che, and then Juan. Pete's standing had declined to that of Dompe near the bottom, whereas Lalo's ascent continued owing to his considerable sport skill and cooperativeness.

Norms Regulating Behavior

Many of the boys' strong preferences reflected those of their community or, more typically, their own selective emphasis of cultural elements available within it. They were sports enthusiasts in the U.S., not the Mexican, sense. They preferred popular U.S. music to the available Mexican tunes and Hollywood to Mexican movies. In television shows as well as within their community, their admiration was strong for clever defiance of the law—a good example of their own selective preference in a community where crime was frequent but not the rule for everyone. Much more than other youth in the community, their behavior together and in public was boisterous, rough, and tough—to a degree that made them conspicuous and the observer highly uncomfortable to be with them on more than one occasion.

Entire clusters of specific actions and reactions of the boys over time become meaningful if we look at those issues that became central in importance for their major activities and survival as a unit. At the positive pole, loyalty to community and more particularly their group was prized so highly that the bounds for conforming behavior were quite narrow. (As we saw, the boy who ran when the group was jumped by another group was ostracized, despite the fact that he ran from another boy with a knife.) Winning in sports, attending practice, and doing whatever necessary to win became the concrete focus of such loyalties. (The boys experienced shame at loss and dread at community response to it. Juan willingly dampened his own assertiveness in the interests of victory, not once but repeatedly. Dompe, needed for his skill, was shamed continually for his inconstancy in attending practice.)

The consequence of conforming to these positive values was mutual appreciation and reward, and the invariant counterpart for deviating from them was negative reaction (even punishment).

Parallel to the vital axis of loyalty was a cluster of actions that, to greater or lesser degree, were anti-authority. The rough, tough boisterousness of these boys was accompanied by the firm belief that anything that they could get away with, without police detection, was a small victory. To be sure, they were habitually without money or means for many needs that middle-class youth would have regarded as necessities. Their talents at petty theft were prodigious.

Since having a good time meant escaping adult surveillance (including their own parents), the nighttime hours were the best to them, hanging out at Perez' Place, whose rear entrance would open to them even after official closing hours. All of the members over 16 except Wero had left school, which was regarded as detested authority that interfered with the late night schedule since it robbed the pupil of morning sleep. The steady derogation of school by high-status members had already produced firm intentions on the part of Tony and Pinto (the two 15-year-olds) to quit at 16. Despite his normal intelligence, Wero left school as an eleventh-grader and Lalo (whose three older brothers had graduated) was continually vacillating.

There was, in short, a cluster of norms rewarding certain "delinquent" actions, such as cutting school and participating in a variety of small crimes. At the same time, however, the avoidance of "trouble" became a positive virtue. The boys were not labeled "delinquent" by authorities because of their successful adherence to this norm, their cleverness, coordination, and mutual help in avoiding potential conflict. The observer reported numerous instances, including a hilarious account of their painful but patient strategy to use the public restroom at a drive-in movie while avoiding confrontation with members of a rival group located between their car and the facilities—a procedure that delayed urination by half an hour. As the foregoing account of the group structure indicates, avoidance of conflict with other fellows or the police became a necessary positive virtue as interest in sport competition increased, since confrontation would have eliminated the boys from the city league. Those members most prone to violent reactions (Juan and Pete) were patiently restrained by other members and praised for their self-control.

Despite their cohesiveness and mutual identification, these boys were not *formally* organized and took a name only when they entered league competition. Unlike similar groups in other large cities, they did not recognize status differentials with titles (for example, "First Runner," "Second Runner," and so on, as in Philadelphia). Their environment almost required that they be together frequently and regularly if they were to have meaningful personal ties, particularly since most had left school. With respect to the existence of structured interpersonal relations and of group norms, however, the group is not distinctive. In upper-class and middle-class neighborhoods of urban areas and suburbs, we found networks of social ties with these properties among youth recognized by each other only as "friends," and by adults only through the most visible examples of pairs or threesomes who were frequent companions (Sherif and Sherif, 1964, 1965). In fact, adults in middle-/and upper-class neighborhoods denied that there were groups, which they equated with "troublemakers."

GROUP NORMS AS REGULATORS OF INDIVIDUAL DIFFERENCES

Individual differences are a universal fact of life in any group. Only in the most formal, traditional, and ritualized situations do a group's norms prescribe exactly how individuals should behave. We can go far off the mark by conceiving norms as "pressures toward uniformity" that erase individual variations. More generally, individual differences are encouraged within a range or latitude defining what is desirable and acceptable. This range of acceptable or tolerable variation may be narrow or broad, clearly defined or vague. At times the limits are defined only when a member takes a step way out of bounds. Thus, reactions by members to deviation from the acceptable latitude are one of the best indications for the existence of a group norm.

Once established, norms tend to persist among members even in the face of attempts by individual members to change them. This resistance to alteration is not very surprising when we realize that the group norm need not represent the adding or averaging of so many individual opinions, but instead represents *mutual* agreements and accommodations that link individuals together in dealing with the matter at hand. Such persistence of norms in the face of individual effort toward change was neatly demonstrated in groups of preschool children observed by the Hungarian psychologist Ferenc Merei (1949). Each group played together, developing a little tradition of its own in favored activities. For example, games were created, a certain order of events became preferred, and certain procedures became standard for distributing and sharing play materials. Once he ascertained that each group had indeed developed its own norms, a new child was introduced in each. The new child was somewhat older, larger, and, furthermore, had been selected as being particularly effective and assertive in play. Would the new child be able to change the group customs?

At first, none of the new children succeeded in "leading" the groups into new customs or procedures. Each became a regular member, adopting the traditions already established, and in some groups the new child was simply absorbed into the existing scheme. Others adopted the group customs, but slowly were able to assume a directive role (distributing play materials, for example). Those few children who succeeded in changing the established norms did so by first following them and then modifying the rules or procedures slightly. Some of them were then able to introduce altogether new customs.

Norms Count in Activities That Matter

The concept of group norms is sometimes severely overworked. Groups engage in a variety of activities, enjoy some novelty, and may live in a highly variable and changing environment. They need not have norms for every occasion. However, in any group, norms will be found or will be developed in those activities that are frequently engaged in and in those matters that have considerable consequence for individual members and their relationships. I recall a student challenging this generalization by telling of a commune he had visited where there "are no norms—anything goes." On closer questioning, however, he revealed that he had not been accepted fully because he was "too square." Their norms were merely different, and his behavior was "out of bounds."

As noted in the illustrative case study, the bounds for acceptable behavior and the consequences of deviating from them are most clearcut in matters of considerable importance to the group. In matters such as being loyal, behaving "properly" with respect to outsiders, and pitching into activities considered significant for group members, the range of tolerable individual differences becomes very narrow and the consequences for the deviant very serious. The boy who was ostracized for running away in the face of danger became a lonely, pitiful figure in the neighborhood.

In 14 months of observing 7 informal groups of high school girls, Merrilea Kelly and I found, for example, that norms for dress and hair styles were very important and clear-cut whereas norms governing choices of activities after high school were much hazier. The differing clarity of norms in these two respects was revealed by individual girls totally outside of their group contexts. They judged clothing as "right" or "wrong" very definitely, but were more noncommittal about a girl's choice of future plans (Sherif, Kelly, et al., 1973).

Male-female relationships are a matter of considerable importance for many groups, including the groups of adolescents we have studied. While Juan, Rogelio, and the boys were interested in girls (especially sex), they kept them at arm's length in their own activities, scorning Dompe, who could not. However, depending on the socioeconomic class and cultural context, we found wide variations in male-female relationships. One group, also Chicano, had its parallel in a girls' group where the girlfriend of the male leader was leader in the girls' group. Elsewhere, heterosexual groupings were more common, at least in certain activities.

The Interesting Case of Sex

Sexual activity is regulated in any human society through the organization of kinship ties and legal and social prescriptions. Any individual or group is influenced by this cultural regulation, and there is no intent here to suggest that what goes on in a particular group fully escapes its impact. Within the cultural framework, the feeling is that sex is a "private" affair, yet the study of groups in different settings within society is convincing evidence that norms shared by members do exist and do differ from one group to the next.

For example, Whyte's street corner boys (1955) had a rather elaborate system for classifying girls and determining "proper" sexual behavior. A "good girl" was the type that these fellows hoped to marry. She was to be treated with respect even when, as in one instance, she became intoxicated to the point that she could have been taken advantage of. "Lays" were subdivided into "one-man girls," the proprietary rights of that member being strictly respected; promiscuous girls, who were fair game for any of them; and prostitutes, who could even be swindled as far as members were concerned. Relatives of members were out of bounds no matter what classification they fell into otherwise.

Among groups of poor southern whites transplanted to Chicago, any white girl was fair game for members, but status with fellow members was enhanced by "overcoming the largest possible number of inaccessible girls," as contrasted with "pigs" (Rosenberg and Bensman, 1973, p. 125). Despite the fact that these boys regarded a "fox" (date) ultimately as a sexual target, they did differentiate between treatment of a fox and a pig. Some respect was due a fox who offered some resistance: "If I have to work real hard I think a lot of them. If they give it to me right off I think they're pigs" (p. 114).

Such normative classification of females, implying different treatment and recognition for conquest, was also found in other lower socioeconomic settings populated by quite different cultural groups (for example, blacks in Washington, D.C., and Puerto Ricans in New York); however, the definitions of the female classes, the situations in which girls were encountered, and the consequences of sexual behavior were quite different (Rosenberg and Bensman, 1973).

Whereas the poor southern white had "dates," but otherwise seldom interacted with girls, the Puerto Rican youth did not know what was meant by "date." With his peers, he arranged "sets" (parties) for the purpose of "scheming." While a boy boasted to fellow members about sexual activities at sets, there was tacit agreement to "protect" a girl's name, which was self-protection as well, as we shall see. If a girl shifted partners, reactions were mild. (In contrast, a girl could be physically assaulted if suspected of "squealing" about male activities that would get them in trouble with the police.) Sexual relations with a streetwalker brought almost no prestige with one's fellows. On the other hand, if a girl acceptable to a boy's group became pregnant, the members fatalistically accept the "necessity" of marrying her. Hence, while males bragged of conquests to one another, there were advantages in concealing names and times.

I know of practically no evidence about the normative regulation of sexual behavior among the adolescent girls who participate with and in heterosexual groups. However, the study of poor youth mentioned above refers to girls' hopes for husbands who "won't be unfaithful," "won't drink," "will be nice," and "will work hard." Such views lead me to suspect that the girls operated in considerable ignorance of the norms accepted among males. I suspect that it may be true that young women are more generally uncommunicative about sexual norms, although this seems to be changing.

Traditionally, of course, virginity was the prize a girl held for marriage, but it has also long been true that both female and male groups valued a young woman who was sexually attractive and desired, while negatively sanctioning the "prude." As long as a girl was rewarded for sexual appeal, but sanctioned for both loss of virginity and prudery, she was on safer grounds by not discussing her sex with other females. Being ignorant of the norms among males that rewarded conquest, she often relied solely on a partner's verbal expressions of affection or love as the key to "how far to go."

Research on sexual norms among college students suffers, with a vengeance, from the difficulties noted in discussing the Clark and Tifft study utilizing the "lie detector." Nevertheless, there is evidence in survey data on college students in the United States that while students talk about sex publicly much more than formerly, females may be following the traditional path of keeping quiet about their own sexual behavior. For example. in one study, 57 percent of female students (sophomores and juniors) found premarital sexual intercourse acceptable when a woman is in love, but only 28 percent thought their close personal female friends would agree. Over 80 percent of males indicated approval of sexual intercourse "with love." About half of the males approved of sexual freedom for men, with or without love, but the same males indicated disapproval of such freedom for anyone they might marry or for their own sister (Kaats and Davis, 1973). These males were classifying females much as the lower-class males who differentiated "good girls" and "lays."

Such data suggest strongly that males, about half adhering to the double standard, are more aware of norms for sexual behavior prevailing among their own-sex groups whereas females are in a state of collective ignorance. Of course, such ignorance can work either way. Recently, when Richard Bord reported data indicating that different studies estimate female virginity on college campuses between 40 and 60 percent, one woman student in the class objected in astonishment: "That can't be right. Everyone is doing it!" If "everyone" were defined in terms of the bounds of her groups, she may have been correct. Such an impression of universality is good evidence for the existence of norms, which endow whatever is acceptable in one's group with qualities of naturalness and universality and what is not to be done ("not doing it") with overtones of the absurd. Particularly at times when cultural norms are changing rapidly, we find small groups with different norms, each convinced of the correctness of its own ways.

POSITION IN THE GROUP AFFECTS
THE KIND OF CONFORMITY EXPECTED

Conformity means bringing one's behavior within bounds defined as acceptable by group members and doing one's best to meet their expectations. As already noted, the acceptable range for individual differences in conforming behavior is narrowest for matters high in the group scheme of things, notably those affecting its maintenance and unity in the face of outside threat (from other groups, authorities, or external circumstances affecting members). Such strictures apply to all members, but are most pronounced for individuals whose roles in the group are most highly regarded and whose status carries the most power to affect the group. With respect to such major or central norms, therefore, the more powerful members including leaders are, if anything, less free than other members (Sherif and Sherif, 1965).

For example, when money is scarce and important activities hinge on having money, a leader is expected to contribute more than others, as Juan did. He runs the risk of being called stingy if he does not. If a high-status member misses group meetings, he or she may be the subject of great concern. ("Is anything wrong?" "Does she think she's too good for us?") A lower-status member might not be missed. With respect to major group norms, those with high status are expected to be exemplary.

Members with lower status, while risking disapproval or even loss of membership for deviating from the bounds of acceptable behavior, are nonetheless tolerated for "slips" that would destroy the standing of a more important member. For example, in one group of boys we studied, high-status members with cars were expected to have them available for group activities, and conflicting plans on their part brought forth cries of "he thinks he's too good for us." On the other hand, a low-status member could beg off from sharing his car on the grounds that his sister needed it, or that he'd spent too much money on gasoline, with no more than a few mumbles of "what do you expect from *him* anyway?"

Nevertheless, it is members with lower status who are likely to be the butt of frequent reprimand, nagging, being "left out" on occasion, or being laughed at by others. How can this be the case? We found that members of lower status were being corrected for deviation much more than members of high status for infractions of less important norms. Matters of etiquette, style, skill, and minor rules of procedure within a group can, in fact, be violated with impunity if one's status in the group is high enough. But let a low-status member perform the same deed, and everyone else expresses astonishment or indignation at such a gross deviation. I recall a low-status member of a girls' group being severely criticized because her underslip showed. On matters of minor importance, particularly those relating to routine matters, the bounds of conformity are narrower for low than higher status members (Sherif and Sherif, 1965).

Such differentiation in the expectations for conformity according to the importance of the group norm and the standing of members make issues of conformity and deviation in groups much more complex than they appear at first thought. In order to understand such differentiation, we need to look more closely at what it means to attain a particular status in a group.

ROLE-STATUS OF MEMBERS

Give-and-take among members of a group is personal. Often the individual member sees it strictly in individual terms. In speaking of herself, a student told me: "I'm not a group person. I'm a pair person. I think of myself with my mother, or with my father, or with my brother, or with one friend at a time." Since her family came into the picture, one immediately can see that her phenomenal perspective is too narrow. Her dealings with her mother could not always in all matters be independent of those with her father, or of her father's with her mother, or her mother's with her brother, or her brother's with her father, and so on. A family living together, as hers was, is a good example of the need for perspective on the relationships among all members in order to understand the give-and-take between any pair.

When we take such an enlarged perspective on relationships among individuals in a group, we have to abstract certain key aspects from them, thereby neglecting much of the richness that accompanies personal relationships of some duration and significance. In short, we are forced to construct a model of the relationships in some respect that, we hope, will best aid us in understanding what happens among the individuals, For example, patterns of liking and dislike, affection or hate, are very important, but nevertheless only one aspect of the relationships. Social power need not be perfectly correlated with patterns of affection. We may love one family member and hate another, but in order to understand what happens when we interact we may also need to know the power relationships among the three of us. Power refers to "effective initiative" in group life.

One advantage of dealing with the power dimension in terms of *effective initiative* exhibited in important activities is that we need not make assumptions about sources of power or the manner in which it is achieved. Both of these issues are, of course, important in the analysis of specific groups and in any attempt to change its power structure or norms. Power may flow from control over resources vital to the group, from skills possessed by some members, from accumulating and dispensing the means to reward, threaten, and/or protect members. Similarly, the manner in which power is achieved may vary all the way from supplying necessary information or friendly persuasion to bald coercion of others through reward and punishments to institutionalization in the form of formal positions or offices (see Collins and Raven, 1969). While the source and basis of power are absolutely essential to understanding power relations in concrete events, their discussion too frequently gets bogged down because they are identified with the bald *exercise* of power. Thus, in common parlance, we seldom talk of power unless we are threatened with loss of job, physical force, or a gun.

To illustrate the confusion, consider some words used in discussing power: dominance–submission, or "the pecking order." These terms reflect older models of power from psychology and biology.

Power, Dominance, and "Pecking Order"

The "pecking order" model was based on a study of chickens, which found that chicken dominance is associated with sexual prowess, high energy in social contacts, and behavior that led to "chickening out" by other fowl. In a flock, the most dominant (chicken A) could dominate all others, chicken B everybody but A, chicken C everybody but A and B, and so on. Now, in chicken life, if you can dominate chickens B through Z in food, sex, and space, you've just about got it made.

Human beings do set up *institutions* that appear to do about the equivalent, for example, military and some religious hierarchies. How-

ever, these are elaborately built and regulation-laden human constructions that could not be maintained *solely* through interpersonal domi-
nance-submission. Even within such formal organizations, the number
of rules, subgroupings, service units, and other complexities defy the
simplicity of a pecking order. "Pecking order" is not a good model of
human power relations.

Any human group that engages over time in a diversity of activities
becomes highly differentiated with respect to the relative effectiveness
of initiative displayed by its members in different activities. Members
heed and accept suggestions made by certain members in certain
activities, but not necessarily in others. For example, members heed
and accept suggestions made by certain members in sports more frequently than they do when the same members engage in activities
emphasizing quite different skills, say cooking a meal. Part of the role
differentiation in groups relates to such differing resources, skills, and
capacities of members relative to various activities, including their
interpersonal skills in providing good humor, adjusting interpersonal
difficulties, and so on.

Military research developed situational tests of effective initiative in
various activities in the hope of having a better basis for choosing
officer candidates (Gibb, 1969). Since it had proved impossible to
devise a paper-and-pencil test of ability or of personality that could
predict who would and would not do well as a military officer, the aim
was to bring candidates to several problem situations, ask them to solve
the problems, and see who, in fact, was most effective. For example, the
problem might be getting a delicate instrument across a stream, or
getting around an obstacle. There was one difficulty, however. Indeed
the men exhibited differences in effective initiative in each problem
situation, but the man who was most effective differed from one problem to the next. They had been hoping to find chickens A, B, and C, but
they found instead men whose rank was sometimes A, B, C; sometimes
B, C, A; sometimes C, A, B; and so on.

What specific *kinds of behavior* are effective in achieving status in a
particular human group varies considerably from one group and one
environmental context to others. Certainly we may find groups in
which assertive dominance characterizes such efforts. Interestingly one
such example is emotionally disturbed adolescents in a hospital ward,
where such behaviors were a primary means of gaining status (Rafferty,
1965). On the other hand, in another ward for male schizophrenics "it
is often the absence of overt dominance acts that reveal high status"
(Esser, 1970, p. 42). Despite that fact, "even severely disturbed patients
recognize possession and each other's status most of the time" (p. 43).
The closest correlate of status (and the relationship was almost perfect)
was the "ability for *sustained* social contact" that is the composite of
several observations on *duration* of social contacts among the patients.

In other words, higher status among these patients was associated with "getting better," having social contacts without attempts at dominance. Thus the peck-order analogy is a poor one even for disturbed, institutionalized adults. For normal human beings in a more varied and varying environment, the possible determinants of power and its behavioral manifestations are infinitely more complex and variable.

LEADERSHIP IN INTERPERSONAL RELATIONS

When individuals interact repeatedly in a variety of tasks, as they often do in human associations of great personal significance, the words and actions of certain individuals come to count more than those of other members in a variety of different situations and activities. In part, this generalization of their power occurs because persons in important relationships share problems other than the simple performance of tasks and the attainment of specific goals. There are problems of how members relate to one another, of how outsiders are to be treated, of how individual actions are to be coordinated. Individuals become acknowledged as more or less effective in these respects. The "power" is thus reciprocal and need not involve sheer "domination" of will or force.

Leadership in groups is, therefore, a reciprocal power relationship among members, much more than an attribute of a particular person. When an individual is recognized as the "leader," what is recognized is the person's status at the top of the power hierarchy. In a formal organization with officers, the office carries with it certain powers. Even in such formally organized groups, however, a power structure may arise that does not coincide entirely with the formal one. In such cases, effective initiative may be exercised by persons other than the president and other officers when important decisions are to be made and activities to be planned and executed. Similar discrepancies between traditional formal structure and how things actually happen are also found in families.

If you are patient, you can learn a great deal about the power aspect of interpersonal relations in groups by observing and noting the relative frequencies with which the members make suggestions, give and take advice, make decisions, and choose activities, and by noting the ways important activities are conducted. Whose words, actions, and efforts *count* more in what happens in your family, among your friends, in a club or committee? This question is different from our usual questions, which tend to be concerned with who talks the most, who gets more attention from others, who is most attractive, and who is liked most. At times, the answers will coincide, but such often is not the case. The exercise can be an eye opener.

There are important reasons why groups that associate for any length of time are likely to develop an overall power structure. First, because groups form when individuals' motivations are conducive to prolonged interaction, their activities tend to become specialized in directions related to the reasons they came together, emphasizing some abilities rather than others (for example, sports, verbal abilities, social skills, business acumen). Second, the process of achieving higher status includes the growing capacity to have more and more "say" in deciding what activities the group will engage in, and high-status members are likely to encourage activities in which they excel and discourage those in which they do not. (Juan's decline in power occurred, in part, because basketball was the league activity and could not be changed.) Third, interpersonal relations in any group present problems that have to do with coordination of the members, with enhancing unity among them and building solidarity. Members who help to achieve such ends are recognized, particularly in a small group, and are likely to achieve high status.

LEADERSHIP ROLES AND TECHNIQUES

We have come nearly full circle from the discussion in Chapter 3 about whether a differentiation of roles in a group always includes a "task" leadership and social-emotional roles, as many people inferred from Bales's research. The last section concluded that social-emotional and coordinating functions typically are performed by a leader in addition to whatever specialized skills that person has. Other members also perform these functions in varying degree. This conclusion is based on observational studies of many small, informal groups. Now, however, a different question arises: Will a leader who attends more to the social-emotional problems affect a group differently than one who does not, but instead focuses singlemindedly on effective task performance by the group?

A deluge of studies on this question followed the pioneering studies in the late 1930s of Kurt Lewin and his students at the University of Iowa. Lewin, Lippitt, and White (1939; Lippitt and White, 1965) were directly interested in the manner in which adults supervised clubs of 11-year-old boys. They set up clubs for handicraft activities and systematically varied the techniques used by the adults, so that each club operated for a time with each of three "leadership styles" in succession. The order of the three styles was varied for the several clubs (so that it could not be said that all effects depended solely on which was experienced first, for example). Several adults used each of the different techniques (so that it could not be said that a particular adult personality was solely responsible for the outcome).

The adult leadership styles were carefully specified, briefly, as follows: (1) The adult determined policy, procedures, and activities for the group, keeping his distance physically and socially from the boys and treating them in a matter-of-fact (none-too-friendly) manner. This technique was called authoritarian. (2) The adult encouraged members to participate in decisions and activities, gave technical assistance, and suggested procedures as needed, behaving in a friendly, helpful manner. This technique was called democratic. (3) The adult pretty well withdrew from the activity, keeping his own initiative and suggestions to a minimum and letting the boys pursue activities as they would. This technique was called laissez faire. (It seems to have been included because one adult leader misinterpreted the "democratic" role and kept "hands off.") Since the tasks were not very high in intrinsic interest for the boys and adult skills were needed, the hands off policy did produce quite different results.

The experiment demonstrated clearly that these three styles affected the behavior of members and group functioning, despite individual differences among boys within the groups and despite personality differences among the adults. The order in which a group experienced the three leadership styles did make a difference, however. For example, one club at first reacted passively to the authoritarian treatment; but after experiencing a "democratic" leader, its members were quite discontent with a return to the authoritarian style. Another club first had the laissez-faire treatment. As one might expect for 11-year-old boys not very absorbed by the tasks presented to them, they established a noisy, rowdy atmosphere in which nothing much got done. They maintained this rowdy behavior throughout most of the study, despite changes of adult leadership. There were also interesting individual differences in reaction to the different adult treatments. For example, whereas most boys greatly preferred the democratic style, the son of a military officer preferred the "authoritarian" adult.

The overall result was greater satisfaction among the boys with the democratic style, better interpersonal relationships, *and* more productivity in handicrafts. Other outcomes were more difficult to interpret, particularly those relating to interpersonal aggressive behaviors. In some cases, as noted, the authoritarian leader produced quiet, submissive boys whereas in others aggressive behavior increased. It is interesting that the latter occurred for the club that had experienced the hands-off adult first and had, as noted above, developed its own norms encouraging rowdiness anyway.

In the decades that followed the research, a flood of studies came out of industrial, business, workshop, and school settings that attempted to replicate the Lewin, Lippitt, and White experiment with adults. No doubt the world struggles in World War II and its aftermath provided fertile ground for repeated demonstration that leadership techniques bearing the title "democratic" would be superior to those labeled "authoritarian" or autocratic. Indeed, it is almost necessary to remove those words from the research to understand the problems that the findings raised. If we can agree that the *manner* in which leadership functions is only one of many possible issues in deciding whether a group is democratic or authoritarian in structure, we can see what these problems were.

In reviewing many studies on leadership style, Anderson (1963) concluded that almost all of the studies in different settings (industry, classroom, and so on) did show that members were happier and their morale higher when the leader encouraged member participation in a friendly manner, confining his directiveness to needed technical assistance. Groups with distant, cold, directive, and (in some cases) harsh leaders did not like the experience. However, the outcomes of this research in other respects were highly inconsistent. For example, there was no consistent superiority in how much a group produced or how effectively it performed the tasks presented to it with the "democratic" style.

LEADERSHIP STYLE IS CONTINGENT ON
OTHER ASPECTS OF THE GROUP SITUATION

The problem will become meaningful, I believe, if you ask yourself whether, under any circumstances, you function better with a leader who is highly directive in organizing and instructing performance in a task than with a leader who encourages you with other members to solve the problems, giving help when you ask for it. (Let us assume that there is not a striking difference between the styles with respect to the harshness of the leader in dealing with members, as cruelty is almost never appreciated.) This question has some practical importance for, as Fiedler (1968) pointed out, "millions of dollars and thousands of man hours each year are spent on management development and on leadership recruitment, selection and training" in business, government, and education (p. 362). Is one style or the other so superior that all people that are to be placed in leadership positions ought to be trained to use one style or the other, or that individuals should be selected on the basis of how well they perform one style or the other?

Fiedler conducted extensive research on a variety of different kinds of groups—athletic teams; work teams in business, research, and production; and military units in the United States and Belgium. Most of them were natural groups, not formed expressly for the research. He focused on the effectiveness of the group in task performance (productivity), which could be assessed, for example, by a sport team's wins or losses or a work group's time and quantity of output.

Fiedler found that persons who habitually took a highly directive role in getting tasks done differed from persons who customarily focus on maintaining a positive flavor in interpersonal relationships in the manner in which they rated coworkers. Specifically, he found that directive, task-oriented leaders tended to rate their "least preferred coworker" much more negatively than the less directive, social-emotionally oriented leader. The evidence that leaders who rate their least preferred coworker more harshly also exercise more directive leadership, as well as the reasons why, are weaker links in the Fiedler research. Nevertheless, using such ratings as the primary basis for assessing leadership style, Fiedler has shown quite convincingly that leadership style does not bear a simple direct causal relationship to the effectiveness of group performance.

Fiedler considered three factors other than leadership style: (1) whether leader-member relations were "good" or "poor," as indicated by their mutual liking; (2) whether the leader, by virtue of his or her formal position, had strong or weak power (authority); and (3) whether the tasks undertaken were structured or unstructured (as defined by how many correct solutions there were, how clear the steps to be taken by each member, and how many correct procedures there were to perform the task). He collected data on performance by 800 groups, some with directive, task-oriented leaders and some with leaders more concerned with positive interpersonal relationships (as defined by their own ratings of their least preferred coworkers). Some with each brand of leadership had good and some poor relations with other members, and some leaders of each brand had high authority (power) and some weak. For each combination of those two factors, some groups performed structured tasks and some unstructured tasks.

You can see that Fiedler's research was an ambitious attempt to assess the effects of leadership styles on performance within the context of the specific group situations in which they occurred. Would a highly directive leader always produce less effective performance? Would a more social-emotionally oriented leader always produce more effective performance? The answer to both was "No, it depends."

The more directive leadership style was associated with better performance when relationships with followers were *good* and the task was *structured*, regardless of whether the leader's authority was strong or weak. The directive leadership style was also more effective in unstructured tasks when leader-member relations were good and the leader had strong power. The leader's friendly relationships with members boosted his or her authority, making his or her directives effective in the members' performance of the unstructured task.

What about the person-oriented leadership? It was associated with better group performance when the task was structured and the leader had strong power, but leader-member relations were not good. Presumably, Fiedler commented, such a leader has to be "diplomatic and concerned with the feelings of his men" (1968, p. 372). Similarly, person-oriented leadership is advisable when the leader is liked, but has little authority, and faces an unstructured task. He "must, therefore, depend upon the . . . cooperation of his members." In the situation where all of the dice are loaded against good performance (namely, the leader has weak power, poor relations with members, and faces an unstructured task) the directive leader seems to achieve the better results more often (provided, of course, that he and other members do not simply throw up their hands in despair). As in Milgram's research (Chapter 1), sheer authority was not sufficient, however, to produce compliance to directives in all circumstances.

The important outcome of Fiedler's research is that the effectiveness of leadership *style* for group performance depends on other important factors in the group—how well the leader gets along with other members, the power his or her position provides, and the kinds of tasks to be tackled. Leadership alone does not "determine" a group situation. This realization permits more careful analysis of specific groups, for example, small classroom groups (Hardy, 1971). One's aim might be setting up learning situations most favorable for a particular style of leadership or, conversely, selecting a leader whose style is most appropriate for a particular classroom situation. Since there is no leadership style that is "always best," Fiedler turns a jaundiced eye on "leadership training" and suggests attention to what is called for in particular group situations.

THE LEADER AS A GROUP MEMBER

Fiedler's research is, I believe, the clearest exposition of why social psychologists these days get very squeamish about talking in terms of "personality" of leaders. It would be nonsense to say that a leader's personal qualities and style of interacting with members have no importance, for the leader's higher power makes these more significant than for any other single member. But researchers are aware, as Fiedler's research shows, that leadership qualities and their effects in a group are, like those of other members, dependent on the entire group context: what the members do, what is important to them, the norms they develop, particularly with regard to the conduct of daily affairs, and the group's relationships with outsiders. Such awareness is contrary to our common sense notions about leaders and leadership, which are frequently endowed with almost mystic qualities and powers.

Nevertheless, the more complicated view of leadership as a role within a specific group context was forced on researchers before Fiedler by the utter failure of research into personality characteristics of leaders. As assessed by psychologists, leader personalities vary as much as those in a random sample from the normal population. While the leader typically excels other members of the group in some respect, a long line of research on leadership revealed that it is not possible to predict *what* respect that will be without knowing about the activities, the other members, and the values or norms of the group context (Gibb, 1969). The most comprehensive reviews of leadership conclude with some such statement as Gibb's, that leadership "is a function of personal attributes and social system in dynamic interaction" (1969, p. 270).

In this chapter the emphasis has been on various properties of the social system (group) that regulate its dynamics. If the extensive research on leaders was forced to such conclusions about the personality and styles of *leaders*, how much more important it becomes for us to recognize and fully accept their implications for understanding the behavior of other, less powerful members.

GROUP SOLIDARITY, UNITY, OR COHESIVENESS

As noted in the last chapter, there have been many theories about the "cement" binding members together as a group. In order to describe how closely members stick to one another, how distinct their social unit is, and how strong their feeling of "we-ness," a variety of terms have been used, including group "solidarity," "cohesiveness," and "integration."

The importance of a group's cohesiveness or solidarity can hardly be overestimated, particularly since we are concerned about individual experience and behavior in group situations. Clearly, the unity of the group is in itself an important boundary for the impact of its normative and power system. I wish, therefore, that clear-cut evidence were available about what produces group cohesiveness and about its effects on member behavior.

Almost all research on the effects of varying cohesiveness on member behavior has utilized the practical availability of sociometric techniques and defined cohesiveness in terms of how much members *like* one another or, at times, in terms of member ratings of how attractive the group is (Cartwright and Zander, 1968; Collins and Raven, 1969; Lott and Lott, 1965). However, members' attractiveness to one another and members' ratings of the attractiveness of the group as a whole are not necessarily closely correlated. Apparently, we can be fond of certain members, but rate the group as a whole as a lost cause. Conversely, the group can be attractive to us even though individual members are not liked all that much. To complicate the picture, liking of members for one another does not necessarily relate closely to two very important outcomes of high cohesiveness, namely, agreement among members on the group norms and agreement among members on mutual role expectations (Feldman, 1968).

When we observe natural groups in real life, it quickly becomes apparent that the unit character of a group is a complex product related

to how stable relationships among members are, the degree of agreement as to group norms, the proper exercise of power, and a host of
outside conditions over which the group, as such, has very little direct
control. These latter include how important the group is in the lives of
its members compared with other groups, the scope of its activities in
the members' lives, how long they have associated or can associate, and
the relative successes or failures encountered in coping with problems
or in achieving mutual goals (Sherif and Sherif, 1969, Chapter 8).
Furthermore, such conditions can produce high cohesiveness among
members even when they choose each other from mutual necessity, not
mutual attraction. Individuals sometimes do find themselves in the
same boat, whether they like it or not.

Most of the research studying groups that vary in their cohesiveness, however defined, shows that members of more cohesive groups
influence one another more, react more strongly to deviation, and are
more responsive to group norms (Collins and Raven, 1969, pp. 122–
124). There is also indication that highly cohesive groups are apt to
influence the behavior of members even when they are not in the actual
presence of the group (Sherif and Sherif, 1964). But we would expect
such to be the case.

One reason that there is not very much more to be said at this point
about group solidarity or cohesiveness is that the concept is one of
those whose study requires cooperation from both sociologists and
psychologists. When we are looking for what makes a group more
cohesive, we need social scientists to study factors affecting the group
as a whole. When we ask questions about the effects of varying cohesiveness on members, on the other hand, we are asking a social-
psychological question that presumes we know what it is about the
group that makes it cohesive. Our need for more input on the sociological aspects becomes obvious when we realize that some of the clearest
evidence about conditions affecting group cohesiveness does not pertain directly to members' liking of one another or their attraction to the
group at all. This evidence indicates that, in many circumstances,
threats, dangers, or problems from outside produce increased group
solidarity or cohesion. Since many such threats or problems are
posed from outside by another group, it follows that we may learn a
great deal more about the impact of a group on member behavior by
considering relationships *among* groups, which we do in the next
chapter.

When Persons Belong to Different Groups

A fish, it is said, is the last to recognize the existence of water. We human beings are so much a part of the stream of daily life that we seldom become aware of the stream itself. What composes the stream, its origin, where it is leading, the directions of the currents become matters of concern when something momentous or frightening compels us to consider them.

We attend to affairs *between* groups—intergroup relations—chiefly when there is "trouble." "Trouble" usually means that members of the respective groups are by that time lining up on opposite sides of the 50-yard line with their backs toward their own goal lines, ready to charge. The rules have been set already. We face the showdown. It is small wonder that government commissions and textbooks on education, community problems, and urban sociology use the phrase "intergroup relations" as synonymous with "something that needs improving."

Before we can find "answers" to troubling problems of intergroup relations, we have to learn to ask the right questions. When "trouble" arises between groups, the first questions that are usually asked concern the particular individuals involved: How can those people *act* that way? What gets into a person to behave like that? The tendency to ask such questions may be "natural," but it has been strongly reinforced by traditions of individualistic psychologizing that ask questions about a person as though he or she were in a vacuum.

Such psychologizing often justifies its focus on the individual through crude analogy with the physical sciences: If we want to understand the structure of matter, we have to know about atoms. An individual is the social atom. To understand an atom, we first have to identify it: Is it oxygen or carbon? However, we really won't understand an oxygen or carbon atom unless we find out something about subatomic particles—neutrons, protons, and the like. Isn't that same procedure the best one for studying individual behavior? Then, we need to search for something *inside* the individual, such as a motive, a need, a drive.

Such analogy with models of physical science forgets some elementary chemistry lessons: A carbon atom "behaves" quite differently in charcoal, in a diamond crystal, or in air (where it may link in various molecular arrangements—carbon dioxide, carbon monoxide, and so on). Far more than a carbon atom, the human individual is an "open" system. Tremendously dependent upon the social milieu from birth, capable of developing abilities to reflect and to act on both self and the social milieu, the human being's actions cannot be understood in a vacuum as though no ties with others exist.

Relationships among groups and the histories of those relationships (as well as personal histories) permeate the "here and now," whether an individual is aware of the fact or not. Relationships between persons, among group members, and between members of different groups are not the same, however. Each may be "good" or "bad"; each may be pleasant or unpleasant; each may be constructive or destructive. Still, they are not the same. It makes a difference whether the relationship occurs within the warm, comfortable bounds of one's own group or across its boundaries with members of another group, even when the two groups are friendly.

This chapter deals with intergroup relations as a process with a history of its own that bounds the experience and behavior of individual members in the respective groups whenever they have dealings across group lines. By intergroup relations, I mean interchange (face to face or indirect) between two or more groups and their respective members. The groups may be small or large; their relations may be friendly or hostile. However, they are *groups*, as defined in the last chapter.

Therefore, an act of love or hate, friendship or aggression, collaboration or antagonism is *intergroup* behavior when it occurs between an individual (or individuals) belonging to one group and an individual (or individuals) belonging to another group, either or both of them acting in terms of their respective group membership (with its standards for loyalty, established views of the other group, goals, etc.

A lot of love and hate, friendly and aggressive action, help and hindrance occur that is *not* intergroup behavior. When such behaviors occur in an intergroup context, however, they cannot be understood apart from the relations between the groups in question. We cannot understand aggression between members of different groups in identical terms with a man beating his wife or a parent abusing a child. The feelings and the actions may be similar; the context and the "causes" are not. A plan for preventing or changing one can, therefore, be inappropriate for the other.

I am making a point of these distinctions because they fly in the face of much modern folk wisdom. For example, there are today many reports on social violence that lump together child abuse, homicide, assault, "juvenile delinquency" of the most varied acts, interracial riots, prison riots, protests, and war. These are certainly all social problems. They are just as surely not all to be understood in identical terms. Many of these "problems" involve intergroup relations; others do not.

This chapter summarizes experiments on intergroup relations that are among the more fascinating in social psychology. Just as the last chapter oriented us to interactions *within* groups, so this chapter tackles intergroup contexts of behavior in a general way. The experimental model of intergroup relations can provide orientation for later chapters that deal with specific examples of prejudicial attitudes, stereotyped images, and hostility between groups of many different kinds in real life (Chapters 10, 13). Such a model is particularly useful for intergroup relations since each of us is on one side or another of racial, ethnic, sex, religious, political, and national group boundaries that often we can view only from our own side.

We need not pretend that the experiments to be summarized, naturalistic though they were, are exact models of those intergroup relations that concern each of us most. In fact, they are not. For one thing, many of the most consequential intergroup relations occur between groups standing in dominant-subordinate relations, with associated notions of superiority-inferiority. Such differentials between groups in terms of power, of economic, cultural, or educational level properly concern us, and they immediately enlist our sympathies on one side or the other. The experiments to be summarized do not, for the groups were equal in almost every way. We can forestall personal identification with one or the other in order to understand the logic and the process of what transpired between them. We can seek to understand, not in order to forgive but to learn more realistically, what steps must be taken to change what goes wrong in intergroup affairs.

REMINISCENCE OF AN EYEWITNESS:
HOW THE RESEARCH HAPPENED

The experiments summarized in this chapter were created and directed by Muzafer Sherif. Three separate experiments were conducted between 1949 and 1954, each lasting three weeks and each taking place at a summer camp organized and run solely for this research. Together with recruitment of research staff, selection of participants, detailed planning, and, later, compiling and reporting what happened, each experiment involved months of hard work by many individuals.

The research is not "typical" in social psychology, but it strikes me as an interesting case study on how research happens to be done. In my mind, there is no doubt that the experiments were labors of love that came to rank almost as an obsession for those deeply involved in them, notably for their director, but also for O. J. Harvey (now at the University of Colorado), the late W. R. Hood, Marvin Sussman (now at Case Western Reserve University), B. J. White (now at the University of Utah), and me.

Any research worth doing starts with questions or a puzzle that plagues the researcher and that, it seems, can be clarified by seeing what happens in concrete circumstances that are planned so that the researcher's hunches about possible answers can be tested. Such tests rule out other possible explanations as much as possible.

Surely it is no accident that these particular experiments on intergroup relations should take shape in the mind of a Turkish social psychologist in the United States as the conflagrations and tragedies of World War II smouldered, who had married an American. We were keenly aware that our marriage was an intergroup affair. Had we not been, we would have soon learned.

Item: My husband was the invited guest speaker at a state psychological convention. We met the hospitable and charming woman who had planned the event. Shortly, officers of the state association joined us and she introduced me: "This is Mrs. Sher-*eef*." (Strong accent on the last syllable, thus definitely a "foreign" name.) Turning to my husband, she began: "And this is our speaker. . . ." Silence. For nearly a minute the woman was speechless. Finally, he stepped into the breach, stating his name and shaking hands all around. What had happened? She had just spoken *his* name in introducing me, but she "forgot" the name of her invited speaker. (This American girl simply could not have the same name as the Turk who stood beside her!)

Item: At a dinner party given by a Turkish student, I sat across the table from the chic, elegant wife of a Turkish businessman. Since I spoke no Turkish and she no English, any conversation had to be translated, while each of us spoke to others in native tongues. I could not help noticing that she repeatedly glanced at me and then made short comments that were not translated. Later I learned that they went like this: "I know a girl in Istanbul who has her coloring. . . . That girl is better looking. . . . She plays the piano very well. . . . She speaks German as well as English and French. . . . Why do you suppose Muzafer married this American?" (After our marriage, my husband learned that he was considered to have "resigned" his professorship in Turkey for having married a "foreigner.")

Recent item: Bill Hosowaka, American born and educated associate editor of the Denver *Post* (whose father had emigrated from Japan), was introduced at a cocktail party to a rather important political figure, who began a conversation: "Mr. Hosowaka, how long have you been in our country?" Noting the politician's youth, Hosowaka replied, "Sir, I think I have been in our country ten or fifteen years longer than you" (New York *Times*, August 8, 1973, p. 33 M).

Recent item: Dr. Donald Granberg, of the University of Missouri, was showing the baby he and his wife had adopted to interested students. The infant girl was a war orphan of Vietnamese and black American parentage. While discussing the circumstances of the adoption and her development, one university student asked: "Will she speak English with an accent?"

Each of these incidents would be puzzling, even illogical if the participants had not been members of different groups, drawing lines or making invidious comparisons that reflected the singular perspective of their own group. When we met, as well as today, there were sharp divisions within and between countries along political, racial, ethnic, economic, and religious lines. Then, as now, the most pressing human woes are tied to problems between groups and their actions toward one another, so ruthless as to stagger the imagination if assessed by the standards of justice or decency accepted for treating others *within* the groups in question. Then, as now, we found it puzzling that the most prevalent views purporting to "explain" intergroup behavior and attitudes seemed to end up merely denouncing them as bad, as irrational, as uncontrollable.

Example: Aggression is a biological instinct that must and will be expressed from time to time in action (see, for example, Freud, 1930; Lorenz, 1963). As instinct, it is by definition irrational. If so, why are some groups more aggressive than others? Inbreeding, you reply? Then how do we account for wars of liberation by peoples once characterized as "passive"? Why were black youth thirty years ago less "aggressive" than their children are today?

Another example: Frustration as the individual strives toward individual goals leads to aggression. Aggression is therefore an irrational response unless aggressive behavior removes the source of frustration (see, for example, Dollard, Doob, Miller, Mowrer, Sears, 1939). Why, then, do some white Americans aggress against native Americans, whose potential to thwart their goals was effectively removed a hundred years ago? Why, indeed, are even now only a small proportion of native Americans at all aggressive since surely their lives are persistently frustrating?

Variation on the last example: Aggressive responses to frustration that cannot be expressed owing to inability to attack the actual frustrator are stored up until a weaker, less powerful target for aggression is found as the scapegoat (see, for example, Allport, 1954). But who picks the scapegoat? *Why* is the target invariably designated by the most powerful in the society—are *they* the most frustrated? In the century following the Civil War why didn't poor white southerners concentrate on lynching other poor white southerners, who were equally as powerless as black southerners if the powers-that-be had decided to permit their lynching? The "scapegoat" theory is inadequate in answering many questions of this kind (Berkowitz, 1962).

In 1947 when the first notions of the intergroup experiments began to take shape, the predominant theories of intergroup prejudice and aggression focused on the motives of individuals. Each, in its own way, laid the onus on the individual, seeking remedies through altering the ways children might be frustrated by their parents, psychotherapy, or appeals to individual morality. Often the image of the prejudiced person that emerged was one of a neurotic, a deviant compelled by inner complexes to aggress against others until a miracle from psychotherapy could relieve their pressure.

Muzafer Sherif was now Research Fellow at Yale, finishing his *Outline of Social Psychology* (1948). We were both reading furiously on intergroup conflicts of all kinds—between racial, ethnic, religious, labor-management, and national groups. The various reports shared common themes concerning intergroup relations, and it was from these common themes found in actual life that hypotheses for the experiments were drawn. Here, somewhat abridged, is the summary on the "psychology" of intergroup hostility, negative attitudes, and prejudice that appeared in that book:

A "we" and "they" delineation is one of the main products of group formation—with positive values becoming invested within the "we" formation, the "we" including the members of the group (small or large). The "we" thus circumscribed has real or fancied qualities and values to be upheld and cherished dearly. Any offenses from without and deviations from within are reacted to with appropriate corrective, defensive and at times offensive measures. "They," from the point of view of the group . . . are invested with a set of values, "traits" (favorable, unfavorable, or various combinations thereof). The favorable or unfavorable properties or "traits" attributed to "they" groups and, inevitably, to their individual members in a rather absolutistic way are determined by the *nature of positive or negative relations between the groups in question.* If the interests, directions, and goals of the intergroup relations are integrated or in harmony, the features attributed to "they" groups are favorable. If the activities and views clash while the interacting groups pursue their peculiar interests and goals, the features are negative. . . . Even in . . . spontaneously formed little groups, feuds and corresponding negative attitudes arise which in time tend to become standardized, if the gangs last. This appeared in the experimental study by Lewin and his associates [see Chapter 4]. Once groups of boys were more or less delineated in their "democratic" and "laissez-faire" atmospheres, *without any integration of the groups,* insulting words were hurled spontaneously at members of the opposite group and fights broke out. The members of the "democratic" group did not stop to resolve the friction by democratic methods. *Democratic procedure was something to be practiced among themselves* (the in-group) in making masks.

Even these simple illustrations lead us to the generalization that positive or negative attitudes in intergroup relationships are the outcome of integration or lack of integration of the interests, goals and the resulting views of the groups in question. Once "in-group" and "out-group" delineations take place, attitudes necessarily arise that define the reciprocal positions of the groups. If one group takes the stand that the other is in its way, interferes with its goals and vital interests, or should be working for its interests, all sorts of "traits" are attributed as inherent qualities of the out-group to justify the stand taken, and the existing or contemplated actions. All racial superiority doctrines are, deliberately or unconsciously, justifications of this sort. The attributed inherent "traits" are labels standardized to perpetuate certain practices advantageous to the interests of the dominant group. (Sherif, 1948, pp. 357–358)

Beyond what was said about the "logic" of intergroup attitudes and behavior, this summary suggested further hunches about their change. It followed that changes in attitude and behavior of individuals could be achieved not by so many discrete individual efforts, but by altering the external conditions so that the "interests and goals" of the various groups would be integrated, not conflicting.

How on Earth to Test the Picture?

The notion of an experimental test became more and more vivid and, early in 1948, we began to speak of it in earnest. Lewin, Lippitt, and White's experiments with boys' groups gave the notion that such experimentation was possible; but they had some disadvantages, too. In the first place, those groups had met for short periods in experimental rooms. Such a plan was not advantageous because we suspected that a rather continual immersion in group life and intergroup relations would be necessary. Whatever happened in a couple of hours could readily be countered by events that occurred outside of the experimental situation. Besides, we felt that young boys would be reluctant to behave in ways that might incur adult disapproval if they knew that their every move was being observed, recorded, and judged. The plan would work, theoretically, only if their activities together had strong motivational appeal. Where and how could such an experiment be done?

I had had experience for several years as a counselor in summer camps and suggested such a possible location for research. Muzafer was not acquainted with such camps, so he spent a good part of the summer of 1948 visiting a variety of camps run by the New York *Herald Tribune* Fresh Air Fund to find out how they were organized, what activities were typical and possible, and what boys liked to do there. (Later we checked favored activities of the boys who actually participated in the camp experiments, using their choices as the basis for what was done.) Then, the first experiment was planned for the summer of 1949 in Connecticut. Boys were to be 12-year-olds, because boys that age are well developed physically and intellectually, and they usually adore camping.

EXPERIMENTAL PLAN

The plan of the experiment was clear from the theoretical account:

1. We had to have (at least) two groups—real groups as defined in Chapter 4.
2. The groups had to come into functional contact in situations where their interests and goals were not integrated, but conflicting. It seemed that this could be arranged through activities where one group could attain its goals only by defeating the efforts of the other group and where one group would, by its actions, frustrate every member of the other group *because of* their respective group memberships.
3. Finally, the aim was to change conditions between the groups so that their goals were not conflicting, but integrated, such that the efforts of both groups pointed in the same direction. If the theory was correct, their intergroup relations should change and, gradually, the attitudes and behaviors of individual members.

But what about other explanations that could be made if, indeed, groups formed, developed hostilities, and came into conflict? For one thing, it seemed clear that if the boys knew one another beforehand, their *past acquaintanceships* would affect what happened. All right: Each boy could be chosen from a sixth-grade class in a different school. We would check to see whether they knew each other before accepting them at camp. In each experiment 22 to 24 boys were selected who were not acquainted before the experiment.

For another thing, it seemed obvious that preexisting *differences in background* might well be a basis for invidious comparisions before camp even started. Therefore, let the boys be as similar in that respect as possible. We chose from Protestant, middle-class respectability to ensure that no one could say that there was a prior basis for discriminating among the boys or that they, as individuals, had had experiences of being discriminated against.

What about the psychological theories that worried us at the time? Well, we could ensure that no one could make a case for attributing what happened to severe or undue frustration in their life histories by selecting boys from stable, middle-class families, average or above in achievement in school and in acceptance by their age-mates in school and neighborhood. We could even (and we did) have psychological tests to ensure that we had a very normal, healthy population and medical examinations to ensure good health. No one could conjecture, then, that anything occurring during the experiment was a direct manifestation of severe individual frustration, neuroticism, or deviancy.

In the experiments themselves, we controlled the possibility that one or another group would have advantages through differences among the individuals composing the groups. The boys who ended up in, one group were matched as closely as possible with those in the other, according to physical size, pertinent skills and interests, and known past accomplishments. In short, we ended up with two groups in each case as similar as possible in terms of the individuals composing them.

Finally, as spelled out in Chapter 3 in some detail, there was the possibility that group formation merely involved mutual attractions among persons who liked one another, hence bred distrust for those in another group toward whom initial attraction had not been as strong. In the first two camp experiments, this possibility was eliminated, you may recall, by first allowing mutual attractions to develop freely and then deliberately splitting the incipient friendships when the camp was divided into two cabin groups. In the last experiment, the groups never saw each other until after they formed.

HOW THE EXPERIMENTS DIFFERED
FROM ANY OLD SUMMER CAMP

You will recall the concerns that led to choosing summer camps as the locations for the experiments: The boys could be together continuously over a period, isolated from outside influences including their families, and could engage in activities of high motivational appeal to them in a natural way. The boys were not to be aware that they were "guinea pigs," that their words and deeds were being observed, or that any of the sequence of events was proceeding through a plan other than their own preferences.

Parents were informed of the study purpose of the camp. Any awareness that the boys might have had of being research subjects was allayed from the start by having research personnel on the scene in regular jobs to be found in any summer camp: camp director, senior counselors, junior counselors (who were really experienced campers under orders of the researchers), and so on. Sherif also appeared on the scene in a camp role: In the first experiment, he was the camp caretaker, which permitted him to roam far and wide without anyone paying attention to him. (In fact, by coincidence, we met one former camper about six years afterward. He told us in detail about the terrific summer camp he had gone to, recalling names of the director, counselors, and campers; but even though he talked for the better part of an hour with the camp's caretaker, he failed completely to recognize him. Some social roles succeed in making a person "invisible"!)

All data were collected without arousing awareness of the boys. Observers made notes and ratings immediately after leaving the boys. Reliability and validity were checked through a combination of different methods, of the kind outlined in Chapter 4. In addition, the major findings up to the final stage of the last experiment (to be discussed later) were replicated in three separate experiments at different locations, involving different boys.

How then were these studies experiments? As already noted, the selection of boys was one aspect of the design. The other major feature was that during the three weeks of camp, the *activities* engaged in and the *conditions for contact* among the boys were systematically controlled and then changed. This experimental control of activities and conditions forms the basis for what was predicted about the boys' behavior over time. It is important to note that while the researchers indeed were controlling and changing the *kinds* of activities and the contacts among the boys, this experimental control was achieved through giving the boys much more leeway than they would have had in the usual summer camp to state their preferences for activities and to plan and execute them themselves. That is one reason why the boys developed such strong identifications with their groups and felt that what happened in the camp was of their own planning and their own doing.

IF IT'S INTER*GROUP* BEHAVIOR, THERE HAVE TO BE GROUPS

Reading the summary of these experiments, you may readily conclude that the outcomes are so clear that they should have been "obvious." I can assure you that, at the time, the predicted outcomes were not obvious. At the time, many novel problems were facing the researchers.

Theoretically, the study of intergroup behavior required the existence of at least two groups, but the research plan called for individuals who were unacquainted at the outset. How could we determine *when* we could call the individuals a group?

This question led us to face the problem of what a group is and what criteria could be used to decide *when* a collection of individuals becomes a group. In Chapters 3 and 4, the background of our efforts to solve these problems was given, including the criteria (status-role relations, a set of norms, and we-feelings). In the experiments themselves, we started with a simple hypothesis: A group will form when unacquainted individuals interact over time in series of activities that have common appeal value to them and that require their interdependent efforts in order to attain their goals.

The initial experimental conditions were, then: The boys assigned to a cabin were encouraged to choose and plan activities with each other that involved all of them, while contacts with the other cabin were discouraged through geographical separation, different schedules for meals, and so on.

In all three experiments, as reported in Chapter 3, groups did develop—each with its own small power structure and each with its own miniature culture. The culture included assorted nicknames epitomizing member roles, special procedures for performing tasks, jargon, special jokes, secrets, and definite preferences for particular places, many of which they named. (For example, after killing a snake near the creek, one group dubbed it "Moccasin Creek" and thereafter preferred to swim there, rather than any number of better locations nearby.) They referred to themselves as "us," "we," and even called their cabins "home." Wayward members who failed to do their bit in activities, who bullied other members, who did not do things "right" (as their norms defined it) found themselves receiving reprimands, ridicule, "silent treatment," and even penalties exacted by members of higher status with the approval of the others. (The latter were typically threats or, in one group, a standardized penalty of removing heavy stones from the stream to raise the water level for swimming.)

In each study, the groups eventually adopted names, but this occurred when they were anticipating sport competition. The names, each providing a glorified handle for the in-group, reflected the ecology and the general culture of the small groups. For example, in the 1949 study near Yale University in Connecticut, one group called themselves Bull Dogs (the Yale mascot) and the other Red Devils (Sherif and Sherif, 1953). In 1953, in the woods of upstate New York, the group names adopted were the Panthers and the Pythons (Sherif, White, and Harvey, 1955). In the 1954 experiment—conducted in Oklahoma at Robbers Cave, a famous hideaway reputedly used by the outlaws Jesse James and Belle Starr, the groups took the names of Rattlers and Eagles (Sherif, Harvey, White, Hood, and Sherif, 1961), inspired by the snakes and hawks native to the region.

From this point, the summary will be clearer if we stick chiefly to one pair of groups and what happened between them. Therefore, most of my account will be taken from the 1954 experiment at Oklahoma involving the saga of the Rattlers and the Eagles. (Later, I'll also refer to the Bull Dogs and Red Devils from the 1949 study in Connecticut.)

"IRRATIONAL" BEHAVIOR BY NORMAL PERSONS

Let us suppose that you are a visitor to the camp at Robbers Cave one morning about a week after the camp started. Your hosts take you to the baseball diamond, and here is what you see:

One small group is on the field, each wearing a T-shirt labeled "Rattlers." The boys are clustered around a partially burnt piece of cloth, on which a few letters and the picture of a snake are still visible. They are excited, shouting, conferring. Now, down the path another group appears, bearing banners labeled "Eagles." One boy from the Rattlers strides up to them, followed on each side by other red-faced Rattlers with clenched fists. The boy holds out the flag, asking who burned it. The Eagles proudly claim: "We did! Who did you think?"

At that one Rattler darts out to one of the Eagle flags, wrests it away, and runs down the road with Rattlers and Eagles behind him in pursuit. Meanwhile, other Eagles run onto the field to seize a Rattler flag standing in the field. Rattlers turn to defend it, but the Eagles succeed in ripping it to shreds. A Rattler grabs an Eagle in a wrestling hold, demanding: "Which one of you guys burned our flag?" The captured Eagle shouts: "We *all* did!"

Fist fights break out. The Rattlers who had captured the Eagle flag returned, followed by the Eagles who had pursued them and who are now red-faced with angry tears in their eyes. One yells out for a Rattler "my size" to beat up, and a Rattler volunteers.

At this point, the adult camp staff has intervened to prevent further fighting and to start the game. The game goes on furiously with members of each group jeering each other ("Stinkers!" "Cheats!" "Damn niggers!" "Communists!"—the latter epithets hurled in the adult world at the time). When the game is over, there is a half-hearted cheer from the winners to the losers ("good sportsmanship" was not completely dead).

You follow the Eagles down the road. They are praising one another for their victory in the game, one boy saying that they had won because they had prayed to win. Another agrees, saying the Rattlers lost because they use swear words all of the time. Everyone agrees and then one boy concludes that since the Rattlers were such stinkers, poor sports, and "bad cussers," the Eagles should not even talk to them again.

This episode occurred only a few days after the two groups came into contact for the first time. If you had been invited to the camp later, you would have seen repeated episodes of name calling, mutual anger, attempts to fight, destructive raids on each other's cabin, and finally the furious Eagles demanding certain possessions stolen by Rattlers, and the Rattlers scornfully replying that the Eagles could have them if they fell to their bellies and crawled! What would you think of these boys?

An outside observer who walked in at this point, with no information about what had gone on before, might have concluded that these boys were disturbed, vicious, and cruel. The behaviors warrant such descriptions; yet these boys had been chosen from the "cream of the crop" in their own localities, had known one another only a little over a week, and had seen the other group for the first time only a couple of days previous. Was there any logic at all to these emotional, hateful scenes?

WHAT IS *SUFFICIENT* CAUSE?

We were interested in conditions sufficient to arouse hostility, negative evaluations, and aggressive behaviors among members of different groups. If we could show that normal, healthy boys as similar as peas in a pod would, under specified conditions, behave in these ways we could say that those *conditions* were *sufficient* to produce these behaviors. (Other factors might, of course, be involved in actual intergroup relations in real life, such as dominating exploitation of one group by the other, leadership bent on selfish interests, cultural differences, religious differences, differences in skin color or appearance, and so on.)

What were the sufficient conditions? Here was our prediction: Hostilities will arise between members of two groups when they come into contact in a series of activities in which each group urgently desires to attain goals that can be won only at the expense of the other group.

To translate these conditions into daily activities, the camp staff yielded to the requests from each group of boys that they would like to compete in sports with another group. (The cultural context has to be stressed to grasp the urgency of their desires. Mexican peasant boys, for example, might not express such a desire spontaneously.) The adults further cooperated by asking the groups to choose the activities in which they would like to compete and by arranging a schedule of events and offering prizes to the victorious group in the entire tournament.

Thus, the competitive structure of games, which permitted successive wins and losses by each group, was transformed into a prolonged series of events in which victory for one group meant loss for the other group, including the loss of the much admired awards (a loving cup and elaborate camping knives for individual members). To emphasize this total victory-loss relationship, charts placed in the dining halls daily recorded *cumulative* scores gained by each group.

As the tournament of games began, the two groups encountered each other for the first time. They were very evenly matched in terms of individual participants. Like good boys brought into the sport complex of their society, they knew and practiced good sportsmanship. At first, courtesy and appreciation to the other group were evident. As we saw, by the second day, the code of good sportsmanship had begun to erode. In the end, it was dead as a doornail.

The events that you saw as a visitor happened quite spontaneously as a result of the Eagles' actions the previous night in burning the Rattler flag. The first day, the Rattlers had won the first baseball game and, after supper, a tug-of-war. Although the Rattlers had developed a "culture" of rough-toughness and cursing, they also attributed their victories that day to their appeals for divine guidance. The prayer at their evening meal was as follows: "Dear Lord, we thank Thee for the food and for the cooks that cooked it, and for the ball game we won today."

The dejected Eagles (whose loss was attributable to their poorer team coordination) speculated that those guys must be "at least eighth-graders" (that is, a couple of years older than they). On their way past the ballfield, they noticed the Rattler flag on the backstop. The Rattlers had placed it there because they had improved the field and considered it theirs. Suddenly, an Eagle scaled the backdrop and pulled the flag down. Others ran and tried to tear it, which failed. Then someone set it afire. What was left of the burned flag was put back up. The Eagles sang "Taps" in mock solemnity and the boys left, their leader saying, "You can tell those guys I did it if they say anything. I'll fight 'em!" Everyone felt better and began to talk and plan for the contests of the next day.

Isn't that a good example of aggression stemming from frustration? Yes, it is; but it was not individual frustration irrationally responded to. The Rattlers had thwarted the Eagles as a group, and as group members the Eagles engaged in aggressive insult calculated as symbolic expression for their lack of respect and to rattle the Rattlers. As we saw, they succeeded. The Eagles won the baseball game the following day. They developed a strategy that enabled them to tie in the second tug-of-war. There was a great deal of planning activity involved in these events.

When the second tug-of-war started, the Eagles sat down and dug their heels into the ground, on prearranged signal. The Rattlers stood pulling to no avail. The rules had not specifically barred such tactics, so the contest continued for about 7 minutes at a stalemate. Finally, the Rattlers adopted their rivals' strategy, sat down and also dug in. Both groups tugged away for another 33 minutes, at which time a limit of 15 additional minutes was announced. The event ended in a tie as the Rattlers kept their last man from crossing the line.

Divergent Experiences from Group Viewpoints

After the tug-of-war each individual in each group was asked how long the contest had lasted after both groups sat down and dug in. Every Eagle gave the time estimate in minutes, whereas Rattlers estimated the duration from 1 to 3½ hours. The largest Eagle estimate was 45 minutes and the smallest was 20 to 25 minutes. On the average, to experience that contest as an Eagle meant to underestimate its duration by 18 minutes, whereas to be a Rattler mean to overestimate the time by 12 mintues. Time duration, which is subject to considerable error, here reflected the boys' experiences as group members.

Intergroup Conflict Heightens In-group Solidarity

We had predicted that one effect of intergroup conflict would be to heighten the unity of each group. However, as the Eagles had earlier experienced considerable depression at their own losses until they united to burn the Rattler flag, the Rattlers now experienced low morale.

After their baseball loss, the Rattlers began to blame one another for actions that led to the loss. Two boys threatened to write home to ask permission to leave, and only the joking flattery of the clever Rattler leader persuaded them not to. They tore up their letters amid great hilarity. After the tug-of-war tie, the Rattlers complained bitterly of the unfair tactics used by the Eagles, deciding at last to raid the Eagles' cabin that night after dark, which they did.

The next morning, the Eagles muttered darkly of revenge, which they translated into a raid on the Rattlers after breakfast. Meanwhile, the Rattlers—so woeful after their loss—were buoyed by their nocturnal raid. They arrived at breakfast in high spirits. When they later discovered the Eagle raid, they cursed the Eagles to a man. After a rain shower, during which the Rattlers made posters and "raiding flags" with vengeance, they plunged into a touch football game with much verbal abuse of the Eagles, and they won by a narrow margin.

The Eagles, now defeated in touch football but victorious in the third baseball game, retired to their cabin area, discussing the possibility of retaliation by the Rattlers for their morning raid. They collected a bucket of stones, "just in case" of a raid.

On the next morning, the Rattlers, now one point behind the Eagles on the last day of the tournament, decided at breakfast to post flags on "everything that's ours," including "home," "the swimming hole," "our upper camp," "our baseball diamond," and the Stone Corral, which was used for campfires. They won the last tug-of-war, but lost decisively in a tent pitching contest. Thus, the two groups came to the final event nearly tied. This event was a group treasure hunt. The Eagles won the treasure hunt, hence the contest, which they proclaimed in voices loud enough to be heard for a mile, some crying and a few jumping in the water with their clothes on to celebrate. The Rattlers were glum and quiet.

What did the Rattlers do facing their final defeat? After the Eagles left for a victory swim, the Rattlers raided the Eagle cabin, stealing the prizes the Eagles had won. Thus, their defeat was turned into an aggressive show of unity and defiance. The returning Eagles, horrified at the vandalism and theft, ran to the Rattler cabin. Challenges were hurled back and forth to fight, but at the showdown the Eagles began to retreat. The Rattlers followed, jeering all the way, and fighting began.

The camp staff intervened, forcing the Rattlers back to their cabin.

As the Rattlers were forced up the trail toward their own cabin, Eagles followed, yelling about what cowards Rattlers were. Later, they bragged to one another how they had chased the Rattlers and won another victory. The groups talked of each other as "poor losers," "bums," "stinkers," "sissies," "cowards." They no longer wanted to eat in the same dining room with each other. When taken to a nearby beach where tourists were also present, each group kept to itself, paying no attention to outsiders, even other swimmers their own age.

Thus, while defeat brought discouragement and even recrimination within each group, the invariant "solution" was new aggression against the other group, which action bound the in-group members even more closely. At the same time "social distance" between the groups was expressed more and more in terms of personal preference to have nothing further to do with the other group or its members.

Intergroup Relations Affect Relations *Within* Groups

One consequence of important intergroup relations, it was predicted, would be their impact on relations within each group. Such was the case. Not only was solidarity heightened among members within a group, but also the preoccupations of members were increasingly directed toward the out-group. The groups no longer turned to their own separate interests when apart. Every hour was filled with some thought of the other group, even when the tournament was completed. One's own group had to be justified, praised, excused, and vindicated, while the behavior of the out-group was condemned as reprehensible. Plans were made about how to overcome or humiliate them.

The Eagles, braggarts within their own confines, cautioned each other not to brag in the presence of the Rattlers. Within each group a host of norms arose specifying proper treatment and behavior in the presence of the other group.

In the Eagle group, a change of leadership actually occurred during the period of conflict. Craig, the leader who had emerged as the group formed, was a good coordinator and peacemaker within the group; but he did not relish the competitive atmosphere of the second stage. On a couple of occasions, he walked away from his group when they were in danger of losing. When scuffling and fighting broke out, Craig withdrew or hid to avoid them. As his magic was fading, the vigorous and competitive boy who "coached" the Eagles in baseball (Mason) began to take over leadership and, by mid-tournament, was acknowledged leader. Craig was just another one of the boys (where indeed he seemed to be more comfortable under these circumstances).

Similar shifts in the status structure within groups had been observed in the Rattler group, too. In this instance, Big Red—a boy who had been put down by his fellows for his tendency to bully smaller boys—emerged as a hero (though not the leader) of his group on several occasions during intergroup conflict.

At the lower echelons of the status structure, previously mild-mannered boys often were the ones to use the most extreme language about the other group, to cry most vociferously for raids and other action against them. These actions were, by now, well within the bounds of acceptable behavior toward the out-group, hence were displays of unity and loyalty to the group. However, it should be noted that aggressive actions and actual raids never occurred solely at the instigation of these lower-status boys. Invariably they were approved and actually led by higher-status members.

In-group and Out-group Images Justified Aggressive Acts

At the conclusion of the tournament, each boy individually indicated his appraisal of his own group and the other group with respect to whether "All of them," "Most of them," "Some of them," "A few of them," or "None of them" are brave, friendly, tough, sneaky, smart alecs, or stinkers. These terms had actually been used by the boys talking about themselves and the out-group. You have probably guessed the outcome. The preponderance of their ratings showed that all or most of their own group were brave, friendly, and tough. All or most of the out-group were sneaky, smart alec, and stinkers (few being brave, friendly, or tough).

The intentions of the out-group were not friendly. Their free choices of friends in the entire camp excluded members of the other group. The friendly, helpful, and democratic ways they practiced within their own warm circle were clearly inappropriate for their ilk. In fact, the other group deserved the treatment accorded them, in their view.

Using the guise of another contest for which the winning group would receive a sum of money, the invidious comparison between own group and out-group was shown independently. In this context, individual performance was judged by the boys in a situation that did not permit wholly accurate appraisal. It was predicted that each boy would rely on his expectations about his own group and the other group, even when encouraged to be as accurate as possible, thereby make errors in predictable directions.

The game consisted of having each group separately pick up dried beans scattered within its own area, the object being to pick up the most beans in one minute. Each boy was given a paper bag, its opening surrounded by a piece of rubber hose which was wide enough to drop beans in conveniently, but which effectively prevented anyone from counting his own beans.

Afterward, as a part of the contest, each boy estimated the number of beans purportedly collected by each other boy in camp. To speed this process up, the contents of each sack were emptied beneath the lens of an opaque projector and the image shown on the screen. The image was projected only five seconds (on the grounds that otherwise the process would take too much time, but actually because we had found that this interval was long enough to *seem* adequate but was too short for counting). Every time 35 beans were actually shown, arranged differently on each occasion. The winner of the bean toss was that group with the best record in *accurately* estimating the number of beans for each boy.

The boys' judgments erred systematically: Boys in each group significantly overestimated the number of beans collected by their fellow members and minimized the number of beans collected by boys in the other group (even to the point of underestimating the out-group's performance). Here we see properties of one's group, namely, its self-glorified image and its standardized derogation of the out-group, reflected in judgments written down by individuals and made under instructions to be as accurate as possible in order to gain the money prize. The Rattlers won this contest, chiefly because they over-estimated themselves less. They had, after all, lost the tournament.

THE SUFFICIENT CAUSE FOR INTERGROUP HOSTILITY AND PREJUDICE

To summarize, we know that these individuals were selected in ways that rule out explanations for their intergroup behavior on the basis of differences in backgrounds, of unduly frustrated individual experiences, or personal instability. No matter what personal, socioeconomic, or cultural differences may be associated with specific cases of intergroup hostility, prejudice, and derogatory attributions, we have found that a sufficient condition is simply that two cohesive in-groups, valued by their members, come together seeking prized goals that only one group may attain and only at the expense of the other group's loss.

The conditions of interaction *between* groups, not the "nature" of the individual participants singly, produced nastiness sufficient and consistent enough to resemble real-life prejudice and hostility. To say that the seeds of "evil" were already in each boy says very little, for these seeds would not have sprouted except for the conditions set up in the experiment. Furthermore, if it were true that all that we saw had burst from an aggressive instinct, it should not be possible to change that state of affairs. As we shall see, the groups did change and so did the behavior of these same boys, later in the experiment.

The logic of what appears to be irrational lies in the perspectives of members, which are based on the premises of their own group with respect to the intergroup relationship. They desired, even felt that they deserved, to win their goals. More and more the other group's actions frustrated that desire but became threats in other ways as well. The Eagles won the tournament, hence were eventually frustrated less. The Rattlers, in stealing their prizes, not only thwarted them again but confirmed the Eagles' worst judgments about the Rattlers. Though victorious, the Eagles were even more vehement and unanimous in their hostility than the Rattlers. The hostile acts and derogatory images of the other group became crystallized for each group as negative attitudes and stereotypes that justified completely the stance of one's own glorious group in the intergroup situation. The strength of these convictions was shown by the ultimate desire on both sides to cut all contact, to have nothing to do with the out-group.

The *particular* activities (competitive sports) serving as vehicles for the spiraling intergroup hostilities were, as noted earlier, culturally induced values for these boys. For individuals with different cultural experiences, we would expect the same outcomes when their groups interact with another group in activities equally high in motivational priority. Available experimental evidence supports this expectation: Avigdor (1952) found equally nasty images arising between groups of girls competing to produce plays to raise money for club jackets. In addition, her study showed that when two groups *cooperated* in producing their respective plays, their images of one another were not nasty, but favorable. Blake, Shepard, and Mouton (1964) reported an impressive number of T-group workshops for students and mature adults that replicated our findings with startling clarity when their groups competed in "solving" important human relations problems. What irony that in the process of "solving problems" of human relations, they generated their own!

CHANGING INTERGROUP RELATIONS AND CHANGING INTERGROUP ATTITUDES

From the first experiment, our interest in demonstrating the sufficient conditions for conflict and hostility between in-groups was sparked by a desire to shed light on conditions necessary for individual participants to change their attitudes and behavior toward one another, once conflict had assumed the upper hand. The logic seemed clear: If all of the antagonistic behavior flowed from confrontations between two groups aimed toward goals that only one group could attain, goals of the groups would have to become compatible before the considerable prejudice and social distance between them would change. In 1949 in Connecticut, the intense efforts of conducting the experiment left very little time or energy to make a systematic attempt to test this notion. However, determined that the boys should not leave camp bearing hostility toward one another, we tried what seemed a surefire expedient because history was full of examples of its temporary success.

The Common Enemy

Uniting in the face of a common enemy has brought together strange bedfellows in the past. In the first experiment (1949), along with admonitions from adults to cool it, a common enemy was introduced to the hostile Bull Dogs and Red Devils. An outside group was invited to the camp to compete in sports with campwide teams selected from the Bull Dogs and Red Devils. The visitors were a welcome novelty and, despite Bull Dog and Red Devil preference not to associate, the competitions were successfully undertaken. The groups cooperated to defeat the outsiders and hostile interchange between them was reduced. However, the Bull Dogs and Red Devils, when left to their own devices, strongly preferred to the end to be with their "own kind" and to keep their distance from each other.

I have found to my amazement that some readers of these experiments have been unable to see why we never again introduced a common enemy for purposes of inducing intergroup cooperation. One reason was that historical examples suggest that old intergroup conflicts reappear once a common enemy is vanquished, but there was a more compelling reason.

When hostile groups unite against a common enemy, the reduction of conflict between them is achieved at the expense of creating conflict on a much larger scale between them and the enemy. The world has witnessed the logical progression of such enlarged circles of conflict twice in the form of world wars. So the issue arises: Is there nothing but threat and confrontation by another group that will unite human beings?

William James wrote of the problem in an essay, "The Moral Equivalent of War." He marveled at the sacrifice and noble human qualities displayed within a nation bent toward war and wondered if there were not an equivalent force toward unity directed toward morally justifiable ends. The question assumes that warfare is immoral, a judgment that some of humanity appears to be unwilling to make, at least if their own group and its honor are at stake.

Nevertheless, James's question remains: Is it possible for people to unite to overcome a threat or to gain a prize that does not involve immoral means or ends? His own suggestions were directed toward overcoming the forces of nature, which, while not always as inimical to man as he suggested, certainly do pose problems far exceeding the grasp of one small portion of humanity. Like James, we wondered whether human struggles with problems other than their own intergroup rivalries could unite enemies.

WHAT KINDS OF HUMAN CONTACT WILL REDUCE CONFLICT?

Social distance between groups becomes an obstacle to any change. How can you get people together who won't speak to one another or who will be together in only certain situations and not in others? Such schism between groups, so common in social life, was abundantly evident between the small groups of campers. Something had to bring them into contact, but what kind of contact would ease the tension between them?

Desegregation in Pleasant Circumstances

One major psychological theory of learning states that need satisfaction and the pleasantness accompanying it will become associated with circumstances occurring simultaneously by chance or design. Thus, theoretically, if candlelight accompanies satisfaction of hunger, we start to value and like candlelight, even though candlelight has nothing directly to do with satisfying our hunger. In real life, such theory is implied when we say: "Get human beings together in pleasant circumstances and they will come to like each other." In addition, of course, such translation of "contiguity" theory to social affairs usually adds "bring them together *as equals* in pleasant circumstances," recognizing full well that it is not particularly pleasant to feel *less* equal than other participants.

In order to test this hypothesis, a series of situations at camp was arranged in the third experiment at Robbers Cave in which the Rattlers and Eagles had to be together if they were to participate in activities highly pleasant to each group. These situations did not involve any interdependence between the groups. Each participated side by side as equals. For example, the meals in camp suddenly became superb. A movie was shown that each group wanted to see. To shoot off fireworks in celebration of July 4, it was necessary to leave the camp, which was on state property. The two groups were taken together. There were, altogether, seven such planned contacts as equals in pleasant activities during three days.

Far from reducing conflict, these desegregated activities served as occasions for the rivals to berate and attack each other. Waiting for meals, they shoved to be first in line, the losing group insulting the group at the head of the line with "Ladies first!" At meals they threw paper, food, and vile names across the dining room in what they came to call "garbage wars." The way things were going, someone was likely to be hurt. There was no evidence whatsoever that contact as equals in pleasant activities would reduce the conflict. Some contact is necessary, of course, but it is not sufficient.

SUPERORDINATE GOALS IN REDUCING INTERGROUP CONFLICT

A corollary to our formulation of intergroup conflict seemed most promising: If conflict develops when groups try to reach incompatible goals, common goals requiring joint action should promote cooperation. Clearly, not just any common goal would do, particularly when joint action was the last thing in the world members of either group would contemplate. We had to think long and hard about what conditions and activities would promote joint actions involving both groups.

The conditions that were arranged were given a name, to distinguish them from other possible common goals: *superordinate goals*. These were to be problem situations in which goals compelling and appealing to each group could be attained *only* through the efforts and resources of both groups. It is important to note that superordinate goals, by definition, are not merely verbal agreements or abstractions defining "good" for each group. They could not be imposed on either group since, by definition, they arouse the efforts of both groups. Also, it will be clear that it is hypocritical to speak of superordinate goals in circumstances where one group holds another in its grip with the intention of bullying it into submission, no matter what.

There are, however, many situations in real life where deadly rivals, as well as powerful and less powerful groups, are interdependent for the solution of problems facing all. Modern urban life is one example. Problems of health, weather warning, food supplies, education, and environmental pollution are others.

Specifically, we predicted that superordinate goal conditions would lead to *cooperative activities* between groups and that a *series* of superordinate goals would have the *cumulative* effect of reducing conflict, hostility, and antagonistic actions among the members.

Would Superordinate Goals Promote Cooperation?

The staff called the entire camp together in Robbers Cave at four in the afternoon to announce the failure of the water system, an announcement that had been preceded by an earlier warning that something seemed amiss. Water came in pipes from a tank over a mile away, which was fed from a reservoir. All of the boys had been in that area. Immediately, they volunteered to investigate the entire water system, for it was very hot and no outside help could be secured until morning. The groups organized teams, as groups, to traverse the entire area, exploring the water system. Over an hour later, everyone met as agreed at the tank, having found nothing wrong in the pipes or at the reservoir. By this time, the boys were very hot and thirsty.

In inspecting the entire tank, boys from both groups mixed for the first time. When at last they found the obstacle preventing the flow of water, it was a hard job to remove it. Rattlers, Eagles, and staff labored until, with great rejoicing, the water began to flow. Yes, they had cooperated and they had succeeded together. Did tension between the groups disappear? No, they returned to camp for supper and another garbage war.

Would a Series of Superordinate Goals Have Cumulative Effects?

The second planned project concerned renting another motion picture, an entertainment that all the boys wanted but that was "too expensive" for the camp or either group alone. The discussion of this problem shows the heavy hand of their past that continually thwarted their attempts to cooperate. (An important aspect of the changes that eventually occurred was learning how to cooperate as equal groups.) The film rental was $15. With the camp offering to pay some part, suggestions about fair contributions came in from all sides. An Eagle said the camp should pay $5, the Rattlers $10, and the Eagles nothing. A Rattler suggested that the Eagles pay $5, and the Rattlers $2. Eventually, a suggestion put forth by the Eagles was adopted: Each group paid $3.50 and the camp the remainder. Within each group, members then calculated the individual contributions required.

Still there lingered strong preference within each group to do things separately when possible. An overnight camp-out on a lake some miles away was arranged only when each group had been assured that each could go in a separate truck, taking their own camping gear. The food and supplies, however, were carried in one truck which was parked some distance from the lake. They arrived at the lake, hot and sweating, and ran to plunge into the cool water. At the end of the swim, the hungry boys found that a staff member was trying to start a truck to go fetch food for lunch, but the truck stalled repeatedly. (This event required great skill by the driver.)

At first, the boys ran to try to push the truck, which was headed up hill. It was too big. Lying on the ground among their gear was the huge tug-of-war rope. A Rattler had the brilliant idea of having a "tug-of-war against the truck." The rope was fed through the front bumper to form two lines for pulling. At first the Rattlers pulled on one line and the Eagles the other. To coordinate their pulling, they chanted "heave, heave" in rhythm, at last moving it, and the truck started. There was mutual rejoicing and backslapping: "We won the tug-of-war against the truck!"

While waiting for the food to return, there was talk within each group about whether they should eat together or separately. In fact, when the truck arrived, they were so hungry that discussion ceased, and both groups plunged into preparing a desegregated meal.

Later on this same trip, the groups found that tent poles and accessories were mixed up, requiring that parts be swapped before the tents could be pitched. Both this exchange and another tug-of-war against the maverick truck were achieved cooperatively in matter-of-fact fashion.

The cumulative effect of superordinate goals was gradual, involving at first such matter-of-fact transfer of practices that had been effective on one occasion to a new problem situation. For example, the undependable truck was sent home, requiring that both groups ride in the same truck, an activity involving loading and seating that was accomplished with dispatch and some enjoyment. On returning to camp, the first meal at the dining hall witnessed the disappearance of shoving to be the first group in line. The groups started "taking turns" to be first in line. Quite on their own, members of one group approached the others to share an evening campfire, at which they took turns entertaining each other with jokes, songs, and skits that had become favorites in each of the separate groups.

Finally, on the last day of camp, the boys agreed that they would go home together on the same bus. As they piled in, the group lines were not kept in all seating arrangements. During a stop for refreshments, the Rattler leader suggested that the Rattlers use the $5 they had won in the bean toss game to treat everyone to milk shakes, despite the fact that (at that time) this sum would have been sufficient for the Rattlers alone to have also had sandwiches. The Rattlers discussed the latter possibility, but treated the Eagles, nonetheless.

Before they left the camp, a follow-up on data collected at the height of conflict revealed that boys' views of one another had indeed changed. Sociometric choices shifted significantly from exclusive in-group preference to include members of the other group in nearly one-third of their total choices. When asked to rate their own and the other group as to whether members were brave, friendly, stinkers, and so on, a significant shift occurred. About three-fourths of their ratings of the out-group were now equally as favorable as those of their own groups, respectively. And, it is important to note, that ratings of their own groups had not changed significantly. They were still highly favorable.

WHAT INTERGROUP RELATIONS CAN TELL US ABOUT CHANGING INTERGROUP BEHAVIOR

The conclusion was that change in the relationships between hostile groups (namely, efforts toward goals producing integration of efforts rather than clash) has a cumulative effect over time on the viewpoints and behaviors of members. This finding has important implications for understanding why efforts to alter *individual* attitudes and behaviors without regard to the prevailing relationships among groups are apt to fail. Here let's consider a few of the typical proposals for such individualistic change. Any or all of these proposals may be highly effective when intergroup relations are in the process of changing, but are severely limited when they are not.

Information Campaigns

Certainly a common belief is that people in different groups dislike one another because they lack accurate and favorable information about one another. In the experiments, Sherif attempted to use his role as a nondescript person at the camp to convey such information to members of one group about the other. He was told, simply, that the information was not correct, that he did not know the others as "we" do. On a larger scale, Hyman and Sheatsley (1947) long ago pointed out some reasons "why information campaigns fail," namely, that most persons who expose themselves to information are those already most interested and favorably disposed toward it. Those not favorably disposed *interpret* the "facts" differently, as we shall see in more detail when discussing communication in Chapter 12.

Conferences and Discussions of the Conflict

There need be no question that groups can settle differences between them if they are willing to surrender decision power to a body more powerful than either of them. With no such surrender of group power, attempts to "talk out" problems between groups face severe difficulties. During the first experiment in Connecticut, a high-status Bull Dog decided at the height of conflict to go to the Red Devil cabin to negotiate better relations between the groups. He was greeted by a hail of green apples from the Red Devils, chased down the path, and derided. Returning to his own group, he needed and probably expected sympathy. He received none. In fact, he was rebuked for an attempt that, his fellows believed, was doomed to failure. "What did you expect?"

In a series of studies done among adults in human relations workshops, Blake, Shepard, and Mouton (1964) verified that our findings in summer camps were not merely "child's play" and extended the study of intergroup negotiation between conflicting groups. Each group selected a negotiator to represent it in discussions to decide which group had the best solutions. Before the negotiations started, the representatives were rated by other members of their own groups as "mature, intelligent, independent, and well intentioned." The behavior of the negotiators was interesting since each did his or her level best to push the group's proposal, very few of them backing down to compromise. If their representative lost the decision, members of losing groups rated their representative as less intelligent, mature, and well intentioned than formerly, and even as a traitor. Representatives who won were treated as heroes by their own groups. The leader or representative who acts for his or her group is limited by constraints from the group, defining what is acceptable to other members and what is not.

When a "neutral" outsider was brought in to pass judgment concerning the group proposals, the rival groups initially saw the "judge" as competent and impartial. They maintained this evaluation of the judge provided he decided in their favor. When the judge did not, group members saw the judge as "biased, unfair, and incompetent." The judge was criticized as showing "no grasp of the problem," "not knowing enough," "not intelligent enough" or not "taking enough time" to arrive at a "fair" decision.

Psychologically, many of these reactions reflect differential perception and recall of facts about one's own group and of the other group. In the workshops, members were given objective tests to see if they could accurately recognize proposals that had been put forth by their own group and the rival group. They recognized the proposals made by their own groups better and, further, made exclusive claim on many points that were also in the proposal of the other groups. In short, their focus was on the superiority of their own proposals to the extent that they were unable to recognize common grounds and overlaps between the groups.

The psychological dynamics of such blatant bias in favor of one's own group when it is in conflict with another are not as mysterious as they may seem. First, we have to take personal loyalty to one's own group seriously. Its values and its norms serve as anchors for one's appraisal of the other group and its proposals. As mentioned in Chapter 2 in discussing the perception and judgment of other persons, one principle in the relativity of judgment is that increasing differences between one's anchor and what one is appraising become more and more exaggerated.

Dawes, Singer, and Lemons (1972) clarified this process between groups in studying judgments by University of Oregon students who were outspokenly "hawks" (pro) or "doves" (anti) toward U.S. military intervention in Vietnam. Using a total of 9 hawk and 9 dove statements, they asked 50 pro-war and 50 anti-war students to make a judgment of which of two statements presented to them on each trial was more "extreme." They did not ask whether the students agreed or disagreed with the statements, but only for an objective judgment of the relative extremity of two statements at a time.

By statistical analysis, they showed that the hawks regarded dove statements as more extreme than hawk statements and that doves regarded hawk statements as more extreme than dove statements. Each group was pushing their opponents' viewpoints as far away from their own as possible, viewing them as "crackpot." They regarded their own position as reasonable and more moderate than statements made by their opponents.

Next hawk and dove students were asked to write statements that they believed were typical viewpoints of hawks and doves, respectively. Later, they were presented these statements written by members of their own and the other group and asked to indicate whether they agreed with each statement. If they did not agree, they were asked why. Doves rejected dove statements written by hawks on the grounds that the statements were too strong and extreme. Doves, on the other hand, wrote hawk statements that hawks were likely to reject on the same grounds. Again difference between one's own views and those of opponents were greatly exaggerated. Such a contrast effect provides a basis for failing to understand opposing views and rejecting them.

A Small But Important Object Lesson

An important implication of the social-psychological obstacles to settling difficulties between groups is that what seems rational and logical to members of one group may see irrational and illogical to members of the other. The groups proceed from different premises and view each other through lenses that exaggerate their differences. Similarly, ingroup self-righteousness leads to attributing blame for the entire state of affairs on the other group. Thus, neither party is in a position to "clear the deck" or "start anew." We know that this vicious spiral can continue to the point of mutual destruction.

I am not proposing that in intergroup affairs there is no blame, no responsibility, no cause and effect, but only that the two groups involved are often the worst possible judges of these matters. What our small experiments showed is that, despite this dilemma and the vicious circle of blame casting, intergroup relations can change when other problems the groups face are sufficiently compelling to all that joint activity toward dealing with them is necessary. As groups and their members cooperate in reaching superordinate goals, the viewpoints and the typical treatment of out-group members do not change overnight. However, the changing intergroup relations eventually affect members through the very group processes that brought member attitudes into existence in the first place. Within their own groups, members who make efforts to support the group in intergroup endeavors win recognition and approval. Now, the member who clings to old ways becomes a deviate in his own group, risking disapproval as an old fogey.

These experiments on behavior in intergroup situations were not intended to provide models for every possible case of intergroup behavior. There are real differences between them and many consequential relationships among groups in real life. In real life, the use of power by one group to dominate others is the typical, not the unusual, case. Their past histories hold members like a vise. Still the experiments convincingly show the reality of intergroup relations for whatever goes on *within* groups, including the attitudes and behaviors of members toward individuals in the other group. Let's not forget that finding later in the book when we discuss social attitudes (including those toward other groups) and social movements, which define new groups bound toward social change and thus, inevitably, confront other groups whose members oppose the change.

MACHIAVELLIANISM, SMALL-SCALE AND LARGE-SCALE

Usually, we think of social "manipulation" or control when some persons or a propaganda message attempts to sway our interpretation of a situation or to influence our decisions. If the individual can recognize the attempt to persuade, he or she is free to reject such manipulation. When such intent is hidden and obscured, we call it Machiavellian and often find it objectionable. Many people fear such "hidden persuaders," as well they might. I believe that the camp experiments suggest other forms of hidden control.

In the camp experiments, hidden persuasion was not used: Adults seldom tried to persuade the boys to do one thing or another. The boys gained the strong feeling that what was happening was *their* doing, *their* business, and *their* choice. Their experience of opportunity to exercise their own initiative seemed unusual to them. However, all of this experienced freedom was limited by the particular range of activities and the kinds of contacts among the boys at each stage of the experiment, which were established in advance by the researchers. Such indirect and impersonal manipulation is by no means unusual in the lives of boys this age. For adults as well, control over the conditions in which human beings interact is surely a larger and more consequential manipulation than the attempt to persuade.

In actual social life, interaction within and between groups is controlled through ecological conditions that need not originate in preference or free choice of individuals living within them. Through the control of geography, resources, and facilities, such large-scale Machiavellianism is translated into hard facts of life, such as where families can live, the kinds of schools children can attend, the kinds of work people can engage in, who they see, what they do together, and the opportunities they have to change their lives, geographically and socially.

The researchers became manipulators of the camp environment for experimental purposes by modeling such circumstances of real life. It would not have been done if harm could have come to the boys, who, in fact, emerged from the camp with considerable personal satisfaction over their experiences. The research purpose of advancing knowledge about human behavior will have been well served if you, the reader, see this kind of manipulation as a parallel to that most potent in shaping your own views of people in other groups. The phenomenal appearance of the "here and now" can be extremely misleading as a basis for conclusions about why we feel and act as we do. Nor is the petty Machiavellianism of the hidden persuader necessarily the largest influence affecting our outlook and actions toward other groups. Hidden persuaders are most effective in arousing distrust of other people, in painting images of them as monsters, when wedges have already been driven between groups in the form of conditions viewed as "hard facts of life." When such wedges are removed, fewer people listen to the demagogue. By removing such wedges, people gain greater power in deciding for themselves and in controlling their own destinies.

Asking Questions About the Human Person: Ape, Angel, or Cultural Robot?

WHERE WE'VE BEEN AND WHERE WE'RE HEADED

The first steps in getting one's bearings in social psychology are to start recognizing the complexity of any social situation and the outstanding features of different kinds. We've been taking such steps in the last four chapters, focusing on the relationships among participants as one of their key features. Starting with brief encounters among strangers (Chapter 2), we went on to social situations in which the history of interpersonal ties has to be considered: the beginnings of mutuality (Chapter 3), the structural properties of those ties that we call a "group" (Chapter 4), and intergroup encounters (Chapter 5).

Of course, we could go on exploring social situations indefinitely since we certainly did not exhaust the possibilities (for example, large organizational or institutional work settings, bureaucracies, collective audiences and meetings, warfare). However, those we have considered can serve as models, or prototypes, that can be used in understanding a large number of other situations, providing we take into account their specific locations, how many and what kind of other people are present, and what they are doing. At this point, I feel impatient to get on. We've only started finding out what social psychology is about.

From now on, the focus will be more directly on the human individual. After all, the individual's personal experience and behavior in social intercourse is what

141

social psychology studies and tries to understand. I hope you will note that I'm not promising a magic key to the mysteries. But in this chapter we start trying harder. The next four chapters focus on concepts that relate directly to the human person, and the last three concern personal change.

YOU AND I AS EVERYDAY SOCIAL PSYCHOLOGISTS

If you or I were to try to sketch what we mean by a "human person," it would be impossible to leave the paper blank. You have lived long enough to read this book, and I long enough to write it. We've had to develop some working assumptions about ourselves and about other individuals in order to live this long. In this sense, we are all social psychologists every day of our lives.

Where did we get our ideas about human beings? Well, each of us has observed ourselves and others. We have some notions based on what we've experienced and seen. All to the good. The difficulty is that we also have all kinds of notions accumulated along the way that we have not or cannot check with direct personal experience or observation. Some of these are clichés or stereotypes picked up as we grew into our own particular families, neighborhoods, schools, churches, and national groups. Others we adopted more deliberately to fill gaps in our own thinking as we encountered new problems and new people. These may have come from diverse sources: ancient philosophies, religions, political ideologies, and (not the least) psychological theories—older and recently popular ones.

One of the reasons that we all have "gap-fillers" from diverse sources is the very human tendency to try to understand why we and others act as we do. The urgency we feel to find a "cause"—preferably a simple one—is understandable. Faced with an important but puzzling human problem, the most difficult feat is to postpone judgment. It is uncomfortable, even painful, to remain in suspense. In such a dilemma, we are sitting ducks for an idea that seems to tie things up in a neater package. And there are certainly a lot of puzzles in daily life.

Neither you nor I can single out all of our assumptions about "what a human being is like." We cannot weed out in one stroke all those that are not based on firsthand evidence or that are down right false, even if we wanted to. However, there are big issues that divide thinking about the human person that we need to become aware of. One such issue concerns the place of human beings in the evolutionary scheme. A closely related one concerns the importance of biological determinants for social behavior, particularly when compared with the impact of the social environment.

By now, you've probably figured out how this chapter got is subtitle: "Ape, Angel, or Cultural Robot?" Psychologists have discussed the issues with a great deal of dignity, of course, under such headings as nature versus nurture, instinctual versus learned behavior, or biological versus cultural determinism. It would be handy if we could say "Now this is nature and that is nurture" or "This much is instinctual and that much is learned." It would be convenient if we could settle the whole matter by declaring that biology has nothing to do with social behavior (which could leave us with either an angel or a cultural robot). Our problem is not that simple.

There is no agreement on what is meant by nature, nurture, instinctual, or learned. Probably there is more agreement on what is meant by angel, and even more that human beings are not in that class. Yet some common assumptions suggest that they are. For example, do you think that society "spoils" human individuals, who would be "basically good" otherwise?

This chapter stirs up some long-standing issues about the human individual as a means of clearing the way for chapters to come. That does not mean that I am going to try to push you into agreeing with everything I write. On the contrary, I hope that we will come out at the end of the chapter prepared to ask better questions.

Asking questions in either-or form about these issues has led us down garden paths choked with weeds. Once in the weeds, we have lost sight of whether we were on the right path. Instead, we have been forced to heed and to follow the most expert or technically equipped weed-killers in our midst. Let's try to avoid those garden paths by remembering that there are questions that cannot be answered by any amount of evidence when posed in either-or form. Here are some examples: Is the egg or the sperm more important in the creation of a human fetus? Which is more important for fire: increased temperature or oxygen?

In what sense, if any, is there a human nature that defines the human condition? What are the implications of that nature for social psychology?

WHAT IS HUMAN NATURE ANYWAY?

If human nature is to mean anything at all, we have to agree on some rules about what is to be included as "natural" and what is not. By human nature, most people seem to mean what is more or less universal in the human condition, hence difficult to foresee as changing soon. Social behaviors and relationships that differ according to the social context in which individuals develop could conceivably be changed by modifying the social context. If this is our interest, I propose that our rules for including something within human nature should be (1) that it be universal in human species in all known societies, and (2) that it have a specifiable basis in the anatomy or physiology of the human organism. We know that the latter change slowly indeed, in comparison with changes in the organization of social life.

Since our interest here is in social behavior, I have not included a familiar biological dictum: that the appearance of an activity in species just below the human on the evolutionary scale is strong presumptive evidence that it is also part of human nature. I am deliberately leaving out this dictum. If anything, our ignorance about the social behavior and social relationships of other animals is even more appalling than that about human beings. True, systematic observations on animal behavior outside of cages are beginning to accumulate. Between C. R. Carpenter's observations on New World monkeys in the 1930s to Jane Goodall's foray into the African environment of chimpanzees, the comparative study of animal social behavior in their own environments interested few students. Meanwhile, biologists, naturalists, psychologists, and popular writers have made pronouncements that supported their own pet theories on human relationships and societies, with the flimsiest kind of evidence on animal social behavior.

When comparative data can be obtained on both human beings and their near-neighbors in evolution, the demonstration that a social activity has a common and identifiable physiological basis is impressive evidence for continuity among the species. Unfortunately, the ceremony in which an academic committee baptizes a student as a biologist or ethologist or comparative psychologist does not remove common errors in thinking that have plagued the comparative study of behavior. The most common were documented a good many years ago by T. C. Schneirla (1946, 1951). Schneirla bemoaned the paucity of comparative studies of social behavior. He noted the unfortunate tendency of his colleagues to draw analogies between human and other animal behavior based on anecdotes, neglecting both species differences and the concrete environments in which behavior occurred. He cautioned that similar *actions* by human and other animals could not be attributed to similar "causes" merely because they (1) "look alike," (2) appear to serve similar functions or ends, or (3) are equally adaptive in dealing with their respective environments. My impression is that more and more investigators are heeding such cautions. Meanwhile, wild speculations flourish. Let's remember that many critical issues of human social behavior would not even arise if human beings were really domesticated laboratory rats, or "naked apes," or were endowed with the conceptualizing capacities of the porpoise or the chimpanzee.

Rules for the Human Nature Game

The two rules for the human nature game that I propose (universality and physiological basis) are surely minimal, yet they are often neglected in arguments over human nature. I don't believe that I have ever heard human nature used to explain that all human individuals will breathe during the next few minutes. Yet breathing certainly qualifies as an indication of human nature by these rules, as do eating, drinking, urinating and defecating, being active and resting, avoiding extremes of cold or heat, attempting to avoid bodily injury, and engaging in sexual activities. All of these have definite physiological bases and they are universal in the human species—almost.

The "almost" begins to creep in, for example, when we include sexual activity. No one can doubt its physiological basis, but the universality rule gives us trouble. Some individuals and some small groups of individuals have taken considerable pains to avoid sexual activity. Otto Klineberg (1954) recognized such dilemmas in seeking universality. He proposed that we look for human nature in terms of probabilities. If you were to observe a human being anywhere on the globe, you could make a fairly safe bet that he or she would sooner or later perform certain actions that have a physiological basis—breathing, eliminating, trying to drink and eat, and so on. Such activities and the processes underlying them are, in Klineberg's terms, highly "dependable" parts of human nature.

Being "dependable" as a part of human nature does not mean that the activity is unaffected by the environment or by the individual's interactions with it. Ways, means, and goal objects for dependable activities have to be learned. Any mother who has breast-fed a child knows that the primitive sucking reflex of the newborn undergoes considerable learning after birth. Interestingly enough, such learning includes the mother's developing skills in locating baby, breast, and body for optimal performance. The child's learning is not a one-way adaptation, but a two-way process. Later, the early sucking actions are wholly inadequate in consuming a garden salad. Adults cannot eat without food and, when none is available for a prolonged period, they stop trying. When foodstuffs are available, what is eaten, when, and under what circumstances are enormously dependent on learning in a social environment. Clearly, then, even the most "dependable" aspects of human nature cannot be separated entirely from conditions in the individual's environment or learning about them.

Therefore, sexual activity is not unique in its considerable dependence on learning and on environmental circumstances. It is less dependable than eating or drinking in that the latter are essential for individual survival. Shall we leave sex out of human nature? Well, that would seem foolish. Those individuals who engage in no sexual activity of any kind are exceptions in any human society.

If we admit sexual functioning as part of human nature, then by the same logic we are forced to admit other, less obvious human capacities into the realm of dependable human nature. For example, speaking a language of some kind is quite as universal among human groups as sexual activity. But, you may object, what about the other rule? There also must be a physiological basis for attributing something to the nature of the human individual. In speaking a language, where are the organs, the hormones, the tissue states, and so on, that are so prominent in other things we have included as dependable?

LINGUISTIC PROCESS AS HUMAN NATURE

There are physiological bases for the universal appearance of language activity in every human group. Clearly, these bases do not reside merely in the eyes and ears, or in the mouth, tongue, and vocal cords. Language activity can develop without these through use of other parts of the body. No, the physiological capacities are centered in the human nervous system and especially the brain. The physiological capacity for conceptual and linguistic activities inheres in normal human development quite as dependably as the growth of the body and its other parts, including the development of sexual functions (Brown, 1965; Chomsky, 1965; Lenneberg, 1967; Lewis, 1963).

Languages, on the other hand, are clearly social constructions. A *particular* language has no more status as part of human nature than a particular technology that a people develop in dealing with the environment. It is not necessary to assume that verbal behavior or speech in a particular language is the required indicator of the capacities to which I refer. Only a human being can deliberately take a "vow of silence" or transfer linguistic behavior freely to other parts of the body (hands, feet, a pencil held in the mouth) or a mechanical device. Only a human being can train another animal (the chimpanzee is the favorite) to perform hand signs or punch a computer outlet to signal words in a human language. (The mass media and some psychologists become so excited at such accomplishments by chimpanzees that they neglect the enormous human accomplishment.)

No, what we call linguistic activity or conceptualizing, for want of better words, is only one sign of pervasive and general cognitive capacities of human beings that distinguish human nature from other animal natures. Am I saying that animals are stupid or that there are no signs of the development of such cognitive capacities lower in the evolutionary scale? Of course not! Anyone who has lived with other animals respects their brands of intelligence, including the ability on occasion to outwit and baffle the human brand. The research literature is full of examples of evolutionary trends in abilities to delay reaction to a desired object in the absence of visual cues (Maier and Schneirla, 1963), of problem-solving, of symbolic actions such as the use of poker chips for exchange (Yerkes, 1943), of tool use (see, for example, Köhler, 1929), and of forming abstract concepts, such as "triangularity."

Animals just below man on the evolutionary scale come out looking very well on a variety of tests of their symbolic and conceptual capacities. However, even at the age of 2 years, a human child forms concepts (for example, triangularity) that exceed the limits of a bright chimpanzee (Hebb, 1966). Apes and chimpanzees devise simple tools from objects in their environment, but not the wheel or pulley. Chimps learn to use and value tokens, but do not open savings accounts, play the stock market, or fight over tax laws on inheritance. They solve difficult problems well, but not the problem of how to grow their own food. They delay reaction without visual cues for a few minutes (Yerkes and Nissen, 1939), but never for an object they have not seen or smelled, such as a new social circle, a vision of a new house, a "home land," or a god.

Much of what is "human" in human nature derives from the structure of a nervous system considerably developed and elaborated beyond those of other animals. Many psychologists in the past were reluctant to regard such differences as quite as "natural" as the differences between human and simian appendages (where monkeys and the higher apes have the great advantage in climbing and swinging). Their caution is understandable. In the past, human beings glorified their capacities for thought and reasoning to make themselves godlike creatures, their unique capacities mental and spiritual, hence unobservable. However, if we keep our eyes on observable data—human behavior and the environmental conditions in which it occurs—we need not fall into such vanity. We should study those human behaviors that are distinctive to human beings with as much care and as great interest as those that are not. Otherwise, we reduce the problems of human behavior to those that are directly comparable to behavior of other animals. Thereby, we eliminate most of the significant problems for social psychology.

Human Development Without Language

The best workers investigating the human nervous system are the first to declare our vast ignorance. We do know, however, that its normal development is one precondition for those cognitive capacities of which conceptual-linguistic behaviors are one sign. The human nervous system is not mature at birth and its growth continues well into the childhood years. Interruption of the process by disease, malnutrition, or injury retards or prevents the acquisition of language. (Of course, the same is true for other aspects of human nature included earlier.)

So far as we know, every normally developing human nervous system can attain a human level of conceptual functioning, including acquisition of the prevailing language, provided that the individual interacts with other human beings who communicate and respond linguistically. Most of what we call "human" in a person depends heavily on such interactions, as shown by the few reliable studies of children totally deprived of them from birth. (Fortunately, most parents value their children too much to volunteer them for a critical experiment: their physical care by adults who neither respond to their infant vocalizations nor speak to them. This fact alone should convince us that we are dealing with *human* characteristics. There would be little point in attempting such an experiment with chimpanzee parents.)

The best-documented case was reported by the sociologist Kingsley Davis (1947). Isabelle was discovered when she was 6½, confined in a darkened room with her mother, a deaf-mute who had borne Isabelle out of wedlock, to the shame of her own parents. There was very little "human" about Isabelle to the psychologists and physicians who examined her. She was fearful of others and new surroundings (as are other animals similarly confined from birth). She made only croaking sounds. She reacted in many ways like a deaf child. The "sociability" that we are likely to assume *is* human nature was lacking.

Fortunately, a team of specialists went to work. It took a speech therapist a week to get Isabelle to respond vocally. By patient effort, her progress thereafter was astounding. She started to utter words and to form simple sentences in 2 months. After 11 months she could identify printed words and simple sentences. In 2 years, she was talking and had a vocabulary of nearly 2000 words, an achievement that typically takes 6 years when begun at birth. By age 8½, she performed normally for her age on standard intelligence tests. By age 14, she had completed elementary school. This accomplishment by Isabelle and her helping team would not have nearly the significance that it does if the changes involved only intellectual and cognitive performance. In fact, her behavior at 8½ and at 14 years was described as that of a "normal" child. She came to relate to other people, to want the things that others wanted, to see herself as both a private person and as a social person to others—all accomplishments revealed in school work, play, and social interchange, yet all absent without linguistic interaction.

Supporting evidence comes from study of deaf children, who are typically retarded in speech, conceptual development, and social interchange by the age of 2 unless compensatory training is started before that age (Lewis, 1963). But, as we know, with compensatory training, deaf, blind, and deaf-blind children can learn to speak and read and to share in other aspects of "humanness" (for good or evil). Social development, the setting of standards for self and others, cooperation as well as competition, desires for social interchange and specific social objects are all contingent on the development of linguistic-cognitive capacities. These *capacities* are as much a part of human nature as eating and sexual activity. All such broadly defined aspects of human nature are contingent both on their physiological bases and on the environmental conditions of development and functioning.

What about human sociality or affiliation? Isn't that human nature? Well, by now, that very question begins to become meaningless. Human infants are forced into a social environment at birth by their tremendous dependency on others for survival. Their dependency continues longer than for other social animals, in part because the human environment is so complex. Sociability or affiliative tendencies presume the human environment, as well as human cognitive capacities. I can see no advantage in continuing the human nature game at this point. A better question is needed, a question that focuses on how human beings become what they do become.

Human Nature and Human Learning

Nothing that has been said so far should suggest that this or that particular way of behaving, this or that particular desire, this or that particular goal is given by human nature. On the contrary, the cognitive capacities referred to in the last section involve a great deal of learning, as well as maturation. They are channeled and shaped by the concrete environment in which these occur. In the realm of social behavior, the inevitable outcome is that the specific actions, the experienced desires, the beliefs, and the values vary enormously according to the opportunities, the valued modes of interacting with others (for example, cooperatively or as rivals), and the goal objects defined as valuable in the sociocultural context where the individual develops. The range of variation in these respects is so great in known human groups that it becomes difficult to catalogue specific social behaviors that are truly universal to all.

What is considered "work" or "play" differs enormously in different cultures and historical periods. In the realm of preferences, even for such basic functions as eating and sexual activity, the range is truly enormous. "There is no accounting for tastes, said the old lady as she kissed the cow." What makes it possible to account for tastes is that every cultural grouping limits the *range* of their variation among its members. The relative speed and the exactitude with which societies achieve such prescription of preferences among their new generations are among the best evidence for the importance of human learning on a conceptual level. For a language, which must be learned itself, is also the primary medium for socialization into the larger society.

Unfortunately, most theories on human learning proceed from quite different premises about the importance of conceptual functioning. A glance at the history of learning research shows why this is the case and why the most highly developed theories are of limited value at present in social psychology. The major models for research into learning were developed for study of animal behavior, including, for example, Pavlov's conditioning model, Skinner's instrumental, or operant, conditioning, Thorndike's trial-and-error model for cats in puzzle boxes and rats in a maze, and models for studying discrimination or choice. These and others were simply "adapted" to human subjects, preferably children. Every one of them restricts the social-learning situation and the use of conceptual capacities in ways dictated by their original purposes for studying animal behavior.

One difficulty with theories of learning based on animal behavior is that necessarily they assume that the animal learns inductively and cumulatively from concrete experiences in definite stimulus situations that the animal is dealing with directly. Generalization or transfer of learning to new situations is presumed to occur only after the initial responses are learned in that concrete situation. However, there is considerable evidence that human children also begin to learn in other ways, particularly with the development of linguistic activity. Pavlov noted this, especially in his later writings with reference to a "second order signal system" in human learning. Luria (1961), while recognizing the accomplishments of his fellow-countryman, nevertheless presented research with children to support his conclusion that the "laws of conditioning" while "fundamental beyond doubt" do not apply in "full force" when the learning process of human children is studied (p. 32).

Any specific situation or reinforcement, he observed, is processed by the human child with reference to a "system of generalized information" (that is, conceptual schema that may also be verbally formulated). The child's subsequent reactions to that specific stimulus situation or reinforcement "depend more on the system it is taken into than on its physical properties." Thus, while learning in animals develops gradually and is not easily changed or eliminated, human learning may short-cut the slow inductive process by "incorporating the given signal [stimulus] into or excluding it from an existing system" of conceptual schema (or "generalized information," p. 45).

What all of this amounts to is that a significant bulk of human learning is not inductive in any strict sense, after the age of 2 or so. Conceptual schema or rules are learned, and the appropriate response to a specific concrete new situation is generated from that schema or rule. The process is deductive. The more recent research on imitation of adult "models" seems to require that such deductive principles be operative (Bandura, 1965; Bandura and Walters, 1963). For example, when a child opts to imitate the actions of a socially powerful adult, but not a less powerful one, the "rule" might be something as follows: What that sort of person does always makes things happen. Bandura (1974) has taken a strong position stressing such "cognitive" activity in human learning.

The significance of deductive conceptual learning for social psychology is immense. A child of 5 years has already picked up an incredible knowledge about his sociocultural milieu. It would be impossible to have accomplished the feat through the slow inductive processes of classical or operant conditioning alone, or trial and error alone, or direct experience of contiguous events and circumstances alone, or even direct imitation alone. The child of 5 has known for two or three years that he or she is a boy or a girl, and a member of such-and-such a group (for example, family), a child and not an adult, with a host of rules, prescriptions, and values that accompany each of these major differentiations. The broad category "adults" is differentiated into subclasses (mommies, daddies, teachers, TV stars, and so on). He or she has learned to cooperate in pretty consistent fashion, to compete with others, to show consistent sympathy with others' distress (rather than laughing), and a great deal of social etiquette. If the society in which he or she lives places the child's group in an enviable or a pitiable plight, a child of 5 typically knows this social fact, revealing it in numerous specific discriminatory responses and manifestations of preference. He or she learns to discriminate among specific objects that can be classified into verbal categories in less than a tenth of the time or number of trials needed when no such categories exist (see, for example, Pyles, 1932). The child follows many rules of conduct voluntarily—through "self-control" rather than constant surveillance by adults.

Human Learning and Human Interaction

Much human social learning occurs in interaction with other human beings. Therefore, it becomes extremely important to bring the properties of human interaction into the picture. Unfortunately, the two are seldom considered together. In Chapter 2, we found that what a person notices, how others in the situation are sized up, and significance of the location and activities in progress all involve psychological processing. The visible features of the others, the situation, and the relationships among participants are sized up with reference to the person's conceptual schema. Are the four sets of factors in a social situation described in Chapter 2 applicable in the analysis of a learning situation? In learning, is the individual responding to the *relationships* among the various aspects of the situation?

Apparently not all learning theorists think so. Some have made a considerable point that conditioned responses can occur in social interaction automatically and that the individuals need not be aware of interaction properties (Thorndike and Rock, 1934; Staats and Staats, 1958; Staats, 1969; Greenspoon, 1955; Taffel, 1955). So popular is this theory that I have heard from both colleagues and students a story of the role reversal to delight all students—namely, that members of a class "conditioned" their professor to stay in one restricted corner of the classroom, by administering reinforcements in the form of smiles, alert looks, and questions when he was there. (I regret to say that every time I hear this story, it is immediately attributed to an inaccessible source: at Cornell, to a professor on leave for the year; to a professor at Harvard, who said he heard that it happened in Arizona; to a Pennsylvania professor, who said he heard that it happened in Illinois. Since I can find no published report, I am forced to conclude that its reality is about equal to that of the cartoon in which Skinner's rat reports to fellow rats how well he has trained the experimenter to deliver food pellets everytime he pushes a lever.)

One of the most frequent research models, testing "automatic conditioning," involves the experimenter's approval ("mmm-hmmm' or "right") when the subject uses certain verbal responses, for example, personal pronouns or plural nouns. In another, the experimenter presents nonsense syllables paired with bipolar adjectives (for example, "good" or "bad"), with the result that the nonsense syllables are rated later as positive or negative depending on the adjective with which each had been paired.

By now, there is considerable evidence that acquiring the response intended by the experimenter is anything but automatic. On the contrary, subjects see the entire procedure as a "game" in which their task is to find out what made their responses "good" (Holmes, 1967). They increase the frequency of the desired response when they discover the "rule" governing the experimenter's approval (see, for example, Spielberger, 1962; Spielberger and DeNike, 1962, 1966; DeNike and Spielberger, 1963) and, furthermore, want to "do well" in the experiment (Page and Dahlke, 1965; Page, 1969, 1970, 1972). It helps if the research subject also has a generally positive attitude toward psychological research (see, for example, Adair, 1973). If a researcher queries a subject to find whether or not the subject is aware of some rule, what the researcher learns depends on how the questions are put and the length of the inquiry; but the subject may also actually deceive the researcher (Levy, 1967; White and Schumsky, 1972), reporting no awareness of a rule even when the researcher knows that the information was given out prior to the experiment. In that event, the person apparently had some notion about how one "should" behave as a research subject.

The upshot is that it is safe to assume that the human individual is sizing up a research situation with as much awareness and conceptual skill as he or she would any other social situation. Thus, the properties of human interaction have to be brought into the psychology of human learning, which typically occurs as information is processed at a conceptual level.

Learning and the Expectations of Others

When the study of human learning is separated from its social context, we eliminate an important feature of much social learning, namely, that we continually react to social situations in terms of the expectations that important other people have for us. What and how we learn is not simply a function of our human capacities or individual abilities, but also a function of the expectations that others have for us.

The sociologist Robert Merton (1948) recognized in social interaction a process that he called the "self-fulfilling prophecy." When we expect or think others expect, for example, that we will succeed or fail, this belief regulates the interaction process. We behave "as if" the expectation were true, thereby affecting what we do and the responses of others, until—lo and behold—our prophecy comes true through our own collaboration.

In 1968, Rosenthal and Jacobson published a book called *Pygmalion in the Classroom*, in which they proposed that a teacher's expectations for a student's performance could affect the level of the child's achievement in school. In the research reported, they gave a group intelligence test to grades one to six in a lower socioeconomic level school district. Then they randomly selected one-fifth of the pupils and told their teachers that the test results indicated that those children showed the potential for increasing their IQ markedly during the school year. In the first three primary grades (but not the others), they reported that this was exactly what happened, despite the fact that the children were randomly selected and were no more likely to gain than the others.

Although several researchers attempted to replicate or extend the Rosenthal and Jacobson findings, the results were not clear-cut. Furthermore, no one had shown that a teacher's expectations might be either beneficial or detrimental to a child's learning. W. B. Seaver (1973) studied the possibility in a natural and unobtrusive way that could not possibly work to the detriment of the children involved. In brief, the basis for a teacher's expectations about a child was having previously taught that child's older brother or sister in the first grade. If the older sibling had been bright, it would be reasonable to think that the teacher would expect the younger child to be bright also. If these expectations did affect the younger child's learning in first grade, the outcome would be that children with bright older siblings would perform better at the end of first grade than comparable children who did not have their older brother's or sister's teacher. Conversely, those with less than bright older siblings should be performing more poorly than comparable children who did not have their older brother's or sister's teacher.

Seaver looked up first-graders in elementary schools in a well-to-do Chicago suburb who had an older sibling previously in the first grade in the same school. Then, he identified those children who had an older brother or sister no more than three grades advanced in the same school. Of these 79 sibling pairs, 27 first-graders had been assigned to the same first-grade teachers who had taught their older siblings.

(Seaver calculated that this proportion was just about what might be expected on the basis of chance, although he had no control over possible bias in the assignment of children to teachers.) The remaining 52 first-graders served as a control, in that their teachers had not taught older brothers or sisters, hence presumably had no expectations based on their performance in the first grade.

The first-graders were divided into children whose older siblings had, in fact, exhibited higher or lower performance in first grade. The division was made by judges who sorted the older siblings' performance on the basis of IQ, scores on the Stanford Achievement Test, and teachers' grades. Seaver assumed that teachers of those first-graders whose older siblings were in the "high" category would have higher expectancies for their performance, whereas teachers of those whose older siblings were in the "low" category would have lower expectancies for their performance. ("Oh, dear! Not another Joey Smith!") However, if learning performance simply "runs in families" and the teachers' expectations had no effect, those children with the same first-grade teachers as their siblings should do no better or no worse than children with different first-grade teachers.

At the end of the school year, Seaver compared the performance of first-graders with the "same teachers" to that of first-graders assigned to different teachers than their older siblings. He compared performance on six subtests of the Stanford Achievement Test (word meaning, paragraph meaning, vocabulary, arithmetic, spelling, and word study) and teacher-assigned grade averages from the winter and spring school terms. If teachers' expectancies for the children actually affected the children's performance, he would find that first-graders for whom hopes were high scored significantly higher than children whose teachers had not taught their bright older siblings. Children of whom less was expected would score lower than the control children who had different teachers than their older siblings'.

That is exactly what Seaver found. First-graders whose teachers had taught their bright older siblings did better than would be expected by chance. Those whose teachers had taught their not-very-bright older siblings did worse than expected by chance. The differences between the "high" and "low" children taught by their older siblings' first-grade teachers and those taught by other teachers were in the predicted directions for all comparisons and were statistically significant for four of the achievement subtests (word meaning, paragraph meaning, vocabulary, and arithmetic). One might think that blatant teacher bias would be revealed most clearly in the grades they assigned. The differences were in expected directions but were not statistically significant.

Clearly, the teachers' expectations did not affect the children by magic. Somehow, they conveyed their notions in their actions, the time spent with the children, or by their reactions to the children's performance. Seaver's research is the most impressive evidence that significant effects on learning are associated with the high or low expectations of others during social interaction.

MALE AND FEMALE "NATURES" AS A CASE STUDY

So far, the rules adopted for defining human nature have led us to include activities, capacities, and their consequences for a human environment that are common to all human beings. However, humanity is everywhere distinguishable as male or female. Every human society has recognized this important biological differentiation through division of work, practices, and norms that affect the lives of individual males or females in virtually all of their human relationships. Controversies about male and female "natures" reveal the sheer nonsense of talking about human nature as though it were biologically "given" once and for all. We cannot account for sex differences in social behavior without accepting human conceptual capacities as essential to the nature of both sexes. It is these capacities that enable the developing male or female to learn so rapidly and so categorically the outlooks and behavior patterns deemed appropriate to his or her sex. They also are essential for the development of such wide variation in what is deemed appropriate in different human societies.

Until recently, most of our textbooks in biology and psychology taught us that sexual differentiation occurred at the moment of conception. The chance meeting of the female's egg with a male sperm bearing a Y chromosome, we read, produced a male. Chance meeting of egg with a sperm bearing an X chromosome produced a female. The XY or XX combination appeared in every cell during fetal growth and that was it.

Now, there is evidence that the meeting of sperm and egg may not be altogether chance—that the intrauterine environment affects the probability that X- or Y-bearing sperm reach the egg. We know that the XY or XX combinations are not the only possibilities, as XYY, XXY, and other combinations are discovered. Moreover, to understand the formation of the distinctive anatomical structures of the two sexes, we cannot stop with the moment of conception. The interplay of genetic and environmental events proceeds in such a way that they cannot be separated in either-or fashion (Money and Ehrhardt, 1972).

At first the cell groupings that will become sexual structures are undifferentiated—neither male nor female. The identical groups of cells later differentiate into male or female gonads, male penis and scrotum or female clitoris, vagina, and labia, and so on. In the usual course of events, such differentiation is programed so that increased levels of androgens (male hormones but not absent totally in normal females) lead to differentiation of male structures. Without such androgenization, the fetus becomes female, regardless of chromosomal combination.

It sometimes happens that the usual course of events does not occur. For example, there have been cases of chromosomal females whose mothers have received medication during pregnancy that raised the androgen levels of the fetus. According to Money and Ehrhardt (1972), such female children are typically tomboys, by which they seem to mean that the little girls are more oriented than a random sample in the same culture to rough-and-tumble activity, masculine sports, and so on. On the other hand, the sample they studied also had unusually high IQs, a finding that by no means goes with masculinization, as we shall see. (One suspects that the clinical sample was biased in other unknown ways.)

Equally interesting is the finding that the chromosomal programing and hormonal balance can go awry so that the newborn infant is ambiguous in sexual differentiation. For example, external genitalia of both male and female may be present. Naturally, this poses a problem for adults, particularly as the sexual organs of the newborn are small. According to Money, who has seen a good number of such cases as children or youth, the identifying sexual label adopted at birth (male or female) then determines the child's gender identity as male or female. In actions, preferences, and so on, the child behaves and identifies self as male or female, as the case may be.

This brief and sketchy account of sexual differentiation cannot stand, however, without reference to the important bodily changes before and during pubescence (signs of sexual maturity). As body and sexual structures grow dramatically, the hormonal concentrations and balances of the two sexes alter sharply toward those typical of sexually mature males or females. (Unless parents or doctors are alert and find appropriate medical facilities earlier, the child with ambiguous or mixed sexual structures ordinarily faces severe problems at this point, even though his or her gender identity is socially established as male or female.)

As Money's work suggests, the social identification of sexual gender proceeds from simple labeling at birth to the variety of treatments, customs, and opportunities that define the social role and status of a boy child or girl child in that society. Even a casual reading of comparative anthropology (see, for example, Mead, 1955, 1967) or comparative accounts of the status and roles of men and women in contemporary societies (see, for example, Seward and Williamson, 1970) can readily convince doubters of the great variety of arrangements, customs, preferences, and personal identities fostered for males and females in different societies at different times. There is no doubt whatever that much of what you or I might conceive as typically masculine or feminine is a reflection of the concrete experiences and notions we pick up in our own particular society.

On the one hand, then, we may say that the most pronounced sex differences in social behavior that we observe in ordinary daily life are not, strictly speaking, signs of male or female "nature." Depending on the sociocultural environment, most of them could turn out differently. On the other hand, we may protest with considerable justice that there must be differences in social behavior associated with the biosocial differentiation that starts at conception and continues, with ever-enlarging environmental influences, through intrauterine and child-adolescent development. I believe that such a viewpoint is justifiable. However, a search of the relevant research literature for several years, with the enormous stimulation and help of participants in a graduate research seminar organized for this purpose (see Baer and Sherif, 1974) revealed very little that can be said about such differences, based on acceptable scientific evidence.

There are several reasons for the current lack of evidence on differences in social behavior associated with male or female "natures." The first has to do with the gross neglect of sex differences in the actual research practices of investigators, along with faulty theoretical orientations to the problem by many psychologists and social scientists. The second concerns complex problems of social organization relevant to the two sexes, a matter that I will take a stab at later in this chapter.

How Sex Clarifies Other Controversies: The "Intelligence" Hassle

The neglect of sex differences in research practice and the faulty orientations to theory can perhaps be illustrated best if we start with the intelligence testing movement (Anastasi, 1966). Binet and Simon produced the first "intelligence" test in France, with the laudable aim of singling out children who were having difficulties in the usual school environment. Before that, a number of investigators had tried to develop intelligence tests. This early movement was associated with Sir Francis Galton's work testing visual acuity, sensory discrimination, and a variety of other discrete performances by different cultural-national groups in the then rampant British Empire.

Whatever its other intentions, there is no doubt that the earlier testing attempts were conducted by persons with racist concerns about keeping their own more powerful, hence "superior race" pure and uncontaminated. We need not weep at the failure of their attempts to assemble a "workable" intelligence test. However, we should note that the testing movement that did produce tests in the United States, inspired by Binet's success, can scarcely claim freedom from the taint of ideological influences (see Cronbach, 1975).

Intelligence testing as developed by Terman and his associates at

Stanford University relied on the Binet model. A series of tasks was selected that children who succeeded in a particular level of school could perform, a battery of such tests being assembled for each age level. A child's "score" represented nothing more or less than the sum of his or her performances that met the criterion, which was based on task performance by children of various ages who were succeeding in school. The principal and still the most impressive evidence for validity of the test score was its correlation with school performance.

Now we come to ideology: In standardizing the tasks for the intelligence tests, researchers did find sex differences on performance on some tasks. However, they could not and did not say that such differences meant males or females were more or less "intelligent." For one thing, girls were (and still are) equally as successful in elementary school and high school as boys. The test had to predict equal school success for both sexes. For another, there was already in the United States among educated middle-class professionals a belief that male and female "intelligence" was equal (even though females did not have the vote when the first widespread use was made of intelligence tests in World War I).

In any event, the practice of *discarding test items that sh*owed large sex differences produced intelligence tests incapable of studying sex differences in overall intelligence as measured. (Certain subtests do reveal fairly consistent sex differences. Why this is so or what is the theoretical or practical significance of the differences is not known; see Baer and Sherif, 1974).

Note, on the other hand, that the standardizers of intelligence tests did not discard items that discriminated among members of different socioeconomic classes or racial or ethnic groups. The retention of such items was entirely in keeping with the status quo in society, where members of subordinated groups had less access to high-quality schools and less chance of succeeding in or out of school.

"Intelligence" tests were standardized by human beings who made certain decisions about where they were willing to discriminate and where they were not. While test scores correlate reasonably well with achievement in current school systems, no one has shown clearly that such achievement is related to other accomplishments in life, except (here more weakly) level of occupational success. Occupational success is clearly related to other variables, such as one's socioeconomic class, race, and sex. For example, occupational success and female intelligence test scores correlate poorly and the reasons are fairly obvious: Most women have traditionally become mothers and housewives—occupations with almost zero value on the occupational scale. (I am not saying that these occupations should have near zero value. They are simply not recognized "occupations" in the work world of our society.) Even today, the increasing numbers of working women are disproportionately to be found in low-paying, low-prestige jobs.

For a moment, suppose that the standardizers of "intelligence" tests had used occupational attainments as their criterion instead of school performance. They would have produced tests on which men would score higher than women, middle-class men higher than workingclass men, white men higher than blacks, native Americans, or Chicanos, on the average. Would you be willing to contend seriously that such a test was "fair"? Would you accept a conclusion that such a test revealed very much about an individual's genetic make up at birth?

Let's go one step further: Ideological and practical concerns resulted in tests that equalized male and female "intelligence scores" so that each would correlate with school achievement. It is extremely difficult to see how there could be *no* ideological or practical basis for the repeated insistence by some testers that the test scores of blacks and whites are indicative of inborn "genetic" differences, rather than indicating something about schools and society. The only strong evidence that test score differences relate to hereditary differences pertains to data on parents and children and on siblings and twins. The highest correlations are found for test scores by those family members who are most similar genetically—identical twins. This finding could be considered evidence of a high heredity factor in test scores provided it holds when twins grow up in environments that are poles apart in advantage. This has not been demonstrated: There is no "scale" to measure environments or to compare them in this way. Disregarding this lack, the tester committed to a hereditary interpretation goes right ahead. He proceeds to use a mathematical formula developed to deal with variations in *physical* characteristics *within* kin groups, applying the formula uncritically to explain differences in "intelligence" test scores *between groups* of differing ancestry, social position, and cultural milieu. Typically, such a tester has been highly involved in education and testing. That is where he has become "expert."

As I write, public controversies have arisen once again over the interpretation and the use of "intelligence" test scores. They are not over the question of whether performance in today's school system is a good criterion, or whether the school systems are adequate for the needs of a diverse student body. The real issues in the controversy are not over theoretical formulas or technicalities, much as testers might like to keep them that way. Documenting some of the controversies over "mental testing," including the blatantly racist and class-biased statements of earlier testers, Cronbach (1975) protests that "Our greatest difficulty is our innocence," by which he means the testers' failure to consider "the consequences of testing for the social structure—a sociological problem that psychologists do not readily perceive" (p. 12). Such an "innocent," says Cronbach, "is not trained to realize that he does not know all the questions" to ask (p. 12).

Clearly, "innocence" of the kind described could also be called ignorance or callous indifference to the needs of others. Not all psychologists are "innocent" about such questions. In 1968, the Association of Black Psychologists called for a "moratorium" on intelligence testing in the schools because they saw it as a social mechanism to "penalize minorities, supply inaccurate information . . . and assist the white establishment" in resisting changes in the structure of education, work, and decision-making opportunities in this country (Jackson, 1975, p. 92).

Historically, the very questions asked by researchers seeking to assign so much weight to "genetic" and so much weight to "environmental" factors in accounting for group differences in test scores (to which they have assigned the glorified term "measured intelligence") were prompted by racist and social class biases. These biases do not disappear simply because a particular tester swears that he is not racist, or even when his other actions belie that epithet. The biases are built into the questions, no matter who asks them, as long as groups of individuals develop in environments that are blatantly unequal. New and different questions are needed.

"Tests" of Sex Difference in Social Behavior

Intelligence tests were introduced in this chapter because almost all psychologists would agree that they are the "best" tests of psychological "characteristics" that have been developed by psychologists. If some intelligence testers can forget that they are dealing with samples of human behavior in specific social situations, small wonder that testers of personality and social behavior can also forget. They, too, are sampling behavior in highly specific situations that they themselves have constructed. Because they labeled a situation as a "test" of "intelligence," "dominance," "submissiveness," "aggression," or "impulsivity," they interpreted the behavior as indicating that individuals *had* "so much" of *something*. The theoretical error was in ignoring the profound effect of social situations on behavior. Test performance was seen as measurement of a "trait" or "essence" that the individual possessed in some degree apart from that test.

There are consistent differences in adult males and females in our society in responses to personality tests or test situations designed to assess social behavior. All such consistent differences clearly reflect the social roles prescribed for male and female adults in the society, hence tell us little about sexual "natures," except that societies are moderately successful in shaping them. So, let's look at early childhood. Pick up a textbook in child psychology written before about 1970. You will find conclusions that boys under the age of 2 are more likely than girls to be aggressive, to maintain a higher activity level, to be more dominant, and are more likely to wander from an adult caretaker and to persist in getting around barriers keeping them from a desired toy. Surely such conclusions must reflect *solid* evidence that early sex differences in social behavior are indicative of differences in male and female natures.

Unfortunately, the data do not, for the most part, warrant the sweeping generalizations printed in textbooks. We are indebted particularly to the work of Eleanor Maccoby and her associates at Stanford University for systematically examining the actual data in the older studies to which the conclusions referred, as well as for undertaking new studies of very young children in search of sex differences. Before the age of 2, Maccoby (1972) found no sex differences in level of physical activity, in persisting to circumvent a barrier, in passivity, in exploratory behavior, or in reactivity to social or nonsocial stimulation. However, Maccoby and Jacklin's survey of literature led them to regard differences in aggressiveness between little boys and girls as likely to be differences in male or female "nature" (see Maccoby and Jacklin, 1974a, 1974b).

The evidence on aggressiveness of boys and girls raises other issues in interpretation: Different investigators have used different situations to study aggressiveness, so different that the specific actions labeled "aggressive" range from hitting a doll that was designed to be hit and recover its balance, to throwing toys, calling nasty names, and hitting another child. Are all of these behaviors sufficiently similar that we are justified in labeling them signs of a trait called "aggressiveness"? If they are, how are these behaviors related to actions labeled aggressive by society later in life? In fact, no one knows. There is no factual basis for assuming that hitting dolls, throwing toys, or hitting another child develop into the kind of aggressiveness that society may associate with adult "manliness." It is even less clear that such acts are related to male dominance in social institutions, where fighting or throwing objects could lead to immediate discharge.

The obvious physiological sources of adult sex differences pertain to the rhythms culminating in ejaculation and female orgasm, the menstrual cycle, the reciprocal copulatory and reproductive roles of the sexes. Now shrouded in myth and convention, the social and personal ramifications of such differences should be studied. Even if specific activity can be linked to hormonal levels, an undefined "aggressiveness" in early childhood can scarcely bear the burden of adult sex differences.

If there must be a conclusion at this point, it has to be that there may well be early sex differences in social behavior revealing male or female natures. However, the available data chiefly suggest such differences, particularly in activities that adult researchers choose to categorize as "aggressive." No one has been able to show that there is continuity between such sex differences in early childhood and those that appear so strikingly between the sexes later in life.

Naomi Weisstein (1971), a young psychologist, wrote an article as a contribution to the developing feminist movement, which she entitled "Psychology Constructs the Female, or the Fantasy Life of the Male Psychologist." She argued that the tradition of "trait" attribution in psychology, and the lack of interest by male psychologists in research that disconfirmed their own stereotypes about women, had produced a psychology with little value for the topic at hand. Essentially, I agree with Weisstein's critique (see also Shields, 1975).

It appears that many male psychologists as well as male and female college students entertain full-blown, negative stereotypes of women. Broverman, Vogel, Broverman, Clarkson, and Rosencrantz (1972) compared samples from these populations who rated the characteristics of an adult male, a "normal, healthy adult," and an adult female. They found that psychologists and male and female students alike rated an adult male higher than an adult female on more desirable characteristics. Further, the stereotype of the adult male resembled that of a "normal, healthy adult," whereas that of an adult female resembled that of a less than healthy and normal human being. If these stereotypes are prevalent in society, it follows that in formulating studies of behavior in early childhood, the investigator may well be guided by bias in what he or she looks for, what is assessed and what is ignored, and how the findings are interpreted. This state of affairs is a major reason why, at present, we can find more about sex differences in social behavior by looking at social arrangements and practices in societies than by looking at available research on little children in one or a few societies.

Male and Female "Natures" in Society

Despite the great differences among known human societies in various respects, including the roles of males and females, there are two complementary features common to all of them. First, a highly disproportionate number of persons with high social power and prestige in their major institutions (family, religious, political, economic, and so on) are male. Second, only women bear children and women are disproportionately represented in those who care for children, particularly when they are very young.

In most societies today, the social status of females is, on the whole, lower than that of males. In many it is still defined as "inferior." Doesn't the greater social power of males suggest that male "nature" is more aggressive, more achieving, more power-oriented? We do not need explanations in terms of male or female "natures" to explain the social positions of men and women. The latter have to do with institutionalized controls over the means for sustaining and creating life which cannot be understood in psychological terms alone. As long as these controls are dominated by one sex, we would expect men and women to develop and to behave quite differently. They spend their days in "different worlds."

However, societies are changing. Most women in the world work, many leaving their children for shorter or longer periods. Modern methods of contraception make possible decisions about whether or when to have children. Modern social organization (particularly in countries such as Sweden, China, or the Soviet Union) can provide alternate means of child care to the mother tied perpetually at home. More and more women are becoming educated in schools and in community settings. The former bastion of male supremacy and female subservience, China, has declared the aim of liberating females and males alike for full community participation. In Western countries, social movements of women are pressing for change in legal, occupational, marital, and financial customs that keep them in disadvantaged positions. The continued practice of warfare by predominantly male governments produces shortages of adult males and more single females. Improvements in standards of living have not been sufficient to support the ever-growing population of children in many countries. Traditional forms of marriage and family life are changing. In this country, more young people are deciding not to have children.

To an important extent, men and women become persons that their societies prescribe that they become, within ranges of individual differences in their feelings and behavioral characteristics that accompany their respective sex roles. Can the traditional norms for maleness and femaleness survive the changing conditions that I mention above? Or, on the contrary, is it possible that changing societies will violate the "fundamental" natures of males or females so that new social practices will lead to total homogenization of the sexes?

In my opinion, neither possibility is likely. My reasons hinge not on hormonal or structural differences between the sexes, but on their equal human nature in conceptual functioning. The basis for my futurism lies in social-psychological research that asked the general question: Can society make anything "right"?

CAN SOCIETY DEFINE ANYTHING AS "RIGHT"?

The issues raised by the question of whether society can define anything as "right" are related to discussions of human nature. Students in my social psychology class once concluded that there wasn't anything "natural" in human nature—that whatever society declared it to be, the individual would become. There are some experiments in social psychology that bear on this general question. They suggest qualifications to the students' conclusion.

Admittedly, the experiments I shall summarize represent highly abstract analogies to the problem at hand. They do not embody the full force of circumstance, persuasion, coercion, reward, and punishment that societies can bring to bear on one of their members. They do not concern issues of life or death, of triumph or defeat, of frustration or longing. They do, however, demonstrate that there are limits to the power of social influences in shaping behavior. They suggest useful analogies for thinking about the more complicated problems in life. They will serve to make us cautious in concluding that the human individual is nothing but a cultural robot.

To tie these experiments to earlier discussion of social influence, let's recall the Sherif experiment on norm formation using the autokinetic setup (Chapter 3). You will recall that in that highly unstructured situation, individuals were strikingly influenced by each other in their judgments over time. However, no one was intructed to attempt deliberately to influence another.

Subsequently, Sherif (1937) used the autokinetic situation to show that a highly unstructured situation is ideal for the would-be manipulator or transmitter of a norm. He instructed a confederate to make judgments of movement with a naive subject within a range that he prescribed ahead of time. The ranges were quite narrow, starting from 1 to 3 inches for the first subject, 2 to 4 inches for the second subject, and so on, up to 7 to 9 inches for the last subject. As expected, the naive person came to make judgments within the prescribed norm used by the confederate. On another day, each naive subject made judgments again, this time alone. Each adhered to the norm prescribed earlier by the confederate. In fact, conformity to the prescribed norm was closer than when the confederate had been present. The receiver of the norm became "more royalist than the king himself." Despite this, the subjects said that they *felt* more independent on the second day when alone; they did not believe that their judgments reflected influence of their previous interaction with the confederate.

As noted earlier, the important finding is that social influence in the form of suggestions from others is *maximally effective when the stimulus situation to be sized up lacks objective structure.* The person had no means at hand to check on the correctness of his or her responses, except that they agreed with judgments made by another person. Subsequent research has shown clearly that such "power of suggestion" is dependent on the variety of feasible responses to a situation. The effectiveness of social influence *decreases as the objective characteristics and relationships in the situation become more clear-cut* (Coffin, 1941; Luchins, 1945; Thrasher, 1954; Tajfel, 1969).

Thus, it becomes a matter of considerable interest whether or not it is possible to influence behavior when the suggested influence completely contradicts what a person can see or hear very clearly. This issue was studied in a series of experiments by Solomon Asch (1956). It is interesting that Asch began the research in the 1940s when it seemed to many people that leaders of the Axis powers, among others, were succeeding beyond their wildest dreams in convincing their people that Great Lies were truth. The experiments were not published until the early 1950s when, in the United States, a wave of conformity to the red-hunting and Cold War policies of self-appointed watchers over patriotism was sweeping the country. No doubt this wave created considerable interest in Asch's experiments. Today I find it difficult to convey what Asch studied and what he actually found since so many people have "heard of" the experiments in ways that seriously distort the findings. So, please, read with caution!

When the Big Lie Fails

Put yourself in Asch's experiment, and let's see what happened: You and seven other students come to the laboratory as volunteers for an experiment that, you are told, concerns judgment of the length of lines. On each trial, you will be shown a line to use as your standard on that trial. Then you will be shown three lines of varying lengths. Your task is to choose the one line among the three that matches the standard line, announcing your judgment aloud.

The trials start. The first standard line is 10 inches long and the three comparison lines are 8, 10, and 8¾ inches. The judging starts. Each person, including you, chooses the middle line. On the second trial, the standard is 2 inches, with comparison lines of 2, 1, and 1½ inches. Again, no one has difficulty in choosing the first line as the match.

On the third trial, the standard is 3 inches and the comparisons are 3¾, 4¼, and 3 inches. The first student to speak chooses the first comparison (3¾ inches), as does the next. Now it is your turn. Oh well, probably those fellows had a lapse, hmmm? Certainly the correct line is the third one, so you call it that way. But, wait a minute. The next student and everyone after that picks the 3¾ inch line as the correct match. Are they kidding? No, the same thing happens on the next trial when the standard is 5 inches and every single one of the other students picks a "match" that is obviously shorter (4 inches). What goes on here?

The same thing happens on 12 of the total 18 trials in which you are trying to pick the correct line. It's against the rules to question why, and the researcher keeps right on presenting one trial after another. How would you react?

It is important to point out that the differences between the correct match and the incorrect matches chosen by the majority were easy to detect. The lines were clear-cut and their relationships easily discriminated (high stimulus structure). When subjects judged them alone, errors were practically nonexistent.

Now let's pause a moment. Try to predict what percentage of the students' judgments (overall) were errors in the majority direction. Would you expect about 25, 33, 50, 66, 75, or 85 percent to be errors toward the majority? (I'll tell you why I'm asking you to guess shortly.)

Asch found that slightly *less than one-third* of the total "matches" made by all naive students in his experiment were incorrect choices in the direction of the errors made by the majority (who had been instructed to make mistakes). The majority of these errors was made by a minority of the subjects (22 percent of whom made 6 to 9 errors and 8 percent of whom [4 students] made 10 to 11). Twenty-six percent of the subjects made no errors; 30 percent made 1 to 3 errors; 14 percent made 4 to 5 errors.

Now I'll tell you why I ask you to guess. For several years, I have been asking students to predict that answer. Some of them said they had heard about or read the Asch study (some of the latter, unfortunately, were taking my examination). Invariably, the great majority have overestimated the frequency of errors, usually by 40 to 50 percent. Why? I believe there are two reasons: Asch's study is sometimes referred to as the classic experiment on majority influence, so people *expect* that a *lot* of influence was demonstrated. In general, I believe the overestimation also reflects an assumption that social influence will *always* be great, regardless of circumstances.

In analyzing the trials on which the errors occurred, Asch found that errors were more frequent when the line chosen by the majority differed from the correct line comparatively less, but infrequent when the difference between correct and majority choice was larger. Further, he showed that the frequency of errors decreased if there was one other naive subject who tried to "call them like I see them."

When Asch talked to the students afterward, he found that almost all of the subjects were quite aware that the majority judgments were wrong. Those who had made no errors said that it had been an uncomfortable experience to be contradicted at every turn. Those who made errors agreed that the situation was uncomfortable, but some had found a good "explanation" for what was happening: they blamed their eyesight, or imagined that the others were experiencing some visual illusion to which they themselves were not subject. A more frequent explanation of errors, however, was the admission that it seemed more comfortable to agree with the majority of other students than to give differing judgments.

Later studies have shown that whether we "feel more comfortable" going along with the majority in judgments that contradict our own senses or sticking to what we see depends in part how we size up the whole experiment. Since an experiment is a cultural event, it is interesting that the cultural background of the subjects plays a part (see, for example, Milgram, 1961; Whittaker and Meade, 1967). Probably, if the majority were significant other people in our eyes, we might follow their absurdities more closely. Conversely, an interesting study by Pollis and Cammalleri (1968) found that a woman student and her "best friend" amid an erring majority practically ignored all of those making wrong judgments.

Certainly, cultural definitions and pronouncements that contradict our senses or concrete experiences are apt to flow from persons important in our eyes. The presence of others also willing to be independent of a cultural prescription enhances our own determination to react as accurately and adaptively as we can on the basis of what we can see or learn. Asch's study shows, I believe, how important the actions of other people are in an attempt to "make anything right." However, it also shows that Big Lies completely contradicting the senses fail more often than they succeed. Even for those who "went along" in the situation, the compelling evidence of their senses prevailed once the others were gone. Arbitrary cultural prescriptions should succeed better, therefore, when people cannot check the evidence so directly and immediately with their own eyes.

The Transmission of Arbitrary Norms Through Generations

The problem of whether "the mores can make anything right" is an old one posed by William Graham Sumner (1906). Jacobs and Campbell (1961) set out to test whether the dictum was true for the transmission of norms formed in the autokinetic setup (highly unstructured) over successive generations of subjects.

They used a small laboratory room in which individuals judging autokinetic movement alone distributed their judgments around 3.8 inches, seldom reporting large movement. Wishing to study a very "arbitrary" norm in this situation, they started the experiment with one naive subject and three confederates, who gave judgments averaging 15.5 inches. The naive subject conformed to this highly arbitrary norm. At the next session, one of the confederates was missing, another naive subject replacing him. At the third session, a second confederate was withdrawn, and a third naive subject added. By the fourth session, all four subjects were naive, but all four conformed to the norm around 15.5 inches introduced by the original three confederates. This successive replacement of confederates, and of the experienced naive subjects in turn, by a fresh naive subject introduced at each session was their model of cultural transmission.

In brief, Jacobs and Campbell found that as successive generations of subjects judged autokinetic movement with the highly arbitrary standard, the arbitrary norm was at first transmitted. On the average, its influence was seen in the judgments of naive subjects four or five generations after all confederates of the experimenter had left. Thereafter, the norms formed during 30 judgments at each session declined toward the much lower judgments (3.8 inches) that subjects gave spontaneously without a confederate's influence. The decline was gradual but complete by about the eighth generation.

MacNeil (1965) elaborated the design in the Jacobs and Campbell study to determine whether the decline from the arbitrary norm was inevitable, or was a function of the very large norm they had introduced. ("Arbitrary" here refers to the extent of the *difference* between a norm formed naturally by subjects in the particular autokinetic situation and the norm introduced by confederates. The greater the difference, the more arbitrary is the norm introduced.) In his study, the "natural" norm was 5 inches, within a range of 4 to 8 inches. The most arbitrary norm was between 15 and 21 inches, with most frequent judgments around 18 inches. The less arbitrary norm was set at 9 to 15 inches, with the most frequent judgments around 12 inches.

MacNeil found that both arbitrary norms were accepted during the early sessions when a confederate was still present. However, for the most arbitrary norm (18 inches), the percentage of conforming judgments fell to 63 percent in the first generation after the confederates were removed. The norm declined rapidly toward the "natural" norm for this situation (5 inches), bearing no trace of the extremely arbitrary prescription by the third generation after the confederate's departure.

The less arbitrary norm (12 inches) was conformed to more frequently and for more generations. Conformity remained above 50 percent of the judgments in the fifth generation. The norm declined slowly (to about 8 inches) over 8 generations.

Weick and Gilfillan (1971) extended the same research plan by using a simple game that could be varied both as to the arbitrariness of customs introduced in playing it and as to the relative ease or difficulty of playing the game according to those customs. The game required that each of three subjects pick a number between 0 and 10, the sum of their numbers to equal a target number given to them. They could not communicate with one another and therefore had to develop a strategy for calculating what number each should contribute to match the target number.

There were at least 25 different strategies that could be used to play the game successfully; hence the assignment of any one strategy to the subjects was regarded as "arbitrary." On the other hand, some of the strategies were quite easy, whereas others were difficult, involving many formal rules of a more complicated nature. The experimenters arbitrarily assigned either an easy or a difficult strategy to three male students, who played the game according to the strategy assigned. Then one man was removed and another subject instructed in the strategy was added. This procedure was followed through 11 generations of subjects.

The outcome was that the difficult and arbitrary strategy was abandoned in favor of an easier one by the fourth generation. Those assigned an arbitrary but easy strategy maintained it throughout the experiment, even though they might readily have adopted another strategy equally as easy.

All in all, this line of research suggests that cultural norms can be transmitted arbitrarily through several generations when the situation lacks clear objective guidelines, but that actual experiences with the matter at hand also affect cultural transmission. Thus, if a norm is extremely discrepant from what is more "natural" for the person (in terms of the situation itself), its influence declines through repeated experience by the same individuals and during transmission to new members. Such decrements also occur if the custom is needlessly difficult in dealing with the problem at hand. However, in these unstructured situations, somewhat less arbitrary choices were easily perpetuated through several generations.

Arbitrary Definitions of Human Nature and Their Change

Clearly, an organized society has a better opportunity than an experiment to enforce its prescriptions through power, punishment, reward, and through limiting the opportunities of those to whom it assigns an inferior or undesirable human nature. When these prescriptions concern the personal styles, the motives, the capacities, or the "character" of individuals, they pertain to highly unstructured matters. We cannot see feelings or motives. Such personal characteristics as "dependence," "slyness," "emotionality," or "submissiveness" have to be inferred over time in a variety of complex situations. There is always room for error, for expecting behaviors, hence finding them. It is understandable that notions about the "nature" of different groups or of the sexes can be perpetuated over many generations, even though the evidence is slim. Furthermore, by complying to the norms set by dominant groups, subordinate groups collaborate in fulfilling the prophecy about their "natures."

On the other hand, if those to whom "inferior" traits are assigned come to realize that they may have collaborated with the cultural prescriptions by behaving in ways that yielded validating evidence, they are likely to participate actively toward changing their condition. They may deliberately act in ways at great variance with the prescriptions. To the extent that they succeed in showing the arbitrariness, even the inhumanity, of the character assigned to them, the cultural prescriptions will be transmitted with increasing difficulty to each succeeding generation. The capacity to change social values or norms is as uniquely human as the ability to learn those prevailing in a society at a particular time.

Thus, while human nature is truly amazing in its flexibility at adapting to different cultural conditions, it need not be true that society can make anything right or that cultural norms go on forever. The conceptual functions of human beings lend distinctive character to the human social environment. It is impossible to understand any aspect of the human person apart from those functions. It is impossible to develop general principles of the psychological functioning of individuals in isolation from the nature of the human environment.

The Self-system: Organization of Social Learning and Anchor for Experience

I am writing to you and to myself. I want my words to be more yours than print on paper that you purchased. Now, it is lonely, writing. It will be months, perhaps years, before you read these words. What will they mean to you? What will my husband, my other colleagues, and my students think of them? I find myself looking for reasons not to write. Yet, I must. Otherwise I cannot face myself.

Make no mistake, these are human problems: thinking of our own actions, pondering ourselves, taking into account what others may think of our actions, trying to grasp the viewpoint of another person, having the urge to convey private experience to others. They trouble no other species. Religious, philosophical, ethical, and psychological literature over the centuries has grappled with them. They have been cloaked in labels of mystery and self-glorification: Soul, Mind, Spirit, Consciousness, Ego, or "I."

If mystery refers to our ignorance, much remains when social psychology tackles problems of self. But tackle them we must. No matter what topic we turn to in social psychology, we run smackbang into active individuals behaving in fairly consistent ways from one day to the next in a variety of social situations. Their reactions to certain kinds of events and people are sufficiently predictable that we regard them as characteristic. We cannot help noticing that several individuals in the same situation attend to quite different aspects of it: They are tuned selectively to different wavelengths. In seeking the springs of conduct, we find that the human individual strives toward standards, goals, and ideals that are not represented concretely in the immediate environment. Though others may scorn these same standards, goals, or ideals, the person who embraces them can become sick with worry over whether and how they can be attained. Regret at their loss is personal loss.

The concept of *self-system* is inferred by the social psychologist from such consistent, characteristic, selective, motivated behaviors by the human individual (verbal or nonverbal). What we infer is that social learning by an individual developing in a cultural environment becomes *organized*. The study of social learning has provided support for a basic tenet in social psychology: Social actions are learned and they can be modified. However, social learning is not accumulated as a ragbag of discrete habits and specific responses.

The concept of self-system is useful in referring to the constellation of those past experiences that relate the individual to his or her own body and to the persons, objects, groups, institutions, social values, beliefs, and controversial issues arising in the environment (see Sherif and Cantril, 1947; Sherif, 1968). Such "connectedness" between the person and the social environment is laden with affect (motivational-emotional) and becomes *conceptual*.

It appears that we are taking on a large order, doesn't it? Many psychologists have thrown up their hands at such problems, often in justifiable reaction against the wholly subjective and mystical accounts of self inherited from centuries of speculative thought. Many are also highly critical of research on the self-system that relies on the person's own words reporting what or how well he or she thinks about self (see Wylie, 1961). Words can be used to mislead as well as to inform. Nor do we always act as we say we will.

Both criticisms are warranted, but they justify neither throwing up the hands nor ignoring the problems. Scientific study of problems related to the self-system has to be tied to observable events: actions by the individual (verbal and nonverbal) in concrete situations over time. There are "solid" data for the concept of self-system in experimental psychology and in the study of human development in different cultures. The price we pay for ignoring them is high: reams of research reports on specific kinds of behavior that bear no apparent relationship to one another. The chief value of a concept of self-system lies in the coherence it brings to findings collected on a variety of specific topics in social psychology.

When we psychologists wander from our own specialties into other research areas, we keep bumping into evidence that signals the self-system. In this chapter, I will point to such evidence. Admittedly, my choices are selective. Equally good ones can be made from other areas in experimental and social psychology. Then, we will look at evidence on the formation of self-system, indicating some variations attributable to the social context of development. That social context is so crucial that I deliberately delayed discussion of self until after the earlier chapters introduced major structural properties in any social environment—interaction processes within and between human groups, with their role-status relationships and normative products. Until the "reality" of such properties for the individual is grasped, I believe that discussion of the self-system is bound to run in circles: The self is the self is the self.

Of course, what each of us really wants to know is about *myself,* or someone else who is important in our lives. I believe that generalizations in social psychology can be useful in finding out about ourselves and others. They can guide us in learning about *whose eyes* we take into account in viewing ourselves as good or lousy, *what* standards we use in deciding whether "I'm okay and you're okay," how *important* different parts of ourselves become, and whether the personal problems we face are self-generated or are, in fact, related to the social circumstances in which we are enmeshed. Such problems are discussed in the chapters that follow. First, let's get a notion of how the "objective" psychologist goes about studying the "subjective."

BUMPING INTO SELF WHILE STUDYING "COGNITION"

In psychology, the cognitive processes refer to psychological activities concerned with "knowing" about the world. Traditionally, textbooks and courses cover them separately as perceiving (processing stimuli here and now), remembering, judging, thinking, reasoning, and so on. The traditional division between cognition and motivation-emotion reflects ancient views that sliced the human organism into a disembodied Mind with its Rational Faculties and an unruly Body stuffed with Irrational Drives and Emotions.

Even though such divorce between Human Mind and Body is not acceptable in scientific circles now (see Hebb, 1974), its categories linger in the vocabulary and working practice of psychologists. Strange to say, human *learning* is not often placed in the cognitive categories. That, too, is a historical accident. Early behavioristic psychologists (and some contemporary ones) threw out Mind, then proceeded to concentrate on movements of the Body, often highly specific, simple movements that were easier to measure or count. In protest, other psychologists insisted on the importance of central neural processes in more complex forms of behavior. Today, the latter are often called "cognitive" psychologists. In a scene where self-conscious "behaviorist" and "cognitive" psychologists still exist, it is difficult to find unbiased words to make the following simple point: The human being is an organism with species-specific capacities for knowing that are not unrelated to its states of arousal or its past experiences, any more than the latter are unrelated to its knowing. The only way we can learn about either or both is through observing how the individual acts. Neither our "knowing" nor our "motives" nor our actions remains static: They change during a lifetime as a consequence of concrete life experiences.

In short, our organisms are human. Each of us is one piece, not a collection of separate filing cabinets. It is hardly surprising, then, that evidence of a self-system pops up in research on cognitive processes. Let's consider some well-researched examples.

REMEMBERING

The classic tradition in research on remembering stems from the work of Ebbinghaus, a German psychologist who reported his studies fifteen years before the turn of this century. In order to control the effects of past experiences, he taught himself lists of nonsense syllables (for example, RAD, IZK, DET) and studied his recall of them over time. Ebbinghaus assumed that by using simple nonsense syllables, he was eliminating the effects of past experiences and simplifying the memory process to its most elementary level. Clearly, the first assumption holds only for certain nonsense syllables, as you can quickly find by composing a series that starts with the consonants in the alphabet, followed by UK (BUK, CUK, and so on).

Ebbinghaus' assumptions were challenged by Bartlett (1932), a British psychologist. Through a series of researches in the laboratory in England and in field situations in Africa, Bartlett showed quite convincingly that the individual uses as much past experience as possible when faced with the problem of recalling nonmeaningful stimuli. Furthermore, he showed that the simplicity of the stimulus need not mean that the memory process itself is simple. For example, a simple arrangement of curved lines was remembered with near-perfect accuracy by one of his subjects because it reminded him of the graph for a mathematical function. Remembering occurs with reference to neural organizations of past experience that Bartlett called "schema." Interestingly enough, contemporary work on memory supports Bartlett's general conceptions on the role of "schema" and their constructive utilization in remembering (Cofer, 1973).

Now, where does the self-system figure in all this? If we look at research in which certain schema are more important, more arousing, more salient for the person than others, we start bumping into the evidence. While in Africa, Bartlett heard that the Swazi had marvelous word-perfect memories. He confirmed this by asking an illiterate herdsman to list and describe all the cattle purchased by his employer the previous year (a list that could be checked by written records). Although it was the morning after a "beer drink," the herdsman quickly rattled off the list of 12 animals, complete with the seller, the purchase price and descriptions—correct in all but two small details. On the other hand, when Bartlett tried to test the Swazi memory by carefully reciting twice a 25-word message he had composed, asking that it be delivered to another person (in 2 minutes), he found that the Swazi natives were no more or less accurate than English natives to whom he gave the same test.

Bartlett found that Swazi feats of memory depended entirely upon their memory for cattle, which they recalled because "most Swazi culture revolves around the possession and care of cattle" (Bartlett, 1932, p. 249). Comparing his field and laboratory investigations, Bartlett concluded that what is salient in perceiving an event and what is subsequently recalled "are, at every age, in every group, and with nearly every variety of topic, largely the outcome of tendencies, interests and facts" that are personally valued as a result of the individual's past experiences in a social context (p. 253).

Involvement of the self also enhances short-term retention. The social psychologist Kurt Lewin observed many years ago that waiters in German restaurants did not write down customers' orders, but were able to recall each order of the several patrons at a table while they ate, talked at leisure, and ordered more coffee and pastry individually. However, the same waiters completely forgot the orders as soon as the bills were paid. One of Lewin's students, Bluma Zeigarnik (1927), studied this remarkable short-term memory for "interrupted" activities as compared with that for completed tasks. As every student knows, truly remarkable feats of short-term memory are possible when something important to one's self is at stake. Materials memorized letter perfect for an examination can be forgotten as we leave the room. Unless the materials themselves have personal import, the slate is clean when we attain what *really* counts: a passing grade in the course or, for the German waiter, payment of the restaurant check with tip. Superior recall for interrupted tasks undertaken by one's group has also been demonstrated, provided that the member accepts the group decision to undertake them or otherwise contributes personally to their execution (Horwitz, 1960).

We Remember What Is Personally Significant

Today, there is ample evidence for this important generalization: When the materials involve some aspect of the person's self-system, they are remembered better (see Smith and Jamieson, 1972). For example, Kamano and Drew (1961) presented a short personality description to college students, telling half of them merely that they would be asked to report on the description later and the other half, in addition, that the description was an evaluation by a clinical psychologist of their own performance on a personality inventory. Each student was asked to reproduce the passage immediately after reading it and again two days later. To control for individual differences in ability to recall, the personally involved students and the simple-recall students had been matched on the accuracy of their previous recall of a different neutral passage. As expected, immediate recall was superior to delayed recall. However, the students who were personally involved in the material actually recalled more of the passage after two days than the simple-recall students did immediately.

. . . But Not Necessarily What Bolsters Ourselves

One common hypothesis about important memories is that we recall better those things that enhance us, favor our own viewpoints, or fulfill our wishes. In the psychological laboratory, Kamano and Drew found the reverse. The personally involved students remembered *unfavorable* information about themselves better than favorable information, both immediately and two days later. In fact, the "wish-fulfillment" or self-enhancing hypothesis in memory has not fared particularly well in its simplest form. Some research has supported it (see, for example, Levine and Murphy, 1943), but other findings contradict the bald notion that we remember "what I agree with" or "what favors my beliefs" (see Smith and Jamieson, 1972).

Balance and Personal Involvement

Feather (1969, 1970, 1971) proposed that the schema involved in memory are more complex than simple positive or negative connections between the information to be recalled and our own views. The material to be recalled can be either favorable or unfavorable to our views. In either case, however, the person may or may not agree with the material. For example, a person who supports a strong defense establishment can disagree with a speech favoring it that proposes increasing the military budget.

Accordingly, Feather proposed that recall be assessed in terms of whether or not the material to be recalled "balanced" or was consistent with the person's existing schema. In one study, he asked people to recall the arguments they could remember on a social issue. He found that they did indeed list more arguments that were balanced—for example, arguments favorable to their viewpoints and with which they agree, or arguments unfavorable to their viewpoints and with which they disagreed. They put forth fewer arguments that were inconsistent or "unbalanced" in these respects—for example, arguments favoring their viewpoints but with which they disagreed or positions unfavorable to their own positions but with which they agreed.

The idea of "balance" or "imbalance" of relationships seems pretty complicated until it is made concrete. Let me try: Suppose I love a man who says that he believes strongly in shared responsibility between partners. I agree with that view, therefore, the structure of relationships between us and our beliefs on that matter is "balanced." On the other hand, suppose he says that he favors male authority in all important decision making. I would disagree and the structure would be "unbalanced." However, he might say that he favored shared responsibility *because* that meant that he need not be as loyal to me as he would have to be otherwise. I disagree with that statement, even though it favors shared responsibility, so things are out of whack again (unbalanced). If I could persuade him to disagree on the loyalty bit, as I do, then the whole deal is balanced: on both the loyalty and the responsibility issues. Now, all other things being about equal, which kind of structures—balanced or unbalanced—would I be most likely to recall at a later time?

This little soap opera and the question illustrate the issues that Rand Spiro and I (1975) set out to explore in the study of selective recall. We particularly wanted to study persons with varying personal involvement since we thought that the answers might depend on how committed a person was to the relationships in question. So we studied students who were supporting Nixon for president just before the 1972 election. The method used for assessing attitudes toward the candidates enabled us to divide the students into those more personally committed to Nixon's victory and those less involved (see Chapter 9 for details on this method).

Instead of asking the students to generate their own arguments on the election (the procedure Feather had used), we constructed arguments for the students to read and, later, to recall. There were 16 statements, 4 on each of 4 major issues in the election (the Indochina war, the economy, and so on). The statements concerned how the candidates would deal with each issue or the consequences of their particular positions. Two statements on each issue pertained to Nixon, one favorable and the other unfavorable. Two other statements on each issue pertained to McGovern, one favorable and the other unfavorable to him. The student read each statement, then indicated whether he or she agreed or disagreed with each. Later in the same session, he or she was asked to recall as many of the statements as possible.

We were interested in several questions:

1. Would the Nixon supporters generate more balanced than unbalanced structures from the statements by *agreeing* with those favorable to Nixon or unfavorable to McGovern, and then *disagreeing* with those unfavorable to Nixon and favorable to McGovern?

    Finding: Yes, they did. The students formed twice as many balanced as unbalanced structures at the outset, as indicated by their agreement-disagreements with the 16 statements. This tendency was significantly greater for the more personally involved students.

2. Who would remember the most statements, the students more or less involved in the election?

Finding: The more involved students recalled significantly more statements, as expected.

3. Would the students recall more statements that favored Nixon's re-election over his opponent than statements that were unfavorable to his re-election?

Finding: No, they did not.

4. Would they recall more statements that they *agreed* with than statements they disagreed with?

Finding: No, they did not.

5. Would the students recall more balanced than unbalanced *structures*?

Findings: Yes, they did. However, we also knew that the students had established a larger number of balanced than unbalanced structures when they originally agreed or disagreed with the statements, before being asked to recall them. They had a larger pool of balanced structures at the outset from which to recall. Feather seemed to be correct about the "self-serving" tendency to have more balanced than unbalanced structures in mind. However, neither his research nor ours, to this point, had shown a *selective* tendency to remember balanced structures *better* or *selective forgetting* of unbalanced structures.

6. Given the tendency to agree and disagree with statements favoring and opposing the candidates in ways that created more numerous balanced structures, hence also the likelihood of recalling more balanced structures (especially if one is personally involved), would we find any selectivity in the recall process *itself* that favored either balanced or unbalanced structures? Does memory sift out the unbalanced or seize on the balanced? We looked at the findings in a different way: *Relative* to the number of balanced and unbalanced structures each student had created (by agreeing-disagreeing), what *proportion* of each did that student actually recall?

Lo and behold, we found that the students recalled *proportionally more unbalanced than balanced structures*, particularly students who were more committed to the candidate. *Proportional* to the number that were unbalanced for them, the more avid Nixon supporters remembered over 60 percent of their unbalanced structures, a record high proportion of recall under the conditions of this experiment. In general, then, there was a selective tendency in recall that, relatively speaking, favored better recall of *unbalanced* structures.

Especially to the more involved students, the few sour notes struck in arguments over the election resounded stubbornly in memory. We do not know whether they would continue to do so for periods longer than our experiment. I suspect that depends on how sour they are and how important the issue is in one's scheme of things.

Experimental research on memory has much to discover about such issues. Meanwhile, I would not like to leave the impression that involvement of the self-system in recall is confined to *improving* recall. Bartlett's research and studies on the "psychology of testimony" are full of systematic errors in recall shaped by personal bias. In addition, studies on the origins of erroneous rumors (see, for example, Allport and Postman, 1965) point to the determining role of strong personal commitments in creating and compounding inaccuracies in the recall of events. Such personal commitments sometimes reflect social values, discriminations, or prejudices that are accepted in the individual's social environment. For example, a quick view of a white man holding a straight-edged razor while arguing with a black man was recalled by prejudiced whites as a black man with a razor arguing with the white man. In this case, the social stereotype had become a *personal* schema affecting both how the individual processed "information" and recalled it. Needless to say, such a transformed recollection is changed even further as it passes along to other persons, each of whom interprets the rumor in terms of personal expectations, suspicions, or fears.

CAN WE MAKE "OBJECTIVE" SOCIAL JUDGMENTS?

The early studies of judgment, like those of memory, concentrated on discrimination of abstract qualities and quantities of objects or events. Again the rationale was to reduce cognition to simpler "elements" and their attributes (pitch or loudness of sound, weights of objects, lengths of lines). Human judgment and its errors were compared with the invariant baselines of physical measurements (sound frequencies, grams, centimeters). As individuals made repeated judgments of such abstract dimensions, the evidence showed that they formed psychophysical scales corresponding, on the whole, to the properties of stimuli being judged—with certain "constant errors" reflecting the human equation and variable errors associated with individual differences among the judges.

While teaching psychophysics at the University of Chicago, the psychologist Thurstone found many of the students monumentally bored by research on judgments of physical dimensions. To liven up things, he began using examples in social judgment. No doubt he had other aims as well because shortly he developed methods for constructing psychosocial scales as the basis for assessing social attitudes. In 1928, he published a paper that announced triumphantly in its title "Attitudes Can Be Measured"!

Thurstone proceeded from the research model developed in psychophysics: The major lack in studies of social judgment was any sort of baseline comparable to the physical measurement units used in psychophysics. There is no yardstick for measuring how favorable or unfavorable a particular statement is toward war. Why not form a psycho*social* baseline by asking human judges to compare or categorize statements related to a social attitude (say toward God, religion, or war)? Thurstone assumed that judges' errors would be normally distributed around a statement's "true" social value. Then, he could take their median judgment of a particular statement as the scale value of the statement (provided the spread of individual judgments around it was not too great).

For example, he asked judges to sort a large number of statements on an issue into 11 categories, distributing the statements into categories fairly equally according to whether each was more or less favorable to the attitude object (for example, war). Calculating the median of the category numbers assigned by the judges to each statement, he selected a series of statements with scale values distributed from 1 to 11, located at "equally appearing" intervals from one another. (Later, the resulting Thurstone scale would be given to subjects in attitude research, with the request that they indicate which statements they agreed with. Their "attitude" was represented by the average of the scale values assigned by the judges to those statements that they endorsed.)

There was one rub: In psychophysical judgment, the judges seldom have any attachment to one weight or line or sound over another. Such is not the case for statements about different positions on a controversial social issue. Therefore, Thurstone had to assume that the persons who judged the statements would not let their own commitments to a position on the issue influence their judgments. He stated specifically that if the judges' own attitudes strongly affected their judgments of the statements, his procedures were not valid since different judges would produce different scale values for the same statements (Thurstone and Chave, 1929).

Thurstone's assumption that judges' attitudes would not affect their "objective" judgments (of how favorable or unfavorable a statement was on an issue) was tested by several investigators. The findings were not unequivocal, but several textbooks stated that the assumption was a safe one. When the late Carl Hovland, of Yale University, brought that conclusion to the attention of a colleague in his Communications Research Program in 1948, it was quite a blow. That colleague (Muzafer Sherif) had proposed to Hovland that they develop an "indirect" method for attitude assessment based on systematic differences in the way people judge the position of attitude statements. Sherif believed that individuals with different attitudes would judge the same statements differently.

The authoritative pronouncement in respected sources that a person's own attitude would not affect judgments sent Sherif into a frenzy of reading. "If that's right," he said, "then everything I know about human psychology is wrong." (The self gets involved in scientific work, you see.) At last, his reading of the earlier research suggested a solution to the puzzle, which Hovland proposed they test. When we moved to the University of Oklahoma in 1949, research on the problem began in collaboration with Hovland at Yale.

Solving the Mystery

The key to the puzzle was the discovery that Thurstone had considered a judge "careless" who piled 30 or more statements (out of 100 or so) into a single category, since instructions requested the judge to use 11 categories fairly *equally*. The most impressive support for the Thurstone assumption was a study by Hinckley (1932) in which black and white college students judged statements about the "status of the Negro in the United States." Following Thurstone's carelessness criterion, he had discarded those judges who placed 30 or more statements in any one category. He reported that a disproportionate number of these judges were black.

Suppose that the discarded judges were *not* careless. In fact, it seemed reasonable that they might be precisely those most personally involved with the issue. Accordingly, the new research compared judgments of Hinckley's statements made by unselected white college students, black students at a segregated black college, the first black students at a white university the year following a Supreme Court decision ending segregation, and the white students at the same university who had been most active in demonstrating against segregation.

The overall "collegiate" norm favoring the end of segregation made it difficult for the researchers to locate anti-Negro whites at the same university. On tests directly questioning them about their attitudes, white students came out smelling like roses, despite the fact that anti-Negro remarks could be overheard in fraternities and dormitories when the same students were with friends. At last, Sherif sent his (then) graduate assistant, O. J. Harvey, to Georgia in the attempt to secure anti-Negro whites at Emory University. Neither was satisfied that the small sample had anything like the personal involvement in the issue that they found among the white activists and black students in Oklahoma.

When Hovland and Sherif (1952) eliminated those students who placed 30 or more statements in a single category, the scale values of the statements resembled those obtained by Hinckley closely. However, as they had suspected, the subjects who were thereby eliminated were the highly involved black and anti-segregation white students.

Accordingly, they examined the judgments made by each of their samples separately.

The scale values of the same statements differed widely for the highly committed and less involved students. Specifically, the statements that were intermediate to the extremes (1 and 11) for uninvolved students were placed toward the extremes by the blacks and white activists. The frequencies with which statements were placed in each of the 11 categories showed clearly what was happening: The highly involved students with extreme stands seldom used the intermediate categories; to them, a statement was either close to their own pro-black view or strongly against it. When Sherif and Hovland (1953) allowed the students to decide how many categories were needed to judge the material, instead of imposing 11 on them arbitrarily, these same students simply eliminated most of the 11 gradations. Typically, they used only 3 or 4 categories. The Thurstone assumption did not hold for persons who were personally involved in the issue they were judging.

The distribution of judgments by the black and pro-black white students were distinctive: The stack of statements they regarded as anti-black included about 40 percent of the statements. Another 25 percent were piled into one or two favorable categories; the remainder were sorted in between the extremes. The judgments by the anti-Negro white students were not so strikingly bimodal. Indeed, replications of the research in the United States from that day to this (see, for example, Selltiz, Edrich, and Cook, 1965; Upshaw, 1962; Zavalloni and Cook, 1965) have found the same thing about anti-Negro white students—a conclusion that led some to conclude too hastily that a personal commitment *for* something has different consequences in judgment from a personal commitment *against* it.

I believe that Eiser (1971) hit on the more nearly correct interpretation. He pointed out that the prevailing norm in U.S. colleges (at least since the early fifties) has been favorable to an improving position for blacks. Those opposed to such improvement were deviating from that norm. However, to disagree with the norm and to take actions to oppose it are two different things. Local chapters of the Ku Klux Klan did not flourish on college campuses. If that analysis is correct, the anti-Negro whites in the research were not as personally involved in the issue as the pro-black students who were, at the time, actively supporting the norm favoring desegregation.

Eiser made the point nicely in his own research comparing judgments made by students at the London School of Economics on statements about the use of drugs. At the time, the prevailing student norms were quite permissive in this regard, opposing legal restrictions. The "deviant" student was one who *favored* restrictions on the use of drugs. As Eiser predicted, it was the students *opposed* to restrictions on drug use whose judgments assumed the strikingly bipolar distribution found by Sherif and Hovland. They judged permissive statements as more permissive and restrictive statements as more restrictive than did students who favored restrictions. Ironically, those students most "tolerant" about drug usage saw the drug issue in black and white terms, with very little gray, a view corresponding to the student norm.

The alternative hunch to explain the Sherif-Hovland findings does not seem reasonable: It amounts to suggesting that being *against* something or someone produces greater objectivity in judgment than being strongly in favor of it. Although neglected in the literature on the topic, Katherine Vaughan's research in southern Texas showed that this need not be so. Anti-Chicano Texans displaced statements about Chicanos in a direction precisely the reverse of the displacements by pro-black students in the Sherif-Hovland research (see Sherif et al., 1965, pp. 118–122). Since they were *against* Chicanos, they piled up many statements in categories favorable to Chicanos at the end opposite their own commitments. To them, a disproportionate number of statements were *pro*-Chicano. The distribution of their judgments forms a mirror image of that by Sherif and Hovland's personally involved pro-black subjects. Eiser's hunch still holds, however: At the time, it was not considered at all deviant for southern Texans to hate Chicanos.

Assimilation-Contrast Effects Relative to Our Own Commitments

All right: When a part of the self-system is aroused, our judgments are affected. Judgments of highly involved persons differ strikingly from those who don't care about the matter. But why? The answer is relatively simple: Even though told to be as objective as possible and to make judgments solely in terms of how pro or con a statement on the issue really is, a highly involved person cannot help using those views that are *personally* acceptable as the anchor in judging the other statements. The person cannot *help* agreeing or disagreeing with the statements, even though that is *not* the task requested. The effects of the personal anchor are twofold: Statements close to it are *assimilated* toward it, while those increasingly discrepant from it are *contrasted* away from it. (Compare these effects in social judgment with the assimilation-contrast noted in Chapter 2 in sizing up other persons.)

Assimilation-contrast effects in social judgment relative to the person's own commitment are *not* found only in one particular procedure for studying social judgment. In a study on judgments by Scottish university students about the favorableness-unfavorableness of statements concerning organized religion, Fraser and Stacey (1973) compared four *different* procedures and methods for data analysis. Male students were explicitly told to judge objectively without regard to their own agreement-disagreement with the statements. With some variations related to these methods, they found that, in each, the students' own views toward the church anchored their judgments. As a result, the more favorable a student was to the church, the higher his ratings of statements expressing favorable opinions (assimilation to one's own view), and the lower were his ratings of statements expressing "neutral" or unfavorable views toward the church (contrast relative to one's own view). When several different research methods yield similar results, we can have a great deal more confidence that self-anchoring leads to consistent displacements in our judgments.

I have to restrain my impulse to plunge further into the research on social judgment and fine points in its interpretation, as I am personally involved in it myself. This introduction to self in social judgment will serve us well when we consider problems related to the setting of personal standards, the people whose reactions to us count in our eyes, our attitudes, and their change. Meanwhile, here is a list of further readings on personal involvement in social judgment: Eiser and Stroebe, 1972; Kiesler, Collins and Miller, 1969, Chapter 6; Shaw and Costanzo, 1970, Chapters 11, 14; Sherif and Hovland, 1961; Sherif, Sherif, and Nebergall, 1965; Sherif and Sherif, 1967; Sherif et al., 1973.

ATTRIBUTING CAUSES FOR OUR OWN AND OTHERS' ACTIONS

Why do I act as I do? Why do others around me behave as they do? Human beings ask such questions and arrive at answers about "causes" sufficiently satisfactory that they can function from day to day with the belief that social events sometimes "make sense." The self-system as formed at the time clearly anchors the process of arriving at such decisions. Fritz Heider (1958) called for more study of such "naive" psychologizing. A number of social psychologists began experimenting on what Harold Kelley, of the University of California at Los Angeles, called "common sense" assumptions about behavioral causality (in Jones, Kanouse, Kelley, Nisbett, Valins, and Weiner, 1972).

We touched on such problems in the last chapter in discussing controversies over human nature. That discussion reminds us of the powerful influence that ideologies passed down from older to new generations have in determining our "naive" or "common sense" assumptions. On the whole, the research on causal attributions for behavior has neglected the person's prior beliefs, as Kelley noted (1973). In fact, we may know more about the influence of psychologists' prior beliefs on their decisions than about those of persons supposedly uncontaminated by psychological theories.

For example, Spohn (1960) reported significant associations between psychotherapists' assessments of patients' mental health and their own value commitments. Freudian analysts in his sample tended to be more conservative in sociopolitical and economic views than non-Freudians. Freudians also attributed higher "mental health" to patients who agreed with their political biases than those who disagreed. Since the psychotherapists believed that poor "mental health" causes disturbed behavior, their attribution of causality is clearly related to their political and theoretical commitments.

Interestingly enough, research has shown that many beliefs entertained by psychologists are also shared by college students. In the last chapter we found that clinical psychologists and college undergraduates agree in attributing personal characteristics to females that diverge from their own views of what characterizes a "healthy, mature adult" or an adult male (Broverman et al., 1972). Both clinicians and undergraduates tend to interpret certain responses on "projective" (unstructured) tests as "caused by" the same feelings or personal problems (Kelley, 1973). It is at least possible that both have been exposed to older psychological theories that permeate our culture as "truth."

The Trap of Attributing "Traits" to Others

The theory that a person's social behavior is "caused" by his or her personal "traits" has had a long opportunity to be tested through research. A "trait" is thought to be some quality or quantity *within the person:* He or she *has* it because that is the kind of person he or she *is.* Many psychologists today agree that research tests are far from positive (see Mischel, 1968). Why?

Certainly one reason lies in the erroneous assumption that what a person says about himself or herself in response to direct questions on a "personality test" can be taken as evidence of a general "trait" that would characterize that person in any relevant situation. Allen Edwards (1957b) showed that such responses are significantly and highly correlated with what the same individuals regard as the "socially desirable" way to be. In the United States (where the bulk of data was collected), the great majority of persons respond in ways that keep them near the "average," with few test results falling at the extremes. Thus, although the tests were designed to study traits like introversion-extroversion, ascendence-submission, adjustment-maladjustment, aggressiveness-shyness, the responses of most people fall well between the two poles and only a few give responses suggesting they clearly "have" such traits (Murphy, 1947, p. 740). Finally, the correlations between responses by the same person to different "tests" for the same "trait" are so low and variable that definitions of personal traits made in one circumstance have poor predictive value for how the person will behave in another.

All of these failures of "trait" psychology in locating "causes" for behavior solely within the person reflect an astounding naiveté. Typically, the trait psychologist *describes* a person's responses with an adjective (as "aggressive," "submissive," "dominant," "nurturant") and then literally attributes that adjective to the person as the *cause* of behavior. Long ago, Woodworth and Marquis (1947, p. 88) pointed out that such "adjectives [trait names] are properly adverbs" describing *how* not why a person acts!

In order to escape from the vicious circle of describing behavior and then attributing its *cause* to the description, the individual's past experiences, organized in self-schema, have to be studied in interaction with the *circumstances* and *situations* where he or she acts over time. As Kelley (1973) pointed out, nonpsychologists, including children, are more charitable than some trait psychologists. They do, at times, take considerable account of the *circumstances* of behavior and of whether behavior is consistent over *time* in *various situations* when they attribute causes to a person's actions.

When researchers look at a person's actions in specified *kinds* of situations, interacting with others to whom that person is related in specified ways (for example, superior-inferior, love-hate), they do find consistencies in behavior. As a well-known trait psychologist concluded long ago, such consistencies occur when the matter at hand and the people in question are personally involving for the individual. When they are not, considerable inconsistency is reported (Allport, 1943).

What lends consistency to social behavior, therefore, is not some "essence" inside the person apart from anything else, but the situational arousal of conceptual schema defining that person's ties with his or her social world. We are dealing with person-environment *relationships,* not "traits." Owing to the person's past experiences, some of these schema are more important, more "central," or higher in priority than others. In social psychology, such arousal of self-schema by ongoing events and situations is referred to as personal (or ego) involvement.

Explaining Our Own and Others' Behavior

A particularly suggestive finding from research pertains to differences when we "explain" our own behavior and that of other people. Jones and Nisbett (in Jones et al., 1972) suggested a general hypothesis that we tend more frequently to attribute our own actions to the requirements of situations we find ourselves in and how others treat us, but to refer more frequently to personal traits or dispositions in "explaining" the actions of others. (If psychology is defined as the study of behavior by "other persons," the inference is clear that some psychologists may be committing this bias daily.) Most of the research confirming their proposition has been conducted in the laboratory, where a person's awareness of being evaluated and of what others may expect of him or her is heightened. In short, the research situations may promote a tendency to appear in the best possible light in relatively brief encounters.

In addition to Jones and Nisbett, Storms (1973) has shown that the predicted tendency does occur during an experimental discussion. However, it can be partially reduced by showing the subject a videotape that focuses on the behavior of the others present, leaving the subject out of the picture. Under these circumstances, the viewing subject attributes more importance to the situation itself in explaining why others acted as they did. Presumably we ourselves might take more responsibility for our own actions if we were exposed to such separate views of others and of ourselves. Yet, Storms cites other evidence that viewing our own behavior may not yield the countervailing corrective to accept ourselves as "cause" for behavior in social interaction. For example, alcoholic patients shown a film of their behavior when intoxicated became so upset that they could not view the film: They could not accept their own behavior as belonging to themselves. They ceased trying to understand "causes."

Investigations on the attribution of causality in interpersonal events will gain by considering more systematically the role of self in the "causal schema" the person has built over time. Attributing our own behavior to events, but the other person's to personal traits or motives sounds like a tendency to pass the buck while excusing ourselves. But, we can think of exceptions. For example, school girls, more frequently than school boys, attribute their failures in academic tasks to themselves, rather than circumstances (Stein and Bailey, 1973). Some of us may have such low opinions of self that we actually refuse signs of acceptance and approval from others. By our refusal, we engage in the "self-fulfilling prophecy" of acting like lousy persons, which encourages others to treat us as lousy, thereby confirming our belief that *they* think we are lousy, too. The psychiatrist R. D. Laing (1967) has depicted vividly such treacherous spirals of self-defeat.

However, attribution of causes for our own behavior and others' behavior need not tend in directions that are consistent with the self-schema as formed. If such were the case, none of us would change during our lifetimes. Instead, I am suggesting that networks of interpersonal links and mutual bonds are the significant framework for attributing causality to behavior (see Chapter 3). As a dramatic instance, let us look at the attribution of causes when individuals belong to antagonistic groups.

Sizing Up Behavior by Members of an Antagonistic Group

The boys in the camp experiments (Chapter 5) were quite certain about what caused their difficulties: It was the impossibly hostile behavior and degraded character of the boys in the *other* group. Shortcomings in their own behavior were merely responses ("natural" ones, they believed) to the incredibly irresponsible behavior by the other group. Yet we, as outsiders, can see that members of both groups behaved atrociously because each became hopelessly involved in struggle between the groups for goals that only one could attain. When that circumstance between the groups changed to those requiring interdependent actions, their views of each other also changed.

Once the singular perspective of one's own group becomes a *personal* perspective, individual perceptions of self and others are firmly anchored by that personal investment. As reported in Chapter 5, Dawes et al. (1972) provided an excellent example on the University of Oregon campus during the controversies among student groups supporting and opposing the Vietnam war. Soliciting "doves" and "hawks" as volunteers through the student paper, they compared their objective (paired comparison) judgments of statements on the war. As expected, doves judged pro-war statements to be more extremely pro-war than hawks judged the same statements. Hawks judged anti-war statements to be more extreme than doves did.

These pronounced contrast effects in judging the others' position were coupled with an interesting assimilation of one's own views to the American norm of "moderation." As every citizen of the United States is taught, it is all right to take a personal stand, but it is not all right to be an "extremist." That's too far out. Don't be a crackpot! So, students on each side judged statements supporting their own commitment as more moderate than the same statements were judged by their opponents.

The implication is clear: Even though I volunteer as a strong supporter of one side or the other on the war, I am "more reasonable" since I am not a crackpot extremist like my opponents. The cultural norm becomes apparent when we compare the results of Dawes et al. with those of Diab (1967) in his studies of Arab nationalism in Lebanon. There, persons taking extreme views were extremists—no ifs and buts.

When, over time, we have built expectations about others, and they about us, these mutual expectations are bound to affect our explanations of our own actions as well as theirs. When another person is mutually and positively linked to self, as lover or friend, for example, more similar causes may be attributed to self and the other than when, as in the above example, the link is hostile. The search for general principles governing perception and judgment of actions by self and by others may be facilitated by concentrating on the person's important role relationships rather than on transitory encounters in the laboratory or in public. In the latter, we may indeed see ourselves as isolated vessels adrift in a sea of circumstance (see Bem, 1967; Jones and Nisbett, 1972, p. 83).

Such orientation follows logically from what we know about the formation of the self-system. The self emerges concordant with the formation of personal ties with other human beings.

WHERE DOES THE SELF-SYSTEM COME FROM?

Before we became parents of three babies whom we could watch ourselves, I had the opportunity to explore the literature on infant and child development in search of answers to that question, while assisting Sherif and Cantril in their work on *The Psychology of Ego-Involvements* (1947). While wishing that they could successfully introduce a new word, they referred to the concept as *ego*—the Latin word for "I." The term *ego* has become so identified with the Freudian ego concept that I have by now largely abandoned it. However, when I refer to self-system or involvement of the self, I am speaking of the same concepts that Sherif and Cantril called "ego" and "ego-involvement." (Psychologists are among the more guilty in changing vocabularies while not changing what they are talking about. My best advice is to keep your eyes on the *problems* and the variables psychologists are *studying*. These are likely to be around for a long time, even though the words used to refer to them may change with remarkable speed.)

In my search, I was astonished to find that careful and detailed observations of infant development had been recorded as early as 1787 (by Dietrich Tiedemann; see Murchison and Langer, 1927). After Darwin's "Biographical Sketch of an Infant" (1877), a number of psychologists wrote down regular observations of children, usually their own or relatives (see, for example, Baldwin, 1895; Moore, 1896; Preyer, 1890; Shinn, 1898, 1907). More recently, Gesell and his associates at Yale University had systematized longitudinal observations from birth to puberty (Gesell, 1938; Gesell and Thompson, 1934; Gesell and Ilg, 1943).

In all of the observational literature, there is agreement on several points. First, there is no evidence for a self-system at birth or during the early months of human life. Nor does the evidence suggest the "awakening" of some primitive inborn intuition. Infants literally have to learn to differentiate between their own bodies and other objects as they develop and move out into the world.

Second, the earliest signs of self are nonverbal, namely, the gradual differentiation between one's own body (and somewhat later its "possessions") and other objects. The lack of such discrimination during the early months is revealed by the infant's inability to localize body sensations and to differentiate between the consequences of one's own actions applied to other objects and to one's own body. The mistakes made by children in the first year of life are amusing evidence for the gradual attainment of that differentiation. For example, Preyer (1890) reported that his year-old son discovered the excitement of biting hard objects with his new teeth, then of clacking his teeth together to make noise. But one day, holding onto his bed railing, he bit his own bare arm—so hard that teethmarks showed for some time afterward. Preyer reported that the boy did not make *that* mistake again.

Such "double sensations" (pleasurable as well as painful) and the increasingly active exploration of one's body combine in the growing discovery that there is a big difference between acting on other things and acting on one's own body. Even in the second year of life, Preyer noted that his son made mistakes in this regard: "The child had lost a shoe. I said, 'Give the shoe.' He stopped, seized it, and gave it to me. Then, when I said to the child, as he was standing upright on the floor, 'Give the foot,' . . . he grasped at it with both hands, and labored hard to get it and hand it to me" (Preyer, 1890, p. 190).

The emerging body self is also revealed in the infant's reactions to others. By about 2 months, the baby smiles at a human face—*any* human face. By 6 to 8 months, different reactions are made to familiar faces and to strange faces. Strangers may evoke worried looks or crying (particularly if the child has not been around a number of other people). By about a year or so, most babies display considerable interest when they see other babies—a fact that is extremely difficult to understand if we believe that we become interested in other human beings only because they reward or otherwise reinforce us. No doubt, such interest in others like ourselves is related to the slow process of self-identification.

For example, a baby's first glances at the self-reflection in a mirror are usually sober affairs, but soon become interested inspection as though looking at another child. Delight and eventually "self-conscious" preening before one's own image follow the discovery that there is not another person in the mirror—that the image is oneself. At about the same time a child with shutter-happy parents starts to pose or mug for the camera. The Kellogs (1933), who raised their son Donald and the chimpanzee Gua together, made movies of the two. By about age 2 Donald had become a ham before the camera, while 2-year-old Gua went merrily on his way, oblivious of an image problem.

The crucial importance of interaction with other people in the process of differentiating the bodily self was summed up by James Mark Baldwin (1895), a remarkable and often neglected psychologist who observed his own children: "The ego [self] and *alter* [other] are thus born together. Both are crude and unreflective, largely organic, an aggregate of sensations, prime among which are efforts, pushes and strains, physical pleasures and pains. . . . My sense of myself grows by imitation of you, and my sense of yourself grows in terms of my sense of myself. Both ego and *alter* are thus essentially social" (p. 338).

Body Self Becomes a Cognitive-Motivational System

Entering the third year of life, a child usually has a pretty good sense of "me" (or my name) as a body. However, the child's social behavior is often inconsistent. The conceptual distinctness of one's body is wholly identified with how that body feels, what it sees, and what it wants from moment to moment. Thus, social behavior at about this age was described by Piaget (1932) as "autistic" and, more recently, by Jane Loevinger (1966) as "impulse ridden." Freud had the same facts in mind when he referred to "His Majesty, the Baby." (He could, of course, have referred to "Her Majesty" as well.)

The imperious, inconsistent baby becomes a conforming, socialized child, at least by 5 to 7 years of age, if not earlier. The remarkable transition in social behavior during these early years cannot be understood apart from the *conceptual-linguistic* developments of that period, to which I referred in the last chapter. One sign of these developments is simply the rate of vocabulary increase: About the first birthday, what adults call "words" start to appear. New words are added so slowly at first that an observant adult can keep fairly accurate count. For example, one early study reported an average of 22 different words used by children of 18 months (Smith, 1926). Sometime during the last half of the second year, something remarkable starts to happen. The *rate* of vocabulary increase becomes the most rapid that it will be ever again in life. The same early study found the average frequencies of different words used by individual children were 118 at 21 months, 272 at 24 months, 446 at 30 months, 896 at 3 years, and 1222 at 42 months. The floodgates of speech open.

Naming Self and Others

The important discovery that "things have names" is the step toward a series of cognitive changes that transform the primitive "body self": Speech becomes *instrumental* for the child as an accompaniment and a substitute for action (for example, for pulling at mother's clothing to get attention). Words are combined, at first two or three at a time, as statements or demands and then as questions (Brown, 1973). The questions display clear evidence that the child actively seeks the *names* for objects, an event easily misinterpreted by parents as a demand for the object itself. The child points or says "Eh-eh-eh!" "Dis?" "Dat?" "Whassat?" and is quite satisfied when a name is supplied. (Knowing this saves a parent from a lot of useless "No-you-can't-have-that.")

However, it is not only the length, the syntax, and the complexity of speech that changes. The *meaning* of words changes rapidly during this period. The earliest words are so broad and flexible that their meanings bear little resemblance to those in adult language. At a little over a year, our Sue learned "joos" for orange juice and applied the word to anything to drink and any liquid, including a swimming pool. Lewis (1963) traced the fate of a word first used by his son at 21 months when he called his cat "tee" (Timmy). Within the next month, the boy also called a cow and a small dog "tee." Meanwhile, he learned "goggie" for his toy dog, correctly assimilating a real small dog to that label. Shortly afterward when he saw a horse, he called it "tee," to which his father replied, "No, horse." So the child said "hosh." About a month later, he saw a St. Bernard, exclaiming "hosh." When his father said that was a dog, the child said "biggie goggie." Henceforth, only cats were "tee."

The meanings of concepts *develop* in the process of *assimilating* new objects to a label and then differentiating the global concept into different discrete categories of like things and experiences. So, too, the little child has started the journey of defining self and others. The effects of categorizing as "me" and "mine" involve both *assimilation* ("my foot," "my toy") and *contrast* between things put in different categories ("you," "yours"). Such contrast is so characteristic of linguistic behavior that linguists sometimes refer to language as a "system of contrasts" (Dinneen, 1967). Thus the "meaning" attached to self and to others is a developing, changing system of reference that depends jointly on the child's conceptual development and life experiences in a concrete social environment.

The "meaning" of self during the second and third years of life (like that of other concepts) is "too broad," instrumental above all, and closely tied to specifics, that is, *literal*. Vigotsky's early studies (1939) showed the literal meaning of such early labels by attempting to persuade a little child to speak, say, of a dog as a cow. At about 3, such persuasion is difficult: a dog is a dog. When a child was persuaded, the transfer of labels was also literal: the dog (now "cow") gave milk, had horns, and so on. The literalness of self at this period is even more striking: A little boy named Cliffie called himself "Ningi" until he was about 2½. At about this time, he distinguished between his own enunciation and that of adults, beginning to say "Kiffie." A month or so later, he was asked if he was "Ningi," and he answered, "No, my name Kiffie. Ningi 'nother little boy" (Sully, 1895, p. 445).

One such literal designation of self during this period is one's sex. The literature agrees that children learn their sex before age 3, well before many children are aware of physical sex differences and before they know what it means socially to be male or female (Money and Ehrhardt, 1972). In any society, the early and *literal* categorization of self as male or female is bound to anchor subsequent observation, experience, and elaboration of what it means to be one or the other. The literalness of the various *contrasts* between the sexes will be greater if the contrast is strongly emphasized in the child's social environment from an early age. In the United States, for example, it should come as no surprise that 3-to-5-year-old girls asked what they want to be when they grow up confine their choices of adult occupations largely to being mothers, teachers, or nurses, whereas boys of the same age choose from a wide range of possibilities (Kirchner and Vondracek, 1973). Children want for self what they observe is defined socially as female or male, one of which (for them) is quite literally a classification of *self*.

The process of self-differentiation into a motivational-cognitive system is notably speeded by the development of children's grammar into an increasingly elaborate, flexible, and culturally conventional vehicle for socialization. The structure of language, both grammatical and semantic, becomes the prime vehicle for categorizing self and others, linking them to events and objects encountered in daily experience. The social psychologist Roger Brown (1973) and his associates at Harvard as well as a growing number of sociolinguists and psycholinguists are providing a substantive basis for the study of self-formation as a social-cognitive-motivation system within the context of language development.

The Emergence of Consistency in Social Behavior and "Self-control"

Alas, although becoming a "blabbermouth," developing apace in "literal" self-definition, motor skills, and cognitive competencies, the child of 3 is only beginning to exhibit consistent patterns of social behavior in interacting with others. A child of this age conforms to rules that adults impose but readily lapses from them when adult authority is absent. After catching the little darling with hands in the cookie jar or crayons on the wall, a parent realizes that an older child or adult is the only reliable insurance for "good" behavior or the prevention of serious "accidents" (for example, taking pills). Increasingly, however, directive control by adults becomes less necessary. The 5-year-old child has become a conformist, who takes the "rules" literally as *true*. Those rules are out there, they are "right," and I follow them because I am a "good" girl or "good" boy.

Rigid conformity to external standards in order to be "good" and escape penalty does not disappear with adulthood. For example, in following traffic rules many adults regard "the law" as absolute and "given"—"that's the law." However, social life in any known human society requires more than simple, blind conformity to external standards imposed by others. Interpersonal relations that we regard as human and "meaningful" require *self*-regulation in matters of mutual importance on a voluntary basis. In every known human society, children not only learn social values and rules, but accept them *personally* as their own, at least in elementary matters such as the conduct of give-and-take with significant others. I no longer follow the rules because *they* are right or because I want a pat on the head, but because *I want* to act this way. This shift from external toward internal control brings consistency to the person's social behavior.

How on earth does the shift from external social control to voluntary conformity through *self*-regulation of behavior occur? We now know that important cognitive changes facilitating the shift occur during early childhood. For example, much of the child's early speech concerns his or her own activities, feelings or events from his or her viewpoint (hence "egocentric" speech). The internalization of such verbal processes facilitates both the focusing of attention and voluntary control of his or her own actions (see Vigotsky, 1962; Luria, 1961).

Piaget and his coworkers (notably Barbel Inhelder) have shown that "knowing" about the physical world is a cumulative process, culminating just before adolescence in the attainment of "formal operations" in logical thought, involving abstract concepts and rules (see Piaget, 1950). There is reason to suspect that such cognitive advances in successive stages are correlated with changes in knowing about self and others in the social world, but systematic explorations have only started (see Flavell, 1968; Feffer, 1970; Quarton, 1976).

Back in the 1920s, Piaget (1932) was studying the transition from conformity via adult control to voluntary self-regulation in children's moral judgments. He proceeded from earlier suggestions by James Mark Baldwin and the social philosopher George Herbert Mead by observing how children learn to follow the "rules of the game" in play and in making decisions about "right" and "wrong" behavior. His findings supported the notion that knowing about social rules (including moral precepts) advances through several stages of development— a proposition that has been studied extensively in the United States by Kohlberg and his associates (1963).

THE ROLE OF AGE-MATE INTERACTION IN SELF-REGULATION

In the early studies, Piaget pointed to the importance of the child's increasing interactions with other children for the transition from learning rules as absolute truth imposed by adults toward their inner acceptance by the child. Through playing with others like oneself, Piaget believed, the little child learns for the first time that following rules is not simply a burden adults impose, but can be a give-and-take affair with others of approximately equal power. Through such give-and-take, the child appreciates, for the first time, that others also have a point of view. This realization, Piaget wrote, marks the beginning of a change in the child's conception of the rules themselves: Rules are not absolute realities in themselves, comparable to the rising and setting sun. They are *two-way* affairs. I follow them and you follow them so that the game can be played. I follow them out of consideration for *you*, another human being. If we agree, we can even change the rules ourselves!

I confess with sadness that neither developmental nor social psychology has really gotten down to the work needed to examine Piaget's hypothesis about the crucial importance of age-mate interaction in self-development. Yet, our review of what it means to form "ties that bind" with others (Chapter 3) and to become a group member (Chapter 4) would indicate that *self*-regulation concordant with social norms is part of those processes. Family and friends are certainly important ties. Psychologists in the United States have, by and large, focused so exclusively on the role of parents in socialization that we are not as clear as we might be about the actual impact of peer interaction in self-formation. The bulk of available research concerns interaction among preschool children, despite the fact that increased age-mate interaction *and* increasing self-regulation of behavior are most prominent during the elementary school years (Hartup, 1970). Nevertheless, there are several converging lines of evidence suggesting that Piaget was correct. Let's examine a few of them.

Cooperation, Competition, and Other Consistencies in Interaction

Studies of little children's play (see, for example, Parten, 1932, 1933a, 1933b) show a trend over time from predominantly solitary and side-by-side play toward increasingly social play involving simple role enactments ("You be mommy and I'll be daddy"). By about the age of 5, cooperative play together becomes the most frequent form. At about the same time, the patterns of preference and association among children in nursery school studies become more stable, suggesting the beginnings of group formations among them (Hartup, 1970). *Consistently* competitive interactions between individuals and between small groups appear at about the same time (Greenberg, 1932; Leuba, 1933; Hirota, 1951).

By *consistently* cooperative or competitive interactions, I mean pursuing an activity with others over time in such a way that our actions continue to mesh with the (cooperative or competitive) structure of the task at hand. The difficulty in sustaining such structure in interaction can be illustrated by two 3-year-old boys carrying a long board across our backyard toward their sand pile. Neither could carry the board alone. Their cooperation was consistent as long as each held on to his end of the board and walked in the proper direction. In fact, each in turn was repeatedly distracted by the sight of things on the ground. One dropped his end, leaving his companion holding the other, to explore among the leaves. He picked up his end and they proceeded, but then his companion stooped to pick up a rock.

Although they made it to the sand pile with the board, the short walk took ten minutes.

Similarly, a competitive activity requires a child to regulate his or her own actions over time so that they head, in this case, toward meeting some standard (for example, getting there "first") or goal. Younger children do not compete consistently and may, in fact, be so distracted through social give-and-take with another child that the competitive structure falls into shambles (Hartup, 1970). If it seems contradictory that consistency in *both* cooperative and competitive activities develops at about the same time, think for a moment: In order to compete, cooperation and agreement on rules is necessary. In order to cooperate, each individual has to regulate behavior in terms of some minimum standard of his or her own performance.

We know by now that the child's social class and cultural milieu affect the appearance, frequency, and consistency of cooperative and competitive behaviors. Middle-class white American boys are more frequently rivalrous than girls in games presented by adult experimenters, in the sense of putting down a rival at any cost (Kagan and Madsen, 1972). White American boys are more competitive than boys in Chicano families or in Mexican villages (Madsen and Shapira, 1970). In short, more than sheer maturation is involved since the variations reflect differences in the children's social milieus.

At about the same time that children can sustain consistently cooperative and competitive interactions with peers, they also begin to be more consistent in reacting to another child's distress with *sympathy*, especially if that child is a favored companion (Murphy, 1937). This development is important in indicating that the child can "put on the other's shoes." Therefore, it is particularly significant that, at about the same time, children raised in an adult world where blacks are discriminated against also begin to exhibit *consistent* invidious prejudices against black children (see Horowitz, 1936; Horowitz and Horowitz, 1938; Goodman, 1952). At the very time when sympathy with another person becomes possible, the self is set apart from *certain* others defined by adults as undesirable—not like self. Black children, in turn, begin in these early years to express preferences for white or light skin color, unless their world is insulated from white discriminations or pervaded with the message that "black is beautiful" (see Clark and Clark, 1947; Horowitz, 1939; Jones, 1972, pp. 90–95, for a review of the research literature).

What could all of these diverse "consistencies" in social behavior possibly have in common? Some of them (for example, competitiveness, prejudice toward blacks) clearly reflect adult society. Even within the United States, children growing up on the Hopi reservation did not compete to outdo one another in school and games because Hopi adults gave primacy to cooperative endeavors (Thompson, 1950). So I am not suggesting that any of the specific behaviors pointed out here are "inevitable."

What I am suggesting is that all of them, for good or evil, are signs of "attainments" in self-formation. They are signs that the child has begun to categorize self and others. They are signs of activities *locating* self in the social world and of grasping the abstract notions that *certain* others have viewpoints and feelings like one's own and *some* people are "inferior" or "superior" to oneself, if society so defines.

Practical Tests of Piaget's Hypothesis About Age-Mates

Piaget's hunch that interaction with age-mates is crucial in self-development is not tested adequately by the developmental trends I have noted. Real-life events suggest, however, that Piaget's hunch was correct. It has been tested in practice by educators who very likely did not read Piaget's work.

For many years, the guiding philosophy of education in the Soviet Union has been to utilize the power of children's ties with one another in developing self-regulation of social behavior that accords with values or norms desired by adult institutions (see Makarenko, 1951). Such fostering of children's "collectives" (groups) starts at an early age and continues throughout childhood. According to collaborative research in the Soviet Union and the United States directed by Urie Bronfenbrenner, of Cornell University (1970), one result is a congruence in the Soviet Union between children's views of one another's actions and adult evaluations.

Bronfenbrenner believes that socializing influences from adults and age-mates in the United States reflect schisms between the generations that are built into the arrangements for daily living. The child's world is segregated from adults in the "split level" house, in preschool through high school, by sharply age-graded arrangements. As a result, children's responses in the United States indicated that they more frequently expect age-mates to "excuse" their lapses from socially desirable behavior, even when they knew that adults would not. In the Soviet Union, children's responses more frequently indicated that age-mates and adults equally value the same socially desirable behaviors.

The significance of such findings is, I believe, that children both in the United States and in the Soviet Union are highly sensitized to age-mates. In the Soviet Union, the deliberate aim is to foster children's groups whose norms are in harmony with adult values as the context for the individual child's growing self-regulation of social actions. Recent reports by psychologists and educators who have visited China support the impact of similar planned interaction among peers during the preschool years. Regardless of our opinions about the merits of the economic-political systems in these countries, there is evidence that

Piaget's hypothesis about the importance of age-mate interaction for the internalization of social values and standards is being confirmed in practice.

In the United States, the impact of age-mates on self-development is less anticipated and much less planned. With important exceptions, preschool and elementary classrooms are not places for fostering age-mate groups (which are viewed as "troublesome"). They are places where large numbers of individual children are to be "taught." At least by elementary school, children form norms among themselves inside and outside of classrooms that adults know about chiefly from an occasional recollection of their own childhoods. Such age-mate norms reflect adult practices and values, of course, including their diversity among different socioeconomic and ethnic populations. They also may run counter to adult rules, often rising specifically to circumvent them. Thus, the rare child in elementary school who would "betray" age-mates by reporting on their behavior to adults becomes virtually nonexistent by junior high school. Because teachers were themselves socialized in the same fashion, they sometimes reinforce primary loyalty to age-mate norms by chiding the "tattler" who violates them through ignorance or a desire to win adult approval.

My aim here is not to suggest that either adult or age-mate influences on the developing self-system are always for the better or worse, but that both are parts of its context. The extent to which psychologists and educators in the United States focus on adult interactions, adult "shaping" of children's behavior, and adult "models" when they study socialization amounts to wearing blinders that shut out one part of that context.

CONSISTENCY IN SOCIAL BEHAVIOR AND CONSISTENCY IN SOCIAL SITUATIONS

The monitoring of our own social behavior could never, by itself, lead directly to consistency in our actions. There are numerous reasons for this bold assertion. One set of them pertains to the formation of the self-system: It is not a simple, unitary structure. It forms over time in relation to a variety of personal ties, public and private situations, group and institutional contexts, and social values. Its components are not "traits" of the person or only specific "habits" that are simply tapped by specific situations; they are conceptual-affective schema that, when aroused, orient the person, affect selectivity in what is attended to, and bias choices. Though interrelated, various schema of the self-system may be mutually contradictory when aroused simultaneously. The self-system may contain parts formed at one period of life or in one context that are no longer appropriate for a person in his or her present stage and station in life. Some of its parts are more salient, more quickly aroused than others, an important distinction to which I shall return in chapters to follow.

The other set of reasons carries us back to the earlier chapters in this book: The individual does not act in social situations directly or solely through the promptings of internal influences. The frame of reference for studying social behavior, or any behavior, includes the immediate stimulus situation as well as the person's past experience. Unless one is asleep or unconscious, the properties of the social situation itself, notably the structure of relationships among its participants, inevitably become anchors for personal experience and behavior (Chapter 2).

These principles are particularly significant for understanding consistent patterns of social behavior related to the self-system. In its very formation as well as in its maintenance, the self, in Erving Goffman's term (1959), is a "collaborative manufacture." To an important extent, consistency in dealings with others arises because the individual develops and moves in a social environment where events, objects, and other persons exhibit regularities. Such regularities include definitions of standards for performance, bounds for acceptable behavior, socially defined locations and tasks, desirable goals, and mutual expectations among persons concerning how one is treated and treats others.

The continuing dependence of social behavior on such external regularities throughout life becomes obvious when, for one reason or another, the usual grooves of living are disrupted. Novel social events become problems for the person, requiring conscious adjustments and choices, even when pleasurable, as they often are. If they also run counter to deeply cherished ties related to self and others, such social disruptions also shake the self. As a result, social disruption is experienced *personally* and leads to highly inconsistent actions.

In the usual run of things, however, growing up as boy or girl, as white or black, as Christian or Jew or Mohammedan, as lower or middle or upper class, as American or French or Chinese means *both* classifying oneself and others in these terms *and* growing up within a social environment that continually supports and defines them more elaborately. To be white, middle-class, male American means continually finding oneself in situation after situation where tasks, activities, and expectations of others point toward competition with other white, middle-class male Americans. The aim is to be "first" or, at least, to win the best of limited awards available.

To be Samoan male, on the other hand, used to mean being brought into situation after situation where the aim is cooperative interaction in family and community, where to "act above your age" was the greatest error (Mead, 1943). Every community and family line had more titles for individual recognition than it used in a generation. The developing individual moved from one situation to the next playing a diversity of roles, with differing statuses, so that he might be *giver* of recognition in one and *receiver* in the next, higher in rank in one and lowest in rank in the next. He "knew his place" in each. The result of this continual movement from one role to the next in diverse situations was a highly flexible person, cooperative above all, whose "personality" could not be characterized as "dominant" or "submissive," as "authoritarian" or "compliant." The occasional individual who was unusually competitive or aggressive within that context was viewed as deviant.

Expectations and treatments from others are as critical to the maintenance of self as any values or standards "incorporated" within it. For example, young black males in the United States who refrain from competition with white males are not necessarily lacking personal motives and standards for achievement. As research has shown, white males have grown up in ways that lead them to be more aggressive and domineering in interaction with blacks. When the competitive situation is truly "open," the black male is competent, and the whites in question *are shown* his competence (he instructs *them*), their interactions with him become less dominant and he, in turn, strives to achieve (Cohen and Roper, 1972). In all likelihood, a similar sequence would be necessary before larger numbers of women become willing and able to display competence in nontraditional interactions with men.

If, as Baldwin proposed, our conceptions of self and of others are "born together," it is equally true that they exist together throughout life. Most of the "others" are those with whom we spend our lives, but some are not. We each have had some others who—as "idols," as categories or "kinds of people," or as actual groups—have affected our views of what we want to be and become. The next chapter introduces a concept linking the self-system to such significant others, significant whether we are actually in direct contact with them or not, because of their impact on our own experience and actions.

Reference Persons and Groups: Social Anchors for Self

When do you think about yourself the most? At moments when you are calm and content? Or, like me, do you ponder about self more when lonely, miserable, uncertain, or concerned with the future? It is ironic that preoccupation with self is more likely at those times when a cool look at our life circumstances and relationships with others might be more helpful. At such times, self-concerns loom so large that talk about "social anchors" sounds uncaring, even diversionary. "Look," we say, "it's *me* I'm worried about." Or, if we think of others, it is likely to be in the search for causes of what we experience: "Sure, *they*'re to blame, but how does that help me now?"

Neither wallowing in private experience nor seeking targets to blame for it is a road to understanding. We need a wide-angle lens that captures both sides of the self-system: the subjective side as related to the outside—to the social world. But everyday language does not provide ready-made concepts to use in talking about such relationships.

In this chapter, we examine conceptual tools developed in social psychology to deal with the social connections of self. Early in the book, we found that becoming related to others makes "something happen" *among* individuals that affects the personal experience and behavior of each (Chapter 3). The connections we form in our families, with friends, with others at work or school and in the community are patterned affairs (Chapter 4). Part of ourselves is linked to the role and status relationships that compose those patterns. Participating with our groups in keeping with their major values and norms also affects our dealings with persons belonging to other groups (Chapter 5). We could not begin to understand ourselves without a grasp of the social patterns that include us and our interpersonal ties.

Understanding ourselves within that framework would be simple if, in a lifetime, we belonged to only one human group. It would not be too difficult if we had just one set of close interpersonal relationships, such as the family, nested within larger institutions (school, work, play, government, and so on) that all reinforced those personal ties and values. If such were the case, the most parsimonious way to learn about individual participants would be first to study that small group (as in Chapters 3 to 5), specifying its major criteria for role and status relationships, its norms and other properties. By discovering how the individual relates to this scheme, we would know enough about the social guidelines for his or her actions to delve in depth into the strictly individual differences between that individual and others. It is an understatement to say that the problem is not that simple.

Every one of us has participated in varied groups and institutions. Their directions and norms need not be harmonious; they are sometimes contradictory. The person's status and role may be high and rewarding in one, but low and humiliating in another. Societies are changing, many rapidly. People move, geographically and within the social structure. "Moving up" in occupational level, education, prestige, and personal comfort is idealized in our society. Downward movement occurs daily, through loss of job, tragedy, aging, or personal failings.

THE CONCEPT OF REFERENCE GROUPS

We human beings are conceptual as well as social animals. We carry our membership in one group with us as we move into another. We dream about and aspire to belong with people and ways of life that are not the same as those in which we move from day to day. We try to learn more about their ways and values. We even try to become like them. We read, watch television, listen to radio and records. Their images are alive within us. In such a scene, explanations of social behavior solely as conformity to the group in which the person moves, or of self-system solely as residue of one early group membership (for example, the family), are bound to be incomplete.

I am not a bad case to illustrate the point: Here I am—mother in a family whose husband and daughters influence me even when I am not with them, even though they are not at home. I teach in a large university; I am a researcher and a writer. I belong to several professional organizations beyond the campus. I go to conferences and meetings and give lectures. It would bore you to hear a fraction of it.

Each of these settings has its own established grooves, and you could learn a great deal about me by knowing what they are and how I stand in each. I cannot pretend that none of them affect me, even as I chafe against some of their strictures. If I felt no loyalty at all to this world or some of its parts, I could not survive personally.

The different parts of my world are by no means in good fit. Being wife and mother do not mesh automatically and neatly with me at school or writing, and vice versa. By definition, I am "different" in a large psychology department that just now has only two full-time women faculty on a basis that is not tenuous. I am by no means comfortable being a "token" woman appointed to university committees at a time when federal laws tell universities they ought to have a few. Once in awhile, I speak my piece in settings almost bizarre—for example, as the only woman speaker at a plenary session of the Scientific Congress held before the 1972 Olympic Games—a bastion of the masculine sports world. Surely, amid such contradictions, I as a person must be very "independent."

Nonsense. It has been my experience that "independent" persons—male or female—have more collaboration from certain other people. I will be the first to tell you that apart from the standards and values shared in my family, you could not know me. In addition, I have social links that you cannot find easily by watching me from day to day. That unseen part of my world contains some groups in which I am not a registered member, but I feel one with them. Part of that world is not, properly speaking, groups or institutions at all. There are individuals whose words I heed though I don't know them. There are "kinds of people" whose values and ideas on human worth I treasure, whose actions I silently applaud and try to emulate. In my world, the actions and opinions of some people with whom I associate count more than others. There are others whom I do not see, but whom I aspire to be counted among.

In social psychology, it is convenient to have a generic term for such social anchors, namely, reference groups. When these are groups in the sense defined in Chapters 3 and 4, that fact suggests an appropriate research strategy: We can learn a great deal more about the person's self-system by knowing the person's relationships in the status (power) structure, norms, and intergroup relationships of that group (whether the person actually is a member or not).

However, some social anchors for self are not human groups. They may be reference persons—certain individuals with high prestige in our eyes who personify the standards we esteem and our own aspirations. Still others are "kinds" (categories, or sets) of people, of whom we can name representatives. Such reference sets are seldom identical with the broad categories used by demographers, census takers, or pollsters (for example, women ages 16 to 45, black males under 25, heads of households). They are more likely to be smaller sets defined by multiple criteria—for example, "respectable" parents in my community, other blacks working for my people, women working for equality of the sexes, college students who oppose war, young people who accept Christ, conservative Republicans. They may be members of a profession that the person plans to enter: Much of the ritual in professional and graduate schools is best understood as methods of incorporating novices into a reference set.

To the extent that such reference persons and reference sets refer to actual representatives, *their* actions and pronouncements are relevant to our own actions, whether we are in face-to-face contact with them or not. (There are interesting questions: For example, is my conception of them accurate? Am I living in a dream world that can be shattered when I really get to know them?)

The concept of reference group (or reference set) is social-psychological, in the sense that it refers to *relationships* between person and social world. When we focus on the personal side, we speak of the self-system. If we study the social anchors themselves, we are studying the social behavior of other individuals, groups, or institutions with their status and normative structures. The concept of reference group or set provides a bridge in specifying individual-group-society relationships, which are the central problem in all social psychology. Research clarifying the concept will aid us in steering through the morass of literature on social attitudes and their change.

Who Am I?

In some societies simpler than our own, personal relationships were nearly synonymous with kinship ties. The individual defined self in terms of his or her kinship with others, often by criteria much more complex and different from our own definitions of "relatives." In such a society, an individual "may be at a complete loss how to treat a stranger who falls outside of the established rubrics" of the kinship system (Lowie, 1925, p. 8).

Noting the striking differences between kinship in Melanesia and on the British Isles, the anthropologist Rivers (1926) spun a delightful fantasy on the "psychologizing" that a Melanesian man might have indulged in when observing English natives. The Melanesian would have a conception of self as belonging to his own generation, strongly linked in kinship with other generations. The terms of kinship were so elaborate that his relationship with each person depended on the exact kinship link. On hearing English people use the single term *cousin* to refer to persons of various ages, sexes, and relationships to their own parents, the Melanesian would have regarded the English as strange creatures indeed. Could they really believe that a person could belong to two generations at once, or that the offspring of mother's brother and father's sister were the same? Rivers speculated that the Melanesian might very well conclude that "the English people, in spite of the splendor of their material culture, in many ways show signs of serious mental incapacity" (p. 45).

In the United States today, kinship is a more restricted link for self. Personal ties beyond parents, sisters and brothers, possibly grandparents, and a few aunts or uncles may depend on chance and personal liking. Social arrangements outside the family are highly complex and often discretely compartmentalized for special kinds of activities (work, school, fun, and so on). It is exceedingly difficult to see ourselves as parts in an organized system with a clarity comparable to the kinship system in Melanesia of fifty years ago. For this reason, it is significant that when people are asked to answer the question Who am I? they typically start with labels that indicate where they stand and what they do in the social structure. As noted in Chapter 2, the same tendency to categorize occurs in our first encounters with strangers, as we seek to find out how to place them relative to us.

Kuhn and McPartland (1954) asked college students to answer for themselves the question Who am I? They found that the first responses were social categories designating a role, status, or group membership: "girl," "husband," "Baptist," "premed student," and the like. What they called "subconsensual" categories followed: "pretty good student," "happy," "bored," "troubled." More recently, Gordon (1968) asked the same question of 156 high school students. The most frequent answers were age (82 percent), student (80 percent), and one's sex (74 percent). Since each was asked to list 15 responses, it is amazing how many of them pertain to *relationships* with peers: Fifty-nine percent referred to how they got along with others, 58 percent to their activities and their roles in them (for example, "football player"), 36 percent to their appearance (for example, "good looking"), 28 percent to how others react to them (for example, "popular"), and 5 percent to material possessions (for example, "car owner") that say quite a bit about their status. Strictly private feelings, experiences, and opinions of self were included—for example, on how they usually felt or acted (52 percent), reference to their independence (23 percent), feelings of self-worth (22 percent), and experiences of personal harmony or conflict (5 percent, for example, "mixed up").

Leigh Shaffer and I (1973) used the Who am I? question in two situations: a college classroom and a psychological laboratory, where the experiment was identified as a study of "personality." In the "personality laboratory," two interesting things happened: First, the students wrote much longer and more detailed responses. Second, the great bulk of the answers were of the "subconsensual" kind: "I'm a sensitive person," "shy," "not very sure of myself." I was reminded of an incident related by the social psychologist turned clinician, S. S. Sargent. He asked a woman who had come to him for help to respond to Who am I? She replied: "Oh, I'm just a big fat slob." One is unlikely to say that in a classroom or at the supermarket.

Such variations in presenting oneself should not surprise us. They are consistent with what we have learned about the impact of social situations and about the self-system. They suggest great caution in talking about a person's "real self" or "true self" on the basis of that person's behavior in a single situation. William James's notion that a person may have several "selves" suggests what is closer to the truth: The self-system is not unitary, cut of one piece, but differentiated and anchored in different reference persons, groups, or sets in relevant situations.

Am "I" Also "We"?

In discussing the concepts of self, of "I" and "me," in social psychology, Wade W. Nobles (1973) criticized the undue focus on the contrast or opposition between the person and others—the self as "'individually' unique and different from other selves" (p. 23). He observed that in other cultures (he referred specifically to African societies) what is self is extended—"oneself and one's people . . . are more than simply interdependent and interrelated, they are one and the same" (p. 24).

A society such as ours praises "self-reliance," "independence," and "self-actualization." An identity merged with one's people in the broadest sense is rare. Nevertheless, research shows that, even in such a society, each individual self contains "we" as part of "I." When activated, that "we" produces unmistakable earmarks of behavior that is personally involved. In fact, the individual may "try harder" when "we" is aroused than he or she would otherwise. One way of showing this is to challenge the person to endure some discomfort.

Lambert, Libman, and Poser (1960) compared the level of discomfort that women students were willing to tolerate in an experimental situation when it appeared a test of each individually, and when each was told what members of her own reference group had done in such a situation. The students were either Jews or Protestants. In the control situation, a pressure cuff with sharp projections inside was placed on the arm, and the pressure increased until the student asked that it be stopped. Each student participated in two sessions. The measure of pain tolerance was the *difference* in the pressure reading from the first to the second session. On the average, the control subjects tolerated *less* pain in the second session. There was no difference in the average drop for Jewish or Protestant women (about −6 units).

In one experimental condition at the second session, the Protestant women were told that Christian students (their reference group) tolerated *less* pain than Jewish students. Conversely, Jewish women were told that Jewish students tolerated less pain than Christian students. In both cases, the women significantly *increased* the level of pain endured (19 units more for Jewish women and 15 units more for Protestant women).

Suppose, however, that they had been told that their own reference group bore *more* pain than the comparison group. The researchers tried this procedure. Christian women responded as though each had been personally patted on the back: Their average increase in pain tolerance was 22 points. Jewish women also responded with increased pain tolerance (9 points), though not as strikingly as when they were told that Jews were inferior in pain tolerance.

The importance of the findings is that, in either case, arousal of an important "we" in the self-system significantly increased the tolerance level. Nor should we overlook that the extra effort occurred when one's own reference group was compared with another group with a long history of less than friendly relationships (to put it mildly).

Which "We" Is More Important?

A few years later, Buss and Portnoy (1967) speculated that the striking increases in pain tolerance in the Lambert et al. study might reflect the rivalrous and hostile relationships between the women's reference groups and the comparison groups (the other religion). In addition, they suggested that *how* hard the person will try depends on how salient the reference group has become for that person.

To test these hunches, they first had students at the University of Pittsburgh rank, in order of their importance to them, a variety of possible reference sets. Of course, there was variability in the students' rankings. Three were chosen that, on the average, differed in importance for the students. The first was being American (average rank: 2.3), the second one's sex (average rank: 3.3), and the third being a Pittsburgh student (average rank: 5.3).

Next they selected groups for comparison: The opposite sex seemed the only feasible comparison for one's own sex. For national and school comparisons, they selected one comparison for each that Pitt students regarded with considerable rivalry and hostility, namely, Russian (national) and the Pennsylvania State University. In addition, they selected national and school comparisons that in recent history were not considered as hostile rivals (Canada and Carnegie Tech).

Buss and Portnoy used steadily increasing electric shock, measuring the *difference* between the levels the individual tolerated at a first and a second session. Control subjects again showed a *decrease* in shock level at the second session. What about those students who were challenged to arouse the "we" in the self-system? Those who were challenged by comparison to a nonrival (Canada or Carnegie Tech) increased their shock tolerance slightly (about 1 milliampere on the average). The difference was statistically reliable; one could *feel* the difference. However, their showing was nothing compared with that when a rival to their reference group was introduced.

Let's start with the reference set lowest in importance: Pittsburgh students when compared with Penn State students. Again, the increase was significant (average 1.9) and large enough that one would definitely prefer the first level of shock. Now, the more salient reference set of one's sex: On the average, its arousal and comparison to the opposite sex produced an increase in shock tolerance of 2.8 milliamperes. Finally, when challenged as Americans by Russians, the average *increase* was 3.9 milliamperes. If Russians were tough, Americans could really *hurt*. This study was done at a time when Americans were being encouraged to support increased spending for both defense and education because the "Russians were doing it." Some wiseacre remarked that if it were announced that Americans had less solid waste to be disposed than the Russians, someone would take the position that we should try for more.

Why Don't Losers *Try* Harder?

In the early 1960s, before the civil rights movement became the black movement in this country, a number of white researchers provided research evidence demonstrating what many people already "knew" to be true: Even when told or given evidence of equal ability with whites in a competitive task, Negro males (as then termed) became compliant in interaction with whites or refrained from competition. They were not motivated to "try harder" by comparison with performance by whites. In both paper-and-pencil and performance tests of "achievement motivation," Negro males responded in ways that white researchers interpreted as efforts to avoid failure or as feeling a lack of personal control over their own performance. Lefcourt and Ladwig (1965) conducted an experiment with black prisoners at a correctional institution that raised serious questions about interpreting such results through attributing their "cause" to the "loser."

Lefcourt and Ladwig reasoned that earlier studies had all placed the black males in a situation where they had come to believe that their chances of winning in competition with whites were considerably less than fifty-fifty. Suppose, they thought, that the prisoner had good reason to believe that the task was related to his performance in a reference group where he was succeeding. In that event, might he not persist in competition with a white male, even in the face of failure?

They chose three samples of prisoners similar in age, intelligence, social class, and types of crimes committed, but who differed in one respect: A third of them were participants in the prison jazz club, which met regularly and also entertained the other prisoners, although only two had played publicly outside the walls. The second sample were men who had joined the jazz group, but had quit after a few meetings. It was assumed that the jazz club was not a reference group, though they were interested in jazz. The control sample had had no interest in joining the jazz club.

At a first session, the prisoners were given several psychological tests. Then the control sample was merely told that they would be called again. Both the control and the two other samples showed up on these tests looking like "losers" who don't try and believe they have no personal control over whether they win or not. However, the two other samples were also interviewed about their interest and experience in jazz, favorite musicians, and so on. They were told they would be called again to test skills related to being a jazz musician.

At the second session, each prisoner played a game against a white stooge, separated by a screen so that he could see only the white man's hands. The game consisted of picking up matches from a number laid out in rows, each partner selecting one or more in turn until one match remained. The partner left with the last match was the loser.

The secret of winning was to pick up matches in certain odd-even combinations, and the white player had memorized the correct combinations to win in every game. Thus, the black prisoner was doomed to failure. He was told that either partner could quit at any time. Each had 20 chips exchangeable for cigarettes and the penalty for quitting was that only half the value of his remaining chips would be his. In fact, the prisoner could win the greatest value of chips by quitting as early as possible before his failures took many chips from him. That is exactly what prisoners in the control sample did: On the average they played only about 5 games out of the 20 possible.

The prisoners who had quit the jazz club persisted a few more games, on the average 8.3 (which was not significantly more). The jazz club members, on the other hand, persisted on the average about 12.5 games, significantly more than either of the other samples. Follow-up interviews showed that they kept at the task longer in the face of repeated failure and greater loss of reward because they became more interested in the task itself. The researcher's interest in jazz and in their performance on a related task was seen as appreciation of their reference group and of them.

The researchers made an important point: "Losers" try and persist in the face of failure when their performance as a member of a significant reference group is in question. The practical implications are considerable. Rather than pronouncing a "loser" as hopelessly unmotivated and "lazy," look for reference group ties and related activities in which trying seems worthwhile—more worthwhile than maximizing immediate rewards. Kidder and Stewart (1975) reported real-life cases where affirmation of important reference groups, combined with joint efforts among people treated as "losers" by society, have transformed the motivations of individual participants.

It may bother you that the researchers tricked the prisoners in order to make their point. Those interested in jazz at least had a pleasant and instructive conversation during the experiment. Perhaps we should reserve our sympathy for the control sample, despite their greater reward in cigarettes. The proceedings must have appeared to them as just one more instance where powerless inmates became guinea pigs. Indeed, more recently, prisoners who have been "guinea pigs" in research on problems much more hazardous than this little game (for example, drug research) have protested that, for them, the offer of payment for their "voluntary" services is coercive, since money is something they seldom have. Some states have forbidden the practice.

In my opinion, researchers and other citizens should remove procedures that systematically dehumanize prisoners, including their use as unwilling "guinea pigs." I cannot help feeling that Lefcourt and Ladwig's research demonstrates one important reason why: Human effort and aspiration require meaningful personal ties and activities with others. A human institution or a motivational theory that ignores such links is dehumanizing by definition. While Lefcourt and Ladwig cannot be accused on that score, prisons and much research within them can be. Those prisoners who band together in an attempt to change their dehumanized environment can teach us a lesson: Once individuals recognize that they are all in the same rudderless boat, they can forge a human anchor together (see Chapter 13).

WHEN DOES THE "WE" MOVE ME?

Commenting on the human tendency to set standards for our own actions, William James (1890) proposed that how we feel about ourselves is determined by a *ratio* between our actualities and our supposed potentialities. We are moved to bring the two into line: The closer the ratio approaches unity, the better our "self-feeling." James called the numerator of the fraction "success," making it clear that he meant our actual performance as viewed by others who *count* in our own eyes (not necessarily the whole society's standards for "success"). As an example, he observed that he personally was content to "wallow in the grossest ignorance of Greek" but "mortified if others know much more psychology than I" (pp. 310–311).

The denominator of James's fraction was our pretensions—the level of attainment that we seek. Thus, being moved toward personal effort was not a simple motive or individual trait for James, but a process involving comparison (a social judgment) between ourselves and our social world. If my performance falls below my pretensions, I feel badly, particularly if I cannot blame others, the circumstances, the riskiness or difficulty of the task, or "fate." If the matter at hand is important, I can try harder to increase my performance. Or, as James suggested, I can lower my pretensions. "To give up pretensions is as blessed a relief as to get them gratified . . ." (p. 311).

In Germany of the 1920s, Kurt Lewin and his students began research into personal experiences of success and failure that was concerned with conditions affecting levels of aspiration or pretensions (see Lewin, Dembo, Festinger, and Sears, 1944). Experiments in the United States stimulated by their work quickly showed that giving up pretensions is by no means a simple matter: J. D. Frank (1935), later a well-known psychiatrist and social psychologist at Johns Hopkins University, found in his doctoral dissertation at Harvard that despite poor performance, there was a tendency to keep aspiration level high—to stick by our pretensions. Later, Robert Holt (1945) showed that most of us can be quite flexible in this respect when the task at hand is trivial or unimportant to us. Then, we adapt our pretensions more closely to the ups and downs of our actual performance. However, when the activity is personally involving, our levels of aspiration are less flexible. A similar rigidity occurs when an experimenter "rigs" the task in such a way that, hard as we try, performance is unpredictable—bouncing up and down for no apparent reason that we can control (see Feather, 1967).

Over periods of time, each of us learns about our "supposed potentialities" through effort and actual performance. When our performance improves steadily, our aspiration levels also tend to rise steadily. As performance levels off, our aspirations level off. We "know" just about what we can do on the basis of past experience and settle our pretensions near the level of our performance.

Therefore, the most opportune situation to learn about where our pretensions come from is one in which we face a novel task or in which, for some reason, we have little reliable basis for anticipating our own accomplishment. For example, Chapman and Volkmann (1939) asked college students to indicate how many correct answers they expected to make on a 50-item test of "literary information." On the basis of a sample item, the students estimated a little over half, on the average. To other experimental samples, the researchers gave more information: To one they announced an average score supposedly attained by literary critics, and to another the same score attributed to workers in the Works Progress Administration (a program during the Roosevelt administration for unemployed workers, many unskilled). The information provided some basis of comparison for the students to establish their own expectations on the task, namely, their own social-intellectual standing relative to literary critics, on one hand, or WPA workers, on the other. "I'm a college student, so I can certainly do better than a WPA worker!" Those students set higher aspiration levels, significantly above those in the uninformed sample. "Literary critics, ye gods! A college student can't possibly do as well!" Those students had lower pretensions.

The conditions affecting our expectations for self are not a social vacuum. We compare ourselves with other individuals and with people in other groups. If we have had experiences in a similar activity, we take that experience into account in judging ourselves, as well as the standing of our reference sets relative to others. Hansche and Gilchrist (1956) showed this very clearly by asking students in introductory psychology classes to state their expectations for performance on a test of general knowledge in psychology whose maximum score was 100. The students had little reason to think that they knew much about psychology at the time, but they had taken a lot of tests. So, when the experimenters told students in different experimental conditions that an average score on the test was 84.4, the students expected a lower score—on the average about 72. The information that 54.4 was an average score led the students to set aspiration levels at 59.4, somewhat higher than the comparison. For an intermediate comparison (69.4), the students' estimates corresponded more closely (66.9 average).

Because a large number of students were given the test, Hansche and Gilchrist were able to assign one of the three comparison averages (randomly) to students informed that the score had been attained by each of three samples: high school students, college sophomores, or first-year graduate students. (Statistical analysis of variance enables a researcher to sort out what portions of the differences in responses are associated with the three different student comparisons and the three levels of comparison scores in this kind of a research design.) Most of the students were college sophomores, so it is not very surprising that when one-third of them were told that college sophomores had made 54.4, or 69.4, or 84.4 (respectively), their average aspirations were 70.1—just about on the median button. With the same three scores, the students' aspirations were higher when the comparison set was high school students (73.8) and lower when the comparison set was graduate students (only 54.7).

Such experimental results make sense only if we appreciate that "we" (college students, in this case) already stand in a known relationship to "they," whose scores are given for comparison. We can be content aspiring to a score of 54.7 knowing that, relative to the performance of an obviously "advantaged" group (graduate students), our own reference set (introductory students) would define "success" at a lower level. There is little reason to have pretensions exceeding those defined as "successful" by others who count in our eyes, particularly when every one of us is "disadvantaged" relative to the only standard available to us for comparison.

What Success or Failure Does to Our Pretensions

Wait a minute! If what others in my reference group think of my performance is so all-fired important, those studies are just a little unrealistic: I don't know what score I made and neither do they (at least those who *count*). That's the real rub in lowering my pretensions, as James suggested. I can't ignore what *they* think. Suppose I try and try, even improve, while all of the time the people who really count for me define "success" way above what I've done? That can happen any place, but it is particularly common in childhood when there really aren't many options. In elementary school, for example, teachers and parents define academic success in terms of grades. Schoolmates are likely to do so as well.

By late elementary school, children have had enough experience to know about where they stand relative to classmates as "successes" or "failures," and they certainly know how adults define "success." What happens when researchers tell fifth-graders how they are doing in an activity and ask them to state their aspiration levels? Whether they are given the class average (Anderson and Brandt, 1939) or their class standing (Hilgard, Sait, and Magaret, 1940) on a specific task, the high standard of adults is reflected in the children's aspiration levels. The poorer performers set aspirations *above* their performance, near the class average. They are bound to experience failure. The better performers, on the contrary, reveal that the reactions of age-mates are important in addition to the high adult standard. They typically set aspiration levels nearer the high adult standard but a little lower than their actual performance (toward the class average). By performing above the aspiration levels they set, they can experience the warm glow of success continually, as well as knowing that they meet adult standards.

Pauline Sears (1940) showed that several years of success and failure by school children produced systematic differences in their "pretensions" and their reactions to social approval or disapproval. Children in grades four to six with uniformly high academic standing were compared with those uniformly low, and with children who were "successful" in reading but unsuccessful in arithmetic. The tasks were reading and arithmetic, given as speed tests. With no special treatment, the children's aspiration levels reflected their past experiences in such tasks. Those who had experienced success in reading but not arithmetic showed that they knew it.

What happened when Sears began to praise the children, regardless of whether they actually succeeded or not? The successful children glowed, but those who had a history of failure in the task lit up: Their pretensions fell closer into line with those of successful children. Telling the children that they made lots of mistakes and went slower than others produced wide individual differences among the children. Successful previously or not, the invidious comparison with others like themselves jarred them. Their feelings of insecurity showed in their shaky expectations for themselves.

Accurate information about how one stacks up relative to others in one's reference group can motivate improvement in actual performance. Several studies have shown that, on the average, children's performance actually improved more over time when they knew their relative standings in class than when they did not (see, for example, Anderson and Brandt, 1939; Strong, 1963). However, such individual competition is likely to be hardest on the very children most in need of improvement—those at the bottom. When "being best" or getting As is the adult standard, it is also likely to put brakes on efforts by those in between the top and bottom.

Probably these are among the reasons why even greater improvements in performance occur when children work toward raising the achievement level of their entire reference group (for example, class or school). In one study of physical fitness tasks (in which performance can be measured pretty objectively), grade school children improved their performances *more* when the aim was to raise the performance level of their *entire reference group* than when competing individually or when trying to reach a personal standard, set individually as "realistic" for each child (Waterman, Northrop, and Olsen, 1967). Actual improvement was less marked for those children who were doing very well or quite poorly at the outset; however, it was general. The largest number of children, those in between the initial extremes, were the ones most affected by working for their reference group.

At the University of Michigan, Alvin Zander (1974) has been exploring relationships between aspiration levels and performance when goals are for the individual and for the group. He has reported, in general, more realistic aspirations, greater effort, and more achievement when group members take the responsibility for setting and for reaching a performance level together. Concerned that so much of the available research concerns strictly individualistic motivations to achieve, Zander and his associates have studied work groups in government and business as well as high school students in the laboratory. The findings suggest that "a strong sense of group involvement can overcome personal fear of failure or lack of achievement motivation."

For us as individuals, efforts toward accomplishment by our reference group can change the meaning of personal "success" or "failure." It is no longer a question of "personal worth" based on a comparison with attainments of other individuals or some abstract standard for performance. Succeeding becomes a question of our contribution to the achievements of our reference group. "Doing my best" then has personal merit. We can "succeed" personally even when the group does not, and even though group failure may be felt as keenly as personal failure. "Failing" is failure to contribute our best effort, not failure to perform at standards attained by other members.

When I Get Involved in Your Pretensions

It is easy enough to see that self is involved in comparing our performance with others and in setting our own aspiration level. It is not as easy to appreciate that our self-system may become involved in sizing up other people's performance and in *their* pretensions. In fact, research has shown that in stating our expectations about the performance of complete strangers, for whom we have no preconceptions, we can be paragons of objectivity, doing our best to adjust our expectations to the ups and downs of that person's actual performance on a task from one attempt to the next (McGehee, 1940). However, let's consider what happens when we become related to another person over time, in friendship or in rivalry. We have expectations of the other person, and we may actively attempt to raise or lower his or her own aspirations.

That thought occurred to us in Connecticut the fall of 1946, perhaps because we were wrapped up in one another and expecting our first baby in the spring. I set up a dartboard at one end of our dining room and started recruiting husbands and wives as well as parents and their children to stand in our living room and throw darts at the board through the double doors. I told them that I was studying eye-hand coordination. To keep one of the pair occupied while the other threw darts, I asked him or her to write down what score the thrower would make, just before each trial. Then I asked the person throwing what he or she expected to make. In that way, each person estimated his or her own performance as well as the partner's.

I found that the person throwing darts usually kept his or her estimates of future performance well above actual performance, holding firm until performance clearly exceeded expectations or fell far below the announced level for several trials. With such marked discrepancies, the estimate on the next trial went up or down, then stayed there until performance changed markedly again. However, in estimating the partner's performance (spouse, parent, or child), the individual reacted the same way. There was little evidence of "objective" tracking of the ups and downs of performance from one trial to the next. The person had pretensions for the partner as well as for self.

Dart thrower and observer expressed delight at good performance and regret at poor. If anything, the observer was more expressive than the thrower: "Don't tighten up!" "You're taking it too casually, dear." "Get that yellow! Get it for Daddy!" "I *knew* you could do it!" No one apologized to me for performing poorly, but several "explained" their partner's failures. One husband said that his wife had not felt well all day. A mother remarked that her daughter was not terribly well coordinated in games, but was a marvelous flute player (which was true: the little girl later played with the Rochester Symphony Orchestra!).

After we went to Oklahoma, O. J. Harvey (1951) did a better job with my dining room experiment, by introducing in the laboratory fascinating variations: pairs of college students who said they were in love, high school students who were "going steady," high school students who were friends, and high school students who had either recently had a public fight or were known by peers to be competing for the same boy or girl friend. As you might expect, the pairs of lovers overestimated one another, much like the relatives in my study. The pairs of friends also judged themselves and each other in similar ways, though less strikingly than the lovers. The rivals judged themselves and their partners quite differently, their expectations for each other revealing devaluation of performance and failure to support the rival's pretensions.

From that research on estimates of *future* performance, it was only a step to devising a task whose outcome would be sufficiently ambiguous that judgments of the performance itself would reveal a person's affective ties with the performer, such as status in one's group (Chapter 3) or membership in a hostile group (Chapter 5). What all of this research may teach us is that our ties with others who count—whether in love or hate—are woven firmly into the self-system, as personal as our private dreams. My pretensions and aspirations for you affect yours, and yours affect mine.

All of this sounds quite nice, until we consider that, like the high school rivals, I may hope that *you* fail. Or, like some parents, I may want you to meet standards as high in playing baseball as in playing the flute. Since such collaboration enters into our experiences of success and failure, we need to learn more about the standards set by others and how they affect our own pretensions.

SOCIETY SETS REFERENCE GROUP STANDARDS

Individuals who interact over time while dealing with consequential problems invariably develop criteria for assessing their respective statuses. Within a society, the status criteria of the more powerful groups are likely to affect all groups within the society. Whether these criteria be economic, political, hereditary prestige, or individual merit, their use by the more powerful groups affects the life conditions, the opportunities, and the aspirations of others *less* powerful.

The effects of a society's major criteria for status are plainly evident in research on standards and goals prevailing within groups of varying status in the society. In a country like the Philippines today, where disparities related to socioeconomic class are striking, researchers concluded that "most of the differences in the aspirations of our respondents could be explained in terms of their social class" (Guthrie et al., 1970, p. 56). In a country as large, complex, and changing as the United States, the relationship between socioeconomic class and personal aspirations is also well documented. The United States is particularly interesting since upward mobility through individual merit is officially encouraged, especially for the young.

In research on naturally formed groups of adolescents (mentioned in Chapter 4), we were interested in the realities of social life faced by youth in urban neighborhoods differing in socioeconomic level (Sherif and Sherif, 1964, 1965). Through analysis of census tract statistics, the neighborhoods where groups lived could be characterized reliably as high, middle, or low in socioeconomic rank; and the ethnic backgrounds of the populations could be specified. Within each area, we conducted surveys in the high schools to discover the standards young people used in evaluating their standing as well as their aspirations in a variety of respects important in society (for example, educational, occupational, financial).

Both the myths and the opportunities of the expanding prosperous society of the 1960s were apparent in the findings. For example, relative to the realities of life in their own areas, youth in all socioeconomic areas were "ambitious." In the lower-class areas, about 42 percent aspired to occupations at levels of income and prestige above their own fathers'. The "sweet smell of success" as defined in the 1960s permeated their hopes. Yet, the most interesting discovery pertained to the differences between the various residential areas in how "success" was conceived. The standards were different.

We asked a series of questions to ascertain the prevailing standards for the minimum that young people conceived as "necessary" or "enough to just get along," the top limits that they set for a person to be "really well off," and what they hoped for and expected to attain in life. We found that the *range* within which hopes and expectations were set differed significantly in high, middle, and low socioeconomic classes.

Such differences can be illustrated quickly through their conceptions of income. Males in lower socioeconomic areas thought that, on the average, less than $50 a week was sufficient income to subsist, a significantly lower sum than males in other areas considered sufficient. Their idea of being "really well off" was about $100 a week, and their aspirations for ten years hence were to earn that amount (although they *expected* a somewhat lower figure). In contrast, males in upper-class areas thought that a weekly income close to $350 a week defined being "really well off," though their expectations and aspirations were nearer $250 a week. Males in middle-class areas were intermediate in all respects. (None of them knew, any more than we did, that within a decade the dollar would be worth a fraction of its value at that time.)

The conceptions of black and Chicano youth in the areas we studied reflected their socioeconomic class (middle or low). The one exception was with respect to blacks' high standards for education (though not most Chicano youth at the time, whose highest aim was to complete high school). The civil rights movement had already had its impact on black youth in low-rank areas. They identified a college education as the necessary step to success, nearly half of them aspiring to it, despite lower expectations for what they might realistically achieve.

The limitations placed on our conceptions and aspirations by our reference groups are illustrated even more strikingly by the high school girls in the research. In every respect except educational level, young women viewed their world within a more restricted range of possibilities. Their conceptions with respect to occupations and income were constricted caricatures of those prevailing among the male youth in their own areas.

More recently, Haller, Otto, Meier, and Ohlendorf (1974) reported research on over 34,000 high school students in all regions of the United States. The students responded to eight questions about their conceptions, expectations, and aspirations with respect to work when they finished school and ten years hence. Statistical analysis showed that an individual's responses to the various questions were highly and significantly correlated—in other words, the students had fairly stable and consistent conceptions about a "worthwhile" range of occupations and set their aspirations within their range. The "limited range of points on the occupational prestige hierarchy" that youth considered worthwhile was significantly higher for middle-class than blue-collar youth and significantly lower for females than males.

Since one's own generation is particularly salient during adolescence, it is not surprising that youth's conceptions and aspirations are also affected by the composition of the student body in the schools they attend. For example, a boy from a lower socioeconomic class is more likely to aspire to a higher educational level if he attends a school populated chiefly by students from a higher socioeconomic background than his own, rather than chiefly by those with the same background (Wilson, 1959). If there is a choice, high school students are likely to prefer friends and social circles (reference groups) within a student body whose members have similar standards and goals for achievement (Haller and Butterworth, 1960; Bell, 1963; Turner, 1964).

These are among the "hidden" processes tending to make schools that segregate students in terms of socioeconomic class, race, or ethnic origins by virtue of where they live into powerful buttresses of the status quo. Being similar in background, the students are likely to accept each other's standards for achievement and ambitions. Of course, there are other obvious difficulties: As long as the school budget is determined by tax monies obtained from the same residential areas, the schools drawing students from socioeconomically depressed areas will be at a great disadvantage educationally as well.

Aspirations, Attainments, and Their Social Context

Conceptions and aspirations of white males about occupations are significantly related to the work they actually do, checked from 7 to 15 years later (Haller et al., 1974). No comparable data have been presented for females, and small wonder. As noted earlier, occupation housewife and mother is not rated as an attainment in the world of work. The swelling numbers of young women with low-paying, low-prestige jobs are actually widening the disparity in incomes paid to male and female workers even while "equal pay for equal work" becomes the legal norm (New York *Times*, February 2, 1974, p. 10). When the economy shrinks, women are among the first to become unemployed. Similarly, despite their lower aspirations on the whole, I would not expect high relationships between ambitions and actual attainments by the 22.5 million black Americans or the 10.59 million Americans of Latin American origin—male and female.

Any theory of social motivation that fails to make explicit both the personal impact of reference group standards and the realistic opportunities or barriers to achievement in society is bound to be *sociocentric*. By that term, I mean that the theorist uses standards prevailing in his or her own reference set to judge others and, therefore, sees "normality" as conforming to those standards and values. When this occurs, the theorist's main effort is to explain why *other* people do not exhibit the behaviors prized in his or her reference set. If the prized behaviors have been attributed to particular "motives" or psychological characteristics, the theorist starts to fabricate other "motives" or psychological traits to explain why other people do not exhibit them. Such sociocentrism can be illustrated on the basis of a survey of research on achievement motivations in males and females (Stein and Bailey, 1973).

During the recent decades, researchers on individual achievement motivation seemed to be asking the question that Shaw put into Professor Higgins' mouth: "Why can't a woman be like a man?" Neglecting the social context of women's lives, some psychologists had gone their merry way building theories about the development of individual achievement motives during childhood in industrial, capitalistic societies. The theories did not predict how women behaved, although they worked well enough for men. Specifically, "tests" of the achievement motive did not predict how women behaved when challenged by tasks and instructions that sent most males into active and persistent attempts to achieve.

Stein and Bailey found that the criteria for achievement and the particular activities used in such research to arouse "achievement motives" were those traditional for middle-class males. In studies of children, activities defined socially as "feminine," or tasks in which the criteria for success did not include being a male, did elicit females' efforts to reach standards of excellence (that is, to achieve). Such findings show that females also exhibit motives to achieve, but in different activities and facing different challenges than males.

Still, it has been difficult for some male researchers to label such efforts and strivings by females as "achievement" motivation. A lot of the activities in which females tried harder had to do with skills in interpersonal relationships. Some male researchers had difficulty in calling *that* achievement at all. To them, "achievement" meant striving to excel at what men should want to do. Those should be the standards used in a "general theory" of achievement motivation, especially since they are related to "success." Rather than studying the social contexts in which individuals become men or women, they proceeded to improvise additional motives for women that would "interfere" with that kind of achievement motivation. Greater anxiety, "fear of failure," "fear of success," and "need for affiliation" have all been proposed as such "interfering" motives, though the research evidence for each is far from clear (Stein and Bailey, 1973).

For a long time, our society has encouraged females at every age to regard being a wife and mother as The Goal, their success being a function of attaining these roles and performing them well, preferably with a husband of high status. Opportunities to achieve in work outside the home were, and still are, largely available through occupations termed "woman's work" (for example, librarians, typists, nurses, elementary school teachers, child care workers, and household workers) and invariably low in status. In all these realms, many women have and do strive to achieve. Therefore, I am puzzled why psychologists have felt the need to dream up "motives" that "interfere" with women behaving like men when challenged to achieve in traditionally male areas. Until recently, only a tiny proportion of women were allowed to climb over the walls enclosing masculine domains. Most of the "motives" fabricated to "explain" why women are "not motivated to achieve" would appear to me as more likely *products* of a woman's actually trying to achieve in male domains (for example, anxiety, fear of failing, fears about the "price" of success, need for social support).

Simpler explanations for lack of strivings by women to achieve in traditionally male areas according to male criteria for success are possible: Many were not allowed to try. Both men and women were brought up to believe that it is unimportant and/or unwise for them to attempt it. This state of affairs explains why attempts to achieve in a male-dominated field are regarded as absurd or "deviant," a woman who would try to do so being seen as necessarily unhappy, flawed, or hopelessly "odd" (see Horner, 1970). I can see no value in imputing to the persons who make such judgments a "fear of success" since achievement in a male field is not defined as success when the achiever is a woman.

The social context is not merely an initiator or a "complication" in understanding social motivation. The individual's social context must be part of the theory. Fortunately, that context is changing. A growing number of men as well as women are casting critical eyes at the ways that "achievement," "success," and "failure" have been defined in society for men and for women, for white majorities and ethnic minorities. Some are suggesting that we need to reevaluate what has been considered worth achieving and to seek new definitions. Others are insisting that opportunities be afforded for achievement. Such efforts are needed if an individual's aspirations and goals are to correspond to actual achievements later in life for any but a small proportion of white males.

PERSONAL SATISFACTION AND CHOICE OF REFERENCE GROUPS

In a study that introduced the term *reference groups,* Hyman (1942) conducted intensive interviews to find how people conceived their own standing relative to others in a variety of respects (for example, socially, intellectually, economically, personally), whom they compared themselves with, and when they experienced satisfaction with the comparison. He found it quite rare for individuals to compare themselves with the total population: "Far more important are their friends, people they work with" (p. 24). Comparing oneself with other members within such reference groups also brought the most personal satisfaction.

In comparing themselves with persons outside of their reference groups, satisfaction with their own status depended to an important extent on their reference group's standing in the larger social scheme. Those whose reference group was high on the social ladder thought everything was fine. They were like the college students comparing themselves with WPA workers on a literary test: It felt great. Below that pleasant view from the top, the lower the standing of one's reference group, the greater was one's personal dissatisfaction. There were exceptions: Individuals who rejected the criteria for status established in the social order expressed little *personal* dissatisfaction with the low status of their reference groups. In effect, such persons refused to be drawn into the rat race, gaining their satisfaction within their reference group or possibly devoting themselves to trying to improve *its* status as a group.

Now suppose that I am a member of a black family in the United States and find that in 1972 our combined income is only 76 percent of that gained by an average white family (New York *Times*, February 2, 1974, p. 10). Being very "realistic," I could say, "Well, really I ought to compare myself with other black families I know and feel good that I am so well off." Although the disparity between white and black income was even greater before World War II, many black citizens had little choice but to find satisfaction through comparisons within their own reference group, which the larger society defined as both separate and inferior.

However, more recently, large numbers of blacks have not rejected the status criteria of the larger society, particularly the importance of education. So, suppose that I am a black male college graduate today and find that my income is less than the average white high school graduate (Kahn, 1974). Wait a minute! Education is important, isn't it? My standings in two very important respects are way out of line. It happens that education and income are linked criteria in the larger society: they told me I'd earn more as a college graduate. My own reference group declares its rights to equality of treatment.

Such dilemmas as these illustrate why social psychologists have to be more cautious than many have been in the past in proposing that cognitive consistency or balance is a primary goal in psychological functioning or, conversely, that cognitive imbalance or dissonance is akin to a "drive state" so overpowering that the individual will go to almost any lengths to reduce the psychic tensions (see Festinger, 1957; Abelson et al., 1968). For young black college graduates, the feasible ways to reduce dissonance are sharply limited. It is doubtful that lashing out at those who define their reference group as "inferior," hence unworthy of equal economic rewards, will reduce dissonance for long. If they could ignore or completely discredit the value of higher education, consistency could be gained in that respect, but what about others?

Dissonance will not be reduced at any price, nor will any old consistency do. If, in fact, they accept the larger society's high value placed on education and the rights of their reference group to equal economic rewards, the only way to reduce dissonance is through long-term efforts with others to bring the socioeconomic status of their reference group into line. Such efforts seldom promote "peace of mind." The promise of "tension reduction" is necessarily distant.

The individual caught in dilemmas created by a larger society with several *contradictory criteria* for status is bound to experience dissonance as long as he or she accepts them all and finds his or her own statuses in various respects highly discrepant or unequal. While the individual will try to resolve the dilemmas by making efforts to bring the statuses into line with one another, this effort will be in the direction of bringing lower statuses into line with *highest* status (see Benoit-Smullyan, 1944; Fenchel, Monderer, and Hartley, 1951). The reverse trend is unbearable. The person who sees these efforts as individual affairs, based solely on individual merit and its recognition by others is in for shocks and more psychic conflict. Let's consider one of the possible dangers.

SOCIAL AND PSYCHOLOGICAL MARGINALITY

The most frequent circumstance for social marginality occurs in societies that allow persons from groups lower on the ladder of power and prestige to improve their status through individual efforts, hard work, talent in some specialized field, educational achievement, or financial good fortune. The individual who takes the challenge to improve his or her status, or possesses talents prized by the status criteria, may win some of the promised rewards, including recognition by people in the magic circles of power and prestige.

However, because the society has several criteria for acceptance into its magic circles, the person may not be recognized as having equally high status in all respects. Some of these criteria are, in fact, likely to pertain to the individual's "lowly" origin with respect to race, religion, socioeconomic class, cultural values, and so on. To be fully accepted by the magic circle that anchors the person's aspirations, he or she may try to break ties with those "lowly" origins in every way possible. Family and former companions are rebuffed. At times the person goes to great lengths to obscure the past, changing manners, speech, appearance, or even name in the process.

In earlier periods in the United States, such upward mobility and attempts to change identities were particularly likely to be successful when the person had only to escape an immigrant family from Europe, to change religions, or to alter manners and speech. In many cases, the attempt was not successful and social marginality was the result. Social marginality is likely when skin color, national origin, ethnic identity, or language are important status criteria in the society.

As others in the individual's group of origin watch him or her being drawn upward in fact or in pretensions, they may become suspicious, wondering if the person has "forgotten who he is." He or she, in turn, may react with dislike and scorn, attempting to divorce self from them. Soon the individual may be seen increasingly as a "traitor" to his or her religion or social class or people. Today, the person might be called an "Oreo" or "Apple" (both white on the inside, but black or red outside). At best, he or she is marginal in the affairs of that group.

At the same time, the more privileged groups to which the person aspires may confine their contacts with the individual to activities and relationships in which recognition was accorded (for example, financial, political, artistic, athletic, or intellectual). The intruder may even be lionized in those special spheres. But the magic circle closes otherwise. The person finds himself or herself limited—excluded as companion, friend, lover, or relative.

Psychologically, the marginal person is caught betwixt and between the contradictory demands of both groups, a state of uncertainty that is compounded by frustrated ambitions for full acceptance. The dissatisfaction, even bitterness, of the marginal person is documented in literature and the social sciences. Some earlier writers saw marginality as potentially creative: One who has seen the view "from the outside" may be capable of utilizing the contradictory experiences in social criticism or artistic production (Stonequist, 1937). Others saw growing dislike for the reference group of one's origin coupled with rejection by the dominant group as producing "self-hatred" (see, for example, Lewin, 1948). There are other possibilities, as we shall see.

Marginality and the Phenomenon of "Relative Deprivation"

A person who sizes up himself or herself according to criteria of dominant groups in society, finding his or her capabilities approaching their standards but nevertheless being barred from their magic circle, need not become psychologically marginal. He or she may reaffirm membership in the group of origin while seeking to raise the status of that group.

This outcome was increasingly frequent among black Americans during the 1960s when, in fact, the doors to education, public accommodations, and (much more slowly) economic gains were opening wider than they had for the past hundred years. It was fostered by interactions among persons for whom social marginality in the interstices of black and white America gave glimpses of the lonely, hopeless futility of psychological marginality. They declared "Black is beautiful." The affirmation of one's black reference group was not a strictly individual affair: It occurred within a swelling social movement.

To many white Americans, some demands of the Black movement in the realm of education and income were startling: "What's the matter with them? They're better off than ever and better off than Negroes any place in the world." Such whites may have been correct, given the comparisons they made. What they failed to grasp was the reference groups used by black leaders in assessing their own status. Both in the civil rights movement and the later Black Power, the reference group that anchored self-assessment was the larger society with *its* criteria for status, with the exception of black "inferiority." Affirming their membership in that society and in their black reference group simultaneously, the leaders looked at the discrepancy between blacks and whites in *present* income, educational and community facilities, housing, and so on. To emphasize that the standards for comparison were not the status of blacks in the past or that of other black people around the world, social scientists coined the somewhat awkward term *relative deprivation*. The term is awkward because it was designed to communicate to whites what reference scales black citizens were using in sizing up their own situation. Relative to the standards of white society (which demanded their services and the ultimate sacrifice, if need be), black citizens were deprived. (Many were also deprived "absolutely," that is, in physical terms, of food and shelter.)

Reactions to the women's movement today reveal a similar need to clarify the standards being used in judgment. "What are women griping about? Women never had it so good any other time or place." Perhaps not, but past times and other places are not the relevant standards for many women today. They compare themselves here and now with men of comparable status in other respects and find appalling gaps in opportunities, legal and financial status, and treatment accorded the two sexes.

It would be quite wrong to leave the impression that contemporary social movements are simply trying to adjust the status of their reference groups in terms of accepted criteria of the larger society. Many participants also try to alter some of those criteria, and some aim at changing the structure of society itself. Chapter 13 concerns the formation of new reference groups within social movements.

Life's Transitions and the Marginal Experience

The experience of being betwixt and between is not unique to persons caught in socially marginal circumstances as they swim upstream in the social currents or to women as they move between kitchen, bedroom, and place of work. Since modern societies do not arrange definite steps and rituals for the various stages of the life cycle, many individuals find themselves in similar limbo at some time during their lives. The vaguely defined periods between childhood and adulthood as well as between maturity and old age are transitions full of ambiguities and contradictions.

Such transitional periods encourage, even require changes in the self-system. While not inevitably an "identity crisis" (Erikson's well-known term), the changes often reach critical proportions. The increase in "situational" and drug-induced breakdowns (alcohol included), depressions, and suicides among late adolescents and among women and men during their "middle years" are well documented. Feeling alone or lonely, abandoned or adrift, headed nowhere or lost are self-experiences that reflect weakening ties with former reference persons and groups, with no stable anchors for self readily available in their place.

The transition between childhood and adulthood is particularly revealing as a case in point. For the sexually maturing and growing young person, ties with parents, other family members, or teachers are no longer sufficient. The adolescent can no longer feel and act like a child, nor do adults desire that. Yet Society does not accord him or her full adult status, nor clear guidelines toward it. The dilemma is often prolonged for years by economic and social dependence on adults. Facing it, young people move with great intensity toward one another.

They are encouraged by the "split level" organization of schools and social life as well as a venal commercial enterprise sustained by their consumption. Their reference persons are often commercial images— their idolatry revealing the intensity of longing to reestablish their own personal identities. They actively *create* new groups among them-selves—within, cutting across, and outside of the established orga-nized forms provided by adult society (see Sherif and Sherif, 1964).

For good or for evil, their "solution" to the dilemma of being a *person* is linked to their relationships with peers. With them, prefera-bly in informal rather than institutional settings, the young person finds others who "really understand." This turning toward peers out-side institutional settings is not confined to the United States or west-ern Europe. A recent survey of youth in Leningrad revealed that 99 percent preferred to spend their leisure outside of school and 93 percent outside their own home, 79 percent specifying primarily the company of peers (Kon, trans. by DeLissovoy, 1973).

SELF-ESTEEM: DO I LIKE MYSELF?

Research on self-esteem has encountered difficulties by attempting to measure self-esteem as some *quantity* that each of us *possesses* and that sustains us in a variety of situations. One problem with these attempts is that most of us tend to put on smiling, confident faces when a researcher asks us directly to evaluate ourselves in a global fashion. Research with children (Coopersmith, 1967) and adolescents (Rosen-berg, 1965) exposes only a minority who confess general misery with themselves, while most self-esteem scores fall within a fairly high range.

William James cautioned that self-esteem depends in part on *whose opinions count* for us. The caution is at no time more important than during the adolescent period. How much I like myself depends on which part of me I'm considering and whose scale of values is impor-tant to me in that respect. In a study of 598 students 16 and 17 years old in five suburban high schools near Minneapolis, Gecas (1972) assessed self-esteem in three respects, relative to five different social contexts. By comparing ratings of self in all of these, he found that individuals tend to maintain a fairly characteristic level of self-esteem, but that significant and interesting differences occur according to one's reference persons in different situations.

Gecas found that adjectives used in research to describe oneself fell into different clusters: "general" self-esteem (a sort of "good–no good" cluster), "power" (for example, powerful, confident), and "self-worth" (for example, dependable, honest). He had the students rate themselves in each of these respects in five different social contexts: in the classroom, with "my family," with "my group of friends," with a member of the opposite sex, and with adults (in general).

An average correlation of 0.54 (1.00 is perfect) supported significant but moderate consistency in self-esteem across the social contexts and in different respects. There were also significant differences. The students' different ratings of self-esteem were more highly correlated within those contexts where reference persons evaluating them were adults (in the classroom, family, or other adults) and within contexts where peers were involved (friends and the opposite sex). The relationships between their ratings *across* adult and peer contexts were much lower.

On every measure of self-esteem, both male and female students liked themselves best in contexts with friends and the least in the classroom context. The second highest ratings for both males and females were with the opposite sex, the one exception (understandably) being in "power." Interestingly enough, "self-worth" (honest, dependable) was as low in the family as in the classroom.

Gecas also related the level of self-esteem in all of these respects and contexts to the students' reports on parental support and parental control. His findings are particularly interesting since one of the most careful studies of younger children (Coopersmith, 1967) reported a relationship between high self-esteem and parental treatment (warmth, acceptance, persuasion rather than physical punishment, and so on). The adolescents' reports on how well they felt that parents supported them were correlated with their self-esteem in the context of family, classroom, and with other adults. Parental support was *not* related to their ratings of self-esteem with friends or with the opposite sex, however. Parental *control* was consistently unrelated to any of the measures of self-esteem.

In interpreting results based on correlations between different variables (for example, self-esteem and parental support), we have to be very careful not to imply that one "caused" the other, especially when both are based on responses by the same students. We can say, however, that students responded in ways indicating that, in their eyes, how much they liked themselves when with peers had very little to do with their parents or other adults.

The "turning toward" peers for value scales and for evaluation is a well-documented phenomenon during adolescence. However, the turn is not toward just any old peers, but those with whom the adolescent can seek and ideally find acceptance and a circle of warmth. Which reference persons and groups are chosen is crucial, for it is *their* activities, status criteria, and norms that become matters of great personal importance. For example, in research on the use of marijuana, Jessor, Jessor, and Finney (1973) found that reports on support from reference peers (friends) was the single best predictor of whether high school and college students *would* use it during the next two years. Other important personal attitudes related to its use (for example, being critical of adult society or low achievement motivations in school) contributed to improved prediction in high school. However, in college all other influences were swamped by the overwhelming frequency of peers actually using marijuana (72 percent of their college sample).

The Importance of Things and Our Reference Groups

In a massive study of 5000 high school students in New York state, Rosenberg (1967) found that students' self-esteem varied depending on the personal significance they attached to different personal qualities and skills. Selecting 16 such qualities rated as "most important" by the majority of students, he examined the self-esteem of students who rated themselves as possessing those qualities little or not at all. Wouldn't you expect that confessing a lack in some quality that most students value would be equivalent to having low self-esteem? Rosenberg found that many such students rated the missing qualities as "unimportant," and 80 percent of them were moderate or high in self-esteem. They were marching to a different drummer—reference persons or groups who shared their view that being a "good student," "honest," "law abiding," or "reliable" were not very important matters.

To an astounding degree, the turning-toward-peers "solution" to dilemmas of the adolescent transition provides an insulating wall from adult society and the matters deemed important in it. It is this insulation that yields the image of alienated youth so widely publicized in popular literature. Such literature often fails to ask "What are youth alienated from?" In the United States, there may be a minority of youth who reject adult society and values altogether and an even smaller fraction drifting in an isolated state. Many are alienated from family, certain institutions, or values in adult society. What is called "alienation" on a large scale is often merely unconcern with the adult world, while accepting many of its assumptions. Such lack of concern is a by-product of belonging to another reference group (peers) that insulates its members, defining what is important in its own terms. Many young people are absorbed in worlds of their own with peers, where adults are simply not very important until they intrude, usually as "hassles."

Thus, young persons often seem a mystery to adults who neglect to find out who or what is important to them. Actually, the problem is by no means unique to adult-adolescent relationships. Killian (1952) pointed out a good many years ago that many individual actions in social situations are difficult to interpret unless one knows the individual's social anchors outside of the situation. Such knowledge is particularly important when the situation has consequences beyond the moment. In emergencies, Killian observed, individuals frequently confront dilemmas that force them to choose the people, in their whole lives, that are most important, or which of their responsibilities shall come first. He reported actions by individuals in emergencies and disasters that seemed very strange indeed until one knew what reference persons or groups the individual had chosen. That sounds rather grim. Perhaps I'd better note that knowing a person's reference set also helps to understand what that person regards as funny (La Fave, 1972).

The concept of reference persons or groups brings into focus the issue of *who* and *what* we care about, and *how much* we care. For this reason, it will help us in the next chapters as we grapple with problems that social psychology has treated, historically, under the heading of "attitudes."

People's Attitudes and Their Involvement

I first became interested in social psychology through puzzling over people's attitudes and their commitment in actions. Prior to U.S. entry into World War II, my fellow students and friends at Purdue University had expressed varied opinions on the possibility of U.S. entry into the growing global conflict. Yet, soon after the Japanese attack on Pearl Harbor, every one of them became ready, willing, and even eager to participate in war. How did it happen?

Two years later at the University of Iowa, fellow graduate students, the faculty, and townspeople believed that the war was being fought for freedom and human rights. Why, then, were Afro-Americans complacently denied the right to enter restaurants and other public places in Iowa City? In research for a master's thesis, I studied the considerable influence of white students' attitudes in their recall and reproduction of information about Afro-Americans (Wood, 1944).

Then I set out for what was, for me at the time, the "big world." I took a job in the East as assistant to the research director of a commercial survey research organization that claimed to be "measuring public opinion." The organization sold glossy packages labeled "scientific research" to newspapers, political candidates, advertisers, and businessmen. Convinced that the survey organization was interested in selling their packages, not in searching to understand people's attitudes, I decided to return to graduate school. But I got a research assistantship at Princeton University, whose graduate school wouldn't look at a woman's application at that time.

Sherif and Cantril, at Princeton, had just completed a long article on the psychology of attitudes for the *Psychological Review*. Their major points made direct hits on some problems I had puzzled over. Having an attitude, they said, is being personally set for or against something. That "something" may be my own body, certain other persons, groups, an institution, a value or ideal, a flag, a system of beliefs. Or, it could be automobiles, a political party, motion pictures, or a social issue. Whatever the "something" is, my preferences or antagonisms have little consequence apart from my ties with others, apart from my reference persons and groups, apart from "our" relationships to the other parts of society, apart from its cultural premises. So, the study of an attitude is above all the study of the person's psychological relationships with his or her social milieu.

As though they had not made the study of attitudes complicated enough, Sherif and Cantril went on: A person's attitude is inferred on the basis of how that person acts. Yet, the way a person acts is responsive to the immediate social situation as well as the inner promptings of an attitude. So, *that* accounted for what I had felt so keenly when interviewing on the streets for the survey organization. Those New Jersey citizens were responding to me, a stranger, and to the novel experience of being "polled" quite as much as to the questions prepared back in the office. Yet only I had a glimmer of how they were responding to me asking questions. Their answers to the questions were all that were counted and analyzed.

I learned about attitudes while working with Sherif at Princeton and then on his projects with Carl Hovland and others at Yale and in Oklahoma. Meanwhile, we became a family of five. I still had not completed graduate studies for the doctorate. Thirteen years after my initial commitment to that action, my husband became visiting professor at the University of Texas so that I could do so. Perhaps this personal experience tells us something about attitudes and the importance of interpersonal ties for committing them in action. I was searching for better ways to study attitudes. I still am. This chapter and those that follow tell some of the things I've learned.

THE ATTITUDE CONCEPT IN SOCIAL PSYCHOLOGY

The sociologists W. I. Thomas and Florian Znaniecki (1918) and the psychologist Gordon W. Allport (1935) declared in historically important writings that the attitude concept was one of the most important concepts, even *the* central concept, in social psychology. In terms of the problems that concerned these authors, they were right. Thomas was concerned with how the individual's ties with society, especially with its social values, affect "definition of the situation" (that is, social perception). Allport was interested in attitudes as "states of readiness" to respond favorably or unfavorably in a situation (that is, social motivation). The social psychologists Daniel Katz and Floyd H. Allport (Gordon Allport's older brother) had pointed in 1931 to the importance of attitudes in voluntary conformity. They found that the attitudes of individual members in a group were not distributed in the bell-shaped normal curve so often found for physical differences, but as a J-shaped curve in which most members conformed with the beliefs normative in their respective group.

More recently, some psychologists and social scientists have asked whether the attitude concept is necessary or even useful (see Abelson, 1972). They usually cite the undeniable fact that a single measurement index for an attitude may not do a very good job of predicting a person's specific actions in a future situation relevant to the attitude. The criticism is warranted, and the challenge to social psychologists to "put up or shut up" about attitudes is serving as a healthy corrective in several respects.

Correctives are needed, in part, because the technology of attitude measurement has been oversold as "scientific" in both public and academic circles. Attempts to predict actions on the basis of existing measurement techniques at best resemble a shotgun blast rather than a well-aimed bullet. Sophistication in measurement technology has developed chiefly at the stage of processing and analyzing data. The data themselves are usually verbal responses to direct requests made by researchers during brief encounters in the classroom, on the street, in short visits to homes, by telephone, or through the mail.

A recent conference of survey researchers and statisticians called by the American Statistical Society found that individuals in increasing numbers are simply refusing to answer questions or to return their research forms. Organizations that in the 1960s were completing from 80 to 85 percent of the interviews they requested are now reporting completion rates as low as 60 to 65 percent (*ASA Footnotes*, 1974). Such a sharp decrease in cooperation doubtless reflects public concern over larger issues involving invasion of privacy by government and other large organizations. However, it is not an isolated reaction to such research sponsorship. In universities as well, student reactions indicate growing skepticism and unwillingness to respond in the straightforward fashion assumed by the measurement techniques. If for no other reason (and there are others), researchers need to reexamine the rationale underlying attitude measurements and predictions based on them.

However, the issue of whether or not the attitude concept is useful is not merely technical. Its answer does not depend solely on whether existing measurement techniques are adequate or inadequate for predicting behavior. Nor is such prediction the most important criterion for a concept's utility at the present stage in social psychology. We have far to go in understanding the determinants of social actions.

The very notion that behavior can be predicted solely from attitude measures alone suggests unwarranted faith that the determinants of social behavior are really quite simple. As we have seen (Chapters 2 to 5), the social situations in which we find ourselves also have a great deal to do with what makes us tick, how we act, or whether we act at all. Such findings are quite in keeping with the *problems* for which the attitude concept was originally considered important—how a person sizes up the situation, what the person moves toward or away from, and the person's conformity to the normative patterns shared by other reference group members. Therefore, the real challenge from critics of the attitude concept is to return to the *problems* that made the concept important in the first place.

To address the problems, we need guidelines for deciding what kinds of experience and behavior the concept refers to. Such experiences and actions will not disappear merely by abolishing the label "attitude." Unfortunately, one of the worst ways to look for leads is to survey what behaviors are included as "attitude research" in the vast literature.

Attitude Research and Attitude Problems

The house of attitude research is a house of disorder. Quite literally, it shelters studies of everything from judgments on the similarity of geometric forms, on autokinetic movement, and on such statements as "The Bonda fossil was a bird," through opinions on the state of the economy, the future of atomic submarines, or preferences for a mouthwash, to reactions by a homeowner to a black family's moving next door, approvals and objections to an undeclared illegal war, and evaluations of personal worth. This strange conglomeration arose in large part because techniques of attitude measurement achieved "success" as salable products in the commercial, government, and academic marketplaces.

When we have tools, there is a terrific urge to use them, particularly if financial support is available. It is easy to become so intrigued with the tools that we forget what they were supposed to be used for. Many a researcher succumbed to the temptation. If asked what an attitude is, such a researcher answered "that which is measurable by my attitude scale" (Triandis, 1967, p. 228). (As you probably know, this tool game is the same one psychologists played for a good many years with the concept "intelligence," which became "what my intelligence test measures.")

On the other hand, much theoretical literature points very clearly to the *problems* that the attitude concept refers to. Despite diverse theoretical positions and terminology, major authors writing on attitudes agree much more than they disagree on the kinds of behavior that indicate a person's attitude (see, for example, Campbell, 1950, 1963; Katz, 1960; Kelman, 1974; McGuire, 1969; Rosenberg, 1950; Sherif and Cantril, 1947; Sherif and Hovland, 1961; Sherif and Sherif, 1969; Smith, 1969; Triandis, 1970; Zimbardo and Ebbesen, 1969, pp. 6–8). It cannot be charged that these theorists are "armchair" speculators. Those cited above have been among the active researchers as well.

Behavior from Which Attitude Is Inferred

Attitude is a concept referring to psychological processes inside the person that a social psychologist infers from that person's behavior in relevant situations. Thus, when we speak of attitudes, we are talking about "internal" factors in the total frame of reference for studying behavior (see Chapter 2).

Attitudes are inferred from the person's characteristic, consistent, selective modes of behavior directed *toward* (for example, preferring, favoring, wanting, or approaching) or *against* relevant objects, situations, events, persons, groups, institutions, and social values (including concepts such as God, my country, or freedom).

Not all characteristic, consistent, or selective modes of behavior imply an attitude. Use of the attitude concept should imply decisions about the origins, the relative frequency and duration, and the properties of such *behaviors in social situations*. The standards for such decisions need to be quite explicit if the concept is to be "useful." For example, the description of behavior as characteristic, consistent, and selective would also be applicable to the coordinated movements of sphincter muscles during elimination, the sucking patterns of a newborn infant, and many motor habits, such as going up and down stairs. We need some guidelines, or criteria, for deciding when characteristic, consistent, or selective modes of behavior imply an attitude and when they do not.

Criteria for Behaviors Indicating an Attitude

Attitudes Are Not Innate, but Learned

Attitudes are not transmitted through the genes. The concept came into being to deal with problems of human motivation, emotion, and cognition that arise from socialization in different sociocultural environments (Thomas and Znaniecki, 1918). The concept is not needed to deal with why human beings get hungry, seek food, and eat.

But why does a vegetarian become ill at the sight of a steak that sets me salivating? Why did some Catholics trapped by an airplane crash in the impenetrable, snow-covered Andes Mountains starve to death rather than eat the flesh of dead companions? Why did others become able to eat only by recalling that Christ also gave His body for them? Why is it upsetting if our beautifully coordinated sphincter muscles function without warning before other people? Why does a man go into a deep depression from the sudden knowledge that he cannot mount and descend the stairs? Attitudes are involved.

As indicated in Chapter 6, the acquisition of language accelerates and then transforms the learning process, notably in learning about things beyond the child's reach. The acquisition of likes and dislikes began earlier during satisfying and distressing experiences related to bodily needs and sensory-motor explorations, but these, too, are transformed. Social psychologists who call themselves "symbolic interactionists" have correctly stressed that things and people acquire symbolic value or stigma through the vehicle of language. As their outstanding theorist George Herbert Mead (1934) emphasized, human attitudes and the interaction process itself thereby become increasingly referable to future plans, intentions, and consequences. The child begins to form attitudes that encompass his or her future as an older male or female, as parent, worker, or student, member of "superior" people or "inferior" people and so on.

Including this criterion means that an account of the learning process underlying attitude formation will have to be included in an adequate psychology of attitudes. I plead guilty in this book to a substantial gap in this respect. My reason is simple: Despite what you may have read to the contrary in texts or in popular magazines, there is no generally accepted theory of learning that adequately accounts for attitude formation.

Learning theories are highly controversial at present, especially between rivals who call themselves "behaviorists" and those who call themselves "cognitive" psychologists. Some of them are beginning the kinds of research that should eventually permit an adequate theory. Meanwhile, I deprive myself of the convenience of referring to positive and negative "reinforcements," the trademark of behaviorists. Such terms are useful when they refer to well-defined events or objects that a researcher knows will increase or decrease the probability of a particular response. Unfortunately, such precision has not been reached in research on the formation of attitudes. Even though we do not know just how learning occurs, we can identify learning when it happens. That is all that this criterion requires.

Once Formed, Attitudes Endure Beyond the Immediate Time and Place

Attitudes endure for weeks, months, years, or even a lifetime. Their expression is not confined to the particular circumstances in which they formed. Attitudes are applicable to a wide variety of situations, including novel ones.

In emphasizing, let's not exaggerate. Since they are products of learning, attitudes can change and they do. However, it is quite misleading to identify attitudes with learned responses that are temporary adaptations to specific situations, hence readily altered by changing those situations. For example, in a laboratory experiment, it is possible to produce consistent responses to an object based on a person's temporary expectations or "sets." Such sets may be established by rewarding certain responses and punishing others, by telling the person what to expect or by demonstrating the desired behavior. Some such responses may exhibit motivational-affective components (preferences or avoidances, agreeing or disagreeing, choosing or rejecting). Unless it can be demonstrated that such behavior endures beyond the laboratory situation itself, or that it recurs in other laboratory situations, we have no business suggesting that attitudes are being studied.

Many of our expectations in social situations are based on more lasting premises about "that kind" of situation or "those kinds of people," as we found in Chapter 2. Such expectations arise from past experiences and are consequential over periods of time in a variety of specific situations. They also endure because our ties with other people and the social environment in which we act do not ordinarily change overnight. (When they do, we may cling to our attitudes more desperately in the effort to be sure that "I am me.") Thus, the "expectancies" that are so important in research on "person perception," "impression formation," attribution of causality, and interaction processes (Chapters 2 to 5) reflect our attitudes, *when they are characteristic or consistent for the person in other situations over periods of time.*

Another body of research to which this criterion is relevant is "opinion research." Unfortunately, opinions and attitudes are sometimes treated as though the terms were interchangeable. Opinion surveys often give no basis for our determining whether the matter at hand is of any concern to people, or even whether they have heard of it previously. Giving our opinion on a topic need not imply an attitude.

For example, Sharon Houseknecht (1974) asked male and female college students to give their opinions on whether or not they intended to have children in the future. Three questions were asked, and she selected only those students who said they were fairly or highly certain one way or another to all three. When the women came later for interviews, most of them stuck firmly to the opinions they had given, elaborating them in great detail throughout a lengthy interview. But a majority of the male students who had stated unequivocally their opinion that they would *not* have children decided at the interview that, well, possibly they would. Very likely, they had answered in the negative in the first place because the matter was of very little current concern in their lives. Their opinions at different times were not consistent.

We know quite a bit about the conditions affecting human judgment on matters of little personal concern. Giving an opinion is a judgment, and we human beings pass such judgments at the drop of a hat. We know that opinions on uninvolving topics are highly dependent on the stimulus context in which the judgment is made, as well as on the range of information to which the person has been exposed previously (see, for example, Helson, 1964). The same stimulus can be judged quite differently in two situations, depending on the context in which it appears. (For example, our opinion on the height of a man 70 inches tall could be "medium" in Minnesota but "very tall" in Japan.) Conversely, as Volkmann (1951) pointed out, consensus on opinions by different individuals can be achieved readily on matters of little personal concern by exposing each individual to the same range of factual information. All such findings illustrate the *relativity* of our opinions to the stimulus context in which they are made.

The relativity of opinions to the stimulus context is also found in judgment of objects and persons related to our attitudes. However, in this case, our attitude is also part of the context for the opinion we render. Depending on its importance to us (as well as the way we size up the situation in which our opinion is requested), the attitude may become the major anchor for our judgment. Whether we have an attitude remains to be proven, not to be assumed. Most "opinion research" provides little evidence that the behaviors studied satisfy this criterion, namely, that attitudes are (more or less) lasting and are not specific to a single situation.

Attitudes Refer to Stabilized Person-Object Relationships

A person's attitudes are experienced as personal, private, subjective; but they are not self-generated—spun of thin air. Formed during interaction with the environment (including its objects, persons, values, ideas, intergroup controversies), they have an "objective" side that can be studied independently of one particular individual who relates to that environment. Otherwise, scientific study of attitudes would be impossible.

The *relationship*, or tie, formed by the individual with the object of attitude is personal or psychological, whether that object be a controversial social issue, another person, a group, a symbolic object like Plymouth Rock, or women's breasts. What I have dealt with as "self-system" is a constellation of such psychological ties with the environment.

It follows that the *degree* of importance or the priority of a particular attitude in the self-system is a major issue for attitude research. Repeatedly, conclusions about attitudes in the research literature are qualified or made dependent on the attitude's "intensity," "salience," "relevance," "importance," "personal meaning," or "centrality" to the person. All such terms point to the question of the strength and stability of the person-object relationship. Any general conclusions about attitudes and behavior have to include answers to that question, which I shall discuss as the question of personal (ego) involvement.

As succeeding criteria will make clear, the person-object relationship means that we are *not* studying personal "dispositions" or "traits" when we study attitudes. "Traits" such as aggressiveness, submissiveness, dominance, or dependence are attributed as dispositions of the person (see Allport, 1937). Attitude refers to person-object *relationships*. There may be excitable and calm Communists, dominant and submissive Republicans. Attitudes refer to attachments or aversions to *something,* not personal "style" or temperament.

Attitudes Have Arousing (Affective-Motivational) Properties

The person-object relationship stabilized in an attitude is not "neutral." The relationship is directional: The person is *for* or *against* the object, wants it or detests it, seeks it or avoids it—and in varying degrees. Such directionality is an earmark of motivated behavior, which is invariably accompanied by positive or negative feelings (emotions). Such feelings are the most immediate personal experience we have that an attitude is aroused. It is important, therefore, to recognize that such affect is a corollary to the self-object relationship stabilized in the attitude, not the whole of the attitude.

It should not surprise us that what we learn is good or bad, flattering or derogatory to ourselves arouses feelings and emotional states. The self's egocentrism or autism has a long history. It is more difficult to understand that feelings and emotions are also generated from the "thou shalts" and "thou shalt nots" prevailing in our reference groups. The emotional accompaniments can be experienced quite personally. As we shall see in the next chapter, what we attribute to the objects of our attitudes serve in large part to maintain our existing relationship to them while expressing, at the same time, our feelings *about* them. The very words we use to describe the object reflect emotions of love, scorn, or disgust. How closely our feelings are tied to the "shalts" and "shalt nots" of our reference groups is readily apparent from such attributions: The labels and adjectives are often common to members of our reference groups. My glowing or nasty descriptions express my feelings and emotions about others, but they also reveal my acceptance of the images standardized in my own group (stereotypes).

Clearly, the level of emotional-motivational arousal associated with an attitude is a major problem in attitude study. One way of attacking the problem is through specifying the *degree* of personal involvement with the attitude objects in question. High personal involvement is associated with intense feelings.

Attitudes Have Conceptual (Cognitive) Structure

As we shall see, the typical methods of attitude measurement ask us to agree or disagree with statements of belief, to judge the correctness or incorrectness of statements about something, to attribute to the object certain descriptive characteristics, or to choose among desirable-unde-sirable alternatives. All such social judgments require cognition at a human, conceptual level of functioning. Of course, firsthand experi-ence with the attitude objects often occurs during attitude formation. But attitudes are also formed without direct personal contact with the objects, that is, through their symbolic representation. Such attitudes may be maintained with all of the fervor and emotional arousal that we ordinarily think of as reserved for immediate personal concerns. Indi-viduals can become quite aroused and take coordinated actions relative to detested objects (for example, "Reds," "homosexuals," "women's libbers") or to highly desired objects (for example, "God," "freedom," "liberty") with no direct contact or firsthand experience with the referents of these concepts.

To say that attitudes have conceptual structure does not mean that we have no attitudes toward a single object or person. However, a strong attraction to another individual involves comparison of other persons as less desirable. In fact, it is at least reasonable to suppose that all attitudes imply a categorization process that differentiates objects into classes and subclasses, at once denoting their similarities and differences as well as our *evaluations* of them. This is one reason why a person's preferences are not always sufficient to represent his or her attitude. People differ with respect to what they categorically reject as well. The clarity of acceptable-objectionable categories also varies. It is possible to have both a preference and a pet hate, but to be noncommit-tal toward other objects in the same domain.

The more consequential social attitudes that we acquire represent our relationship to entire classes of social objects, persons, institutions, values, and beliefs. Their categorization into *evaluative* subclasses indicating our positive or negative relationship to each is an essential cognitive activity underlying response to any particular representative of the class. When we see an object or person, the most frequent and quickest reaction is to name or label what we see. When these are persons, we employ labels that are, in fact, social categories important in our lives and the society in which we live (man-woman, black-white, rich-poor, loser-winner). This chapter and the next explore the cogni-tive-affective structure of attitudes more thoroughly.

WHAT IS AN ATTITUDE?

Let's stand back a moment to see what has been accomplished so far in this chapter. Since the attitude concept is important in social psychol-ogy historically, it seemed worth our while to indicate what kind of problems made it important. These problems have to do with socializa-tion process in the individual's sociocultural setting, with what aspects of the environment come to attract or repel him or her, with personal preferences or rejections, and with the sociocultural premises about "what kind of a world it is." These person-object ties give rise to expectations about people, places, and things in particular social situations. Let's not forget that other persons are usually the most salient aspect of the social context. Therefore, the person's private experiences inevitably reflect ties with others, the associated patterns of role relationships with others, and the value emphasis (norms) conveyed in give-and-take with them.

A peculiarly American phenomenon made it necessary to be as explicit as possible about the kinds of behavior from which attitude should be inferred. That phenomenon is the commercial and political success of public opinion research, whose pale reflection in the experimental laboratory produced tons of projects and doctoral theses on opinions treated as equivalent to attitude research. The "success" of which I speak is measured by standards having very little to do with advancing our understanding of public opinion, and even less of individual attitudes. I mean marketplace success: Opinion research is big business. A lot of people work at it. The product is consumed avidly. It no doubt influences commercial and political decisions. It is painful to observe that social psychologists are not immune to confusing those standards of success with the successful efforts to reduce our collective ignorance about what makes individuals tick.

Therefore, I have had to stress that opinions do not necessarily equal attitudes, nor "opinion research" equal "attitude research." An *opinion* is a social judgment reported by an individual in a specific social situation. It may be shaped chiefly by a person's attitude. It may be chiefly responsive to the immediate social situation. That is a major reason that I discussed in detail the guidelines needed to make decisions about when a person's behavior does or does not indicate an attitude.

Since I will be discussing attitudes henceforth on the basis of those criteria, let me sum them up: An attitude is a cognitive-affective structure relating the person to a class of objects and specific representatives therein (for example, individuals) that directs the person's dealings with them consistently in selective and biased ways (*for* or *against*). It is formed in the course of interaction with the environment (through dictum and example as well as reward and punishment). Its structure is revealed in the ways the person categorizes, evaluates, feels, and acts toward objects within that class.

It follows that attitudes are the stuff of which the self-system is formed. The issue of what and how much of the self-system becomes involved when a person's attitude is aroused is a crucial question, if prediction of the person's actions in concrete situations is our eventual aim. Therefore, there is no clear basis for distinguishing sharply between "personal" and "social" attitudes, except in terms of their objects. Individuals form attitudes toward physical as well as social objects. Some may be highly idiosyncratic; others may be quite frequent among members of the same group. All are "personal," in that all are personally arousing and experienced with varying degrees of affect or emotion. All are "social," in that they form in a social context.

The psychological principles governing the formation of attitudes and their incorporation in the self-system cannot be altogether different merely because some psychologists call themselves social psychologists and others call themselves personality psychologists. Both have been guilty of ignoring the other's work. Fortunately, many problem areas are being viewed more and more as common to them both (see Bieri, 1967; Jessor et al., 1973). As noted in the last chapter, the person's self-esteem and the attitudes such self-evaluations imply are important in human personality and are also related to the standards in one's reference groups. Similarly, attitude formation is involved in growing up as "male" or "female." If social psychologists ever should decide to abolish the attitude concept, investigators of human personality would probably reinvent it.

HOW ARE ATTITUDES MEASURED?

Let's start answering this question in terms of the traditional methods that comprise the great bulk of attitude research. These are direct confrontations by a researcher asking us to reveal what we believe or how we feel. Our responses to the researcher's requests are the raw staff used to infer our attitudes. No amount of juggling and statistical manipulation of our responses can add to their significance, make them more candid or more representative of our behavior than they are when we make them.

The attitude data are almost invariably judgments of some kind about beliefs—either our judgments of belief statements or attributions to something or somebody that we "believe" to be true. For example, in Thurstone's method (Chapter 7), the researcher gives a series of belief statements chosen on the basis of other people's judgments to represent the range of beliefs about an object (for example, war) and gradations between the extreme positions. We are asked to read them and to indicate with which statements we agree.

In the semantic differential technique developed by Osgood, Suci, and Tannebaum (1957), we are given a concept, say, "normal adult men." Below that concept is a series of rating scales, each with a pair of adjectives representing opposites. On each rating scale, we are asked to place a check to indicate what we believe to be true of that concept. For example, one scale might be:

strong __ __ __ __ __ __ __ weak

Another might be:

emotional __ __ __ __ __ __ __ unemotional

We are attributing characteristics to men that we believe to be true.

Another widely used technique was developed by Rensis Likert (1932), and comprises a series of belief statements that are strongly worded to represent clear *pro* or *anti* positions about an issue, people, or groups. Half of the statements are *pro* and half are *anti*. For each statement, there are five alternative responses: Strongly Agree, Agree, Undecided, Disagree, Strongly Disagree. The respondent checks one response for each statement.

There are other techniques, some of which will be introduced later. Here I am concerned that in all of them, what can be inferred about our attitudes depends on how well the researcher has selected the belief statements or bipolar adjectives and how well our responses represent our attitude.

Selecting Attitude Items

There is no doubt that Thurstone gave the most careful consideration to the problem of what to present to individuals in order to secure samples of behavior from which their attitudes could be inferred. In Chapter 7, we reviewed Thurstone's method, which starts with a thorough survey of what people were saying and doing about the attitude object to be studied. After collecting a wide range of verbal statements from the press and other mass media, from interviews or observation, the researcher presents them to some "judges." It is assumed that the judges can reach reasonable consensus on how "favorable" or "unfavorable" a belief statement is about its object (for example, the "status of Negroes"), irrespective of their own attitudes.

Then the researcher analyzes the judgments, considering the median judgment of each statement as the "scale value" for that statement. From the total, a smaller set of statements is chosen for the attitude "test" that (1) represent the entire range of positions on that issue from one extreme to the other, (2) are judged with the least variability, and (3) are substantively pertinent to the issue in question. When the respondent chooses the beliefs he or she agrees with, the researcher already has these scale values for each statement. The researcher *averages* the scale values of all statements agreed with, which represents the respondent's attitude henceforth.

As we know (Chapter 7), the judges' attitudes may dramatically affect their judgments of belief statements, hence the scale values. This does not mean that Thurstone's method for selecting statements is wholly worthless. On the contrary it is the best we have. It does mean that *any* "scale" developed to measure an individual's attitude is a *relative* affair. At best, it is relative to the range and structure of beliefs prevalent in a society at the time. For example, an attitude scale constructed forty years ago on the seriousness of various crimes by the most exacting of Thurstone's methods is not directly comparable to one constructed more recently (Coombs, 1967). This means that a social psychologist who wants to assess attitudes has to be a careful student of the society in which he or she lives.

In the Likert technique, the researcher starts as Thurstone did, but selects only strong, unequivocal statements on both sides of an issue. These tend to be quite extreme statements since one invariant finding is that moderate statements are judged with greater variability by different individuals than extreme statements. Such equivocal statements are eliminated in standardizing the final attitude test, which uses only those statements to which persons with extreme pro and anti attitudes respond quite differently.

In view of the importance of selecting items that represent the attitude domain in question, it is disappointing that many researchers are quite careless about this stage. That is why, no doubt, one search of the literature for tests of social attitudes with demonstrated reliability yielded few enough to fit between the covers of a single book. Shaw and Wright (1967) made the search and warned their readers that even those included do "not warrant application . . . as measures of individual attitude." They recommended their use only to compare similarity or differences in attitudes prevailing among different *groups* of individuals.

Similarly, Dawes (1972) warned the readers of his book on attitude measurement that "current attitude measurement techniques are not so good" that findings can be taken at face value. One of the reasons he gave for writing a book on the logic and methods of attitude measurement was to "generate skepticism" as an antidote to "sweeping and fallacious beliefs about people's attitudes" (pp. 2–3). One wonders again why attitude measurement techniques are regarded as "successful."

Giving Numbers to a Person's Attitude

Each of the traditional measurement techniques aims at combining the individual's opinions on various beliefs in order to assign a single number to represent the individual's attitude. Once the researcher has assigned a number to each person, he or she can make interesting comparisons: for example, how pro or anti individuals are toward another group or on a social issue. The researcher can compare the average scores in two groups. There are several techniques for accomplishing such ends (see Edwards, 1957a; Dawes, 1972).

The advantages of being able to give one number to each individual are great. However, we should understand what is being done so that we can properly evaluate the significance of the data that come out of the computer. Let's take a concrete example using the Likert technique. Suppose that I want to study attitudes toward the impeachment of the President. I choose 30 statements about the issue, half favoring impeachment and half against it. Here are two such statements, representing beliefs at opposite extremes that were frequently stated before ex-President Nixon revealed evidence showing his role in covering up wrongdoings and resigned:

The evidence leaves no doubt that President Nixon himself was the principal instigator of the whole sordid mess of Watergate crimes and invasions of privacy.

Scoring	Strongly Agree	Agree	Undecided	Disagree	Strongly Disagree
	5	4	3	2	1

All the loose talk about President Nixon's personal participation in the Watergate affair or its coverup is nothing but shameful partisan politics on the part of his enemies.

Scoring	Strongly Agree	Agree	Undecided	Disagree	Strongly Disagree
	1	2	3	4	5

Observe that in scoring the response to each statement, the alternative most favorable to impeachment is given a score of 5 and that against impeachment is given a score of 1. By reversing the numbers assigned to the alternatives for pro and anti impeachment statements, a pro-impeachment choice will always be given the larger number.

By adding the numbers assigned to each alternative you choose, I have a large number (for example, 30 items $\times$ 5 = 150) indicating that you are all in favor of impeachment or a small sum (for example, 30 items $\times$ 1 = 30), indicating that you oppose it. When your responses actually represent such consistently extreme alternatives, I have a pretty good basis for concluding that you have an attitude, one way or another.

However, what can I conclude about a person who receives a score of, say, 90 between the extremes of 30 to 150? One could obtain such a score by checking the "undecided" alternative for each of the 30 statements. There are other ways. The person could check alternatives numbered 2 on half of the statements and those numbered 4 on the other half, or various other combinations of numbers adding to 90. In that case, the meaning of the person's "score" on the attitude test becomes difficult to interpret, particularly if I am interested in how that person will act or react in another situation.

The effort to assign a *single* score to the attitude obscures any patterns in the various responses to the items, unless the person is perfectly consistent in selecting extremely pro or extremely anti alternatives. Yet all traditional measurement techniques represent the individual's attitude with a single score (a sum or average) or, alternatively, several scores each representing different aspects of the attitude (for example, beliefs, affective reactions, predictions about future behavior).

All such methods also confront the person with the bald fact that his or her attitudes are being studied. On some matters, including public issues, it is socially acceptable to speak out regardless of how one may appear to others or how much one might tread on their toes. However, such candidness need not be the rule. For example, in Schuman and Hatchett's study of black citizens' attitudes toward white people in Detroit black interviewers elicited answers indicating distrust of whites more frequently than did white interviewers (1974). Who asked the questions made as much as 8 or 9 percent difference in the frequencies of response. The differences were sufficiently large that they compared with those associated with changes detected during the study (1968–1971), which overall indicated decreasing trust of white authorities and institutions.

All of us have some matters that we consider private business. To an "outside" investigator, we are likely to respond in terms that ensure against possible unfortunate consequences in the future. We want to appear in a fair and reasonable light, or at least not make a spectacle of ourselves as a nasty person in the situation. What do the numbers we receive on an attitude test mean then? Perhaps they count the number of times we put our best foot forward.

What Do We Need to Know about a Person's Attitude?

I do not raise issues about attitude measurement because I dislike numbers. The single scores, sums, and averages used to represent a person's attitude are unsatisfactory because they do not help in answering some of the most important questions about a person's attitude. Here are some of these questions:

1. What is the position *most acceptable* to a person within an entire range of possible positions *for* or *against* some object? What other points of view will the person *also accept,* or at least tolerate? Individuals upholding the same stand do differ in the range of their tolerance. Conversely, they differ in what they find *objectionable.* Some people take offense at almost anything opposed to their own viewpoint. Others reserve their wrath for particular objects, viewpoints, or groups that they reject. Are all "moderates" also tolerant? If not, what are they intolerant of? Such questions pertain to the cognitive-affective structure of a person's attitude.

2. If the individual is *for* or *against* something, how important is this stand amid the other things that concern him or her? We need to know

how personally involving the attitude in question is for the individual if we want to understand how strongly it will be aroused in specific situations when the person has other business than tending to that attitude. To the degree that the matter is personally involving and the person has become committed to accept certain things and reject others, we would expect the business at hand to interfere *less* with expression of that attitude in word and deed. We would expect the person to be *less* susceptible to attempts to change his or her cherished views and beliefs. We would expect the person to be *more* responsive to attempts at enlisting active support on his or her own side. These issues pertain to the arousing (motivational, affective) properties of the person's attitude. However, as we shall see, they are also closely related to its cognitive (categorical) structure.

While discussing research that bears on these questions, we also must face the issue of the impact of the research situation itself on the person's responses. Research situations are unusual in the individual's life. They often imply that he or she is being evaluated as a person. When social attitudes are in question, such evaluation may portend practical consequences, such as getting or losing a job, being watched or arousing suspicion. Later in the chapter, I discuss some indirect, nonconfrontive ways to study attitudes. I am strongly opposed to their use when the findings are used to evaluate the "fitness," "normality," or "worth" of particular individuals. Such methods were designed and should be used only for better understanding of behavior. Knowing something about them, you will be in a better position to decide when, with whom, and with what sponsorship their use is warranted. Meanwhile, I turn to research on the structure of attitudes that were freely and publicly expressed.

ATTITUDE STRUCTURE: LATITUDES OF ACCEPTANCE, REJECTION, AND NONCOMMITMENT

Beginning in the late 1940s and early 1950s, I participated in a series of researches continuing to the present day on the cognitive-affective structure of attitudes. The research has concerned a wide range of public issues and other attitude objects, most of them selected because they were current at the time and important to people with differing attitudes.

The research invariably started with learning as much as possible about the social context of the attitudes, in order to represent the total range of beliefs and the differentiated positions people adopted. For example, by the 1950s the state of Oklahoma had had several referendum campaigns to repeal the state's law prohibiting the sale of all alcoholic beverages except "light beer" (Jackman and Sherif, 1959).

The most extreme prohibition groups published statements like the following: "Since alcohol is the curse of mankind, the sale and use of alcohol, including light beer, should be completely abolished." The logical opposite was as follows: "It has become evident that man cannot get along without alcohol; therefore, there should be no restriction whatsoever on its sale and use." Published accounts revealed three increasingly more moderate positions favoring repeal. Likewise, there were three positions favoring prohibition but decreasingly severe in restricting sale and use of alcohol from the "curse of mankind" statement above.

The following statement was written to represent dead center on the prohibition issue: "The arguments in favor and against the sale of alcohol are nearly equal." The total series of nine statements (four pro-repeal, four anti-repeal and one dead-center) was reliably ranked by judges as representing clear gradations between the extremes.

It is unlikely that any of the nine alternatives will excite you, but they certainly did many residents of Oklahoma as the referendum campaign proceeded, which is why Hovland, Harvey, and Sherif (1957) chose to study the issue. This paraphrase of the actual instructions tells roughly what you would have been asked to do if you had participated in the research:

Read these nine statements giving different views on the prohibition issue, then check the one position that is most acceptable to you. Now turn the page. Here are the same nine statements. Read them again. Are there any other statement or statements that are not objectionable to you? Indicate any that you also find acceptable. Now, on the third page, choose the one statement that is most objectionable to you. On the last page, if there are other statement(s) also objectionable, indicate them also.

Such instructions define what Sherif called "needed concepts in the study of attitudes" (1967), namely, the latitudes of acceptance, rejection, and noncommitment:

1. Latitude of acceptance: the person's most acceptable position plus any other positions also acceptable.
2. Latitude of rejection: the position most objectionable to the person plus any others also objectionable.
3. Latitude of noncommitment: those positions that the person neither accepts nor rejects when left free (as in the above instructions) to accept or reject as few or as many as desired. (In other words, this latitude is indicated by default after the person has accepted and rejected what he or she wants to.)

The extraordinarily simple Method of Ordered Alternatives outlined above has been used to assess attitude structure on a variety of social issues—including the choice of candidates in presidential elections

(1956, 1960, 1968), domestic and foreign policy issues, a labor-management issue, and more personal issues related to sex roles (Sherif and Hovland, 1961; Sherif, Sherif, and Nebergall, 1965; Whittaker, 1967; Diab, 1967; Elbing, 1962; Tittler, 1967). The following generalizations are supported by findings on these quite different issues obtained by different investigators:

1. The more extreme the position that the person chooses as most acceptable, the larger is the person's latitude of rejection (more positions rejected).
2. The more moderate the person's most acceptable position, the larger is the person's latitude of noncommitment.
3. As the most acceptable position becomes more extreme, the latitude of rejection becomes disproportionately greater than the combined latitudes of acceptance and noncommitment.
4. The more moderate the most acceptable position is, the more nearly equal the sizes of the latitudes of acceptance, rejection, and noncommitment.

On a variety of issues it has been shown that these generalizations hold equally for persons taking extreme and moderate positions on *both* sides—pro and anti, or favoring one outcome over its opposite. In fact, the patterns of response by extremely pro and anti prohibitionists or by strong Republicans and Democrats look like mirror images of one another: Each party accepts two or three positions on its own side and rejects five or six positions, including all positions on the opposite side, the "undecided" or "neutral" position, and at times even a moderate statement supporting its own side.

Using A for acceptance, R for rejection, and O for noncommitment, here are the patterns for typical extremists on opposite sides of an issue, the underlining indicating their most acceptable and objectionable positions on the same belief statements:

$\underline{A}$ A A O R R R R $\underline{R}$ $\underline{R}$ R R R R O A A $\underline{A}$

For comparison, here are typical patterns for persons choosing more moderate pro or con positions as most acceptable:

O A $\underline{A}$ A O O R R $\underline{R}$ $\underline{R}$ R R O O A $\underline{A}$ A O

What is the relevance of attitude structure for the person's behavior? Suppose that the two extremists above start talking about the issue in question. Clearly, an argument will result: There is no overlap in positions the two accept. Where one is noncommittal, the other rejects. The two moderates, on the other hand, have three positions in the middle that would not arouse immediate disagreement. In a discussion, they are much more likely to reach some compromise agreement (see Sereno and Mortenson, 1969). Chapter 12 discusses research relating the structural properties of one's attitude to how susceptible or resistant one becomes to social persuasion and other attempts at changing one's views.

On Extremism and Personal Involvement

The picture of persons with extreme attitudes that emerged from the research could be characterized as "negativistic," "narrow-minded," or "close-minded." Such uncomplimentary adjectives are commonly attributed to persons upholding extreme stands, especially those opposed to our own. They suggest that such persons are not very "normal," "healthy," or "well balanced."

An alternative hypothesis is feasible: Perhaps the person who adopts an extreme position is simply more personally involved in the issue, in the sense that the attitude has quite high priority in that person's self-system. Data from survey research indicate that on a variety of social issues, people who take extreme stands rate the strength of their own attitudes as greater than those who prefer moderate positions, on the average (Cantril, 1946). In our own research, we knew that most of the people who adopted extreme positions were active participants in organized groups or campaigns supporting their side.

If high personal involvement produced the categorical rejection and low noncommitment among extremists, then high involvement with a moderate position should produce a similar attitude structure. A highly involved moderate should reveal a latitude of rejection greater than the latitudes of acceptance and noncommitment. Where could we find people taking intermediate positions on a controversial issue who were also, demonstrably, highly involved in the issue? If such persons existed, we knew what to predict about the structure of their latitudes of acceptance, rejection, and noncommitment.

Can a Person Be "Extremely Moderate"?

A unique opportunity to test the relationship between latitudes of acceptance, rejection, and noncommitment, on one hand, and personal involvement, on the other, arose in Texas prior to the 1966 election for U.S. Senator. The Republican incumbent was known as a conservative. The Democratic nominating convention chose a candidate who was even more conservative than the Republican, with the result that the liberal Democrats bolted the convention. Don Beck and Roger Nebergall (1967) seized the opportunity to study the disaffected Democrats. They found that many of them decided to "sit this one out," becoming inactive politically. Others, however, continued to be politically active. Some refused to endorse either candidate; others gave moderate support to the Democrat or the Republican.

Beck and Nebergall compared the latitudes of acceptance, rejection, and noncommitment on the election issue for the politically inactive (less involved) and politically active (more involved) Democrats. Among those who chose the middle "undecided" position on the election as most acceptable, there were striking differences between the politically active and inactive: On the average, the politically active rejected 6.4 of the 9 statements and their latitude of noncommitment approached zero (less than 1, on the average). In contrast, the inactive rejected only 2.6 statements, on the average, remaining noncommittal to 4 of the 9 statements.

In short, while supporting *neither* side, the highly involved "unde-cideds" behaved like "extremists" in categorically rejecting most positions on both sides (saying, in effect, "a plague on both of your houses"). Those who resolved their dilemma through moderate support for one candidate or the other also differed according to their involvement: The politically active, though lukewarm in their support, rejected significantly more positions than the politically inactive. I believe that these findings have wider implications. Despite the most extensive propaganda in history to "get out the vote," voter turnout in 1972 was the lowest since 1948 in a presidential election. Low voter turnout is popularly attributed to "apathy." Perhaps these findings indicate that low voter turnout can also reflect failure to support either of the candidates on the part of highly involved citizens dissatisfied with all available alternatives. The genuinely "apathetic" may be those with extremely large latitudes of noncommitment (for example, the "inactive" Democrats in Texas).

In addition to the Beck-Nebergall study, other research using different procedures for assessing attitude shows that the *relative sizes of the person's latitudes of acceptance, rejection, and noncommitment indicate the degree of that person's involvement in the attitude object*, whether the person's preferred position is extreme or moderate. Some of that research is summarized later in the chapter. Here, I am going to stick my neck out to conjecture on what such findings suggest about people who take extreme positions on social issues.

Extremism, Personality, and Culture

Since World War II, a number of attempts have been made to classify persons upholding certain extreme positions in terms of personality syndromes. The best-known of these was directed toward persons who, on the one hand, held extremely negative attitudes toward certain minority groups and, on the other, accepted beliefs typical of fascist ideology. Such persons, it was said, had started early on the road to becoming "authoritarian personalities" (Adorno, Frenkel-Brunswik, Levinson, and Sanford, 1950). Parents so repressed and frustrated them that they came to idealize father and other authority figures, while venting frustrations through aggressive hatred of the weak and helpless.

Although serious technical deficiencies were found in the scales for assessing the authoritarian personality, the most devastating critiques of the theory were research findings that showed the dependence of the extremist attitudes on the sociocultural setting. In the southern United States, persons scored higher in prejudice toward blacks than in other regions, but no higher in acceptance of fascist beliefs than in other regions. In the Middle East, scores on fascist beliefs were higher than in the United States, but not scores on prejudice (see Ehrlich, 1973).

Milton Rokeach (1960) attempted to eliminate some obvious deficiencies in the authoritarian personality research, including its exclusive focus on extremism of the "right," by developing a scale that he believed assessed "closed-mindedness" or "dogmatism" without regard to a person's politics. However we may evaluate the evidence for that claim, it is impossible to read the statements on the dogmatism scale without noticing their ideological content. The high dogmatist would uncritically accept beliefs that are "conventional" in certain strata of our society.

Alan Elms (1972) has written an excellent critique of such approaches, insofar as they attempt to link political extremism to personality disturbances. In his own studies of right-wing extremists in Dallas, he found signs of mental disorders no more frequent than in the larger adult population. Except for their political views, he was unable to detect signs of "imbalance" or extremism in other respects. Commenting on the tendency "to conclude that psychological health leads naturally to a particular political stance," he observed that even scientists are guilty of "an unvoiced assumption that the perfectly normal individual is perfectly moderate in his politics, neither too liberal nor too conservative, seeing a little good perhaps in both sides but The Good in neither" (p. 98). He asked whether "a person [who] insists on his moderation with great passion, berating any who diverge from the middle of the road because he sees all positions to left and right as falling in the gutters," might not be guilty of "extreme moderation." Elms's "extreme moderate" resembles the picture of the politically active "undecideds" and moderates in the Texas election studied by Beck and Nebergall. It is a picture of high personal involvement.

As Elms correctly points out, matters of personal "adjustment" and "coping" are inevitably related to the social milieu to which one must adjust or cope. There are social milieus in which extreme stands on social, political, or religious issues are the norm. Conformity implies extremism. In Dallas, he found, most right extremists were brought up to "honor" conservative values. Like Daniel Katz (1960) and Brewster Smith (1969), Elms found himself unable to understand their political views without recognizing that a person's attitudes "help express his own sense of himself and what he most highly values." Attitudes, he concludes, "are an essential part of our identity" (p. 85).

In viewing the latitudes of acceptance, rejection, and noncommitment as indicators of the *degree* of personal involvement, I am essentially agreeing with Elms's orientation. Such an orientation also enables us to understand why some research has reported significant correlations between high scores on Rokeach's dogmatism test and the size of the objectionable latitudes on certain social issues (see, for example, Powell, 1966; Larsen, 1971). One reasonable possibility is that the dogmatism test assesses uncritical conformity to highly conventional "truisms" in certain reference groups.

For example, Mormon students who scored higher on dogmatism also rejected more belief statements than students with low dogmatism scores when the beliefs concerned central values of Mormonism such as anti-communism and prohibiting the sale of liquor (Larsen, 1971). However, the relationship between latitude of rejection and dogmatism was quite low for attitudes toward television, on which the church position is less important. Thus people highly conforming to dogmatic beliefs in their group are also more involved with central norms (reject more deviant positions) than with peripheral ones (television).

Rather than searching first for personal quirks or foibles related to social attitudes, it seems to me less prejudicial and more efficient to search first for the person's reference groups. High personal involvement in issues concerning one's reference group may indeed close one's mind on those issues. It need not follow that the mind's shutters are closed on issues not closely tied to one's identity. This possibility is suggested by Eagly and Telaak's (1972) finding of no significant correlation between the sizes of latitudes exhibited by college students on several unrelated social issues (birth control, legalization of marijuana, and gun control). On the other hand, choice of issues closely related to one's reference group (say, issues of birth control, legalized abortion, and population growth) might yield significant correlations in tolerance-intolerance across issues (for example, for a Right to Life group or a Zero Population Growth group).

In the next sections, we will find members of the League of Women Voters, strongly committed loyalists to a Third World country, and high school girls with "closed minds" on matters closely related to their group affiliations. The high school students were, above all, moderates in their preferences (for clothing styles). Still, the more involved they were, the less tolerant they were of deviations.

A PERSON'S OWN CATEGORIES FOR EVALUATION

When a person has formed an attitude, a set of categories is available to use spontaneously in discriminating, comparing, and evaluating incoming stimulation related to the attitude. In fact, as Sherif and

Hovland learned (Chapter 7), the involved person cannot help using his or her own categories even when specifically instructed to concentrate on objective judgments (for example, how favorable or unfavorable belief statements were on the issue). If the issue is related to how the person sees self and others, the person cannot help agreeing-disagreeing with or accepting-rejecting beliefs at the same time.

The result was that persons highly involved in the issue neglected to use intermediate categories when instructed to sort beliefs into 11 piles. They concentrated their judgments into the extreme categories with which they personally agreed and extreme categories with which they disagreed, piling a disproportionate number of statements into that waste bin of rejection. When permitted to generate any number of categories they chose, highly involved persons sorted 114 beliefs into only 3 or 4 piles, and less involved persons discriminated more finely, generating 5 or 6 categories, on the average.

These findings suggested that Sherif's original hunch had been correct: A person's attitude could be studied indirectly through the ways "objective" judgments are made. It would not be necessary to ask the person outright what his or her attitude is on the topic. Instead, the request is for "objective" judgments as to how favorable-unfavorable a belief statement is to its object. The person is given a stack of cards, each with an item on it, and asked to sort the cards into piles. It is made clear that the person is to decide how many piles are needed so that the statements within each pile "belong together," and how to distribute the cards into the piles (categories) thus generated.

The items to be sorted are chosen to cover the entire range of beliefs, from one extreme to another, with a large number in between, preferably totaling 50 to 100 items. The intermediate statements are crucial since they are often more ambiguous than statements of extreme positions. In fact, many ambiguous intermediate statements are included deliberately since individuals with different attitudes (categories) place them in contrasting fashion (La Fave and Sherif, 1968).

What happens as an individual sorts through and reads the cards? Typically, the extreme statements are sorted out early to serve as standards of the end categories. Statements that the person finds objectionable are quickly stacked into one pile. Particularly if the person is highly involved, many items in the objectionable pile will be statements originally selected as "intermediate." Using the acceptable latitude as an anchor, the person displaces many ambiguous items *away* from it (contrast), hence piles them up as "objectionable." Other less discrepant intermediate statements are assimilated to acceptable categories. The person may generate a number of intermediate categories, which are accepted, rejected, or not evaluated. (The total frequencies of the cards in categories with the same labels indicate the latitudes of acceptance, rejection, and noncommitment.)

This Own Categories technique has been tested on a variety of personal and social issues, with the following not-so-obvious results:

1. The more highly involved the person is in the issue, the fewer are the categories generated. This means that highly involved persons discriminate less keenly among the items. They scarcely discriminate at all among items objectionable to them. Typically they lump all objectionable items into a single pile.

2. The more highly involved the person is in the issue, the less evenly are items distributed into the categories. Using fewer categories, the highly involved person is "choosy" in placing items into acceptable categories, while piling up objectionable items indiscriminately. The result is that the person's latitude of rejection is disproportionately greater than the latitude of acceptance. Noncommitment is infrequent. In short, the Own Categories technique confirms the findings stated earlier about the relationship between personal involvement and the latitudes of acceptance, rejection, and noncommitment.

One might reasonably expect that if a person *cares* a great deal about something, finer discriminations would be made related to it. In fact, that happens when the individual is asked to categorize objects that are all acceptable to him or her in varying degrees (Sherif, 1961). The person becomes much more "choosy," using many more categories for the objects than he or she does when the same items are presented with an equal number of objectionable items.

Do the Findings Indicate Involvement or Ignorance?

Couldn't the findings reflect some difference between the more and less involved persons other than their personal involvement? One possibility was checked by Reich and Sherif (1963), who compared the categorizations of mature women (35 to 50 years old) whose median educational level exceeded four years of university study. One sample was composed of active members of the League of Women Voters, which had taken as its major study project the issue of legislative reapportionment. A sample of schoolteachers was matched to league members as closely as possible for age and education. The women in both samples favored reapportionment, but the schoolteachers had taken no active steps to support it. The league members also had more information on the topic than the teachers, which one might think would lead them to discriminate more finely.

Each woman judged 60 statements about reapportionment, about half of these selected as intermediate and the other half equally divided between extremely pro-reapportionment and extremely anti-reapportionment statements. The instructions were to sort the statements according to how pro- or anti-reapportionment the statements were. On the average, the league members placed over half of the 60 statements in the *anti*-reapportionment extreme; 74 percent of them used 4 or fewer categories to sort the statements. In contrast, 74 percent of the teachers used *more* than 4 categories, and they distributed statements into those categories much more equally than league members.

Another way to check whether the few categories and unequal distributions of items into them reflect personal involvement or some other characteristic of the person is to compare the *same* individuals when categorizing materials that are more or less involving to them. I made such comparisons as a part of research on my doctorate dissertation (Sherif, 1961). I was primarily interested in predicting differences in the Own Categories used by Navaho and non-Indian high school students on the basis of prevailing norms in the two cultures. I did a cultural survey on prevailing values before the experiment, including measures to find out what was more and less personally involving to the students. Four sets of materials were sorted in the experiment: (1) names of ethnic and national groups (most involving), (2) brief descriptions of teenage behavior (involving), (3) price tags with the dollar values indicating clothing prices (less involving), and (4) the same series of numbers without dollar signs (not at all involving). As predicted, the number of categories used by the same individuals *increased* in that order (from most to less to not at all involving).

Fred Glixman (1965) also checked the effect of increasing involvement on the categorizations of the same individuals (college students) by asking each to sort (1) descriptive statements of themselves, (2) statements on a social issue, and (3) a set of familiar objects (paper clip, chalk, and so on). As in my research, there was a low positive correlation (about 0.35) between the number of categories used by the same persons for the three sets of items. However, significantly fewer categories were used for self-descriptions than for the familiar objects, despite the fact that there were more self-descriptions than objects to be sorted.

Glixman also compared the distribution of items into the person's own categories, concluding that the distribution of the different items could not be accounted for by a person's "cognitive style," but reflected attitudinal differences toward the contents. Interestingly enough, more recent research into statements for attitude scales shows that statements with personal reference are more subject to assimilation-contrast effects than impersonal statements (Schulman and Tittle, 1967). Such displacements produced the skewed pattern Glixman found, with a greater pile of objectionable than acceptable descriptions but very little in between.

Koslin, Waring, and Pargament (1965) had Peace Corps volunteers categorize series of statements on five issues to check whether the relative sizes of the latitudes of acceptance and rejection differed for the same individuals in terms of their relative personal involvement in the five issues. The relative frequencies of items placed in objectionable categories increased from the least involving issue (housing in India) to the most involving issue (segregation in the United States). By having Peace Corps volunteers sort two equivalent sets of statements on two occasions, Koslin (1966) also showed that reliability of the Own Categories technique is quite high (0.95) when individuals are personally involved. (They sorted statements about their motives in joining the Peace Corps.)

Do these findings prove that personal involvement is the *only* determinant of the person's own categories? In my opinion such a conclusion would be foolish since there is every reason to suspect that education, cognitive concreteness-abstractness (Harvey, 1967), cognitive complexity (Bieri, 1967), and developmental level (Escovar, 1975) also affect the ways that individuals classify objects, events, and beliefs. One's familiarity with the object domain is also important and clearly varies in different social classes and cultures. However, categorizations by children, of preschool through elementary school ages, reveal that equally familiar objects are categorized quite differently as early as 4 years of age, when one set is highly involving (toys) and the other less involving (common household objects). Using fewer categories for the toys, both younger and older children also revealed strong preferences for sex-role appropriate toys and less striking developmental changes with age than when categorizing the household objects (Escovar, 1975).

What the findings show rather clearly is that the degree of personal involvement cannot be ignored. The *efficient* way to investigate other possible determinants of the person's categorizations will be to assess degree of involvement before studying other determinants.

THE DEGREE OF INVOLVEMENT IN
A PERSON'S REFERENCE GROUP

Studying attitude through a person's own categories helps us to understand better what is meant by personal involvement (or ego-involvement). When a situation arouses an attitude high in personal priority, the individual is not only aroused, but also processes incoming information relative to his or her distinctively patterned own categories. In short, to say that the individual is personally involved in a situation is to comment on cognitive process as well as the level of affective-motivational arousal.

In previous chapters, I emphasized that those parts of the self-system related to one's membership and other reference groups were likely to be particularly arousing. The Own Categories technique affords the opportunity to investigate both the cognitive and emotional arousal associated with reference group ties. Gian Sarup (1969; Sherif et al.,

1973) compared judgments made individually by Indian students in the United States on beliefs about their native country. All of the students (median age, 28 years) had favorable attitudes toward their country, rating it positively as a place to live and to pursue their chosen profession. Despite their favorable attitudes, however, some students were more closely identified than others in Indian affairs. Would these students, with favorable attitudes toward India, but differing in national involvement, categorize beliefs in the same way?

Sarup observed Indian students at a large state university, noting those who regularly read Indian papers and journals, attended meetings, and so on, and thereby selecting a criterion sample of publicly committed nationalists. Both these highly committed nationalists and other Indian students were asked to serve as judges for items to be included in a study on the "brain drain" of Indian students. Sarup presented each student with 50 statements about India to sort into their own categories as to how favorable or unfavorable each statement was about India. After completing the judgment task, each student was asked to label any categories acceptable and objectionable to him or her.

The committed nationalists used, on the average, only three categories, put fully 30 of the 50 statements into an objectionable category and accepted only 16. The less committed students used significantly more categories (more than 4, on the average). They rejected only about 15 of the 50 statements, accepted about 22, and remained noncommittal to 13 statements, on the average.

The Indian students ranked their family as their most important reference group. The committed nationalists ranked their nation a close second, whereas other students rated it lower. In addition to observed activities, the more committed students differed in reporting that more of their friends were willing to return to India on completing their studies than did the less committed students. Otherwise, self-reports by the two samples were remarkably similar. Behaviorally, however, the highly involved nationalist saw less need to differentiate finely among beliefs about his or her country (using fewer categories) and was much more prone to reject categorically statements that might impugn it. You may have heard other nationalities react in a similar way (for example, "America: Love It or Leave It!").

THE DEGREE OF INVOLVEMENT AND THE IMPORTANCE OF REFERENCE-GROUP NORMS

If individuals form personal attitudes relative to the norms of their reference groups, then the importance of different norms in their groups should be reflected in the individual's judgments of stimuli related to them.

As a part of our research on natural groups of adolescents, an observer (Merrilea Kelly) made observations unobtrusively in a large high school over a period of 14 months (Sherif, Kelly et al., 1973). Solely on the basis of the frequency and regularity of their interaction, seven informal groups of girls were identified, each with 7 to 8 members. The observations also provided a basis for identifying two areas of normative concern to all groups. One such area was personal appearance and dress. From observation, this area was clearly important to all the groups. The other had to do with the girls' plans for the future, which became more salient as their senior year in high school began, but in general were less pressing than their appearances from day to day.

The naturalistic observations (see Chapter 4) were used as the basis to rank the seven groups in terms of how important each normative concern was to the respective members. For example, a group we called the "governors" (because of their school activities) was ranked first in concern over the future, in terms of time spent discussing it, activities centered around college planning, and so on. On the other hand, a group we called the "wild ones" was ranked last in concern over the future, but first in concern with personal appearance. A group we called the "long hairs" (avant garde at the time) was ranked third for concern about the future but last in concern about appearance (ranking below the "sports" group in that respect).

Quite unrelated to the observations, 48 of the members participated in a judgment experiment. Sets of pictures were prepared representing (a) clothing and hair styles ranging from fashionable to unfashionable, (b) young women engaging in different kinds of activities after graduation from high school (work, school, marriage, and so on), and (c) abstract geometric forms that had nothing to do with any group activities. Each girl sorted each of the three sets of line drawings, using the Own Categories instructions. When she was done, she was asked to label her categories as to her own acceptance or rejection of them. We used the frequency of items *not* labeled (noncommitment) as an indicator of personal involvement: the greater the frequency of noncommitment, the less the involvement. The rationale here was that normatively regulated behaviors are subject to sanctions (positive or negative), hence *lack* of acceptance-rejection could be interpreted as lack of concern.

Significantly fewer categories and less noncommitment were found for the students in judging the personal appearance items than the pictures of future activities. We expected this because personal appearance was a more important normative concern generally. The critical question was whether the members of the different groups would reflect, in their individual judgments, the *relative* importance of the two normative concerns (personal appearance and the future) in their own group. If so, we should be able to rank the number of categories and the relative frequency of noncommitment by individual members and come up with the same ranks obtained when the *groups* were ranked on the basis of observed concern with the normative issue. High and significant correlations were obtained. For the relationship between observed concern and number of categories used, the correlations were 0.93 (appearance) and 0.96 (future). Between observed concern and noncommitment, correlations were lower (0.75 and 0.78), but still statistically significant (perfect correlation = 1.00).

For example, the individual members of the "long hairs," who were third in observed concern over their futures, used fewer categories for the future items than the "wild ones," who were ranked last and who used the most categories and exhibited the most noncommitment. On the other hand, the "wild ones" used the fewest categories and had the least noncommitment for the personal appearance items (their observed concern was ranked first). Members of the "long hairs" used the largest number of categories and showed most noncommitment on the appearance items (in which their group was least concerned). The fact that there was no relationship between group membership and judgments of the geometric forms strengthens our conclusion: The ways the individuals "sliced" the other pictures into categories reflected their personal involvements as members of groups in which these normative issues differed in importance.

BRIEF ENCOUNTERS AND ATTITUDE ASSESSMENT

This book started with an overview of what social psychologists have learned about individual experience and behavior during brief encounters (Chapter 2). Most attitude assessment occurs during brief encounters with a researcher. There is plenty of evidence that the research situation may have a profound effect on the individual's responses from which attitude is inferred.

It *does* make a difference whether an interviewer is from the same or a different social class background, race, or sex as the respondent (Cantril, 1944; Cannell and Kahn, 1968; McClelland, 1974). In research situations, individuals *do* tend to agree or disagree with belief statements in ways that they think will be "socially desirable" (Edwards and Walker, 1962). Oklahoma college students in the early 1950s were sufficiently aware of the anti-segregation views of faculty to respond to standardized attitude tests as great "liberals," despite the fact that observers in their dorms reported many of them making highly prejudiced statements to friends (Chapter 7). Shirley Weitz (1972) reported that "liberal" Harvard students who rated a potential black laboratory partner *most* favorably on a paper-and-pencil test were *more* likely to be cool, condescending, and withdrawn when anticipating actual social interaction with the black partner. Clearly, we cannot simply take measurements made in a research situation at face value.

The problem was pinpointed by Donald Campbell (1950) when he called for research methods in attitude study "which do not destroy the natural form of the attitude in the process of describing it ... [that study attitudes] without making respondents self-conscious or aware of the intent of the study" (p. 15). Whether in the laboratory or on the street, the person who knows that his or her attitude is being studied may well be apprehensive about being evaluated by the researcher (Rosenberg, 1969). The "social psychology of the research situation" is not confined to the experimental laboratory (see Rosenthal and Rosnow, 1969; Adair, 1973). We are talking about the impact of any social situation in which a researcher "investigates" another person.

INDIRECT AND UNOBTRUSIVE TECHNIQUES

The Own Categories technique is one example of an "indirect" way to assess attitudes without arousing awareness of the researcher's intent. The most widely used "indirect" measures have been the so-called projective tests, in which the person is asked to tell a story about a picture or to narrate a story started by the researcher with an opening sentence (see, for example, McClelland, 1955; Horner, 1968). It is assumed that the person deals with such an unstructured task by "projecting" inner needs or attitudes. The persistent difficulty with such techniques is that the researcher has to *interpret* the responses. The possibility is real that the researcher will "project" his or her own attitudes or research hypotheses onto the ambiguous verbal responses produced by the subjects. There are continuing controversies among researchers over the reliability of the ways data are categorized (Entwisle, 1973; Tresemer, 1974). Psychologically, the problem of reliability becomes one of the effects of the researcher's own categories upon interpretation of responses to the projective tests. The Own Categories technique eliminates this problem by having the person generate categories for objects prestandardized as relevant to his or her attitude. The researcher analyzes the *person's categories*, instead of using his or her own to classify verbal responses to projective tests.

One obvious answer to the impact of the research situation is to eliminate the researcher or to place the researcher in natural settings as a "people watcher." For example, Milgram and his associates (Milgram, 1972) "lost" stamped letters addressed to organizations with known political stands at public locations in several neighborhoods, with the result that the frequencies of letters actually mailed from the different neighborhoods reflected the pro or anti views of their residents. Heussenstamm (1971) placed Black Panther party stickers on the cars of 15 black, white, and Chicano students to study attitudes of police. These stickers were sufficient to elicit 33 citations from police for alleged traffic violations by the 15 students within 17 days in Los Angeles of 1969, even though the students drove carefully. Webb, Campbell, Schwartz, and Sechrest (1966) compiled a large number of such "unobtrusive" techniques for obtaining data about social behavior, many of them pertinent to social attitudes.

Such unobtrusive research methods are invaluable for "people watching," particularly in determining regularities in social behavior (see Chapter 4). Yet they are bound to be insufficient in themselves when we ask psychological questions about attitude functioning. Such questions include those asked earlier in this chapter: What is the structure of the individual's attitude? How personally involving is its arousal?

Observation and other "unobtrusive" methods for ascertaining the regularity and frequency of a person's behavior over time will be more useful when combined with methods for investigating the psychological structure of the person's attitude and the degree of his or her involvement. Such a combination of methods yields several measures of the person's attitude. If the various measures agree, or converge in their support of an inference about the person's attitude, we have much better grounds for making statements about the attitude. Each method, in turn, may supply different kinds of information. Multiple methods for measuring attitudes are needed if one's aim is to predict the person's behavior at a later time. However, attitude assessment alone need not be sufficient for that purpose, for reasons that we will discuss next.

PREDICTING SPECIFIC ACTIONS RELATED TO ATTITUDE

The prime criticism of the attitude concept has been the ostensible failure of traditional verbal reports of attitude in predicting specific actions related to the attitude (see Deutscher, 1966). In fact, scores obtained from tests requiring endorsement or rejection of highly general belief statements do not correlate well with an action arbitrarily chosen by the researcher to check the relationship (Tittle and Hill, 1967). The correlations are lowest for those scales that systematically eliminate personal reference from the belief statements (Schulman and Tittle, 1967).

Why should we expect otherwise? In addition to the problems of adequate assessment, we know very well that a person's actions in any social situation are never a direct outcome of an attitude or another internal factor alone (Chapter 2). The prediction of action in a specific situation has to include other internal factors aroused in the situation (including other attitudes), the person's relationship to other persons present, to the location, the activities at hand, and the possible consequences of the action in the person's life.

Within the last few years, numerous significant research attacks have been made on these problems (Liska, 1974). As a result we can say now that the bald statement that attitudes are unimportant for the way a person acts is simply wrong. The research is contributing constructively in identifying other attitudes, reference group ties, social norms, and situational factors that influence whether or not the person does take specific actions congruent with his or her attitudes.

Multiple Methods for Attitude Assessment

The most notable successes at prediction attained by public opinion surveys have been in forecasting voting in national elections (Abelson, 1968). What is seldom mentioned in connection with these efforts is that they are dependent on the outlay of unprecedented effort, repeated assessment over time, and checking survey responses against past voting records in election districts. The research effort before elections far exceeds any other assessment efforts in either public opinion surveys or academic research. The polls would go out of business if they predicted elections incorrectly, hence the great effort unmatched in their other surveys. The more sophisticated research in voting prediction has, for some years, shown that better predictions result from assessing several attitudes toward candidates, salient public issues, and political parties than from any single attitude (Campbell, Converse, Miller, and Stokes, 1960; Goldberg, 1966; Jeffries and Ransford, 1972; RePass, 1971).

It is hardly surprising then that one advance in research methodology has involved the measurement of several related attitudes, often weighted as to their relative importance. For example, Triandis (1967) has emphasized the value of specifying attitudes toward several important social characteristics of persons (for example, race, sex, occupation) rather than a single blanket categorization (for example, race) in predicting a person's intentions to interact with others. Similarly, Rokeach and Kliejins (1972) reported that their attempt to predict college students' absences from classes was substantially improved when the students themselves weighted the importance of two attitude measures: one toward class cutting itself and the other toward the professor whose class was to be cut.

Fishbein and his associates (Fishbein, 1973; Ajzen and Fishbein, 1973) have shown that prediction of an action is greatly improved by assessing both the person's attitude toward that action and the person's beliefs about the normative expectations of others (reference persons or groups). Further, they found that the person's "motivation to comply" with such normative expectations by one or several reference persons or groups *multiplies* the weight assigned to those others' expectations in their "prediction formula." In short, high involvement with one's reference groups increases the relationship between normative expectations of others and one's behavior. Their formula has worked best in studies in which the researcher had greater control both over the persons and the situations in which attitudes and actions were assessed.

What all of these efforts have in common is the use of several attitude measurements and the choice of attitudes specifically related to a future situation and/or action, rather than highly abstract, general, and impersonal belief statements. Fendrich (1967) showed that when students are asked to commit themselves personally to an action *before* responding to belief statements, substantial and high correlations were obtained between their attitude scores, their commitment to act, and their actual action. Without such prior commitment, correlations were low and insignificant. The act of committing oneself to an action has been found consequential in a variety of social-psychological research (see, for example, Kiesler, 1971). Similarly, Fishbein (1967) has persistently emphasized the person's commitment to an "intention" to act as the crucial linkage in predicting actual behavior.

What we are finding, then, is that attitudes relate to a person's actions when the self becomes involved in ongoing activity. In view of this, it is rather surprising that there is only one study in the research literature to date (to my knowledge) that has inquired both into the person's attitudes and how involving they are, with reference to the likelihood of a concrete future action.

Personal Involvement and Social Pressure to Act

Merrilea Kelly (1970; Sherif, Kelly et al., 1973) studied the likelihood of personal engagement in actions related to three attitudes differing in their priority (importance) in the self-systems of college women. She believed that a person would be more likely to engage in action relative to an attitude with high personal priority than one with lower priority. Furthermore, she was concerned about what happened between the time of a person's commitment to action and the actual event, reasoning that busy college students may need social encouragement or pressure to engage in any actions beyond their heavy commitments to courses, campus, and personal activities.

Rather than arbitrarily selecting an action situation, Kelly did extensive pilot research to select three issues clearly different in how involving they were for students enrolled in introductory psychology classes. As we have also found in several other studies, the most involving topics for college sophomores are seldom the sociopolitical issues studied in the majority of research on these problems. Kelly found that issues of personal-social development and adjustment were uniformly most involving for students. At the time (the spring of the U.S. invasion of Cambodia), two issues confronting all students on the campus were also involving, but considerably less so than the personal adjustment issue: the social and civil rights of black students and the relevance of intellectual achievement in the university. After surveys in which students ranked a variety of issues as to their personal importance, Kelly also had students construct their own categories on these issues. The fewest categories and most rejection were found on the personal adjustment issue (highly involving), and the most categories and least rejection on the educational issue (least involving).

Two hundred and fifteen women participated for one point of research credit, which they received simply for coming to the first session. At that session, each student completed attitude tests on the three issues. Then, as predetermined on a random basis, she was asked to sign a statement committing herself to attend a meeting on one of the three topics (personal adjustment, black student status, or educational achievement). From one to three weeks later, each student received a letter informing her of the time and place of the meeting. She was asked to attend or to return the letter indicating a time when she could meet the researcher to learn what had happened.

On the personal adjustment topic, the meeting concerned opportunities to participate in human relations (sensitivity) training. The meeting on the black issue concerned organized attempts on campus to increase interracial understanding. The meeting on education concerned a series of tutorials geared to topics of relevance to undergraduates. These meetings were held at scheduled times, with small attendance, which was not particularly surprising on a campus where student unrest was growing to the point that pass-fail grades in courses were given at the term's end. On the most involving issue, about 22 percent showed up, as compared with about 7 to 8 percent on each of the other two.

Meanwhile, Kelly called all students who had not showed up or returned her letter, scheduling new appointments. She called once more if those were missed. By this series of encouragements and pressures, the following total percentages actually took action on the three issues: Highly involving (personal)—63.3 percent; involving (black rights)—48.5 percent; moderately involving (education)—38.3 percent. Conversely, the totals who took no action were, in the same order: 36.7 percent, 59.5 percent, 61.7 percent. Interestingly, the great majority of those who did not act (28.3 percent, 47.1 percent, and 53.3 percent, respectively) stated on the letter they returned or by phone that they were not interested in attending the meeting, thus behaving consistently with their stated intentions. The remaining students (4 to 8 percent) kept "intending" to come but missed two appointments made with Kelly.

The frequencies of those attending the meeting, of those attending with social encouragement, and of those not attending differed significantly in the direction predicted: More action and more responsiveness to pressure occurred with greater involvement. What about the effect of specific attitudes on these topics? The women's attitudes on these three issues were all favorable, ranging from strongly favorable to moderately favorable. Within this small favorable range, the extremity of the individual's attitude bore no relation to the probability of taking action.

When Attitude Conflicts with Expectations of Reference Persons

Kelly's students with favorable attitudes were consistent when they responded to social encouragement and acted, but not all combinations of attitude and action situations lead us to expect action. For example, a person who was against interracial interaction would refuse a request to attend an interracial meeting. Suppose, however, that the person has a favorable attitude, and is asked to have his or her picture taken with a black student (DeFleur and Westie, 1963). The person may agree, but refuse permission for the picture to be used on the campus or in his or her hometown. Research has shown that the reasons for such refusals invariably refer to what important reference persons (fraternity brothers, family, and so on) would "think." In fact, social norms instruct us on what *not* to do as well as what to do, at times more explicitly forbidding action than explicitly instructing *how* to act.

The most interesting research on what happens when the individual's attitude conflicts with the normative expectations of reference persons has been stimulated by DeFleur and his associates (DeFleur and Westie, 1963; Linn, 1965; Warner and DeFleur, 1969; Acock and DeFleur, 1972). Such situations are most likely to occur in times of rapid social change, often involving generational conflict. The prediction of action from knowledge about a person's attitude requires much more systematic attention, along lines started by DeFleur, to the social situation in which the action or inaction occurs and to the consequences foreseen.

Campbell (1963) pointed out quite correctly that social situations differ significantly with respect to how conducive they are for expressing one's attitude. He suggested that situations might be "graded" in terms of their "ease" or "difficulty" in such respects. The recognition that significant others have normative expectations running counter to one's own proclivities would constitute a "hurdle" for expressing one's attitude in their presence, in Campbell's terms.

Leigh Shaffer (1974) completed his doctoral research at the Pennsylvania State University on the problem of committing oneself to action and following through when the commitment involves persuasion of other persons whose attitudes differ from one's own. He defined situations with "easy" or "difficult" hurdles in terms of *whom* an individual pledged to persuade, a person potentially sympathetic or one probably hostile to the message. Studying members of a religious organization, Shaffer arranged that some members were requested to persuade a series of target persons in conformity with either a major group norm (personal evangelism) or a less important group norm (bringing recruits to a public meeting). High-status members and novices with lower status were assigned randomly to one or the other request.

The higher-status members (with huge latitudes of rejection for opposing views on religion) committed themselves to action about equally on both norms, acting in line with their commitments about equally for "easy" and "difficult" target persons, particularly if (as requested) they actually named such persons in advance. The lower-status members, who were also significantly less involved, were more likely to commit themselves in line with the more important norm than the less important one. Furthermore, they were more prone to follow up the commitment with persons they regarded as "easy" to approach.

Shaffer's main finding was that the more involved members both committed themselves and acted in line with their attitudes more consistently, without regard to situational hurdles. The fledglings were responsive to the importance of the norm and the situational hurdles. This outcome bears an important message about when actions can be expected to follow from a person's attitudes and when, indeed, there is more talk than action.

Attitudes Toward "My Kind of People" and "Those Others"

The most consequential attitudes are those defining just how, as an individual, one relates to other human beings. That is why, back in Chapters 4 and 5, I made such a fuss about differentiating between social situations within the cosy bounds of our own group and interactions among members of different groups. Whether we are aware of it or not, the past history among us, or between "us" and "them," intrudes into the give-and-take of the moment through our respective attitudes. It makes a great difference whether that history is "ours" or whether it is between "us" and "them."

The definitions of in-group and inter-group behavior (Chapters 4 and 5) are basic to what this chapter is all about. However, they are a bit narrow in the sense that "we" and "they" do not always refer to human groups, as defined in Chapter 4. When they do not, they refer to social classifications, status categories, or strata representing differences in social power. Now that the concept of reference group is familiar, we can expand the definition of intergroup behavior in Chapter 5.

When two or more individuals interact in terms of their belongingness to different reference groups, or reference *sets*, we have an instance of intergroup, or inter*set*, behavior. It follows that attitudes toward members of other groups and social categories differing from our own are inferred from such behaviors or from what we do or say about "them." An example may clarify this expanded definition.

At a convention of psychologists, a publisher's representative asked if I had read a book published by a rival company and written by a woman. I praised the book, expressing interest in meeting its author. Did he know her? "Oh yes," was his reply, "but she's not my dish. Too pushy, too ambitious. She set out to write a best seller and put everything in that book to make it sell." Then he added: "I like women a little soft." This was in reply, remember, to my praise of a book and my interest in meeting its author.

The publisher's reactions reflected intergroup attitudes in part: sour grapes toward a potential best seller from a rival company. They also reflected a definite attitude toward a person in the broad social category woman. If the author had been a man, the aims attributed to him might have won the publisher's grudging admiration. Certainly the sour grapes would have been expressed quite differently than through his preference for a "soft dish." In terms of his reference set, behaviors that might be quite appropriate for a man were defined as "pushy," "too ambitious," not "soft" enough for a woman—just plain out of place. His reply, of course, was quite irrelevant to my inquiry.

Human societies are organized in terms of power relationships among different groups, strata, and status classifications. Human beings are recognized as belonging to these different social categories through signals ranging in their concreteness from physical differences (for example, sexual, racial), dress, speech, place of residence, or activity to complex verbal accounts of ancestry, beliefs, or ideology. From all of the possible criteria that could serve as significant signs for differentiating one set of people from another, we learn certain signs because they are associated with the power relationships in our society or between our own nation and others. These signs of our "position" and where "they belong" include those related to socioeconomic status, occupation, race, ethnicity, nationality, religion, and, invariably, sex as a social as well as biological fact. The lines of such social categories crisscross throughout society. At times, two or more social categories intersect and prevent the formation of groups among individuals, within a given social category, whose overriding common interest would seem to promote unified actions, otherwise. Thus, the poor or powerless may see themselves as black or white, male or female, protestant or Catholic rather than as one in their deprivation and suffering.

Any attitude establishes a relationship between self and "something" in the environment. It makes a great deal of difference in personal experience and action whether that "something" is another person defined as "my kind of people" or as "that kind of people." It makes a great deal of difference whether relationships between "my kind" and "those others" have been defined as complementary and cooperative, on one hand, or as relationships between the powerful and powerless, between rivals, between conqueror and conquered, between "superior" and "inferiors," on the other. Such differences have to be fully understood if ever there is to be a theory of attitudes that applies to all human attitudes.

In fact, books on social psychology are filled with "theories" of attitudes and interpersonal expectations that are not applicable at all when applied to interset attitudes and expectations. Many "theories" of intergroup attitudes, on the other hand, propose wholly unique psychological processes and principles for dealing with the facts of "prejudice" and "stereotyping." For this reason, I will start with a caution about pitfalls that are quite common in thinking about attitudes toward people in social categories other than our own.

"EXPLAINING" BY DEFINITION: THE CASE OF PREJUDICE AND STEREOTYPE

We need to define terms in social psychology in order to point clearly to what we are studying and what we are not. When a definition also "explains" what it refers to, it precludes alternative explanations. Such definitions are marks of "scientific maturity" when alternative explanations have been studied and discarded as inadequate. Definitions that "explain" are blinding, however, when alternative ways of looking at the problem have not been examined. They shut our eyes to the alternatives and send us in search of "facts" that support our definition. One example is the definition often used in social psychology to "explain" hostile attitudes toward members of other groups.

The underlying assumptions were simple and reasonable: The most obvious difference between attitudes toward those near and dear and toward those in social categories quite different from our own is that we have much more firsthand experience with our "own kind." In a society like the United States of fifty years ago, the segregation of human lives according to race, residence, sex, socioeconomic class, or religion at home, in school, work, and leisure practically guaranteed that difference. The difference was quite obvious when attitudes toward distant nations and cultures were considered. Thus, each child had "to be carefully taught" what "outsiders" were like, when dealings with them were "in order" and when they were not. What a child in a dominant group learned from elders about those classified as "inferior," according to the argument, was a derogatory image of them so unpleasant that dislike, hostility, or abhorrence was a logical consequence.

Intent on reforming *what* was taught, many social psychologists proceeded from those assumptions to define unfavorable attitudes toward other groups and categories quite differently from other attitudes. For example, one influential definition was "antipathy based upon a faulty and inflexible generalization" (Allport, 1954; see Ehrlich, 1973, pp. 3–4, for other examples). Such attitudes were given a special label: prejudice. The definition "explains" prejudice in terms of a "faulty and inflexible generalization" that the individual has learned.

What was that "faulty and inflexible generalization"? It was a generalization *about* what "those people are like," a stereotyped "picture in the head" learned in the absence of sufficient or accurate information *about* them. The term stereotype came into the social sciences directly from the influential book *Public Opinion* (1922), by the journalist Walter Lippmann. An exposé of the ethnocentric nationalisms in political and international dealings during the World War I era, the book emphasized the importance of such "pictures in the head" in the interpretation of current events. Social scientists began to collect data on the images held toward this or that group, often with little reference to the actual relationships among the people in question. The latter was probably not intended by Lippmann, who started his journalistic career as hand-picked apprentice to Lincoln Steffens, an older journalist known early in the century for his exposés of the "shame of the cities," of state governments, and of U.S. oil and banking interests in Mexico just before World War I.

Once into the pitfall of defining negative attitudes as "prejudice" based on "stereotypes," let's see what the consequences are. First, consider the practical consequences: The logical way to change "what has to be carefully taught" is to correct the "faulty generalization" through information or firsthand experience that is both accurate and favorable to the other party. However, if the generalization is also "inflexible," what happens when a prejudiced person meets a living, breathing individual whose behavior contradicts the image he holds of the social category? "Well, there are bound to be some *exceptions*. Thank heavens they aren't *all* the same." How is favorable information received? "Well, no one's *all* bad." Or worse still: "Where do you get those facts? Not a word of truth in them. Now I can tell you a hundred true stories about. . . ." And so forth.

When the people in question have been the victims of discrimination or maltreatment, there are genuine ironies in the best-intentioned efforts to change "faulty generalizations" through favorable information about them. Twenty-five years ago, advertisements in mass-circulation magazines in the United States pictured black persons (when they did at all) as unskilled, subservient workers (94 percent of blacks were so portrayed; Shuey, King, and Griffith, 1953). Thanks to the efforts of reformers and no doubt the dollar wisdom of salesmen, the proportion of blacks pictured as unskilled workers in such ads had shrunk to 29 percent by 1968 (Cox, 1970). Had the proportion of unskilled black workers in the United States shrunk so dramatically as well?

Similarly, children's books winning the prestigious Caldecott and Newbery medals, and others classed as best sellers from 1967 to 1971, pictured a child's world overpopulated with males in a sex ratio of 3:1 (Weitzman, Eifler, Hokada, and Ross, 1972). The male to female ratio for adults in the books was 1:7 for "service" activities, but that for "leadership" activities was 5:0 and that for "rescue" activities was 4:1. There is a worthy effort being made to change the man's world pictured in such image-making media. Will women's roles in activities at home and at work change, too? The irony is that, if they do not, the women pictured in the media will be "exceptions to the general rule" that plague practical efforts to change attitudes solely through favorable information.

There are also theoretical consequences to the pitfall in which we have become trapped: If "prejudice" is defined as antipathy based on faulty generalizations about others, how is it possible for the stereotypes "in the head" to remain inflexible in the face of clear, concrete experiences that contradict it? The psychology of rational or adaptive mental processes offered no explanations. Logically, there were two alternatives: Either the person's antipathy is utterly "irrational" (he is "mixed up in the head" or "sick") or maybe there is a "kernel of truth" contained in the stereotype. The definition of "prejudice" restricted the search for explanations to these two hypotheses.

Both of the alternative hypotheses have been discussed widely, with the "irrationality" or "sick" explanation generating by far the most frequent and popular research. Since that approach was discussed in Chapters 5 and 9, I will note here only that the amount of research activity generated by a theory need not be a good index of how "fertile" or "seminal" the theory is. The alternative hypothesis, suggesting that a kernel of truth supports faulty, inflexible generalizations, has generated more talk than research. Most of the talk has implied that "Well, that's the way *they* really are, y'know" or has protested that the way we see people and things could not be merely a projection of pictures in our own heads. The lack of research reflects hesitancy to tackle the problem of how a kernel of truth could maintain a faulty generalization, even in the improbable event that we could define and measure a kernel of truth. It is possible to demonstrate differences between different categories of people, but to find in such differences a kernel of truth about them that "explains" a faulty, inflexible picture in our heads is another matter.

The pitfall of explaining prejudice by definition has become a quagmire. Our best course is to get out of it by rejecting the definition of prejudice that has restricted the search for explanations to two dead ends.

ATTITUDES AS SELF-OTHER RELATIONSHIPS

To avoid the practical and theoretical pitfalls, let's consider "prejudice" toward others as a special case of attitudes toward people placed in a social category other than one's own, namely, those attitudes that are negative and unfavorable. Let's remember that favorable attitudes toward others in certain "different" social categories are not only possible, but, in fact, are frequent. So the problem is *what* differences are responded to negatively and why.

In the last chapter, we learned that attitudes are not merely cognitive generalizations *about* their objects, nor concepts *of what "they are like."* Foremost, attitudes forge links with others in our reference groups or sets, and barriers from others if the norms of our reference group so dictates. The overwhelming fact about both favorable and hostile attitudes toward persons in "different" social categories is that they represent voluntary conformity to social norms specifying *what differences are important*. They are not "deviant" behaviors, nor idiosyncratic preferences and dislikes.

Attitudes are relationships, involving the self-system *with* others or keeping us *away from* others. The psychological processes in attitude formation are simultaneously cognitive and motivational-emotional, entailing the placement of others into categories that differentiate "me" and "us" from "them" while also evaluating where "we" stand relative to "them." Their earliest signs in development are *preferences* and dislikes for certain differences, and labels for the people, not generalizations *about them*.

As time goes by, we learn beliefs about them and attribute traits to them that also express feelings about them and that justify the particular *relationship* between self and "them." What we observe about them is filtered through the aperture of that *relationship*. That is why what we notice, what we emphasize, and what we say about them are such feeble "facts." For example, if we learn that we are "superior" to a people and then see some of "them" resting before their broken-down house, we say they are "lying around." Not asking what they have been doing or what they have eaten, we call them "lazy."

The self-other categorization that is primary in directing us to emphasize *certain* differences among human groupings while ignoring others usually reflects social categories established long before we were born. Its primacy is indicated by researchers' measurements of different aspects or components of our attitudes. Our beliefs about others, the nice or nasty qualities we attribute to them, our feelings about them, and our expectations of how we should treat them are positively correlated (see McGuire, 1969; Ehrlich, 1973, pp. 101–108). Though not always perfectly congruent with each other, our beliefs, attributions to others, and our feelings form a pattern in harmony with the self-other relationship. When the research concerns attitudes toward another human grouping with whom our reference group has had long-standing hostile relationships, correlations between different "components" of our attitudes are quite high (Ansari, 1956).

In short, what has to be carefully taught about people in other social categories is what our *relationship* with people in that category *should* be. Therefore, it is specious to seek the "roots of prejudice" solely within the individual or solely in how the individual perceives others. What has to be carefully taught stems most immediately from the norms of our own reference sets, but the roots of prejudice do not stop on our native soil. The taproot springs from the actual relationships in the past and present *between* people and was planted by the power exercised by one over the other, the conflicts and struggles *between* different parts of society and between societies.

Institutionalized in the way we live our lives, the relationships between groups, status levels, and nations contain the roots of prejudice. One supreme irony of our own times is that those who would foster "tolerance" are often among those most reluctant to change the social arrangements that nourish those roots or to endure the confusion and struggle that such changes would necessarily entail.

SOCIAL DISTANCE FROM OTHER PEOPLE

Where do you live? What kind of facilities do you have for living and working? Who has authority over you and in what respects? Whom do you associate with and why? Whom do you *not* associate with?

Answers to such questions give the most immediate indication of the effects of social structure and power relations on our own lives. The vast differences and the nearly unbridgeable gaps between groups and categories of people arising from their respective environments within the social structure have been documented in historical, economic, and sociological research. Within such social realities, social norms arise prescribing social distances among persons belonging to different groups and strata.

Robert E. Park (1924) was a journalist, and then public relations man for the Tuskegee Institute in the days of Booker T. Washington, before he joined the sociology faculty at the University of Chicago. Observing social distances between groups, he suggested that personal relationships between their respective members might be graded, as a consequence, into varying "degrees of understanding and intimacy." A younger sociologist, Emory S. Bogardus (1925), applied the concept by developing means to assess norms for social distance between racial and ethnic groups and different nationalities. Social distance is among the few concepts in social psychology with a cumulative research history of half a century.

Bogardus (1967, 1968) collected data over a forty-year period (1926 to 1966), providing impressive evidence that white, middle-class norms for maintaining social distance from various ethnic and racial groups are as American as the Thanksgiving Day turkey. His respondents were college students—representatives of the "bright hopes" of society's future. In his four surveys, a total of 8333 responded.

THE BOGARDUS TECHNIQUE FOR ASSESSING SOCIAL DISTANCE NORMS

Bogardus (1925) developed his methods after he had interviewed college students and found them willing to rate how intimate or how distant they preferred to be with various ethnic and racial groups. They responded readily to the groups "in general," without any specification of particular individuals who belonged to them. However, Bogardus realized that attitudes toward general categories of other people had little meaning apart from the circumstances in which the persons were to be encountered. Furthermore, he intuitively did what more recent researchers have had to "discover": He asked the individual to express *personal* willingness to interact with others in each of a series of situations representing increasingly intimate role relationships.

The technique is disarmingly simple: The respondent receives a sheet of paper with the names of 30 to 40 groups or categories of people listed alphabetically down one side—from Armenians, "U.S. white Americans," Canadians, Chinese, and Czechs; on down through Indians (American), Indians (of India), Irish, Italians, Japanese, and Jews; to Russians, Scots, Spanish, Swedish, and Turks. Beside each name is a row with seven spaces for responses. These spaces are labeled across the top of the page as column headings, as follows:

1. Would marry into group.
2. Would have as close friends.
3. Would have as next-door neighbors.
4. Would work in same office.
5. Have as speaking acquaintances only.
6. Have as visitors only to my nation.
7. Would debar from my nation.

The respondent is asked to give first "feeling reactions" to each group listed down the side, in terms of the "chief picture . . . you have of the entire group," working as rapidly as possible and checking "as many columns for each group as you can." The social distances listed above are those used by Bogardus from 1926 to 1966. Other researchers have modified them to suit their research purposes, as we shall see. Note that the first five alternatives represent decreasing intimacy, and the last two are degrees of rejection.

The responses obtained from individuals were analyzed to find the average rating given to each of the groups (with a possible range from alternatives 1 to 7 above). Bogardus then ranked these average ratings for the various groups in order, from the groups rated the closest (on the average) to those kept at greatest social distance. What we learn from such an analysis is more pertinent to the prevailing social norms than to particular individual attitudes. What have we learned about norms of social distance maintained by young, white, middle-class college students in the United States?

The Stability of Preference Order

The order of the various groups, ranked in terms of the average ratings for social distance accorded them, is remarkably stable over the forty-year period studied: At the top (closer intimacy) come other "U.S. white Americans," Canadians, English, Irish, French, Swedish, Scots, "Hollanders," Norwegians, Germans—all from northern Europe. At the very bottom ranks (greatest social distance) we find Asians (Indians from India, Koreans, Japanese, Chinese), Negroes, Turks, and Mexicans. In between the top and bottom is an assortment of middle and southern Europeans (for example, Spanish, Czechs, Poles, Greeks), Jews, Armenians, and American Indians. The rank order correlations between the lists obtained from 1926 to 1966 range from 0.92 to 0.98 (when 1.00 = perfect).

Intergroup Conflicts and Changes in Preference Order

Changes that occurred over the past forty years in the ranks for specific groups clearly reflect changed intergroup relations during those years: There are no surprises. Between 1926 and 1946, the intervening World War II produced greater distance toward Germans, who quickly regained the loss by 1956. Similarly, the Japanese, already low in rank in 1926, slipped to the bottom rank in 1946, but regained their erstwhile low status by 1956–1966. The Italians, intermediate in rank in 1925, slipped down by 1946, but moved up strikingly in 1956 and 1966, when they ranked among the more intimate with the Norwegians and Germans. The rank accorded Jews inched steadily, but slightly upward through the middle ranks. The red-hunting of the early 1950s and the Cold War were reflected in lower ranks accorded nationalities with socialist governments, most notably Russians who plummeted from a high middle rank in 1926 and 1946 to sixth from the bottom in 1956 and 1966.

Is Social Distance Decreasing?

From 1926 to 1966, the average social distances accorded to groups in the middle and lower ranks steadily decreased. The overall decreasing social distance was reflected in more groups receiving more intimate ratings and in the smaller *difference* between the most intimate (average) rating and the most distant ratings (the *difference* decreasing from 3.9 in 1926 to 2.6 in 1966). These shifts may reflect the greater interaction among diverse groups, especially in work and public situations, during the forty-year period. They may also reflect increase in students' sophistication at responding in terms they believe are "socially desirable" to the researchers. The possibility that more recent findings reveal no normative pattern of social distance, but merely a conglomeration of various uniquely individual personal preferences, was tested through factor analysis and rejected (Ames and Sakuma, 1969). A patterned order of preference for social distance still exists.

Social Distance Norms and Individual Attitudes

Individual attitudes of college students reflect the prevailing social distance norms, with only small proportions of them desiring great social distance from all groups but their own or rejecting social distances from any groups (Hartley, 1946). There is evidence that those conforming most closely to the prevailing social distance norms are also more conforming to their reference groups in other respects (see Hartley, 1946; Triandis and Triandis, 1965; Ehrlich, 1973).

Hartley (1946) found that some 55 percent of the college students he studied in 8 northeastern universities exhibited rather consistent individual differences in the general amount of social distance they preferred to other groups. Their average social distance ratings for 32 actual ethnic groups correlated from 0.78 to 0.85 (high and positively) with their ratings of three fictitious groups that he inserted in the list (Pirenean, Wallonian, and Danirean). The other 45 percent did not respond to the fictitious groups (see Ehrlich, 1973, p. 129). A later finding by Prothro and Melikian (1953) in Lebanon suggests that keeping a general level of social distance from all groups other than one's own may be distinctively American. While their students at the American University in Lebanon (mostly Arabs) preferred considerable social distance from certain groups (for example, Turks), 93 percent refused to respond to Hartley's fictitious group names.

In 1960, I had high school students in Oklahoma and Navaho students at a government school sort 50 to 100 names of ethnic and national groups according to social distance preference, using the Own Categories technique (Chapter 9). About 10 percent of the Oklahoma students and 15 percent of the Navaho students placed all groups in a single category, indicating that they did not want to make invidious comparisons among them. Approximately 85 percent of the combined samples generated at least one category composed of groups for which they rejected social contacts of a friendly nature (Sherif, 1961).

Women's Roles and the Social Distance Norms

Men and women in Bogardus' research ordered the various groups as to preference for intimacy or distance in much the same way (correlation of 0.98). However, the average social distances accorded by women were consistently greater than those accorded by men (excepting toward other "white Americans," of course). The difference between the sexes was greatest for groups kept at considerable social distance by both. Between 1956 to 1966, the size of the consistent sex differences decreased markedly. Two studies failed to find males more "liberal" than females (Kelly, Ferson, and Holtzman, 1958; Turbeville, 1950). Obviously, whether or not a sex difference would be found depends in part on which men and women are studied.

Nevertheless, the obtained differences and their decrease remind us that the role relationships included on the Bogardus scale and its various adaptations may have quite different meanings for traditional men and women. The "double standard" for men and women does not apply only to sexual relationships. The traditional female role centered solely within the family and immediate circle of father's or husband's friends. Any deviation from social distance norms subscribed to by that narrow circle immediately threatened a woman's standing. A man could maintain the same norms in that circle, while readily being more "tolerant" in the wider and separate world of work and public leisure. As long as such a double standard prevailed, with women's "worth" defined only in the home sphere, it is hardly surprising that women showed up on the social distance test as more conservative than men, even when one took into account differences in women's ages, marital status, educational level, and amount of contact with members of the "out-group" in question (Williams, 1964).

The male double standard is seen quite clearly if we consider, as Elyce Milano did (1973), what would happen if the Bogardus technique were adapted to study social distances that men prefer from women. Of course, most men would accept women for marriage, in their neighborhood, and in the same office, at least as secretaries (though perhaps not as the boss). Some men would have difficulty in accepting a woman as "close friend" or to their sport or social club (where she could pop nude out of a cake, however). Certainly, we have to be careful in defining social intimacy as sexual intimacy since men who might not dream of marrying a woman from another ethnic or racial group might welcome her in bed.

As women's lives gain centers other than the home, we may expect further changes in the sex differences that have been reported in response to social distance questions. Alternatively, more women as well as men may reject the pattern of preference and invidious distinction established by social distance norms, as some have already done.

Social Distance Preferences of the Powerful and the Powerless

Norms of social distance flow downward from the more powerful and dominant groups in society to the less powerful, not vice versa. When dominant groups in society successfully maintain social distances from others through the required social arrangements, all groups in society are affected. As long as dominant groups managed to epitomize for others the "good life," and were the only source of "good things" for the others, some members of subordinated groups ranked other groups in society in much the same preference order as the dominant groups. The exception was the lowly status of their own group, which they moved up near the top (Hartley, 1946; Williams, 1964).

Such a reflection of the "superior" groups' snobberies is not universally found, doubtless because the discriminated groups are by no means homogeneous in their experiences (see Ehrlich, 1973, Chapter 8, for a review of available evidence). Perhaps the experience of being marginal in one's membership in a "lowly" group, while rejected by the dominant group, might serve to open one's eyes about what the social distance norms can do in preventing diverse "lowly" groups from recognizing their common fate. From the viewpoint of the dominant groups, passing their social distance norms down to "minorities" represents effective use of a principle as old as Caesar: Divide and conquer. Thus marginal persons may reject the social distance norms *in toto*, forming new reference groups with others of like mind.

WHITE NORMS FOR KEEPING BLACKS AT A DISTANCE

The most thorough documentation of what representative samples of the U.S. white population say about social distance concerns white norms toward black Americans. In assessing their verbal reports, we have to compare them with the institutional arrangements that continue to separate white and black Americans in the most important aspects of living, working, studying, and playing. For all but a more prosperous minority of black Americans, such arrangements also spell lack of privilege and opportunity.

Suppose that we compare the responses by white Americans on national surveys to statistics indicating possibilities for actual contacts with blacks as equals in neighborhoods, schools, and work. The conclusion is inescapable that many white Americans talk more permissively than they act. For example, 53 percent of the white populations in 15 major U.S. cities said in 1968 either that they "would not mind at all" if "a Negro family with about the same income and education as you moved next door to you" or that they already had black next-door neighbors (Campbell, 1971). Forty-four percent said they *would* mind, and 51 percent opposed laws to prevent racial discrimination in housing. Yet, 75 percent of a nationwide white sample reported that they lived in wholly white neighborhoods.

Campbell (1971) reported similar discrepancies between actual conditions and "liberal" attitudes concerning school desegregation. While 75 percent of whites nationwide favored school desegregation in 1970, the overwhelming majority also reported that the grade schools nearest their homes were all white (36 percent) or "mostly white" (44 percent). Forty percent of a nationwide sample of blacks reported that the grade schools nearest their homes were either all black (13 percent) or mostly black (27 percent) (Campbell, 1971, p. 144).

Most grade schools are populated by children from the immediate neighborhood. The response by 53 percent of whites who said they "would not mind at all" having a "Negro family with about the same income and education as you move next door" was interpreted as "tolerance." It does not necessarily mean that none would succumb to a real estate salesman who warns them with an eye to his own profits that their property values will fall when the black counterpart moves in. Furthermore, a moment's thought will tell us that proportionally more black than white families have low incomes. Realistically 53 percent of the nationwide white sample could not have black neighbors "with about the same income and education as you," especially since there are many fewer black than white families to start. Thus, logically, it is impossible for white Americans to separate their attitudes and actions concerning their residences from issues concerning school desegregation, as much as some people may try. The 75 percent who state that they favor school desegregation must include a sizable minority whose actions belie their words, in one way or another.

Nevertheless, white Americans' stated preferences about contact with black Americans have changed dramatically since 1942, when the National Opinion Research Center started asking representative samples their opinions. In that year, only 44 percent of the white population in the North and less than 4 percent in the South favored desegregation of public transportation. Only 40 percent in the North and 2 percent in the South favored desegregation of the public schools (Hyman and Sheatsley, 1964).

In 1963 and 1970, the center adopted a modified Bogardus technique to secure information on social distance norms (Greeley and Sheatsley, 1971). That period spans the first prominence of the civil rights movement in the South, the subsequent rise of more militant Black Power groups within the black movement, and incidents of mass protest associated with race relations in 126 U.S. cities—75 of them officially classified as "major" (Philadelphia *Inquirer,* January 7, 1968).

The survey results show that by 1970, 88 percent of the nationwide white sample accepted desegregation of public transportation; over 80 percent accepted desegregation of parks, restaurants, and hotels; and

75 percent favored school desegregation. Increasingly more intimate social contacts followed: Over 50 percent said they would *not* "object strongly" if a family member wanted to "bring a Negro friend home to dinner" (which is hardly the same as a welcome). Nearly 50 percent *disagreed* that "white people have a right to keep Negroes out of their neighborhoods if they want to, and Negroes should respect that right." About the same proportion *disagreed* that "there should be laws against marriages between Negroes and whites." All of these percentages represent an increase over those obtained in 1963, both in the North and in the South. Yet one cannot help but reflect how carefully these items were worded to "protect" white "sensibilities" and privilege in defining their own "privacy."

The final question was perhaps the most interesting: Would you agree that "Negroes shouldn't push themselves where they're not wanted?" In 1963, 75 percent of the white sample agreed with that statement and, by 1970, about 80 percent agreed with it. Perhaps some of them justified their agreement in terms of etiquette: Isn't it a norm for human conduct that "no one should push themselves in where they're not wanted?" In fact, that is a norm against "intruders" into an "ingroup."

I am saddened by the collapse of white pretensions at being "fairminded" when given a loophole like that question. I can remember not being wanted as a woman in activities some men thought were not "my place." So I wish that I could ask the 80 percent who agreed that "Negroes shouldn't push themselves where they're not wanted" just what kind of "privacy" for self they were protecting. Were blacks welcomed into the buses of Montgomery, Alabama, side by side with whites? Was the red carpet rolled out for black children after federal decisions desegregated white schools in 1954? Were the college freshmen who sat for hours at the lunch counter at the Woolworth store in Greensboro, North Carolina, without being served "pushing themselves where they're not wanted?" Can you recall any change in social arrangements for living that did *not* involve someone being where "they're not wanted?"

Young people under 25 were apparently more susceptible than others in the nationwide sample to such reflections. Slightly over 40 percent of them rejected the proposition in 1963. However, the percentage rejecting it among white young people *declined* by 1970, along with that for every other age group, size of community, income level, educational level, and religion (Greeley and Sheatsley, 1971).

WHAT DIFFERENCES AMONG PEOPLE BECOME IMPORTANT?

In the study of how we see things, one of the most common pitfalls was called the "stimulus error" by early psychologists. The "stimulus error" consists of trying to "explain" *how* we see something by *describing what* we are looking at. It is a treacherous error in the study of social perception. Our most immediate experience is that we observe a person with certain physical features, who expresses certain ideas and acts in such and such a way. We are likely to conclude that we respond as we do *because* the person *possesses* those characteristics.

In fact, such observations of the other individual tell us about that person's *social classification relative to* our own. Similarities symbolize common reference groups, and those similarities are more important for us than merely matching one another in terms of skin color, eye shape, or an isolated idea. Differences may signal fundamental conflicts between the vital and the selfish interests of our respective peoples, historically or at present.

Just what similarities or differences among people are emphasized as the basis for defining "my kind of people" and those to be kept distant? They vary historically and from one society to the next. The emphasis can change relatively quickly as societies change or as social movements emerge. For example, Dodd (1935) reported that religious differences were a primary basis for social distances in Lebanon some forty years ago. Less than two decades later, Prothro and Melikian (1952) found that students at the same university discriminated instead on the basis of nationality, a shift reflecting the rise of Arab and other nationalisms in the interim. The one clear conclusion from research is that *any* detectable differences between members of different groups can become signals for hostility when their groups are engaged in conflicting relationships (see Sherif and Sherif, 1953; Sherif, 1966; LeVine and Campbell, 1972).

Triandis and Triandis (1960, 1962, 1965) compared the social distance preferences of college students in the United States, Greece, West Germany, and Japan to determine the group differences that received greater emphasis in these countries. They chose four social criteria that might affect social distance responses—namely, race (for example, Negro-white), nationality, religion (same or different from one's own and socioeconomic rank (represented as occupations with high or lower status). They composed a series of very short descriptions of persons by varying the four characteristics systematically. For example, one description was a "Portuguese white physician of the same religion as you." The Portuguese physician appeared later in the list with a different religion, then as a Portuguese black physician of the same religion or a different religion. The same combinations were made with occupation changed to truck driver. Finally, another nationality was inserted and separate descriptions were composed by varying race, religion, and occupation.

Each student indicated willingness to associate or not with the person described in ten role relationships (from "I would marry" to extreme social distance). Suppose, for example, that a U.S. student accepted a white American physician of the same religion to marriage, while accepting a Negro American physician of the same religion no closer than as resident in the same apartment house. The same student permitted a white unskilled laborer of the same religion as "close kin by marriage," but wanted no contact at all with a Negro unskilled laborer of the same religion. The student was responding to occupational differences consistently, but it is easy to see that the racial label was the more salient.

By making such comparisons, Triandis and Triandis (1965) found that U.S. students stood out like sore thumbs from those in other countries in the importance they accorded to race. In Greece, religion was emphasized more than race, which was followed by occupation and nationality. German students emphasized occupational level, followed by religion, race, and nationality. Japanese students responded first to the person's occupational level, then to race, followed by nationality, with religion receiving least emphasis.

These findings do not mean that there are no racists in West Germany or religious bigots in the United States. In fact, during the 1950s, white college students in the North and South revealed that conformity to a belief in God could be more important than whether a person was black or white (Rokeach, Smith, and Evans, in Rokeach, 1960). The data were collected following that period in American history often called the "McCarthy era." Belief in God had been linked with being a patriotic American, and "atheist" had become a bad word associated with "Godless communism" through an unprecedented use of mass media (including television). The students were given a series of descriptions composed only of a person's race ("Negro," "white person") and religious beliefs ("believes in God," "atheist") in several combinations. A student rated each as to the *probability* of being friends with that person. It was hardly surprising that the probability was higher for a God-loving Negro than any kind of atheist.

I have always had great difficulty in understanding why Milton Rokeach felt that his findings supported his passionate belief that "man" has a "basic psychological predisposition . . . to organize the world of human beings in terms of the principle of belief congruence" (1961, p. 187). Having lived through the period in which those data were collected, I recall how many public exposures, witch-hunts, trials, and persecutions of innocent people were necessary to produce a generation of college students who believed that atheists were pariahs. A great deal of political and economic power contributed to the organization of that "congruence in belief."

Apparently willing to believe that the United States is a racist society, but not that individual white Americans had racist beliefs, Rokeach (1961, 1966) took issue with the Triandis' research showing that U.S. students discriminated according to racial classification. I think that fifty years from now the controversy will be regarded as a tempest in social psychology's teapot.

The evidence to date is clear that the research subjects (mostly white college students) respond to the social situation in which the decision is made. In institutional settings prohibiting segregation both legally and normatively (for example, in a university or public hospital), white subjects were asked to select two partners from two black and two white individuals. One of each race had agreed and one had disagreed with the subject in a discussion on topics unrelated to race. Nearly all subjects selected *desegregated pairs,* also including at least one person who had been agreeable enough to support them previously in the discussion (Rokeach and Mezei, 1966; see Dawes, 1972, pp. 128–129). In research situations where their opinions are solicited on paper-and-pencil tasks for "eyes only" of researchers, white students on the whole avoid racial differences in favor of other available criteria (see, for example, Stein, Hardyck, and Smith, 1965; Hendrick, Bixenstine, and Hawkins, 1971). The students expect researchers to disdain a racial preference and they make more "socially desirable" responses.

However, when increasingly intimate associations are suggested, racial membership becomes salient to white students, who often discriminate despite researchers' norms (Triandis and Davis, 1965; Hendrick et al., 1971; Goldstein and Davis, 1972). Somewhat similarly, whether a black confederate of the experimenter influences a white student's judgments in an Asch-type set-up depends on how intimate or personal the matter is that is being judged, being *least* when personal identity is at stake (Boyanowsky and Allen, 1973). All of these findings make sense if we keep in mind that students attend to differences in social situations as well as to the "presentation" of self.

WHAT KINDS OF BEHAVIOR MAKE
ROLE RELATIONSHIPS "INTIMATE"?

By securing judgments on how intimate or how distant certain role relationships were considered, Triandis and Triandis (1965) found that those listed on a Bogardus-type social distance test are not ordered universally in the same way. For example, "a family friend" in Greece was considered a quite intimate relationship, more so than a "close kin by marriage." But, in the United States, a family friend was judged as only slightly more intimate than being a neighbor, both of which represented greater social distance than a "close kin by marriage."

Triandis (1967) has done yeoman's work in comparing the sort of behaviors associated with different kinds of interpersonal relationships in several cultures. Using composite descriptions of people that vary their social characteristics of the kind described earlier (for example, nationality, religion, sex, occupation), he has collected data from several cultures indicating the kinds of behaviors that are considered appropriate with various people. Some of these are common across cultures, but there are important differences between cultures as well.

Generally speaking, the two most intimate role relationships pertained to persons with social characteristics (socioeconomic status, race, religion) as nearly like self as possible, with one difference: sex of the other person. *Interpersonal intimacy with sexual intent* included such relations as falling in love, serious dating, physically loving, or marrying. The intimacy of *friends* as near equals (being a partner with, eating with, gossiping with, accepting or giving a favor, being a close friend, and so on) was largely reserved for the same sex.

A cluster of behaviors that Triandis called *respect* had to do with deference given a person with high status in one's own reference group. In addition, he found role relationships implying important status differences in society: Triandis called these *superordination*, meaning *authority* to command, reprimand, and so on, with its reciprocal actions indicating *subordination*, deference, and, in some societies, attempts to gain acceptance by "superiors." He suggested that "social distance" amounted to excluding a person successively from each of the foregoing degrees of intimacy and confining the person to the subordinate role in authority relations.

If you will look back at the Bogardus items early in this chapter, you will see that only the first two items (marry and "close friend") imply much intimacy. There is a great distance between the intimacy of friends and simply having someone as a neighbor, particularly today. Triandis' work suggests how narrow a range of people is included within intimate give-and-take and the gaps between people that social distance implies. Similar attitudes and values are likely to arise within the narrow range defined as "us." The vast body of research demonstrating the greater likelihood that persons with similar attitudes and values are mutually attracted to one another has to be interpreted within that framework (see, for example, Byrne, Ervin, and Lamberth, 1970).

Many college students these days, as well as other Americans, are keenly aware of problems imposed on them by what Triandis called superordination or authority relations. To many, these become less and less intimate, more and more impersonal—even faceless—as they proceed into the large educational, work, and political institutions of modern life. Add to such problems those of *exclusion* according to one's racial or ethnic origins, socioeconomic background, sex, political beliefs, or life style. Then the full impact of research findings on social distance will become more vivid.

ATTITUDES TOWARD "OTHER KINDS" AND
THE PSYCHOLOGY OF SOCIAL JUDGMENT

In order to act in ways indicating differential intimacy with or distance from others, a person has to make comparisons, decisions, or choices— in short, social judgments of others and the situations in which they are encountered. One of the most general and well-established principles in psychology is as follows: When stimuli (including nonsocial kinds) are judged as belonging in the *same category* in some important respect, they are viewed henceforth as *more similar* to one another in a variety of *other* respects than to stimuli placed in a different category. In fact, differences between stimuli placed in different categories are exaggerated (see Brown, 1965; Bruner, 1957; Tajfel, 1959; Eiser and Stroebe, 1972).

The principle holds in judgments of other people. For example, Secord (1959) had prejudiced whites judge the personal characteristics of individuals in photographs whose physical appearance (skin color, features, and so on) ranged from Negro to Caucasian. The striking result was that, despite the physical differences, those faces categorized by the whites as "Negro" were assigned personal characteristics composing the then-conventional Negro stereotype. The findings indicate a categorizing process, not merely a bit of confusion engendered by overgeneralizing from one's perception of one black-skinned person to the next. The traits were attributed just about equally to all faces *labeled* Negro, dropping off entirely for faces labeled white. Tajfel, Sheikh, and Gardner (1964) reported similar minimization of differences within a category and emphasis on differences between categories in a study dealing with Canadians and Indians.

Consider now a set of social categories for people in one's own society and in other societies. There is at least one important difference between such categories and those used in classifying neutral stimuli such as weights, lines, rocks, or plants: One of the categories for people includes oneself and others within one's reference group. Inevitably, our personal investment in that category means that it will be used as an anchor in judging other people. Furthermore, our anchor category is defined in terms of our *relationships* with people in the other categories. What are some of the consequences?

First, we use the standards defining membership in our own category for sizing up other people. Whatever those criteria are, we react to similarities and differences of other people relative to them. We assimilate others judged similar in those terms, friendly in those terms, helpful in those terms, supportive in those terms. Differences between us and them are exaggerated and emphasized more as *their* aims, status, and activities become increasingly different from our own. In short, the use of our own category as anchor results in assimilation-contrast effects in our judgments of the others' characteristics, behaviors, values, and purposes.

Second, to the degree that our own category becomes the exclusive anchor in sizing up others, all other people and the characteristics attributed to them are divided into those assimilable to our own and those unlike it, *period*. Such sharp division into "those who are for us" and "those who are against us" is considered paranoid if it occurs *within* the bounds of our own groups. Across group lines, such division of humanity into those "like us" and those "beyond the pale," hence beyond our own morality, is not so unusual as to be bizarre. This is what racism, ethnocentrism, class hatred, religious bigotry, or sexism is all about. Labeled as "misguided" or "overzealous loyalty," a similar phenomenon confronted the American public in 1973 when aides to the President of the United States testified to criminal acts committed, they said, because anyone opposing the White House came to be seen as "enemy" against whom extraordinary measures appeared justified in their eyes.

Third, since judgment is always relative both to the anchor we use and to the people being judged at a particular time, it follows that we react quite differently to the *same* people depending on the context in which they are considered. In a study of high school students' own categories in judging ethnic groups (1961), I found that they became highly discriminating whe all of the groups being judged were, in fact, fairly similar and acceptable to their own. When the same groups were judged in the context of an equal number of quite different groups, however, the same groups were viewed as much more similar. In short, what we call "similar" on a given occasion depends in part on how great a range of differences we consider at the time. Conversely, if we are confronted by a choice between a few groups whom we have categorized as thoroughly detestable, the *least* detestable group is judged more favorably than would have been the case otherwise (see, for example, Diab, 1963 a, b).

The advantage of viewing attitudes toward other persons as embodying a set of evaluative categories defining "our" relationships to "them" is that a variety of otherwise puzzling reactions start to make sense. The category including self and one's reference set establishes the premises for the way our other categories "carve and slice" the rest of humanity. Understanding these premises is essential for understanding our feelings about others and the traits we attribute to them.

REFERENCE GROUP PREMISES AND HOW PEOPLES ARE CATEGORIZED

A study using procedures similar to the Own Categories technique reveals quite a bit about premises for social distance in the United

States. Jones and Ashmore (1973) asked Rutgers University students to sort 50 cards, each bearing the name of a national, racial, or religious group, according to *similarities* among the groups within each category they constructed. Any number of categories could be used. In addition, another sample of students rated each group on semantic differential scales (Chapter 9). Their ratings supplied some of the labels given to the premises discovered through analysis of the similarity judgments. (The labels will be given with their findings on similarity.)

Analysis of the students' categorizations focused on how frequently a particular group was placed into the same category as each other group. By determining these relative frequencies, the researchers were able to specify "clusters" of groups reflecting the premises the students had used in constructing their own categories.

The students were at no time asked for their own *preferences*, but only for similarity judgments. Therefore it is significant that the clusters obtained bear striking resemblance to those in a factor analysis of Bogardus 1966 data on social distance (Ames and Sakuma, 1969). Although cluster analysis gave no order of preference, I will list them in the Bogardus preference order, indicating representative groups included in each cluster. Note that the clusters are not merely geographic:

Anglo-Saxons (English, Irish, Scots, Canadians, and *Americans!*)
Western Europeans (French, Italians, Germans)
Eastern Europeans (Armenians, Greeks, Russians, Poles)
Spanish (Spaniards, Mexicans, Cubans, Brazilians)
Middle Eastern (Israelis, Arabs, Turks)
Orientals (Indians-Asians, Japanese, Chinese, Indonesians)
Dark-skinned (American Negroes, American Indians, Ethiopians, and
    so on)

In addition, one cluster was composed of Baptists, Catholics, Jews, and Quakers, usually categorized together as native religions.

It is important to note that not all students put the 50 groups in these general "clusters" consistently. For example, a student might categorize the French or Germans with other groups in the "Anglo-Saxon" cluster. Or, a student might put Russians and Cubans in the same category. By analyzing such variabilities in putting groups together, Jones and Ashmore attempted to specify several premises used in making the Own Categories.

At the most abstract level, the students divided the groups into two broad classes as "Western" or "non-Western" cultures, which was statistically synonymous with the criterion "economically advanced" or "underdeveloped" (p. 432). Next, the students distinguished reliably between "communist-noncommunist" groups. Thus, for example, East Germans might be grouped with Russians, rather than with West

Germans and Dutch in the Western European cluster. The researchers called the next basis for distinctions "Christian–non-Christian," but it was statistically synonymous with "good-bad." This may explain why Israelis were often differentiated from other Middle Eastern peoples on this premise. Finally, within these divisions, students persistently differentiated between groups according to skin color, for example between Chinese and Indians-Asians within the Oriental cluster.

The students' categories reflect the premises of the most technologically developed country in the world, which has waged cold wars with communist countries and hot wars in "underdeveloped" countries while struggling for supremacy over other such "lowly" peoples (some Spanish, some Oriental, some dark-skinned) as well as their own minority populations. I have the distinct impression that these premises for "similarity" are precisely what some people in other countries object to when they see American treatment as exploitive and racist. The racism is not revealed merely in a dark-skinned category but also in others (for example, Oriental). The resemblance to the social distance norms strongly suggests that these are premises based on "superiority" doctrine.

Personal Involvement in Ethnic Identity and Social Distance

There is a widely shared notion that social distance from others is a direct outcome of high personal involvement in one's own group, thereby "explaining" norms for social distance in terms of loyalty to one's own group (see LeVine and Campbell, 1972, for discussion of several versions of this notion). The notion can be examined by comparing the social distance preferences of groups whose members differ with respect to the degree of their personal involvement in their own group.

Joan Heller Rollins (1973) made such a test in Rhode Island, a small state with a diversity of ethnic and national groups. She selected 120 students who were all second-generation Americans with four grandparents born in Poland, Italy, Ireland, Canada (French Canadian), Portugal, an eastern European country (Jewish), or four grandparents with Anglo-Saxon last names of protestant religion born in the United States ("Yankees"). Rollins thought that such "pure" cases would be likely to think of themselves as "hyphenated Americans." Students from each select background sorted statements concerning the social status of their own ethnic groups using the Own Categories technique. Rollins counted the number of categories used as a measure of degree of involvement in one's own group, fewer categories indicating higher involvement (see Chapter 9). In addition, each student responded to a Bogardus-type social distance test relative to each of the other groups.

There was no relationship between involvement in the status of one's own group and the amount of social distance accorded to the other groups. In fact, the Portuguese-Americans (most involved) accorded less social distance to other groups than any group excepting the Irish Americans (least involved). Rollins found almost the reverse relationship: High involvement in the status of one's own group was associated with greater social distance accorded to one's group *by the others.*

Individuals using the fewest categories in judging their own group's status were accorded the *most* social distance by the others. (The correlation between the two was negative, therefore: −0.77.) The least involved group members (Irish) received the least social distance from others. The most involved group members (Portuguese) were accorded considerable social distance from others, a response reflecting their very low status in the eyes of other groups.

The Portuguese situation may be compared, perhaps, with that of black Americans until fairly recently. The low status accorded by whites meant that most of them were highly involved in their group's status; however, they did not reciprocate in large numbers by according great social distance to high-prestige whites. The increasing minority of black Americans who prefer separatism from all whites is a product of certain factions in the black social movement, rather than an inevitable outcome of high levels of identification with one's group. Social distance norms are an outgrowth *of relations between groups,* not simply a "natural" outgrowth of "consciousness of kind."

Personal Involvement in Intergroup interactions and Social Distance

The civil rights movement of the sixties raised many questions about how black students reacted to interacting with whites. Within that context, we had the opportunity in 1966 and 1967 to study how black students sized up interracial encounters on the college campus. We asked them to judge how advisable or inadvisable it was for a black student to interact with whites in a variety of different situations (Sherif, 1973). The situations ranged from highly formal contacts in classroom and other institutional settings to highly informal and more intimate interactions with white peers of the same and opposite sex. The opportunity arose primarily through the collaboration of the sociologist Estella Scott Johnson and her students and of two graduate students, Edith Grey and Ken Roy.

The hypothesis was quite simple: I predicted that personal involvement in black-white interactions would be greatest for those black students who were *least* insulated from them socially. Accordingly, I expected members of black social fraternities and sororities to be less involved than unaffiliated "independents" and more hair-splitting about what was advisable and what was not. Furthermore, I thought that men would be more involved than women, simply because women in general were more restricted in their social encounters than men. Finally, I compared students on the campus of the Pennsylvania State University, which had very few black students at that time, with those at Cheyney State College, a predominantly black institution, thinking that the latter were more "insulated." As it turned out, the overall differences between samples on the two campuses were not statistically significant, largely because the differences between fraternity members and independents and between men and women were so great on the Penn State campus.

Using the Own Categories technique, we asked each student to sort 50 brief scenarios describing black-white contacts. The situations described were collected through interviews by Edith Grey from black students themselves. Each scenario was incomplete in that it required a decision by a black student as to whether or not to continue interacting with the whites in the situation. The student's task was to sort the scenarios into any number of piles needed, in terms of how advisable it would be for the black student to continue interaction, so that scenarios within each pile were about equally advisable or inadvisable.

For example, one scenario read as follows: "A black student has a white roommate who is friendly and congenial. Just before Dad's Day when their fathers are coming to see their room, he suggests that they take turns showing the room to their fathers, since his father doesn't know that his roommate is black. The Dad's Day schedule allows only half an hour for room visits." Black students agreed that the student should not interact with that white roommate.

The scenarios were made equivalent for the male and female students (total 315) by changing sex of other participants and obvious sex-related descriptions (for example, Dad's Day was changed to Mother's Day). Incidentally, we found that, for these black students, the decision to interact or not had very little to do with how formal or how personal the role relations with whites were in the scenarios. Instead, their major standard was how the whites in the scenarios behaved. Quite intimate role relations were viewed as advisable if the whites revealed nondiscriminatory and nonracist attitudes. The sole exceptions were (1) for heterosexual interactions with whites leading to intimacy, for which judgments were highly variable, with women's implying greater social distance than men's; and (2) for interacting with whites to the neglect of black associates or for status-seeking in white campus organizations at the expense of less participation with other blacks.

The main findings confirmed expectations, in that independent students used fewer categories and were less noncommittal in their judgments than fraternity members. Males were more involved than females by the same measures. The contrast was greatest on the large state university campus where independent males, on the average, used only 2.8 categories for the 50 scenarios, but fraternity males used 4.7 categories. Similarly, independent women used 3.5 categories on the average, and sorority members used 5.6 categories. More categories were accompanied by more noncommitment in evaluating the scenarios. On the small college campus, noncommitment was particularly high. Although independents and fraternity members and males and females differed significantly as predicted, the differences among them were smaller there than at the large university.

What did this mean? Members of fraternities and particularly of the sororities were insulated from black-white interactions by their groups and prone to distinguish finer gradations of appropriate social distance from whites than the independents. The latter (men even more than women) had formed quite clear-cut criteria for choice: Some interactions were clearly acceptable, a few suggested need for caution, and the rest were simply not to be pursued. Interestingly enough, it was chiefly males and independent students, rather than fraternity-sorority members, who organized the first meetings of the Black movement on the university campus the year after our research, requesting white students to stay away. When reverberations of the Black movement hit the small, predominantly black college, student action was directed primarily against its own black administration rather than black-white problems.

White university students asked to sort the scenarios as if they were black had great difficulty in doing so. Typically they used quite a few categories (4 to 5 on the average) and were more noncommittal than black university students. Their reactions were in marked contrast to those of the white students studied later by Charlene Wenckowski (1973) for her honor's thesis, when there were more black students on the campus and an Equal Opportunity Program supporting some of them. She revised the scenarios to bring them up to date. White students significantly underestimated the frequency of situations where black students, actually, had indicated great uncertainty as to whether interracial interaction was advisable. On the other hand, for those situations where they correctly estimated black students as judging "advisable" or "inadvisable," the white students significantly underestimated the *intensity* of the black students' responses. In short, to white students, the black students appeared more certain and decisive than they were on some issues. At the same time, white students failed to appreciate how strongly black students reacted on others.

ATTRIBUTING TRAITS TO "THOSE OTHERS": SOCIAL STEREOTYPES

The "reasons" given by members of one group for their relationships with others almost always have to do with the others' "character," their personal traits, or their behavior. As we learned in Chapter 7, such attribution of *cause* to others is not confined to intergroup or interset relations. When particular traits applicable to most or all of the individuals in a social category are standardized, then (and only then) are we justified in calling such attributions "social stereotypes."

The attribution process can and does occur in the absence of consensus among individuals as to which traits are assigned to others. When consensus on details is lacking, it may still be that the various individual members attribute traits that are chiefly positive or chiefly negative in affective tone. They are pleasant or nasty, while varying in details. Thus it is entirely possible to have a favorable or an unfavorable attitude toward others without a clear social stereotype.

Research findings support the above conclusions, which have major importance for our understanding of attitudes: Contrary to some theories and to some practical efforts to change attitudes, attributions to others are not the basic "causes" of negative attitudes or of discriminatory actions. Psychologically, the basic processes involve categorizing others into social classifications whose premises make unfavorable comparisons inevitable. Such classifications arise when one set of people seeks to dominate, to subdue, to exploit, to vanquish, or to claim greater merit than another set of people. Once achieved, the classifications are handed down to newcomers, who can readily discover for themselves the "reality" of the *relationship* by their own observations. If consensus on a social stereotype has also been achieved during the interactions, its attribution to others aids in "explaining" and maintaining the relationship. *They* are to blame.

How Have Stereotypes Been Studied?

Two general methods have been used for studying stereotypes. One stems from the early studies by Daniel Katz and K. W. Braly (1933, 1935) at Princeton University. They presented a list of adjectives or traits (for example, "happy-go-lucky"), then asked students to choose five that were most appropriate for each group on a list. The other method is closely related to the semantic differential technique (see Chapter 9). A group or category name is presented, and the person is asked to rate that group or category on a series of scales. Each scale consists of a pair of bipolar adjectives (good–bad, strong–weak, very emotional–not at all emotional, clean–dirty, and so on). The person indicates how much or in what degree one or the other adjective characterizes the people in question. Alternatively, rating scales may consist of single adjectives, with the request for ratings of how much or how strongly one agrees that each adjective applies to the group, or of how many members it is characteristic (for example, "all of them"–"none").

The findings are usually presented in terms of the percentage of a given sample who choose a given adjective for the same group or make particular ratings on the adjective scales. Average ratings are also used. As noted above, we have no business calling a pattern of such attributions a "social stereotype" unless persons in the sample agree significantly in their choice of adjectives or in their ratings. Researchers have been careless at times in establishing rules for deciding when there is consensus and when there is not. The few who have looked for consensus in terms of the number of *individuals* who agreed in attributing a *particular configuration* of adjectives to others have not always found consensus. For example, Ehrlich and van Tubergen (1971) reported that they found three distinct configurations of consensual traits attributed to Jews in a sample of 91 business school students. About half of the same sample displayed one of two consistent stereotype patterns for atheists, and 43 selected attributes in individually unique patterns.

Some Puzzles About Social Stereotypes

I am resisting the temptation to regale you with tales of the particular images such and such a group has of so and so. Such lists are readily available (Ehrlich, 1973). While the reference just cited is an exception, I am struck by the misleading and sometimes erroneous conclusions drawn about stereotypes in textbooks. It is important to clear up a couple of them.

Are Stereotyped Images More Likely for Unfamiliar Groups?

The conclusion is sometimes offered that stereotyped images form in the *absence of information* or face-to-face encounters with others. It would follow that traits attributed to unfamiliar peoples should be agreed on as frequently as traits attributed to familiar groups, if not more. In fact, one recent book attributes the following finding to Katz and Braly's early study: "For groups actually quite unknown, such as the Turks and the Japanese, there were as vivid stereotypes of as high consensus as there were for more familiar groups such as American Negroes" (LeVine and Campbell, 1972, p. 168).

Katz and Braly (1933, 1935) reported the percentages of Princeton students choosing given adjectives to describe each group. Their procedures were repeated at Princeton later by Gilbert (1951) and by Karlins, Coffman, and Walters (1969). In none of this research was consensus on traits selected to describe Turks or Japanese anywhere the equivalent of that for Negroes. The highest consensus was in 1933. The highest percentage agreement for Turks was 47 percent ("cruel") and no other single trait was accepted by more than 26 percent. The highest agreement for Japanese was on "intelligent" (45 percent) and "industrious" (43 percent, which increased to 57 percent in 1967); no other agreement exceeded 24 percent of the students. Agreement on attributions to

Negroes in 1933 exceeded 75 percent on two traits ("superstitious," "lazy") and was consistently higher for other traits than agreement on Turks or Japanese.

Another way of looking at how "vivid" or crystallized the stereotypes were is to count the number of *different* adjectives that account for one-half of the choices made by the students, each of whom chose 5 adjectives. This rough index of consensus also fails to support the notion that unfamiliar groups were stereotyped as vividly as familiar groups. In 1933, a minimum of 4.6 adjectives accounted for half the total choices made regarding Negroes and 5.5 for Jews, another familiar group. For Turks, the index was 15.9 in 1933, 32.0 in 1951, and 25.6 in 1967 (Karlins et al., 1969). A "vivid" stereotype would include fewer adjectives.

Looking at other research, I find no evidence contrary to the conclusion that *consensual* stereotyped attributions are *more* likely for *familiar* groups than unfamiliar ones. The highly consensual stereotypes attributed by the sexes to their own and the other sex also support such a conclusion.

Despite low consensus and uniformity in trait attribution to Turks, Karlins et al. (1969) regarded the "greatest enigma in these three related studies" at Princeton to be "the persistence with which the subjects have harshly characterized the Turks" (p. 8). Apparently, despite low agreement on *particular* adjectives, the Princeton students did agree that anything to be attributed to Turks should be nasty, as one might expect for a group so low in the order of preference on the Bogardus social distance scale. It is possible to hold an unfavorable attitude toward a group without necessarily entertaining a consensual social stereotype of traits attributed to them.

Do Stereotyped Traits Reflect How Favorable-Unfavorable Our Attitude Is?

Ehrlich (1973) treated stereotypes as "cognitive" components of attitudes, that is, "beliefs about" people, whereas Triandis (1967) treated them as "affective" components. If the traits attributed to a group mirror our evaluations of them, both are correct. The probable reason for confusion on this question is that no satisfactory method has been devised to assess how favorable or unfavorable a stereotype is, taken as a whole. The same separate "trait" may be favorable when applied to "our own kind" and "unfavorable" applied to "them" (see Vinacke, 1956).

The Katz-Braly research (1935) had students rate how favorable or unfavorable each trait, by itself, would be when used to describe a friend. Karlins et al. (1969) asked for similar individual ratings of adjectives "as normally used to describe people." In both studies, the favorableness of a stereotype was computed simply as an average of all the ratings given to adjectives that students attributed to a group. The outcome was rather strange at times: For example, the stereotype of Negroes in the Karlins et al. study came out with a favorability rating of nearly zero, when actually it included both positive and negative attributions. The average favorability ratings for Japanese, Germans, and Jews were all higher than those for English or Americans. Yet it is possible that many individuals who rated those groups included a single negative trait that achieved little weight in the average. For example, it is one thing to believe Germans are "ambitious, industrious, efficient, intelligent" (as the students did) and quite another to add to this list a trait like "conceited" or "treacherous." The composite image appears different.

As we learned in Chapter 2, personal qualities attributed to others are not merely a serial list of discrete traits. Some traits (for example, "warm" or "cold") serve as anchors to others, affecting their meaning and hence their favorableness. Vinacke (1956) pointed to the need for assessing the favorableness of total configurations, but not much has been done about it. On the other hand, Centers (1951) gave trait lists attributed by Princeton students to students at the University of California (Los Angeles), asking them to "guess who" each list described. He found that the great majority of California students could match the groups and trait lists correctly. Seventy-five percent correctly recognized the 1933 attributions to Japanese, Chinese, and Turks, and 95 percent correctly identified those of English and Jews. Since percentages agreeing on trait attributions are much lower, the California students must have been able to detect key traits and affective tone that guided their correct identifications. For example, the single adjective "cruel" could have anchored their recognition of Turks.

What all of this means is that stereotype attributions *by themselves* are quite poor signs of favorableness-unfavorableness of attitude at present, owing to "technical difficulties." However, if we look at the order of groups according to social distance preferences, we can certainly conclude that in general we attribute much nicer qualities to those we invite to intimacy than to those we keep at arm's length.

Does Firsthand Contact Change Group Stereotypes?

This question is obviously related to the first one about familiarity, but here we have some evidence on different amounts or kinds of face-to-face dealings among people. I should preface it by noting that there have been numerous studies on the kinds of contacts between racial groups in the United States associated with more favorable attitudes on the part of whites (see Williams, 1964). While those studies did not concentrate on stereotypes, they seem to show that the most propitious circumstances for intergroup contacts involve associations as equals, particularly when members of the respective groups work toward a common goal (see Chapter 5).

A great difficulty in comparing stereotyped attributions among people with differing amounts of contact is that there is seldom any way to equate their attitudes before contact begins. Triandis and Vassiliou (1967) compared American stereotypes of Greeks among samples of Americans with little or no contact (students in Illinois), with medium contact (U.S. servicemen in Greece), and high contact (U.S. officials and businessmen in Greece). The Americans with medium and especially high contact had much more consensual and negative stereotypes of Greeks than American college students. The U.S. officials and businessmen regarded the Greeks as "bad coworkers" and attributed other characteristics indicating dissatisfaction with their Greek subordinates. The Greek counterparts—namely, those they worked with—saw Americans in turn as more "haughty" and "dogmatic." However, the Americans' experience with Greeks did one thing: It bolstered their own images of Americans way above that held by college students at home. (Or, perhaps, their image of Americans was more favorable to start with; we cannot know.)

Greek university students in Athens who had little contact with Americans had quite unfavorable images of Americans. The Greeks who worked for Americans had a better image, as did Greek students in the United States, However, it is entirely possible that the Greek students who came to the United States had a more favorable image at the outset.

Somewhat better controls for initial attitude were used in a study by Gardner, Taylor, and Santos (1969). They compared stereotype ratings attributed to Filipinos and to Filipino students by U.S. teachers who had not been in the Philippines with those attributed by teachers who went there for nine weeks and who made ratings at the beginning and end of their visit. The teachers in the Philippines lived with Filipino families of diverse socioeconomic status. It is to that considerable diversity of experience that the researchers attribute one principal finding: Consensus on traits attributed to Filipinos decreased significantly over the nine-week visit. Such changes did not occur for teachers who stayed in the United States. On the other hand, after teaching Filipino students, the teachers arrived at *greater* agreement in their attributions to students, reaching consensus on more traits and increasing the extremity of their ratings somewhat. In other words, their attributions (though favorable on the whole) were more stereotyped following their common experience teaching. For example, they saw students as significantly more religious, as poorer, as more emotional, but as somewhat less difficult students than they had at the outset.

The two studies together suggest that stereotypes do change with contact, in the direction of greater consensus if contact experiences are similar but toward decreased consensus when contacts differ considerably. The greater consensus was toward more negative stereotypes when attitudes were not favorable at the outset and toward qualified acceptance when they were favorable.

MUTUAL ACCEPTANCE OF STEREOTYPED TRAITS: THE REMARKABLE SEX CASE

If some people have a stereotyped image of another "kind of people" and the latter agree to that description of themselves, does that mean that the stereotype is "true"? Do such findings mean that they *do* act as described *because* they are "that kind" of people? The first question could be answered yes only if we could also have some independent account of how the people in question *actually* act. If indeed the stereotype represents at least part of the "truth," then we are ready for the second question. It is this "explanation" of behavior by stereotypes that I want to examine while presenting the remarkable case of mutual acceptance of stereotyped traits by the two sexes.

A team of researchers has summarized their respective efforts over the years in studying the trait attributions by the two sexes to their own sex and the other sex (Broverman, Vogel, Broverman, Clarkson, and Rosenkrantz, 1972). They reported a "strong consensus" on attributions considered typical and even ideal for men and women by both sexes. That means that men and women were in accord concerning their attributions to each sex. The consensus was found among college students, people of different ages, religions, marital statuses, and educational levels. Notably, mental health workers (psychiatrists, clinical psychologists) agreed with the attributions made by college students.

Both men and women attributed traits they regarded as favorable to their own and to the opposite sex. However, the cluster of attributes regarded as "male" was rated as more "socially desirable" and as more "healthy" by both students and mental health workers. In fact, when asked to rate a "normal, healthy, socially competent adult person" (without regard to sex), the psychiatrists and psychologists made ratings that closely resembled those they gave to an adult man.

The striking comparison between the stereotyped image of males and females, shared by both, turns on personal characteristics entailing competence, rationality, and assertive behaviors. These were reserved almost exclusively for males. More frequently than males, though not with exclusive possession rights, women were pictured in terms of personal warmth, gentleness, and expressiveness. The negativity and "unhealthiness" of the female stereotype reflect the additional finding that it is topheavy with traits such as "dependence," being "very submissive,'' "very excitable," "illogical," "sneaky," "easily hurt," and "lacking self-confidence."

Individuals whose mothers had worked did not emphasize the categorical differences between men and women as strongly. Cross-cultural comparisons by Jeanne Humphrey Block (1973) indicate that the sharp division in terms of competent assertive behaviors for men and dependent emotionalism for women is *not* as striking in some other societies (for example, Sweden) as in the United States.

Let us suppose that you set out to explain why a person behaved in ways that could be described as "dependent," "submissive," "excitable," "sneaky," "easily hurt," and "lacking self-confidence," though warm, gentle, and expressive. I should think that the first questions you would ask would be "on *whom* is this person dependent? To whom is she submissive? About *what* is she excitable? *When* and *whom* does she try to deceive? *Who* can easily hurt her? *When* does she lack self-confidence?" You would be looking for someone who takes responsibility for a dependent, someone with authority to whom she submits, someone who is so unresponsive to her wishes that she plots to fulfill them, someone whose word is important to her (hence who can hurt her), but does not support her attempts at activities other than those that express her warmth, gentleness, and expressiveness. Is that someone a man?

My point is that the social stereotypes of men and women in this country describe a *role relationship* in which the behaviors described (true or not) cannot occur independently of another person. The male traits that describe competence and assertiveness represent the value placed on man as a working creature responsible for others, but deemphasize activities at home that could make such responsibility and authority tolerable to another person. The female stereotype is negative because of its emphasis on dependence in a power relationship with men. Any competencies and responsibilities that women display simply do not appear in the stereotype, perhaps because they do not carry cash value.

Now back to the question raised earlier: Do these mutual stereotypes accepted by both men and women "explain" behavior by men or by women? Since the attributions refer to behavior that could not possibly occur apart from the role relationship between men and women, we really have not proved that males or females are "that kind of people." We have merely described a relationship, caricatured by its inordinate emphasis on males' awful responsibilities as "sole breadwinner" and female dependence in the power relationship. Although "trait" theories of behavior appear to be more sophisticated, they end up making similar attributions to individuals on the basis of behaviors that can occur only during interaction in human relationships. It is to the relationships *between* men and women that we must turn to understand their behavior, including that of agreeing on sex stereotypes.

Do "Victims" Accept Images Attributed by Aggressors?

In discussing research on this issue, as in that preceding on men and women, it is important to recognize that derogatory stereotypes are seldom *entirely* unfavorable (Erhlich, 1973; Karlins et al., 1969). The appearance of social stereotyping in children begins well *after* unfavorable categorization and the beginnings of social distance from others (Horowitz, 1936). At first they make wholesale use of unflattering adjectives, but the images are later "refined" by additions of a few "saving" traits that adult stereotypes usually include (see Blake and Dennis, 1943). Thus, when a "victim" accepts the attributions of an aggressor, a modicum of self-esteem may be guaranteed by selective emphasis on a "saving grace."

In his autobiography, Nehru (1941) wrote of being educated in the late nineteenth century "entirely from the British imperial viewpoint," where the numerous failings of the Indian people were contrasted to the "virtues and high destiny of the British." Most Indian intellectuals of that day, he wrote, accepted the British judgment. They assuaged their self-esteem by the sure knowledge that, at least, the Indians were superior to the British *spiritually*. Similarly, African children on the Gold Coast before independence described "natives" in the derogatory terms used by children of European colonialists, while speaking admiringly of the latter (Jahoda, 1961).

It is really not surprising, therefore, that only a few decades ago, research reported that black college students in the United States accepted the deprecatory stereotypes attributed to Negroes by whites, as well as some of the unfavorable stereotypes standardized in white society for other ethnic groups (Bayton, 1935; Meenes, 1943; Bayton and Byoune, 1947). To be sure, some of the students made it clear that they were rating "other Negroes"—not themselves, their teachers, or families to whom such terms as "lazy," "superstitious," and possibly "musical" did not apply.

Bayton, McAlister, and Hamer (1956) later asked white and black students to rate upper-class and lower-class Negroes, as well as upper-class and lower-class whites. The striking result was that both white and black students selected quite different configurations of traits for lower-class than for upper-class Negroes. Further, although frequencies of endorsing particular traits did differ, their ratings of lower-class Negroes were consensual and similar. (Negro students added that lower-class Negroes were "loud.") Negro students had more consensual stereotypes of lower-class whites than did the white students, whose level of agreement on any one trait did not exceed 20 percent.

The black sociologist Franklin Frazier (1957) had accused middle-class blacks of doing just what the Bayton et al. study revealed. The "Black Bourgeoisie," he wrote, accepted white, middle-class definitions of self while attributing to poor blacks the white stereotypes of Negroes. Thus, cut off from a black world, with which it was impossible to identify, and barred from the white middle class, the Black Bourgeoisie lived in a "world of make believe" without roots (p. 24).

In an address to the seventy-sixth annual convention of the American Psychological Association a few months before his assassination, Martin Luther King (1968) returned to the point: "There has been significant improvement from the days Frazier researched, but anyone knowledgeable about Negro life knows its middle class is not yet bearing its weight. Every riot has carried strong overtones of hostility of lower class Negroes toward the affluent Negro and vice versa. No contemporary study of scientific depth has totally studied this problem" (p. 183).

Since then, Minako Kuokawa Maykovich (1972) reported data from large samples of college students, adults, and school children in California that suggest considerable change in stereotypes on the part of both blacks and whites. Black students attributed such traits as "musical," "aggressive," and "straightforward" to blacks, a cluster also endorsed by white students, who added such negative traits as "grasping" and "revengeful." Black and Japanese-American students (particularly a group of political activists) agreed with white students in seeing whites as "materialistic, pleasure-loving, and aggressive," while adding negative characteristics such as "deceitfulness" and "conceit." The same trends in attribution were also found, though to lesser degree, for adults and elementary school students.

Maykovich's research also compared attributions to Japanese Americans by a sample of conventional students and a sample of activist Japanese-American students. Both samples attributed a stereotype that included "traditional, industrious, reserved, and quiet." However, unlike the conventional students, the activists rated these characteristics quite unfavorably. They disclaimed such an image for themselves, indicating that they hoped to change that kind of behavior on the part of other Japanese-Americans. The "thin line" between declaring oneself an "exception" to derogatory stereotypes and devoting oneself to changing the human relationships that give rise to the stereotype is actually a giant step in attitude change. Its importance may far exceed the psychological significance of the stereotyped views.

GLORIFYING STEREOTYPES INTO "SCIENTIFIC EXPLANATIONS"

Stereotyped images of other groups become standardized in a group to "explain" and, ideally, to justify what has been going on between them. A stereotyped image of one's own group need be no more "accurate," for its function is also to promote behaviors in accord with the values and practices of the group. In fact, what the "self" images held by different nationalities have in common is their favorable character (see Buchanan and Cantril, 1953; Hofstätter, 1957). I wonder why psychologists do not even bother to wonder whether *these* stereotypes are "true."

Coupled with a laudatory self-image, the attribution of unfavorable stereotypes to other groups or classes of people speaks to the exercise of power and to power struggles among people. The purposes of such stereotypes are not to compare human beings "objectively," but to "explain" one's own "superiority" and dominance. Past superiority doctrines have included almost every conceivable rationale for this purpose, including one's race.

As the anthropologist Ruth Benedict wrote: "The first lesson of history . . . is that when any group in power wishes to persecute or expropriate another group, it uses as justification reasons which are familiar and easily acceptable at the time" (1942, p. 41). In the modern world, "science" has become the familiar and prestigious reference for such purposes. Race doctrines have used "science" to elaborate stereotyped attributions through selective "facts" and jargon borrowed from biology or the social sciences. The same charge can readily be filed against male superiority doctrines, whether biological or sociological in construction. The issue is not whether groups or the sexes differ, but whether the differences justify racial or sexual dominance relations.

These are among the reasons that in studying attitudes toward other peoples, social stereotypes must be understood within the framework of invidious categorizations for people that reflect "our place" and "their place" in a larger scheme of human relationships. Stereotyped attributions are only part of the cognitive-affective structure of our attitudes, which, in turn, never "determine" our actions single-handedly, apart from the social environment. Unless we understand that environment, including the use of social power in human relationships, the study of attitudes has very little value in explaining behavior of human beings as they interact with one another.

Stability
and Change
of Attitudes
and Actions

These days, almost everyone wishes that it were possible to change someone *else's* attitude toward something. Naturally, it would also be nice if that could be accomplished fairly quickly and without very much effort. Perhaps this is one reason why many people are willing to believe that there are quick techniques to change a person's attitude. On the other hand, many people express a fear that someone will try to "change *me*," implying that there are also "dirty" techniques that can be used against their own wishes. Science fiction, horror movies, and tales from far-off lands abound in wonders accomplished by quick techniques for attitude change that are both "dirty" and "scientific."

There certainly are dirty techniques of attempting attitude change in this hard world, dirty in that they rely on extreme coercion, torture, imprisonment, and threat of death. However, there is nothing scientific about them. Most are not quick.

Social psychology has no magic techniques for changing someone else's attitudes—dirty, quick, or otherwise. In fact, I believe it unlikely that you or I will ever change anyone *else's* attitude single-handed. Other hands are needed, especially those of the person who has the attitude. Somewhere along the line, that person has to collaborate in the effort. In that sense, the person is changing himself or herself, quite as much as "being changed" by someone or something.

Let's remember what we are talking

about: Attitude change means change in those kinds of behavior from which we infer that a person has an attitude. These are among that person's more consistent, characteristic, and selective modes of behaving toward or away from (for or against) certain objects, persons, places, situations, institutions, social values, or other aspects of the social environment (Chapters 9 and 10). The only way that we can tell whether a person has changed an attitude is through changes in these kinds of behaviors (verbal and nonverbal). That is why, in the long run, it is futile to talk about attitude change apart from changes in the person's actions.

The next three chapters are about attitude change, and they are related. This chapter starts with the attempt to find out some of the ways that stability and change of attitudes are related to stability and change in the social environment. Within the context of social change, the rest of the chapter concerns research in which interactions among individuals is the context for attitude change. The next chapter concerns research on communications directed toward persons to change their attitudes when interaction with the communicator is not possible. Finally, Chapter 13 considers developing social movements as the context for attitude changes among participants and nonparticipants.

One word of caution before we start: There is a great deal of research in social psychology that carries the label "attitude change" that will not be included because it presented no clear evidence that the persons studied had attitudes in the first place, as defined above, or lacked evidence that changes observed were anything other than a *temporary adjustment of behavior or opinions* by the persons. If you explore the research literature further, you may find it useful to keep these two criteria for attitude change in mind. Much of the research that does not meet them becomes interesting when considered as studies of how a person sizes up a social situation, circumstances affecting the passing of an opinion, or the beginnings of attitude formation, instead of attitude change research. The confused state of affairs in the literature did not arise because an "honesty in labeling" agency was needed, but because of genuine confusion in the field about attitude measurement. As noted in Chapter 9, there has been widespread belief that anything measured by an "attitude scale" was an attitude. Unfortunately, that belief did not ensure that the persons in question had attitudes; therefore it represented a genuine obstacle to research on attitude change.

STABILITY AND CHANGE IN THE SOCIAL ENVIRONMENT

One way to grasp the magnitude of the problems involved in attitude change is to ask why attitudes and patterns of action do *not* change. When we look around the world, we cannot help being impressed by the regularity, stability, and persistence of the ways people conduct their daily affairs among themselves and in dealings with others. We are struck by the enduring devotion that we see to values, myths, ideals, and institutions (like the family). Differences between societies in these respects are striking, as they often are between groups, strata, and the sexes within the same society. The persistence of such differences is astonishing.

Such stability over time and persisting differences between peoples in different places reflect in part stability in the social environments of the people in question. Certainly the most significant condition for the stability of individual attitudes is a stable social environment.

It is fashionable to phrase the problem of attitude change as the converse: Behavior changes when the environment changes. Yet having said this, we have said rather little. Which parts of the social environment change and which do not? The environment can change quite a bit while people cling to old attitudes and patterns of acting. At times, resistance to change can be proportional to the onslaughts of environmental change. For example, the mother in Tennessee Williams' *The Glass Menagerie* still felt and acted the southern belle as she struggled in poverty to find security in the shape of a husband for her crippled, withdrawn daughter. Many an American visiting in another culture has returned feeling and acting more "American" than before the journey began. At times, a person clings to the past in order to feel "that I am still *me*."

Looking back a few generations, we can readily see that changes have occurred. In some countries, the difference between today and yesterday is so great that the present generation feels part of an entirely different world from that of their own parents. Such sharp breaks in outlook signal exceedingly rapid and sweeping social changes directly affecting at least part of the population, and particularly its youth. The scope and rate of social change are dramatic in some newly founded nations and in the wake of successful revolutionary overthrow of "old orders" (for example, in the Soviet Union after World War I, in other eastern European countries after World War II, and in Cuba or in China during the last twenty-five years).

It is customary to speak of the United States and many other countries as devoted to "evolutionary" change—that is, gradual change achieved through reforms, progressive shifts of emphasis, or increases in quantity or degree, rather than sharp and sudden breaks with the past. What actually happens within such a framework is that the rate of change differs enormously for different aspects of the social environment.

The "evolution" in work and the organization of work, in communicating, traveling, and other aspects of living produced by technological change in this country has created geographical, social, and psychological mobility on a scale that breaks sharply with the past. Changes in marriage customs and the family, in religious and educational institutions, in living arrangements, and in a host of values have not proceeded at a comparable pace. What we see instead is people trying to do the same or more of the same, with increased frequencies of failure. (For example, marriage is still a thriving institution; there are simply more divorces, remarriages, child desertions, and so on. The recent trend toward marriage contracts, being studied by the sociologist Marvin Sussman (1974), is a fascinating attempt to reform the institution from within.)

Let's look more closely at how stability and change in different parts of the social environment are related to problems of attitude change, starting with those in which change has been most rapid.

TECHNOLOGY AND THE RADIUS OF THE SELF-SYSTEM

Technology refers to the palpable physical tools and facilities, as well as the methods and techniques, that human beings use in work, keeping track of events in time, communicating, traveling for business or pleasure, and the varied activities of human living. Social psychologists have, by and large, neglected the study of how technologies affect human outlook and action or how their change promotes changes in attitudes. There are exceptions, however.

In Chapter 3, I mentioned research comparing the norms and attitudes of residents in five Turkish villages selected as increasingly remote from contact with modern technology (Sherif, 1948, pp. 369–401). In each village, residents were interviewed about what places and people were "near" or distant and "strange" and about what it meant to be poor or rich. In the most isolated villages, concepts of time and distance were highly imprecise. Attitudes toward what was distant and strange included almost every place and every person outside of walking distances. A few men who had been away in military service firmly believed that places to which they had walked were more distant than even more remote places they had reached by train. Most outsiders seemed incredibly wealthy because the villagers' conceptions of creature comfort were limited by the few possessions and crop surplus of the most fortunate in their own village.

Residents of villages increasingly in contact with the tools and products of modern technology lived (psychologically) in worlds encompassing an increasingly larger radius from home. In the least isolated village (a seacoast town), only "foreigners" were really strange to the residents. Their wants and desires also were much more varied than those of residents in the more isolated villages.

Lest you think that these findings are peculiar to the culture and religion of Turkish peasants, consider a similar comparison made by the psychologist Mandel Sherman and T. R. Henry about ten years earlier (1933). They studied four "hollow" communities and a small rural town in the Virginia mountains, less than 100 miles from Washington, D.C. In the most isolated hollow, the self radius of residents with respect to distances and outsiders was as restricted as in the most isolated Turkish village. Children in Colvin Hollow did not know different days of the week or holidays since "all days are practically alike" there (p. 135). When asked "What do you want to be when you grow up?" most children had no idea what was meant. When the question was explained, the usual answer was "I want to be what I am" (p. 104).

Sherman and Henry also found that the range of desires and the wants of Hollow residents increased from the most to the least isolated community. They attributed the differences to contact with modern technology, trade, and work methods. However, even if a resident *wanted* what the outside world had to offer, leaving the community was another matter. One literate man left Needles Hollow to work in a sawmill in West Virginia. He returned because there was "no gettin' up with a whistle and eating with a whistle here" (p. 196).

Sherif believes that material culture and technology, in particular, limit the radius within which the self-system is related to other people, things, and places in a variety of ways. The psychological "limits" are analogous to what happens when a person is asked in the psychological laboratory to judge a series of physical objects, weights, lengths of lines, or sound frequencies. The most extreme stimuli in the series (for example, lightest and heaviest) become anchors in judging the others in between (see Volkmann, 1951). The person develops a psychological reference "scale" over time that enables him or her to judge other objects between the extremes pretty accurately, on the whole. Such a "scale" is psycho*physical* in the sense that it reflects physical realities. However, one's reference scale is strongly anchored by the extremes of that particular series and is, in that sense, "limited."

In the laboratory, a person who has formed a psychophysical scale for judging a particular series has difficulties (makes errors) at first when the series of objects to be judged is changed or expanded. Nevertheless, after a lag, the person's reference scale adapts to the new series. Such relatively rapid adaptation to change in judgment of physical objects is analogous to that of persons exposed to new tools or means of transportation. Technological change often accomplishes tasks better or with less effort than means previously available, and the results can be observed directly.

Much of the social environment, however, is not as readily perceived and sized up as its technology. There are scales of values, of statuses (for example, of occupations or groups), of preferences (for example, for physical beauty or food) whose "reality" lies in social consensus among people (agreements) that we have learned over the years. These pertain to our intimate affairs (for example, treatment of others, sexual conduct, family responsibilities); to intergroup relations; to religious, legal, political, or other social beliefs. It is these aspects of society, psycho*social* scales, that change more slowly than its material culture through "evolutionary" process.

Technological Change and the Role of Persuasion

Much has been made of "resistance" to technological change, particularly by "backward" peoples confronted with changes proposed by technologically advanced nations. It is important to understand what such resistance is all about and when "persuasion" in the form of propaganda need not be necessary for attitude change. To an important degree, modern technology represents power, which explains both why new nations seek it so eagerly and why, at times, it is resisted.

There is evidence to support the analogy between a person's relatively quick adaptation of psychophysical scales and attitudes toward new technology when the innovation represents a more efficient or easier way to accomplish a familiar task. For example, no one has to tell a peasant struggling with an overloaded donkey that a truck can transport his goods to market more efficiently and with less effort. A sturdier, sharper steel tool is readily accepted to replace a wooden one (Foster, 1962). In such cases, seeing is believing.

Such acceptance of new technology can occur even though other attitudes do not change. Peasant women in an unusually successful new maternity hospital in Ecuador complained to researchers from the Smithsonian that the hospital forced them to eat foods, sleep with windows open, take daily baths, and clean their fingernails—all breaks in custom that they believed endangered their babies. Why, then, had they come to the hospital? Because, they said, they had seen that babies came from the hospital much healthier than those born at home (Foster, 1962, p. 237).

Olga Lang (1946) studied Chinese peasants who had "heard very little, if anything, of modern ideas" back in 1935–1937 when they were starting to work in modern industry in large numbers (p. 337). Nevertheless, their work experiences started significant attitude change, particularly with respect to the traditional respect and submission accorded to parents and husbands. In remarkably short time periods, young women and men began to assert their independence from fathers whose authority had been unquestioned previously. They sometimes even neglected older parents as a result. Their newly won wages and "worldly" experiences brought new respect and authority to them as well. One wife explained that she made most of the important family decisions because "I have worked in the factory since I was very young and I know more of the world than my husband, who has never left his native village" (p. 206).

When the social psychologist George Guthrie set out to study attitudes related to technological innovation in the rural Philippines, the literature on "modernization" had led him to expect that "traditional" attitudes must "be changed" through programs of persuasion before the standard of living could be improved. In fact, he and his Filipino collaborators (Guthrie, Azores, Jaunico, Luna and Ty, 1970) found certain "modern" attitudes prevalent among a majority of peasants both near Manila and as far as 400 kilometers away. However, they also found attitudes of suspicion toward landlords, middlemen, and tax collectors, and well-developed interpersonal strategies for "collective survival" in poverty that were inimical to campaigns of "persuasion" to adopt technology. The strategies were reflected in expectations that people who managed to gain above the low living standard should share their margin with relatives and friends, on penalty of theft (which was not infrequent).

Guthrie concluded that innovative projects would succeed only if introduced on a sufficiently broad scale, so organized that all, not a few, would benefit directly and promptly. "Projects may fail, on the other hand, when tenants feel that their gains go to landlords or middlemen, when a new project has no developed market, or when chickens or vegetables are stolen or shared with neighbors, so that no return is experienced by the one who has done the work" (p. 122). "Social approval and acclaim" for change, he thought, should follow successful programs, not precede them. Unfortunately, the sponsors of technological innovations are too frequently not as unselfish or as sensible as Guthrie believes that they must be.

Today, we in the nations with the most highly developed technologies can appreciate the cautions of peasants thoroughly accustomed to being "taken." There is a century-old faith in the inevitability of progress through technological innovation, or simply in the inevitability of technological change. However, we are beginning to realize that new collective strategies—interpersonal, group, and institutional—may be necessary to resist not technology per se, but those of its users who promote change without regard to its toll on the physical and social environment, on human lives now and in the future.

PSYCHOSOCIAL SCALES AND ATTITUDE CHANGE

Many of our attitudes about ourselves and other people are referable to psychosocial scales. Their existence is predicated on consensus among people in the past and at present about what is ideal, good, bad, or wicked. Such agreements are embodied in social norms or values, in institutional and organizational arrangements backed by all manner of social, economic, and political power. To different individuals and groups of individuals, the various "positions" on such psychosocial scales represent cherished beliefs and ideals, collective positions taken, and "last stands" upheld by themselves and by other peoples.

Psychosocial scales pertain to our most intimate as well as our most ritualistic public affairs. In contrast to psychophysical scales, their change often proceeds quite slowly. The United States can produce and adapt to a man on the moon more quickly than a black woman in the White House as president.

The positions on a psychosocial scale carry loads of emotionally charged value for those who uphold one or more of them. The extreme positions set "limits" to the radius of self that are perhaps more tenacious than those in a psychophysical scale. The "middle-of-the-road" position acquires salience that it does not have at all in judgment of physical objects (see Volkmann, 1951) because it marks the divide between opposing camps. Ostrom and Upshaw (1968) asked college students to write statements supporting various positions about prayer or about college fraternities. The students reported greater ease in writing extreme and "neutral" positions than on other positions in between. In addition, those with favorable attitudes on the issues reported greater ease in writing statements on the favorable extreme than the unfavorable extreme, whereas those with unfavorable attitudes found it easier to write about the unfavorable extreme (see Chapters 7 and 9).

When a new position is added at the extreme of a psychosocial scale (say a new group appears supporting a more radical position), it may be assimilated to our old category for extreme positions on that matter, providing that it is but a "step away" (Pollis, Pollis, and Rader, 1971). Reactions to new extremes that are more discrepant from the old scale ("three steps" away in the experiment cited) emphasize the "far out" character of the proposed innovation (contrast effect). A new extreme category is created. The upshot is that what was once "extreme" is now not the extreme. Pollis et al. found changes in people's endorsement of what was most acceptable to them following judgment of an extended scale of beliefs. They propose that attitude change may occur similarly, over time, simply by being exposed to an increasing range of extreme positions. Something of the kind may have occurred, for example, in reactions to positions taken by new women's groups. "Equal pay for equal work" by women aroused indignation, laughter, or a great many ifs and buts a decade ago, but is generally acceptable today, in part because new extreme positions on women's rights have been clearly stated during the decade.

On the other hand, we should not forget that, on some issues, a new extreme three or four "steps" away from the old represents an actual or perceived threat to some powerful group in society. Then, a "far out" new extreme category is not merely a judgment contrast to the usual range of differences in opinion. The outrage that accompanies such contrast effects in highly involving issues is powerfully reinforced through publicity, fear arousal, and attributions to the innovators. For example, once the small groups called Black Panthers were stigmatized as "way out" in the late 1960s, their ruthless suppression and the murder of members was accomplished without great public outcry on a scale comparable to protests of brutality during voter registration campaigns in the South a decade earlier. Since whites as well as blacks were mistreated and killed in that earlier repression, there is probably also a basis for the contention that some white Americans have two scales for assessing brutality—one toward whites and the other toward blacks.

CULTURAL LAGS AND CONTRADICTIONS

One of the most incisive accounts of the relatively rapid impact of technological change and the lagging rate of change on psychosocial scales was the "hypothesis of cultural lag" first proposed in 1922 by the sociologist W. F. Ogburn (1964). He defined a cultural lag as a contradiction developing between two related aspects of culture when one changes "before or in greater degree than the other part does, thereby causing less adjustment between the two parts than existed previously" (p. 86). Although not confining the hypothesis to technological change, Ogburn emphasized that technology and the physical sciences in our times have been "the great prime movers of social change" (pp. 90–91), thus are likely to create the "lag."

When such lags increase and accumulate in a society, he wrote, the outcome is that increasing thousands of individuals are affected by their contradictions in daily life. The powers that be soon discover that their society is ridden with "social problems," as well as small and large "crises." The individuals affected experience personal tragedies, misery, psychological turmoil, conflict, or great disaffection from those people or institutions that they see as most directly responsible for them. Particularly in a culture stressing individualism and "self-reliance," or in cases when blame for one's plight is not readily affixed on specific other persons or groups, the individual frequently blames himself or herself. "I was careless or irresponsible; I am incompetent, stupid, sinful. There must be something wrong with me." When the person realizes that similar things happened to others, he or she becomes less willing to assume the entire burden of guilt.

Ogburn documented a number of cultural lags carefully. For example, with the growth of factories using complex large equipment, increasing numbers of serious industrial accidents occurred in the

United States. Yet common law concerning accidents had been formulated when tools were simpler and ordinarily used on one's own
premises (or by a person who had no legal rights anyway). Between
1870 and 1910, several hundred thousand accidental injuries and
deaths occurred in factories, bringing pain, deprivation, and misery to
affected workers and their families. At last, the first employers' liability
and worker compensation laws were passed in 1910. Safety regulations
are still at issue in many work settings—for example, mines.

Today, such lags and contradictions as well as "social problems"
they create are rampant. Consider that a man is still measured in large
part by his competence and wage-earning capacity, which is also the
ultimate basis for his traditional authority in the family. Yet, increasing
automation of work can permanently remove a man from his occupation or make his relationship to the work situation so impersonal that
working becomes a misery (Faunce, 1960). As women in increasing
numbers have had to become self-supporting, as single individuals or
single heads of families, they face a host of contradictions in legal and
financial regulations designed long ago for women wholly dependent
on (or "owned by") fathers and husbands. Informal and institutional
pressures on women have diminished little since the psychologist Leta
Hollingworth (1916) wrote "Social Devices for Impelling Women to
Bear and Rear Children," yet social concern grows about increasing
population—a phenomenon that is a product more of improved agri-
cultural and health technology than reduced frequency in mass killing.

Such contradictions produced by cultural lags affect different
groups and strata of the population in different ways, providing fertile
grounds for attitude change as well as moves to prevent it.

THE POWER OF A NEW REFERENCE GROUP:
BENNINGTON COLLEGE STUDENTS

The 1930s found the United States loaded with culture lags and contradictions. The most prosperous country in the world found itself in
severe economic depression; war blazed in China and Spain while
smoldering in other parts of Europe. By 1936, the first graduating class
of a new women's college was leaving the isolated village of Bennington, Vermont. The new college was devoted to participatory learning
through student-faculty interchange and projects of the kind advocated
by "progressive education." Theodore M. Newcomb was a member of
the young, politically concerned faculty, and he initiated research on
this "natural experiment" that is one of the most significant studies of
attitude change in social psychology.

Bennington students came, by and large, from well-to-do, conservative families, leaving their homes in late adolescence to spend all but
one weekend a month during the academic year in a closed academic

community of about 250 students with a faculty markedly more "liberal" than their families. Newcomb constructed Likert tests (see Chapter 9) for attitudes on nine controversial sociopolitical issues on which strong conservative, liberal, and radical positions were being taken in the country at the time. He administered the tests each year for four years to the members of each class, subsequently following several classes through 2 to 4 years of college (Newcomb, 1943). In addition, he followed the graduating classes at intervals over a 25-year period by mailing questionnaires to their members (Newcomb, 1950; Newcomb, Koenig, Flacks, and Warwick, 1967).

Newcomb found that the women's attitudes became progressively more liberal, on the average, during 4 years of college, the changes being statistically significant for 6 of the 9 issues. Lest you think that these shifts toward faculty attitudes were simply "indoctrination," remember that interaction, discussion, and project work were the principal methods of instruction and note well the following: The women who were the most active in the college community and who had higher prestige for other students also became the most liberal. The changes signaled not merely shifts in a couple of attitudes, but the adoption of a new reference group—which involved change in numerous related attitudes, beliefs, and interpersonal attachments.

The importance of the reference group concept in handling the results of his study became apparent to Newcomb when he analyzed those women who did *not* change their political attitudes while at Bennington. Newcomb made this analysis when his friend Muzafer Sherif asked if he would prepare a summary of the research for inclusion in a book he was writing. Newcomb (1948) came up with an astounding conclusion: The individuals whose sociopolitical attitudes did not become more liberal also did not take the college community as their reference group. A few of them became involved in small, informal groups of classmates who did not concern themselves with political matters. Their friends "insulated" them from the liberal political community. Most of the others maintained strong ties outside of the community with family or male friends whose attitudes were much more conservative than the Bennington norms. Their reference groups for political attitudes were outside the community, some of them experiencing considerable discomfiture as a result (for example, "Family against faculty has been my struggle here"). A few women became defensive about their parents' views, contrasting the liberal political norms at Bennington to them and committing themselves more firmly to conservative positions.

In his follow-up of graduates, Newcomb found that persistence of the attitude change after the Bennington experience was, in part, a function of students' length of residence in the college community (1950). However, over a period of many years, persistence of liberal sociopolitical attitudes and actions (for example, voting) depended on choices the women made about their own careers, friends, and, especially, husbands. Those who married men with similar sociopolitical views or who worked in careers where they were likely to interact with others similarly inclined were the ones whose "Bennington" attitudes persisted (Newcomb et al., 1967).

But "Being a Member" Counts, Even If It's Not Our Reference Group

The importance of one's reference group as well as of actual daily associations with others not in one's reference group was shown some twenty years after Newcomb's study by Alberta and Sidney Siegel (1957). They selected a sample of women students who all aspired to live in the most prestigious dormitories on a college campus (because they were located along "fraternity row").

The researchers assessed sociopolitical attitudes at the end of the freshman year among women who had been assigned (randomly) to their chosen dormitory, those who had been assigned elsewhere but *still* wanted to live on the prestigious "row," and those who had decided to remain in the lower-prestige dorms by preference. Women in the "row" houses displayed the most conservative attitudes, and those who had "made it" had become more conservative.

Women who still held to the prestigious, conservative reference group, but had lived elsewhere were somewhat less conservative in attitudes than those who "made it." The women who decided to stay in low-prestige, assigned dormitories, thereby adopting them as their reference groups, were the least conservative of all. Both those whom we associate with and whom we aspire to associate with affect our attitudes and outlooks.

THE IMPACT OF THE "THE TIMES" ON COLLEGE STUDENTS AND OLDER FOLKS

Bennington College was unusual in its small size, isolation, and relative homogeneity of faculty and students. Most studies of college students in more "open," more diverse settings show neither uniform change nor unidirectional change in sociopolitical or other attitudes during the college experience, though several have reported trends toward liberalism from freshman to senior years (Feldman and Newcomb, 1969). The choice of a college, of a field of study, and of other reference groups are important in what kind of changes occur or whether they occur at all. On the other hand, research also shows decided differences in the attitudes and values endorsed by students at different periods in our history since the 1930s.

Incoming college students (mostly males in the studies) reflect the impact of their own times more clearly than seniors or alumni. Follow-ups of the same students through middle life indicate, however, that older folks also change their attitudes in response to major events and crises in society (Hoge and Bender, 1974). The finding that the individuals do not necessarily become either more rigid or more conservative in their attitudes as they grow older flies in the face of the keen experiences of "generation gaps" by many younger and older persons. In fact, such gaps in attitudes are found, but their size and scope differ appreciably from one generation to the next.

The years of the Generation Gap in recent journalism can be readily understood from the research. College students of the early 1950s reflected a "nationwide movement to political and social conservatism beginning in about 1939 and peaking in the [Joseph] McCarthy movement of 1952–54," notably in increased emphasis on economic goals and on conventional religiosity (Hoge and Bender, 1974, pp. 578–579). At that time, there was no unsurmountable gap between college and the then older generation. The young conservatives leaving college in the mid-1950s did exhibit changes in value emphasis and attitudes, particularly up to their middle or late thirties, while men were more mobile socially and geographically in their work. However, by the late 1960s, some rather striking social events had occurred (for example, the civil rights movement, urban "riots," the assassination of President Kennedy, the enlargement of the Vietnam war, the murder of Martin Luther King, the demonstrations and "police riot" at the 1968 Democratic convention in Chicago). College students of the late 1960s, entering a world so different, found their viewpoints miles apart from many of their elders (even those age 30 or so who had graduated a decade before). The older generations had not (by and large) changed *that* much.

The impact of actual events on attitudes, as well as their *relative* stability over time, were apparent in Thistlethwaite's analysis (1974) of data collected from college men in 25 major universities around the country in the summers of 1969, 1970, and 1971. The elaborate attitude questionnaires were mailed to students' home addresses, and the analysis reported only on those who responded to all three. The researcher quite properly emphasized that the samples were biased in the direction of overrepresenting conservative, more conventional, and less politically active students (p. 229).

War-related and race-related protests on college campuses were frequent by the summer of 1969. The spring of 1970 witnessed the public announcement of the U.S. invasion of Cambodia by an administration elected two years earlier on a platform of ending the war and reaffirming "law and order." The latter was conceived in the eyes of many students as indiscriminate killing and wounding of students at Kent State University and Jackson State University.

The rank orders of the same students' attitude "scores" were significantly correlated from one year to the next from 1969 to 1971. That finding supports the general stability of individual attitudes, in that differences *between* individuals were similar from one year to the next. However, there were striking and significant *changes* in attitude positions by the students as a whole, especially following the spring of 1970. These changes were in the direction of being more anti-war, more in favor of free speech, civil rights, and domestic welfare programs; greater disaffection from authorities; less inclination toward U.S. involvement in anti-communist foreign policies. The changes from 1969 to 1970 were much more pronounced for younger undergraduates than for seniors.

From 1970 to 1971 the greatest changes were toward greater alienation from society, including renewed distrust of faculty. In order to understand these signs of disillusionment, it may help to recall that in the spring of 1971, the administration's "law and order" activities led to the arrest without warrants of thousands in Washington, D.C., many of them students there to demonstrate against the war. The wholesale arrests and fingerprinting continued until court officials let it be known that they could not consider the cases. Nevertheless, many students became keenly aware that "innocent bystanders" were not exempt from arrest and police or FBI "records."* Nor was the end of the Indochina war in sight.

During the period, nationwide surveys of the adult population also reported increasing estrangement from and distrust of government from 1964 to 1972 (ISR Newsletter, 1974, pp. 4–5). The index was a ratio between the proportion in the population expressing distrust and the proportion expressing trust. The plunge toward increasing distrust was precipitous among black Americans after 1968, the balance tipping in that direction by 1972. The growth in this index of estrangement affected all age groups in the white population as well, being greatest for people under 25 and over 50. A related finding is that the proportion of eligible voters who voted in the 1972 presidential election fell to its lowest level since 1948, despite an unprecedented propaganda campaign from all quarters to vote. The "landslide victory" of the Republican candidate therefore represented the votes of about one-third of the total electorate.

Something had happened to many people's attitudes, all right—their attitudes toward those who governed. The issue of major importance for social psychology is that a person's attitudes and actions on sociopolitical issues are not unrelated to attitudes toward other persons and groups, particularly the person's reference sets. Losing faith in others with high status and power can lead to withdrawal on such

*The illegal arrests resulted in court decisions awarding "damages" of about $10,000 each to over 2000 persons.

matters, particularly if force operates to prevent protest. Our attitudes are not unrelated to our ties with others, as Newcomb's Bennington study showed long ago.

Attitude Change When Reference Persons "Betray" Us

When actual events demonstrate undeniably that members of a reference set or a reference idol have acted within one's own latitude of rejection, sudden and sharp change on related attitudes may occur. Sherif (1970) gave an example reported on the University of California campus in the spring of 1969. Touring Republican congressmen were conversing with moderate students as militant activists demonstrated nearby protesting the closing of a "people's park." The moderates sympathized with the militants' protest, though deploring their tactics. Instead, they trusted authorities as reasonable men, susceptible to friendly persuasion. As they talked, a National Guard helicopter began spraying tear gas over the heavily populated campus. According to the congressmen's report, the moderate students "were radicalized that moment" (Evans and Novak, 1969). Their sympathy moved to the militants and away from authority.

In August, 1974, a county cochairman of the 1972 Committee to Re-Elect the President sat with his wife and a reporter waiting to hear the President speak on television. Four days earlier, the President had disclosed that since June, 1972, he had lied in denying any role in covering up illegal acts by his subordinates. The cochairman and his wife had been strongly against the President's impeachment or resignation until that disclosure. They had seen the evidence presented by the House Judiciary Committee on the President's activities as "indecisive," as had ten committee members, whereas others regarded the same evidence as clearly warranting impeachment. Here were the cochairman's words:

I've . . . we've . . . always felt close to Nixon, to the man. . . . This all came as a helluva shock . . . the revelations he made Monday, well I was terribly disturbed. . . . If I had known then what I know now, I would not have been cochairman . . . what I've been thinking of is during the War in the prison camp. One day the German guard came up to us and told us "Roosevelt is dead." All at once everything was silent and then the tears welled up to my eyes.

Then the President spoke on television, announcing his resignation. "Jesus, I guess that's the end of something," was all the once cochairman could say (Pennsylvania *Mirror*, August 9, 1974, p. 1). That, too, is attitude change. (The President was not impeached. He resigned, accepting a "full pardon" from a new President whom he had appointed.)

Older Folks Change Reference Groups
and Attitudes: The Baby Doctor

Dr. Benjamin Spock, now in his seventies, pediatrician and author of
the best seller *Baby and Child Care* (26 million copies), was certainly
no radical to mothers of my generation who used his book. It gave
practical information and advice cheifly designed to reassure young
parents that their judgments about their babies could be trusted. It
bothered me that its author could not "understand" why a young
mother would want to work, but why complain about a book that could
help me find out whether my child was getting the chicken pox or
dying?

Conventional and somewhat conservative by tradition and personal
taste, Dr. Spock was against military intervention in Vietnam and voted
for Lyndon Johnson as president in 1964. He felt increasingly betrayed
as that administration poured troops, bombs, defoliants, and devastation into Vietnam. He and his wife began to join meetings and demonstrations against the war, marching alongside students and "hippies,"
as their old friends called them. According to Dr. Spock, it was not
until 1968 that his baby book got blamed for the "state of our youth" by
the Reverend Norman Vincent Peale, Jr., during a sermon in his New
York church. He charged Dr. Spock with seducing a generation of
parents into giving their babies "instant gratification," which
explained to the Reverend Peale why so many youth were acting in
ways of which he heartily disapproved. As it happened, the attack on
the baby book followed Spock's indictment on a conspiracy charge by
the federal government in connection with demonstrations at the 1968
Democratic convention in Chicago. (I cannot believe that Peale and I
read the same book.)

At that point, Dr. Spock said, those of his old "establishment"
friends who remained began to find him and his wife "incompatible"
as friends. He began to get nasty letters about his book from strangers.
He was convicted and sentenced to two years in jail, a decision later
overturned by a higher court. Meanwhile, as a result of their activities
and the trial, he and his wife continued to acquire a "whole new set of
friends." Spock then became candidate for the presidency in 1972 on
the People's Party ticket, an advocate of "democratic socialism," and at
latest report was revising his baby book to correct his self-admitted bias
as a "male chauvinist" (Bartlett, 1974). Quite a bit of attitude change for
the Spocks, and a lesson to us on the importance of new reference
groups for attitude change at any age.

BACK TO THE THIRTIES: MORENO'S
ROLE-TAKING AND ROLE-PLAYING

Being part of a reference group or set is not simply being stamped into a
mold, significant as membership is. The individual also develops

mutual expectations and patterns of give-and-take with others—that is, *role* relationships—that are closely related to his or her attitudes. For example, one of the interesting studies of attitude change concerned those changes that happened when workers were promoted either to foreman or to union shop steward (Lieberman, 1956). The foremen's attitudes changed most, in the direction of management to which their role was attached. In cases where demotion owing to an economic recession occurred, new changes were found, back to attitudes shared by other workers.

In recent years, there has been some research and a great deal of applied activity on such effects of role enactment (for example, a policeman or a prisoner). The grandfather of such research was Dr. J. L. Moreno, whose work on sociometry was discussed early in this book. Moreno, who died recently at an advanced age, began his work on role-playing as a young psychiatrist in Vienna after World War I. In part, he was inspired by the "living theater" developed by actors on the streets spontaneously portraying events of the time—a theater that also appeared in the United States in the 1930s after Moreno came here and again in the 1960s. Each of these were periods of social protest.

Moreno's group therapy included enactment of a ready-made role (for example, one's own or a character in a script), improvised role-playing in *a* role (for example, *a* mother), or playing *my* role or a role "I'd like to play." His aim was role-creating, that is, spontaneously developing new mutual expectations and reciprocal actions with others. Other participants might also be role-playing as "auxiliary egos" instructed to play the person's mother, boss, and so on. The varied and flexible training exercises, programs, and procedures developed in Moreno's institutes were called "psychodrama." They pervaded the "group dynamics" movement that developed in the 1950s (Chapter 3). You may have seen demonstrations on television under a variety of labels ("encounter," "sensitivity training," and so on). Later, parts of the women's movement incorporated some of Moreno's notions about the roles one "received" from society and "spontaneity" in action.

Moreno's aims were to change the self, which he saw as partially a product of role enactments. Thus, attitude change was expected: "psychodrama . . . developed in a rapidly changing world in which many roles have become worn and have either to perish, to be revitalized, or to be replaced" (Moreno, 1960, p. 85).

A funny thing happened to Moreno's concepts in academic research on role-playing and attitude change of the 1950s and 1960s. They got dissected or boiled down to the question of whether a person's attitudes would change when he or she was *assigned* by a researcher to play a role. That assignment might be to act like a person supporting legalization of marijuana, to be a paid stooge of the researcher passing on erroneous reports to other subjects, or simply to be a "subject" performing tasks for an experimenter without question. What was then studied was why the person did or did not change evaluations made about the researcher, another person in the experiment, or the task itself. Elms (1972) gave an insightful review of such role-playing research (pp. 247–270), which is sometimes included in discussions of attitude change in social psychology books. It seems more reasonable to me to interpret most of it as the individual's adaptations to brief encounters in a research situation. Researchers and subjects alike were "playing the game" (see also Bem, 1967).

There were important exceptions. For example, the research by Irving Janis and Leon Mann (1965, 1968) studied role-playing as a means to encourage women students to stop smoking. The research was more in keeping with Moreno's analysis. The women reported smoking at least 15 cigarettes a day, the average being about 25 cigarettes. Each was asked to pretend that she had come to a doctor's office with a persistent bad cough. An "auxiliary ego" dressed in a doctor's white coat showed her an X-ray of a messed-up pair of lungs, saying they were hers, that immediate operation was indicated with "moderate" chances of success, and discussed the link between smoking and lung cancer. He urged her to stop smoking immediately and then called the hospital to arrange for her admittance.

Now all of this was obviously a "game," but the role-playing experience shook the women considerably, some taking the vow to stop smoking immediately. Follow-ups by telephone at intervals of 7, 8, and 18 months later brought reports that the women had significantly reduced cigarette consumption, on the average, to fewer than 15 cigarettes a day (Mann and Janis, 1968). The role-playing episode was powerfully supported by the Surgeon General's report linking cigarettes and cancer, which appeared 8 months after the episode. However, those who role-played reported less smoking than two samples of other students whose reports were solicited at the same time. There was certainly evidence that the role-playing experience had an impact, whether or not we wish to regard the outcome as attitude change. The role being played was "me . . . myself." And that makes all the difference in the world.

Role-playing and Attitude Change

What do we know about role-playing and attitude change? First of all, we should not expect much attitude change from playing an assigned role contrary to our own attitudes. Many theories and practical programs for change emphasize the development of "empathy" for the person in a different role. Very likely, empathy (putting oneself in the other's shoes) is possible in proportion to the degree of similarity in two persons' reference sets or groups, or to a compelling life experience that one has in common with the other person. For example, it is difficult for many men and women to attempt to enact the role of a

person of the other sex, despite the fact that some are adept at caricatured gestures and mannerisms of the other sex.

We would expect such difficulty in "empathy" from what we
learned about the problems that white students had in anticipating the
reactions of black students in interracial situations (Chapter 10), about
the greater ease in constructing arguments to support positions about
prayer on one's own side rather than the other side (earlier in this
chapter), about the caricatures that resulted when "hawks" were asked
to write "dove" statements, and vice versa (Chapter 7). The limitations
of role-playing and empathy are to be found in the state of *relationships* between the roles. That is probably why Moreno would not have
approved of casting a person in the role of someone with an opposing
attitude in order to change: "Taking the role of the other is a dead end.
The turning point was how to vitalize and change the roles . . ." (1960,
p. 85, emphasis in original).

Alvar Elbing (1962) compared attitude change following role-playing on one's own side and on the opposite side of a controversial social
issue. He found much less change in the latter case, particularly if the
person was involved in his or her own position. On the other hand, he
found that role-playing on one's own side produced significant shifts
toward becoming more extreme than one was at the outset. There is a
good deal of other evidence that actions in line with one's attitude can
make one more extreme or intensify one's convictions.

For example, Kiesler (1971) reported a field study in which women
favoring the distribution of birth control information in a high school
were first asked to sign a petition of support. Of those who signed, half
later received information attacking the plan, while the other half did
not. Subsequently, all of the petition signers were asked to volunteer in
distributing birth control information. After signing the petition, all of
the women indicated more favorable attitudes toward birth control
information. Those who were confronted by information critical of
their stand actually volunteered more frequently (40 percent) than
those who had not received the attack (10 percent).

The key concept in understanding all of this is the self-system. One's
attitude on one matter is not altogether discrete and isolated from the
rest of the self. Attack is an attack on me as well as my view on the
topic. A hint of what goes on is conveyed by research on what happens
when a belief tangential to self is attacked strongly, for example, the
"cultural truism" that we should brush our teeth three times a day.
Quite contrary to an attack on attitudes, an attack on such a truism can
weaken it severely (McGuire, 1962, 1969; McGuire and Papageorgis,
1961). One way to prevent such weakening is to provide the person
with a defense (for example, reasons why regular tooth brushing is
valuable) since in all probability he or she has simply never questioned
why.

However, the more effective way to prevent a cultural truism from crumbling resembles what probably goes on when a person has an attitude more personally important. In the research, the best way was to give the person some notion in advance of what an attack on the truism might be, in addition to counterarguments to refute an attack. Such an "inoculation" procedure was effective even when the counterarguments provided by the researchers were *not* directly pertinent to the actual attack subsequently made on the belief. Apparently, the *person* got involved in something that had never been at issue before, thus was able to "fend for himself" in the face of attack.

When a person has an attitude, the matter *has* been at issue before, particularly when it concerns relationships with others or controversial social issues. Already "inoculated" against attacks, the person's commitment to action involves more of the self-system than merely that issue. The person's reference persons and groups are also at stake, including their expectations that he or she will "put the body where the mouth is."

We are now close to another line of research on attitude change that has been linked with the problem of norm formation. As suggested in Chapter 3 this process is not unrelated to Moreno's concern with creating new roles.

THE POWER IN DECIDING TO ACT TOGETHER

The more recent research on committing oneself to take actions proceeds from earlier experiments by Kurt Lewin and his associates (Lewin, 1953, 1965), which started during World War II and are usually called "group decision" studies. At the time, there were short supplies of meat for civilians, whose consumption of certain meats was rationed in order to supply vast numbers of military personnel. The U.S. government was concerned that meat rationing not cause nutritional problems unnecessarily, particularly since certain less preferred meats were cheap and not in short supply. But how could housewives be persuaded that liver, kidneys, pancreas, hearts, and other less popular parts were both nutritious and delicious when properly prepared?

What Lewin did was in keeping with the message of his earlier experiments on participatory leadership with boys' groups (Chapter 4). He set out to show that information and appeals to do something contrary to one's attitude were more likely to lead to action when the individuals themselves participated in deciding to act than when they were simply told why it was "best for you." Instead of telling them "try it, you'll like it," his idea was to provide a setting where individuals could decide "let's try it, maybe we'll like it." There is no doubt that the problem was a challenge. Lewin jokingly compared the women's reactions to the particular meats with the horror and aversion aroused by a neurotic phobia.

The first experiment involved six groups of women who worked as Red Cross volunteers, 13 to 17 women in each group. If my mother's experience in such work during World War II was representative, these were women who knew one another and worked together several times a week. Forty-five minutes were available for either a lecture or a discussion, three groups being assigned to each. The lectures were attractive, exhorting the women to use the neglected cuts and linking the appeal to the war effort as well as nutritional concerns. Their health value and economy were emphasized. Attractive ways to prepare them were presented, along with mimeographed recipes.

In the other condition, a social psychologist and skilled group worker, Alex Bavelas, introduced the problem in much the same way. Then he opened the discussion to "see whether housewives could be induced to participate in a program of change without . . . any high-pressure salesmanship." The discussions included airing obstacles to using the meats—objections from husbands and children, cooking odors, and the like. The same preparation techniques and recipes were provided. Then the women were asked to decide whether or not to use some of the foods, committing themselves by a show of hands.

The outcome was striking: Only 3 percent of the women who heard lectures later reported that they had included in their menus one or more of the food items that they had not used before. In the discussion groups, 32 percent reported they had started to use new cuts of meat. The experiment served as a model for many other studies, although, surprisingly, some recent researchers on closely related problems appear to have forgotten them.

In order to rule out the possibility that the first results were chiefly an outcome of Alex Bavelas' charms as compared with the lecturer's, Marian Radke Yarrow conducted another study with housewives living in the same neighborhoods, this time working within the latitude of acceptable foods in the attempt to increase use of both fresh and evaporated milk. The same person (not a professional lecturer or group worker) conducted both the lecture and discussion sessions. The use of milk was checked two weeks afterward and again four weeks after the sessions. Again, the contrast between the lecture and the discussion was great: After two weeks, between 40 and 50 percent of the housewives who participated in discussion-decision sessions reported increased use of milk, as compared with 15 to 30 percent of those given the lecture (the higher percentages in each case applying to the less used evaporated milk). Furthermore, the change persisted after four weeks.

Meanwhile, Alex Bavelas (in Lewin, 1953) brought group decision to a factory, where a group of sewing-machine operators decided in January, 1943, to increase the level of their production from an average of about 75 units to an average of 87 to 88 units, which they then maintained from February through August. Shortly after the war, Coch and French (1953) did a field experiment in the same pajama factory in Virginia, which employed mostly young women workers. They compared unit production per hour when more efficient work procedures were introduced by one of several methods: (1) the management simply told them about the changes, the chief rationale being the highly competitive market for pajamas; (2) the problem was presented and, with agreement of the workers, certain operators were chosen to try the new procedures and then instruct the others; (3) all workers participated in active discussion of the problem, general agreement was reached (though no "group decision" was requested), and all workers participated in the training. The outcome was an overall increase of approximately 15 units per hour for the total participation group (the increase persisting for the month studied). There was an initial decline in production in the special operator condition (2 above), but a gradual increase thereafter almost reaching output of the total participation workers after half a month. There was a steady, much lower output by those who were simply told what would happen (1 above).

The procedures of earlier group decision studies were captured somewhat better in Levine and Butler's study (1953) of male foremen in a diversified industrial setting. The researchers noted that in the original experiments only the discussion sections had been told that their behavior would be checked later. Therefore, they compared changes following decisions made together with those after lectures when no forewarning of a follow-up was given in either. Furthermore, the actions of interest were studied without asking the person directly to report his own actions.

They studied 29 supervisors in a factory, randomly assigned to a control, lecture, or discussion session. The problem presented was one in social judgment: The supervisors were charged with rating workers' performance at regular intervals, but their ratings showed a persistent tendency to overrate workers in higher job grades and to underrate workers in low job grades. The matter was serious since supervisor ratings affected what wages a worker would get. The lecture session gave loads of information about performance rating, laid out the problem, and supplied the remedy: Rate each man's work without regard to job difficulty or level. In the discussion session, the problem was presented; an hour and a half discussion ensued, in which the participants came to the same conclusion and decided to try it. No session was held for the control sample.

The supervisors' subsequent ratings of workers were checked, without telling them about it. Levine and Butler found that the control sample's ratings continued to show a bias according to the worker's job grade. Those supervisors who heard the lecture did also, although they corrected their bias somewhat by lowering performance ratings for the very highest grade. Those who participated in discussion and decision reduced their bias to an insignificant level, on the average.

Whatever Happened to Group Decision Research?

In the 1940s and 1950s, the *techniques* of discussion leading to a group decision were seized by people in a good many different circumstances as a *means* of changing *other* people's attitudes. As "techniques" they were promoted and "oversold." At times some of the essentials in Lewin's model were forgotten, particularly that decision making had occurred among people who had interacted previously, who were not unaccustomed to discussing problems of mutual concern, and who faced problems that, while requiring distasteful actions on occasion, did not require violation of *shared norms* for mutual conduct. Pars Ram and Gardner Murphy (1953) reported from India that the "discussion technique" was ineffective among high school boys there in changing attitudes toward different castes. In fact, the boys were unaccustomed to open discussion of such attitudes and their change required gross violations of their reference set (caste) norms.

Researchers began to ask questions such as the following: "Now what *is* it in the 'technique' that produces attitude change and action: the discussion itself, the decision itself, the fact that other people see one commit oneself, or the fact that others are observed to commit themselves?" To vary all of these "elements" in an experimental design meant having a total of nearly 500 subjects, which also meant that certain essentials of Lewin's earlier work were ignored.

Edith Pelz (1965) performed such a study on "getting" students to volunteer for psychological experiments, which was not a common problem for them. Nor had the students interacted in the past. She found what we would expect on the basis of our analysis of the sets of factors in a transitory social situation (Chapter 2): None of the "elements" in the original Lewin experiments had a significant effect (not discussion versus lecture, not public or private commitment, not whether a decision was made or not). The only discernible trend was that more students actually signed up in classes where decisions to volunteer were requested and also where a high proportion of students decided to volunteer (for reasons unknown). By breaking down the "technique" in parts, while ignoring the context in which it had proven effective, the problem under study had been transformed to that of the impact of other persons in a brief encounter.

So, into the 1960s, the power of persons deciding together to cope with a common problem was neglected in academic research, just at the time when many people in small and larger gatherings outside were actually doing just that. Roger Brown (1965) wrote his lectures at Harvard and MIT as a delightful and ingratiating text in social psychology; his chapter on group dynamics contained not one study in which interaction proceeded beyond "brief encounters" among strangers (see Chapter 2). Lewin's group decision studies were not to be found in the book. Instead, he built the "group" chapter around a master's thesis at MIT on a phenomenon that was called "the risky shift"—a tendency for an individual to make a more cautious decision alone than that reached when instructed to arrive at a consensus with several other persons. (In fact, as Brown pointed out, the converse was also found. At times consensus was more cautious than individual decisions.)

Risk and Polarization in Collective Decisions

Perhaps one reason that social psychologists and students found the "risky shift" notion so interesting was that some important social psychologists had equated "conformity" with "yielding to pressures toward uniformity." Others saw group norms as invariably "leveling" individual differences to "mediocrity" (or the arithmetic average of individual differences). Perhaps such definitions of "conformity" were not surprising for American psychologists emerging from the oppressive political atmosphere of the 1950s whose pressure "not to rock the boat" they had felt. However, equating "conformity" with "averaging" contradicted a great many research findings: Sherif (1961) had insisted that while norm formation reduced individual differences, it could result in changes that were *either* more or less "extreme" than the arithmetic average of initial individual differences. Moreno had demonstrated that new mutual expectations and patterns of behavior could develop through interacting with others. Lewin's group decision studies had *not* involved intense "pressures" but voluntary enlistment to do something out of the ordinary. The boys at Robbers Cave were not pressured to hate members of the rival group, but moved together toward an extreme (not average) antagonism and stereotyped view of others, at times risking their necks in the process (see Chapter 5).

By the late 1960s, researchers on "risky shifts" found themselves bogged down in a morass of conflicting findings. That probably was an inevitable outcome of the attempt to find decision-making principles for "groups" by studying transitory brief encounters (see, for example, Pruitt, 1971; Fraser, Gouge, and Billig, 1971).

Meanwhile, researchers in a France that was stunned by massive student protests in 1968 demonstrated what must have been patently obvious in daily life: When people (French students) have attitudes toward what they are deciding about (toward De Gaulle or North Americans in the research), the effect of reaching a decision collectively with others of similar inclination is often change in the direction of the most extreme positions taken among them (Moscovici and Zavalloni, 1969). This "polarization" toward extreme attitude positions, more extreme than the arithmetic average of prior individual judgments, is harmonious with the conception of norm formation (Chapter 3): "Something happens" *among* individuals, the most influential by no means always being exemplars of "mediocrity" or the arithmetic average of individual attitudes.

Doise (1969) confirmed the "polarization" of group decisions by having French architecture students at a private "progressive" school make judgments individually on the characteristics of their own group (stereotypes) and then having four at a time reach a collective decision on them. In one condition, they were confronted with the presumed opinions about their school by students at another architecture school that was its arch rival. The collective decisions about their own group were more extreme than the average of individual judgments made previously.

Furthermore, especially when faced with the rival's evaluation, group decisions represented shifts toward the judgments made by those individuals with the most extreme opinions initially. In Doise's research, these more extreme persons were also accorded more favorable interest by others (sociometric choices). Doise suggested that such extremists actually behaved in more consistent and confident fashion than the others during discussion. He compared their impact with that of a highly consistent minority on the other less assured participants (see, for example, Faucheux and Moscovici, 1967).

Doise emphasized the context of intergroup relations (in which a decision by a group is merely one incident) and the dynamics of the discussion itself in understanding when a collective decision may be more extreme than the attitudes of individuals. Group decisions are not made in a social vacuum. For example, Coffman and Harris (1974) reported that white students agreed on more favorable trait attributions to blacks after discussion in a research situation, whereas discussion among black students led to less favorable attributions to whites. The conclusion that the outcome was an inevitable "polarization" phenomenon in group discussion would be a vast oversimplification. We need to consider the current state of relationships between blacks and whites as well.

What "polarization" research shows very clearly is that individuals interacting toward group decisions respond to all the sets of factors in any social situation (Chapter 2), the relationships among the participants becoming primary when they are members of a group (Chapter 4) or are confronted by opposing groups (Chapter 5). Thus, some researchers are sounding wise cautions against premature attempts to "explain" all group decisions by a single theory about psychological propensities or about group effects on individuals (Myers and Lamm, 1975). Others call for more detailed descriptive studies of the conditions under which polarization of attitudes occurs (Cvetkovich and

Baumgardner, 1973, p. 162), correctly noting that such research should aim at greater understanding of individuals' relationships with their reference groups. In brief, if we would understand attitude change occuring within the context of group decisions, we must study group processes and intergroup relations as well as individual attitudes.

GROUP DECISIONS ABOUT *WHOSE* PROBLEMS?

In the research on nutritional problems, Kurt Lewin could assume that, given wartime shortages, the proposed decision to use nutritious and inexpensive foods was, indeed, in the best interests of housewives and their families. In many circumstances, however, alternative steps and other decisions might be more advantageous to the persons involved in decision making than those proposed by the sponsors of research. If parties are in conflict, is it invariably in the best interests of one side to decide to cooperate with the other? Will the sponsors of the research be content with decisions reached by participants that address their own problems effectively, but that were *not* the decisions preferred by the sponsors? Such questions quickly become apparent when social scientists attempt to apply their findings in life situations where different groups of people are highly unequal in social power.

In an address on receiving the Kurt Lewin Memorial Award, Morton Deutsch (1969) phrased such problems in terms of conflicting interests "between those groups who have considerable authority to make decisions and relatively high control over the conventional means of social and political influence and those groups who have little decision-making authority and relatively little control over the conventional means of influence" (p. 32). He noted that a frequent rationale justifying the positions of those "who are satisfied with their roles and the outcomes of the decision-making process" is that those with less power and authority are "incapable and so deficient in morality and maturity" that *their* decisions are not to be trusted (p. 32). The less powerful in turn may become so accustomed to accepting "superior" authority that they lack experience in reaching their own collective decisions and faith in their own capacity to do so.

He suggested that social scientists consider for a moment what their advice would be if

we were consultants to the poor and weak rather than to the rich and strong. . . . Let me note that this would be an unusual and new position for most of us. If we have given advice at all, it has been to those in high power. The unwitting consequence of this one-sided consultant role has been that we have too often assumed that the social pathology has been in the ghetto rather than in those who have built the walls to surround it, that the "disadvantaged" are the ones who need to be changed rather than the people and the institutions who have kept the disadvantaged in a submerged position. . . . Let us not lose sight of what and who has to be changed, let us recognize where the social pathology really is! (p. 33)

The relevance of his cautions and questions was illustrated later by Marcia Guttentag (1972) in documenting what can happen when a less powerful group is "allowed" to make decisions toward changes whose very success is seen as a threat by more powerful groups. Parents and school personnel in three poor and congested school districts in Harlem (New York City) interacted on the difficult problems involved in their children's education. They decided to institute "community control" over their schools by locally elected school boards and to involve parents, teachers, and students in activities to improve both the educational level and the atmosphere of the schools. Guttentag presented convincing data on the effects of these processes. Parents visited and helped at school at much higher rates than previously or in comparable districts. Children regarded their school with new eyes; they learned more and different lessons than children in comparable districts. Despite these successes, the entire plan was abolished by decisions at a higher level. The school district was incorporated into a larger one governed by a remote central board.

INSTITUTIONAL DECISIONS AND PERSONAL DECISIONS

My purpose here is to raise questions about the roles of social scientists, practitioners, and other citizens in programs to change attitudes and actions of *other* people. These include issues about the use of power to promote local initiative in decision making and actions toward change while reserving the right to squelch those efforts. Invariably, the latter occurs as self-righteous concern over "keeping *them* from making mistakes" or "saving others" from the changes. Shouldn't the power to decide and act together carry the power to make mistakes as well as to achieve? I believe that such questions need to be pondered.

Marcia Guttentag (1972) is one of a few social psychologists who have cast such problems in terms of the power structures and ideologies (belief systems) of the groups involved in change. Referring to teacher-pupil interactions and improved "achievement" scores, she stressed that what happened in the classroom could not be understood apart from the system of community action involving parents and school officials alike: "it is the social and ideological system within which these interactions are embedded which provides the truest and most general explanation for the observed interactions" (p. 19). The very banding together of people in the district represented opposition to the central school board (p. 19), which had concerns other than whether children learned to read or what the schools meant to adults in the community. It is their "social and ideological system" that provides the most general explanation for what happened: abolition of the community-controlled district.

This kind of analysis has implications both for critics who charge that social science findings "don't work" when applied in real life and for uncritical enthusiasts who have difficulty in comprehending why social psychologists are not "out there" solving everyone's problems.

WHEN A SOCIAL PSYCHOLOGIST BECOMES A TECHNICIAN OF ATTITUDE CHANGE

The charge that social science is a tool for manipulating people is quite true if the social scientist becomes merely a technician serving the interests of those who want to manipulate people. The social psychologist may be in particular danger in this respect since the tools of the trade are most appropriate for small-scale study of individuals interacting in well-defined social milieus. It is very easy to confine our focus to specific individuals or small groups in the here and now, neglecting the impact of anything outside on those individuals or on the here and now. The upshot may be that the "causes" of observed behavior are sought only in the persons or only in their immediate environment.

Yet, we have seen in this chapter that powerful means of attitude change lie in the interactions among individuals who face a common problem that is unlikely to arise solely from *within* their closed circle and decide together to take actions they think appropriate to remedy the problem. As we learned in Chapter 5 in discussing Sherif's experiments on groups in summer camps, the moment that relations *between* groups are involved in processes of attitude formation or change, the power of any one group on its members can become a force toward hostility and destruction or toward effective solving of problems of mutual concern to both groups. The problem of assessing the *outcomes* of group processes becomes even more complex when one group, in fact, is more powerful than the other. That is why, in real life, the most crucial issues about attitude change quickly become issues about the structure and the uses of social power.

Some social and clinical psychologists have either thought very little about such problems or are quite willing to put whatever skills they possess in the service of those groups and institutions with the means and the power to use them. The greatest hue and cry being raised these days about "interventions" to change behavior is directed at a very broad movement toward "behavior modification," composed chiefly of psychologists trained in experimental laboratories or clinics, which are the worst places in the world to find out about problems of the kind raised here. Otherwise, it would be unthinkable that "reasonable" people could contend that their technical services in prisons have nothing at all to do with the institutional purposes, regulations, and cultures of the prison (*APA Monitor*, 1974).

Jerome D. Frank of Johns Hopkins University is one of a rare breed, a social psychologist (Ph.D.) who is also a psychiatrist (M.D.). In a fascinating assessment of the history and outcomes of various kinds of psychotherapy, Frank (1972) recognized the problems of being a mere technical expert when the patients' problems are, in fact, closely related to social problems in human relationships. Patients come, or are brought to therapy, he believes, when they have become sufficiently "demoralized" that they can no longer cope with life problems through their customary means, when they have become isolated from or are in deep trouble with interpersonal relationships, or when their group ties and traditional beliefs no longer serve as adequate guides for coping.

What a therapist provides, he believes, is a trusting human relationship, an enthusiasm as well as prestige for a rationale toward recovery, thus faith that the actions taken together will bring improvement. In short, Frank sees the therapeutic process as an interpersonal or, increasingly, a group process in which decisions, commitment to action, and mutual support are aimed toward sufficient change in attitude and action that the individual can "cope" once more.

Issues of social power arise when one asks, as Frank did, what happens if therapy aims at leading the person to cope with the world exactly as he or she finds it. In effect, therapeutic techniques then become a means to ensure that the housewife totally dependent on a dominating husband submissively accepts the situation, that a man forcibly retired at middle age resigns himself to being a replaceable part in industry, that a black youth is grateful for a job that brings him significantly less income than that he could attain if he were white. Neither Frank nor any of the psychotherapists whom I know personally would accept such an outcome as an adequate definition of "coping," but it has been only a short time since such "adjustment" was the expected outcome. The issues raised here about psychotherapy are pertinent to many other attempts to promote attitude change.

Increasingly, in my opinion, social and other psychologists will have to recognize that the use of their skills within the communities and institutions of society raises issues far more significant than whether or not their techniques "work." In the long run, what "works" will have to work in the interests of the broadest possible circle of human beings, not merely in the interests of those groups intent on controlling others for their own benefit. Otherwise social psychologists would become "part of the problem," breeding new dilemmas through their efforts to cope with the old ones.

Reactions to Communications When We Can't Answer Back

Every day our lives are flooded with communications over television, radio, in magazines, newspapers, classrooms, and meeting rooms. Much of it is designed to persuade us through information, emotional appeals, propaganda, or, what is more likely, all three. We listen. We turn it off. We go to the woods to get away from it all. Even there, we're likely to be asked "Did you hear what they said on the radio?" All of this communication is just for us, and we can't answer back.

This chapter is about research on various reactions to such communications, especially those designed to change attitudes. Social-psychological research is an important aspect of the problems related to persuasive communications if only because the media, sponsors, and speakers turn to research to justify their decisions. As a social psychologist, I am considerably more concerned with you and me. It's important that we understand when we are and are not most susceptible to being influenced and the circumstances conducive to our attitudes changing in response to such "one-way" communication.

Research on one-way communication is a huge mass, accumulated through years of activity. Without some orientation as to what is important, a person can sink into it, losing sight of what is important. Therefore, we have to find out something about what's been going on, then concentrate on the important issues.

HYPOCRISY ABOUT RESEARCH IN HIGH PLACES

We owe it to William McGuire (1969), the Yale social psychologist, for pointing out that communication campaigns designed to change attitudes represent an investment of about $20 billion a year in the United States, which ten years ago made them "our third largest investment of national resources, in a distant but respectable third place behind expenditures to support the military establishment and to conduct formal education." If McGuire didn't include the part of the military budget that is spent for propaganda, he was underestimating. Because of this huge outlay, McGuire concluded, "those who are directly or indirectly engaged in this enterprise are loathe to accept . . . at face value" the fact that research has yielded "little evidence of attitude change, much less change in gross behavior such as buying or voting" (p. 227).

The mass media downplay the lack of evidence for attitude and behavior change when "selling" a client or when pouring their own dollars into the research budget, but they positively jump on it when anyone uses research to attack their agencies or policies. They feel free to use "research" to justify their own arbitrary decisions about what is to be seen and heard on the air, but they rush to congressional hearings or public forums to deny research evidence that watching actions on television (for example, aggression or violence) can have a connection with their occurrence in real life.

Most people in the United States today spend more time watching television and listening to the radio than they do eating, talking with friends, participating in community efforts, or making love. The mass addiction is particularly true of young children, but also of adolescents and adults (Cole, 1970). Of course, the content of the media can and do affect us. They are a major part of the social environment, filling hours of daily life, conveying what life is like, what is important, and what dreams are made of. To suggest that they have no effect on us amounts to suggesting that what we see, hear, and the way we spend our time are of no importance.

On the other hand, the fact that media content is part of our daily lives makes it difficult to offer proof of the kind that people in high places insist on: "Show us actual cases where someone committed a crime, killed or brutalized another person, raped someone, or got drunk because they saw it on television." Researchers should call their bluff on that one. It is seldom possible to show that any one incident "caused" behavior when that incident is, in fact, part of a pattern in the person's life. Against the background of what we can see on television, one more brutal death, one more "I Love Lucy," or one more deodorant ad may seldom move a person to jump up immediately to kill, to hatch a plot to outwit her husband, or to spray more deodorant under the arms. Quite the contrary, the repetitive background may deaden immediate impact of a particular show. It is the impact of that background that should be studied, not this or that hour of pictures and sound.

Social psychologists should make the following challenge to the media: The only way to detect the direct impact of media programing is to alter it completely and then to see what the consequences are. For example, against the background of the usual television fare offered to children, an interesting program promoting positive forms of social action and kindness should provide such marked contrast that children's behavior with one another would be significantly affected. Aletha Stein and Lynette Friedrich (1975) reported such research. Gorn, Goldberg, and Kanungo (1975) found evidence for enhancement of the unusual in television viewing, such that minority children portrayed attractively were actually preferred by 3 to 5-year-old Canadian children over children more typical in their own surroundings or in usual television fare.

The long-time director of research at CBS, Joseph Klapper (1960, 1967) regarded attempts to link exposure to specific program content and specific actions of individuals with some cynicism. Certainly he is correct that many researchers have not comprehended the difficulties of pinning down specific "causation" for a single action. In the United States, he felt, the mass media serve primarily to reinforce existing values and things as they are (1967). Individuals selectively tune in what is congruent with their attitudes and tune out what is not. We get more of the same because the media "give the public what it wants." The klinker in this argument is that those who plan and program the media and their sponsors also selectively choose what is to be featured and what is not. Public "fairness" doctrines operate only within the narrow range of *their* choice. The selectivity of viewers, listeners, and readers is hardly sufficient to deal with the problem of bias in the media. The audience has too narrow a range to choose from.

THE SELECTIVITY OF AUDIENCES

The problem of selectivity in tuning in or tuning out communication is not nearly as simple as the notion that we receive what pleases us and tune out what does not. Such selectivity does occur. For example, a telethon sponsored by Republicans to convert Democrats on an election eve was viewed by two Republicans to every Democrat (Schramm and Carter, 1959). A campaign to win supporters to the United Nations was heeded almost entirely by persons already favorable toward and well informed about the UN (Star and Hughes, 1950). Similarly, a readership study in Lebanon at the time when Arab Unity was a great issue showed selective choice of newspapers and magazines in line with the readers' attitudes, but such selectivity was by no means exclusive (Diab, 1965, 1967). For example, those opposing or "undecided" on the issue read more anti-unity literature than pro-unity, but supporters of Arab unity read a wide range of pro and anti literature.

Selective choice in line with our own attitudes was only one of the reasons cited in the still popular article "Some Reasons Why Information Campaigns Fail" (Hyman and Sheatsley, 1947). Experimental research suggests, in fact, that we are more likely to expose ourselves to communications on matters of more personal import than on unimportant topics, whether their bias fits well with our beliefs or not. The direction of selective bias (favoring or against our stand) varies depending on whether the information is novel or a rehash of what we have heard a million times, whether or not we need the information for practical use, and how strongly we are committed to our own stand (Brock and Balloun 1967; Clarke and James, 1967; Freedman, 1965; Sears, 1965; Sears and Freedman, 1965).

Much more research is needed on the selectivity problem, particularly since that done by the media and advertisers is so inadequate. Neither a record of the channel to which a TV set is tuned when it is on nor a retrospective report on what someone has watched gives more than a very rough notion of what particular individuals actually attended to. (Our family received a request for a weekly diary of our TV watching and faithfully filled in the shows that week that we hoped would be kept on the air, whether we had watched them or not.) On the other hand, most laboratory research suffers from the fact that the selectivity problem is ignored. An audience is "captured" in a classroom or laboratory to listen to whatever the researcher chooses to present.

WHO SAYS WHAT TO WHOM, HOW, AND WITH WHAT EFFECT: A RHETORICAL QUESTION

Aristotle really should share no blame for what has happened in research on communication, despite the fact that it is considered scholarly to attribute the formula in the heading above to that worthy Greek. Aristotle was thinking about how best to present an argument face to face with an audience of fellow countrymen. He was quite aware that the speaker and the message were always related to the audience's cultural background, emotions, and knowledge (which is what the concepts of ethos, pathos, and logos were about).

It took American social scientists to decide that *the* problem in communication was the one-way impact of a message on its target. *Who* delivered the message and *how* it was done became the main problems. The communication situation was seen as something like a shot in the arm, the main problem being what you put in the syringe, who inserted the needle, and the bedside manner with which it was done.

There was one thing to be said for researchers in the 1930s and 1940s: Most of them really did study persons with attitudes toward something. They tried to change those attitudes through a variety of communications, including speeches, motion pictures, high school and college courses, and pamphlets. By the end of that period, it was evident that most studies in the already voluminous literature had succeeded in shifting the *average* attitude test scores before exposure to communication toward the direction proposed in the communication (see Murphy, Murphy, and Newcomb, 1937; Williams, 1947).

True, as Murphy, Murphy, and Newcomb (1937) observed, there were puzzles about people's responses in different experiments. They noted that, at times, the average change represented a shifting of the entire distribution of individual attitudes toward the position conveyed in communication. At other times, however, different individuals either "side with the speaker or against him. He puts his appeal over to the hearer, or if he fails by a hair's breadth, he may fail altogether and create against his position feelings which he never suspected" (1937, p. 875).

When we surveyed the research literature about twenty-five years ago, we found that in the great majority of studies, there were individuals who changed toward the communication, some who did not change at all, and some who changed in the direction completely opposite to that intended by the communicator (see Sherif and Sherif, 1956). The problem of why this happened was seldom the focus of research before the mid-1950s, although some researchers presented "change scores" separately for those initially favorable and unfavorable to the message. Researchers in the prestigious Yale Communications Research Program routinely presented their findings in terms of the concept of "net change." Net change was the difference between percentages of people changing toward the advocated position and away from the advocated position, ignoring those who do not change at all. Why didn't they change? Why did some change toward and some away from the communication? Most of our research has concerned this puzzle.

Retreat to the Psychological Laboratory

After World War II, study of the "one-way" flow of messages from a communicator to "recipients" retreated to the laboratory to ask the kinds of questions that a distant sponsor (for example, a government agency, a business, or an advertiser) might ask in preparing a communication. Should I confine myself to *my* message or should I recognize that "another side" exists? How important is it to be "first" in getting my message across, or is it better to be last? What kind of a communicator is best for my purposes? Will it help to frighten them about the consequences of *not* doing what I propose? Indeed government agencies and foundations gave numerous grants to support "attitude change" research, as did businesses.

The huge outpouring of laboratory research on such problems was reviewed by McGuire (1969). As he noted, the increase in such research after the war was attributable in part to Carl Hovland's research program at Yale, whose own interests grew from his work during the war in assessing the effects of government propaganda on troops (Hovland, Lumsdaine, and Sheffield, 1949). Hovland's accomplishments as competent experimental psychologist account in part for the considerable prestige that "opinion change" research began to acquire. Hovland was enormously supportive and helpful to researchers with a wide range of theoretical positions.

However, much more than Hovland's prestige was sending research on attitude change back to the laboratory. In part, the trend reflected the efforts of social psychology to gain the respect of other psychologists as "academic establishment" folks. There was a painful consciousness of being and of indoctrinating one's students as "*experimental* social psychologists," as though experiments had never been done in social psychology. There was much talk praising "manipulation" of variables in preference to studying naturally occurring differences in attitudes or situational factors. Research participants were described as being "run" through procedures (as though they were rats). As a result, many experiments were labeled attitude-change studies when one simply could not speak of participants having an attitude in the first place. The rationale was that one could detect the impact of "experimental manipulations" better and that there was less "confounding" of what one was studying if one started with a clean slate.

All the while, increasing numbers of graduate students were working on advanced degrees and many of their theses reflected the above rationale. When Carl Hovland (1959) gave his Scientific Contribution Award address to the American Psychological Association in 1958 he was only three years from his untimely death. He took a critical look at research on communication effects and came up with an astounding conclusion: Looking at laboratory research and then at surveys done outside the laboratory, he saw a "marked difference in the picture of communication effects obtained in each" (p. 8). In the laboratory experiments, high frequency of change was the rule; in survey research, little change or very slow change was the rule.

Among the significant reasons Hovland cited for this outcome, two are of particular interest here. The first was the kind of attitudes studied. In the experimental research, we "usually try to find types of issues involving attitudes which are susceptible to modification. . . . In the survey procedures ... socially significant attitudes which are deeply rooted in prior experience and involve much personal commitment are typically involved." In short, issues studied in the laboratory were often "relatively uninvolving" whereas those of sufficient importance to be studied in real life were typically highly involving to the person. In addition, he noted, communications studied by survey research "usually involve reaching the individual in his natural habitat, with consequent supplementary effects produced by discussion with friends and family" (p. 11).

How a Research Situation "Confounds" the Study of Attitude Change

The traditional plan in the experimental study of attitude change in response to communication was, first, to assess a person's attitude (or secure an opinion) on a topic chosen by the researcher. Sometime later (anywhere from 15 minutes to a couple of weeks), the researcher presented communications (speech, pamphlet, movie) carefully designed and attributed to some other source (for example, with high or low prestige). Afterward, the attitude assessment was repeated. Change was measured as the difference between the measurements before and after the communication. Typically, the person was either alone in the laboratory or in a highly formal audience (for example, classroom) situation. It all sounds very neat and "controlled."

Now let's recall the main points of Chapter 2: Individuals always respond to the properties of a social situation, even a casual one, and a research situation has special properties of its own. When the person has no attitude on the topic of communication, or when it is a matter of slight concern or of great uncertainty to the person, we would expect him or her to size up the situation to see what is the expected or desirable behavior and to react accordingly. Unless the individual becomes resistant to the research for some other reason (for example, for being an unwilling captive or having an antagonistic attitude toward researchers), he or she is exceedingly likely to notice and act on cues as to what the researcher expects: "Hmm, some change in responses on the attitude or opinion questionnaire must be expected." As described above, in the before-after design with low levels of personal involvement in the topic at hand, people respond to what is expected: Opinions change all over the place, typically toward the communication (Kerrick and McMillan, 1961; Sherman, 1967).

However, participating in research can arouse other self-concerns, in addition to any attitude that is being studied. Thus, volunteers solicited and paid for research are significantly more likely to change toward the position advocated in a before-after research design than students captured in their classrooms (Rosnow and Suls, 1970). Informing research subjects of what change is expected after pretesting their attitudes is more likely to produce some resistance to change (Lana and Menapace, 1971). The effect of such a "warning" is significantly greater when the person is, in fact, more involved in her own position at the outset (Apsler and Sears, 1968).

Brehm (1966) and his associates have repeatedly found differences in responsiveness to the research situation depending on whether the student sizes up the situation as allowing some choice in reacting or feels "mouse-trapped" into responding a particular way. Brehm calls the feeling that oneself is coerced "reactance," meaning that the person reacts *against* the attempt at manipulation. Such self concerns may explain results such as these: Patients at a rehabilitation hospital embarking on recovery programs after heart or lung ailments were given a test on their attitudes toward self and the outside world and were told that these would change following therapy. They actually changed less after four to six weeks of therapy than those who were simply pretested (Lana and Menapace, 1971). Surely such attitudes were highly involving to the person and the feelings accompanying them very real. A researcher telling a patient at that time that "you're going to change and I'm going to check up on it" could arouse resentment for "lack of understanding of how I feel," and "telling me what I'm going to do."

Now, these kinds of responsiveness to the research situation can also affect reactions in the only kind of survey research that studies attitudes of particular individuals over time, namely, the "panel" studies testing and retesting the same persons' opinions at intervals. However, we cannot attribute the lower frequency of change and the slowness to change in survey research that Hovland remarked on solely to such procedures or the resistance they arouse. The impact of the research situation itself on attitudes would be expected to vary with the degree of the person's involvement in his or her own stand (Chapters 7 and 9).

Demand Characteristics of Research Situations and Personal Involvement

When involvement in the topic that is the subject of the communication is low, almost any procedure in the research situation increases the general level of arousal. Several procedures (for example, committing oneself to a position when requested by the researcher, reading a communication advocating a clear-cut position, or changing one's ratings) may in themselves heighten involvement temporarily (Rhine and Polowniak, 1971). Thus, the impact of research procedures appears to be at a maximum when personal involvement in one's stand is initially quite low and the situation is defined as "research."

Such notions were tested in an experiment by Tittler (1967, Sherif et al., 1973) in which he compared the precommunication to postcommunication changes in attitude tests (the Method of Ordered Alternatives) on issues that he had previously selected as high and low in involvement for college students. Communications on topics of low involvement to students were easily selected, since Tittler was interested in the findings of an earlier study by Janis and Field (1959) that women were more prone to change their opinions on a variety of issues than men. He selected two of the issues they had used as likely to leave college students totally unconcerned: the merits of General von Hindenburg as a historical figure and the probable success of an unknown comedian named O'Keefe! Then through a series of interviews and ratings by college students on the importance of various issues to them, Tittler chose two that were highly involving to students, one concerning the male and the other the female sex role. As expected, Tittler found that students were significantly more noncommittal on the less involving than the more involving topics (see Chapter 9).

Communications were prepared that were opposite to the positions taken initially by students on each of these topics, but did not represent the most extreme stands on the issues. Afterward, the students' attitudes were checked again. Aware of the "demand" effects of the research plan for students who had volunteered and were concerned to "do well," Tittler gave half of the students completely irrelevant communications (for example, on the merits of flu vaccine). Changes after these communications, he felt, would reveal general tendencies for students to shift their responses simply to comply with the researcher's before-after tests to study "change." In fact, about one-quarter to one-third of the students changed their most acceptable positions on attitude tests following these irrelevant communications, responding to what they thought the researcher expected of them.

If we follow Tittler's logic and subtract the percentages who changed following an irrelevant communication from the percentages who changed following persuasive communications pertinent to the issues at hand, we find that the "net change" attributable to the communications themselves was only about 25 percent of the men and women on the sex role issues and nearly 50 percent on the less involving issues. (In absolute terms, about 50 percent changed on the sex role issues and about 80 percent in response to communications on Hindenburg and O'Keefe! Evidently, the research situation "demanded" change quite strongly.)

Tittler found no evidence that the women were more likely than men to change on all four issues. However, the one sex difference that he did obtain clarifies why Janis and Field (1959) found a consistent tendency for women to be more susceptible to influence than men. On the historical merit of General von Hindenburg, more women (88 percent) changed than men (73 percent). Since the women's latitude of noncommitment was also greater than men's on this issue, it seems reasonable that women were simply less involved in the military figure. Janis and Field found consistent sex differences toward the greater "persuasibility" of females chiefly because all of the several topics they studied were of very little personal concern to females.

The important conclusion is that the impact of a research situation and of a persuasive communication are functions of how involving a person's stand is in the first place. With very low involvement, we are studying the impact of the research situation much more than the person's attitude or its change. The considerable change found by Tittler on sex role issues also reflects the impact of the research situation, but its significantly lower frequency reflects the students' involvement in the issues and in their particular stands.

COMMUNICATION FLOW: IS IT ONE-WAY, TWO STEPS, OR SEVERAL?

Hovland's critique was properly concerned that laboratory-type research on attitude change restricted the person to a communicator's message while shutting the doors to his or her communication with anyone until the researcher got the "goodies" in the form of evidence for change. Way back in the 1940 presidential election, the sociologists Lazarsfeld, Berelson, and Gaudet (1948) made an interesting discovery in their "panel survey" study of voter preferences and behavior: Individuals who changed their choice of candidates seldom mentioned the mass media as sources of influence or information that led them to change. Those most frequently mentioned were friends, family, or acquaintances.

Furthermore, change was significantly more frequent among those persons who initially preferred the candidate from a political party other than their own or a candidate not chosen by close relatives and friends. People involved in such "cross pressures" changed from August to the October preceding the election much more frequently than those whose candidate preferences coincided with own party choice. Of the 24 individuals who had initially preferred the candidate of the other party, all but 2 decided to vote for the candidate of their party's choice. A person's reference group (here probably both party and family or friends) has considerable impact on his or her decisions.

Subsequent research studied diverse attitudes and actions of considerable importance to the persons: other voting decisions, magazine preferences, fashion changes, new products, and innovations (for example, the use of new drugs by physicians) (Merton, 1949; Berelson, Lazarsfeld, and McPhee, 1954; Katz and Lazarsfeld, 1955; Coleman,

Katz, and Menzel, 1959, 1966; Rogers, 1962). Together these studies on the influence of mass communication, advertising, or innovation recast the problem of attitude change through communication.

The notion that communication flows from mass media directly to the target person, who is affected or not, was simply wrong. Attitude change and change in behavior patterns seldom followed promptly on receipt of communication, as their study in the short-range experiment demands. They seldom occurred prior to interaction with reference persons or groups appropriately concerned with the matter at hand (for example, women friends for fashion, other doctors for drugs). In view of this finding we wonder at experimental procedures that *prevent* such interaction as "messy," "unpredictable," or "confounding" the purity of the research design.

Elihu Katz (1965) summarized the research on the "two-step" flow of communication (which may involve many interchanges). He pointed out that even when a message reaches everyone at the same time, those who first alter their actions as a consequence are individuals who are more interested in the topic at hand, who deliberately expose themselves and receive more communication on the topic, who are socially active with respect to the topic, and who are regarded by others as being competent in those activities. Such "opinion leaders" are also more likely to "know" first and more about the topic than others.

"Opinion leaders" sound at first like an elite, but studies of who opinion leaders are show that they are scattered throughout the population. Who they are depends on the attitude being studied. They are differentiated from others in the population chiefly in ways that indicate higher status in a formally or informally organized group (see Chapter 4). Here is the way Katz (1965, p. 205) characterized such "opinion leaders":

1. They "personify" certain values (that is, they represent ideals and other norms of their particular group to other members).
2. They are regarded as "competent" with respect to the matter at hand (that is, others have seen in the past that they perform related activities well, that they "know what they're talking about," that their initiative has been effective and trustworthy).
3. They are "strategically located." (They interact with greater frequency within a definite social circle and, in certain cases, serve to link its members with other circles and groups.)

In short, the descriptions of who "opinion leaders" are indicate that they have higher status in "interpersonal networks" within communities, in and between organized groups, in institutions and within social, professional, occupational, political, or religious organizations (Katz and Lazarsfeld, 1955). The effectiveness of communication from outside of these networks is not a one-way process to each of the separate individuals. Earlier or later, individuals talk to, observe, question, or otherwise interact with opinion leaders (directly or secondhand). All this means is that social interaction among members of reference sets or groups is part of the process through which outside communications do or do not exert their influence. The higher-status individuals exert relatively more influence in receiving, evaluating, and disseminating a message, as indeed they do in any matter of some importance to their groups.

How Social Networks (Reference Sets)
Affect Persistence of Change

Recalling Newcomb's finding about the importance of friends and families on political attitudes, we can see that the "two-step" or many-step flow of communications that reach members of a reference set would affect the persistence of any change that occurs. One thing people in a reference group do is to talk about and rehash issues of concern to them.

Cook and Insko (1968) showed the importance of such "reexposure" to a position presented in communication and, in addition, the importance of linking its message to several, rather than one or two, salient concerns or values. They started in the laboratory with an experiment on "person perception" that simply served to distract students from their real purpose. Then they presented to different samples of University of North Carolina students one of two tape-recorded speeches arguing that the President of the United States should be elected by Congress. (This was, of course, before the United States had had both a President and a Vice President selected by their predecessors and approved by Congress.)

One communication tied the argument to only two important concerns: strengthening the checks and balances provided in the Constitution between the executive and legislative branches and better ensuring that a competent person would be chosen. The other communication pulled out four additional supporting values for the argument (adding to the dignity of elections, savings, ensuring cooperation with the Congress, and so on). The researchers then sent cards the next day to three groups of these same students asking them to arrive 4, 7, or 11 days later for a second session of the experiment at a certain time and place. Half of these cards also contained the reminder that in part of the first session they had heard an argument that the President should be elected by Congress.

Cook and Insko avoided the "demand" character of a before-after measurement of attitudes by randomly assigning students to have their attitudes assessed only once, either without a communication or *after* the communication (immediately or 4, 7, or 11 days later when they returned for the second session). Such a procedure is possible when we can assume that everyone has about the same initial attitude and that the random assignment to different experimental conditions will guarantee that individual differences will be distributed by chance throughout the various conditions.

Since the issue was probably not highly involving, it was not surprising that the immediate effect of the communication was significant change toward the position advocated. Students who received cards with no messages reminding them of the speech were *less* favorable, their favorability toward the proposal *decreasing* with the length of delay between the two sessions.

The trend over time for students who received the reminder about the speech on their card and were tested 4, 7, or 11 days later was the opposite: Those who had kept their little appointment cards with the "reminder" for longer periods were *more* favorable to the proposal than those who had had their cards for shorter periods. Furthermore, the effect of looking at the card a few times (which is what the researchers think happened) was greater for those who had initially heard the argument linked to everything to be desired (six values) than only a couple of values.

I find this experiment intriguing because it appears to show the effects of two influences that occur naturally when reference group members interact: repeated statement of the "right" view and linking that "right" view to all of the group's values and ideals, or as many as possible. I believe that Cook and Insko are correct that natural environments (mass advertising repeating the same message daily by the hour or interactions with reference groups) support attitude change more through reminders of the "correct" position and links to important values than by reminding the person of all the detailed reasons why the position is "correct."

WHEN IS A PERSON LIKELY OR UNLIKELY TO CHANGE?

As noted earlier, one impact of the one-way flow model on communications research was to lead researchers to neglect the issue of what kind of attitude the person had in the first place and what a communication was, in effect, asking the person to do. As we have seen (Chapter 9), the structure of a person's attitude that is highly involving differs from that of a less involving one: The highly involved person has a much broader latitude of rejection, compared with the acceptable latitude, and is noncommittal about very little. The less involved person is much more noncommittal.

Public opinion pollsters learned the hard way that when a large percentage of respondents answer "don't know" or "no opinion," they are fertile targets for the influence of events, propaganda, and persuasion (see Marks, 1949). They learned this lesson in 1948 when some incorrectly predicted that Thomas Dewey, not Harry Truman would be elected President chiefly by assuming that the noncommitted either would not vote or would divide up about fifty-fifty between the two. They did not: a substantial percentage decided to vote for Truman, who won the election.

In our own work, we have found repeatedly that persons with large latitudes of noncommitment are more likely to respond positively to persuasive communication and/or to change in the course of natural compelling events (Sherif, Sherif, and Nebergall, 1965; Sherif and Sherif, 1969). On controversial social issues, such as an election outcome, such individuals are more likely to take moderate than extreme positions. For not one, but several reasons, persons taking extreme positions are likely to display less noncommitment and more rejection (see Chapter 9). These reasons include the likelihood that the person is a member of a group that takes the position and that upholding an extreme stand means that the person is exposed rather more frequently to attack from others. Being attacked by moderates on the same side of an issue frequently occurs, for example when the respective parties represent warring factions within a social movement or when, as in the United States, "extreme moderation" is prized, at times with a vengeance. In any event, such experiences mean that the person has to justify, nourish, and support the extreme stand in order to maintain it.

However, high involvement and extremity of stand on the spectrum need not go together. Regardless of his or her position, including "absolute noncommitment," a person whose attitude is high in the priorities of the self-system is resistant to change. Changing such an attitude means, for the person, not merely shedding an opinion, but changing a part of the self that is intertwined with many other important values.

Such an attitude may concern issues that are, in the broad scheme of things, pretty trivial. If having a fast car and driving like a fool is manly adventure, and I am an adventurous man, don't tell me I can't drive my car over 55. If my long, shiny hair is important to me as a woman, I'd feel stripped of femininity if it were shaved off. If to be a self-respecting, decent person in my community is to be a Republican or a Democrat, I can withstand all kinds of shenanigans in my party and all kinds of propaganda before I'll think of switching parties.

Such involvement in images of self relative to other people "who count," in values, ideals, and modes of conduct is no abstraction floating around in a person's head: Typically, relevant commitments are made daily in our normal social life, in whom we see and don't see, how others react to us and us to them, what we do and don't do, what we listen to and don't listen to. So attitudes high in priority in the self-system do get reinforced, both from our own actions and through interactions with others. When, in addition, our attitudes pertain to the major norms or values of a reference group, to change them means suffering the scorn or loss of what is, to most people, the most important thing when the chips are down: affectional ties with other human individuals.

If we begin to doubt, if events contradict what we so earnestly expect, if others who *matter* betray or abuse us, if we desire one thing but our friends oppose it, if we act in ways that violate our own most cherished values, we will experience a most discomfiting state, which Leon Festinger (1957) referred to as "cognitive dissonance," and which he conceived as analogous to "a state of drive or need or tension" that demands "action to reduce it just as, for example, the presence of hunger leads to action to reduce the hunger" (p. 18). Such an analogy treats bodily tensions and inner conflicts involving the self-system as equivalent. Of course, psychic conflicts involve states of bodily tension. When they do, we do not rid ourselves of the mental and emotional anguish at any price, though we may do something to temporarily alleviate the tension. Depending on our values, we are much more likely to swear, to jog three miles, to take a drink or smoke a joint, to turn to a pleasant activity, to pray or do Yoga exercises than we are to change the self-attitudes and allegiances that are at the heart of the dissonant experience. We do not reduce the bodily tension or resolve the cognitive dissonance at any price in order to restore equilibrium. On the contrary, we may seek or expose ourselves to more serious inner conflict, in order to avoid making those changes in our precious selves or in our ties with precious others that would bring relief.

For a time in social psychology, "cognitive dissonance" became a catch phrase to explain almost any change in a person's attitude or behavior, probably contrary to the wishes of Festinger or his students. It was picked up by advertising men. I last saw the phrase in an article written by one of ex-President Nixon's former advisers, and I don't doubt its appropriateness. Perhaps it was such overextension that led Festinger to cease active research on the problems referred to in his book, in which attitude change was a rather minor one. His former students appear to have concluded, by and large, that the theory became imprecise in part because it had not been related explicitly to problems in the stability or instability of the self-system (see Aronson, 1968; Elms, 1972; Sahakian, 1974). It is with similar concern that I point out here that moment-to-moment attempts to restore "consonance" or "psychic equilibrium" are much more likely if there is no issue of changing important attitudes. The more parsimonious accounts of the research on cognitive dissonance center on the person's self perceptions during transitory encounters (Bem, 1967).

Since the great majority of research on cognitive dissonance has not concerned attitude change as I have defined it, I have made no attempt to review it here. When a state of dissonance, inner conflict, shame, or guilt is aroused that does relate to important attitudes, Festinger was certainly correct that the person may be ripe for attitude change. Such change is most likely to occur over a long period of time, however. Sustained "dissonance" in the self-system almost always precedes the rare "sudden conversion" or switch of reference groups (Frank, 1972). Such issues will be raised in the next chapter.

SIZING UP COMMUNICATIONS DISCREPANT FROM OUR ATTITUDES

In order to change our own position on a psychosocial scale, a communication from another person or a group has to propose a position differing from our own. The issue that was raised by Sherif and Hovland (1961) was *how* different a position was likely to be effective. The *discrepancy* between the person's latitude of acceptance and the position advocated is the term applied to this problem in the research literature.

In their earliest study on the discrepancy problem, Hovland, Harvey, and Sherif (1957) compared reactions by active supporters for the repeal of prohibition laws in Oklahoma (wets), active members of anti-repeal groups (drys), and moderately pro-repeal college students at the University of Oklahoma. They presented pro-repeal, moderately pro-repeal, and anti-repeal tape-recorded messages to persons taking each of nine positions as their "most acceptable" stand. (The fact that there were large numbers taking each of these positions was the main reason they studied that issue at all.) They asked those exposed to the communications to judge the position advocated in the message by marking the position on a straight line whose ends indicated "extremely pro-repeal" and "extremely anti-repeal." Then they calculated the average distance from the extreme ends of the scale of the marks made by the respondents for each of the three communications.

In judging the extremely pro- and extremely anti-repeal messages, almost everyone correctly placed them at or very near the extremes, regardless of their own position on the issue. However, in judging the moderately wet communication, statistically significant differences in judgment occurred according to its discrepancy from the person's own position. Those whose acceptable latitude was quite close to the communication judged it quite accurately as leaning just a bit to the "wet" side. With somewhat larger discrepancies, however, the message was slightly displaced by wets *toward* their position (assimilation effect). As the discrepancies became increasingly larger, the position advocated in the message was contrasted to the person's own position. The "drys" (WCTU members) judged the communication as much wetter than it was (contrast effect, away from their own position). The wets at the pro-repeal extreme, judged the communication a bit more to the dry side than it was (a contrast tendency).

A correlated result was that the proportions of persons upholding each attitude position as their own who liked the message and who found it fair and unbiased became smaller and smaller as the discrepancy increased. The further away a communication was, the more it was judged unfair, biased and propagandistic, and the more it was disliked. In a later study on the same issue (since repeal had not succeeded), Norman Jackman and I (1966) presented a series of statements for and against repeal as well as moderately dry statements to pro-repeal and anti-repeal partisans. These statements were stated as facts. We asked them to rate how true or false they were. As you might expect, statements on the opposite side of the issue were regarded as downright false, whereas those on the person's own side were rated, on the whole, as pretty true. Interestingly enough, the quite factual moderately dry statements (for example, some traffic accidents are caused by drinking) were rated as significantly more true by drys than by pro-repeal supporters.

Carl Hovland's program at Yale supported this second prohibition study and another study on judgments of communication about the 1956 presidential election on the grounds that attitude change was being studied. Each was planned to measure attitudes about two weeks before and just after a person received one of the communications. Frankly we never believed that changes found could be attributed to the communications alone since active election campaigns were going on outside all the time. Still, I'll give you the figures for the prohibition study to compare with other studies I've already reported. Among pro-repeal and anti-repeal activists, percentages of change after listening to the extreme opposite communication were practically nil (4 percent in each case). They consisted of accepting somewhat more moderate positions on the same side. Among the initially less committed students (most of whom were a trifle wet), 28 percent changed toward the pro-repeal communication. None of these changes amounted to changing sides. Fourteen percent who heard the anti-repeal communication shifted in its direction. Quite a difference from the percentages in Tittler's study on Hindenburg!

We repeated similar procedures for the issue of the choice of candidates in the 1956 and 1960 presidential elections with more communications (for example, presenting a moderate communication on each side of the issue and one that gave no conclusion at all; Sherif, Sherif, and Nebergall, 1965). In the 1960 election, we analyzed the judgments by persons more or less involved in the outcome of the election separately and found that whether assimilation or contrast affects occurred was closely related to the degree of a person's involvement as well as to the apparent discrepancy of the communication. People who were not highly involved showed a great capacity to assimilate discrepant messages over a broad range of positions. Those who were involved contrasted messages only slightly discrepant from their own stands.

More recently, Janet Marzolf (1973) studied judgments of communications for or against the women's movement that had been designed to be quite moderate. Introductory psychology students appraised them as moderately favorable or unfavorable to the movement. However, members of a women's studies course judged both messages as *extremely* anti-movement, and wanted to know where on earth we obtained such anti-movement messages. In the earlier research the messages were not attributed to any particular source so that people would be concerned mostly about the message, not the source. However, in both the 1960 election study and the second prohibition study, we found a strong and significant trend for people with strong attitudes to attribute communications even moderately opposed to their attitudes to the "opposition." So these women were no more suspicious than highly involved people in earlier studies.

Now let me sum up what we know from these and a number of other studies of communication:

In the first place, the discrepancy between a person's stand and a communication is not a fixed absolute quantity. Above all, it depends on the degree of the person's involvement in the issue, in two ways: (1) High personal involvement makes a person's attitude a stronger anchor in comparing the position of the message. (2) High personal involvement also means that the person will have a broader latitude of rejection and less noncommitment relative to the acceptable latitude. As a consequence, the same message presented to highly involved and less involved persons may fall in the latter's latitude of noncommitment but in the highly involved person's latitude of rejection.

In the second place, there is comparatively little variation in sizing up the stand taken in an extremely partisan message, despite the fact that its extreme opponents may, indeed, exaggerate its extremely (Chapter 7). What this means is that a communication strongly advocating one extreme end position can be assimilated only by persons already leaning toward that side. Proportional to the discrepancy from their own stand, others dislike the communication, see it as biased propaganda and probably as a pack of lies. There is usually no question of attitude change and there is also no experience of "dissonance." It simply makes them angry that there should be such bone-headed people around. Thus, extreme advocacy is largely effective in rousing supporters to action or, occasionally, in spurring "leaners" or noncommitted people from their lethargy by involving them in the issue (which may eventually lead to attitude change). Advocacy of extreme positions may also eventually extend the range of positions that others will even consider, as noted in the last chapter.

Consequently, questions about the effectiveness of moderate communications in short-range attitude change are more interesting, particularly in the United States where being moderate is akin to cleanliness (which is next to godliness). One reason that moderate communications evoke interesting reactions is that, by and large, they are more ambiguous as to just what position they do represent. In fact, in research, one can go quite mad in attempting to secure consensus among judges on the position of some moderate communications because judges with differing attitudes interpret them so differently.

In part, we can understand such variability in judgments of moderate messages in terms of psychological selectivity: For example in the 1960 election, we presented a totally balanced communication composed of the arguments each party made on five issues, but which drew no conclusion. There was a strong tendency for people favoring both Republican and Democratic candidates to emphasize selectively the arguments on their own side, hence to assimilate that totally unbiased message to their own position. Similarly, both Republicans and Democrats judged the famous debates between Nixon and Kennedy as giving the edge to their own candidate, the assimilation being directly proportional to the extremity of their most acceptable stands on the election outcome (Sherif et al., 1965).

Even the simple announcement that one is neutral or "absolutely noncommittal" may leave room for doubt. Such a stance falls in the latitude of rejection of highly involved persons with extreme stands and they have been known to denounce neutrality as "immoral" (Secretary of State Dulles during the Cold War years of Eisenhower's administration).

How Moderates Use Extremists: The Double Anchor

When a communication does attempt seriously to present a clear and moderate position on one side or the other of a controversial issue, the communication is assimilated or contrasted to the person's own position, depending on its discrepancy from and how involved the person is in the attitude. The person who upholds a moderate stance on a controversial matter (whether a social issue or personal dispute) pleases others who are also moderate since they can assimilate the message toward their own latitude of acceptance. However, the moderate seldom receives gratitude from highly involved, more extreme proponents in a controversy. Each side contrasts the message to its highly discrepant stand (the major anchor in judging it), thereby pushing the speaker's position away from it and making it less acceptable.

Suppose that you wanted to advocate a moderate position on one side of a controversial issue, but hoped to avoid being damned by extreme advocates on your own side or by those taking the opposite extreme. By itself, your message stating your moderate position will be contrasted to their strong views by extremists on both sides. If, however, you couple your moderate message with the extreme view on your own side, you have provided an additional anchor that may affect the judgments of those on the opposite side of the issue in a felicitous fashion. In contrast to the extreme position on your side, the opposition will find your position *closer* to their own than they would if they only heard your viewpoint. The extreme on your side provides an additional anchor for their judgments. We have a "double anchor," rather than just one.

Just after the turn of the century, some suffragists were quite upset by the extreme positions taken by certain feminists on women's issues, notably by Charlotte Gilman, who thought herself a socialist (though not all socialists agreed). The suffragists wanted to confine their aim to securing the vote for women. Charlotte Gilman was rocking the boat by demanding much more. However, one suffragist wrote to her seeing an advantage to the suffrage movement in her extreme position: "After all, I think you will do our cause more good than harm, because what you ask is so much worse than what we ask that they will grant our demands in order to escape yours" (O'Neill, 1971, p. 132).

Martin Luther King (1964) also appreciated the value of emphasizing the extreme stands in the black movement toward equality after he had been put in Birmingham jail and criticized by white religious leaders for "extremism" in the form of civil disobedience: " . . . I stand in the middle of two opposing forces in the Negro community. One is a force of complacency. . . . The other is one of bitterness and hatred and comes perilously close to advocating violence" (pp. 72–73). He attempted, thereby, to get the religious leaders to place him correctly as a moderate whose "small" deviation from their own "sympathy" for civil rights might lead them to assimilate his civil disobedience into their latitudes of acceptance or, at least, noncommitment, when compared with black leaders even more extreme.

A test of the effectiveness of coupling a moderate message opposed to the person's attitude with a statement of the extreme opposition was made by Helen Kearney (1975). In a field study, she gave moderate messages opposing the extreme stands taken, respectively, by members of one group actively advocating strong anti-abortion laws and members of another supporting liberalized abortion laws. On a random basis, some members in each group received the message moderately opposing their own views in the context of an irrelevant communication (irrelevant to these individuals, but not to Puerto Ricans, whose independence the message concerned). The others received the same moderate message in the context of a message advocating the extreme opposite to their own positions on the issue. Kearney wanted to see whether the contexts of the messages, one providing an additional extreme anchor, would affect judgments of the moderate communication.

Without the extreme anchor, individuals on both sides of the issue judged a message moderately opposing their own position as more extremely opposed to it (contrast effect). There was a tendency for judgments of the moderate messages to be *less* extreme when the extreme opposite message was also given; however, the differences were not statistically significant. With high personal commitment to a stand, that stand is such a salient anchor that providing another at the opposite extreme makes only a slight difference, at best, in judgments of moderate messages.

However, in a laboratory study with women students, the added (extreme opposite) message was effective in shifting judgments of the moderate message in the moderate direction. These women all had attitudes favoring liberal abortion laws, but some were more highly involved in the issue than others, as indicated by their latitudes of rejection and noncommitment. (The researcher had hoped to include men in the study as well, but found too few male undergraduates taking sufficiently extreme stands or involved enough in the issue.) By and large, the more involved students were not as strongly committed to their stands as the activists in the field study, notably lacking experience in public activities promoting their own views.

As expected, the more involved women judged the moderately opposed message as *more* opposed in the context of an irrelevant message (contrast effect), than the less involved students. However, the introduction of the additional extreme message produced significantly different judgments for both more and less involved women. The moderate message was judged as *more* moderate in that context, indicating that both anchors were used: the woman's own stand and the position of the opposite extreme message.

Politicians have used a similar technique to bring less than enthusiastic sympathizers to regard them as more "like" themselves (that is, to assimilate their position). In this case, the extreme anchor to be contrasted with the person's own stand is not that on the same side, but that on the opposite (enemy) side. Here, the appeal is equally to the moderates and extremists on his or her own side. The technique is to repeatedly contrast the speaker's position to the opposite extreme, thereby emphasizing his or her nearness to anyone remotely on the same side of the issue. Thus, before the Nixon administration declared that the United States was withdrawing from Vietnam, the President's assistant, H. R. Haldeman, wrote enthusiastic approval to proposals that "hippie" anti-war demonstrators be allowed to shout obscenities at the site of a presidential address in a southern state. The effect of the demonstrators on an audience friendly to Nixon could only be to minimize any differences they might see between their views and Nixon's policies—in contrast to the huge gap between Nixon and the demonstrators.

Whether you take a moderate or extreme position on an issue, these strategies for controlling assimilation-contrast effects in judgments of communication are important to recognize. If you are a moderate, you may be hoodwinked; if you take an extreme position, you may be "used" either by the opposition or by others on your own side.

WHAT DO WE KNOW ABOUT ATTITUDE CHANGE IN RESPONSE TO DISCREPANT COMMUNICATIONS?

From the viewpoint of the person exposed to communication designed to influence, the problem is "what range of communications discrepant from my own stand am I likely to assimilate, hence likely to regard favorably enough that I may change as a consequence of the message?" Conversely, "beyond what difference from my own position will a communication turn me off so that its intended influence is either lost or has the reverse effect, that is, makes me more convinced or even more extremely entrenched in my side of the story?" The most important circumstances determining answers to these questions center on (1) the degree of the person's involvement in the matter at hand, (2) communication discrepancy (3) the clarity of the alternative positions (and their consequences for the person), and (4) the individual's relationship with the communicator (for example, is the latter credible?). As we shall see, these are not unrelated matters.

The Degree of Personal Involvement

The available research is quite clear that when the person has little personal investment in his or her own position, increasingly discrepant communications can be assimilated and may produce increasing changes in behavior, given that other aspects of the social situation are compelling. By a compelling social situation, I mean that the location, the activities, the other people, and the communication define clearly what the person is expected to do, and present no obstacles to the expected action. In research situations, the unconcerned subject obliges.

Thus, Hovland and Pritzker (1957), Zimbardo (1960), and many other experimenters have found that research subjects confronted with issues of little personal concern change increasingly toward proposals attributed to a majority of their peers, an "expert," a friend, or another preinstructed subject in a research situation. Invariably, the research situation and procedures have given clues that change is expected, and change they typically do.

The issue at hand has invariably lacked clarity in some respect (as to the value and consequences of alternative positions). Often it was not very familiar to the subjects. Often, alternatives were indeterminate, hypothetical, or predictions of the future (for example, whether Washington or Lincoln was a great President, how a juvenile delinquent *should* be treated, or whether protective tariffs *should* be reduced).

Whittaker (1963, 1967) repeated the Hovland and Pritzker study, confirming their findings of increased change with increasingly discrepant communications attributed to peers on the uninvolving and abstract issues those investigators studied. (Note, however, that while they were uninvolving and abstract to college students, they might very well appeal to someone else and be seen as real problems.) On issues somewhat more involving to students (for example, whether there should be curfews for male students), the most discrepant communications produced no change at all, despite the compelling research situation. Similarly North Dakota farmers exposed to communications advocating greater government controls in agriculture either did not change or shifted more toward their initial stand opposing government control.

Bochner and Insko (1966) also looked at the discrepancy problem in the college classroom, where either a Nobel Prize winner or a YMCA director was said to have advocated anywhere from 8 to 0 hours of sleep a night. Students who received the message advocating 7 or 8 hours in a "reader comprehension" test dutifully responded, on the average, that about 7½ hours was the most desirable, whereas those receiving messages advocating 6, 5, 4, or 3 hours a night reported increasingly less sleep as desirable. With messages advocating only 3 hours (the YMCA director) or 1 hour of sleep (the Nobel Prize winner), the students responded, on the average, with 6 to 6½ hours as desirable, an amount perhaps more nearly their own custom. Advocacy of 0 hours of sleep brought an abrupt decline in message influence, as students responded with about 7 hours. Meanwhile, the students indicated by their ratings of the messages that they thought the messages were increasingly nonsensical, unreasonable, and so on, as they advocated less and less sleep, and that the communicators were decreasingly credible.

Norman Miller (1965) did a careful study showing different reactions to extreme communications opposing individuals' own stands on an issue, depending on how personally salient their stands were made in the research situation. He studied high school students chosen from a large number as being extremely for or against fluoridation of public water supplies. Half of the students were first told how important the issue was, particularly to high school students. They were also assured that the sponsoring organization "feels the way you do," were asked to state reasons for their own position, and were asked to commit themselves to distribute materials on the issue. These procedures were calculated to heighten personal involvement in their own pro or anti position. Indeed they did.

Very slight change, if any, and some change away from the position advocated in the extreme opposite communication was found for highly involved students. Those not aroused changed their positions significantly toward the position advocated in the communication, particularly if their stands were initially favorable to fluoridation. This latter result may be related to the frightening consequences contained in the extreme anti-fluoridation message, which emphasized fluoride's poisonous potential. All the pro-fluoridation message had to offer was threat of more cavities.

In summary, available evidence indicates that a person with little involvement in the issue at hand can be moved by communications increasingly discrepant from his or her stand, when such change is clearly expected. However, extreme discrepancies are unlikely to be assimilated; hence the message is likely to be ineffective. Persons who are involved in their stands on the issue assimilate and are affected by messages over a much narrower range of discrepancies. They are unlikely to be moved to change merely by one widely discrepant communication.

The Problem of How Discrepant a Message Is

There have been very few studies asking how discrepant a message can be from the person's latitude of acceptance and still produce attitude change. As I noted earlier, this problem is complicated by the fact that the discrepancy of the message is a relative matter, relative to the person's latitude of acceptance, noncommitment, and rejection. Peterson and Koulack (1969) attempted such a study by choosing 72 students with identical responses to an attitude test (Method of Ordered Alternatives) on the Vietnam war. These students at Washington State University at that time all supported continued "escalation" of the war in Vietnam in order to "force Vietnam to seek peace," also accepting the need to "stop communist aggression" there. However, they also agreed on the need for time to see if the war would "have any value." They were asked to role-play by writing an essay on positions increasingly against the war.

After writing the essay, their attitudes were assessed once more (three weeks after the first assessment). The researchers found the greatest change among students who had written on a position two steps removed from their latitudes of acceptance, namely, that the "price of war . . . is growing too high to continue." Amount of change declined with increasingly discrepant positions to nearly zero for positions suggesting withdrawal from Vietnam.

Eagly and Telaak (1972) conducted a similar study of male and female students at the University of Massachusetts who favored birth control. They carefully designed communications slightly, moderately, and greatly discrepant from students' pro-birth control attitudes and assessed their judgments of these discrepant communications. They found that the students assimilated the least discrepant message and increasingly contrasted the more discrepant messages opposing birth control. The only significant attitude change occurred among students who judged a message as within their latitude of acceptance, and such changes were very small, on the average (average of less than one position). When the researchers divided the students into thirds according to whether their initial latitude of acceptance was "narrow," "medium," or "wide," they found that significant attitude change occurred only among those with "wide" latitudes of acceptance (which also implied smaller latitudes of rejection, hence less personal involvement). Among these "tolerant" and less involved students, the greatest attitude change was found for the moderately discrepant communication and the least for the most discrepant communication.

The Ambiguity of Alternatives (the Lack of Structure)

Early in this book, we found that social influence from others is greatest when there are many ambiguous or equally feasible alternatives (Chapter 3). On the other hand, we learned that, even here, the "sky is not the limit" in how discrepant that influence can be from a scale or position that the individual accepts (Chapter 6).

These conclusions were clearly supported in an experiment by Nemeth and Markowski (1972), who utilized a notoriously weak sensory capacity of human beings—their sense of taste. Specifically, they had subjects taste lemonade mixtures varying in sweetness from no sugar to considerable sugar, asking them to rate their relative sweetness-sourness. After securing their individual judgments of five drinks, three preinstructed confederates started announcing aloud judgments of the sourest drink that diverged from the person's initial judgment of it by 2, 3, 4, or 5 units on the sweetness scale. It is important to remember that after tasting a bit, the taste buds "adapt" so that our judgments are really not so accurate. Several alternatives are possible, even though the amount of sugar is an "objective" fact. Finally, each person judged the sour drink again by himself or herself.

On the average, discrepant influences were increasingly effective on the person's judgments in the presence of the others up to the 4-step discrepancy, but declined to almost 0 with the greatest discrepancy between sour and sweet drinks. However, these averages masked what really happened: With increasingly discrepant social influence from others, individual variability in judgments regularly and significantly increased. The number of individuals who were affected at *all* declined from 14 (out of 15) with the smallest discrepancy to only 6 (out of 15) in the most discrepant. In addition, the subjects became increasingly suspicious as the discrepancy increased about the experimenters' intentions to influence or trick them.

When they later judged the sour drink alone, most subjects in all conditions judged the sourest drink sweeter than initially (which might be expected through adaptation). Their average change privately was *inversely* related to the discrepancy of the planted judgments they had been exposed to—that is, the more discrepant the messages they had been exposed to, the less change.

This study tells us quite a bit about how suggestible we become when uncertain of ourselves, particularly in the presence of others. But it also tells us clearly what other studies have shown: Increasingly discrepant influences from others lose their magic, particularly when we are no longer in their presence. In real life, we are frequently confronted by ambiguous or indeterminate alternatives. It is then that we are most likely to be keenly influenced by others in an immediate situation, provided that the proposal is not too discrepant from our own position. However, out of the others' sight, the comparison process leads us to be less affected and more suspicious of the increasingly divergent proposals made by others.

The Source, Where the Source Stands, and Our Involvement

There is a great deal of evidence showing that a communicator chosen for expertness and prestige in the matter at issue is more effective than a less prestigious, less competent communicator (see for example, Hovland and Weiss, 1951). Furthermore, there is good reason to believe that the prestigious communicator's message affects our immediate judgments on uninvolving matters over a much greater range of discrepant positions than a less prestigious one (see, for example, Aronson, Turner, and Carlsmith, 1963; Bochner and Insko, 1966). With increasingly discrepant messages, research subjects more frequently become suspicious and, furthermore, increasingly discredit the message.

Researchers have been rather arbitrary in studying communicators, in that they have not explicitly recognized that our judgments of a communicator hinge not only on his or her general reputation in society at large, but also on his or her position within or outside of our own reference groups. The social context in which we see a communicator as "one of us" or "not one of us" and the importance of the topic of communication are not independent: We may regard the person as "credible" on an issue of little importance but incompetent on a matter that concerns us personally and on which our reference group takes a divergent stand. For example, Sereno (1969) found that a high-prestige source (Dr. Jonas Salk) influenced persons highly involved in birth control issues less than students less concerned about the issues.

Lewis Rodgers (in Sherif et al., 1973) studied this problem by securing judgments on the credibility of a number of well-known public figures (for example, Nixon, Johnson, Humphrey) on controversial issues of varying concern to members of the Students for a Democratic Society (left wing) and of the Young Americans for Freedom (right wing) in 1967–1968. He chose particular issues because he learned, through attending the meetings, that both groups were highly concerned about the Vietnam war but that the SDS was also highly concerned about race relations, whereas YAF members were less concerned. Furthermore, YAF members spent a great deal of energy discussing economic issues (for example, the "gold drain" from the United States), whereas SDS did not.

Rodgers had members of each group rate the "credibility" of ten public figures on each of the three issues (Vietnam war, race issue, "gold drain" issue). The communicators were well known and varied from a "liberal" to "conservative" stance in their public image. As expected, members of the two groups differed almost diametrically in whom they regarded as "credible" or as inveterate liars. Of those each group rated as "credible" on the three issues, each also perceived little divergence between their own positions and those of the credible communicators.

The question is how they perceived the positions of communicators whom they rated as *not* credible on the three issues. We might think that any message from communicators judged not credible would be perceived as highly discrepant from our own stand before the communicator even opened his or her mouth. That was the case with those issues of great concern to the respective groups. The greatest *difference* between one's position and that of a communicator judged as *not* credible was on the issue most important in one's own group and more involving to one personally (Vietnam war for the SDS and the *gold drain* issue for the YAF). In these issues, the respective members of the two groups saw an unbridgeable gap between them and the communicators they had rated as not credible.

On the other hand, SDS members saw a very slight difference between their own positions and the position taken by communicators they had rated *not* credible on the gold drain issue (which they were not highly involved in). YAF members saw little discrepancy from those communicators they found not credible on the race issue. In other words, if Hubert Humphrey addressed SDS students on the Vietnam war, he might as well have stayed at home; but if he talked to them on the gold drain issue, he would have had very little gap to overcome between his views and theirs. Conversely, Lyndon Johnson could not have had a meeting of minds with YAF members on the gold drain (economic) issue, but would very likely have found a common ground in discussing race questions, in which they were less involved.

Communicator Prestige, Personal Involvement, and Message Discrepancy

Research that has looked simultaneously at communicator prestige, degree of personal involvement in the issues, and at the discrepancy of communication as these together relate to attitude change is sparse. The first study was done by Ramon Rhine and Lawrence Severance (1970) at the University of California (Riverside) on one issue very low in involvement for the students (park acreage to be alloted in Allentown, Pennsylvania!) and one issue that aroused them quite a bit, namely, the increased university tuition then being advocated in California. They assessed attitudes only after a communication was presented, comparing them with those of control samples receiving no communication to see if the communications produced significant differences between students' attitudes randomly assigned to the research conditions. Different communicators were said to have given the messages on the two issues, but for each issue, one was selected as high and one as low in prestige. Messages advocating different positions from the students' average preferences were presented over a wide range of discrepancies to different student samples in the experimental design.

Rhine and Severance found, as predicted, that students changed more on the less involving than the involving issue, regardless of the "prestige" they had attributed to the source. Students getting messages on the less involving issue (park acreage) changed their positions in amounts increasing directly with the increasing discrepancy of the amount advocated (up to 240 acres). Those highly involved in an issue (tuition) did not change significantly but, if anything, were less affected by the more discrepant proposals. At the same time, derogation of the messages was greater among more involved students, increasing when the messages were increasingly discrepant.

Gerald Gorn (1971) studied the same problems with a slightly different research plan, whose advantage was that the same communicators and the same messages could be presented while varying degrees of the recipients' involvement in the issue. Gorn chose the issue of Quebec separatism in Canada, which was then highly salient owing to the political activism of separatists, a recent kidnapping, and martial law, which had been lifted only shortly before the research began. In Montreal, there was no doubt that students were highly involved in the issue. By choosing students at McGill University (an "English" school), Gorn also ensured that those he studied would all be opposed to separatism. To secure students also opposed to separatism, but less involved in the entire issue, he traveled far west of Montreal to Calgary. To both sets of students, he presented one of three communications, carefully designed to differ from the students' anti-separatism stand in three increasingly discrepant steps. For half of the students, the communications were attributed to a prestigious but nonpartisan authority, and, for the other half, to a student at a university of much lower prestige than either McGill or Calgary. Gorn pretested the prestige and credibility of these communicators, and also found that the students whom he actually studied regarded them as differing in credibility.

Gorn found no significant change under any conditions for the highly involved (Montreal) students. The less involved (Calgary) students did shift their most acceptable position significantly toward the moderately discrepant, but not the most discrepant, message. The messages were rated unfavorably when attributed to a low-prestige source, particularly those more discrepant from the students' stands.

Together, these studies indicate that degree of personal involvement in a person's stand, discrepancy of the position advocated, and prestige of the communicator are all important determinants of whether attitudes change in response to communication and of how the communication is evaluated relative to the person's own attitude. Degree of involvement emerged in both studies as the strongest determinant of whether attitudes changed or not. Message discrepancy was important relative to the degree of involvement. That communicator prestige was less important suggests that we need to learn a great deal more about what makes another person's words count on different issues and occasions. As indicated earlier, it seems likely that communicator (source) credibility will also turn out to hinge on the communicator's relationship to the person and the person's reference groups. In order to rule out preexisting attitudes toward well-known communicators, both studies in this section used fictitious figures, carefully designed to appear high or low in credibility to their participants, but lacking the "halo" that a real leading figure in our reference groups may acquire. Nevertheless, both studies settle a lot of dust by showing very clearly (1) that personal involvement in one's stand is the critical factor determining whether one-shot communications will be effective or not and (2) that with low or moderate involvement, the greatest change in own position occurs with messages *moderately* discrepant from one's stand, not diametrically opposed to it.

WHAT DO WE KNOW ABOUT ATTITUDE-COMMUNICATION DISCREPANCY?

The discrepancy of a message from a person's stand on the issue is no more "absolute" than whether that person regards the communicator as someone to be heeded. The discrepancy that is perceived by the person depends on how involved he or she is in the issue at hand and how committed to the position taken. Degree of personal involvement indicates the structure of the attitude—namely, the relative sizes of the latitudes of acceptance, rejection, and noncommitment. Hence, the critical discrepancy is relative to those latitudes, namely, where the message and the communicator are placed within them.

The implications of the research are decidedly practical, whether we want to guard against propaganda or attempt to persuade others. If we have little personal involvement in our stand or in the issue presented in a communication, we are sitting ducks for a high-prestige communicator, who can potentially influence us to change our preferred position over very large ranges of discrepancy. One way that a communicator can increase that range of influence is to emphasize the ambiguity and lack of clarity in the real world. Practical politicians utilize prestige and the ambiguity of the issues at hand for such purposes frequently. For example, during the mid-sixties certain politicians and journalists repeatedly emphasized that the Vietnam war was taking place in such a distant, strange land and had so many complexities that only someone with "all the facts" could decide what course to pursue (presumably the President). Even then, however, there were limits to the decisions that could be advocated, limits imposed by their extreme discrepancy from stands taken by large numbers of people. The most extreme messages (for example, using nuclear weapons or attacking China) gained few adherents. Even with low personal involvement, attitude change increases as communications become increasingly discrepant only to a point. Over time, the tragic consequences of the point to which such persuasion was effective on many people subsequently heightened their personal involvement in the war, leading many to reevaluate and again to change their stands.

If we are personally committed to our position on an issue, the wily communicator will not attempt to persuade us on the spot through a highly discrepant message. (If he or she does, the evidence is clear that the attempt will fail and that we will react negatively to it.) Again, the probability that we will change is related to the clarity of the alternatives, being greater when the options are numerous, unclear, and their outcomes uncertain. Increasingly discrepant messages may sway us, particularly from a person we esteem highly, until they begin to fall well within our latitude of rejection, when we will react negatively in proportion to their discrepancy from our stand.

In real life, persons moderately or highly committed to a stand are more likely to be moved by discrepant messages repeated over time, particularly if "opinion leaders" and other reference persons are also concerned and exposed to them. As field research has shown, one's reference persons and groups are critical in whether or not communications are effective in real life. Unfortunately, research models for experidental study of attitude change, especially in the laboratory, have precluded the possibility of considering such critical interactions. Most of them have focused on one-shot attempts to persuade an isolated person through communication. However, I do not think that such criticisms need to arouse despair. After all, it was not long ago when some researchers were also ignoring the degree of personal involvement or commitment to one's stand in attitude change research, usually on the grounds that it was thought to be a "sloppy" or "confounded" variable. As we have seen, experimental research has "captured" that variable in several ways, with the result that we now know it to be the most significant of all in the communication process.

PERSONAL INVOLVEMENT AND SUSCEPTIBILITY TO CHANGE

In this chapter, personal involvement has been defined in terms of commitment to a person's stand on the matter at hand, hence as related to the structure of the person's attitude. In those terms, it has become easy to understand why a person with low involvement is susceptible to attitude change over a wide range of discrepancies. However, our vision of the world around us would have to be narrow indeed if we were to conclude that this is all there is to say about susceptibility to attitude change or about personal involvement.

For example, suppose that a person is highly involved in an issue, but very uncertain as to which stand to take on it. Or, suppose that a person has been committed to a stand, perhaps taking it as a "natural" and "normal" part of self, but then begins to experience instability or disaffection from those reference persons and groups who also regard that attitude as "natural" and "normal." Add to either or both of these a set of life circumstances in which alternatives suddenly increase, the future is ambiguous, or the usual grooves of daily living are upset. People who find themselves in such plights are likely to be highly involved in a personal way, and they may also be ripe for change. Such individuals are found in growing numbers in periods of rapid change with massive contradictions and cultural lags. The times are full of us.

At this stage in the development of social psychology, we are unlikely to learn about such problems best within the ordered confines of the laboratory. The natural laboratory for studying them is the world around us, particularly its social movements.

Social Movements as Generators of Social and Personal Change

This book started by discussing social psychology in challenging times. The overriding challenge to humanity was flung at Hiroshima and Nagasaki by the most powerful nation the world had yet seen. Since then, conflicts over the question of who is to control whom and what on this earth have widened and deepened. The growing cloud of thermonuclear armaments could rain the final answer: No one.

Humanity's common predicament is the issue of whether or not it can survive when human beings produce the means to destroy themselves and the earth as a habitable planet. Our survival depends on joint efforts in attaining workable human relationships that incorporate all peoples into the circle defined by each as "humanity." If the human experience has tested one truth, it is that human beings are capable of inhuman destruction the moment that we place any person, any group, any nation beyond the pale of humanity. Now, by destroying those "beyond the pale" we can destroy life itself.

We human beings are going to have to change the ways and the rules by which we live. In attempting to do so, we are bound to encounter a host of contradictions and dilemmas. Our era is one of exceedingly rapid social change—of uneven spread, distribution, and rate in different aspects of living and for different groups of people. Age-old, centuries-old, generation-old continuities in inequality and restriction proceed side by side with newly won opportunities and freedoms. Gaps between "haves" and "have nots" widen, while the justice of having and the necessity of not having are questioned more urgently. Each of our lives may be more notable for its contradictions than for its consistency.

SOCIAL PSYCHOLOGY AND SOCIAL MOVEMENTS

Social psychology is one human endeavor toward better understanding of human problems. It has chosen to attempt understanding through the human means of the scientific enterprise focused on individuals interacting with one another in the social world as it exists. Social psychology can never write prescriptions to "save" the world. At best, it can provide guides for diagnosing what the problems are and for exploring potentialities for change that are better than blind beliefs about "human nature," superstitions, wishful or fearful thinking.

Like any scientific endeavor, social psychology starts by looking at regularities. Regularities in social behavior, in interpersonal and group dealings, and in procedures and outcomes define the problems that are most readily studied through scientific methods. Their recurrence over time facilitates the development of concepts, research methods and techniques, and other tools whose purpose is to provide a basis for formulating general principles and laws. Consequently, there is a strong tendency in social psychology to concentrate on stability, regularity, and continuity in social behavior. "Lawfulness" is easier to find there.

These are not the only reasons, however, for the tendency to neglect problems of social change. Unlike those engaged in scientific study as a chemist or microbiologist, the social psychologist is inevitably *part* of what he or she is studying. The social psychologist cannot watch dispassionately as two human beings or two groups fight, saying, as a chemist might in combining two chemicals, "Well, what do you know . . . an explosion!" When social change exceeds the bounds of what a social psychologist's own self-system and reference groups define as "normal" or "desirable," it is personally disturbing.

For such reasons, the very words used in discussing problems of change in social psychology carry value judgments—words such as *deviance, de-individuation, breakdown, anomie, anti-social, disequal-ibrium, dysfunctional, hidden hostilities, alienation, collective out-bursts,* or even *collective suicide.* In the late sixties, one social psychologist accused certain black activists of acting like alcoholics who drink the morning after to "cure" a hangover. He did not like their proposals for change.

The dilemma for social psychology is that there can be no valid laws or principles about social behavior that do not accommodate change as well as stability and continuity in social behavior. If change is treated as an aberration, or those who promote change are labeled as "abnormal," it is unlikely that we have understood what we regard as "normal." In fact, change is as "natural" to social life as stability and continuity.

Every human individual changes from childhood through adolescence, adulthood, and old age. Such changes occur because the body and the social environment change, but also because the individual changes the environment. We have seen in earlier chapters that individuals are capable of changing their dealings with one another, forming new rules, and changing their social environment through their own efforts. They form new groups with their own criteria for judging human worth and with their own goals. They adopt new reference groups, changing their attitudes and actions in the process. If the groups they form or the new reference groups they adopt are sufficiently comprehensive in their personal lives, important parts of the self-system change as well.

The natural "laboratory" for studying such social and personal change today is the study of social movements—phenomena whose study in social psychology is not without precedent (see Brown, 1954; Cantril, 1941; Heberle, 1951; Killian, 1964, 1968; Lang and Lang, 1961; McLaughlin, 1969; Milgram and Toch, 1969; Sherif and Sherif, 1956, 1969; Toch, 1965; Turner and Killian, 1972). But the study of social movements is not a matter for social psychology alone. Necessarily, it entails history and other social sciences, including sociology, political science, economics, and social anthropology. In studying social and personal change through social movements, social psychologists can readily see how dependent their own work must be on findings from such related disciplines. Only together can a comprehensive and valid account of social and personal change be achieved.

Social psychology can contribute to the study of social movements within the framework of findings from other disciplines. Other social sciences are better equipped to deal with large-scale events over time, with the structure of society and the distribution of power, living conditions of various segments of its population, comprehensive effects of technological change, and other social forces that are studied more adequately and efficiently without focusing on particular individuals. Within such frameworks, many aspects of a social movement represent social-psychological problems.

Social movements arise through the interactions among individuals, frequently in relatively small numbers, especially in the early phase. They form groups, and they form or join larger organizations. In the process, the individual's attitudes change, at times so fundamentally that a new personal identity takes shape.

Invariably, social movements give rise to attempts at collaboration between groups as well as to confrontation among groups in conflict. Psychological conflict between new and old reference groups often grips some of the participants. Many persons not participating in the movement are affected by its actions and communications, by events during intergroup encounters, and by any changes that its activities succeed in effecting. Social movements are the best context for studying human beings as both active agents and targets of social change.

I am closing this book with the challenge that phenomena of social movements present to our established understanding of human social psychology. Everything covered in social psychology so far can be utilized. No new concepts or principles will be introduced. On the other hand, we will find a rich field for further study and will note that certain common assumptions about human behavior are found wanting when we look at participants in a social movement.

This chapter does not pretend to be a complete treatment of social movements from a social-psychological viewpoint, or of the particular movement that I draw on for illustrative purposes, namely, the women's movement. Instead, its aim is to illustrate how social-psychological concepts can be utilized in this context and to alert us to dangers in drawing conclusions about human experience and action based on findings obtained solely in the laboratory or in the typically stable settings of much field research.

Some historical background has to be included since professional historians proceeded for years as though the women's movement had not happened. Necessarily, the historical material here represents a bare minimum, selectively presented for its relevance to social-psychological concepts. I do not pretend to forecast the future of the women's movement. It is now in an early phase of its reappearance after decades of malignant neglect. Already, the new movement has had significant consequences in changing attitudes and actions of both women and men. Many more nonparticipants have been affected indirectly.

WHAT A SOCIAL MOVEMENT IS NOT

These days, we often hear people say, "Whatever happened to the student movement?" "The black movement of the sixties is dead" or "Thank heavens all those hippies have gone home to roost." The mass media, accustomed for some years to featuring marches, demonstrations, and urban riots, dig frantically for signs of new excitement in the gatherings of religious sects of various kinds. Their news always has room for reports of a collective protest, a kidnapped heiress allegedly "brainwashed" by "movement people," a hijacked plane or other terrorist acts. From the media, we could conclude that only "real nuts" and innocent victims are affected by social movements.

One reason for such questions and for equating "social movement" with "terror and violence" is that many people are at a loss in dealing with social events or phenomena that do not fit readily into the grooves of established institutions and procedures. Many of the people who pronounce the demise of recent movements did not understand where they came from in the first place. Their activities were noticed only when they were sufficiently striking to become a spectacular "story" in the news. Surely it is no accident that what is selected to be a "story" often includes large numbers of people interacting in excited ways and, at times, violent actions. Many people, including the powers-that-be in a society, have nothing to lose and everything to gain if the term *social movement* arouses terror in people's hearts. Wittingly or unwittingly, many people dread change and those who propose it. One tactic to maintain things as they are is through arousing fears.

For such reasons, it is helpful to start characterizing a social movement by stating what it is *not*.

It is *not* simply incidents of violent behavior, individual or collective, although these may be episodes in a movement (even a women's movement). Violent behavior occurs both individually and collectively in contexts that have nothing to do with social movements—for example, in public emergencies, between formally or informally organized groups, or after a soccer game. Historically, social scientists and psychologists have not been exempt from accepting the common assumption that all collective violence can be explained in the same way, regardless of its social context. Such an assumption is simply wrong (see Sherif and Sherif, 1969, Chapter 23).

A social movement is not merely one or a few pressure groups dedicated to legal or other specific social reforms, although such groups may be parts of a social movement. On the other hand, a social movement may, at a given time, focus its unified efforts toward specific reforms. The women's movement was so united during the decades immediately preceding 1920, when the Nineteenth Amendment finally granted women the vote after "a century of struggle" (see Flexner, 1971).

A social movement is not merely sporadic public protest in the form of sit-ins, boycotts, strikes, rallies, mass marches, or riots, although these and many other forms of collective action may occur either as planned tactics or as unplanned (hence "spontaneous") episodes during a social movement.

A social movement is not identical to any one organization formally instituted by its participants, such as the National Organization for Women (NOW) or the Women's Equity Action League (WEAL), although these are certainly part of a social movement. Nor is it some vague entity such as "Women's Lib," a media term applied indiscriminately to the women's movement. The term came from the slogan "Women's Liberation," which was also used by some movement groups as their name. Many women resent the media contraction as derogatory to the slogan; still others participate in the movement but do not equate their aims with the slogan.

A social movement is not merely a set of individuals, small or large, who feel a "oneness" in their attitudes—in noncomformity to certain social norms for dress, for interpersonal behavior, for sexual behavior, for preferences in music or art—and, therefore, feel comfortable together and uncomfortable with "establishment people." While such nonconformity in attitudes and practices, and comfortable feelings of "oneness" do occur within social movements, they do not, in themselves, necessarily signal a social movement. In large, complex societies that permit variability among their subpopulations or generations, such phenomena may occur apart from a social movement, even when those affected see themselves as the "wave of the future."

Then, what is a social movement?

WHAT SOCIAL MOVEMENTS ARE

The following paragraphs summarize the general characteristics of a social movement that we have found useful in defining the term (Sherif and Sherif, 1969; Sherif, 1970).

A social movement refers to a *pattern of active attempts toward social change*, initiated through the interactions of individuals and groups to deal with social problems that have been generated by contradictions and inequities in the ways different aspects of social life are organized. Such attempts are made by individuals and groups of individuals prompted by intense personal experiences of dissatisfaction, which are fed by the persisting social problems. Both they and other persons or groups who throw their lot with them are, over periods of time, attempting or proposing social change through their joint efforts. The pattern of their *efforts over time*, in different places, with different participants; the *protests* they formulate about things as they are; the *ways they propose to deal with the problems* (which may be escapist, visionary, revolutionary, reformist, or retrogressive); the *organizational forms* they develop; the *values* and ideals, the myths and idols they cherish; and the *ideologies* they develop—all of these are parts of the social movement.

Such a social movement represents attempts at social change or innovation whose scope may range from highly *specific* issues to *many* issues. The scope of proposed changes varies from specific reforms affecting only a restricted portion of the population or parts of existing institutions to sweeping changes in many institutions or in the very structure of society. The *means* by which the efforts are made include appeals to the public or to certain groups within it, lobbying and social pressure, slogans that epitomize grievances or goals, symbolic acts and rituals, agitation, education, recruitment and training of new participants, action projects as well as episodes of collective action, and confrontations with those who oppose them that may be fortuitous or planned (for example, strikes, civil disobedience, sit-ins, rallies, boycotts, marches, property destruction, insurrection).

Increasingly, over time, such means become planned tactics of groups or organizations within the movement. Therefore, over time, the occurrence or nonoccurrence of collective interaction and of violence becomes a question of participants' *conformity to the movement's beliefs* about the nature and remedies of social problems and to *group decisions* about planned tactics.

Of course, much also depends on reactions by other groups and by authorities who oppose their aims, for a social movement aimed at social change of any consequence invariably becomes involved in *intergroup conflict*. Its intergroup context also determines how public or secret, how "constructive" or "subversive" a movement becomes. Secrecy or planned tactics for subversion of the establishment are not indigenous to social movements. They are indigenous to *societies* where extraordinarily severe penalties are exacted for attempting social changes of the kind proposed. (The early history of the labor movement in the United States in the decades after the Civil War contains many pertinent examples.)

If this is a social movement, it is no wonder that some social psychologists shudder at the thought of studying personal change within such a context. We are talking about efforts and events that are often far-flung, that may involve at first only a small number of people, and that may proceed over years, with ups and downs and with new participants. Their complexity seems staggering in comparison with the university laboratories, college campuses, summer camp sites, and other locations where social psychologists have done their major researches into attitude formation and change, effects of communication, group decisions and norm formation, inter-group collaboration and conflict, and so on.

WHY SOCIAL PSYCHOLOGISTS CANNOT IGNORE SOCIAL MOVEMENTS

There are at least two reasons why social psychologists cannot ignore social movements, even when working in the laboratory. The first of these concerns the impact of actual social movements on individuals who participate in laboratory research. It was only a few years ago that some social psychology texts typified women as more passive, dependent, persuasible, more "externally controlled" than men. Today, can we study compliance or persuasibility in the laboratory without recognizing that some women are not very compliant or persuasible on such matters? Men, it was said, feared failure. How is an experimentalist studying reactions to failure to deal with the fact that, today, many young men fear failure as the researcher defines it far less than they fear "success" as society has defined that achievement for men?

The second reason pertains to phenomena that are quite common in the context of a social movement, but that are unlikely to occur within a traditional research setting and that cannot, therefore, be understood adequately with the theories and concepts developed within such settings. For example, how are we to deal with the finding that some women exhibit more "internal control" over their own behavior than we might have expected from men and that these women are activists in the women's movement (Sanger and Alker, 1972)? How do we explain such a finding in view of the frequent accounts of social movements that describe participants (male or female) as so many puppets manipulated by strings from outside by the "organization" or by "charismatic leaders"?

How do models of interpersonal interaction developed in the laboratory fare when we try to apply them in the context of a social movement? Several such models conceive of interaction in terms of an "exchange" akin to that in the marketplace. Read the instructions given to participants in nonviolent resistance during the demonstrations, sit-ins, and voter registration drives in the South of the early 1960s to see how such models fare. Those instructions included options that the individual could adopt, such as *not* protecting the body from blows, folding the hands over the skull, protecting the genitals, and so on (Zinn, 1964). Do we have a theory of human motivation that can handle the fact that many black youth chose one of those options, following the instructions? What schedule of reinforcements can lead youth to defy the armed force of authority and imprisonment to resist the draft?

In a changing world, can there be a valid social psychology that neglects its social movements?

SOCIAL PROBLEMS AND THE MOTIVATIONAL BASE THEY GENERATE

Social movements arise when social problems in a society become sufficiently widespread and intense that large numbers of individuals are personally and deeply affected by them. The impact of social problems on personal lives is crucial in the formative phase of a movement. No social movement starts without such personal impact, yet individual motivations are not sufficient to start one, in and of themselves.

Better understanding of the motivational base of a social movement will clarify why, for example, social movements are not necessarily started or formed by those most oppressed, downtrodden, and miserable. One reason is fairly evident: Individuals sorely struggling for the bare essentials of life or severely stressed by circumstances may find the greatest difficulty in summoning the energy or persistence to tackle problems in concert with others, especially when immediate relief for their personal plights is unlikely as a consequence. For example, Barbara Dohrenwend's analysis (1973) of relationships between stressful life circumstances and psychological distress among adult residents of New York City indicated that both were greater for the poor and for women (especially single women) than for middle-class residents and males. For several reasons, it does not follow that the very poor or single women are the most likely participants in a social movement.

In addition, societies and the people affected form cultural definitions about what can and cannot be changed, about who is and who is not responsible for personal dissatisfactions. These include, for example, the Mexican peasant heritage of "fate" explanations, with accompanying admiration for those who accept and hold up well under trying conditions. The common expressions ni modo (What can anyone do? There is no way) and el aguante, which Diaz-Guerrero (1965) translated as "ability to hold well even in face of abuse," became the slogans for resignation. Such cultural explanations for personal experiences of stress and strain direct the individual to cease any search of the environment for causes of personal distress.

As the roles of men and women began to change, the discontent experienced by many women was quickly defined by the most powerful and "intellectually respectable" segments of society in ways that turned the onus for the discontent on the individuals themselves. Especially after World War II, women were told for many years that their individual, personal shortcomings were responsible if they experienced great stress and strain in being women. The messages were contained in textbooks on the family (Ehrlich, 1971), on sociology (Kirschner, 1973), on psychology (Weisstein, 1971), on gynecology (Scully and Bart, 1973), and on the female sex in general (see Friedan, 1963). Women, they were told, should be happy in "expressive" nurturant roles relative to their husbands and children or in work (if work they must). "Natural" happiness came to a woman through being submissive to male decisions, being "considerate" of masculine preferences, and allowing "her husband's sex drive to set their pace," attempting to "gear hers satisfactorily to his" (Scully and Bart, 1973, p. 1048).

If a woman experienced stress in following such dictums, indeed if she was not following the messages happily, the verdict was that she was not a "real" woman. Something was wrong with her. If she could not correct it, psychological or medical help was needed promptly to facilitate adjustment to things as they were, or "coping" with them. As long as a woman took these pronouncements to heart or went to practitioners whose aim was to help her "adjust" or "cope," she was not likely to speak to other women about her problems or to look to life circumstances for their "cause." She was unlikely to take steps with others to start a social movement.

Discontents and Comparison Processes

In order for personally experienced problems to contribute to formation of the motivational base for a social movement, the problems have to be defined as amenable to collective action toward social change. That is why the historical background, available or newly developing systems of beliefs (ideologies), and contemporary examples of successful social actions by others all contribute to such a motivational base.

For example, without the rise of new independent nations in Africa and Asia throwing off centuries of colonial rule, young black students in Greensboro, North Carolina, would have been less likely to try, quite hesitantly at first, to sit in at the Woolworth's lunch counter in the early 1960s. Their actions, in turn, were not lost on other black and white students who then began to mount protests on racial and peace issues. Later, in the mid-sixties, student demonstrations spread like waves as the mass media transmitted their images from Berkeley to eastern universities, the Midwest, to Paris and Tokyo.

Without the growing ferment, the ideas and slogans from the black movement, the peace movement, the diverse aspects of what became a broad student protest, the long-simmering discontent among Mexican-Americans might not have emerged as a Chicano movement. The fragmented, geographically scattered population of native Americans would probably not have seen any hope in the notion of Red Power. Native Americans were perhaps more miserable earlier, but how many would have seen any "point" in attempting to control what had been "allowed" as their lot under the Bureau of Indian Affairs or any hope in attempts to regain anything lost during their conquest? Similarly, after securing the vote in 1920 until the mid-sixties, very few women could see any point in a women's movement.

Many women and men have expressed wonder that women should feel strongly that their personal problems are parts of social problems that must be remedied. "What do those women want now? They're better off than any women in the world. Give them husbands to keep them pregnant, and they'll be all right." Certainly it cannot be contended that women in the United States are the most mistreated, restricted, dependent, underprivileged, and hobbled by custom in the world. However, to understand the motivational base of the women's movement, we have to understand who the participants compare themselves with and the problems that concern them. For this purpose, a little historical background is needed.

BACKGROUND TO THE REVIVAL OF THE WOMEN'S MOVEMENT

In Chapter 8, the concept of "relative deprivation" was introduced, somewhat critically, since in fact *deprivation* is not all that relative a matter. It is when the minimum necessities for bodily maintenance and health are met that we need to speak in relative terms. Beyond that minimum, our satisfaction with our status and that of our reference groups is inevitably a relative affair. It depends on our standing relative to others classified in the same general reference set (for example, our society). From the earliest days of the women's movement in the United States, women derived their general social standing from their fathers or husbands. Thus, they compared themselves and their status with that of men at a comparable socioeconomic level.

This is not to say that the pioneers in the women's movement were uninterested in women or men whose socioeconomic level was lower than their own. On the contrary, many became deeply involved in activities directed toward the abolition of slavery, improvement of the plight of working men and women, and other causes. Elizabeth Cady Stanton, who called the first meeting of women to discuss their grievances at Seneca Falls, New York, in 1848, received her first crushing humiliation when she and other women were prevented from participating on a par with men at a meeting on the abolition of slavery in London. However, the Declaration of Principles adopted from the Seneca Falls meeting was a direct paraphrase of the 1776 Declaration of Independence, proclaiming for women the same rights and freedoms that the founding fathers had declared for "all men."

The fascinating history of the long, courageous work of the early feminists, suffragists, and working women of the nineteenth century makes it very clear that social, economic, and legal equality with their masculine counterparts concerned women in various social classes. In addition, they had varying visions of a better future society freed of slavery, or ruthless exploitation of the newly emerging industrial working class, and of the depressingly isolated state of much of the rural population (see Flexner, 1971; O'Neill, 1971).

What started as a broad, many-issued protest became increasingly focused on the right to vote as the long struggle entered the twentieth century. Narrowing the focus occurred through the necessity of recruiting support from men and other women. The vast majority of both sexes recoiled in horror at movement critiques of the family, sexual mores, and hypocrisy during the super-Victorian period of American history. Yet, for the vote, there was an unprecedented pool of potential support.

By the turn of the century, more women than ever before were active outside the home in "ladies clubs," literary and cultural circles, prohibition societies, home and foreign missionary societies, "lady bountiful" activities in the slums, as well as dedicated social welfare work.

The number of women workers had increased, and there were women labor activists. All of the major women's colleges had been founded. The women's movement became a broad alliance of such formal organizations, two major national women's organizations devoted to women's rights, many informal groups and clusters, male allies, and experienced leadership. The amount of effort, organization, and time that went into securing women's suffrage was prodigious. After World War I (1920), the vote was granted.

The Vote, like any single goal pursued with effort by so many for so long, became larger than life before it was won. To many, it symbolized a turning point for humanity, which then would share and be checked by those feminine virtues that both men and women agreed at the time were endowed to the fairer, gentler sex. They were to be deceived by their own myths. The Vote was to save the world that the United States was supposed to have "made safe for democracy."

Once this single issue was won, there was little left to unite its supporters. "They felt," wrote Carrie Chapman Catt, "a vacancy where for years there had been purpose consecrated to an immortal principle." Only Alice Paul, with the small National Woman's Party that had splintered from the large national organizations to support a many-pronged political attack on women's problems, continued to work for the Equal Rights Amendment to the Constitution. That amendment, worded in the same way, still awaited the final ratifying states' votes over fifty years later.

During the 1920s and 1930s almost every idea or proposal for change in women's position and for relationships between men and women that we can read today had been written or said. However, few women or men took them seriously as cause to get together, to seek "liberation." Again, it was a question of what was compared with what during those circumstances. In the 1920s, women were liberating themselves from long skirts, long hair, and sexual pruderies shared by their own mothers, some of whom had fought for the vote. Youth was freer to enjoy the changes; in comparison their mothers seemed from another age.

In the 1930s, men and women alike were forced into preoccupation with the Great Depression. The period was one of social movements focused on the tragic contradictions, inequities, and suffering of an economic order gone awry, the accompanying political turmoil, war, and the threat of war. Still the change in women's status from 1920 was striking. When World War II engulfed the United States, women were becoming trained and educated, working outside of the home and in the military establishment in unprecedented numbers. As always, in times of war, issues of women's status were submerged in common national cause.

MOTIVATIONAL BASE FOR REBIRTH AND ITS EARLY PHASE

The rise of the women's movement anew between 1960 and 1965 is not readily explained by any single theory or hypothesis advanced in the social science literature. However, two seem pertinent. One is an hypothesis advanced by J. C. Davies (1962) to explain the timing of revolutionary uprisings, which the women's movement decidedly was not. The other was advanced by critics of Davies to predict outbreaks of collective violence, which has been notable by its absence in the women's movement. Nevertheless, a combination of the two does help in understanding the revival of a women's movement in the United States at that time.

Davies' hypothesis was that revolutionary protest is most likely to occur "when a prolonged period of objective economic and social development is followed by a short period of sharp reversal" (p. 5). Let us add to that another hypothesis by Snyder and Tilly (1972), to the effect that collective interaction is more likely to occur when a high degree of national political activity is underway, but is countered by repressive government action. Together, these two hypothesis describe, quite broadly, what happened before and when the women's movement emerged.

It was the period immediately following World War II that brought for women a "period of sharp reversal" in what had appeared to be a prolonged and fairly steady period of improvement in women's status and condition. Many women worked during the war. After the war, women were consigned to roles of homebody, mother, and helpmate both by economic conditions and by a barrage of social pressure. The reversal was reinforced powerfully in the 1950s by the political narrowness, the treatment of nonconformists, the Cold War against the Soviet Union which turned into indiscriminate witch-hunts for domestic "reds and pinkos." In classrooms and the popular press, sexist "theories" were presented as "psychology" or "sociology" to be accepted as "scientific fact."

At least one sociologist, Joseph Folsom, foresaw the propaganda campaign early, writing before the war's end that the glorification of marriage and family as be-all and end-all for women, with its accompanying derogation of any "career," carried dangers. He expressed fears that such messages "cultivated by the schools and colleges, can be used through upper-class prestige and adroit publicity to bring into disrepute the movement for equal opportunity and thus prepare the way for a resubjection of women" (O'Neill, 1971, p. 333). His fears were founded.

During the 1950s white women bore more children than they had before the war, wondered why they had become educated, flattered themselves that they were more cultured and better mothers as a result.

became the avid consumers of a booming postwar economy, watched their sex become a major cultural and commercial commodity, moved with their husbands into suburbia, spent more time keeping house and alone with children than their mothers had, if only because there were so many more products to use and their husbands were gone for longer periods. For black women, the poor, the Indian, and the Chicana, things were pretty much the same.

It is somewhat astonishing to recall that as late as 1962 a group of women who became actively concerned about the dangers of war and thermonuclear testing were promptly regarded as suspect by the House Un-American Activities Committee, which investigated their "alleged peace activities" as part of their search for the "Communist conspiracy." The women were pacifists (Women Strike for Peace). In public hearings they justified their concern over the Cold War and nuclear testing in the name of "the concern and love of mothers for their children" (Toch, 1965, p. 187). The group had started in 1961 under a very broad umbrella ("a belief that mankind deserves a future") for women concerned by the threat of nuclear war. Its very existence was suspect.

In 1961 at the request of Esther Peterson, director of the U.S. Women's Bureau, President Kennedy appointed a commission on the status of women, chaired by Eleanor Roosevelt. What this gesture did, in fact, was to bring together competent and vocal women, leading eventually to the formation of 50 state commissions to study women's status in their states (Freeman, 1973). What the women began to learn was that the status of women had declined in comparison with that of the 1920s. For example, more women were attending college, but proportionally fewer were obtaining degrees or advanced degrees. Proportionally fewer were to be found occupying positions of responsibility.

Such findings might never have had an impact. Meanwhile, however, Betty Friedan published *The Feminine Mystique,* (1963) which expressed for many educated housewives exactly their plight. She had done graduate work in psychology, and made trenchant criticisms of popular writings that degraded women in the name of "psychology" or "science." Her descriptions were closer to the hearts of women readers than the ponderous English translations of the erudite Simone de Beauvoir's *Second Sex* (1953), which many women then decided to read.

Group Formations Within the Emerging Movement

The year after Friedan's *Feminine Mystique* was published, the 1964 Civil Rights Act was passed with equality of sex included, as a "joke" according to some congressmen (Freeman, 1973, p. 798). A few members of the newly formed Equal Opportunity Commission took it seriously, wishing wistfully that there were "some sort of NAACP [National Association for the Advancement of Colored People] for women." By 1966, Representative Martha Griffiths of Michigan was blasting the Commission on the floor of the House for having an executive who called the provision a "fluke" and for ridiculing the law. That June, during the Third National Conference of the presidential commissions on the status of women in the 50 states, a small group of women met in Betty Friedan's hotel room. That informal get-together was the birthplace of the National Organization for Women (NOW), which by 1974 had 591 chapters and 40,000 members (Spokeswoman, June 15, 1974, p. 1).

Meanwhile, during 1967 and 1968, the civil rights, the anti-war, and the student movements were approaching crisis stage. The war against Vietnam had been intensified. War protests grew. The years included a National Conference for New Politics; the assassination of Martin Luther King; insurrections and riots in black sections of major cities; student "take-overs" at Columbia and other universities; the assassination of Robert Kennedy; a summer climaxed by the 1968 Democratic convention, marked by protests and what an official report later called a "police riot"; television broadcasts of student and worker militancy in France, and everyday television pictures of devastation and killing in Vietnam, often in "living color."

There were, in short, both a heightened degree of national political activity under way and governmental as well as other less official efforts at repressing protest, as suggested by the Snyder-Tilly hypothesis (1972). Among those politically active were numerous young women. Even earlier, according to Jo Freeman (1973), there had been women's caucuses called within various anti-war and student organizations. But it was in the tumultuous atmosphere of 1967–1968 that, suddenly, in at least five different cities (Chicago, Toronto, Seattle, Detroit, and Gainesville, Florida) independent groups of women met and organized spontaneously.

They met to share and to protest the fact that, despite their own efforts, women were at best accorded the pleasure of "manning" typewriters and mimeograph machines, bringing coffee, and serving as "chicks" to be "balled" for sport and relaxation. Such spontaneous formations by women seem to have occurred within a short time period in many other major cities (for example, New York, Boston, Washington, San Francisco, and Philadelphia). The issue of which groups were earliest and most active arose chiefly because the national news media focused their publicity a few years later almost exclusively on New York.

In short, the revival of a women's movement began within a very few years and was accomplished primarily through informal interactions among women who defined their common problems as stemming from the social position and treatment of women: older women meeting at first under official government auspices, on the one hand, and on the other, younger women, most of whom had participated in one of a variety of political activities or protests. Together, they formed new reference groups of women, whose status relative to men was at issue in a variety of respects. From the beginning, there were those who questioned that to be "like men" was a desirable goal, but there was no doubt that the inequality of status and respect felt so deeply was that between men and women. They felt that as women they faced many personal dilemmas, stresses, and strains that men did not experience because of their social status.

Susceptibility to Attitude Change in the Context of the Movement

Despite the historical background and their personal experience, it is not immediately apparent why women in the late 1960s were particularly susceptible to changing long-held attitudes and, in some cases, their self-image as women. Such attitudes and self-images are, after all, built up over long periods of time in the process of socialization into society as women. In fact, the events described, plus more personal circumstances related to sexual relationships, the use of contraceptive devices now readily available for women's use on their choice, and marriage and family relationships had combined to create two general conditions in which any human being becomes more susceptible to personal change.

First, ties with reference persons and groups established earlier were often conflicting and shaky. It is no coincidence that the largest source for new participants was young women in or just out of college, in transition from family ties and the collegiate atmosphere. Another source of recruits was among women who earlier had shifted their centers of gravity directly from family and college friends to husbands, only to find themselves "lost" in the process, with ensuing doubts about their marital and parental ties.

Second, and simultaneously, the period of social and political turmoil combined with changing sexual mores presented a highly unstructured social environment. Uncertainty as to "what will happen next," what to decide, what kind of a future was possible in the unstable world about them, a suddenly expanded range of alternatives defining what is "right, just, or possible" meant that established guidelines for action were increasingly questioned.

The combination of these two circumstances—one related to stability of the self-system and one related to degree of structure in the social environment—makes any human being, male or female, highly susceptible to searching for new alternatives. New groups composed of persons with common problems and dilemmas are particularly likely to become reference groups. Changes in specific attitudes and actions occur within the supportive context of like-minded members. Depending on the scope of concern and the ideology of such groups, changes in the person's self can and did occur.

Participants and Their Social Networks

The early participants in the revived women's movement were far from "typical" of the population at large. While every social movement aims eventually to broaden its membership to embrace the majority of those whose cause it champions, early participants are often distinguished in being relatively better educated, more privileged, and more experienced in the kinds of activities engaged in than a cross section of those in whose name they hope to speak.

The older women who started NOW and the Women's Equity Action League (WEAL) were distinguished, many highly experienced in media usage (Freeman, 1973) and in legal or professional affairs. The talents of the young women who met informally in various cities were revealed in outpourings of position papers, researches, books, and creative endeavors of many kinds. Many of the latter were students or graduates of high-prestige universities and colleges.

Participation in a social movement is not, however, a direct function of the individuals' social backgrounds or characteristics. It is equally important to inquire into their past associations with one another. Then we can begin to appreciate the importance of Snyder and Tilly's emphasis on "increased levels of political activity." According to Jo Freeman's study of the early women's groups (1973), there was in every case a preexisting network for communication among individuals that could be "co-opted" into the service of forming the group. Having interacted previously, the first members were tuned to similar wavelengths through common or similar experiences, had keenly experienced the motivational base generated by contradictions in their own lives, and "had the faith" that talking together about the issues was one way of doing something about them.

The importance of social networks that can be co-opted into the formation of a movement group was also stressed in a study of three peace groups of men and women on an Oregon college campus (Bolton, 1972). The researcher concluded that recruitment of new members occurred primarily through the individuals "belonging to social networks, some of whose members already belonged to the peace group" and who recruited them. There was little evidence in the research that new members had deliberately sought out and "chosen" the group. Needless to say, the latter can happen when a group's public activities begin to attract attention and to achieve "results."

The importance of informal social networks among individuals for group formation within a developing movement is critical since movements are unlikely to involve those individuals who have the most efficient means of communication within the grooves of established society. Lance Shotland (1970) demonstrated this obstacle neatly by tracing the progress of a message through existing social networks of students, faculty, and administrators at Michigan State University. He compared the relative ease or difficulty with which persons in each classification could use social networks available to them to pass along research materials to a specific student, faculty member, or administrator. Each person was given research materials with the name of its eventual target. The instructions were to pass the message along to someone whom the individual had talked to personally and who seemed to have a good chance of getting the message to its designated target. The issue was how many intermediaries would be required for the research materials to reach the specific person named.

Shotland calculated the average number of intermediaries that the materials passed through before reaching the target. Administrators readily used existing channels to reach other administrators and faculty, but they required about four intermediaries on the average to reach a specific student. Similarly, faculty reached administrators with fewer intermediaries than they needed in reaching other faculty members or students, which required an average of between five and six intermediaries.

Students themselves were the most generally isolated from administrators, faculty, and other students. In fact, the number of intermediaries required for their materials to reach other students, faculty, or administrators was sufficiently large (averaging over four) that Shotland compared their chances in reaching the targets to those for two people chosen at random from the entire U.S. population. (His estimate was based on previous research by Stanley Milgram, 1969, in which about five intermediaries were needed to reach unknown targets in entirely different states.)

Shotland's research stimulates us to distinguish between having friends and acquaintances, on the one hand, and on the other, being "plugged into" communication channels that can be utilized effectively for specific purposes. An individual need not be "socially isolated" in the former sense, yet be quite remote from networks to reach others with similar orientations and common experiences. The latter serve both to initiate interactions and to recruit new participants.

As in any social movement, the number of registered members in any one group or in its major organizations was less important in the early days of the women's movement than the potential for new recruits. This potential, in turn, depends on how widespread the social problems are that feed the motivational base of the movement. Marlene

Dixon (1971), a sociologist, detailed many of the contradictory circumstances in which many women found themselves, stressing their relation to the rapid spread of new groups and caucuses. By 1969, there were women's groups forming in most professional associations. The organizers of the 1970 march in New York were astounded at the numbers and wide range of women who marched to commemorate the fiftieth anniversary of suffrage. Before and after this event, small consciousness-raising groups initiated by younger women were springing up all over the country among women of various ages. In 1973, the National Black Feminist Organization was born.

Even today, it is somewhat misleading to calculate the size of the women's movement solely on the basis of membership lists of formal organizations. Within the broad movement, many housewives, members of more traditional women's organizations and church groups, college faculty and students, working women and trade unionists are engaging in activities that are movement-related and that they would not have dreamed of a decade earlier. Women participants greatly outnumbered men, but many men have been actively involved in one or more movement-related activity and a few publicly belong to one of its organized branches. Many more men have been affected one way or another by the movement.

ORGANIZATIONAL GROWTH: GROUP FORMATIONS

In the early formative stage of any movement, the theme uniting all participants is invariably what is hurting. Thus, in the early days and months, the airing of personal hurts and even rage is a focus of interaction. The close relationship between the motivational base, the early social networks, and their focus in interaction means that group formation often centers on common protests and gripes. The first agreements and decisions reached by the membership usually represent their "bill of gripes." Thus, early protest meetings and initial agreements are often high points in feelings of solidarity among members. The same events have the appearance of "negativism" to outsiders, who complain "All they can do is say what they are *against!* What are they for?"

The apparent negativism of any movement in its early phase is, in turn, a source of its early tactics and plans. Early protests and actions are symbolic to members of their bill of gripes and newly found unity. To outsiders, they may appear not only negative but outrageous, bizarre, or frightening. The mass media featured sights of young women whistling and shouting sexual evaluations at construction workers, picketing the Miss America contest, bitterly denouncing men, and making other public demonstrations of protests and gripes. The media were selective, of course, in what was considered "news" or entertainment. Many movement participants complained correctly that calm, reasoned accounts of movement aims and activities were not included in the mass media offerings because the mass media preferred the spectacular.

A Bill of Gripes and the Search for Affirmative Programs

Yet, study of the early formative phase in a variety of social movements indicates that groups forming within them are invariably more united, more clear, and concentrate their tactics on what they are *against* than what they are for (Sherif and Sherif, 1969, Chapter 24). Nonpartici-pants, in turn, typically react with astonishment: "What is this outra-geous behavior? They're against everything! What do they want?"

The civil rights and equality movement among blacks, the varied student protests, and the women's movement each faced this reaction, in turn. It is the reverse side of the first coin minted by a social movement: the bill of gripes. From the viewpoint of a participant, clear-cut accentuation of what one is against signifies the broadened latitude of rejection, which is the earmark of heightened personal involvement on controversial issues (see Chapter 9).

Arriving at a positive program of aims and activities for achieving them is a far more difficult achievement, within both developing groups and the movement as a whole. In the two broad segments of the women's movement in the late sixties, it was the somewhat older women in NOW who agreed more clearly what they were also *for*: repeal of discriminatory statutes, abolition of job discrimination, equal-ity of treatment, and so on. The formation of NOW proceeded along lines familiar to women experienced in formal organizations—from the top downward with formal officers, committee structure, dues, creation of task forces, and provisions for forming new chapters (Freeman, 1973). Lacking means and experienced "organizers" at local levels, NOW's more than 500 chapters initially repeated the process of group formation across the country, often on a highly informal basis with weak links to the national organization (Freeman, 1974).

Factionalism as a Product of Search

The difficulties in arriving at a positive program of beliefs and action programs during the formative phase of a social movement are exem-plified by events in NOW's history. Differences among its members in past experience, ideology, and tactical preferences brought the pangs of *factionalism*—conflicts among smaller groupings within the larger organization. (A glance at the history of any social movement will convince you that factionalism is not peculiar to the women's move-ment, but a symptom of the difficulties in gaining unity toward positive aims.)

NOW suffered three splits from 1967 to 1968. The Women's Equity Action League split off early as a more "establishment" group oriented toward specific reforms and legal tests, unwilling to confront the abortion issue that concerned many NOW members, and somewhat disturbed by the life styles of some NOW members (including the prevalence of pants, which were then a new style). (More recently, WEAL has expanded its interests and relaxed its "correctness," at least on local levels.) Later NOW was to suffer but survive further factional splits. The issues were expressed most vociferously by its former leader, Betty Friedan (1973), as fears that the organization would adopt the "anti-male" views of some members and on the issue of whether NOW should treat lesbians as women, hence equal, too. The convention of NOW adopted the latter position. NOW continues to enlist male members.

Consciousness Raising and Redefinition of Self

On the other side of the movement, the early emphasis remained on a bill of gripes, the call for "rage," the development of a new consciousness, and, in some quarters, "total commitment" as feminists (see Dixon, 1971). The younger women organizing spontaneously into fairly small groups were fed up with their treatment in "male" organizations, which at times were identified with any structure or hierarchy. Perhaps influenced by a general distrust of structure fostered in the earlier T-group movement (Chapter 3) as well as ideas from philosophical anarchists, the emphasis initially was on *no* formal structure, officers, or programs. Many participants explained that the formal structures in their experiences had been designed to be dominated by men.

The consciousness-raising groups formed within the movement were recognition of and reaction to male authority throughout upbringing and adult life. Their primary purpose was women's redefinition of themselves as women and, in the process, explicit assessment of their ties to and positions in various reference groups and sets, including males. One manifesto of the Black Power movement had proclaimed: "We must first redefine ourselves" (Carmichael and Hamilton, 1967). Many of the women involved in consciousness-raising groups would have had little use for the first author of that work, whose famous line was that the only position for women in the black movement was prone. Nevertheless, they took the same formula as credo, which indeed any social movement composed of the perenially subordinated must.

Redefinition of selves proceeded in many ways. Dixon (1971) saw the process as a way to overcome the greatest obstacle in organizing women, namely, "women's belief in their own inferiority" (p. 169). In other contexts, consciousness raising was seen as prerequisite to women's making decisions about their personal lives. The redefinitions that emerged varied greatly, often emphasizing women's strength and at times including certain stereotypes that other women sought to change (for example, of a perennially warm mothering figure). Since protest at being used as a sex object was widely shared, norms inhibiting discussion of sexuality among women (see Chapter 4) were crumbled in women's search toward understanding their own sexuality.

Like any social movement, the participants looked for a positive image of themselves by searching the past, not only for its injustices to women but for its heroines, creative geniuses, unsung talents, and myths (including the vain search for the "original" sex). Many groups proceeded from conscious raising to positive actions in the form of historical, literary, artistic, and information-gathering projects (see, for example, Baer and Sherif, 1974). Such productivity raises interesting questions for social psychology, in view of the emphasis placed on lack of structure in most consciousness-raising groups. (In fact, the most frequent criticism of consciousness-raising activities has been that the lack of structure was not conducive for training women to participate in programs and projects aimed at change; Freeman, 1974.)

Group Structure and Group Products

In Chapter 3, it was proposed that interactions and interpersonal relationships invariably become structured among individuals motivated to interact over some time. Did such structure emerge among women who emphasized lack of structure, diversity of values, and individual consciousness? There is considerable evidence that it did: Even in the most "structureless" groups, interaction did not proceed in total chaos. In some groups, time limits were set on the length each person talked. In a few, despite disdain for formal roles or special competencies, structure appeared in the form of drawing lots to determine who would perform an activity or give a talk outside the group. Some observers noted that even in groups whose members derogated structure most vehemently, the interactions among members became implicitly structured over time. Such informal structure gave great advantage to those participants who were able to achieve power by subtle means, but handicapped those who were less experienced and "believed" there was no structure. As noted earlier, W. F. Whyte (1953) had made the same observation concerning the "anti-leadership" norms in T-groups at Bethel, Maine: The experienced observer could detect leadership behaviors that did not violate the norms, hence were not noticed by many participants.

The point is that despite the emphasis on lack of structure, diverse products of interaction did develop in different consciousness-raising groups, including norms, values, and ideals accepted by the members.

However, the informal and "anti-structure" character in this wing of the movement had the advantage in dealing with problems of factionalism: By their very conception, the groups encouraged the formation of new groups from old or from a small nucleus, thereby proliferating separate groups rather than splits within an organization.

The range of ideological persuasions and backgrounds in this wing became quite broad, including neighborhood rap groups among housewives, communes of varying political persuasion, creative workshops, and determined cells of feminists of political and nonpolitical cast. A few regard themselves as "true" feminists, scorning "politicos," by which they appear to mean socialists or particular "brands" of socialists. Some who call themselves "radical feminists" engage in no more radical activities than forming rape counseling services or day-care centers, thus enacting in modern form the "lady bountiful" roles of predecessors early in the century. In short, the older political and social labels apply poorly to the diversity of women's groups that arose within the movement, literally from grass roots.

COUNTERREACTIONS AND INTERGROUP CONFLICTS

No social movement proposing change of any significance has been met with baskets of rose petals strewn at its feet. Counterreactions are inevitable, proportional to the scope and the "seriousness" of the proposed changes, that is, to how much they would disrupt the superiority and privileges enjoyed by others under established conceptions and procedures.

When counterreactions fall short of repression or physical harrassment of participants, they may enhance the growth of the movement in several ways. The "opposition" becomes concrete. As in encounters between conflicting groups (Chapter 5), confronting the opposition can strengthen solidarity within the movement, heightening members' feelings of identity and determination. In addition, the reaction may provide tangible evidence of their bill of gripes, thereby attracting new members hitherto not convinced of its validity. In these senses, overt and blatant expressions of sexism serve the women's movement by promoting women's identification as women, particularly if the expressions come from men of some standing in society.

Ironically, the diversity and generality of the positive aims in the women's movement have protected its adherents thus far from the more vehement onslaughts of counterreaction suffered by other social movements. At the same time, the movement is peculiarly vulnerable to the more subtle opposition through evasion, inaction, and policies of divide and conquer. Within the context of a society legally committed to equality in civil rights, NOW, WEAL, and other groups focused on even more specific reforms (for example, change of abortion laws) have achieved successes with astounding rapidity, but have only begun to face the fact that legal changes can be countered by formal and informal actions that cancel their impact. Pressure groups have formed to reinstate some of the changed laws. Such groups seldom appear as "anti-women" but as "pro" some value or institution that some women in the movement would be reluctant to attack, such as the church, family, or even the economic and mental well-being of young males.

For example, in academia, successful reforms toward affirmative action in admissions and hiring faculty have aroused comparatively little overt opposition, though a few "committees of concern" have appeared. Nevertheless, there is a great deal of expressed concern over "maintaining academic standards," over the need to "choose the best candidate" regardless of sex, and over what the shrinking job market will do to the financial security and emotional problems of young males. Since the increase in numbers of women faculty has been less than 1 percent, despite the proclaimed "success," affirmative action appears to some a victim of evasive practices and the constant reiteration of quality standards a protective strategy. Nor is it satisfactory to young women to suggest that their financial security and sense of worth are necessarily more expendable than those of their male contemporaries.

Divide, Co-opt, and Conquer

The attempt to pit women's aspirations against men's (as represented above) is only one of several versions illustrating the frequent divide and conquer tactics of movement opponents. One such attempt gave wide publicity to the alleged lack of sympathy for the women's movement among black women. To the contrary, the Harris poll (May 20, 1971) reported that 62 percent of black women as compared with 39 percent of white women then favored "most of the efforts to strengthen and change women's status in society." The results were, in fact, more favorable to another version of the same tactic, namely, that "most women" did not support the movement. However, a more recent survey reported that 52 percent of a representative nationwide sample of women favored "women's liberation," and 73 percent favored efforts to change things for women in their family, their jobs, and in government when the term "liberation" was not used (*ISR Newsletter*, 1974).

The kinds of counterreactions to the women's movement that will arise depend a great deal on the positive programs pursued by its varied parts and on larger social forces affecting entire societies. For example, widespread unemployment invariably generates reactions against affirmative action programs aimed at equalizing opportunities for women, as well as for subordinated racial and ethnic minorities. It is also possible, however, that it could bring home to both men and women their common predicament in the labor market (see Baer and Bush, 1974).

Those women who aim primarily at entry into the "man's world" of work and public affairs as equals, changing that world only by their joining it, are likely to see counterreaction largely in forms with which they are long familiar—ridicule, joking derogation, and evasion. However, their heroic "toughing it out" and public exposures of evasion can generate another reaction common in established power centers: "Since we can't fight it, let's take enough women into the system so they're part of it." Thus co-opted, women would soon find themselves on the sunny side of the fence from other women, a circumstance not unknown at present.

Similarly, larger economic and political pressures can readily be utilized by countermovements to pit young men against young women, blacks against white women and vice versa, "intellectuals" against working people. In the United States, social movements have been particularly vulnerable to the twin counterreactions of co-opting their leaders and of dividing potential supporters. Since many women have been brought up to equate avoidance of conflict with being an acceptable woman, they are, ironically, particularly vulnerable to such divisive countertactics. The irony is that by succumbing to divisive countertactics, they would be participating in the deepening of divisions among potential supporters.

MOVEMENT GOALS AND ATTITUDE CHANGE

Within a four-year period, the widespread efforts and publicity of the women's movement in the United States achieved significant attitude change, not only among its participants but among individuals drawn from a cross section of socioeconomic and educational levels of men and women in the country. According to the Roper Organization (Klemesrud, 1974), the changes occurred with respect to both the movement's existence and each of the specific issues widely publicized as movement aims.

Among women, clear positive support for efforts to change or strengthen women's status was voiced by only about 40 percent polled in 1970, but 57 percent in spring, 1974. Those opposed decreased from 42 percent in 1970 to 25 percent in 1974. A larger percentage of men than women has consistently voiced verbal support of this aim, increasing from 44 percent in 1970 to 49 percent in 1972 and 63 percent in 1974. More than half (52 percent) of the women questioned in 1974 said that they hoped to combine work outside the home and marriage, but fewer (46 percent) preferred a marriage "where husband and wife share responsibilities more—both work, both share homemaking and child responsibilities." Thirty-eight percent preferred marriage and motherhood without a career, a percentage corresponding to that reported in another survey to the effect that "most" or "many" women were "happiest when they are taking care of a home or looking after children" (ISR *Newsletter*, 1974, p. 2). An even larger percentage of men (46 percent) agreed with the latter sentiment.

Despite the large and significant variations in verbal responses according to the wording of the questions and the particular issues focused on, there can be little doubt that the women's movement has successfully enlarged the latitude of acceptable alternatives for women's activities and male-female relationships. There is room for considerable doubt about the scope of such changes and about the translation of movement aims into actions, just as there is about the relationship between verbal reports on attitudes and life circumstances of blacks and whites in this country (see Chapter 10). (For example, the word *liberation* decreased verbal support from 73 to 52 percent, as reported on the basis of another recent poll in the last section.)

Such moot questions are not, however, the only reason that we should not rely solely on reports from commercial survey research. Such polls are not particularly well suited to elicit other signs of attitude change that are also widespread among men and women, particularly the young. The women's movement has brought to many participants and nonparticipants a heightened awareness of what it means to be a woman or a man in their own society. One signal of such awareness is the concern with sex-specific language. The drive to eliminate sex bias in language (English being particularly susceptible to it) would be absurd, as its critics repeatedly charge, if it were not also a signal of such heightened awareness, that is, genuine attitude change.

In a recent discussion with a small class of undergraduates on topics not closely related to the women's movement, two students taught me how sex bias in language related to their attitudes. One young man was criticizing a well-known experiment in social psychology for failing to give evidence that reading taboo sexual words was a severely embarrassing experience to the women who had participated in the experiment, evidence needed, he felt, to support the interpretation of the results. "Besides," he added, "the researchers studied women, then described their procedures referring to the research subjects as 'he'." What he meant was that the male researchers had lived in a world that they viewed with entirely different eyes from his own.

In the same discussion, a woman undergraduate complained of her difficulties in planning for future graduate work: Her parents, she said, always tried to treat her brother and herself equitably; but when her brother wanted to go to graduate school, he was encouraged with the assurance that he would receive their financial support whereas she was not. Her parents approved of her goal, but could not see the way clear to help her financially, remarking "That's your baby." Their refusal of financial support was not all that bothered this young woman, as she repeated the phrase three times, adding: "That's what they think I *should* be doing." It is not quite true that "sticks and stones will break my bones, but words will never hurt me" when the words signal so much about what others think of one—even others who one knows love and care.

IDENTITY SEARCH AND THE SCOPE OF CHANGE

Women's heightened consciousness of their status and role relationships in society with others, of the contradictions in them, and thus of the social origin of many inner conflicts experienced as personal has been a deliberate effort and aim in the women's movement. There is no doubt that for many women, particularly young ones facing a crisis-ridden society and uncertain future, consciousness raising has produced attitude change on so broad a scope that it can be referred to as changed identity, even conversion to one of several possible new belief systems. Such sweeping changes in the self-system have occurred over time, particularly among women who have immersed themselves in joint activities and projects directed toward change. The more usual cases, however, involve changes in clusters of attitudes toward specific activities and relationships—in sexual, work, home, or family spheres—which are genuine and important to the women (and men) involved, but fall short of transforming the self-system.

There are good reasons for the wide range of differences in extent of attitude change among participants in the women's movement. Theoretically, we should expect the extent of change in the self-system to parallel the areas of changed activities, changed relationships with men and women, and of joint decisions toward change (see Chapters 8 and 11). Within the women's movement, there is great diversity in aims, programs, and opportunities among its various parts and groups in those respects. A few small groups of feminists attempt to secure "total commitment" from members; however, the women's movement is not, by and large, proceeding along lines of an "exclusive" structure that encompasses all phases of its members' lives. Most informal and formal groups are, on the contrary, "inclusive" (McLaughlin, 1969), attempting to attract as many adherents as possible even though some may participate only in nominal fashion.

For the vast majority of participants as well as those affected indirectly, the women's movement is one aspect of life, important though it may be. Young women searching for some stability and core for the self-concept often become deeply absorbed in movement literature and activities for considerable periods of time. Freeman (1974) has estimated that such absorption is likely to be temporary, lasting two years, on the average. She suggested that such rapid turnover of membership might handicap movement organizations, but it is also possible that erstwhile members move toward other parts of the sprawling movement or engage in other activities that will strengthen the movement in the long run. A follow-up study on white student activists in early civil rights protests in the South (1960–1963) found that ten years later they were more likely to be engaged in social and political activities for related causes than students who had not been protestors (Fendrich, 1974). Such continued involvement by women following activism in the movement is a realistic possibility.

Perhaps more important than sheer length of participation is the question of how "discrete" or comprehensive is the attitude change and commitment among participants. It should not surprise us that, at times, such change is confined to sexual activities or career decisions, both consequential but not total spheres of self-identity. Nor should it surprise anyone but those quite unaware of the facts concerning female socialization that some women may become quite vocal on certain movement issues (say repeal of abortion laws), but hesitate to spring forward to occupy leadership positions and remain quite conventional in other political-social attitudes.

After all, it is exceedingly painful to run risks of losing whatever appreciation our fellow men and women have accorded to us, to cut our ties with those who have been near and dear, and to reorient childhood and newly acquired attitudes within a short time. Such options appear particularly grim within the context of a women's movement that seeks the broadest possible support, yet lacks organizational contexts where women and men are jointly involved in building new reference groups to replace the social ties that could be lost in the process. The fact that more and more women and men are engaging in such activities means that the practical obstacles are not forbidding, though they are formidable.

Currently, the women's movement boldly proclaims, on the one hand, that its aims are no less than transformed human relationships between the sexes, with new women and new men their outcome, while proposing, on the other hand, a series of highly specific changes in laws, in financial regulations, in marriage and divorce arrangements, and in facilities for family planning and child care. Many women do not realize, and most movement literature does not make it clear, that equality of the sexes, if achieved, would mean a very different organization of social life than we now know. Nor do many see beyond the "obstacle removal" stage of planning, to contemplate the contradictions in education, training, work, the economy, politics, and government that are already plaguing men in the "man's world."

Few women or men today are as naively hopeful of the attainments of a movement toward women's equality as were those most optimistic about the fruits of women's gaining the vote during the early 1900s.

Women's votes would, in their eyes, sweep the halls of government clean from its corruption, override decisions to make war, and humanize the world of work. A sympathetic historian, William O'Neill (1971), commented on the striking failure during those years to appreciate the lack of fit between the movement's positive proposals and its ultimate aims. "The greatest weakness of the feminist movement was precisely this inability to appreciate the limits that the organization of society placed upon its larger aspirations" (p. ix).

Many a writer on social movements, particularly those involving subordinated peoples, dwells at great length on their apparent negativism, their lack of agreement on positive programs for change, the rivalry among factions, ideological disagreements, and leadership struggles that often ensue. The weaknesses of the current women's movement in these respects are not distinctive but are, in fact, characteristic of any such movement in its early phases. Charges of failure to examine the implications of translating specific proposals into action programs are typical reactions of outsiders or opponents, as are derogatory labels classifying movement adherents with whatever social, political, or religious bogey that currently arouses the most terror in the heart.

After all, a social movement raises problems that are problems for the larger society and with which society's most powerful participants have failed to deal or to solve. In calling for equality of the sexes, the women's movement is ultimately calling for changes in the basic structure of every known society—the relationships between men and women. Its aims will surely be frustrated if its positive proposals fail to recognize other changes in society that those proposals imply. On the other hand, the women's movement can hardly be expected to provide better or more complete blueprints for the future than have other social movements, which have often left the "woman question" as something to be solved automatically or to be worked out when other aims are realized.

CONFLICT, TACTICS, AND VIOLENCE

Any social movement seeking changes opposed by other segments of society sooner or later comes into conflict with them, and the women's movement is no exception historically or currently. Such social conflict, which becomes conflict between groups over time, poses the problem of what tactics the movement should use in order to proceed toward its immediate and long-range goals while dealing with the opposition. In early phases, such tactics often include dramatic and symbolic actions (for example, meetings, marches, petitions) designed to call attention to the problems that concern participants and to increase the range of possible solutions currently considered. As social conflict increases, such tactics become increasingly risky both because they seldom accomplish the goals singlehandedly and because they may arouse repressive actions from the opposition.

As a movement proceeds, more time and effort is required of participants on organizational activities, fund raising, education, recruitment of new members, and interacting to decide on programs and tactics. Thus, what the newspaper or television public sees of a movement may not represent the level of its activities at a given time. In fact, what the public sees is likely to represent *either* the most spectacular staged events by the movement *or* incidents involving aggressive and violent actions.

In the early attempts by social scientists to deal with social movements, their accounts also focused on public events, rather than on analysis of why the movements had developed, what had preceded the events in question, or what movement goals were. Under the label "collective interaction" or "collective behavior," older sociologists and psychologists gave colorful and even lurid accounts of people gripped by the hypnotic spells of crowds or venting evil impulses (see Sherif and Sherif, 1969). In many cases, such accounts reveal more about the authors' opposition to the people and their aims than they do about why the people gathered or what they hoped to accomplish.

The study of collective interaction, including episodes of property destruction or personal violence, is certainly legitimate and intriguing. However, equating social movements with collective interaction has not helped our understanding of either. The feminist movement before World War I involved many mass demonstrations and episodes of violence, first initiated by authorities then by small groups of women as well. We could not possibly have understood the movement by focusing on those episodes, nor were the episodes understandable apart from the context of the movement and the repressive actions by authorities.

The current women's movement uses tactics of political pressure, legal actions, publicity and persuasion, lawful demonstration, and other nonviolent means. Like the earlier movement and the early civil rights movement in the United States, it is likely to respond to possible repressive actions with nonviolent, passive resistance. When such tactics are adopted by a movement, individual frustrations do not lead to aggressive actions as long as the individual is a dedicated movement member (see Pelton, 1974). Violent actions are most likely to occur when repressive actions by authorities are inflicted on movement participants (see Snyder and Tilly, 1972) or when a group within the movement adopts violent means as the most feasible tactic (and sometimes sees it as the only one) to meet its opposition.

In the analysis of violent actions, which are frequent in contemporary life, we will be wise to insist, as social psychologists and as individual citizens, that the social context in which the actions occur is quite as important as the personal backgrounds of participants. We should not suppose for an instant that there is or can be a general psychological theory of aggressive or violent behavior that ignores the historical and immediate context in which it occurs (see Megargee and Hokanson, 1970).

Such is particularly the case when, as a planned tactic within a social movement, violent deeds are committed. Here pertinent concepts have to include the person's reference group, his or her relationship to other participants, and intergroup relationships with both authorities and victims of the violent actions. For example, during the unorganized collective outbreaks in large U.S. cities in 1968, where most participants were not political activists, the selection of victims for theft and vandalism was not an entirely "chance" affair. It bore some relation to prior intergroup relationships in the areas (Berk and Aldrich, 1972).

This note on tactics and violent actions may seem discordant from a woman writing on the women's movement. However, it is no more than a caution to beware of oversimplified explanations of unusual collective actions that occur within the context of a social movement or in line with its tactics. I can remember when the mere act of writing about the women's movement was sufficiently unusual that all kinds of bizarre and simplistic explanations were given about the writer in the name of "psychology." If she was not an aggressive, "castrating" female engaging in "masculine protest," she must be a barren, frustrated "old maid." A great deal of the popular literature on social violence that occurs within the context of a social movement is just about equally enlightening and is designed for similar purpose.

LAST WORDS

My purpose in this chapter has been to place some major problems in social psychology in the context of some of the major problems of our times. I have not intended to imply that either the issues or the aims of the current women's movement are necessarily more pressing than others. On the contrary, it is now literally possible that any efforts by the less powerful to reduce inequities among human beings can disappear in destruction that even the most powerful cannot control.

In the past, great human effort and energy has gone into understanding and utilizing the physical environment. In order to prevent its destruction along with human lives, we are now faced with the question of whether human beings can understand and plan their own relationships with one another. We have learned that it is possible for human beings to hold some of their differences in abeyance in order to cooperate toward goals genuinely superordinate to the selfish interests of their respective groups and to learn a great deal about one another in the process. Such findings may be suggestive of the kinds of learning experiences that are needed before we can deal with the overriding questions of our times.

In the process, there is bound to be conflict between individuals, between groups, between nations. There is bound to be social change that, as individuals, we may find painful. The conflicts and change will bring decisions for each of us. Under such circumstances, we may be particularly prone to throw up our hands and leave the decisions to those who tell us they "know what is best" because they occupy positions of political, economic, or military power or because they are "experts." It is not inevitable that we do so.

If I had to say what place social psychology has in society, in a few words, I guess that I would say that it can help in understanding what the human problems are, in showing what their impacts upon human beings are, and in analyzing alternative ways that individuals in inter-action go about dealing with the problems, changing themselves and their groups in the process. I say "help in understanding" because the contrubutions of other social sciences are surely needed for a rounded picture. That means that I do not believe that either social psycholo-gists or any other social scientists from another discipline can become "the experts" to tell others all they need to know or "what is best for you." On the other hand, the methods and the findings from their efforts can be and should be part of the information on which decisions are based. This is one reason that I wrote this book: to share what I know with you. Your part in decisions affecting the future is as great as mine, and the future begins today.

References

Abelson, R. P. Computers, polls, and public opinion. *Trans-Action,* 1968 (September), 20–27.

———. Are attitudes necessary? In B. T. King and E. McGinnies (Eds.). *Attitudes, conflict and social change.* New York: Academic Press, 1972.

———, Aronson, E., McGuire, W. J., Newcomb, T. M., Rosenberg, M. J., and Tannenbaum, P. (Eds.). *Theories of cognitive consistency: A sourcebook.* Chicago: Rand McNally, 1968.

Acock, A. C., and DeFleur, M. L. A configurational approach to contingent consistency in the attitude-behavior relationship. *American Sociological Review,* 1972, *37,* 714–726.

Adair, J. G. *The human subject: The social psychology of the psychological experiment.* Boston: Little, Brown, 1973.

Adorno, T., Frenkel-Brunswik, E., Levinson, D. J., and Sanford, R. N. *The authoritarian personality.* New York: Harper & Row, 1950.

Aiello, J. R., and Jones, S. E. Proxemic behavior of black and white first-, third-, and fifth-grade children. *Journal of Personality and Social Psychology,* 1973, *25,* 21–27.

Ajzen, I., and Fishbein, M. Attitudinal and normative variables as predictors of specific behaviors. *Journal of Personality and Social Psychology,* 1973, *27,* 41–57.

Allen, H. Bystander intervention and helping on the subway. In L. Bickman and T. Henchy (Eds.). *Beyond the laboratory: Field research in social psychology.* New York: McGraw-Hill, 1972, pp. 22–33.

Allport, F. H. *Social Psychology.* Boston: Houghton Mifflin, 1924.

Allport, G. W. Attitudes. In C. Murchison (Ed.). *Handbook of social psychology.* Worcester, Mass.: Clark Univ. Press, 1935, pp. 798–844.

———. *Personality: A psychological interpretation.* New York: Holt, Rinehart & Winston, 1937.

———. The ego in contemporary psychology. *Psychological Review,* 1943, *50,* 451–478.

———. *The nature of prejudice.* Reading, Mass.: Addison-Wesley, 1954.

———, and Postman, L. J. The basic psychology of rumor. In H. Proshansky and B. Seidenberg (Eds.). *Basic studies in social psychology.* New York: Holt, Rinehart & Winston, 1965, pp. 47–64.

Altman, I., Taylor, D. A., and Wheeler, L. Ecological aspects of group behavior in social isolation. *Journal of Applied Social Psychology,* 1971, *1,* 76–100.

Ames, R. G., and Sakuma, A. F. Criteria for evaluating others: A reexamination of the Bogardus Social Distance Scale. *Sociology and Social Research,* 1969, *54,* 5–24.

Anastasi, A. *Differential psychology.* New York: Macmillan, 1966, pp. 452–505.

Anderson, H. H., and Brandt, H. F. A study of motivation involving self-announced goals of fifth grade children and the concept of level of aspiration. *Journal of Social Psychology,* 1939, *10,* 209–232.

Anderson, R. C. Learning in discussions: A resume of the authoritarian-democratic studies. In W. W. Charters, Jr., and N. L. Gage (Eds.). *Readings in the social psychology of education.* Boston: Allyn & Bacon, 1963, pp. 153–162.

Ansari, A. A. A study of the relation between group stereotypes and social distance. *Journal of Education and Psychology,* 1956, *14,* 28–35.

APA Monitor. ACLU scores token economy. Washington, D.C.: American Psychological Association, 1974, 5(8), 1, 7.

Apsler, R., and Sears, D. O. Warning, personal involvement and attitude change. *Journal of Personality and Social Psychology,* 1968, *9,* 162–166.

Aronson, E. Dissonance theory: Progress and problems. In R. P. Abelson, E. Aronson, W. J. McGuire, T. M. Newcomb, M. J. Rosenberg, and P. Tannenbaum (Eds.). *Theories of cognitive consistency.* Chicago: Rand McNally, 1968.

———. *The social animal.* San Francisco: Freeman, 1972.

———, Turner, J. A., and Carlsmith, M. Communicator credibility and communicator discrepancy as determinants of opinion change. *Journal of Abnormal and Social Psychology,* 1963, *67,* 31–37.

ASA Footnotes. Survey research problems getting worse, study shows. Washington, D.C.: American Sociological Association, 1974, 2(5), 2.

Asch, S. E. Studies of independence and conformity: I. A minority of one against a unanimous majority. *Psychological Monographs,* 1956, *70*(9).

Atkins, A. L. Own attitude and discriminability in relation to anchoring effects in judgment. *Journal of Personality and Social Psychology,* 1966, *4,* 497–507.

———, and Bieri, J. Effects of involvement level and contextual stimuli on social judgment. *Journal of Personality and Social Psychology,* 1968, *9,* 197–204.

Atkins, A. L., Deaux, K., and Bieri, J. Latitude of acceptance and attitude change: Empirical evidence for a reformulation. *Journal of Personality and Social Psychology,* 1967, *6,* 47–54.

Avigdor, R. The development of sterotypes as a result of group interaction. Doctoral dissertation, New York Univ., 1952.

Baer, H. R., and Bush, T. L. Demographic and economic trends: Social implications for women. Paper delivered at the tenth annual conference of the Canadian Association for American Studies, Ottawa, Ontario, October 12, 1974 (mimeographed).

Baer, H. R., and Sherif, C. W. (Eds.). A topical bibliography (selectively annotated) on psychology of women. *JSAS Catalog Selected Documents in Psychology,* 1974, *4,* 42.

Baldwin, J. M. *Mental development in the child and the race.* New York: Macmillan, 1895.

Bales, R. F. *Interaction process analysis: A method for the study of small groups.* Reading, Mass.: Addison-Wesley, 1950.

———. The equilibrium problem in small groups. In T. Parsons, R. F. Bales, and E. A. Shils (Eds.). *Working papers in the theory of action.* New York: Free Press, 1953.

————. Task roles and social roles in problem solving groups. In I. D. Steiner and M. Fishbein (Eds.). *Current studies in social psychology.* New York: Holt, Rinehart & Winston, 1965, pp. 321–332.

————, and Slater, P. E. Role differentiation in small decision-making groups. In T. Parsons et al. (Eds.). *Family, socialization and interaction processes.* New York: Free Press, 1955.

Bandura, A. Vicarious processes: A case of no-trial learning. In L. Berkowitz (Ed.). *Advances in experimental social psychology.* New York: Academic Press, 1965.

————. Behavior theory and the models of man. *American Psychologist,* 1974, *29,* 859–869.

————, and Walters, R. H. *Social learning and personality development.* New York: Holt, Rinehart & Winston, 1963.

Bartlett, F. C. *Remembering: A study in experimental and social psychology.* New York: Cambridge Univ. Press, 1932.

Bartlett, K. Dr. Spock revising child care book. *Centre Daily Times* (State College, Pa.), August 6, 1974, p. 7.

Bayton, J. A. The racial stereotypes of Negro college students. *Journal of Abnormal and Social Psychology,* 1941, *36,* 97–102.

————, and Byoune, E. Racio-national stereotypes held by Negroes. *Journal of Negro Education,* 1947, *16,* 49–56.

Bayton, J. A., McAlister, L. B., and Hamer, K. Race-class stereotypes. *Journal of Negro Education,* 1956, *25,* 75–78.

Beck, D., and Nebergall, R. E. Relationship between attitude neutrality and involvement. Paper presented to the annual meeting of the Speech Association of America, Los Angeles, 1967. (Data reported in Sherif and Sherif, 1969.)

Bell, G. D. Processes in the formation of adolescent's aspirations. *Social Forces,* 1963, *42,* 179–195.

Bem, D. Self perception: An alternative interpretation of cognitive dissonance phenomena. *Psychological Review,* 1967, *74,* 183–200.

Benedict, R. *Race and cultural relations. Problems in American life.* No. 5. Washington, D.C.: National Education Association, 1942.

Benoit-Smullyan, E. Status, status types and status interrelations. *American Sociological Review,* 1944, *9,* 151–161.

Berelson, B., Lazarsfeld, P. F., and McPhee, W. N. *Voting: A study of opinion formation in a presidential campaign.* Chicago: Univ. of Chicago Press, 1954.

Berk, R. A., and Aldrich, H. E. Patterns of vandalism during civil disorders as an indicator of selection of targets. *American Sociological Review,* 1972, *37,* 533–547.

Berkowitz, L. *Aggression: A social psychological analysis.* New York: McGraw-Hill, 1962.

Berscheid, E., Dion, K., Walster, E., and Walster, G. W. Physical attractiveness and dating choice: A test of the matching hypothesis. *Journal of Experimental Social Psychology,* 1971, *7,* 173–189.

Bieri, J. Attitudes and arousal: Affect and cognition in personality function. In C. W. Sherif and M. Sherif (Eds.). *Attitude, ego-involvement and change.* New York: Wiley, 1967, pp. 178–200.

————, Orcutt, B. A., and Leaman, R. Anchoring effects in sequential clinical judgments. *Journal of Abnormal and Social Psychology,* 1963, *67,* 616–623.

Blake, R. R., and Dennis, W. The development of stereotypes concerning the Negro. *Journal of Abnormal and Social Psychology,* 1943, *38,* 525–531.

Blake, R. R., Shepard, H., and Mouton, J. S. *Managing intergroup conflicts in industry.* Houston: Gulf Publishing, 1964.

Block, J. H. Conceptions of sex role: Some cross-cultural and longitudinal perspectives. *American Psychologist,* 1973, *28,* 512–526.

Bochner, S., and Insko, C. A. Communicator discrepancy, source credibility and opinion change. *Journal of Personality and Social Psychology,* 1966, *4,* 614–621.

Bogardus, E. S. Measuring social distances. *Journal of Applied Sociology,* 1925, *9,* 299–308.

———. *A forty year racial distance study.* Los Angeles: Univ. of Southern California, 1967.

———. Comparing racial distance in Ethiopia, South Africa and the United States. *Sociology and Social Research,* 1968, *52,* 149–156.

Bolton, C. D. Alienation and action: A study of peace group members. *American Journal of Sociology,* 1972, *78,* 537–561.

Bonacich, P., and Lewis, G. H. Function specialization and sociometric judgment. *Sociometry,* 1973, *36,* 31–41.

Bovard, E. W., Jr. Social norms and the individual. *Journal of Abnormal and Social Psychology,* 1948, *43,* 62–69.

Boyanowsky, E. O., and Allen, V. L. Ingroup norms and self-identity as determinants of discriminatory behavior. *Journal of Personality and Social Psychology,* 1973, *25,* 408–418.

Brehm, J. W. *A theory of psychological reactance.* New York: Academic Press, 1966.

Brock, T. C., and Balloun, G. L. Behavioral receptivity to dissonant information. *Journal of Personality and Social Psychology,* 1967, *4,* 413–428.

Bronfenbrenner, U. *Two worlds of childhood: U.S. and U.S.S.R.* New York: Russell Sage Foundation, 1970.

Broverman, I. K., Vogel, S. R., Broverman, D. M., Clarkson, F. E., and Rosenkrantz, P. S. Sex-role stereotypes: A current appraisal. *Journal of Social Issues,* 1972, *28*(2), 59–78.

Brown, R. Mass phenomena. In G. Lindzey (Ed.). *Handbook of social psychology.* Vol. 2. Reading, Mass.: Addison-Wesley, 1954.

———. *Social psychology.* New York: Free Press, 1965.

———. *A first language: The early stages.* Cambridge, Mass.: Harvard Univ. Press, 1973.

———. Development of the first language in the human species. *American Psychologist,* 1973, *28,* 107–128.

Bruner, J. S. On perceptual readiness. *Psychological Review,* 1957, *64,* 123–152.

Bryan, J. H., and Test, M. A. Naturalistic studies of helping behavior. *Journal of Personality and Social Psychology,* 1967, *6,* 400–407.

Buchanan, W., and Cantril, H. *How nations see each other: A study in public opinion.* Urbana: Univ. of Illinois Press, 1953.

Burke, P. J. Participation and leadership in small groups. *American Sociological Review,* 1974, *39,* 832–843.

Buss, A. H., and Portnoy, N. W. Pain tolerance and group identification. *Journal of Personality and Social Psychology,* 1967, *6,* 106–108.

Byrne, D., Ervin, C. R., and Lamberth, J. Continuity between the experimental study of attraction and real-life computer dating. *Journal of Personality and Social Psychology,* 1970, *16,* 157–163.

Campbell, A. *White attitudes toward black people.* Ann Arbor: Institute for Social Research, Univ. of Michigan, 1971.

———, Converse, P. E., Miller, W. E., and Stokes, D. E. *The American voter.* New York: Wiley, 1960.

Campbell, D. T. The indirect assessment of social attitudes. *Psychological Bulletin,* 1950, *47,* 15–38.

———. Social attitudes and other acquired behavioral dispositions. In S. Koch (Ed.). *Psychology: A study of a science.* Vol. 6. New York: McGraw-Hill, 1963, pp. 92–172.

———, Kruskall, W. H., and Wallace, W. P. Seating aggregation as an index of attitude. *Sociometry,* 1966, *29,* 1–15.

Cannell, C. F., and Kahn, R. L. Interviewing. In G. Lindzey and E. Aronson (Eds.) *Handbook of social psychology.* Vol. 2. Reading, Mass.: Addison-Wesley, 1968.

Cantril, H. *The psychology of social movements.* New York: Wiley, 1941.

———. *Gauging public opinion.* Princeton: Princeton Univ. Press, 1944.

———. The intensity of an attitude. *Journal of Abnormal and Social Psychology,* 1946, *41,* 129–135.

Carmichael, S., and Hamilton, C. V. *Black Power: The politics of liberation.* New York: Random House, 1967.

Carter, L. F. Leadership and small group behavior. In M. Sherif and M. O. Wilson (Eds.). *Group relations at the crossroads.* New York: Harper & Row, 1953.

Cartwright, D., and Zander, A. (Eds.). *Group dynamics: Rsearch and theory.* (3rd ed.) New York: Harper & Row, 1968.

Centers, R. An effective classroom demonstration of stereotypes. *Journal of Social Psychology,* 1951, *34,* 41–46.

Chapman, D. W., and Volkmann, J. A social determinant of the level of aspiration. *Journal of Abnormal and Social Psychology,* 1939, *34,* 225–238.

Chomsky, N. *Aspects of the theory of syntax.* Cambridge, Mass.: MIT Press, 1965.

Clark, J. P., and Tifft, L. L. Polygraph and interview validation of self-reported deviant behavior. *American Sociological Review,* 1966, *31,* 516–523.

Clark, K. B., and Clark, M. K. Racial identification and preference in Negro pre-school children. In T. M. Newcomb and E. L. Hartley (Eds.). *Readings in social psychology.* New York: Holt, Rinehart & Winston, 1947.

Clark, R. D., III, and Word, L. E. Why don't bystanders help? Because of ambiguity? *Journal of Personality and Social Psychology,* 1972, *24,* 392–400.

Clarke, P., and James, J. The effects of situation, attitude intensity and personality on information seeking. *Sociometry,* 1967, *30,* 235–245.

Coch, L., and French, J. R. P., Jr. Overcoming resistance to change. In D. Cartwright and A. Zander (Eds.). *Group dynamics: Research and theory.* New York: Harper & Row, 1953 (second printing, 1956).

Cofer, C. N. Constructive processes in memory. *American Scientist,* 1973, *61*(5), 537–543.

Coffin, T. E. Some conditions of suggestion and suggestibility. *Psychological Monographs,* 1941, No. 241.

Coffman, T. and Harris, M. Shifts in stereotypes following upon group discussion. Abstract (personal communication), 1974.

Cohen, E. G., and Roper, S. S. Modification of interracial interaction disability: An application of status characteristic theory. *American Sociological Review,* 1972, *37,* 643–657.

Cole, B. G. (Ed.). *Television.* New York: Free Press, 1970.

Coleman, J., Katz, E., and Menzel, H. *Medical innovations: A diffusion study.* Indianapolis: Bobbs-Merrill, 1966.

———. Social processes in physicians' adoption of a new drug. *Journal of Chronic Disease,* 1959, *9,* 1–19.

Collins, B. E., and Raven, B. H. Group structure: Attraction, coalitions, communication, and power. In G. Lindzey and E. Aronson (Eds.). *Handbook of social psychology.* Vol. 4. Reading, Mass.: Addison-Wesley, 1969.

Cook, T. D., and Insko, C. A. Persistence of attitude change as a function of conclusion re-exposure: A laboratory-field experiment. *Journal of Personality and Social Psychology,* 1968, *9,* 322–328.

Coombs, C. H. Thurstone's measurement of social values revisited forty years later. *Journal of Personality and Social Psychology,* 1967, *6,* 85–91.

Cooper, C. L., and Mangham, I. L. (Eds.). *T-groups: A survey of research.* New York: Wiley Interscience, 1971.

Coopersmith, S. *The antecedents of self esteem.* San Francisco: Freeman, 1967.

Cox, K. K. Changes in stereotyping of Negroes and whites in magazine advertising. *Public Opinion Quarterly,* 1970, *33,* 603–606.

Cronbach, L. J. Five decades of public controversy over mental testing. *American Psychologist,* 1975, *30,* 1–14.

Cvetkovich, G. and Baumgardner, S. R. Attitude polarization: The relative influence of discussion group structure and reference group norms. *Journal of Personality and Social Psychology,* 1973, *26,* 159–165.

Darwin, C. Biographical sketch of an infant. *Mind,* 1877, *2,* 285–294.

Davies, J. C. Toward a theory of revolution. *American Sociological Review,* 1962, *27,* 5–19.

Davis, K. Final note on a case of extreme isolation. *American Journal of Sociology,* 1947, *52,* 432–437.

Dawes, R. M. *Fundamentals of attitude measurement.* New York: Wiley, 1972.

———, Singer, D., and Lemons, F. An experimental analysis of contrast effect and its implications for intergroup communication and indirect assessment of attitude. *Journal of Personality and Social Psychology,* 1972, *21,* 281–295.

DeBeauvoir, S. *The second sex.* New York: Knopf, 1953.

DeFleur, M. L., and Westie, F. R. Verbal attitudes and overt acts: An experiment on the salience of attitudes. *American Sociological Review,* 1958, *23,* 667–673.

DeNike, L. D., and Spielberger, C. D. Induced mediating states in operant conditioning. *Journal of Verbal Learning and Verbal Behavior,* 1963, *1,* 339–345.

Deutsch, M. Conflicts: Productive and destructive. *Journal of Social Issues,* 1969, *25*(1), 7–42.

Deutscher, I. Words and deeds: Social science and social policy. *Social Problems,* 1966, *13,* 235–265.

Diab, L. Factors affecting studies of national stereotypes. *Journal of Social Psychology,* 1963a, *59,* 29–40; Factors determining group stereotypes. *Journal of Social Psychology,* 1963b, *61,* 3–10.

––––––. Studies in social attitudes: II. Selectivity in mass communication media as a function of attitude-medium discrepancy. *Journal of Social Psychology,* 1965, *67,* 297–302.

––––––. Measurement of social attitudes: Problems and prospects. In C. W. Sherif and M. Sherif (Eds.). *Attitude, ego-involvement and change.* New York: Wiley, 1967, pp. 140–158.

Diaz-Guerrero, R. Sociocultural and psychodynamic processes in adolescent transition and mental health. In M. Sherif and C. W. Sherif (Eds.). *Problems of youth.* Chicago: Aldine, 1965.

Dinneen, F. P. *An introduction to general linguistics.* New York: Holt, Rinehart & Winston, 1967.

Dixon, M. Why women's liberation. In M. H. Garskof (Ed.). *Roles women play: Readings toward women's liberation.* Belmont, Calif.: Brooks/Cole, 1971.

Dodd, S. C. A social distance test in the Near East. *American Journal of Sociology,* 1935, *41,* 194–204.

Dohrenwend, B. S. Social status and stressful life events. *Journal of Personality and Social Psychology,* 1973, *28,* 225–235.

Doise, W. Intergroup relations and polarization of individual and collective judgments. *Journal of Personality and Social Psychology,* 1969, *12,* 136–143.

Dollard, J., Doob, L., Miller, N., Mowrer, O. H., and Sears, R. *Frustration and aggression.* New Haven: Yale Univ. Press, 1939.

Dunnette, M. D. People feeling: Joy, more joy, and the "slough of despond." *Journal of Applied Behavioral Science,* 1969, *5,* 25–44.

Eagly, A. H., and Telaak, K. Width of the latitude of acceptance as a determinant of attitude change. *Journal of Personality and Social Psychology,* 1972, *23,* 388–397.

Edwards, A. L. *Techniques of attitude scale construction.* New York: Appleton-Century-Crofts, 1957a.

––––––. *The social desirability variable in personality assessment and research.* New York: Holt, Rinehart & Winston, 1957b.

––––––, and Walker, J. N. Relationship between probability of item endorsement and social desirability scale value for high and low groups on Edwards' SD scale. *Journal of Abnormal and Social Psychology,* 1962, *64,* 458–460.

Ehrlich, C. The male sociologist's burden: The place of women in marriage and family texts. *Journal of Marriage and the Family,* 1971, *33,* 421–430.

Ehrlich, H. J. Attitudes, behavior, and the intervening variables. *American Sociologist,* 1969, *4,* 29–34.

––––––. *The social psychology of prejudice.* New York: Wiley, 1973.

––––––, and Van Tubergen, N. Exploring the structure and salience of stereotypes. *Journal of Social Psychology,* 1971, *83,* 113–127.

Eiser, J. R. Enhancement of contrast in the absolute judgment of attitude statements. *Journal of Personality and Social Psychology,* 1971, *17,* 1–10.

——, and Stroebe, W. *Categorization and social judgment.* New York: Academic Press, 1972.

Elbing, A. O. An experimental investigation of the influence of reference group identification on role playing as applied to business. Ph.D. dissertation, Univ. of Washington, Seattle, 1962.

Elms, A. C. *Social psychology and social relevance.* Boston: Little, Brown, 1972.

Emmers, R. H. All of a sudden, the silence. *Pennsylvania Mirror,* August 9, 1974, p. 1.

Entwisle, D. R. To dispel fantasies about fantasy-based measures of achievement motivation. *Psychological Bulletin,* 1973, *77,* 377–391.

Escovar, L. Categorization in young children: A study in social-cognitive development. Doctoral dissertation, Pennsylvania State Univ., 1975.

Esser, A. H. Interactional hierarchy and power structure on a psychiatric ward. In S. J. Hutt and C. Hutt (Eds.). *Behavior studies in psychiatry.* New York: Pergamon Press, 1970, pp. 25–59.

Evans, R., and Novak, R. Campus revolt hearings changing minds in House. Pittsburgh *Post Gazette,* May 31, 1969, p. 6.

Faucheux, C., and Moscovici, S. Le style des comportement d'une minorité et son influence sur les réponses d'une majorité. *Bulletin du C.E.R.P.,* 1967, *16,* 337–361.

Faunce, W. A. Automation and the automobile worker. In W. Galenson and S. M. Lipset (Eds.). *Labor and trade unionism: An interdisciplinary reader.* New York: Wiley, 1960.

Feather, N. T. Level of aspiration and performance variability. *Journal of Personality and Social Psychology,* 1967, *6,* 37–46.

——. Attitude and selective recall. *Journal of Personality and Social Psychology,* 1969, *12,* 310–319.

——. Balancing and positivity effects in social recall. *Journal of Personality,* 1970, *38,* 602–628.

——. Organization and discrepancy in cognitive structure. *Psychological Review,* 1971, *78,* 355–379.

Feffer, M. Developmental analysis of interpersonal behavior. *Psychological Review,* 1970, *77,* 197–214.

Feldman, K. A., and Newcomb, T. M. *The impact of college on students.* San Francisco: Josey Bass, 1969.

Feldman, R. A. Interrelationships among three bases of group integration. *Sociometry,* 1968, *31,* 30–46.

Feldman, R. E. Response to compatriot and foreigner who seek assistance. *Journal of Personality and Social Psychology,* 1968, *10,* 202–214.

Felipe, N. J., and Sommer, R. Invasions of personal space. *Social Problems,* 1966, *14,* 206–214.

Fenchel, G. H., Monderer, J. H., and Hartley, E. L. Subjective status and the equilibration hypothesis. *Journal of Abnormal and Social Psychology,* 1951, *46,* 476–479.

Fendrich, J. M. A study of the association among verbal attitudes, commitment and overt behavior in different experimental situations. *Social Forces,* 1967, *45,* 347–355.

————. Activists ten years later: A test of generational unit continuity. *Journal of Social Issues,* 1974, *30,* No. 3, 95–118.

Festinger, L. *A theory of cognitive dissonance.* New York: Harper & Row, 1957.

Fiedler, F. Personality and situational determinants of leadership effectiveness. In D. Cartwright and A. Zander (Eds.). *Group dynamics: Research and theory.* New York: Harper & Row, 1968.

Fishbein, M. Attitude and the prediction of behavior. In M. Fishbein (Ed.). *Readings in attitude theory and measurement.* New York: Wiley, 1967.

————. The prediction of behaviors from attitudinal variables. In C. D. Mortensen and K. K. Sereno (Eds.). *Advances in communication research.* New York: Harper & Row, 1973.

Flavell, J. H. *The development of role-taking and communication skills in children.* New York: Wiley, 1968.

Flexner, E. *A century of struggle. The women's rights movement in the United States.* New York: Atheneum, 1971.

Foster, G. M. *Traditional cultures and the impact of technological change.* New York: Harper & Row, 1962.

Frank, J. D. Some psychological determinants of the level of aspiration. *American Journal of Psychology,* 1935, *47,* 285–293.

————. The bewildering world of psychotherapy. *Journal of Social Issues,* 1972, *28*(4), 27–44.

Fraser, C., Gouge, C., and Billig, M. Risky shifts, cautious shifts and group polarization. *European Journal of Social Psychology,* 1971, *1*(1), 7–30.

Fraser, R. S., and Stacey, B. G. A psychophysical investigation of the influence of attitude on the judgment of social stimuli. *British Journal of Clinical and Social Psychology,* 1973, *12,* 337–352.

Frazier, F. *Black bourgeoisie.* New York: Free Press, 1957.

Freedman, J. L. Preference for dissonant information. *Journal of Personality and Social Psychology,* 1965, *2,* 287–289.

Freeman, J. The origins of the women's liberation movement. *American Journal of Sociology,* 1973, *78,* 792–811.

————. The new feminism. *Nation,* 1974 (March 9), 297–302.

Freud, S. *Civilization and its discontents.* London: Hogarth Press, 1930.

Friedan, B. *The feminine mystique.* New York: Dell, 1963.

————. Up from the kitchen floor. *New York Times Magazine,* March 4, 1973, pp. 8ff.

Gaertner, S., and Bickman, L. A nonreactive indicator of racial discrimination. The wrong-number technique. In L. Bickman and T. Henchy (Eds.). *Beyond the laboratory: Field research in social psychology.* New York: McGraw-Hill, 1972, pp. 162–169.

Gardner, R. C., Taylor, D. M., and Santos, E. Ethnic stereotypes: The role of contact. *Philippine Journal of Psychology,* 1969, *2*(1), 11–24.

Gecas, V. Parental behavior and contextual variations in adolescent self esteem. *Sociometry,* 1972, *35,* 332–345.

Gesell, A. *The first five years of life.* New York: Harper & Row, 1940.

————, and Ilg, F. L. *Infant and child in the culture today.* New York: Harper & Row, 1943.

Gesell, A., and Thompson, H. *Infant behavior.* New York: McGraw-Hill, 1934.

Gibb, C. A. Leadership: I. Psychological aspects. In D. L. Sills (Ed.). *Interna-*

tional encyclopedia of social sciences, 1968, *9,* 91–101. New York: Macmillan and Free Press.

———. Leadership. In G. Lindzey and E. Aronson (Eds.). *Handbook of social psychology.* Vol. 4. Reading, Mass.: Addison-Wesley, 1969.

Gilbert, G. M. Stereotype persistence and change among college students. *Journal of Abnormal and Social Psychology,* 1951, *46,* 245–254.

Glixman, A. R. Categorizing behavior as a function of meaning domain. *Journal of Personality and Social Psychology,* 1965, *2,* 370–377.

Goffman, E. *The presentation of self in everyday life.* Garden City, N.Y.: Doubleday, 1959.

Goldberg, A. S. Discerning a causal pattern among data on voting behavior. *American Political Science Review,* 1966, *60,* 913–922.

Goldberg, P. A. Are women prejudiced against women? *Trans-Action,* 1968, *5,* 28–30.

Goldstein, M., and Davis, E. K. Race and belief: A further analysis of the social determinants of behavioral intentions. *Journal of Personality and Social Psychology,* 1972, *22,* 346–355.

Golembiewski, R. T., and Blumberg, A. (Eds.). *Sensitivity training and the laboratory approach: Readings about concepts and applications.* Itasca, Ill.: F. E. Peacock, 1970.

Goodman, M. E. *Racial awareness in young children.* Reading, Mass.: Addison-Wesley, 1952.

Gordon, C. Self-conceptions: Configurations of content. In C. Gordon and K. Gergen (Eds.). *The self in social interaction.* New York: Wiley, 1968.

Gorn, G. Effects of ego-involvement, communication discrepancy, and communicator prestige on attitude change. Doctoral dissertation, Pennsylvania State Univ., 1971.

———, Goldberg, M. E., and Kanungo, R. N. Children's television and prosocial behavior: A ray of light in the tunnel of darkness. Faculty of Management, McGill Univ., Montreal, Canada, 1975 (mimeographed).

Greeley, A. M., and Sheatsley, P. Attitudes toward racial integration. *Scientific American,* 1971, *225*(December), 13–19.

Greenberg, P. J. Competition in children: An experimental study. *American Journal of Psychology,* 1932, *44,* 221–248.

Greenspoon, J. The reinforcing effect of two spoken sounds on the frequency of two responses. *American Journal of Psychology,* 1955, *68,* 409–416.

Guthrie, G. M., Azores, F. M., Juanico, M. B., Luna, M. P. S., and Ty, T. P. *The psychology of modernization in the rural Philippines.* IPC Papers No. 8. Quezon City: Ateneo de Manila Univ. Press, 1970.

Guttentag, M. Children in Harlem's community controlled schools. *Journal of Social Issues,* 1972, *28*(4), 1–20.

Haller, A. O., and Butterworth, C. E. Peer influences on level of occupational and educational aspirations. *Social Forces,* 1960, *38,* 289–295.

Haller, A. O., Otto, L. B., Meier, R. F., and Ohlendorf, G. W. Level of occupational aspiration: An empirical analysis. *American Sociological Review,* 1974, *39,* 113–121.

Hansche, J., and Gilchrist, J. Three determinants of the level of aspiration. *Journal of Abnormal and Social Psychology,* 1956, *53,* 136–137.

Hardy, R. C. Effect of leadership style on the performance of small classroom groups: A test of the contingency model. *Journal of Personality and Social Psychology,* 1971, *19,* 351–356.

Hartley, E. L. *Problems in prejudice.* New York: King's Crown Press, 1946.

Hartup, W. W. Peer interaction and social organization. In P. H. Mussen (Ed.). *Manual of child psychology.* New York: Wiley, 1970.

Harvey, O. J. Conceptual systems and attitude change. In C. W. Sherif and M. Sherif (Eds.). *Attitude, ego-involvement and change.* New York: Wiley, 1967.

————, and Sherif, M. Level of aspiration as a case of judgmental activity in which ego-involvements operate as factors. *Sociometry,* 1951, *14,* 121–147.

Hebb, D. O. *A textbook of psychology.* (Rev. ed.) Philadelphia: Saunders, 1966.

————. What psychology is about. *American Psychologist,* 1974, *29,* 71–79.

Heberle, R. *Social movements: An introduction to political sociology.* New York: Appleton-Century-Crofts, 1951.

Heider, F. *The psychology of interpersonal relations.* New York: Wiley, 1958.

Helson, H. *Adaptation-level theory: An experimental and systematic approach to behavior.* New York: Harper & Row, 1964.

Hendrick, C., Bixenstine, V. E., and Hawkins, G. Race versus belief similarity as determinants of attraction: A search for a fair test. *Journal of Personality and Social Psychology,* 1971, *17,* 250–258.

Heussenstamm, F. K. Bumper stickers and the cops. *Trans-Action,* 1971, *8,* 32–33.

Hilgard, E. R., Sait, E. M., and Magaret, G. A. Level of aspiration as affected by relative standing in an experimental social group. *Journal of Experimental Psychology,* 1940, *27,* 411–421.

Hinckley, E. D. The influence of individual opinion on construction of an attitude scale. *Journal of Social Psychology,* 1932, *37,* 283–296.

Hirota, K. Experimental studies of competition. *Japanese Journal of Psychology,* 1951, *21,* 70–81. (*Psychological Abstracts,* 1953, *27,* 351.)

Hofstätter, P. R. *Gruppendynamik: die Kritik der Massenpsychologie.* Hamburg: Rewohlt, 1957.

Hoge, D. R., and Bender, I. E. Factors influencing value change among college graduates in adult life. *Journal of Personality and Social Psychology,* 1974, *29,* 572–585.

Hollingsworth, L. S. Social devices for impelling women to bear and rear children. *American Journal of Sociology,* 1916, *22,* 19–29.

Holmes, D. S. Amount of experience in experiments as a determinant of performance in later experiments. *Journal of Personality and Social Psychology,* 1967, *7,* 403–407.

Holt, R. R. Effects of ego-involvement upon levels of aspiration. *Psychiatry,* 1945, *3,* 299–317.

Hood, W. R., and Sherif, M. Verbal report and judgment of an unstructured stimulus. *Journal of Psychology,* 1962, *54,* 121–130.

Horner, M. S. Sex differences in achievement motivation and performance in competitive and non-competitive situations. Doctoral dissertation, Univ. of Michigan, 1968. See also Fail, bright women. *Psychology Today,* 1969, *3*(6).

———. Femininity and successful achievement. In J. M. Bardwick et al. (Eds.). *Feminine personality and conflict.* Belmont, Calif.: Brooks/Cole, 1970, pp. 45–76.

Horowitz, E. L. The development of attitudes toward Negroes. *Archives of Psychology,* 1936, No. 194.

———, and Horowitz, R. E. Development of social attitudes in children. *Sociometry,* 1938, *1,* 301–309.

Horowitz, R. E. Racial aspects of self identification in nursery school children. *Journal of Psychology,* 1939, *7,* 91–99.

Horwitz, M. The recall of interrupted group tasks: An experimental study of individual motivation in relation to group goals. In D. Cartwright and A. Zander (Eds.). *Group dynamics.* (2nd ed.) New York: Harper & Row, 1960, pp. 370–394.

Houseknecht, S. K. Social psychological aspects of voluntary childlessness. Master's thesis, Pennsylvania State Univ., 1974.

Hovland, C. I. Reconciling conflicting results derived from experimental and survey studies of attitude change. *American Psychologist,* 1959, *14,* 8–17.

———, and Pritzker, H. A. Extent of opinion change as a function of amount of change advocated. *Journal of Abnormal and Social Psychology,* 1957, *54,* 257–261.

Hovland, C. I., and Sherif, M. Judgmental phenomena and scales of attitude measurement: Item displacement in Thurstone scales. *Journal of Abnormal and Social Psychology,* 1952, *47,* 822–832.

Hovland, C. I., and Weiss, W. The influence of source credibility on communication effectiveness. *Public Opinion Quarterly,* 1951, *15,* 635–650.

Hovland, C. I., Harvey, O. J., and Sherif, M. Assimilation and contrast effects in reactions to communication and attitude change. *Journal of Abnormal and Social Psychology,* 1957, *55,* 244–252.

Hovland, C. I., Lumsdaine, A. A., and Sheffield, F. J. *Experiments on mass communication.* Princeton: Princeton Univ. Press, 1949.

Huston, T. L. (Ed.). *Foundations of interpersonal attraction.* New York: Academic Press, 1974.

Hyman, H. H. The psychology of status. *Archives of Psychology,* 1942, No. 269.

———, and Sheatsley, P. B. Some reasons why information campaigns fail. *Public Opinion Quarterly,* 1947, *11,* 412–423.

———. Attitudes toward desegregation. *Scientific American,* 1964, *211*(July), 2–9.

Inhelder, B., and Piaget, J. *The growth of logical thinking from childhood to adolescence.* New York: Basic Books, 1958.

ISR Newsletter. Change in women's status is approved by both sexes. Ann Arbor, Mich.: Institute of Social Research. 1974, *1*(20), 2–3.

———. Trust in government falls: Independent votes increase. Ann Arbor, Mich.: Institute of Social Research. 1974, *1*(20), 5–6.

———. Recent shifts in black attitudes show growth of race consciousness, militancy, alienation. Ann Arbor, Mich.: Institute of Social Research. 1974, 2(1), 4–5.

Jackman, N. R., and Sherif, M. Group processes and communication on the prohibition issue. *Sociology and Social Research,* 1959, *43,* 265–270.

Jackson, G. D. Another psychological view from the Association of Black Psychologists. *American Psychologist,* 1975, *30,* 88–93.

Jacobs, R. C., and Campbell, D. T. The perpetuation of an arbitrary tradition through several generations of a laboratory microculture. *Journal of Abnormal and Social Psychology,* 1961, *62,* 649–658.

Jahoda, G. *White man.* London: Oxford Univ. Press, 1961.

James, W. *The principles of psychology.* New York: Holt, 1890.

Janis, I. L., and Field, P. B. Sex differences and personality factors related to persuasibility. In C. I. Hovland and I. L. Janis (Eds.). *Personality and persuasibility.* New Haven: Yale Univ. Press, 1959.

Janis, I. L., and Mann, L. Effectiveness of emotional role-playing in modifying smoking habits and attitudes. *Journal of Experimental Research in Personality,* 1965, *1,* 84–90.

Jeffries, V., and Ransford, H. E. Ideology, social structure, and the Yorty-Bradley mayoralty election. *Social Forces,* 1972, 358–372.

Jennings, H. H. *Leadership and isolation. A study of personality in interpersonal relations.* (2nd ed.) New York: McKay, 1950.

Jessor, R., Jessor, S. L., and Finney, J. A social psychology of marijuana use: Longitudinal studies of high school and college students. *Journal of Personality and Social Psychology,* 1973, *26,* 1–15.

Jones, E. E., and Goethals, G. R. Order effects in impression formation: Attribution context and the nature of the entity. Morristown, N.J.: General Learning Press, 1971.

Jones, E. E., Kanouse, D. E., Kelley, H. H., Nisbett, R. E., Valins, S., and Weiner, B. *Attribution: Perceiving the causes of behavior.* Morristown, N.J.: General Learning Press, 1972.

Jones, E. E., and Nisbett, R. E. The actor and the observer: Divergent perceptions of the causes of behavior. In E. E. Jones et al. (Eds.). *Attribution: Perceiving the causes of behavior.* Morristown, N.J.: General Learning Press, 1972, pp. 79–94.

Jones, J. M. *Prejudice and racism.* Reading, Mass.: Addison-Wesley, 1972.

Jones, R. A., and Ashmore, R. D. The structure of intergroup perception: Categories and dimensions in views of ethnic groups and adjectives used in stereotype research. *Journal of Personality and Social Psychology,* 1973, *25,* 428–438.

Jourard, S. M., and Lasakow, P. Some factors in self disclosure. *Journal of Abnormal and Social Psychology,* 1950, *56,* 91–98.

Kaats, G. R., and Davis, K. E. The dynamics of sexual behavior of college students. In A. M. Juhasz (Ed.). *Sexual development and behavior: Selected readings.* Homewood, Ill.: Dorsey, 1973, pp. 214–231.

Kagan, S., and Madsen, M. C. Rivalry in Anglo-American and Mexican children of two ages. *Journal of Personality and Social Psychology,* 1972, *24*(2), 214–220.

Kahn, E. J., Jr. *The American people. The findings of the 1970 census.* New York: Weybright & Talley, 1974.

Kamano, D. K., and Drew, J. E. Selectivity in memory of personally significant material. *Journal of General Psychology,* 1961, *65,* 25–32.

Karlins, M., Coffman, T., and Walters, G. On the fading of social stereotypes:

Studies in three generations of college students. *Journal of Personality and Social Psychology,* 1969, *13,* 1–16.

Katz, D. The functional approach to the study of attitudes. *Public Opinion Quarterly,* 1960, *24,* 163–204.

———, and Allport, F. H. *Students' attitudes.* Syracuse, N.Y.: Craftsman Press, 1931.

Katz, D., and Braly, K. W. Racial stereotypes of 100 college students. *Journal of Abnormal and Social Psychology,* 1933, *28,* 280–290.

———. Racial prejudice and racial stereotypes. *Journal of Abnormal and Social Psychology,* 1935, *30,* 175–193.

Katz, E. The two-step flow of communication: An up-to-date report on an hypothesis. In H. Proshansky and B. Seidenberg (Eds.). *Basic studies in social psychology.* New York: Holt, Rinehart & Winston, 1965.

———, and Lazarsfeld, P. F. *Personal influence: The part played by people in the flow of mass communications.* New York: Free Press, 1955.

Kearney, H. R. Personal involvement and communication context in social judgment of a controversial issue. Doctoral dissertation, Pennsylvania State Univ., 1975.

Kelley, H. H. The warm-cold variable in first impressions of personality. *Journal of Personality,* 1950, *18,* 431–439.

———. The processes of causal attribution. *American Psychologist,* 1973, *28,* 107–128.

Kellog, W. N., and Kellog, L. A. *The ape and the child.* New York: McGraw-Hill, 1933.

Kelly, J. G., Ferson, J. E., and Holtzman, W. H. The measurement of attitudes toward the Negro in the South. *Journal of Social Psychology,* 1958, *48,* 305–317.

Kelly, M. Unpublished manuscript, Pennsylvania State Univ., 1970.

Kelman, H. C. Effects of success and failure on "suggestibility" in the autokinetic situation. *Journal of Abnormal and Social Psychology,* 1950, *45,* 267–285.

———. Attitudes are alive and well and gainfully employed in the sphere of action. *American Psychologist,* 1974, *29,* 310–324.

Kerrick, J. S., and McMillan, D. H. The effects of instructional set on the measurement of attitude change through communication. *Journal of Social Psychology,* 1961, *53,* 113–120.

Ketchum, J. D. *Ruhleben: A prison camp society.* Toronto: Univ. of Toronto Press, 1965.

Kidder, L. H., and Stewart, V. M. *The psychology of intergroup relations: Conflict and consciousness.* New York: McGraw-Hill, 1975.

Kiesler, C. A. *The psychology of commitment: Experiments linking behavior to belief.* New York: Academic Press, 1971.

———, Collins, B. E., and Miller, N. *Attitude change: A critical review of theoretical approaches.* New York: Wiley, 1969.

Kiesler, S. B., and Baral, R. L. The search for a romantic partner. The effects of self-esteem and physical attractiveness on romantic behavior. In K. J. Gergen and D. Marlowe (Eds.). *Personality and social behavior.* Reading, Mass.: Addison-Wesley, 1970, pp. 155–165.

Killian, L. M. The significance of multiple group membership in disaster. *American Journal of Sociology,* 1952, *57,* 309–314.

———. Social movements. In R. E. L. Faris (Ed.). *Handbook of modern sociology.* Chicago: Rand McNally, 1964.

———. *The impossible revolution? Black power and the American dream.* New York: Random House, 1968.

King, M. L., Jr. Letter from Birmingham's jail. In B. Daniel (Ed.). *Black, white and gray.* New York: Steed & Ward, 1964, pp. 62–80.

———. The role of the behavioral scientist in the civil rights movement. *American Psychologist,* 1968, *23,* 180–186.

Kirchner, E., and Vondracek, S. I. What do you want to be when you grow up? Vocational choice in children aged three to six. Presented at the Society for Research in Child Development, Philadelphia, 1973 (mimeographed).

Kirschner, B. F. Introducing students to women's place in society. *American Journal of Sociology,* 1973, *78,* 1051–1054.

Klapper, J. T. *The effects of mass communication.* New York: Free Press, 1960.

———. Mass communication, attitude stability and change. In C. W. Sherif and M. Sherif (Eds.). *Attitude, ego-involvement and change.* New York: Wiley, 1967.

Klemesrud, J. Most women now favor improving status. *Pennsylvania Mirror,* October 11, 1974, p. 4.

Klineberg, O. *Social psychology.* (Rev. ed.) New York: Holt, 1954.

Kohlberg, L. Moral development and identification. In National Society for the Study of Education, 62nd Yearbook: *Child Psychology.* Chicago: Univ. of Chicago Press, 1963.

Köhler, W. *Gestalt psychology.* New York: Liveright, 1929.

Kon, I. S. (trans. by V. de Lissovoy). Soviet parent child relations. *Literary Gazette,* February 29, 1973.

Koslin, B. L. Personal communication, 1966.

———, Haarlow, R. N., Karlins, M., and Pargament, R. Predicting group status from members' cognitions. *Sociometry,* 1968, *31,* 64–75.

Koslin, B. L., Waring, P. D., and Pargament, R. Measurement of attitude organization with the "own category" technique. Princeton Univ. 1965 (mimeographed).

Kuhn, M. H., and McPartland, T. S. An empirical investigation of self-attitudes. *American Sociological Review,* 1954, *19,* 68–76.

La Fave, L. Humor judgments as a function of reference groups and identification classes. In J. H. Goldstein and P. E. McGhee (Eds.). *The psychology of humor.* New York: Academic Press, 1972.

———, and Sherif, M. Reference scales and placement of items with the Own Categories technique. *Journal of Social Psychology,* 1968, *76,* 75–82.

Laing, R. D. *The politics of experience.* New York: Ballantine Books, 1967.

Lambert, W. E., Libman, E., and Poser, E. G. The effect of increased salience of a membership group on pain tolerance. *Journal of Personality,* 1960, *28,* 350–357.

Lana, R. E., and Menapace, R. H. Subject commitment and demand characteristics in attitude change. *Journal of Personality and Social Psychology,* 1971, *20,* 136–140.

Lang, K., and Lang, G. *Collective dynamics.* New York: Crowell, 1961.

Lang, O. *Chinese family and society.* New Haven: Yale Univ. Press, 1946.

Larsen, K. S. Affectivity, cognitive style, and social judgment. *Journal of Personality and Social Psychology,* 1971, *19,* 119–123.

——, Coleman, D., Forbes, J., and Johnson, R. Is the subject's personality or the experimental situation a better predictor of a subject's willingness to administer shock to a victim? *Journal of Personality and Social Psychology,* 1972, *22,* 287–295.

Latané, B., and Darley, J. M. Bystander "apathy." *American Scientist,* 1969, *57,* 244–268.

Lazarsfeld, P. F., Berelson, B., and Gaudet, H. *The people's choice.* New York: Columbia Univ. Press, 1948.

Lefcourt, H. M., and Ladwig, G. W. The effect of reference groups upon Negroes task persistence in a biracial competitive game. *Journal of Personality and Social Psychology,* 1965, *1,* 668–670.

Lenneberg, E. H. *Biological foundations of language.* New York: Wiley, 1967.

Leuba, C. J. An experimental study of rivalry in young children. *Journal of Comparative Psychology,* 1933, *16,* 367–378.

Levine, J., and Butler, J. Lecture vs. group decision in changing behavior. In D. Cartwright and A. Zander (Eds.). *Group dynamics: Research and theory.* New York: Harper & Row, 1953 (second printing, 1956).

Levine, G. M., and Murphy, G. The learning and forgetting of controversial material. *Journal of Abnormal and Social Psychology,* 1943, *38,* 507–517.

LeVine, R. A., and Campbell, D. T. *Ethnocentrism: Theories of conflict, ethnic attitudes and group behavior.* New York: Wiley, 1972.

Levinger, G. Task and social behavior in marriage. *Sociometry,* 1964, *27,* 433–448.

——, and Snoek, D. *Attraction in relationship: A new look at interpersonal attraction.* Morristown, N.J.: General Learning Press, 1972.

Levy, L. H. Awareness, learning and the beneficent subject as expert witness. *Journal of Personality and Social Psychology,* 1967, *6,* 365–370.

Levy, P., Lundgren, D., Ansel, M., Fell, D., Fink, B., and McGrath, F. E. Bystander effect in a demand-without-threat situation. *Journal of Personality and Social Psychology,* 1972, *24,* 166–171.

Lewin, K. *Resolving social conflicts.* New York: Harper & Row, 1948.

——. Studies in group decision. In D. Cartwright and A. Zander (Eds.). *Group dynamics: Research and theory.* New York: Harper & Row, 1953 (second printing, 1956). Also in H. Proshansky and B. Seidenberg (Eds.). *Basic studies in social psychology.* New York: Holt, Rinehart & Winston, 1965.

——, Dembo, T., Festinger, L., and Sears, P. S. Level of aspiration. In J. McV. Hunt (Ed.). *Personality and the behavior disorders.* New York: Ronald Press, 1944.

Lewin, K., Lippitt, R., and White, R. K. Patterns of aggressive behavior in experimentally created "social climates." *Journal of Social Psychology,* 1939, *10,* 271–299.

Lewis, G. H. Role differentiation. *American Sociological Review,* 1972, *37,* 424–434.

Lewis, M. M. *Language, thought and personality in infancy and childhood.* New York: Basic Books, 1963.

Lieberman, S. The effects of changes in roles on the attitudes of role occupants. *Human Relations,* 1956, *9,* 385–402.

Likert, R. A technique for the measurement of attitudes. *Archives of Psychology,* 1932, No. 140.

Linn, L. S. Verbal attitudes and overt behavior. *Social Forces,* 1965, *43,* 353–364.

Lippitt, R., and White, R. K. An experimental study of leadership and group life. In H. Proshansky and B. Seidenberg (Eds.). *Basic studies in social psychology.* New York: Holt, Rinehart & Winston, 1965, pp. 523–537.

Lippmann, W. *Public opinion.* New York: Harcourt Brace Jovanovich, 1922.

Liska, A. E. Emergent issues in the attitude-behavior consistency controversy. *American Sociological Review,* 1974, *39,* 261–272.

Loevinger, J. The meaning and measurement of ego development. *American Psychologist,* 1966, *21,* 195–206.

Lorenz, K. *On aggression.* New York: Harcourt Brace Jovanovich, 1963.

Lott, A. J., and Lott, B. E. Group cohesiveness as interpersonal attraction: A review of relationships with antecedents and consequent variables. *Psychological Bulletin,* 1965, *64,* 259–309.

Lowie, R. H. *Primitive society.* New York: Boni & Liveright, 1925.

Luchins, A. S. Social influences on perception of complex drawings. *Journal of Social Psychology,* 1945, *21,* 257–273.

Lundgren, D., and Miller, D. Identity and behavioral change in training groups. *Human Relations Training News,* 1965, *9* (Spring issue).

Luria, A. R. *The role of speech in the regulation of normal and abnormal behavior.* New York: Liveright, 1961.

McClelland, D. C. Measuring motivation in phantasy: The achievement motive. In D. C. McClelland (Ed.). *Studies in motivation.* New York: Appleton-Century-Crofts, 1955, pp. 401–413.

McClelland, L. Effects of interviewer-respondent race interactions on household interview measures of motivation and intelligence. *Journal of Personality and Social Psychology,* 1974, *29,* 392–397.

Maccoby, E. E., and Jacklin, C. N. Comments on the etiology of sex differences. Paper presented at the annual meeting of the American Association for the Advancement of Science, Washington, D.C., December 28, 1972.

———. What we know and don't know about sex differences. *Psychology Today,* 1974a, (December), 109–112.

———. *The psychology of sex differences.* Stanford, Calif.: Stanford Univ. Press, 1974b.

McGehee, W. Judgment and the level of aspiration. *Journal of General Psychology,* 1940, *22,* 3–15.

McGuire, W. J. Persistence of the resistance to persuasion induced by various types of prior belief defenses. *Journal of Abnormal and Social Psychology,* 1962, *64,* 241–248.

———. The nature of attitudes and attitude change. In G. Lindzey and E.

Aronson (Eds.). *Handbook of social psychology.* Vol. 3. Reading, Mass.: Addison-Wesley, 1969, pp. 136–314.

———, and Papageorgis, D. The relative efficacy of various types of prior belief-defense in producing immunity against persuasion. *Journal of Abnormal and Social Psychology,* 1961, *62,* 327–337.

McLaughlin, B. (Ed.). *Studies in social movements: A social psychological perspective.* New York: Free Press, 1969.

MacNeil, M. K. Norm changes over subject generations as a function of the arbitrariness of prescribed norms. Master's thesis, Univ. of Oklahoma, 1965. Reported in M. Sherif and C. W. Sherif, *Social psychology.* New York: Harper & Row, 1969, pp. 216–218.

Madsen, M. C., and Shapira, A. Cooperative and competitive behavior of urban Afro-American, Anglo-American, Mexican-American, and Mexican village children. *Developmental Psychology,* 1970, *3,* 16–20.

Maier, N. F., and Schneirla, T. C. *Principles of animal psychology.* (Rev. ed.) New York: Dover, 1963.

Makarenko, A. S. *The road to life: An epic of education.* 3 vols. Moscow: Foreign Language Publishing House, 1951.

Mann, L., and Janis, I. L. A follow-up study on the long-term effects of emotional role playing. *Journal of Personality and Social Psychology,* 1968, *8,* 339–342.

Mann, R. D. The development of the member-trainer relationship in self-analytic groups. In C. L. Cooper and I. L. Mangham (Eds.). *T-groups: A survey of research.* New York: Wiley Interscience, 1971, pp. 233–271.

Marks, E. S. The undecided voter. In F. Mosteller, H. Hyman, P. J. McCarthy, E. S. Marks, and D. B. Truman (Eds.). *The pre-election polls of 1948: Report to the committee on analysis of pre-election polls and forecasts.* Social Science Research Council Bulletin, 1949, 60, 263–289.

Marzolf, J. L. Judgments of communications on women's issues as related to attitude. Honor's thesis, Department of Psychology, Pennsylvania State Univ., 1973.

Mausner, B. The effect of prior reinforcement on the interaction of observer pairs. *Journal of Abnormal and Social Psychology,* 1954, *49,* 65–68.

Maykovich, M. K. Reciprocity in racial stereotypes: White, black and yellow. *American Journal of Sociology,* 1972, *77,* 876–897.

Mead, G. H. *Mind, self and society: From the standpoint of a social behaviorist.* Chicago: Univ. of Chicago Press, 1934.

Mead, M. *Male and female.* New York: Mentor Books, 1955.

———. *Sex and temperament in three savage societies.* New York: Apollo, 1967.

——— (Ed.). *Cooperation and competition among primitive people.* New York: McGraw-Hill, 1943.

Meenes, M. A. A comparison of racial stereotypes in 1935 and 1942. *Journal of Social Psychology,* 1943, *17,* 327–336.

Megargee, E. I., and Hokanson, J. E. *The dynamics of aggression.* New York: Harper & Row, 1970.

Meltzer, L., Morris, W. N., and Hayes, D. P. Interruption outcomes and vocal amplitude. *Journal of Personality and Social Psychology,* 1971, *18,* 392–402.

Mercatoris, M., and Craighead, W. E. The effects of nonparticipant observation on teacher and pupil classroom behavior. *Journal of Educational Psychology,* 1974, *66,* pp. 512–519.

Merei, F. Group leadership and institutionalization. *Human Relations,* 1949, *2,* 23–29.

Merton, R. K. The self-fulfilling prophecy. *Antioch Review,* 1948, *8,* 193–210.

———. Patterns of influence: A study of interpersonal influence of communications behavior in a local community. In P. F. Lazarsfeld and F. N. Stanton (Eds.). *Communications research. 1948–49.* New York: Harper & Row, 1949.

Milano, E. M. The implications of ignoring the status of women: A re-evaluation of various concepts within the minority relations field. Master's thesis, Pennsylvania State Univ., 1973.

Milgram, S. Nationality and conformity. *Scientific American,* 1961, *205*(6), 45–51.

———. Behavioral study of obedience. *Journal of Abnormal and Social Psychology,* 1963, *67,* 371–378.

———. Some conditions of obedience and disobedience to authority. In I. D. Steiner and M. Fishbein (Eds.). *Current studies in social psychology.* New York: Holt, Rinehart & Winston, 1965.

———. Interdisciplinary thinking and the small world problem. In M. Sherif and C. W. Sherif (Eds.). *Interdisciplinary relationships in the social sciences.* Chicago: Aldine, 1969.

———. The lost-letter technique. In L. Bickman and T. Henchy (Eds.). *Beyond the laboratory: Field research in social psychology.* New York: McGraw-Hill, 1972.

———. *Studies on obedience.* New York: Harper & Row, 1974.

———, and Toch, H. Collective behavior: Crowds and social movements. In G. Lindzey and E. Aronson (Eds.). *Handbook of social psychology.* Vol. 4. Reading, Mass.: Addison-Wesley, 1969.

Miller, N. Involvement and dogmatism as inhibitors of attitude change. *Journal of Experimental Social Psychology,* 1965, *1,* 121–132.

Mills, T. M. *Group transformation: An analysis of a learning group.* Englewood Cliffs, N.J.: Prentice-Hall, 1964.

Mischel, W. *Personality and assessment.* New York: Wiley, 1968.

Money, J., and Ehrhardt, A. A. *Man and woman, Boy and girl.* Baltimore: Johns Hopkins Univ. Press, 1972.

Moore, K. C. The mental development of a child. *Psychological Review Monograph Supplement,* 1896, *1*(3).

Moreno, J. L. *Who shall survive?* (Rev. ed.) Boston: Beacon Press, 1953 (First ed., 1934).

———. *The sociometry reader.* New York: Free Press, 1960, 1–86.

Moscovici, S., and Zavalloni, M. The group as a polarizer of attitudes. *Journal of Personality and Social Psychology,* 1969, *12,* 125–135.

Murchison, C. (Ed.). *Handbook of social psychology.* Worcester, Mass.: Clark Univ. Press, 1935.

Murchison, C., and Langer, S. Tiedemann's observations on the development of the mental faculties of children. *Journal of Genetic Psychology,* 1927, *34,* 205–230.

Murphy, L. B. *Social behavior and child personality.* New York: Columbia Univ. Press, 1937.

Murphy, G. *Personality.* New York: Harper & Row, 1947.

———, and Murphy, L. B. *Experimental social psychology.* New York: Harper & Row, 1931.

———, and Newcomb, T. M. *Experimental social psychology.* New York: Harper & Row, 1937.

Myers, D. G. and Lamm, H. The polarizing effect of group discussion. *American Scientist,* 1975, *63, 297–303.*

Nehru, J. *Toward freedom.* New York: John Day, 1941; Beacon Press, 1958.

Nemeth, C., and Markowski, J. Conformity and discrepancy of position. *Sociometry,* 1972, *35,* 562–575.

Newcomb, T. M. *Personality and social change.* New York: Holt, Rinehart & Winston, 1943.

———. Attitude development as a function of reference groups. In M. Sherif. *An outline of social psychology.* New York: Harper & Row, 1948.

———. *Social psychology.* New York: Holt, Rinehart & Winston, 1950.

———, Koenig, L. E., Flacks, R., and Warwick, D. P. *Persistence and change: Bennington College and its students after twenty-five years.* New York: Wiley, 1967.

Nobles, W. W. Psychological research and the black self-concept: A critical review. *Journal of Social Issues,* 1973, *29,* 11–32.

Norfleet, B. Interpersonal relations and group productivity. *Journal of Social Issues,* 1948, *4,* 66–69.

Odiorne, G. S. The trouble with sensitivity training. In R. T. Golembiewski and A. Blumberg (Eds.). *Sensitivity training and the laboratory approach.* Itasca, Ill.: F. E. Peacock, 1970, pp. 273–287.

Ogburn, W. F. *On culture and social change: Selected papers.* Chicago: Univ. of Chicago Press, 1964.

O'Neill, W. L. *Everyone was brave: A history of feminism in America.* Chicago: Quadrangle, 1971 (with a new afterword by author).

Osgood, C. E., Suci, G. J., and Tannenbaum, P. H. *The measurement of meaning.* Urbana: Univ. of Illinois Press, 1957.

Ostrom, T. M., and Upshaw, H. S. Psychological perspective and attitude change. In A. G. Greenwald, T. C. Brock, T. M. Ostrom (Eds.). *Psychological foundations of attitudes.* New York: Academic Press, 1968.

Page, M. M. The social psychology of a classical conditioning of attitudes experiment. *Journal of Personality and Social Psychology,* 1969, *11,* 177–186.

———. Demand awareness, subject sophistication and the effectiveness of a verbal "reinforcement." *Journal of Personality,* 1970, *38,* 287–301.

———. Demand characteristics and the verbal operant conditioning experiment. *Journal of Personality and Social Psychology,* 1972, *23,* 372–379.

———, and Dahlke, A. E. Awareness in the classical conditioning of verbal behavior. Paper presented at the annual meeting of the Southwestern Psychological Association, Oklahoma City, 1965.

Park, R. E. The concept of social distance. *Journal of Applied Sociology,* 1924, *8,* 339–344.

Parten, M. B. Social participation among preschool children. *Journal of Abnormal and Social Psychology,* 1932, *27,* 243–269.

———. Leadership among preschool children. *Journal of Abnormal and Social Psychology,* 1933a, *28,* 430–440.

———. Social play among preschool children. *Journal of Abnormal and Social Psychology,* 1933b, *28,* 136–147.

Pelton, L. H. *The psychology of nonviolence.* New York: Pergamon Press, 1974.

Pelz, E. B. Some factors in "group decision." In H. Proshansky and B. Seidenberg (Eds.). *Basic studies in social psychology.* New York: Holt, Rinehart & Winston, 1965.

Peterson, P. D., and Koulack, D. Attitude change as a function of latitudes of acceptance and rejection. *Journal of Personality and Social Psychology,* 1969, *11,* 309–311.

Pheterson, G. I., Kiesler, S. B., and Goldberg, P. A. Evaluation of the performance of women as a function of their sex, achievement and personal history. *Journal of Personality and Social Psychology,* 1971, *19,* 114–118.

Piaget, J. *The moral judgment of the child.* London: Routledge, 1932.

———. *The psychology of intelligence.* New York: Harcourt Brace Jovanovich, 1950.

Piliavin, I. M., Rodin, J., and Piliavin, J. A. Good samaritanism: An underground phenomenon? *Journal of Personality and Social Psychology,* 1969, *13,* 289–299.

Piliavin, J. A., and Piliavin, I. M. Effect of blood on reactions to a victim. *Journal of Personality and Social Psychology,* 1972, *23,* 353–361.

Pollis, N. P., and Cammalleri, A. Social conditions and differential resistance to majority pressure. *Journal of Psychology,* 1968, *70,* 69–76.

Pollis, N. P., Pollis, C. A., and Rader, J. A. Attitude change without persuasion. *Journal of Social Psychology,* 1971, *84,* 225–232.

Polsky, H. W. *Cottage six.* New York: Russell Sage, 1962.

Powell, F. A. Latitudes of acceptance and rejection and the belief-disbelief dimension: A correlational comparison. *Journal of Personality and Social Psychology,* 1966, *4,* 453–457.

Preyer, W. *The mind of the child. Part II. The development of the intellect.* New York: Appleton, 1890.

Prothro, E. T., and Melikian, L. H. Social distance and social change in the Near East. *Sociology and Social Research,* 1952, *37,* 3–11.

———. The California Public Opinion Scale in an authoritarian culture. *Public Opinion Quarterly,* 1953, *3,* 353–362.

Pruitt, D. G. Choice shifts in group discussion: An introductory review; Conclusion: Toward an understanding of choice shifts in group discussion. *Journal of Personality and Social Psychology,* 1971, *20,* 339–360; 494–570.

Pyles, M. K. Verbalization as a function of meaning. *Child Development,* 1932, *3,* 108–113.

Quarton, R. The development of social cognition. Doctoral dissertation, Pennsylvania State Univ., 1976.

Rafferty, F. T. Group organization theory and the adolescent inpatient unit. In M. Sherif and C. W. Sherif (Eds.). *Problems of youth: Transition to adulthood in a changing world.* Chicago: Aldine, 1965.

Ram, P., and Murphy, G. Reported in G. Murphy, *In the minds of men.* New York: Basic Books, 1953, pp. 114–115.

Reich, J., and Sherif, M. Ego-involvement as a factor in attitude assessment by the own categories technique. Univ. of Oklahoma, 1963 (mimeographed).

RePass, D. E. Issue salience and party choice. *American Political Science Review,* 1971, *65,* 389–400.

Rhine, R. J., and Severance, L. J. Ego-involvement, discrepancy, source credibility, and attitude change. *Journal of Personality and Social Psychology,* 1970, *16,* 175–190.

Rhine, R. J., and Polowniak, W. A. J. Attitude change, commitment and ego-involvement. *Journal of Personality and Social Psychology,* 1971, *19,* 247–250.

Rickers-Oviakina, M. Social accessibility in three age groups. *Psychological Reports,* 1956, *2,* 283–294.

Rivers, W. H. R. *Psychology and ethnology.* New York: Harcourt Brace Jovanovich, 1926.

Rodgers, H. L., Jr. Reference groups as determinants of the judged credibility of communicators and their judged position on issues. Master's thesis, Pennsylvania State Univ., 1968.

Rogers, E. M. *Diffusion of innovations.* New York: Free Press, 1962.

Rohrer, J. H., Baron, S. H., Hoffman, E. L., and Swander, D. V. The stability of autokinetic judgments. *Journal of Abnormal and Social Psychology,* 1954, *49,* 595–597.

Rokeach, M. *The open and closed mind.* New York: Basic Books, 1960.

———. Belief versus race as determinants of social distance: Comments on Triandis' paper. *Journal of Abnormal and Social Psychology,* 1961, *62,* 187–188.

———, and Kliejins, P. Behavior as a function of attitude-toward-object and attitude-toward-situation. *Journal of Personality and Social Psychology,* 1972, *22,* 194–201.

Rokeach, M., and Mezei, L. Race and shared belief as factors in social choice. *Science,* 1966, *151,* 167–172.

Rollins, J. H. Reference identification of youth of differing ethnicity. *Journal of Personality and Social Psychology,* 1973, *26,* 222–232.

Rosenberg, B., and Bensman, J. Sexual patterns in three ethnic subcultures of an American underclass. In A. M. Juhasz (Ed.). *Sexual development and behavior. Selected readings.* Homewood, III.: Dorsey Press, 1973, pp. 108–125.

Rosenberg, M. *Society and the adolescent self-image.* Princeton, N.J.: Princeton Univ. Press, 1965.

———. Psychological selectivity and self-esteem formation. In C. W. Sherif and M. Sherif (Eds.). *Attitude, ego-involvement and change.* New York: Wiley, 1967, Chap. 3.

Rosenberg, M. J. An analysis of affective-cognitive consistency. In M. J.

Rosenberg, C. I. Hovland, W. J. McGuire, R. P. Abelson, and J. W. Brehm (Eds.). *Attitude organization and change. An analysis of consistency among attitude components.* New Haven: Yale Univ. Press, 1960, pp. 15–64.

———. The conditions and consequences of evaluation apprehension. In R. Rosenthal and R. L. Rosnow (Eds.). *Artifact in behavioral research.* New York: Academic Press, 1969.

Rosenthal, R. *Experimenter effects in behavioral research.* New York: Appleton-Century-Crofts, 1966.

———, and Jacobson, L. *Pygmalion in the classroom: Teacher expectations and pupil's intellectual development.* New York: Holt, Rinehart & Winston, 1968.

Rosenthal, R., and Rosnow, R. L. *Artifact in behavioral research.* New York: Academic Press, 1969.

Rosnow, R. L., and Suls, J. M. Reactive effects of pretesting in attitude research. *Journal of Personality and Social Psychology,* 1970, *15,* 338–343.

Sahakian, W. S. *Systematic social psychology.* New York: Chandler (Intext), 1974.

Sampson, S. F. The effects of selected social relationships on the resolution and maintenance of dissensus in the autokinetic situation. Paper to the American Sociological Association, Boston, Mass. Based on Crisis in the Cloisters: A Sociological Analysis. Doctoral dissertation, Cornell Univ., 1968.

Sanger, S. P., and Alker, H. A. Dimensions of internal-external locus of control and the women's liberation movement. *Journal of Social Issues,* 1972, *28,* 115–130.

Sarup, G. Reference groups: Some determinants and consequences. Doctoral dissertation, Pennsylvania State Univ., 1969.

Schneirla, T. C. Problems in the bio-psychology of social organization. *Journal of Abnormal and Social Psychology,* 1946, *41,* 385–402.

———. The "levels" concept in the study of social organization in animals. In J. H. Rohrer and M. Sherif (Eds.). *Social psychology at the crossroads.* New York: Harper & Row, 1951, pp. 83–120.

Schramm, W., and Carter, R. F. Effectiveness of a political telethon. *Public Opinion Quarterly,* 1959, *23,* 121–126.

Schulman, G. L., and Tittle, C. R. Assimilation-contrast effects and item selection in Thurstone scaling. *Social Forces,* 1967, *46,* 484–491.

Schuman, H., and Hatchett, S. *Black racial attitudes: Trends and complexities.* Ann Arbor: Institute of Social Research, 1974.

Scully, D., and Bart, P. A funny thing happened on the way to the orifice: Women in the gynecology textbooks. *American Journal of Sociology,* 1973, *78,* 1045–1051.

Sears, D. O. Biased indoctrination and selectivity of exposure to new information. *Sociometry,* 1965, *28,* 363–370.

———, and Freedman, J. L. Effects of expected familiarity with arguments upon opinion change and selective exposure. *Journal of Personality and Social Psychology,* 1965, *2,* 420–426.

Sears, P. S. Levels of aspiration in academically successful and unsuccessful school children. *Journal of Abnormal and Social Psychology*, 1940, *35*, 498–536.

Seaver, W. B. Effects of naturally induced teacher expectancies. *Journal of Personality and Social Psychology*, 1973, *28*, 333–342.

Secord, P. F. Stereotyping and favorableness in the perception of Negro faces. *Journal of Abnormal and Social Psychology*, 1959, *59*, 309–315.

Segall, M. H. Anthropology and psychology. In O. Klineberg and R. Christie (Eds.). *Perspectives in social psychology*. New York: Holt, Rinehart & Winston, 1965, pp. 53–74.

Selltiz, C., Edrich, H., and Cook, S. W. Ratings of favorableness of statements about a social group as an indicator of attitudes toward the group. *Journal of Personality and Social Psychology*, 1965, *2*, 408–415.

Sereno, K. K. Ego-involvement: A neglected variable in speech-communication research. *Quarterly Journal of Speech*, 1969, *60*, 69–77.

————, and Mortenson, C. D. The effects of ego-involved attitudes on conflict negotiation in dyads. *Speech Monographs*, 1969, *36*, 8–12.

Seward, G. H., and Williamson, R. C. (Eds.). *Sex roles in changing society*. New York: Random House, 1970.

Shaffer, L. S. Importance of norms, group structure and situational thresholds in attitude-related behavior. Doctoral dissertation, Pennsylvania State Univ., 1974.

————, and Sherif, C. W. Surveillance gadgetry and task significance as variables in research. Paper to the Eastern Psychological Association, Washington, D.C., May, 1973.

Shaw, M. E., and Costanzo, P. R. *Theories of social psychology*. New York: McGraw-Hill, 1970.

Shaw, M. E., and Wright, J. M. *Scales for the measurement of attitudes*. New York: McGraw-Hill, 1967.

Sherif, C. W. Established reference scales and series effects in social judgment. Ph.D. dissertation, Univ. of Texas at Austin, 1961.

————. Social categorization as a function of latitude of acceptance and series range. *Journal of Abnormal and Social Psychology*, 1963, *67*, 148–156.

————. Social distance as categorization of intergroup interaction. *Journal of Personality and Social Psychology*, 1973, *25*, 327–334.

————, and Jackman, N. R. Judgments of truth by participants in collective controversy. *Public Opinion Quarterly*, 1966, *30*, 173–186.

Sherif, C. W., Kelly, M., Rodgers, H. L., Jr., Sarup, G., and Tittler, B. I. Personal involvement, social judgment and action. *Journal of Personality and Social Psychology*, 1973, *27*, 311–328.

Sherif, C. W., Sherif, M., and Nebergall, R. E. *Attitude and attitude change: The social judgment-involvement approach*. Philadelphia: Saunders, 1965.

Sherif, M. A study of some social factors in perception. *Archives of Psychology*, 1935, No. 187.

————. *The psychology of social norms*. New York: Harper & Row, 1936 (Harper Torchbooks, 1966).

————. An experimental approach to the study of attitudes. *Sociometry*, 1937, *1*, 90–98.

———. *An outline of social psychology.* New York: Harper & Row, 1948.

———. Conformity-deviation, norms and group relations. In I. A. Berg and B. M. Bass (Eds.). *Conformity and deviation.* New York: Harper & Row, 1961.

———. *In common predicament: Social psychology of intergroup conflict and cooperation.* Boston: Houghton Mifflin, 1966.

———. *Social interaction: Process and products.* Chicago: Aldine, 1967.

———. Self concept. *International Encyclopedia of the Social Sciences.* Vol. 14. New York: Macmillan and Free Press, 1968.

———. On the relevance of social psychology. *American Psychologist,* 1970, *25*(2), 144–156.

———, and Cantril, H. The psychology of "attitudes." Part 1. *Psychological Review,* 1945, *52, 295–317.*

———. The psychology of "attitudes." Part 2. *Psychological Review,* 1946, *53,* 1–24.

———. *The psychology of ego-involvements.* New York: Wiley, 1947.

Sherif, M., and Harvey, O. J. A study in ego functioning: Elimination of stable anchorages in individual and group functioning. *Sociometry,* 1952, *15,* 272–305.

Sherif, M., Harvey, O. J., White, B. J., Hood, W. R., and Sherif, C. W. *Intergroup conflict and cooperation. The Robbers Cave Experiment.* Norman, Okla.: Institute of Group Relations, 1961.

Sherif, M., and Hovland, C. I. Judgmental phenomena and scales of attitude measurement: Placement of items with individual choice of number of categories. *Journal of Abnormal and Social Psychology,* 1953, *48,* 135–141.

———. *Social judgment. Assimilation and contrast effects in communication and attitude change.* New Haven, Conn.: Yale Univ. Press, 1961.

Sherif, M., and Sherif, C. W. *Groups in harmony and tension.* New York: Harper & Row, 1953 (Octagon, 1966).

———. *An outline of social psychology.* New York: Harper & Row, 1956.

———. *Reference groups: Exploration into conformity and deviation of adolescents.* New York: Harper & Row, 1964.

Sherif, M., and Sherif, C. W. Attitude as the individual's own categories: The social judgment-involvement approach to attitude and attitude change. In C. W. Sherif and M. Sherif (Eds.). *Attitude, ego-involvement, and change.* New York: Wiley, 1967, pp. 105–139.

———. *Social psychology.* New York: Harper & Row, 1969.

———. (Eds.). *Problems of youth: Transition to adulthood in a changing world.* Chicago: Aldine, 1965.

Sherif, M., White, B. J., and Harvey, O. J. Status in experimentally produced groups. *American Journal of Sociology,* 1955, *60,* 370–379.

Sherman, M., and Henry, T. R. *Hollow folk.* New York: Crowell, 1933.

Sherman, S. R. Demand characteristics in an experiment on attitude change. *Sociometry,* 1967, *30,* 246–261.

Shields, S. Functionalism, Darwinism and the psychology of women: A study in social myth. *American Psychologist,* 1975, *30,* 739–754.

Shinn, M. W. Notes on the development of a child. Vols. 1 and 2. Berkeley: Univ. of California Press, Publications in Education 1898 (vol. 1); 1907 (vol. 2).

Shotland, L. The communication patterns and the structure of social relationships at a large university. Doctoral dissertation, Michigan State Univ., 1970.

Shuey, A. M., King, N., and Griffith, B. Stereotyping of Negroes and whites: An analysis of magazine pictures. *Public Opinion Quarterly*, 1953, *17*, 281–287.

Siegel, A. E., and Siegel, S. Reference groups, membership groups and attitude change. *Journal of Abnormal and Social Psychology*, 1957, *55*, 360–364.

Smith, M. B. *Social psychology and human values.* Chicago: Aldine, 1969.

Smith, M. E. An investigation of the sentence and the extent of vocabulary in young children. Iowa City: Univ. of Iowa Studies in Child Welfare, 1926, *3*(5).

Smith, S. S., and Jamieson, B. D. Effects of attitude and ego-involvement on the learning and retention of controversial material. *Journal of Personality and Social Psychology*, 1972, *22*, 303–310.

Snyder, D., and Tilly, C. Hardship and collective violence in France, 1830–1960. *American Sociological Review*, 1972, *37*, 520–532.

Sommer, R. *Personal space: The behavioral basis of design.* Englewood Cliffs, N.J.: Prentice-Hall, 1969.

———, and Becker, F. D. Territorial defense and the good neighbor. *Journal of Personality and Social Psychology*, 1969, *11*, 85–92.

Spielberger, C. D. The role of awareness in verbal conditioning. *Journal of Personality*, 1962, *30*, 73–101.

———, and DeNike, L. D. Operant conditioning of plural nouns: A failure to replicate the Greenspoon effect. *Psychological Reports*, 1962, *11*, 355–366.

———. Descriptive behaviorism vs. cognitive theory in operant conditioning. *Psychological Review*, 1966, *73*, 306–326.

Spiro, R. J., and Sherif, C. W. Consistency and relativity in recall with differing ego-involvement. *British Journal of Clinical and Social Psychology*, 1975 (in press).

Spohn, H. E. The influence of social values upon the clinical judgments of psychotherapists. In J. G. Peatman and E. L. Hartley (Eds.). *Festschrift for Gardner Murphy.* New York: Harper & Row, 1960, pp. 274–290.

Spokeswoman, June 15, 1974.

Staats, A. W. Experimental demand characteristics and the classical conditioning of attitudes. *Journal of Personality and Social Psychology*, 1969, *11*, 187–192.

———, and Staats, C. K. Attitudes established by classical conditioning. *Journal of Abnormal and Social Psychology*, 1958, *57*, 37–40.

Star, S. A., and Hughes, H. McG. Report of an educational campaign: The Cincinnati plan for the United Nations. *American Journal of Sociology*, 1950, *55*, 389–400.

Stein, A. H., and Bailey, M. M. The socialization of achievement orientation in females. *Psychological Bulletin*, 1973, *80*, 345–366.

Stein, A. H., and Friedrich, L. K. Impact of television on children and youth. In E. Mavis Hetherington, J. W. Hagen, R. Kron, and A. H. Stein (Eds.). *Review of child development research.* Vol. 5. Chicago: Univ. of Chicago Press, 1975.

Stein, D. D., Hardyck, J. A., and Smith, M. B. Race and belief: An open and shut case. *Journal of Personality and Social Psychology,* 1965, *1,* 281–289.

Steiner, I. D. *Group process and productivity.* New York: Academic Press, 1972.

Stevenson, H. W., and Allen, S. Adult performance as a function of sex of experimenter and sex of subject. *Journal of Abnormal and Social Psychology,* 1964, *68,* 214–216.

Stone, W. F. Autokinetic norms: An experimental analysis. *Journal of Personality and Social Psychology,* 1967, *5,* 76–81.

Stonequist, E. V. *The marginal man.* New York: Scribner, 1937.

Storms, M. D. Videotape and the attribution process: Reversing actors' and observers' points of view. *Journal of Personality and Social Psychology,* 1973, *27,* 165–175.

Strong, C. H. Motivation related to performance of physical fitness tests. *Research Quarterly,* 1963, *34,* 497–507.

Sully, J. *Studies of childhood.* New York: Appleton, 1895.

Sumner, W. G. *Folkways.* Boston: Glenn, 1906.

Sussman, M. B. a. Personal marriage contracts: Old wine in new bottles. b. Personal contracts study. Cleveland, Ohio: Institute on the Family and the Bureaucratic Society, Case Western Reserve Univ., 1974 (mimeographed).

Taffel, C. Anxiety and the conditioning of verbal behavior. *Journal of Abnormal and Social Psychology,* 1955, *51,* 496–501.

Tajfel, H. The anchoring effects of value in a scale of judgments. *British Journal of Psychology,* 1959, *50,* 294–304.

———. Social and cultural factors in perception. In G. Lindzey and E. Aronson (Eds.). *Handbook of social psychology.* Vol. 3. Reading, Mass.: Addison-Wesley, 1969.

———, Sheikh, A. A., and Gardner, R. C. Content of stereotypes and the inference of similarity between members of stereotyped groups. *Acta Psychologia,* 1964, *22,* 191–201.

Taylor, D. A. The development of interpersonal relationships: Social penetration processes. *Journal of Social Psychology,* 1968, *75,* 79–90.

———, and Altman, I. Intimacy-scaled stimuli for use in studies of interpersonal relations. *Psychological Reports,* 1966, *19,* 729–730.

———, and Wheeler, L. Self-disclosure in isolated groups. *Journal of Personality and Social Psychology,* 1973, *26,* 39–47.

Thistlethwaite, D. L. Impact of disruptive external events on student attitudes. *Journal of Personality and Social Psychology,* 1974, *30,* 228–242.

Thomas, W. I., and Znaniecki, F. *The Polish peasant in Europe and America.* Chicago: Univ. of Chicago Press, 1918.

Thompson, L. *Culture in crisis: A study of the Hopi Indians.* New York: Harper & Row, 1950.

Thorndike, E. L., and Rock, R. T. Learning without awareness of what is being learned or intent to learn it. *Journal of Experimental Psychology,* 1934, *17,* 1–19.

Thrasher, J. D. Interpersonal relations and gradations of stimulus structure in judgment variation. *Sociometry,* 1954, *17,* 228–241.

Thurstone, L. L. Attitudes can be measured. *American Journal of Sociology,* 1928, *33,* 529–554.

———, and Chave, E. J. *The measurement of attitude.* Chicago: Univ. of Chicago Press, 1929.

Tittle, C. R., and Hill, R. J. Attitude measurement and the prediction of behavior: An evaluation of conditions and measurement techniques. *Sociometry,* 1967, *30,* 199–213.

Tittler, B. I. The relationship between attitude change and ego-involvement and its relevance to sex differences in attitude change. Master's thesis, Pennsylvania State Univ., 1967.

Toch, H. *The psychology of social movements.* Indianapolis: Bobbs-Merrill, 1965.

Tresemer, D. Fear of success: Popular, but unproven. *Psychology Today,* 1974, *7*(10), 82–85.

Tresselt, M. E., and Volkmann, J. The production of uniform opinion by non-social stimulation. *Journal of Abnormal and Social Psychology,* 1942, *37,* 234–243.

Triandis, H. C. Toward an analysis of the components of interpersonal attitudes. In C. W. Sherif and M. Sherif (Eds.). *Attitude, ego-involvement and change.* New York: Wiley, 1967.

———. *Attitude and attitude change.* New York: Wiley, 1970.

———, and Davis, E. E. Race and belief as determinants of behavioral intentions. *Journal of Personality and Social Psychology,* 1965, *2,* 715–725.

Triandis, H. C., and Triandis, L. M. Race, social class, religion and nationality as determinants of social distance. *Journal of Abnormal and Social Psychology,* 1960, *61,* 110–118.

———. A cross-cultural study of social distance. *Psychological Monographs,* 1962, *76,* 1–21.

———. Some studies in social distance. In I. Steiner and M. Fishbein (Eds.). *Current studies in social psychology.* New York: Holt, Rinehart & Winston, 1965.

Triandis, H. C., and Vassilliou, V. Frequency of contact and stereotyping. *Journal of Personality and Social Psychology,* 1967, *7,* 316–328.

Tuchman, B. W. Developmental sequence in small groups. *Psychological Bulletin,* 1965, *63,* 384–399.

Turbeville, G. A. A social distance study in Duluth, Minnesota. *Sociology and Social Research,* 1950, *34,* 415–423.

Turner, R. H. *The social context of ambition.* San Francisco: Chandler, 1964.

Turner, R. H. and Killian, L. M., *Collective behavior.* (2nd ed.) Englewood Cliffs, N.J.: Prentice-Hall, 1972.

Upshaw, H. S. Own attitude as an anchor in equal appearing intervals. *Journal of Abnormal and Social Psychology,* 1962, *64,* 85–96.

Vidulich, R. N., and Wilson, D. J. The environmental setting as a factor in social influence. *Journal of Social Psychology,* 1967, *71,* 247–255.

Vigotsky, L. S. Thought and speech. *Psychiatry,* 1939, *2,* 29–54.

———. *Thought and language.* New York: Wiley, 1962.

Vinacke, W. E. Explorations in the dynamic processes of stereotyping. *Journal of Social Psychology,* 1956, *43,* 105–132.

Volkmann J. Scales of judgment and their implication for social psychology. In J. H. Rohrer and M. Sherif (Eds.). *Social psychology at the crossroads.* New York: Harper & Row, 1951.

Walster, E., Aronson, V., Abrahams, D., and Rottman, L. Importance of physical attractiveness in dating behavior. *Journal of Personality and Social Psychology,* 1966, *5,* 508–516.

Ward, C. D. Ego involvement and the absolute judgment of attitude statements. *Journal of Personality and Social Psychology,* 1965, *2,* 202–208.

———. Attitude and involvement in the absolute judgment of attitude statements. *Journal of Personality and Social Psychology,* 1966, *4,* 465–472.

Warner, L. G., and DeFleur, M. L. Attitude as an interactional concept: Social constraint and social distance as intervening variables between attitudes and actions. *American Sociological Review,* 1969, 153–169.

Waterman, A. D., Northrop, G. W., and Olsen, L. D. Motivation and achievement in the elementary school. *Elementary School Journal,* 1967, *67,* 375–380.

Wax, M. Tenting with Malinowski. *American Sociological Review,* 1972, *37,* 1–13.

Webb, E. J., Campbell, D. T., Schwartz, R. D., and Sechrest, L. *Unobtrusive measures: Nonreactive research in the social sciences.* Chicago: Rand McNally, 1966.

Weick, K. E. Systematic observational methods. In G. Lindzey and E. Aronson (Eds.). *Handbook of social psychology.* Vol. 2. Reading, Mass.: Addison-Wesley, 1968.

———, and Gilfillan, D. P. Fate of arbitrary traditions in a laboratory microculture. *Journal of Personality and Social Psychology,* 1971, *17,* 179–191.

Weisstein, N. Psychology constructs the female or, the fantasy life of the male psychologist. In M. Garskoff (Ed.). *Roles women play: Readings toward women's liberation.* Belmont, Calif.: Brooks/Cole, 1971.

Weitz, S. Attitude, voice and behavior: A repressed affect model of interracial interaction. *Journal of Personality and Social Psychology,* 1972, *24,* 14–21.

Weitzman, L. J., Eifler, D., Hokada, E., and Ross, C. Sex-role socialization in picture books for pre-school children. *American Journal of Sociology,* 1972, *77,* 1125–1150.

Wenckowski, C. Black-white attitudes toward advisability of opposite race interactions. *Journal of College Student Personnel,* 1973 (July), 303–308.

White, H. A., and Schumsky, D. A. Prior information and "awareness" in verbal conditioning. *Journal of Personality and Social Psychology,* 1972, *24,* 162–165.

White, M. J. Effects of room size, status and sex on interpersonal distance. Master's thesis, Pennsylvania State Univ., 1972.

Whittaker, J. O. Opinion change as a function of communication-attitude discrepancy. *Psychological Reports,* 1963, *13,* 763–772.

———. Parameters of social influence in the autokinetic situation. *Sociometry,* 1964, *27,* 88–95.

———. Resolution of the communication discrepancy issue in social psychology. In C. W. Sherif and M. Sherif (Eds.). *Attitude, ego-involvement and change.* New York: Wiley, 1967.

———, and Meade, R. D. Social pressure in the modification and distortion of judgment: A cross-cultural study. *International Journal of Psychology,* 1967, *2,* 109–113.

Whyte, W. F. Leadership and group participation. New York State School of

Industrial and Labor Relations, Bulletin 24. Ithaca, N.Y.: Cornell Univ., 1953 (reissued 1956, 1960).

———. *Street corner society.* (New ed.) Chicago: Univ. of Chicago Press, 1955.

Williams, R. M. *The reduction of intergroup tensions.* New York: Social Science Research Council, Bulletin 57, 1947.

———. *Strangers next door.* Englewood Cliffs, N.J.: Prentice-Hall, 1964.

Wilson, A. B. Residential segregation of social classes and aspirations of high school boys. *American Sociological Review,* 1959, *24,* 836–845.

Wood, C. R. An analysis of changes occurring in successive stages of verbal abstracting. Master's thesis, State Univ. of Iowa, 1944.

Woodworth, R. S., and Marquis, D. G. *Psychology.* (5th ed.) New York: Holt, Rinehart & Winston, 1947, p. 88.

Wylie, R. C. *The self concept: A critical survey of pertinent research literature.* Lincoln: Univ. of Nebraska Press, 1961.

Yalom, I. D. *The theory and practice of group psychotherapy.* New York: Basic Books, 1970.

Yerkes, R. M. *Chimpanzees: A laboratory colony.* New Haven: Yale Univ. Press, 1943.

———, and Nissen, H. W. Prelinguistic sign behavior in chimpanzees. *Science,* 1939, *89,* 585–587.

Young, K. *Source book for social psychology.* New York: Knopf, 1927.

Zander, A. People often work harder for group than for selves. *ISR Newsletter,* 1974, *2,* (3), 2–7 (Institute of Social Research, Ann Arbor, Michigan).

Zavalloni, M., and Cook, S. W. Influence of judges' attitudes on ratings of favorableness of statements about a social group. *Journal of Personality and Social Psychology,* 1965, *1,* 43–54.

Zeigarnik, B. Das Behalten erledigter Handlungen. *Psychologische Forschung,* 1927, *9,* 1–85.

Zimbardo, P. G. Involvement and communication discrepancy as determinants of opinion conformity. *Journal of Abnormal and Social Psychology,* 1960, *60,* 86–94.

———, and Ebbesen, E. E. *Influencing attitudes and changing behavior.* Reading, Mass.: Addison-Wesley, 1969.

Zinn, H. *SNCC: The new abolitionists.* Boston: Beacon Press, 1964.

Indexes

Index of Authors

(*See also* References, pp. 393–422)

Abelson, R. P., 221, 231, 261
Abplanalp, J., xiv
Abrahams, D., 38
Acock, R. C., 284
Adair, J. G., 152, 259
Adorno, T., 249
Aiello, J. R., 86
Ajzen, I., 261
Aldrich, H. E., 391
Alker, H. A., 368
Allen, H., 46
Allen, S., 29
Allen, V. L., 282
Allport, F. H., 24, 231
Allport, G. W., 117, 178, 185, 230, 273
Altman, I., 72, 73
Ames, R. G., 275, 286
Anastasi, A., 157
Anderson, H. H., 212
Anderson, R. C., 107
Ansari, A. A., 272
Ansel, M., 47
Aronson, E., 76, 344, 355
Aronson, V., 38
Asch, S. E., 164–167
Ashmore, R. D., 286
Azores, F. M., 218, 307

Baer, H. R., 157, 385. *See also* Kearney, H. R.
Bailey, M. M., xiv, 186, 218–219
Baldwin, J. M., 188, 199
Bales, R. F., 59–62
Balloun, G. L., 333
Bandura, A., 150
Baral, R. L., 40
Baron, S. H., 56
Bart, P., 369
Bartlett, F. C., 173–174, 316
Baumgardner, S. R., 326
Bavelas, A., 321
Bayton, J. A., 298
Beck, D., 248, 249

Becker, F. D., 31
Bem, D., 187, 318, 344
Bender, I. E., 313
Benoit-Smullyan. E., 222
Bensman, J., 98, 99
Berelson, B., 339
Berk, R. A., 391
Berkowitz, L., 117
Berman, P., xiv
Berscheid, E., 39
Bickman, L., 48
Bieri, J., 37, 240, 255
Billig, M., 324
Binet, A., 157
Bixenstine, V. E., 282
Blake, R. R., 130, 136, 298
Block, J. H., 297
Blumberg, A., 76
Bogardus, E. S., 272, 273–275, 283, 286
Bohner, S., 352, 355
Bolton, C. D., 377
Bonacich, P., 63
Bord, R., xiv
Boyanowsky, E. O., 282
Braly, K. W., 291
Brandt, H. F., 212
Brehm, J., 337
Brock, T. C., 333
Bronfenbrenner, U., 196
Brooks, S., xiv
Broverman, D. M., 184, 296
Broverman, I. K., 184, 296
Brown, R., 146, 190, 192, 284, 363
Bruner, J. S., 284
Bryan, J. H., 48
Bush, T., xiv, 385
Buss, A. H., 206–207
Butler, J., 322
Byoune, E., 298
Byrne, D., 39, 283

Cammalleri, A., 166
Campbell, A., 261, 276–277

Campbell, D. T., 86, 87, 167, 233, 259, 260, 264, 287, 292
Cannell, C. F., 258
Cantril, H., 171, 188, 230, 248, 363
Carlsmith, M., 355
Carter, R. F., 332
Cartwright, D., 110
Catt, C. C., 372
Chagnon, N., 86
Chapman, D. W., 210, 211
Chave, E. J., 179, 180
Chmielewski, D., xiv
Chomsky, N., 146
Clark, J. P., 85
Clark, K. B., 195
Clark, M. K., 195
Clark, R. D., 44
Clarke, P., 333
Clarkson, F. E., 184, 296
Coch, L., 322
Cofer, C. N., xiv, 173
Coffin, T. E., 164
Coffman, T., 293, 325
Cohen, E. G., 199
Cole, B. G., 331
Coleman, D., 9, 10, 11
Coleman, J., 339
Collins, B. E., 102, 110, 111, 183
Converse, P. E., 261
Cook, S. W., 181
Cook, T. D., 341, 342
Cooper, C. L., 76, 77, 89
Cooper, P., xiv
Coopersmith, S., 225, 226
Cox, K. K., 269
Craighead, W. E., 86
Cronbach, L. J., 157, 159
Cvetkovich, G., 325

Dahlke, A. E., 152
Darley, J. M., 42–44
Darwin, C., 188
Davies, J. C., 373
Davis, E. K., 282
Davis, K., 148
Dawes, R. M., 137, 187, 242, 282
De Beauvoir, S., 374
De Fleur, M. L., 264
De Lissovoy, V., 225
Dembo, T., 210
De Nike, L. D., 152
Dennis, W., 298
Deutsch, M., 326, 327
Deutscher, I., 260

Diab, L., 187, 247, 333
Diaz-Guerrero, R., 369
Dinneen, F. P., 191
Dion, K., 39
Dixon, M., 379, 381
Dodd, S. C., 280
Dohrenwend, B., 369
Doise, W., 325
Dollard, J., 116
Doob, L., 116
Drew, J. E., 174–175
Dunnette, M. D., 79

Eagly, A. H., 251, 254
Ebbesen, E. E., 233
Edrich, H., 181
Edwards, A. L., 86, 242, 258
Ehrhardt, A. A., 155–156, 191
Ehrlich, C., 369
Ehrlich, H. J., 271, 275, 277, 292–293, 298
Eifler, D., 270
Eiser, J. R., 181, 182, 183, 284
Elbing, A., 247, 319
Elms, A. C., 10, 250–251, 318, 344
Entwisle, D. R., 259
Erikson, E., 224
Ervin, C. R., 39, 283
Escovar, L., xiv, 255
Esser, A. H., 103
Evans, R., 315
Evans, R. I., 281

Faucheux, C., 325
Faunce, W. A., 310
Feather, N. T., 175–176
Feffer, M., 193
Feldman, K. A., 312
Feldman, R. A., 110
Feldman, R. E., 49
Felipe, N. J., 31
Fell, D., 47
Fenchel, G. H., 222
Fendrich, J. M., 262, 388
Ferson, J. E., 276
Festinger, L., 210, 221, 344
Fiedler, F., 107, 108, 109
Field, P. B., 338
Fink, B., 47
Finney, J., 227
Fishbein, M., 261–262
Flacks, R., 311
Flavell, J. H., 193
Flexner, E., 365, 371
Folsom, J., 373

Forbes, J., 9, 10, 11
Foster, G. M., 306
Frank, J. D., 210, 329, 345
Fraser, C., 324
Fraser, R. S., 182
Frazier, F., 299
Freedman, J. L., 333
Freeman, J., 374, 375, 377, 380, 382, 387
French, J. R. P., Jr., 322
Frenkel-Brunswik, E., 249
Freud, S., 116
Friedan, B., 374, 375, 381
Friedrich, L. K., 332

Gaertner, S., 48
Galton, F., 157
Gardner, R. C., 284, 295
Gaudet, H., 339
Gecas, V., 225–226
Gesell, A., 188
Gibb, C. A., 103, 110
Gilbert, G. M., 292
Gilchrist, J., 211
Gilfillan, D. P., 168
Glixman, A., 254
Goethals, G. R., 36
Goffman, E., 198
Goldberg, A. S., 261
Goldberg, M. E., 332
Goldberg, P. A., 34
Goldstein, M., 282
Golembiewski, R. T., 76
Goodman, M. E., 195
Gorn, G., xiv, 332, 357, 358
Gouge, C., 324
Granberg, D., xiv, 116
Greeley, A. M., 278, 279
Greenberg, P. J., 194
Greenspoon, J., 151
Grey, E., xiv, 288
Griffith, B., 269
Griffiths, M., 375
Guthrie, G., xiv, 218, 307
Guttentag, M., 327, 328

Haarlow, R. N., 68
Haller, A. O., 218
Hammer, K., 298
Hansche, J., 211
Hardy, R. C., 109
Hardyck, J. A., 282
Harris, M., 325
Hartley, E. L., 222, 275, 277. *See also*
    Horowitz, E. L.

Hartley, R. E. *See* Horowitz, R. E.
Hartup, W. W., 194, 195
Harvey, O. J., 57, 115, 116, 117, 122, 215,
    246, 255, 345, 346
Hatchett, S., 244
Hawkins, G., 282
Hebb, D., 147, 172
Heberle, R., 363
Heider, F., 183
Helson, H., 37, 236
Hendrick, C., 282
Henry, T. R., 305
Heussenstamm, F. K., 259
Hilgard, E. R., 212
Hill, R. J., 260
Hinckley, E. D., 180
Hirota, K., 194
Hoffman, E. L., 56
Hoge, D. R., 313
Hokada, E., 270
Hokanson, J. E., 391
Hollingworth, L., 310
Holmes, D. S., 152
Holt, R., 210
Holtzman, W. H., 276
Hood, W. R., 56, 115, 116
Horner, M. S., 220, 259
Horowitz, E. L., 195, 298. *See also* Hartley,
    E. L.
Horowitz, R. E., 195
Horwitz, M., 174
Hosowaka, W., 116
Houseknecht, S., xiv, 235
Hovland, C. I., 36, 37, 179, 180, 181, 230,
    246, 335, 345, 351, 355
Hughes, H. M., 332
Hyman, H. H., 136, 220, 278, 333

Ilg, F. L., 188
Inhelder, B., 193
Insko, C. A., 341, 342, 352, 355

Jacklin, C. N., 161
Jackman, N. R., 245, 246, 346
Jackson, G. D., 160
Jacobs, R. C., 167
Jacobson, L., 153
Jahoda, G., 298
James, J., 333
James, W., 209, 210
Jamieson, B. D., 174
Janis, I. L., 318, 338
Jeffries, V., 261
Jenkins, L., xiv

Jessor, R., 227, 240
Jessor, S. L., 227, 240
Johnson, E. S., 288
Johnson, R., 9, 10, 11
Jones, E. E., 36, 183, 185, 186, 187
Jones, J. M., 195
Jones, R. A., 286
Jones, S. E., 86
Jourard, S. M., 72
Juanico, M. B., 218, 307

Kagan, S., 195
Kahn, E. J., Jr., 221
Kahn, R. L., 258
Kamano, D. K., 174, 175
Kanouse, D. E., 183
Kanungo, R. N., 332
Karlins, M., 68, 293, 298
Katz, D., 231, 233, 250, 291
Katz, E., 339–340
Kearney, H. R., xiv, 349–350. *See also*
   Baer, H. R.
Kelley, H. H., 34–36, 183, 184
Kellog, L. A., 189
Kellog, W. N., 189
Kelly, J. G., 276
Kelly, M., 183, 257, 263
Kelman, H. C., 59, 233
Kerrick, J. S., 336
Ketchum, J. D., 70–71
Kidder, L. H., 209
Kiesler, C. A., 183, 262, 319
Kiesler, S. B., 34, 40–41
Killian, L. M., 228, 363
King, M. L., Jr., 299, 349
King, N., 269
Kirchner, E., 192
Kirschner, B. F., 369
Klapper, J., 332
Klemesrud, J., 385
Kliejins, P., 261
Klineberg, O., 145
Koenig, L. E., 311
Kon, I. S., 225
Koslin, B. L., 68, 254, 255
Koulack D., 353
Kruksall, W. H., 86
Kuhn, M. H., 204

Ladwig, G. W., 207
LaFave, L., xiv, 228, 252
Laing, R. D., 186
Lambert, W. E., 205
Lamberth, J., 39, 283

Lamm, H., 325
Lana, R. E., 337
Lang, G., 363
Lang, K., 363
Lang, O., 306
Langer, S., 188
Larsen, K. S., 9, 10, 11, 251
Lasakow, P., 72
Latané, B., 42–44
Lazarsfeld, P., 339, 340
Leaman, R., 37
Lefcourt, H. M., 207
Lemons, F., 137, 187
Lenneberg, E. H., 146
Leuba, C., 194
Levine, G. M., 175
Levine, J., 322
LeVine, R. A., 287, 292
Levinger, G., 53, 63
Levinson, D. J., 249
Levy, L. H., 152
Levy, P., 47
Lewin, K., 105, 174, 210, 321, 323
Lewis, G. H., 63
Lewis, M. M., 146, 190
Libman, E., 205
Lieberman, S., 317
Likert, R., 241, 242, 243, 311
Linn, L. S., 264
Lippitt, R., 105, 106
Lippman, W., 269
Liska, A. E., 261
Loevinger, J., 190
Lorenz, K., 116
Lott, A. J., 64, 110
Lott, B. E., 64, 110
Lowie, R., 203
Luchins, A. S., 164
Lumsdaine, A. A., 335
Luna, M. P. S., 218, 307
Lundgren, D., 47, 79
Luria, A. R., 150, 193

McAllister, L. B., 298
McClelland, D. C., 259
McClelland, L., 258
Maccoby, E. E., 161
MacDougall, W., 5
McGehee, W., 214
McGrath, F. E., 47
McGuire, W. J., 221, 271, 319, 331, 335
McLaughlin, B., 363, 387
MacLeod, R., 71
McMillan, D. H., 336

MacNeil, M., 167, 168
McPartland, T. S., 204
McPhee, W., 339
Madsen, M. C., 195
Magaret, G. A., 212
Makarenko, A. S., 196
Mangham, I. L., 76, 77, 79, 89
Mann, L., 318
Mann, R. D., 77
Markowski, J., 354, 355
Marks, E., 343
Marquis, D. G., 185
Marzolf, J., 347
Mausner, B., 59
Mead, G. H., 193, 234
Mead, M., 156, 198
Meade, R. D., 166
Megargee, E., 391
Melikian, L. H., 275
Menapace, R. H., 337
Menzel, H., 340
Mercatoris, M., 86
Merei, F., 96
Merton, R., 153, 339
Mezei, L., 282
Milano, E., xiv, 276
Milgram, S., 6–8, 10–12, 26, 166, 259, 363, 378
Miller, D., 79
Miller, N., 183, 352
Miller, N. E., 116
Miller, W. E., 261
Mills, T. M., 77
Minturn, L. See Triandis, L.
Mischel, W., 184
Monderer, J. H., 222
Money, J., 155, 156, 191
Moore, K. C., 188
Moreno, J. L., 64–66, 317
Mortenson, C. D., 247
Moscovici, S., 324, 325
Mouton, J. S., 130, 136
Mowrer, O. H., 116
Murchison, C., 6, 188
Murphy, G., 6, 175, 184, 323, 334
Murphy, L. B., 6, 195, 334
Myers, D. G., 325

Nebergall, R. E., 183, 247, 248–249, 343, 346
Nehru, J., 298
Nemeth, C., 354, 355
Newcomb, T. M., 6, 310–312, 334
Nisbett, R. E., 183, 185, 186, 187

Nissen, H. W., 147
Noble, M., xiv
Nobles, W. W., 205
Northrop, G. W., 213
Novak, R., 315

Odiorne, G. S., 79
Ogburn, W. F., 309–310
Olsen, L. D., 213
O'Neill, W. L., 349, 371, 373, 389
Orcutt, B. A., 37
Osgood, C. E., 240
Ostrom, T. M., 308

Page, M. M., 152
Papageorgis, D., 319
Pargament, R., 68, 254
Park, R. E., 272
Parten, M. B., 194
Pavlov, I., 149–150
Pelton, L., 390
Pelz, E., 323
Peterson, P. D., 353
Pheterson, G. I., 34
Piaget, J., 190, 193–194, 196
Piliavin, I. M., 44, 45
Piliavin, J. A., 44, 45
Pollis, C. A., 308
Pollis, N., 166, 308
Polowniak, W. A., 337
Portnoy, N. W., 206–207
Poser, E. G., 205
Postman, L. J., 178
Powell, F. A., 251
Preyer, W., 188–189
Pritzker, H. A., 351
Prothro, E. T., 275
Pruitt, D., 324
Pyles, M. K., 151

Quarton, R., xiv, 193

Rader, J. A., 308
Rafferty, F. T., 103
Ram, P., 323
Ransford, H. E., 261
Raven, B. H., 102, 110, 111
Reich, J., 253–254
RePass, D. E., 261
Rhine, R. J., 337, 357
Rickers-Oviankina, M., 72
Rivers, W. H. R., 203
Rock, R. T., 151
Rodgers, H. L., Jr., 183, 257, 356

Rodin, J. A., 44
Rogers, E. M., 340
Rohrer, J. H., 56
Rokeach, M., 261, 281, 282
Rollins, J. H., xiv, 287, 288
Rom, B., xiv
Roosevelt, E., 374
Roper, S. S., 199
Rosenberg, B., 98, 99
Rosenberg, M., 225, 227
Rosenberg, M. J., 221, 233
Rosenkrantz, P. S., 184, 296
Rosenthal, R., 29, 153, 259
Rosnow, R. L., 259, 336
Ross, C., 270
Ross, E. A., 5
Rottman, L., 38
Roy, K., 288

Sahakian, W. S., 344
Sait, E. M., 212
Sakuma, A. F., 275, 286
Sanford, N., 249
Sanger, S. P., 368
Santos, E., 295
Sarup, G., 183, 255, 257, 337, 338
Schneirla, T. C., 144
Schramm, W., 332
Schulman, G., 260
Schuman, H., 244
Schumsky, D. A., 152
Schwartz, R. D., 86, 260
Scully, D., 369
Sears, D. O., 333
Sears, P. S., 210, 212
Sears, R. S., 116
Seaver, W. B., xiv, 153–155
Sechrest, L., 86, 260
Secord, P., 33, 284
Segall, M. H., 88
Selltiz, C., 181
Sereno, K. K., 247, 356
Severance, L., 357
Seward, G. H., 156
Shaffer, L. S., xiv, 86, 204, 264–265
Shapira, A., 195
Shaw, M. E., 183, 242
Sheatsley, P. B., 136, 278, 333
Sheffield, F., 335
Sheikh, A. A., 284
Shepard, H., 130, 136
Sherman, M., 305
Sherman, S. R., 336
Shields, S., xiv, 162

Shotland, R. L., xiv, 378
Shuey, A. M., 269
Siegel, A., 312
Siegel, S., 312
Simon, T., 157
Singer, D., 137, 187
Skinner, B. F., 149–150
Slater, P. E., 62
Smith, M. B., 233, 250, 282
Smith, M. E., 190
Smith, P. W., 281
Smith, S. S., 174
Snoek, D., 53
Snyder, D., 373, 375, 390
Sommer, R., 30, 31
Spielberger, C. D., 152
Spiro, R., xiv, 176
Spock, B., 316
Spohn, H. E., 183
Staats, A. W., 151
Staats, C. K., 151
Stacey, B. G., 182
Stanton, E. C., 371
Star, S. A., 332
Stein, A. H., xiv, 186, 218, 219, 332
Stein, D. D., 282
Steiner, I. D., 66
Stevenson, H., 29
Stewart, V. M., 209
Stokes, D. E., 261
Stonequist, E. V., 223
Storms, M. D., 186
Stroebe, W., 183, 284
Strong, C. H., 213
Suci, G. J., 240
Sully, J., 191
Suls, J. M., 336
Sumner, W. G., 167
Sussman, M. B., 115, 304
Swander, D. V., 56

Tajfel, H., 164, 195, 289
Tannenbaum, P. H., 240
Taylor, D. A., 72, 73
Taylor, D. M., 295
Telaak, K., 251, 354
Test, M. A., 48
Thomas, W. I., 230, 233
Thompson, H., 188
Thompson, L., 195
Thorndike, E. L., 151
Thrasher, J., 169
Thurstone, L. L., 178, 179, 180, 242
Tiedemann, D., 188

Tifft, L. L., 85
Tilly, C., 373, 375, 390
Tittle, C. R., 260
Tittler, B. I., 183, 247, 257, 337, 338
Toch, H., 363, 374
Tresemer, D., 259
Triandis, H., 49, 232, 233, 261, 275, 281–283, 295
Triandis, L. M., 275, 281–283
Tuberville, C. A., 276
Tuchman, B. W., 76
Turner, J. A., 355
Turner, R., 363
Ty, T. P., 218, 307

Upshaw, H. S., 181, 308

Valins, S., 183
Van Tubergen, N., 292
Vassiliou, V., 295
Vaughan, K., 182
Vidulich, R. N., 28
Vigotsky, L. S., 193
Vogel, S. R., 184, 296
Volkmann, J., 210, 211, 236, 305, 308
Vondracek, S., 192

Wallace, W. P., 86
Walster, E., 38, 39
Walster, G. W., 39
Walters, G., 293
Walters, R. H., 150
Waring, P. D., 254
Warner, L. G., 264
Warwick, D. P., 311

Waterman, A. D., 213
Webb, E. J., 86, 260
Weick, K., 86, 168
Weiner, B., 183
Weiss, W., 355
Weisstein, N., 161, 369
Weitz, S., 258
Weitzman, L. J., 270
Wenckowski, C., 290
Westie, F. R., 264
Wheeler, L., 73
White, B. J., 115, 122
White, H. A., 152
White, M. J., xiv, 31
White, R. K., 105
Whittaker, J., 57, 166, 352
Whyte, W. F., 78, 87, 89, 382
Williams, R. M., 277, 334
Williams, T., 303
Williamson, R. C., 156
Wilson, D. J., 28
Wood, C. R., 229
Woodworth, R. S., 185
Word, L. E., 44
Wright, J. M., 242

Yalom, I. D., 72, 76, 80, 81
Yerkes, R. M., 146, 147
Young, K., 6

Zander, A., 110, 213
Zavalloni, M., 181, 324
Zeigarnik, B., 174
Zimbardo, P. G., 233, 351
Znaniecki, F., 230

Index of Subjects

Abortion issue, 349–350
Achievement, 153–155, 158–160, 199, 217–220
Achievement motivation, 207–209, 213–214, 218–220, 259
Action programs, 380–383, 387–389
Actions, 260–265
Activists, 248–251
Activities, 37–41, 50. *See also* Task
    appeal of, 119, 121–122
    structure of, 66, 194–195
Adolescence, 193, 224–225
Adolescents, 204, 216–218, 257–258
Adult-child interactions, 196–197
Adult-youth relationships, 226–228
Advertisement, 269–270
Affectivity, 237, 271–272. *See also* Emotional arousal
Affiliation, 219. *See also* Bonding
Affirmative action, 384–385
Africa, 88, 174–175, 205
Age-mate interaction, 193–197
Aggression, 114, 116–117, 123–125
    theories of, 389–391
Aggressiveness, 160–162
Aggressors, 298–299
Agreement. *See* Consensus
    in recall, 175–178
Alcoholics Anonymous, 76, 80
Alienation, 227–228. *See also* Distrust, Reference groups
Altruism, 48–49
Ambiguity, 41–51, 56–57, 164–167, 259, 354–355, 376
Ambition, 216–220
American Indian movement, 370
Anchor, self as, 170–199
Anchoring effects, 34–37, 182–183. *See also* Assimilation, Contrast
Anchors, 50, 83, 236
    double, 348–351
    for self-system, 200–228
Antagonistic group, 186–188. *See also* Intergroup conflict, Out-group
Anthropology, 4–6, 86, 156–157

Anxiety, 219–220
Apathy of voters, 249
Applications of research, 46, 208–209, 328–329
Arbitrary standards, 167–169
Aspiration. *See also* Self-esteem
    level of, 210–215, 218–220
Assimilation-contrast effects
    in judging communications, 345–351, 359
    in judging communicators, 356
    in judging similarities to self, 284–285
Assimilation effect, 36–37, 50, 182–183, 187, 191, 348
Atheists, 281, 292
Attention. *See* Selectivity
Attitude, 22, 230–240
    and conflicting expectations, 264–265
    favorableness of, 293–294
    represented by score, 242–244
    toward research, 152
Attitude-behavior relationship, 247, 260–265
Attitude change, 22, 235, 301–302, 341–345, 348, 351–356
    and changed reference groups, 310, 376–379
    and current events, 312–316
    and group decision, 320–326
    maintenance of, 311–312
    and personal involvement, 357–360
    and psychosocial scales, 307–309
    and role playing, 318–320
    in social movement, 381–383, 385–389
Attitude change research, 244, 331–332
    in the field, 339–341
    and laboratory, 334–339
    needed, 358–360
Attitude-communication discrepancy, 345–351, 358–360
    and attitude change, 351–358
Attitude measurement, 231–232, 240–248, 251–253, 258–262, 302
Attitudes, 183, 366
    in-group, 266, 271–272, 300

intergroup, 117–118, 128–139, 266–300
   needed concepts on, 244–245
   and power relationships, 267
   priority of, 343–344
   in selective recall, 176–178
   in social judgment, 178–183
   social vs. personal, 239–240
   of students-faculty, 311–314
Attraction, 32–41, 53–54, 120. *See also*
   Liking
   and cohesiveness, 64–68
Attractiveness, 110–111
Attribution process, 183–187, 241, 297.
   See also Traits
   in intergroup relations, 117, 128–130,
   135
Attributions
   of blame, 138–139
   by dominant groups, 169
   and self-other, 271–272
   to social categories, 290–291
   ʼof traits to sexes, 160–162
"Authoritarian personality," 249–251
Authority, 6–15, 59, 95, 283
   of leader, 108–109
Autism, 190
Autokinetic phenomenon, 56–59, 164,
   167–168
Automation, 310
Awareness, 151–152. *See*
   Consciousness, Experience

Balance theory, 175–178
Behavior, 12–15
   cause of, 183–187. *See also* Attribution
   violent, 389–391
Behaviorism, 13–15, 234
Behavior modification, 328–329
Belief congruence, 281–282
Beliefs, 256, 271–272. *See also* Ideology
   and attitudes, 237–238, 240–244
   and attribution, 183–187, 381–382
Bennington College study, 310–312
"Big Lie," 164–167
Bill of gripes, 379, 380–382
Birth control issue, 354
"Black Bourgeoisie," 299
Black citizens' attitudes, 244
Black college students, 288–290
Black men, 199
Black movement, 223–224, 278, 370, 381
Black Panthers, 259–260, 309
Black Psychologists, Association of, 160
Black women, 379, 384

Black workers, 269–270
Blame. *See also* Attribution
   in intergroup conflict, 138–139
Bogardus test, 273–277
Bonding, 19–20, 64–81
British imperialism, 298
Bystanders, 41–47

Cambodia, 262–263, 313–314
Categorization, 32–41, 151, 180–183,
   190–192, 237, 251–259, 284–287,
   290–291
Causality, 124–125, 129–130, 186. *See
   also* Attribution
Census tract statistics, 216
Chicano, 182, 217–218, 370
Children, 163, 212–214, 270. *See also*
   Development, Self
China, 163, 196, 306
Chromosomes, 155–156
Cigarette smoking, 318
Civil disobedience, 349
Civil Rights Act (1964), 374–375
Civil Rights movement, 207, 217, 223, 278,
   313, 380
Clinical judgment, 37, 183–184. *See also*
   Social judgment
Cognition, 172–187
Cognitive dissonance, 221, 344–345, 347
Cognitive-motivational system, 189–192.
   See also Attitude, Self
Cognitive psychologists, 172, 234
Cognitive structure, 237–238
Cognitive style, 254–255
Cohesiveness, 20, 64, 95–96, 110–111.
   See also Solidarity
Cold War, 165, 274, 374
Collective interaction, 365, 367, 373–375,
   377, 389–391. *See also* Social
   movements
College students, 99–100, 210–212, 262–
   264, 308, 310–314
Commitment, 179–183, 248–251, 262–
   265, 319–320, 387–389. *See also*
   Personal involvement
Committee to Re-Elect the President, 315
"Common enemy," 131–132
Communication, 22, 330–360. *See also*
   Interaction, Language
Communication flow, 339–341, 378
Communicators, 351–352, 355–358
Comparison group, 206–207
Comparison process, 206–207, 370. *See
   also* Social judgment

Comparative psychology, 144, 146–147
Competence, 59, 199, 340
Competition, 124–125, 130, 194–197, 198–199, 207–209
Concept formation, 146–147, 149–151, 190–192. *See also* Categorization
Conceptual functioning, 163, 169, 237–238. *See also* Linguistic process
Conditioning, 149–152
Conflict
  avoidance of, 95–96
  intergroup, 92–94, 117–128
  interpersonal, 264–265
  intrapsychic, 337–339, 342–345, 347, 360, 376–377
  reduction of, 128–139
Conformity, 20, 92, 94–96, 100–101, 231, 249–251, 271. *See also* Deviation, Norms
Consciousness, 13–15, 16, 70
Consciousness-raising, 60, 381–383, 387–389
Consensus, 58–59, 236, 292–293, 305, 307–309. *See also* Norms, Psychosocial scales
Consistency theories, 221–224
Consistent behavior, 192–199, 226, 233–240, 263
Contact, 132–135, 292–296
Context effects, 226–227, 236, 285, 332. *See also* Social judgment
Contingency model of leadership, 107–110
Contrast effect, 36–37, 50, 137–138, 182–183, 191–192, 308. *See also* Assimilation effect, Social judgment
Cooperation, 194–199
  between groups, 133–139
Co-option, 89, 385
Counter-movement, 383–385
Creativity, 382
Credibility, 355–357
Cultural comparisons, 27–28, 31, 48–49, 195–196. *See also* Ethnocentrism
Cultural lags, 167–169, 309–310
Cultural norms, 49, 98–100, 167–169, 187. *See also* Norms
Cultural roles, 198–199. *See also* Role
Cultural truism, 319–320
Culture, 7, 18–19, 27–29, 94–96, 122, 124, 249–250

Dating, 38–40
Debriefing, 15–16, 43. *See also* Ethical values

Deception, 14–15, 152. *See also* Ethical values
Declaration of Independence, 371
Deductive learning, 150–151
"Definition of the situation," 231
Delinquency, 95–96
Demagogue, 140
Demand characteristics, 337–339, 341–342. *See also* Laboratory, Research situation
Democratic-authoritarian leadership, 105–110
Democrats, 247
Demonstrations, 313–314
Depression (1930s), 310, 372
Deprivation, 224. *See also* Relative deprivation
Desegregation, 132, 180–182, 278–279, 282
Development, 147–149, 186–197, 224–225, 255
Deviation, 20, 92–96, 181–182, 220. *See also* Conformity, Norms
Discrepancy. *See* Attitude-communication discrepancy
Discrimination, 277–279, 291, 380. *See also* Domination, Power, Prejudice
Discussion, 35, 136–139
Distrust, 314–315
Divide-and-conquer tactics, 277, 384–385
Dogmatism, 250–251
Domination, 102–104, 199. *See also* Authority, Power
"Don't know" responses, 342–343
Double standard, 99–100, 276
Drug usage, 181–182, 227

Ecology, 122, 139–140. *See also* Location
Education, 196–197, 216–218
Effective initiative, 67–68, 89–90, 93–94, 101–110. *See also* Power, Status
Egocentrism, 193
Ego-involvement, 188. *See also* Personal involvement
Emergencies, 41–46, 228
Emotional arousal, 12–15, 237. *See also* Personal involvement
Empathy, 80, 319–320
Encounter (brief), 24–51
Environment, 155–157, 159, 302–310. *See also* Culture, Location, Social situation
Equal-appearing intervals, 179
Equal Opportunity Commission, 375

Equal Rights Amendment, 372
Ethical values, 163–169
  and research, 15–18, 45, 209, 328–329
  of children, 196–197
Ethnocentrism, 27–28, 157–158, 160–163,
  284–288, 300
Evaluation, 238, 251–258
Events, 312–316
Evolutionary social change, 303–304
Evolutionary theory, 142, 144–147, 150–
  151
Expectancy, 39–40, 235. *See also*
  Attitude, Expectations, Set
Expectations, 41–44, 199, 235, 264–265
  and beliefs, 271–272
  and learning, 152–155
  mutual, 59–81, 83
  for self, 211–215
Experience, 12–16, 125, 170–199
Experimenter effect, 7–15, 29, 35–36
Experiments, 6–15, 65–69, 114–140. *See
  also* Research as cultural event, 164–
  167
Extreme messages, 348–349
Extremity of attitude, 181, 187, 247–251,
  264

Factions, 77, 380–385
Failure, 186, 212–215
Family, 371. *See also* Kinship
Favorableness-unfavorableness, 177,
  181–182, 293–294
Feminine Mystique, 374
Feminist movement, 383, 389–391. *See
  also* Women's movement
Field experiments, 65–69, 114–140, 152–
  155, 378
Field research, 15, 26, 28–32, 36, 44–49.
  See also Survey research
Filipino, 295–296
Foremen, 322
Formal organization, 96, 102–103, 380.
  See also Groups
Frame of reference, 198–199, 233
Freudian therapists, 183–184
Friendship, 59, 71, 72–73, 96, 166, 215,
  282–283
Frustration-aggression hypothesis, 116–
  117, 119–120, 125, 129–130

Gender identity, 191–192. *See also* Self,
  Sex roles
Generalizations, 11–13, 150–151
Generation gap, 313

Generations, 95–96, 167–169, 196–197.
  See also Attitude change
Genetic differences, 155–160
Goals, 111, 124–125, 133–135, 385–389
Group, 20, 54, 69–70, 82
Group decision, 320–325
  and recall, 174
  and social power, 326–329
"Group dynamics," 75–81
Group formation, 66–81
  during adolescence, 225, 227
  in social movement, 374–379
Group norms, 96–101. *See also* Norms
Group polarization, 324–326
Group products, 382–383
Groups, 97–98, 257–258, 288–290
Group structure, 84, 90–96, 382–383. *See
  also* Norms, Roles, Status
Group therapy, 74–81

Helping, 41–49
"Hollow Folk," 305
Hormones, sexual, 156–157
House Un-American Activities
  Committee, 374
Human nature, 20–21, 143–149
Human person, 141–169
"Hyphenated Americans," 287–288

Identity search, 222, 387–389. *See also*
  Self, Self-system
Ideology, 158–160. *See also* Beliefs
  and clinical judgments, 183–184
  and decisions, 327–329
  and social movements, 380–381, 383,
  387–389
  of T-groups, 78
  unconscious, 142–143
  and violence, 390–391
Impeachment, 243, 315
Impression formation, 32–41. *See also*
  Social judgment
Income differences, 216–218, 221
Indirect measurement of attitudes, 179–
  183, 252–253, 259–260
Individual, 141–169
Inference, 13–15
Information, 136, 269–270, 333
In-group, 117–118, 285, 287–288. *See
  also* Group formation, Solidarity
"Inoculation" procedure, 319–320
Instinct vs. learned dichotomy, 143
Institutional decisions, 327–329
Institutionalization, 272, 277–279

Instrumental roles, 61–63
Integration of group, 110–111
Intelligence, 157–160, 232
Intentions, 262. *See also* Commitment, Personal involvement
Interaction, 19–23, 24–51, 193–197
  effects of, 52–55, 288–290
  environmental effects on, 75–81
  intense, 70–71
  and learning, 145, 151–155
Interaction process analysis, 59–63
Intergroup attitudes (defined), 266
Intergroup behavior, 113–114, 121–125, 135–139, 266
Intergroup conflict, 124–130, 274
  and social movements, 367, 383–385
Intergroup interactions, 288–290
Intergroup relations, 20, 112–140
  and comparison groups, 206–207
  and in-groups, 383–385
  and polarization, 325–326
Internal control, 193–197, 368. *See also* Self
Interpersonal relationships, 19–20, 53–55, 83, 127–128
Interviews, 230
Intimacy, 72–73, 282–283. *See also* Social distance
Involvement. *See* Personal involvement
"Irrational" behavior, 122–124, 270
Issues, importance of, 261, 337–339, 343, 351–353, 356
Italian-Americans, 87, 98

Japanese-Americans, 299
Judges, 137–139
Judgment, 55–59, 164–165, 235–236, 354–355. *See also* Social judgment

"Kernel of truth" hypothesis, 270
Kinship, 86, 203–204, 282–283

Labeling, 58, 191, 238. *See also* Categorization
Labor movement, 367
Laboratory, 6–16, 25–26, 57, 204–205, 367–368
  and field research, 259, 350, 360, 363
Laboratory models, 6–16, 334–339, 359–360
Language, 146–151, 191, 234, 386–387
Latitude of acceptance, 96–97
Latitude of noncommitment, 247
  and change, 337–339, 343
  and involvement, 249, 257–258

Latitude of rejection, 247–248, 263, 380
Latitudes of acceptance-rejection-noncommitment, 244–249, 347–354
Laughter, 28–29
Leader, 75–81, 109–110, 340–341. *See also* Status
Leader-follower relations, changes in, 93–94, 127–128
Leadership, 78, 92–94, 100–101
  defined, 104–105
  instrumental, 61–63
  norms against, 382–383
  style, 105–110
  and task structure, 108–109
Learning, 145, 149–151, 233–235
Legal reform, 384, 388–389
Lie detector, 84–86
Likert tests, 241–244, 311
Liking, 38–41, 53
  leader-member, 61–63, 108–109
  reversals in, 146–152
  and solidarity, 64, 110–111
Linguistic development, 190–192
Linguistic process, 146–152
Location, 9–10, 19, 26–29, 358
  of group interaction, 90–91
  isolated, 73
  and personal space, 31–32
Lost letter technique, 259

McCarthy era, 281, 313
Machiavellianism, 139–140
Male "natures," 155–163
Male superiority doctrines, 300
Management development, 107–110
Marginality, 222–225. *See also* Self, Reference Groups, Relative deprivation
Marriage, 63, 304
Mass media, 300–333, 339–341
  and social movements, 364–365, 370, 374, 379
Meaning, 190–192
Measurement. *See also* Observation, Reliability
  of attitudes, 231–232, 240–248, 251–253, 258–262
  indirect, 179–183
  of stereotypes, 291–292
Men, 155–163, 198–199, 207–209
  and women's movement, 371–372, 381, 384–385, 386, 389
Mental patients, 103–104
Message, 333–336. *See also* Communication

Method of ordered alternatives, 246
Methods, multiple, 89–90, 182–183, 261–262
Model
    experiment as, 6–15, 138–141
    of nature-nurture controversy, 159–160
Modeling, 41–47, 51
Moderate positions, 343. *See also* Attitudes
    judgment of, 345–351
    and personal involvement, 248–251
"Modernization," 307
Moral judgment, 193–197
Motivation, 21–22, 54–55
    and attitude concept, 231, 237
    and cognition, 189–192
    theories of, 218–220, 368
Motivational base
    for group formation, 69–70, 76–77
    of social movements, 368–370, 373–375
Mutuality, 53–54, 72–73

Naming, 190–192. *See also* Categorization, Labeling
National Black Feminist Organization, 379
National groups, 206–207, 256, 273–277, 280, 285–287
National Organization for Women (NOW), 365, 375, 377, 380–381, 383
National Woman's Party, 372
Navaho youth, 254
Negativism, 379–380
Net changes, 334, 338
Nonsense syllables, 173
Nonverbal behavior, 188–190
Nonviolent resistance, 368, 390
Norms, 20, 54–59, 77–78, 94–98, 164, 167–169, 324–326
    assessment of, 84–86
    of maleness-femaleness, 156, 163
    for out-groups, 127–128, 130, 180–182, 273–279
    and personal involvement, 251–258, 264–265
    sexual, 98–100, 371–375, 382, 386–388
    and status, 92–94, 100–101, 340, 382–383

Obedience, experiments on, 6–15
Observation, 59–60, 86–96, 257
Occupations, 158–159, 192, 216–220, 280–281
Opinion leaders, 340–341, 359–360

Opinion research, 235–239, 384–386
Organization. *See* Formal organization, Group, Status
    in social movements, 366–367, 379–383
Out-group, 117–118. *See also* Intergroup relations
Own-categories technique, 181, 251–259, 275, 285–290

Pacifists, 374
Pain tolerance, 205–207
Panel studies, 337
Parent-child expectations, 214–215
Parents, 194, 316
Participant observer, 87
Participants, in movement, 377–379, 380–381, 382, 384–385, 387–388
Participation, 35, 60–63, 87
Passive resistance, 390
Peace groups, 377
"Pecking order," 102–104
Peer groups, 217, 225, 227–228. *See also* Groups
Peer relationships, 193–197, 204
Peoples' park protest, 315
Persistence, 208–209
Personal appearance, 38–41, 257–258
Personal change, 361–391
Personal involvement, 174–178, 185, 214–215, 236, 252–258, 262–265, 336. *See also* Self system
    and context affects, 350–351
    degrees of, 236–237, 245, 351–353
    and "extremism," 248–251
    and judgment of communicators, 355–357
    and social distance, 287–290
    and susceptibility to change, 337–339, 342–345, 360, 376–377
Personality, 10, 103, 109–110, 204–205, 240, 249–251
    ratings of, 35–41
Personality tests, 10, 160–162
Personal qualities. *See also* Traits
    normative regulation of, 68–69
    and self-esteem, 227–228
Personal space, 30–32
"Personal" vs. "social," 74–81, 240
Person-other relationship, 236–239, 271–272
Person perception, 32–41, 235, 341. *See also* Social judgment
Philippines, 216, 307
Physical attractiveness, 38–41

Physical sciences, 113–114
Physiology, 143–147, 155–157
Piaget's hypothesis, 193–197
Polarization, 324–326
Popularity, 78–79. *See also* Liking
Power, 20, 61–63, 83, 101–110, 162–163.
    See also Effective initiative, Status
Power relationships, 68, 105, 267–268,
    277, 291, 326–329
Praise, 212–213
Preference order, 274–277
Preferences, 230, 237, 239
Prejudice, 20, 22, 129–130, 268–300. *See*
    also Attitudes, Intergroup conflict
  and actions, 264
  appearance of, 195
  and authoritarianism, 250–251
Premises, 285–287, 291
President of United States, 176–178, 243,
    247, 339
Prestige of communicator, 355–358
Pretensions, 209–215
Prison camp, 70–72
Prisoners, 207–209
Privacy, 16–18, 74–81, 231, 279
Prohibition issue, 245–246, 345–346
Projective tests, 259
Prosocial behavior, 332
Protests, 379. *See also* Bill of Gripes
Psychodrama, 64, 317
Psychophysical scales, 305–307
Psychophysics, 178–179
Psychosocial scales, 179–183, 305–309
Public opinion surveys, 229–231, 261,
    342–343
Puerto Ricans, 98–99
Pygmalion in the Classroom, 153–155

Quebec separatism, 357–358

Race, 48–49, 244, 280–282
  discrimination, 277–279
  issues, 180–182, 262–264, 355–357
Racism, 33–34, 159–160, 281–282, 285,
    300
Rapport, 87–96
Reactance, 337
Recall, 174–178
Reference group, 21–22, 200–228, 339
  and attitudes, 237, 250–251, 310–312
  change of, 316
  and communicator, 355–357
  as criterion for similarity, 280
  degree of involvement in, 255–256

formation of, 374–376
  norms, 256–258, 264–265
Reference person(s), 21, 200–228. 261–
    262, 264–265, 315–316, 376
Reference sets, 202–203, 266, 340–342
Reinforcement, 56, 151–152, 234, 368
Relative deprivation, 223–224, 371
Relativity of judgment, 235–236, 241–
    242
Reliability, 28, 89–90, 255, 259
Religion, 280–282
Representatives (group), 136–137
Repression, 373–375, 390
Republicans, 247
Research, 16–18, 51, 231–232, 331–333
Research design, 341–342, 357, 336–
    339
Research situation, 86–90, 244
  effects of, 230, 244, 258–259. 282. 336–
    339
  and role playing, 317–320
Research subject, 14–15, 26, 43–44, 121–
    122, 151–152, 209,336–337
Revolutionary social change, 303
  Davies' hypothesis on, 373–374
Risky shift, 324–326
Rivalry, 195. *See also* Competition
Role-playing, 64, 290, 316–318
Role relations, 27–29, 83, 187
  intimacy of, 282–283
Roles, 20, 22, 61–63, 78–79. *See also*
    Leadership. Status. Sex roles
  in group, 91–96. 101–110
  and helping, 48–49
Ruhleben prison, 70–72
Rules, 193. *See* Norms
Rumors, 88, 178

Scale values, 179–183, 241–242
Scapegoat hypothesis, 117
Schema, 50, 173–175, 185
Schizophrenics, 103–104
Schools, 158–160, 217–218
Science, 3–4, 7–10, 299–300
Second Sex, 374
Segregation, 268, 277–279
Selectivity, 29–37, 175–178, 233–240,
    332–333, 348, 391
Self-control, 192–199
Self-disclosure, 72–73
Self-enhancement, 175
Self-esteem, 209–210, 225–228
Self-fulfilling prophecy, 153, 186
Self-hatred, 223

Self-help groups, 76, 80–81
Self-Identity, 203–207, 381–383, 387–389. *See also* Self-system
Self-radius, 304–306
Self-system, 21–22, 170–199. *See also* Attitudes, Personal involvement
    and attitudes, 239–240, 250–251, 271–272, 360
    attributions to, 185–186
    changes of, 381–383, 387–389
    and involvement, 236, 262–264
    and reference groups, 200–228
    stability of, 376–377
Semantic differential, 240–241
Seneca Falls Declaration, 371
Sensitivity groups, 74–81
"Set," 235. *See also* Expectancy
Sex differences (similarities), 10–11, 38–39, 45, 48–49, 63, 155–163, 186, 276, 283, 289–290, 338–339
Sexes, relationships between, 29, 98–100, 206–207
Sexism, 285, 386–387
Sex roles (social), 156–157, 162–163, 191–192, 255
    issues on, 72, 338–339
    and power, 62–63
Sex stereotypes, 33–34, 270, 296–297
    and clinical judgments, 184
Sexual activity, 145–146. *See also* Sexual norms
Sexual attraction, 37, 38–41
Sexual differentiation, 155–157
Sexual norms, 98–100, 371–375, 382, 386, 387, 388
Siblings, 153–155
Significant others. *See* Reference groups, Reference persons
Similarity
    and attraction, 39–41
    criteria for, 280–282
    judgments, 284–287
Sit-ins, 279, 370
Situational factors, 185, 260–265. *See also* Social situation
Slavery, abolition of, 371
Slogans, 365–366
Slum, 87, 90
"Small World" technique, 378
Social categories, 33–34, 204–207, 238, 271–272, 284–285
Social change, 22–23, 100, 169, 361–391. *See also* Cultural lag, Social movements, Technology

Social control, 16–18. *See also* Authority, Conformity, Power
Social desirability, 84–86, 184–186, 275, 282
Social distance, 127, 272–282, 286–287
Social environment, 302–310. *See also* Social situation
Socialization, 192–197, 233–234
Social judgment, 178–183, 215, 238, 240–248
    of communicators, 355–357
    of discrepant messages, 345–351, 353–354, 358–360
    and group norms, 256–258
    of in-group and out-group, 128–129, 136–138
    with Own Categories, 251–258
    of personality, 35–41
    and prejudice, 284–285
Social learning, 145, 150–151. *See also* Attitudes, Learning, Socialization
    organization of, 170–199
Social mobility, 201, 222–225
Social movement, 22–23, 139, 360, 361–391
    "group dynamics" as, 74–81
    "relative deprivation" in, 223–224
Social networks, 96
    and attribution, 186–188
    in forming groups, 377–378, 381
    in reactions to mass media, 340–342
Social norms. *See* Norms
Social perception, 35–41. *See also* Social judgment
    and "stimulus error," 280
Social power. *See* Power
Social pressure, 164–169, 262–264
Social problems, 309–310, 368–370
Social psychology, 1–6
    of research, 51, 182, 258–259. *See also* Research situation, Research subjects
    and social change, 362–364
Social situation, 6–14, 18–19, 83, 141
    and attitudes, 232–233
    components of, 26–29, 31, 37–40
    consistency in, 197–199
    structure of, 41–51, 164–169, 376
Social unit, 66–81, 110–111
"Social" vs. "personal," 79–81
Society
    defining "right," 163–169
    power relations in, 267–268, 389
    and reference groups, 215–220
    and sex roles, 162–163

Sociocentrism, 218–220. *See also* Ethnocentrism
Socioeconomic class, 96, 216 218, 221–224, 298–299, 326–329
Socioemotional roles, 61–63
Sociological analysis, 83–84, 111
Sociology, 4–6
Sociometric choices, 78–79, 110–111
and intergroup relations, 128–129, 135
Sociometric questions, 64, 66–68
Solidarity, 20, 110–111. *See also* Cohesiveness
and intergroup conflict, 126–127, 383–385
Source of communication, 351–352, 355–358
Soviet Union, 163, 196–197, 225
Spanish-Americans, 90–96
Speech, 190–192
Sports, 94, 124, 130
Stability, 274, 301–304
Standards, 210–220. *See also* Anchors
Status, 20, 28–29, 83, 128, 215. *See also* Power, Role
changes in, 93–94
criteria for, 216–224
in groups, 91–92, 101–110, 265
of reference set, 211–212
satisfaction with, 220–224
in T-groups, 78–79
of women, 162–163, 310, 374–375
Status equilibration, 221–222
Stereotypes, 20, 22, 33–34, 290–291
changes in, 294–296, 299
and familiarity, 292–293
favorableness of, 293–294
of in-group, 128–130, 135
and judgment, 284–285
research on, 291–292
of sexes, 162. 296–297
Stimulus, 25. *See also* Social situation
"Stimulus error," 279–280
Stimulus structure, 55–59, 164–167
Strangers, 25–51
Structure
of group, 90–96
of intergroup relations, 124–125
lack of, 50–51, 354–355, 376. *See also* Ambiguity
of social situation, 41–51
"Structureless" groups, 382–383
Students, 363, 370, 378, 388. *See also* College students

Students for Democratic Society, 356
Success, 207–214
Suffrage movement, 349, 371–372
"Suggestion," 164–169
Superordinate goals, 133–135, 391–392
Survey research, 229–231, 333, 336, 337, 339, 384, 386
Susceptibility to change, 337–339, 342–345, 360, 376–377
Sweden, 163
Symbolic interactionists, 234
Sympathy, 195

Task. *See also* Social situation
and leadership, 61–63, 103–109
structure of, 108–109
Teachers' expectancies, 153–155
Technology, 3–5
of attitude assessment, 231–232
of change, 301–302, 328–329
and psychological scales, 57–59
and self-radius, 304–307
Tension reduction, 221, 344
Territoriality, 126
T-groups, 59, 75–81, 89, 381, 382
Threat by "common enemy," 131–132
Thurstone scaling, 178–183, 240–242
Time estimates, 125
Tool use, 147
Traditions. *See also* Norms
persistence of, 96–97
and status, 80–81
Traits, 35–41, 160–163, 169, 237
attribution of, 118, 184–186
favorableness of, 293–294
Trait theories, 184–186
Transitions in development, 224–225
Trust, 314

Uncertainty, 360
"Undecided" response, 243
Unemployment, 384–385
University structure, 378
Unobtrusive methods, 86–96, 120–121, 259–260
Urban life, 42–46
U.S. Women's Bureau, 374

Validity, 89–90. *See also* Reliability
Values, 227–228, 341–342. *See also* Ethical values, Norms
Variability, 242, 347, 355
Verbal learning, 149–152

Vietnam war, 137–138, 313–314, 316, 353, 356, 359
Violent actions, 122–124, 365–367, 389–391
Vocabulary development, 190–192
Volunteer subjects, 336. *See also* Research subjects
Voter turnout, 249, 314

War, 131, 133–135, 137–138, 163
Watergate, 243
We-feeling, 66, 117–118. *See also* Cohesiveness, Solidarity
Western–non-Western cultures, 286–287
Who Am I test, 204
Woman question, 389
Women
    achievements of, 218–220
    changed viewpoints of, 58–59

persuasibility of, 367–368
status, 369, 373–374
Women's Equity Action League (WEAL), 365, 377, 381, 383
Women's liberation, 365–366, 384, 386
Women's movement, 22–23, 224, 347, 364, 365, 369–370
    formation of, 371–383
    goals of, 385–389
    reactions to, 383–385
Women Strike for Peace, 374
Women workers, 322
World War I, 70–71, 269, 317, 372
World War II, 115, 229, 334, 372–374

Yale Communications Research Program, 334–336
Young Americans for Freedom, 356–357

Ziegarnik effect, 174